Black

PCSO Handbook

Second edition

Blackstone's

Police Community Support Officers' Handbook

Edited by
Dr Bryn Caless

Authors
Dr Robin Bryant, Barry Spruce, and
Robert Underwood

OXFORD
UNIVERSITY PRESS

OXFORD
UNIVERSITY PRESS

Great Clarendon Street, Oxford OX2 6DP

Oxford University Press is a department of the University of Oxford.
It furthers the University's objective of excellence in research, scholarship,
and education by publishing worldwide in

Oxford New York

Auckland Cape Town Dar es Salaam Hong Kong Karachi
Kuala Lumpur Madrid Melbourne Mexico City Nairobi
New Delhi Shanghai Taipei Toronto

With offices in

Argentina Austria Brazil Chile Czech Republic France Greece
Guatemala Hungary Italy Japan Poland Portugal Singapore
South Korea Switzerland Thailand Turkey Ukraine Vietnam

Oxford is a registered trademark of Oxford University Press
in the UK and in certain other countries

Published in the United States
by Oxford University Press Inc., New York

© Oxford University Press, 2010

British Library Cataloguing in Publication Data

Data available

Library of Congress Cataloging-in-Publication Data

Blackstone's police community support officers' handbook / edited by Bryn
Caless; authors, Robin Bryant, Barry Spruce, and Robert Underwood.
    p. cm.
  Includes bibliographical references and index.
  ISBN 978–0–19–958022–4
1. Police—Great Britain—Handbooks, manuals, etc. 2. Police training—Great
Britain. I. Caless, Bryn. II. Bryant, Robin. III. Spruce, Barry. IV. Underwood,
Robert. V. Title: Police community support officer's handbook.
  HV8196.A4B542 2010
  363.2'3—dc22

                                                                  2009049065

Typeset by MPS Limited, A Macmillan Company
Printed in Great Britain
on acid-free paper by
L.E.G.O. S.p.A.

ISBN 978–0–19–958022–4

10 9 8 7 6 5 4 3 2 1

About the Authors

Dr Bryn Caless was formerly Head of Human Resources for Kent Police and Director of Kent Police College and is now Associate Tutor in Law and Criminal Justice Studies at Canterbury Christ Church University. He has extensive experience of the strategic management of police and PCSO training, having worked with Dr Robin Bryant on establishing the IPLDP training model in the force and, with Robin, devising and delivering an innovative European postgraduate professional qualification for senior police officers. Prior to this, Bryn worked at the Ministry of Defence where he originated and oversaw training programmes for the civil service and the military, including leadership and management development programmes. He is also a contributor to the *Blackstone's Student Police Officer Handbook*; to *Blackstone's Police Operational Handbook: Practice & Procedure* (ed. Harfield, 2009) and is currently working on a Handbook for the Special Constabulary and a book on chief police officers.

Dr Robin Bryant is Director of Law and Criminal Justice Studies at Canterbury Christ Church University, and was responsible for implementing the first college-based police training model in the UK with Kent Police, as well as helping Bryn Caless to devise professional qualifications in European policing. He is the joint-editor, with his wife Sarah, of the *Blackstone's Student Police Officer Handbook*, and is the author of numerous articles about the police, specializing in 'hi-tech' crime. He is working currently with Bryn Caless on a book about chief police officers.

Barry Spruce is an experienced PCSO trainer and formerly taught with Kent Police. He is now Head of the Extended Police Family Department for Kent Police and joint author, with Bryn Caless, of the 'Neighbourhood Policing' section of *Blackstone's Police Operational Handbook: Practice & Procedure* (ed. Harfield, 2009). He is working with Bryn currently on a Handbook for the Special Constabulary.

Robert Underwood is a former Kent Police officer, who helped to devise the Kent Student Officer Programme. Together with colleagues, he was jointly responsible for the design of the Foundation Degree in Policing which formed the basis of initial police learning in Kent. He is also a contributor to both the *Blackstone's Student Police Officer Handbook* and its forthcoming companion *WorkBook*, and to *Blackstone's Police Operational Handbook: Practice & Procedure* (ed. Harfield, 2009,), as well as working with Bryn and Barry on *Blackstone's Special Constabulary Handbook* (forthcoming). Robert is now an Associate Tutor at Canterbury Christ Church University.

Note: **David Morgan**, who writes a column regularly for *Police Review*, was formerly a police constable training officer with Heddlu Dyfed Powys. He contributed to the first edition of this Handbook.

Foreword

I am delighted to provide the Foreword to this excellent book. I have worked with the Editor, Dr Bryn Caless, for many years. Without question he is a leading authority in police and PCSO training; he talks good, solid, down-to-earth common sense and is someone always worth listening to. I couldn't have thought of a better choice of Editor. On this basis alone I would recommend the book unequivocally. Having actually read it, doubly so!

The role of Police Community Support Officer (PCSO) is relatively new. It marks a significant shift in practical community policing, allowing greater numbers of officers to be deployed, more visibly and with excellent (and so vital!) connections in their local communities. They now form a valuable asset for their police forces. However, their arrival has also had a couple of unexpected benefits too. As one example: the number of minority ethnic officers joining as PCSOs is roughly ten times the number joining as Constables. This is helping to engage with ethnic communities in a whole new way—to great benefit generally, and in countering modern terrorism in particular. You can see, therefore, that the job of a PCSO affects the 'sharp end' very directly.

Many PCSOs now want to progress to full Constables and go on to pursue a very worthwhile career in policing. Skills for Justice has ensured that the competences required of a PCSO dovetail exactly with the somewhat broader set of a Constable, which would allow seamless progression. Modern, forward-looking police forces such as Kent are now taking advantage of this (there's Bryn's work again!), saving some thirty weeks of initial training, and a whole lot of tax-payers' money.

The book is primarily for PCSOs, prospective PCSOs, and all officers responsible for the training and development of PCSOs, including tutor constables and divisional managers. Its coverage of neighbourhood policing may also be of interest to other practitioners involved in this vital area. Good luck! PCSOs are making a big difference in the challenging world of modern policing: go for it!

Dick Winterton
Chief Executive
Skills for Justice

Acknowledgements

The Editor wishes personally to thank

those organizations which gave ready permission to quote extensively from their work, particularly the **Association of Chief Police Officers** (ACPO) and **Skills for Justice**;

all his former colleagues in **Kent Police**, particularly the PCSO trainers in the Personnel and Training Directorate, for support, conversations about policing, and insights into the job;

Peter Daniell and the Law editorial department of Oxford University Press including Katie Heath;

Helen Jacobs for photography and many conversations;

Judy Nokes, Information Policy Adviser at the Office of Public Sector Information (OPSI), for her help with permissions to quote from government publications;

Malcolm Underdown for invaluable Health and Safety expertise;

Dick Winterton, former Chief Executive of Skills for Justice and now CEO of City and Guilds, for many conversations, his friendship, and his permission to quote extensively from the National Occupational Standards and the behavioural competences for PCSOs.

Extra special thanks go to:

esteemed colleagues **Barry**, **Bob**, and **Robin** who put up with my demands, tolerated my enthusiasms, delivered against a tight deadline, and whose support I value so much.

Most of all, my love and thanks to:

my darling wife **Clare** and my super family—**Helen, Wez, Sally, Kit, and Maddy**—for fascinating conversations about society, community, and the law, and for good-humouredly accommodating a phantom PCSO for so long.

Barry Spruce thanks his colleagues in the Extended Policing Family Department of Kent Police, and thanks especially **Emma**, **Phoebe**, and **Joseph** for their much needed support.

Robert Underwood thanks **Vuka Underwood** for everything.

Acknowledgements

Contents

Contents

Contents

List of Figures

List of Photographs

Glossary of Terms Used in Policing

The following is a list which explains many of the common terms in use in policing. It is not exhaustive but this 'Jargon Buster' is designed to help you to get a grip on the acronyms, abbreviations, mnemonics, and other linguistic contortions which form the often impenetrable language of the police 'family'.

ABH Actual bodily harm

ACC *Assistant Chief Constable,* command rank

ACPO Association of Chief Police Officers; sometimes used as a vernacular proper noun for a Chief Officer (qv)

actus reus Latin: 'criminal act', part of the proof of criminal liability, coupled with 'guilty mind' or *mens rea* (qv)

ad hoc Latin: 'for this special purpose', but has elided to mean 'off the cuff' or 'unrehearsed'

ADQ Assessor-Directed Questions (for evidence of competence in meeting the **NOS**, qv in your **SOLAP**, qv)

ADVOKATE An inadequate, but sadly prevalent, mnemonic supposed to help with gathering evidence (see the preferable **SOCRATES**, qv). Its principles were formulated in the wake of the famous case of *R versus Turnbull* (1976). The mnemonic is: A = Amount of time you or the witness had the suspect under observation, D = Distance between you or the witness and the suspect, V = Visibility in the vicinity at the time, O = Obstructions between you or the witness and the suspect, K = Known or seen before, A = Any reason for remembering the suspect, T = Time lapse, E = Errors

AIRWAVE National police radio communication system

Analyst A professional police staff member whose role (usually) is to analyse and assess crime intelligence, and present research

ANPR Automatic Number Plate Recognition system; cameras linked to police and DVLA computers can identify or 'ping' registration plates on vehicles of interest

APA Association of Police Authorities. Every police force has a police authority, which oversees its efficient and effective operation. Together, the Police Authorities ought to carry some clout; in practice the APA tends to be a bit of a talking shop

Glossary of Terms Used in Policing

APEL Accredited prior experiential learning; a means of obtaining credit exemptions (or acceptance on a learning programme) based on previous experience and reflection on that experience

APL Accredited prior learning; a means of obtaining credit exemptions for study or learning already undertaken

arcana Intensely-specialized knowledge (Latin: 'of the (secret) chest')

ARV Armed Response Vehicle

ASBO Anti-social behaviour order

BCU Basic Command Unit (Area, Division)

'bilking' Vernacular term; means making off without paying (such as at petrol stations)

'Biometrics' The use of unique physical characteristics as identifiers, such as the iris of the eye

BMI *Body mass index*, a determination of the fat ratios in the body and their relationship to obesity. Used by forces to determine propensity for things like diabetes and heart problems. Now largely replaced with 'waist measurement' indicators

'Border Agency' A term to describe the Immigration and Nationalities Department, in its role of safeguarding the UK's international frontiers , often rendered as 'UKBA'

'brought to justice' [Often rendered as **'btj'**] a government term to describe the complete process from criminal act through detection to arrest and arraignment for trial. Clearly, to be meaningful, 'btj' ought to include a finding of guilt and a punishment, but purists and jurists argue that 'not guilty' and 'no punishment' equally represent 'btj' outcomes.

'bureau' A fingerprint unit

byelaws Local laws (such as restrictions on parking) enforceable only in the local area itself

case law Precedents set by court decisions

'Cat A' 'B' 'C' Categories of homicide. 'A' is serious/series-impactive 'stranger' killing, **'B'** a serious or cross-force murder where the offender is not known, and **'C'** a local or domestic murder, where the offender is known. All classifications of this type are relative, and factors such as intense media interest can also be used as determinants. Generally, a force's Major Crime Unit investigates 'Cat A' and 'Cat B' homicides and, usually, **BCU Tac CIDs** (qv) will investigate 'Cat C'

caution The formal warning to a suspect under PACE 1984, in three parts, depending on the stage the investigation has reached:

1. *You do not have to say anything*
2. *but it may harm your defence if you do not mention* (**a**) *'when questioned'* or (**b**) *'now'*, *something which you later rely on in court.*
3. *Anything you do say may be given in evidence.*

CAP Common approach path to a crime scene

CCTV Closed-Circuit Television (note the '**d**'; it is *not* 'close-circuit')

CDRP Crime and Disorder Reduction Partnership

Centrex former commercial name for National Police Training, now part of **NPIA** (qv)

cf Compare (Latin: *'conferere'*)

chemical cocktail The combination of chemicals and hormones in a person's body at moments of high tension or stress. Such chemicals as adrenaline and hormones such as cortisol prepare the body typically for *'flight or fight'*

ch(s) Chapter(s)

Chief Officer *A police officer with the rank of Assistant Chief Constable and above; Command rank*

CHIS Covert Human Intelligence Source (informant)

'CJ'(S) A common acronym, referring to some process or unit concerned with Criminal Justice (Systems)

CJI Criminal Justice Inspectorate; a combination announced in late 2006 of earlier, separate inspectorates, such as the Inspectorate of Constabulary (HMIC) and the Inspectorate of Prisons; given legal status in the **Police Justice Act** of 2006

'collar' An arrest (vernacular)

common law The old (then unwritten) law of the land covering such basic crimes as murder, theft, and rape. Much common law is still **extant** (*alive and working*).

'continuity' (of evidence): an audited and continuous trail from crime scene or suspect to court, such that evidential items can be accounted for at all times en route, to obviate interference or contamination

COSHH Control of Substances Hazardous to Health (health and safety programme, leading to a nationally recognized qualification)

CPIA Criminal Procedure and Investigations Act 1996

CPS Crown Prosecution Service

'CRAVED' A neat mnemonic which reminds us what items are 'stealable', that is, attractive to a thief or burglar. The mnemonic is:
Concealable
Removable

AVailable
Enjoyable
Disposable
(see Clarke, 1999)

crime scene That place where a crime is known to have happened, or where it is suspected of having taken place

CSI Crime Scene Investigator (forensic)

'cuff' Police vernacular verb for not doing something which one is supposed to do as a matter of duty or obligation, hence avoidance of a 'proper action'

custody, or custody suite A designated area in a police station (usually where the cells are located), where arrested persons are logged and processed by trained custody staff, usually led by a sergeant

DC Detective Constable

DCC Deputy Chief Constable, number two in the Force

DCI Detective Chief Inspector

DCS Detective Chief Superintendent; command rank

de minimis At the least risk (Latin: from the phrase *'de minimis non curat lex'*, meaning 'the law is not concerned with trifles')

Designation The process whereby a Chief Constable confers powers on PCSOs (we use a capital '**D**' to distinguish this specialist use of the word throughout the Handbook)

DI Detective Inspector

digital Referring to any computer-based equipment which uses binary digits as an encoding process

direct speech The *verbatim* (word-for-word) recording of what someone actually said. The opposite is 'recorded speech'. You should record all things said to you and needed in evidence in direct speech in your **PNB** (qv)

DNA Deoxyribonucleic Acid (genetic 'fingerprint')

DS Detective Sergeant

DVLA Driver Vehicle Licensing Agency

DWP Department of Work and Pensions

ECHR European Convention on Human Rights, which led to European countries adopting common legal principles in defence of individual liberty. It underpins our own **Human Rights Act 1998**

'either way' An offence triable at *either* a magistrates' court *or* the Crown Court depending on its seriousness (such as a financial limit for theft)

et al Latin: 'and others' (*'et alii'*)

EVA Environmental Visual Audit, sometimes known as the 'structured patch walk'; it is a way of noting all the problems in a patrol area, such as drugs' paraphernalia, abandoned vehicles, graffiti, litter, and vandalism

Federation Police 'Union', strictly a Staff Association, covering ranks from Constable to Chief Inspector

'fishing' Police vernacular verb for any speculative attempt at anything, particularly where the intention is to try to get someone else to do the hard work

5x5x5 An intelligence report (**NIM**, qv). The numbers refer to the reliability, access, and other factors about the source providing the intelligence

FLO Family Liaison Officer

FOA First Officer Attending (a crime scene)

FPN Fixed Penalty Notice, a fine for an offence, such as speeding instead of going to court, in an attempt to speed up the criminal justice system. See also **PND**

FPP Force Policing Plan

FY Financial Year (in the police, it runs from 1 April to 31 March of the following calendar year)

GBH Grievous (note *not* 'grievious') Bodily Harm

'Grade' The rank and pay band for **Police Staff** (qv)

HATO Highways Agency Traffic Officer, steadily replacing police major roads patrols in characteristic 'battenberg' vehicles in black and yellow

'hit' A DNA sample which can be 'matched' with an identified person (not always criminal)

HMCE Her Majesty's Customs and Excise, its investigative division is now part of **SOCA** (qv); title changed from HMCE in 2006 to Revenue and Customs

HMIC Her Majesty's Inspectorate of Constabulary (now part of Criminal Justice Inspectorate, **CJI**, qv)

HMIS Her Majesty's Immigration Service (now parts of IS are in SOCA, qv)

HMPS Her Majesty's Prison Service

HMSO Her Majesty's Stationery Office, now known as TSO, The Stationery Office; the government publisher and printer

HO Home Office

HOLMES, HOLMES2 Home Office Large Major Enquiry System; a database (and its successor), geared to large-scale police investigations (eg homicide)

Glossary of Terms Used in Policing

HORT1 Known in police jargon as a *'horty'*, this is a document issued to motorists requesting them to produce their driving documents at a police station within seven days

'hot spot' A location where there is a high incidence of current crime and criminality (linked with crime analysis, also 'hot victim', etc)

ILP Intelligence-Led Policing

indictable-only offences Serious offences tried at Crown Court

INDIS Immigration and Nationality Directorate Intelligence Service (now partly in **SOCA**, and partly in the new '**Border Agency**', qv)

Informant See **CHIS**; an informant passes criminal intelligence to a police source handler.

Inter alia Latin: 'among other things'

Intoxilyser A device used in police stations to analyse specimens of breath from people arrested for drink-driving offences

intranet Police **internal** electronic information system

IPCC Independent Police Complaints Commission, replacing the old Police Complaints Commission, made statutory in Police Reform Act 2002. The IPCC investigates complaints against the police, especially in shootings or deaths in custody

ISP Internet Service Provider

JAPAN Acronym for ensuring that proportionality and justification for an action are considered. JAPAN, and other acronyms like it, including **PLAN**, **SOCAP**, and the like are commonplace in police learning

JRFT Job-Related Fitness Test: a means to determine if a person is able to undertake a job with high physical demands (such as patrol or firearms)

Level 1 Local (BCU) crime signifier (**NIM**, qv)

Level 2 Cross-BCU or cross-Force crime signifier (**NIM**, qv)

Level 3 National or international crime signifier (**NIM**, qv)

LOCARD Forensic database system, named after a renowned scientist

MAPPA Multi-Agency Public Protection Arrangements (part of the joint agency approach to child protection, violent and sex offenders, rehabilitation, managed return of prisoners to the community, etc)

mens rea Latin: 'guilty mind'—one of two things you must prove to show criminal liability (the other is the 'criminal act', or *actus reus*, qv)

MIM Murder Investigation Manual

Ministry of Justice In 2007, the Home Office, which had expanded under successive Labour governments, was split into two; matters to do with policing, immigration and the like remained with the Home Office, whilst matters to do with the judiciary and magistracy were brought into a new ministry of justice. Ironically, the police have as persuasive a claim to be in the Ministry of Justice (as the 'gateway' to the criminal justice system) as they have to be in the Home Office.

'minutiae' Latin: 'of small parts'; the individuality of a fingerprint through examination of its 'ridge' characteristics (anywhere up to 150 characteristics in a single fingerprint)

MISPER Missing person

MO Latin: *'modus operandi'*, 'a (characteristic) way of doing something'

modus vivendi Latin: 'a practical way to co-exist' (between those who differ)

MOD Ministry of Defence

MOU Memorandum of Understanding

MPS Metropolitan Police Service (the 'Met')

'MSF' Most Similar Forces (for comparison), a means for the Home Office and HMIC of comparison between police forces which have similar staff numbers, similar industries, populations, geography, transport infrastructure, and so on. A sound idea basically, it does not always compute in terms of crime incidence or 'brought to justice' figures. Whether intended or not, the effect is to create league tables among police forces

NB Take especial note of (Latin: *'nota bene'*, 'note well')

NCALT National Centre for Applied Learning Technologies, the national on-line police e-learning portal, now part of **NPIA**

NCIS National Criminal Intelligence Service (now part of SOCA, qv)

NCPE National Centre for Policing Excellence (now part of NPIA, qv)

NCS National Crime Squad (now part of SOCA, qv)

Neighbourhood Policing Teams Small, local policing unit, consisting usually of a police sergeant, up to two or three constables and three or more PCSOs, sometimes with Special constables and partner agencies too; all working to local targets and agendas, but integrated with overall BCU targets and priorities

'Nexus' A combined computer database system, linking, for example, local intelligence requirements, a criminal database such as the Police National Computer (**PNC**, qv), the Driver and Vehicle Licensing Agency's database of vehicle ownership and a targeting computer system, such as **ANPR** (qv)

NHTCU National High Tech Crime Unit (part of **SOCA**, qv)

NIM National Intelligence Model

No Number

NO ELBOWS(S) Mnemonic to help you to remember the rules for your Pocket Note Book (**PNB**, qv)

> NO Erasures,
>> Leaves torn out or lines missed,
>> Blank spaces,
>> Overwriting,
>> Writing between lines,
>> Spare pages, and
>> **Statements must always be recorded in direct speech**

NOS National Occupational Standards (held and developed by **Skills for Justice**, qv)

NPIA National Police Improvement Agency, formed in 2006, this amalgamates (and centralizes) a number of support services, including training (**Centrex**) and the Police Scientific Department, Information Services (PITO)

NPP National Policing Plan

NSLEC National Specialist Law Enforcement Centre, a consortium of representatives of national policing bodies which seeks 'excellence' in policing, principally in covert operations

op Operation

p or pp Page or pages

PACE Police and Criminal Evidence Act 1984, PACE 'Codes' are additions for police guidance

PACT Police And Communities Together, an arrangement where key people in a community have regular meetings and agree plans for the neighbourhood with the police

passim Latin: 'everywhere', but used in the sense of 'throughout'

PC *Police Constable*

(P)CSO (Police) Community Support Officer, a title which signifies that the individual CSO is part of the police force, not a community, rural, or parish warden, or any of the associated designations, such as traffic (or parking) warden. PCSOs have standard powers on a national basis, but may have additional powers designated by the Chief Constable of the force in which they operate. PCSOs are under the operational command of their Chief Constable or Commissioner, but are employed by the Police Authority.

PDR Performance Development Review (annual 'appraisal')

PI Performance Indicator (but qv **Policing Pledge**)

PIP Professionalizing the Investigative Process, a national standard for levels of competence for detectives, begun in 2006

pixel A minute (small) area of illumination, in shades of grey (for fingerprints) or colour, from which an electronic image on a screen is composed

PLAN Acronym which, like **JAPAN** (qv), acts as a reminder that police and PCSO actions must be Proportionate, Legal, Authorized and Necessary.

PNB Pocket Note Book

PNC Police National Computer

PND Penalty Notice for Disorder, similar to Fixed Penalty Notice (**FPN**, qv) for low-level public nuisance

POCA Proceeds of Crime Act 2002

police caution A formal warning given by a senior police officer to an adult who has admitted his or her guilt (do not confuse this with a **caution** (such as under PACE) to a suspect)

Police Staff Official designation of support ('civilian') staff, some of whom are operational but who do not have warranted powers like police officers. PCSOs are police staff

Policing Pledge Designed both as a reassurance measure for local communities and as a measure for police performance, the Policing Pledge, introduced in late 2008, has ten commitments to standards of service and delivery, all on a local theme, qualitatively assessed through 'satisfaction' measures

PRA(02) Police Reform Act 2002, which gave the statutory basis for PCSOs, and helped to define their powers. Rendered in our text as 'PRA02'

'precept' The levy locally for police authority funding of the police, it is part of the community charge, but is often expressed in terms of a percentage increase annually. Central government seeks to 'cap' or limit the precept in high-spending councils.

'probationer' A police officer in initial training or the first two years of service; a PCSO before confirmation of appointment and **Designation** (qv); now both are usually called 'student officers'

PS *Police Sergeant*

PSDB Police Scientific Development Bureau, now part of **NPIA** (qv)

PSE See **Police Staff**, above. A weak acronym, which stands for Police Staff (Employee). But the 'E' is retained to avoid confusion with a Police Sergeant

PSNI Police Service of Northern Ireland (was the RUC, Royal Ulster Constabulary, GC). PSNI began recruiting PCSOs in 2007

QPM Queen's Police Medal

qv Latin: 'which see' (*'quod vide'*)

reprimand A formal warning given to a juvenile by a police officer, on admission of guilt for a first and minor offence

RIPA Regulation of Investigatory Powers Act 2000

risk assessment A process of understanding that hazard plus (or 'times') likelihood = something going wrong. Assessing the risk may help you to do something positive about it

'sanitized' Intelligence with identifying features and origins omitted

'shoemarks' Footwear prints which can match a suspect to a crime scene, in the same ways that DNA and fingerprints do

sic Latin: as it is written (*'sic'* = 'thus')

'signal crime' The notion that some kinds of crime act as warning signals about the security of everyday life. Some crimes matter more than others in 'signalling' people's concerns. The theory behind signal crimes is also referred to as 'Broken Windows Theory'

SIU Special Investigation Unit (for child abuse and child protection investigations)

Skills for Justice (SfJ) Developed from the old 'sector skills councils', this is the learning standards and skills 'guardian' for the criminal justice system. As well as devising means whereby the professionalism and qualifications of staff in the criminal justice sector may be recognized, Skills for Justice (sometimes rendered as **SfJ** or **S4J**), holds all **NOS** for the sector and all behavioural competences

SLA Service Level Agreement

SMART(ER) Of objectives; Specific, Measurable, Achievable, Realistic, Timely (and Evaluated and Reviewed) or abstract nouns to the same effect

SMT Senior Management Team (on **BCUs**, it usually consists of the BCU Commander, two CIs or Superintendents (Crime and Operations) and the Business Manager); other combinations will depend on the size of the BCU

SOCA Serious Organised Crime Agency; set up by the government in February 2004, to embrace the work of **NCS**, **NCIS**, the Serious Fraud Office (SFO), and the Investigation and Intelligence Divisions of Customs and Excise and HM Immigration

Service staff. The aim was to create a national unified law enforcement agency. SOCA courted controversy at the outset, because apparently its staff can have any designation which its Director-General may determine. See The Police Reform Act 2002, Schedule 4, section 38, Chapter 1. SOCA has attracted criticism because of its internationalist focus, which leaves gaps between individual police forces and the Agency, allegedly where serious and organized crime goes undetected.

SOCO Outmoded term ('Scenes of Crime Officer') largely replaced by **CSI** (qv)

SOCRATES A mnemonic to remember the nature of evidence-gathering in the wake of *R versus Turnbull* (1976). The mnemonic (more accurate than **ADVOKATE** but less familiar) is:

S = *S*uspect descriptors

O = *O*bservation by witness

C = *C*larity of the witness's observation

R = *R*eason to remember the suspect

A = *A*ppearance of the suspect

T = *T*ime elapsed between observation and identification

E = *E*rrors of fact or mistakes

S = *S*pace (how much distance between witness and suspect)

SOLAP Student Officer Learning and Assessment Portfolio initially used for police officers' learning; now the principles, if not all the content, are applied to PCSOs. You will be expected to sustain a reduced form of SOLAP after training, because a portfolio of evidence of your competence is needed to appraise your performance (see **PDR**, qv) annually

SOLO Sex Offender Liaison Officer

SOP Standard Operating Procedure

'spine point' The placement of an individual on the **Police Staff** (qv) pay scale, determined by grade, experience, responsibility, and length of service

SPOC or spoc Single Point of Contact

Statute law Modern, written legislation

Statutory Instrument Legislation introduced by a government minister on the back of other Acts. The purpose is to avoid going through the consultation and debate process in Parliament for relatively minor things

STR Short Tandem Repeat, a DNA profiling methodology

summary offences Offences which are dealt with at a Magistrates' Court

Tac CID Detective unit on a BCU (Tactical Criminal Investigation Department)

TacOPS Tactical Operations Department, usually includes firearms and public order departments, centrally managed

'tenprint' A fingerprinting process whereby all ten digits of a suspect or other individual are recorded

TICs 'Taken into consideration' offences by a court. These are crimes to which an offender admits, rather than face further charges. Always referred to in the plural

TP Test Purchase

T&CG Tasking and Co-ordinating Group (**NIM**, qv)

uc Undercover (police officer)

Unison Police Staff ('civilian') Association, currently represents PCSOs, but also much larger representation of workers in the public service generally, such as hospital workers

VCSE Volume Crime Scene Examiner (forensic)

VIU Vehicle Intelligence Unit

VOSA Vehicle and Operator Services Agency

WPLDP Wider Police Learning and Development Programme—a particularly elephantine collection of letters to cover **NPIA** learning and development programmes in the extended policing 'family', part of the 'mixed economy' of modern policing

YOT Youth Offending Team; often a partnership group between police and other agencies, in which PCSOs can be involved

The phonetic alphabet

The purpose of the phonetic alphabet is to ensure that there is no confusion over similar sounding letters such as 'p' and 'b' and 'd'; or, more subtly 's' and 'f', or 'm' and 'n', when spelling something out over the radio. The accepted '*sound form*' for each letter in English is as follows:

A	Alpha	J	Juliet	S	Sierra
B	Bravo	K	Kilo	T	Tango
C	Charlie	L	Lima	U	Uniform
D	Delta	M	Mike	V	Victor
E	Echo	N	November	W	Whisky
F	Foxtrot	O	Oscar	X	X-Ray
G	Golf	P	Papa	Y	Yankee
H	Hotel	Q	Quebec	Z	Zulu
I	India	R	Romeo		

Numerals

Only two numerals sound similar: '5' and '9'. These are distinguished in speech by saying '**FIFE**' for 5 and '**NINER**' for 9. This
is important when spelling out a car registration such as **BD59
SFE** (try it and see). However, you need to know other sounds
for numbers: '**0**', often rendered in speech as 'oh' or 'nought', is
always **ZERO** in the Phonetic Alphabet, to distinguish it from **O
Oscar**. The best way to represent the sounds of the numbers is
like this:

0 ZERO	5 FIFE
1 WUN	6 SICKS
2 TOO	7 SEV—UN
3 THUH—REE	8 ATE
4 FORE	9 NINER

Numbers are always given separately in speech. You don't say for
57, 'fifty seven' but '*Fife Sev-un*'; you don't say for 103, 'a hundred and three', but '*Wun Zero Thuh-ree*'. So the motorway 'M 62'
would be 'Mike Sicks Too' in speech.

No confusion of the sounds is possible if this pronunciation
is followed. This system is in universal use where English is the
first or primary language, (apologies to our Welsh colleagues);
all the emergency services and armed forces in the UK use this
phonetic alphabet. Don't worry about some odd spellings which
you might see, such as 'Whiskey', because the point about the
phonetic alphabet is that it is spoken not written. What you have
to do is learn this alphabet by heart and practise it as much and as
often as you can, in conjunction with the 24-hour clock.

Task

Get friends or family to help you by testing your spelling out of words
and numbers (the 'alpha-numeric') in the phonetic alphabet. Practise
relaying information to friends or colleagues on the phone or radio. Try
using cards with the letters on one side and the phonetic name on the
other, to test yourself.

You are expected to be proficient in the use of the phonetic
alphabet and numbers without delay.

Introduction

How to use this Handbook and how to test yourself

Welcome to the Police Community Support Officers' Handbook! As you read through this Handbook, you may notice that it is sometimes as much about the context of policing, what is driving your Force, and what your police colleagues may be doing, as it is about your role. This is because we did not want the Handbook to be merely a reference manual. Your job has meaning only in the context of what your Force is doing and specifically what the Neighbourhood Policing Team alongside you is doing in your community. The role of the Neighbourhood Policing Team itself needs to be understood in the context of where the police service is going and what constitutes 'policing' in the twenty-first century. We try to give that context throughout, but especially in Chapters 2, 5, 6, and 7.

How the Handbook is organized

The Handbook consists of a number of stand-alone sections. Their importance to you as a PCSO will vary according to the job you are doing and the problems that you have to solve. **Each section is divided according to numbered headings**. Each of these heading numbers is referenced in the Index. This means that you can read 'thematically' as well as logically, with close, detailed, textual reference to the nuts and bolts of the job of PCSO. We begin with a chapter about joining the police. This is not for the PCSO who is already employed and busy in a community; rather it is for the person who wants to know what being a PCSO involves and how to go about applying. **We test your understanding of what we have told you and offer particular points for you to note, as well as topics you may care to discuss with colleagues, trainers and assessors.** These are recurrent features throughout the

Handbook—because we have *not* designed the Handbook only for the student PCSO or the new joiner. We have designed it for the PCSO who is serving, just as much as for the new entrant. You may want to refresh your knowledge of your powers (Chapter 3), or check which National Occupations Standards you have to complete each year (Chapter 4), or you may need to understand more detailed contexts of your work, such as how the criminal justice system works (2.9); what the rules of evidence are (5.2); how to handle aggression (5.5); the nature of 'Designation' (2.6); what's involved in going to court yourself (7.5); understanding the community's fear of crime (6.5); what is meant in practical terms by human rights (2.11); what is included in the 'mixed economy' of policing; how '*doing policing*' is a growing industry (7.6); or what the difference is between 'common law' and 'statute' (3.1.2).

Each section of each chapter is complete in itself, but inevitably there is much cross-referencing between the parts of this Handbook. When you come across a term you don't understand, or an acronym you are not sure about (such as JRFT—the job-related fitness test), we have provided a basic **Glossary of police terms**. Your own force is also likely to have a 'jargon buster', so check how you access your local word crib.

Each chapter is distinct: we move in a logical order from **applying to join** (Chapter 1), through **joining up** (Chapter 2); to a comprehensive analysis of your designated **powers** (Chapter 3), a detailed description of the **National Occupational Standards** (NOS), together with the **integrated behavioural competences** expected of a PCSO (Chapter 4). The referential theme is carried on in Chapter 5, which looks at how you respond to and record evidence; how you negotiate, defuse situations, deal with aggression, refresh your safety awareness training, and how you should make a dynamic risk assessment. These are all essential factors in actually **doing the job**. Then we look at the **community** in which you work (Chapter 6) and explain what drives a community, what success factors are, and what kinds of things drag a community down; we look at the fear of crime and signal crimes, partnerships, ethnic and diverse communities, and how the debate about where policing is going affects you.

Chapter 7 discusses the **standards** expected from you and the role of the Professional Standards Department in your Force, before considering **corruption** in the police and the 'dark side' of the job when standards are abandoned. We talk about what being a professional means, and take you through **appearances in court**, from first summons to completing the giving of evidence. We ask where policing, and the PCSO part in policing, may be going in terms of the **'extended police family'** before examining the supervision of PCSOs and the potential for a career structure within PCSO roles. We take a look at the whole **future** of policing.

Finally, we have a chapter (8) which contains ways for you to **test what you have understood**. We appreciate that self-testing can occasionally be a bit sterile, so we've devised an imaginary community, **the town of Tonchester**, for you to visit and to ground your tasks and tests in 'reality' as well as providing a bit of fun. Tonchester gives you a context in which everything that is likely to happen to a PCSO, happens, from teenage drinkers, through the collapse of a building, to a major road collision, and we refer to the town in parts of the Handbook where we need 'worked examples'. If you really want to know how well you have understood something (especially whether you understand your powers, or the NOS, or desired behaviours), Chapter 8 will tell you.

We close the Handbook with suggestions for further reading and provide a **Bibliography** which not only shows many of the sources and authorities we refer to, but also gives you pointers for further and deeper understanding. Whilst **this Handbook is the most comprehensive tool, the most exact explanation, the clearest description and most rigorous analysis of the role of the PCSO in existence**, we never stop learning. The Bibliography helps you to focus where you want your research and learning to develop. A comprehensive **Index** lets you find easily where everything is.

This, the second edition of the only detailed Handbook for PCSOs, is simultaneously a context for policing, an insight into the meaning of what you do, a detailed reference guide to powers and competences, a resource to explain the law, a means of helping you to learn, a challenge for the future, and a friendly, informal but authoritative depiction of what it is like to put on the uniform and go out into the world as a Police Community Support Officer.

Police Ranks

The Police is a disciplined service, with an established hierarchy or 'rank structure'. The ranks, shown below, are designated on the **epaulettes** (*shoulder boards*) of officers' uniforms. The general rule is that the greater the amount of embroidery on the epaulette, the higher the rank (but note the single crown of the Superintendent). This is matched by the peaked hat or bowler worn by uniformed officers. Senior ranks are depicted by the amount of braid, black or silver, on the cap's peak or bowler's brim. Again, the more silver you see, the higher the rank. You will be expected to show formal deference to higher rank. Whether or not you salute the higher rank in uniform depends on your Force policy. Certainly, you should come to attention when addressed.

Whilst the police is structured hierarchically and has ranks like the Armed Services, don't expect discipline to be robotic in any sense, because you are, and will always remain, accountable at law for your own actions. What you do is always down to you to defend or justify, and you cannot hide behind orders, ranks, or silver braid if your judgement was poor.

Some differences from the standard

In the Metropolitan Police and the City of London Police, there are different ranks at the top end of the hierarchy. Broadly, in the 'Met', a Commander ranks as an Assistant Chief Constable (ACC), a Deputy Assistant Commissioner (DAC) ranks as a Deputy Chief Constable, an Assistant Commissioner (AC) ranks as a Chief Constable (as does the Commissioner of the City of London Police). The Deputy Commissioner and Commissioner ranks in the Metropolitan Police are above Chief Constable rank in terms both of salary and resources which they command. The Commissioner rank dates from the very first 'commissioners of police' in London's New Police in 1830.

Detective ranks

You'll be aware that detectives don't wear uniform. They have the same ranks as their uniformed counterparts with the difference that their ranks are always preceded by the word 'Detective' from Constable to Chief Superintendent, so: 'Detective Sergeant' or 'Detective Chief Inspector'. You will be smartly corrected if you get the designation wrong; police officers are always very exact about their ranks and titles. Chief Officers of police, that is Assistant Chief Constables (ACC), Deputy Chief Constables (DCC), and Chief Constables (CC) are always regarded as 'uniformed' and do not use the title 'detective'.

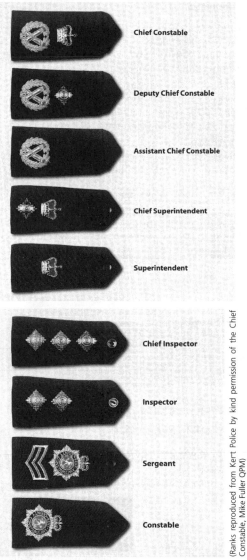

Chief Constable

Deputy Chief Constable

Assistant Chief Constable

Chief Superintendent

Superintendent

Chief Inspector

Inspector

Sergeant

Constable

Insignia of police ranks

(Ranks reproduced from Kent Police by kind permission of the Chief Constable, Mike Fuller QPM)

Ranks for PCSOs?

We do not yet have any rank structure for PCSOs, but we feel that this cannot be far away, as PCSOs grow in experience and service. Our best guess is that PCSOs, when given a rank structure, will have something like this:

Probationer PCSO (first year)
PCSO (second and subsequent years)
Senior PCSO (five years or more and moved up one band)
Principal PCSO (seven years or more and moved up two bands)

Some forces are considering the idea of creating the grade of *'Supervising PCSO'*, where this will replace the police officer supervisor (usually police sergeant, but can be an experienced police constable), yet a review of PCSOs by the National Police Improvement Agency (NPIA) in 2008, concluded that the 'norm' would be that Neighbourhood Policing Teams would be supervised by a police sergeant.[1] As for any designation by badges of rank, all we can do is speculate. The front runner of possibilities is that rank will be designated by silver bars, something like those of special constables, from one bar for PCSO up to three bars for *'Principal PCSO'* or *'Supervisor PCSO'*. Nothing is decided yet, so you can join in the fun of speculating (see also 7.9).

> **Discussion point**
> How would you structure PCSO 'ranks' in harmony with police ranks so that (a) different ranks are clearly marked and (b) there is no confusion with police ranks?

The organization of a typical police force

We have to note that organizational structures vary from police force to police force, and very few are identical. However, in the structure which we show below, the basic functions of:

- BCU level policing
- Neighbourhood teams
- Specialist crime investigation, including serious organized crime and major crime
- Specialist crime techniques, including forensic investigation, surveillance, and covert technical operations

- Information technology
- Force communications
- Finance, administration, engineering (vehicle fleet), and estates
- Human Resource Management
- Learning and Development (Training)
- Traffic
- Firearms and tactical operations
- Public Order
- Dogs
- Helicopter, boat, fixed-wing aircraft, or other specialists such as divers and searchers, cavers, mountain rescue, river police, and 'mounted' (horse) division (for example the City of London)

have to be brigaded together somehow. The standard method for doing this is by creating 'Directorates' commanded by an ACC or equivalent. A smallish police force of fewer than 4,500 might have three directorates such as **Division or Territorial (BCU) Operations**, **Central Operations**, and **Support Operations**. Larger forces, say of 6,000 or more, might have four or five Directorates organized as shown in our structure diagram below.

Don't ignore the 'impact drivers' on the Chief Constable of any police Force: these are partners in the so-called 'Tripartite Arrangement' of the **Police Authority** and the **Home Office** (the Chief makes up the other side of the triangle) but there are also the **Criminal Justice Inspectorate** which includes HM Inspectorate of Constabulary, the **media** and the **public**. All or any of these can call the Chief Constable to account for the actions of his or her Force. If there is impact on the Chief, sooner or later there will be impact on you too.

Task

Look at our diagram (see below). How does your force structure vary from what we describe? Note the differences.

Matched funding and non-government funding

Direct force-based funding is now the principal source for PCSOs, and, with rare exceptions, it is both the largest and the most common default option for police forces and authorities. Not surprisingly, the government, which funded the majority of PCSOs directly until 2008, is keen to encourage other sources

Introduction

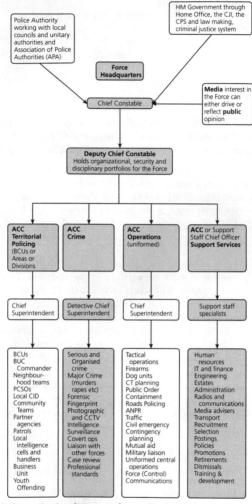

A typical organizational structure for a police force

NB: shading denotes normally located at Force Headquarters.

both of funding and of support, among which it includes local and county authorities, local businesses, consortia of city centre shops, local markets, schools, universities and colleges, local transport providers, and chambers of commerce. Not all of these groups and organizations could afford a full-time PCSO, in which case part-funding is sought, which can then be matched by the police authority. This is called '**matched funding**'. Advertising and sponsorship logos are also ways in which the business community is encouraged to invest in PCSOs, as is an appeal to their vested interests. A PCSO who patrols a bus station, say, at peak times, is likely to bring considerable reassurance value both to the travelling community and to the bus franchise operators. It is common for transport providers to sponsor PCSOs as a result. Indeed, we know of forces where there is an arrangement to carry police officers and PCSOs on the public transport network for no charge, provided that the officers are in uniform and that they will intervene if there is a problem. The incentive for the transport operators is obvious. Finally, the support for locally-sponsored PCSOs need not be confined to ready cash and legal contracts with the police authority; it can be support 'in kind'. This means that, for example, provision of mobile phones, or of a vehicle or bicycle, of premises or accommodation, of lockers or venues for meetings, or use of CCTV; all can help to sustain the viability of a PCSO.

Discussion point

Can you think of any problems and downsides to sponsorship or matched funding?

Questions about sustainability arise from matched funding. At present, we have seen very few matched funding schemes which extend beyond four years. Yet government ministers and senior politicians frequently assure us that PCSOs are here to stay. Are they?

Trust us; we're the government

In case you think that we are unduly sceptical, consider the plans a couple of years ago for the amalgamation of police forces in England and Wales reducing individual forces from 43 to something like 17 or 18. Welcomed by some forces—especially in the east of England—hated by others, the principle was well advanced in late 2005, so that forces were making serious and well-researched bids to justify 'stand-alone' status, or had gone a long way into advanced planning to join with neighbouring forces to produce the elusive 'critical mass' which the Home Office considered important (*'critical mass'* in this context means simultaneously being able to deliver neighbourhood policing teams and to investigate terrorist offences), and which had been recommended by HMIC, Denis O'Connor, in his inspection report (2004).

There was, in May 2006, another in the frequent changes of Home Secretary and an announcement followed from the new incumbent, in July 2006, that amalgamation had been abandoned. Even this message was mixed. Judicial reviews protesting against amalgamation, advanced planning for the merging of force HR and IT systems, and proposals for integrated training suites were all dropped and the whole process ground to a halt. Those who had done a lot of work on amalgamating were devastated, those who had opposed merging from the outset were jubilant. The point of revisiting all this is not to rake over old ground or to recriminate, but merely to point out that, if a week in politics is a long time, years of politically motivated funding for PCSOs may be an unsustainable pipedream. The record of consistency in criminal justice issues among British governments of *any* political hue is not reassuring.

Discussion point

Do you believe that there is a sustainable long-term future for PCSOs?

What do you base your opinions on?

What are the funding pitfalls, do you think?

Where else could funding come from?

What is the appetite for private funding?

What happens if increased funding for PCSOs becomes hard to find or sustain?

The short-term answer may be that fewer PCSOs will be recruited and 'natural wastage' (including application to police forces) may further thin the overall numbers (though see a counter-argument below). But the real and brutal truth is that police forces and their police authorities are stuck with a bill—consisting of your wages, equipment, deployment costs, training, and pension—which they have to pay. Good for you, less so for the long-suffering council tax payer and the police authority which has to seek an increase in the **precept** (*money raised locally from council tax to support the* *police force*). Failing that, or even as well as that, the likely recourse of your police force and police authority will be to slow down **police officer** recruitment. Home Office figures published in early February 2007 showed a fall in police officer numbers for the first time, to 141,873 in England and Wales. At the same time there were 8,517 PCSOs, a rise of 25% over six months. There is no proven causal connection between a fall in police officer numbers and the rise of PCSO numbers, though the Police Federation evidently believes there is one (*Police Review*, 2 February 2007, 6). There has been a steady rise since in the number of PCSOs to about 16,000 currently, but police officer numbers have held pretty steadily; there has been no marked or dramatic decrease. This may change if the UK's economic crises multiply and deepen and authorities are strapped for cash and precepts are 'capped'. The shortfall will be seen in lower and slower recruitment of police officers.

We're sorry if this sounds a little crude, but the plain facts are that, on balance, many police forces would prefer to have more police officers, but cops are much more expensive than PCSOs, so police authorities are hardly likely to ingratiate themselves with their electors if there are massive increases in community charges. You should not expect either police forces or police authorities to continue to recruit additional (as opposed to replacement) PCSOs if the funding streams dry up. This may mean that, whilst the overall numbers of PCSOs may not change, the need to replace PCSOs through turnover will remain something of a constant. Given that a PCSO *is* cheaper, if less flexible than and not as well trained as a police officer, police authorities that are strapped for cash may cut back on the recruitment of police officers in order to sustain PCSO numbers. By doing so, they may retain satisfaction ratings from local communities (something which, as elected representatives, police authority members will be anxious to do), but such a strategy may be in the teeth of opposition from the Police Federation and the media.[2]

The future

It is possible, of course, that the future of PCSOs may become a political imperative, in which case a Labour government would support PCSO funding, though perhaps less enthusiastically. If a Conservative government was returned to power, it might sustain the PCSOs for a short time, such as two or three years, but would only persist with them if there were to be concerted, massive, and vocal local community support, bolstered by support in the news media. We believe that by 2012 the funding for PCSOs will be carried wholly by individual police forces, with or without local partners, at the expense of police officer strength, though a compensating increase is planned in the (unpaid) Special Constabulary to 20,000.[3] Once forces are fully reconciled to the notion of paying for their PCSOs, we may see more imaginative and more extensive partnership schemes in which PCSOs are supported proportionately from other sources that then make use of the PCSO in their own interests. This seems to us to have an inherent danger of 'commercializing' the PCSO and bridging rather uneasily the current divide between 'public' and 'private' policing. What this continues to mean too, is that you need to be aware of these currents, both political and economic, and note carefully what sources of funding underpin your work, particularly if some of those sources seem vulnerable to economic stringency.

References

C. Haynes, 'Authorities hike tax to cover CSO gap', *Police Review*, 16 March 2007, 7

Endnotes

1 See NPIA, *PCSO Review, Neighbourhood Policing Programme*, (July 2008 National Police Improvement Agency, available from <http://www. npia.police.uk/en/docs/PCSO>_Review_Final_Report.pdf>; accessed 1 May 2009)

2 Indeed, in mid-March 2007, nine police authorities sought an increase in the 'precept' to cover the costs of PCSOs in their respective forces (Haynes, 2007). These included Durham, Lancashire, Norfolk, Avon and Somerset, North Wales, Sussex, and the Metropolitan Police (which, with 3,184 PCSOs in March 2007 and about 3,800 currently, is the largest employer of PCSOs); average precept increases were around 6%. Northamptonshire Police employed 25 extra PCSOs, but paid for them, reportedly, through 'a net loss of 11 police officers and 28 other' police staff posts (Haynes, 2007).

3 Announced in the Special Constabulary National Strategy Conference, March 2008, see NPIA, (2008), *A National Strategy for the Special Constabulary* (2008, Strong Worldwide on behalf of the National Policing Improvement Agency), available from <http://www.npia.police.uk/en/docs/National_Strategy>_March_08.pdf>; accessed 10 March 2009

Chapter 1
Coming In

1.1 **So You Want to be a PCSO**

This chapter is largely addressed to the aspiring or enquiring person who is thinking about applying to be a PCSO—**it is not for the already serving officer**, who should press on now to Chapter 2 or whatever else in the Handbook is directly relevant.

1.1.1 **To the person thinking of applying to be a PCSO**

Welcome to the only chapter in the Handbook designed for you and you alone. This chapter will discuss with you your **motivation** for becoming a PCSO and then explore **what police forces are looking for**. This is followed by a detailed examination of the **recruitment** process and gives you the opportunity to consider how you should aim to perform in completing the **application**, attending **assessment**, and performing at **interview**.

1.1.2 **Other elements: ethics, diversity, fitness**

Then we look briefly at **ethics** and **diversity** (these are covered in much more detail later in the Handbook), and consider the **physical fitness** and physical standards required of a PCSO. We hope that, by the time you have worked your way to the end of the chapter, you will have a clear idea of what is expected of you and whether or not you can meet those expectations. If you can, good luck with the application and subsequent stages and, if you are successful, we hope that you enjoy the job. If you don't get in, perhaps you need to consider some life choices, re-applying, or ask yourself whether this job is really for you.

1.2 Why do You Want to be a PCSO?

We don't expect to be able to itemize all the individual motivations of the more than 15,000 people nationally who will apply to
become PCSOs this year. Only about 5,000 of you will get through
to selection and interview, and about 2,500 will survive to final
acceptance. This isn't intended to put you off, but to suggest that:

- It's not easy or automatic to become a PCSO
- Lots of people try, but only the really well-prepared make it
  through the selection process
- It's worth persisting because it is an important and
  challenging job
- Because lots of people want to do it, we have a high standard
  against which to measure you and your motivation
- The fact that you have bought this Handbook (you have,
  haven't you?) means that you must be **serious about applying**
- This Handbook is a **guide**, not a crib—it suggests what you
  should think about, but doesn't give you the answers
- If you really want to become a PCSO then this chapter will
  help to channel your determination into a strategy for success.

1.2.1 Motivation

Let's talk about motivation. Motivation, put simply, is what drives
or encourages you to do something.

When people are motivated, it means that their interest in an
activity or in what a group does is stimulated and they want to
join in. Watch people listening to their favourite music; if their
feet are tapping and bodies are swaying and they move with
the rhythm of the piece, they are probably showing an interest
in dancing. This is a very basic motivation and its behavioural
manifestations are clear and simple. Those motivations involving
career choices are often very complex, made up of overlapping
drives and desires, and may possibly involve sustaining all that
interest over a long period. Think about becoming a doctor or
a professional footballer or a pop idol or a classical musician. To
succeed in any of these callings you have to have two things: the
drive to achieve and the **potential** to achieve. We will talk about
potential later when we look at what police forces want from you,
the aspirant PCSO. We are here concerned with what drives you,
what makes *you* want to become a PCSO.

1.2.1.1 *Reasons to be a PCSO*

It may be that, at this stage, you are merely curious or you could be very motivated indeed and already starting to fill in the application form. Most of you will fall between the two extremes, but you may have a number of reasons for considering the job of PCSO.

What do you think:

(a) **motivates most people to become PCSOs** and

(b) **what motivates *you* to become a PCSO?**

The answers to (a) and (b) may not be the same. *Don't worry.* We all have different reasons for doing what we do and for entering the kinds of occupations which we choose. You need to be aware of **why people do things**, and most importantly (because you will be asked about it) **why you do things**. Look at the following list of statements. Do any of them match your own feelings and desires?

1.2.1.2 *Behavioural statements*

1. I really want to help people in my community because I can see what needs to be done to improve people's feelings of safety and civic pride, and I know that I am capable of helping them.
2. I want to make a difference; looking after people has always stimulated me, but I was never much good at biology and blood and things like that, so I didn't want to go into medicine!
3. I just like being with people and hearing what sort of things amuse them, infuriate them, interest them, and sadden them; I guess you could say that really I'm a people person.
4. What is really important to me is making people do what they should; there's so much sloppiness about with people not caring about the fabric of their community. I'd make them realize that there's a price to pay for ignoring the wishes of other people.
5. I have a strong sense of fairness and justice. I was bullied at school and I hated the helplessness that I felt then. I want to help the bullied to stand up and resist the intimidation or threat or whatever it might be, and to get some pride back, just as I had to.
6. Respect is what it's all about, isn't it? It's *not* to do with 'political' or any other kind of correctness; it's about understanding how people

feel when they're treated as lower or inferior just because they are different. I don't just mean being black or lesbian, I mean respect for old people and their wisdom and experience, or respect for the young and their pride and hope, and it's respect for people who maybe can't always say what they feel or express how confusing life is to them. And respect isn't hard!

7. I was mugged for my Ipod about six months ago and it made me feel sick and small, and very angry. There were three of them, and they just grabbed it and pushed me away. I felt like a little kid, but they were huge and threatening, and laughing at me. I couldn't get the player back from them, and they walked away. Didn't run. They weren't scared, *I* was. I've been a victim and I know what it is like. I know what it means to feel frustrated and, you know, unable to do anything. I can understand how others like me feel; and I want to do something to help them. Not cups of tea and sympathy but really, REALLY doing something to stop this violence and make people aware of the jungle out there and how they need to cope with it.

8. My dad was in the army and he always said that a uniform makes people respect you. Well, I didn't get much respect at school or at work because I'm a bit, well, timid sort of thing and I'm basically shy. I didn't join in things, was never a football or cricket player. Did cross-country though, so I'm pretty fit. So I thought if I had a uniform on, people would look at that, at the police badge, and treat me better.

9. I wanted to be a cop but failed the selection thing and so this is next best.

10. I've never really thought about it much; I mean, my family has all been involved in public service in one way or another—my mum is a teacher, just as I was, and my dad is a staff nurse at the hospital, and my brother is a police officer in the Met in London. So I was always going to do something in the public service, doing things *for* people, and never going to go to the City and making pots of money or anything like that. I've been in lots of organized groups for sport and for charity and I don't think this is going to be that different—whatever you do you have to work as part of a team and be part of a group—because that's how things get done.

11. My parents expected it and that's how it happened. I can remember when my father said that that this was the sort of thing a woman could do with pride and so help all of us and I thought yes, he's right! I *can* do this and it won't matter that I'm a woman and I *can* be independent and make up my own mind.

You may be able to identify your own feelings and motivations with some of these, though probably not all. These statements are all based on comments made by past candidates when asked why they wanted to become PCSOs, but we now need to dig under them, as it were, and think what each of the statements says about the person's ambition and motivation.

1.2.1.3 *I really want to help people in my community because I can see what needs to be done to improve people's feelings of safety and civic pride, and I know that I am capable of helping them*

This is an assertion that the person thinks s/he can make a difference in the community. Since this is fundamentally what a PCSO is about, the candidate is showing strong motivation, but s/he will have to go on and provide evidence that this is how s/he behaves and that the motivation is supported by clear achievements, perhaps through community projects in which s/he has participated, or some other tangible example of what s/he has done to help (or 'improve') the community. Simply making the assertion is not enough (because anyone can say that; the point is to prove it). The candidate would also be expected to explain what s/he means by *'feelings of safety'* and *'civic pride'*, because these are key concepts in understanding the police reassurance agenda and community/neighbourhood policing plans. Lastly, the candidate's comment that *'I am capable of helping them'* would be probed and s/he would be expected to be able to show some ways in which that capability had been demonstrated or evidenced. Perhaps you could think of examples?

1.2.1.4 *I want to make a difference; looking after people has always stimulated me, but I was never much good at biology and blood and things like that, so I didn't want to go into medicine!*

There is a mixture here of the positive and the negative in terms of motivation. The statement that the person wants to make a difference is positive and key to the effective role of the PCSO but s/he should expect to be asked precisely how s/he thought s/he could *'make a difference'*, and in what areas and why. In other words, a candidate should prepare specific evidence to support any general statement such as this. The person should also expect to be asked why *'looking after people'* has been stimulating and what experience s/he has of doing it. Some schools, for example, run activities where people in the community are aided by having small tasks done for them, such as shopping for the house-bound (of any age). Alternatively, candidates may have had a community support element in a previous or current job (teaching, local health administration, social work, and so on). A candidate would be expected to evidence that this *'looking after'* was more than a one-off; it should have happened consistently over a period. The comment on *biology*, *blood*, and *medicine* is refreshingly honest, but a bit negative in terms of motivation. Concentrate instead on the things which *do* stimulate and motivate you, except for brief illustrations of why you haven't done, or stayed with, other occupations. Besides, as a PCSO you may have to assist at accidents or road traffic collisions, or violent crime scenes where there may be an abundance of *'biology and blood'* and you'll have to cope as first on the scene, however squeamish you may feel. This is what we mean about thinking through the effect of your statements.

1.2.1.5 *I just like being with people and hearing what sort of things amuse them, infuriate them, interest them, and sadden them; I guess you could say that really I'm a people person*

This is actually a very coherent and endearing statement from someone who clearly enjoys being with people and being stimulated by their company. Being a good listener and enjoying meeting people are key attributes for the successful and effective PCSO, but you also need to bear in mind that the role is not simply a refuge for the inveterate gossip. Try to avoid using such flat clichés as *'people person'*, which makes you sound a bit artificial or derivative. That said, this person was trying to explain that being with and around people was highly stimulating and enjoyable. There is nothing wrong with that at all and you'll be a poor PCSO if you don't like people. But, and it is a big 'but', as a PCSO, you have to maintain a degree of separation and objectivity in your daily dealings with people. You must be able to stand back from problems and see ways through to solve them, rather than being immersed in the flood of emotions and feelings with which people in the community sometimes invest projects or difficulties. You may have to make judgements between disputing parties; you may have to seek compromises between factions in the community; and you may have to resolve disputes and arbitrate when tempers run high. Simply being a jolly type who enjoys a good chinwag isn't going to help you do any of these things. Indeed, your partiality for one side or another may actually get in the way of your being effective. This candidate would be questioned closely about matters like objectivity and dispassion, as well as about the evidence to support his or her social gregariousness.

1.2.1.6 *What is really important to me is making people do what they should; there's so much sloppiness about with people not caring about the fabric of their community. I'd make them realize that there's a price to pay for ignoring the wishes of other people*

This speaker is a bit of a 'control freak', it seems: *people don't know what the right thing is to do, so I'll make them do it.* This is a form of self-righteous self-importance which anyone wanting to be an effective PCSO (or, indeed, an effective police officer) should avoid at all costs. Of course, there are times when compulsion, or the reasonable use of force, is the only recourse, such as when you have to intervene to prevent an innocent person from being attacked or endangered. But as a PCSO you will spend much more time persuading, cajoling, and encouraging than insisting on the exercise of power. **There is no place in policing of any kind for the exercise of power for its own sake.** So, do not think for a moment that being a PCSO is about your ego. That said, the points about *people not caring for the fabric of their community* and that there is *a price to pay for ignoring the wishes of others* are very telling and may be fundamental to the problems which a community is experiencing. Some anti-social behaviour orders (**ASBOs**) are made precisely because people ignore the obligations and responsibilities that come with being a member of a community. *Making people realize . . .* is not within a PCSO's remit and, although a large part of your behavioural competence (which we explain later) is about respect for the origins, views, and life choices of others, you cannot compel it by force; only by example. This candidate, had s/he made it through to the interview stage, would have been asked in detail about cooperation, negotiation, team work, group identity, and tolerance. Much evidence would have been needed to offset the negative and rather compulsive character depicted here.

1.2.1.7 *I have a strong sense of fairness and justice. I was bullied at school and I hated the helplessness that I felt then. I want to help the bullied to stand up and resist the intimidation or threat or whatever it might be, and to get some pride back, just as I had to*

This comment expresses a series of strong emotions and it is clear that the injustice of being bullied, with its attendant feelings of helplessness and low self-worth, is still quite raw (we do not know how old this person is, nor how long ago this experience may have been). There is nothing amiss with having a well-defined sense of right and wrong, justice and injustice, fairness and unfairness—indeed, such feelings are probably part of the vocational complex which inclines people to public service in the first place—but we have to be careful that this doesn't become a kind of vigilantism. There is a danger that such a person might blind him or herself to the complexity of issues and reduce them to the simple level of good versus bad. Most of life actually consists of shades of grey, rather than this tempting simplicity, and a PCSO, in particular, is expected to be able to make objective judgements about situations and see ways through and around difficulties. This calls for clear vision, not the distorting lens of anger. Of course a PCSO must act decisively to confront bullying, and *'resist ... intimidation or threat'* but, as we see later with attitudes to 'hoodies' and groups of young people 'hanging about', the tendency of the angry and self-righteous can be to demonize others and to label them unfairly. We're all prone to do this at times, which is why the behavioural competences, which we will look at later, address such thinking quite specifically. Certainly, this candidate would have experienced some gentle but thorough probing about anger management, tolerance, respect for others, and clarity of judgement, as well as limits to PCSO powers.

1.2.1.8 *Respect is what it's all about, isn't it? It's not to do with 'political' or any other kind of correctness; it's about understanding how people feel when they're treated as lower or inferior just because they are different. I don't just mean being black or lesbian, I mean respect for old people and their wisdom and experience, or respect for the young and their pride and hope, and it's respect for people who maybe can't always say what they feel or express how confusing life is to them. And respect isn't hard!*

This person understands one of the central behavioural competences of a PCSO: *respect for others' difference*, whether deriving from race or sexual orientation, or gender, or age, or disability, or belief. There is a maturity in this statement which suggests that the speaker has practical experience on which to draw and a deep understanding of the '**respect agenda**' which was strongly espoused by Tony Blair towards the end of his term as Prime Minister (1997–2007). The 'respect agenda' was an attempt to celebrate difference rather than fear it, but it still has some way to go before it is fully effective. Some might disagree with the candidate's last comment, that *'respect isn't hard'*. For many it is very hard indeed, and you may encounter this in the police service as well as in many other walks of life. Nonetheless, many of us have difficulties in accepting that all have a right to be treated with dignity. This is not to say that you condone the crime, but that even the worst people, who do horrendous things to others, *should still be treated by you with respect*. At the interview stage, this candidate could expect persistent investigation into evidence of his or her approach to diversity and how he or she would respond to other people with closed minds or entrenched attitudes.

1.2.1.9 *I was mugged for my Ipod about six months ago and it made me feel sick and small, and very angry. There were three of them, and they just grabbed it and pushed me away. I felt like a little kid, but they were huge and threatening, and laughing at me. I couldn't get the player back from them, and they walked away. Didn't run. They weren't scared, I was. I've been a victim and I know what it is like. I know what it means to feel frustrated and, you know, unable to do anything. I can understand how others like me feel; and I want to do something to help them. Not cups of tea and sympathy but really, REALLY doing something to stop this violence and make people aware of the jungle out there and how they need to cope with it*

There is a distressing story here which informs the speaker's attitude to all victims, but especially with compassion for those who have been subject to a violent assault, because the speaker has experienced this and can empathize with victims. However, the same caveats apply to this series of statements as applied to the speaker who commented on having been bullied at school: care must be taken to avoid distorting one's view of the world. There is something a bit messianic about the speaker's desire to *'stop … violence and make people aware'*. Most people *are* aware of the daily jungle, where the predatory criminals stalk. They rely on people like PCSOs and police officers, as well as the huge 'private policing' industry, to keep them safe. Yet in another sense, the speaker is right to say that there is a responsibility on each of us to be aware of threats and dangers around us; no less from crime than from fire, flood, or other incipient hazards. As for the speaker's dismissive *'cups of tea and sympathy'*, in fact, being a PCSO is often about having a cup of tea and a chat with people, simply to reassure them that PCSOs are approachable and human. The speaker could expect to be challenged at interview (and even subsequently) on how much emotional baggage s/he is carrying as a result of being a victim of crime, lest it prejudices or inhibits the speaker's ability to be an effective PCSO. The speaker's behaviour would certainly be monitored when given training in self-protection, lest there was too much latent aggression which might lead to a form of vigilantism.

1.2.1.10 *My dad was in the army and he always said that a uniform makes people respect you. Well, I didn't get much respect at school or at work because I'm a bit, well, timid, sort of thing and I'm basically shy. I didn't join in things, was never a football or cricket player. Did cross-country though, so I'm pretty fit. So I thought if I had a uniform on, people would look at that, at the police badge, and treat me better*

This person has some real problems about self-esteem and confidence. There is nothing wrong with being shy (all of us experience situations or social events where we feel a bit inhibited) but there is a general expectation that PCSOs have a sturdy, independent confidence and resilience which does not rely on the very tenuous authority of a uniform. In a real sense, this person expects to be able to hide his or her inadequacies behind a badge, and **it won't do.** There are plenty of people in the community who will have little or no respect for a uniform, unless the wearer of it has something of his or her own to bring to the equation. At the same time, there are suggestions here that s/he is a bit of a loner (not a team player) and there is a central illogicality in supposing that a uniform supplies what is lacking in character or experience. The speaker could expect some close questioning on his or her motives to become a PCSO and some detailed probing on 'teamworking'.

1.2.1.11 *I wanted to be a cop but failed the selection thing and so this is next best*

There is a blunt honesty about this comment which is rather endearing, and indeed, as many as 40% of those applying to become PCSOs want to go on to become police officers. However, there is a bit more to being a PCSO than second-best to being a police officer. This person could expect to be asked a number of questions about his or her perceptions of the differences between being a PCSO and being a police officer, and some probing behind the bluntness of (and lack of detail in) the statement itself. In particular, the speaker could expect to be asked about the PCSO role and how much s/he understands about communities, patrol, intervention, and communication. There is another point: what people say on joining and what they say six or eighteen months later, can be quite different. We see this with new police joiners, many of whom want to drive fast cars with two-tones and blue strobes ('lights and music'). Within their first year, because of their exposure to other kinds of police work, the same joiners express preferences for detection work and more specialist areas of policing. The same may be true of PCSOs who express a desire to become police officers (which, *at best*, will be eighteen months to two years after joining as PCSOs). It is likely that the enjoyment of the PCSO job itself will satisfy many, whilst others (about 10%) will have left policing altogether. In our experience (and also using the Special constabulary as a rough guide) fewer than 15% of those who join as PCSOs will end up as police officers within five years.

1.2.1.12 *I've never really thought about it much; I mean, my family has all been involved in public service in one way or another—my mum is a teacher, just as I was, and my dad is a staff nurse at the hospital, and my brother is a police officer in the Met in London. So I was always going to do something in the public service, doing things for people, and never going to go to the City and make pots of money or anything like that. I've been in lots of organized groups for sport and for charity and I don't think this is going to be that different—whatever you do you have to work as part of a team and be part of a group—because that's how things get done*

Many PCSOs used to be teachers, and this speaker is evidently part of that growing tradition. There is more; this person is imbued with the spirit of public service (with education, health, and the police service as influencing factors) and has acquired experience of working within a community through sport and charity events. The behavioural competency of 'teamworking' (in contrast to the speaker before last) is clearly strong and s/he understands the power of individuals doing things together. There is a strength and a maturity about this speaker which suggests that s/he understands the nature of the work. Now, that is not the same as having a clear motivation, and the fact that the speaker admits to not having '*thought about it much*' might lead to some digging about motive and drive rather than understanding or experience. The police service quite clearly does want candidates for PCSO roles to have thought carefully about why they want to do the job and what makes them interested in police activity. This speaker could merely be following a family 'tradition' of service without much in the way of self-analysis or reflection. This would not debar the speaker from being a credible candidate as a PCSO, but acceptance and the consequent investment in training and operational deployment by a police force requires something more tangible than family tradition. The interview team would explore the candidate's experiences and evidence to ensure that the level of commitment was genuine and the drive both sustained and individual.

1.2.1.13 *My parents expected it and that's how it happened. I can remember when my father said that he thought that this was the sort of thing a woman could do with pride and so help all of us and I thought yes, he's right! I can do this and it won't matter that I'm a woman and I can be independent and make up my own mind*

This speaker seems to have an expectation of the role of PCSO as some sort of liberating, emancipating activity in the performance of which she expects to blossom as a person. It could be the case that she has unreal expectations of the nature of the work, or it could be that she is projecting on to the role her own hopes and ambitions. Either way, this could be disappointing for her. Alternatively, her father's comment that being a PCSO is '*the sort of thing a woman could do*' is true enough, but there is implicit in the father's comment an assumption that there is 'women's work' and there are other kinds of work, which might entail a sexism for which there is no place in the policing family. A PCSO is a PCSO: the officer may be a woman or a man, there is no substantive difference. It is the person's **qualities and skills** which matter, not the gender (or any other discrimination). But it may be that we are reading too much into what could be a simple statement of surprised pleasure in the woman's discovery that this seems to be a job which she could do and in which she could assert her pride and independence. If that is the correct interpretation, well and good. However, the speaker would have to be prepared for some detailed investigation at interview and in other situations, where her motivations and drive in wanting to become a PCSO will be followed up. Becoming a PCSO is not something which should be embarked on lightly, certainly never just because one's parents '*expected it and that's how it happened*'.

1.2.2 Summary analysis

We hope that you can understand from our analysis of the 11 motivational (behavioural) statements, which are pretty typical of those who apply to become PCSOs, that candidates' assertions are questioned and their motives are explored. None of us has a single unblemished motive for doing anything; motives are always a messy mixture of conceits, desires, ambitions, hopes, and wish fulfilment, bound up with our relative understanding of the activity itself and its everyday reality. This mixture is always worth examining and teasing apart, so that the most dominant motives can be detected and assessed. We go into this in more detail later, but for the moment you can assume that your motives to become a PCSO will be looked at by assessors and you should prepare yourself thoroughly for the questions which will ensue. **Why do you want to become a PCSO?** is a perfectly reasonable place to start.

1.3 **What Police Forces are Looking For**

You should have some sense of what police forces are looking for in their PCSOs from the analysis and discussion in the previous section. Also, you should have a look at Chapter 4 where we discuss the competences which PCSOs are expected to attain in the National Occupational Standards (NOS) within their first year of service, and against which they are assessed thereafter. You will see the important behavioural competences examined there too (see 4.15 below).

1.3.1 Behavioural competences

You should become well used to these, because large parts of the recruitment process are based on six behavioural competences (see 1.3.1.1 below). Each competence is tested twice during the assessment day's syndicate work (see 1.4.7 below), but it is important for you to understand that you are being assessed as a **potential** PCSO, not as one already in service.

1.3.1.1 *Six behavioural competences*

These are the six behavioural competences, now used across all 43 police forces, but you should note that No 4, **Community and Customer Focus**, is *not* tested in the national selection process (because it is unfair to expect those not yet in the job of PCSO to understand and participate in the delivery of neighbourhood policing plans, among other things):

Six Behavioural Competences

1. **Resilience**
2. **Effective Communication**
3. **Respect for Race and Diversity**
4. **Community and Customer Focus**
5. **Personal Responsibility**
6. **Teamworking**

We shall examine these in some detail in a moment, but you should know now that you will continue to be assessed against all six of these behavioural competences for the rest of your service: they are central to your performance as a PCSO and the bedrock of all police interactions with other people (including your own colleagues in the Force). Firstly though, let's define what the terms mean as far as the competences are concerned.

1.3.1.2 *Definitions of the behavioural competences*

Resilience: Can persist with a plan of action, even if circumstances and situations are difficult; not cast down by lack of success, persistent, dogged, able to withstand disappointment, can change to fit necessary circumstances, flexible under pressure.

Effective Communication: Can communicate instructions, decisions, requirements and needs clearly; has a good vocabulary and can adapt language to circumstances, can speak simply without being patronising, understands how people respond to authority and can adapt to fit the needs of the person or the larger audience; can write clearly and coherently and draft reports, plans and strategies appropriately.

Respect for Race and Diversity: Understands other people's points of view and takes those views into account when responding to them; treating all people, irrespective of their appearance, or what they may have done, with dignity and respect all the time, whatever the situation or circumstance.

Community and Customer Focus: Can see things from the point of view of those who are policed as well as from the point of view of those who do the policing [empathy]; encourages others to empathize, building a good understanding and relationships with all parts of the community that is served.

(Adapted from the original and reproduced with kinc permission of Skills for Justice.)

Personal Responsibility: Makes things happen because of taking responsibility and achieves tangible results; shows motivation to succeed, is conscientious and committed to the role and to making a difference in the community; has a high degree of integrity in all actions and takes personal responsibility for own actions seriously, sorting out any problems that develop; focused on achieving outcomes which assist the community; always willing to learn new things, develop personal skills and knowledge; leads by example.

Teamworking: Works effectively as a team member, supporting colleagues and sharing burdens fairly; not shirking the humdrum or routine tasks, not one to bask in self-glory, a team player, where collective effort always exceeds the lone attempt; a keenly participative member of a team or group, quick to praise others, slow to blame; eager to share.

If you are accepted as a PCSO, these behavioural competences will form part of your **continuing professional development** (called CPD for short), when each competence is assessed at a particular level. You need not be concerned about that now, but the detail is at 4.15 below if you want to understand what is involved. For the rest of this section, we shall look in more detail at the basic competences needed with the five behaviours (remember, we are excluding **Community and Customer Focus** for the time being) and suggest to you how you might evidence your potential in achieving them, as well as suggesting what other characteristics your assessors will be looking for.

1.3.1.3 *Positive and negative behaviours*

Each of these behaviours has **positive indicators** and **negative indicators**. The positive represents the sorts of things which police forces want to see, and the negative the sorts of things which they don't want to see. Study them carefully.

1.3.2 Resilience

You are expected to attain a Category B standard in this competence. The **positive indicators** include dealing confidently with members of the public, feeling comfortable with working alone (without direct, constant supervision), being aware of and dealing with personal stress, but able to accept both criticism and praise. It is also expected that you will exclude your emotions from disputes and disagreements, and be patient in dealing with people who make complaints, although you can say 'no' firmly, when necessary. Above all, you take a 'rational and consistent approach to work'.

Commentary

1.3.2.1 *Work–life balance*

What this means in effect is that you are a self-starter and can be relied on not to get emotionally hung up on issues. Work is important to you but not the be-all and end-all of life: having this in balance means that you do indeed have a rational and consistent regard for your duties.

Negative behaviours

By contrast, the **negative behaviours** involve you not seeing the wood for the trees, where you get upset easily; panic when you confront problems; and need constant reassurance, support, and the comfort of a supervisor in the offing. This can lead you to react inappropriately when faced with rude or abusive and foul-mouthed people, and your way of dealing with this can be aggressive. You moan a lot and give in when pressured. You spend a lot of time worrying about making mistakes which leads you to become risk-averse.

Commentary

You will not be much use as a PCSO if you cannot quietly and effectively get on with the job, referring upwards only when you cannot make that level of decision yourself. The kind of person described negatively here is a liability, always needing a supervisor as a kind of 'comfort blanket' and never making and standing by his or her own decision. Should you show these characteristics at assessment or during your probationary period of service, it is probable that you are not suited to being a PCSO. We describe elsewhere the salient characteristic of resilience in a PCSO is a '*sturdy imperturbability*', where very little can deflect you or put you off.

1.3.3 **Effective communication**

You are expected to attain a Category C standard in this behaviour. The **positives** include the ability and skill to speak clearly and concisely, without hiding behind jargon. You make sure that all your written and spoken communication is well constructed and understood, and you put your points across in a friendly and approachable way, making sure of your facts and trying to keep people's interest. You listen well and pay attention to what others are saying and you clarify issues through apt questions.

Commentary

1.3.3.1 *Positive communication*

You should refer to any of the excellent books on the market on how to write English to help you communicate clearly in writing, if you are not already confident that you can do so adequately. Refer to the box at 1.4.8.2 below for the principles. Speech is less formal but still needs a structure and clarity to ensure that people understand you precisely. This means that you know what words mean, and what ambiguity entails; you know how to select words that people won't feel threatened by, or simply not understand. You do not fall into the trap of using acronyms (abbreviated terms which become words in their own right, like ACPO) to non-police audiences.

The **negative behaviours** are the polar opposites of engagement and clarity. This involves speaking without thinking; not understanding (or caring) about the needs of your audience; rambling, unstructured, diffuse, ambiguous, and inappropriate writing and speaking; ducking difficult questions; and being a poor listener. The most negative behaviour of all is to assume that people understand you without checking to see if they do.

1.3.4 **Respect for race and diversity**

You are expected to attain a Category A standard in this behaviour. We have already looked at some of the issues contained in this misleadingly mild title, and we refer you to 4.15.2 below for fuller discussions and analyses of what this behaviour entails. We shall simply summarize here what the positives and negatives are, with brief commentaries. *Remember that not attaining the desired standard in this behaviour may result in your failure to be accepted into the police family, no matter what your other attainments or grades.* The police service takes positive behaviours in this subject very seriously indeed.

1.3.4.1 *Other points of view*

Positive behaviours include being able to see things from others' perspectives and understanding that there may be different views of the same thing, without threatening your independence of thought. Similarly, you will be polite, tolerant, and patient with people inside and outside the police force, treating everyone with respect and according them dignity, especially when resolving disputes or dealing with people who feel vulnerable. You acknowledge and respect a broad spectrum of social and cultural customs, beliefs, and values within the law and you challenge inappropriate behaviour vigorously. The key words are sensitivity and respect in this behaviour, perhaps particularly when others' values clash with your own.

Commentary

1.3.4.2 *Strong values*

These strong values underpin the essence of behaviour in the police family, and especially so for you, the PCSO, with your daily contact with people in front-line neighbourhood policing. Your positive role model in showing respect and tolerance may impact on the behaviour of others.

Negative behaviours need spelling out, perhaps, so that you understand what actions and attitudes should be avoided. Such behaviours would ignore the feelings of others and deride or belittle their beliefs, customs, and cultures, and would be shown in such actions as not encouraging people to talk about what concerns them, being tactless, dismissive, or impatient with different points of view or attitudes, leading you to overemphasize power and control in inappropriate ways. This includes using humour inappropriately and showing bias or prejudice when dealing with people who are not like you.

Commentary

Negatives in race and diversity could be dismissal offences

We have commented elsewhere in this Handbook that negative behaviours in respect for race and diversity could be dismissal offences. Should you exhibit any such behaviours at the assessment process, you will not be accepted into the police service. If you are serving, you may very well be dismissed. Some of these negatives are actually against the law (racism, sexism, homophobia, discrimination on any of the grounds of race, belief, age, disability, gender, or sexual orientation); which, we should remind you, you are pledged to uphold. We make no apology then, for continuous reference to these standards throughout the Handbook. It is a message that you must take on board, leading you to act positively if you are to serve the community as a PCSO.

1.3.5 **Personal responsibility: doing a good job without supervision**

You are expected to attain Category B in this behaviour. The **positive behaviours** in this competence have to do with your willingness to take responsibility for what you do and that, by extension, you can be trusted to get on with doing a good job without close supervision. You can be relied on to get results in a sensitive, determined, and effective way, mindful of the feelings of others but focused on what you need to do. You keep promises, you don't let people down, you are conscientious, taking pride in your work, and you follow things through without having to be asked to do so. You are open, honest, and genuine, standing up for what is right and not being swayed by expediency or short-term gains at the expense of your integrity.

Commentary

1.3.5.1 *Behaving ethically and responsibly*

This is about behaving ethically and responsibly, showing others that you can be trusted and relied on; you deliver what is needed and go the extra mile to ensure that what is needed is what happens. To do this well, you need to be aware of your own strengths and weaknesses and know when you need the help of others and when you can go ahead on your own. Much of this has to do with confidence and a blend of experience in the role, though you will be expected to deliver on this competence as soon as you join.

1.3.5.2 *Shirking personal responsibility*

Negative behaviours are found in people who are frightened or lazy and who don't want to accept that they are in charge of their own lives, work, and results. Such people ignore issues, hoping that they will go away, or duck issues, hoping someone else will cope, and they put in the minimum effort to get by. They are often cynical, give up easily, and have poor motivation or desire to learn.

Commentary

Showing behaviours of this kind during the recruitment process will probably result in your being screened out early. However, should you make it through selection and begin to exhibit these traits when you are in training or on patrol, you can expect to be challenged and your behaviours brought to your attention quickly and strongly. Persistence in refusing to take personal responsibility will almost certainly result in you being assessed as incapable of being an effective and efficient PCSO.

1.3.6 Team working: supporting each other and pulling together

You are expected to attain a Category C standard in this behaviour. Team working is a core activity in the work of a PCSO. For all that you take personal responsibility for what you do and for all that you are capable of working alone, it is with and through colleagues, and with and through partnerships, that you really get results. The **positive behaviours** are that you actively support the team and individuals within it to achieve the objectives and that in doing so you are cooperative and friendly with others, whom you support. You are always willing to help others, but not afraid to ask for help yourself, and you develop mutual trust and confidence in those with whom you work. You willingly take on unpopular or routine tasks and you take pride in any of the teams of which you are a member.

Commentary

1.3.6.1 *The importance of teamwork to the PCSO*

This is another behaviour by which the success of the concept of PCSOs, and indeed of neighbourhood policing, stands or falls. Results are obtained through mutual and consensual effort, and this means that the effective PCSO is a member of many different teams, both inside and outside the police, and within communities and within partnerships working with those communities.

1.3.6.2 *Being selfish and in it for yourself destroys teamwork*

The **negative behaviours** show high degrees of selfishness and egotism, such as the individual who takes credit for success without acknowledging what others did to help. Such people only do the jobs which are interesting or which will bring them to notice and they have a personal agenda for success which ignores or bypasses teamwork and joint efforts. Such people show very little interest in working with others and are always scarce when a difficult or unpopular job is to be done.

Commentary

These behaviours disrupt teams and made joint ventures fail. The cynicism with which the person promotes his or her own interests is also a factor in destroying the best of cooperative intentions. Such behaviours are often hard to detect, particularly by a supervisor who may not spend prolonged periods with team members, but over time, such selfishness will emerge. If properly evidenced, such behaviours can result in disciplinary actions and in extreme cases, dismissal. It is much better not to employ such people in the first place, hence the importance of detecting any such behaviour at the initial assessment stages.

1.3.7 Summary

These are not the only characteristics that police forces will look for in those who want to become PCSOs, but they are the principal indicators and, between them, they capture many of the manifestations of positive behaviour that forces will look for. The **Community and Customer Focus** behaviours are expected to develop during your initial period of training and in your job performance, and you emphatically will be assessed on your positive achievements here. We talk about the behavioural competences at greater length in Chapter 4 (at 4.15 below) but our purpose in covering the same ground now (though not in precisely the same way) is to ensure that all material relevant to those applying to become PCSOs is available in the same place. Now it is time to look more closely at the recruitment process itself.

1.4 Applying to Join: the Recruitment Process

[We are grateful to the Home Office and the Office of Public Service Information (OPSI) for permission to quote from recruitment documents and summaries of assessments. None of those involved necessarily accepts our commentary.]

As a result of your expressing interest in becoming a PCSO, you will receive a pack[1] through the post (you cannot yet access on-line) that contains:

• A printed *Guide to becoming a Police Community Support Officer*
• An application form to become a PCSO
• An A4 sized envelope pre-addressed to the reception centre for national applications in Bristol
• A candidate registration form
• A printed sheet informing you about assessment centres.

1.4.1 Guide to becoming a Police Community Support Officer

The important and obvious first point to make is that you must read the *Guide* before starting to fill in the application, because the *Guide* explains what a PCSO does. The application booklet specifically requires you to provide examples of how you meet some of the competences, which will enable assessors to judge whether you are likely to have the skills and qualities to be 'an effective PCSO'.

1.4.1.1 *Thinking about your application: conveying 'the true you'*

Another thing that the *Guide* tells you is that if you are unsuccessful in your application, you cannot apply again within six months. This makes it all the more important that your application is carefully thought out and considered before you send it in. It would be a pity if your haste and carelessness resulted in your application being refused when a little forethought and planning would have got you through. This is especially the case, as we shall see in a moment, when you are asked for examples of how you meet a competence. If your examples are poorly considered (they do not illustrate how you performed competently) and weakly expressed, you will not be helping yourself; whereas examples which clearly illustrate how you meet the competence will be effective indicators of your likely performance as a PCSO. It follows that better and more relevant examples mean that you are more likely to be invited to the assessment process.

1.4.2 The recruitment process

The **recruitment process** itself is in three parts:

1. **Applying to be considered as a PCSO**
2. **Attending an assessment centre (so a successful application)**
3. **Passing medical, security, and reference checks (so the assessment was successful).**

(Each of these stages has to be passed before you will be accepted by a police force as a PCSO.)

The *Guide* is quite clear from the outset, indicating that PCSOs have to have special qualities and asking the following questions:

- How would you deal with a group of binge drinkers dancing in the street?
- What would you do to win the trust of housing estate residents scared to give evidence about a violent assault?
- How would you handle kids using a shopping centre as an indoor cycle speedway?
- What would you do to rebuild the confidence of an elderly couple who were burgled last week?[2]

1.4.2.1 *The nature of a PCSO's work*

We have quoted these examples in full, partly because they are eminently practical, but partly also because they go to the heart of a PCSO's work. You will not always be dealing with crimes, but sometimes you will be dealing with conditions that occur as a result of crimes, or actions and events which may precede a crime. For example, using the example above, the binge drinkers could quickly turn violent and cause damage or assault someone. The children cycling could crash through a shop window or knock someone down. A member of the public could try to restrain the children and be injured, or criminal damage could be caused when the children try to turn movable items in the shopping centre into ramps and obstacles. The other two examples are consequences in the wake of possibly serious crimes.

The *Guide* then tells you:

> **You can't arrest anyone. You've got no handcuffs, no baton. All you've got is you. It's down to your ability to get on with some of the most challenging people in some of the most difficult situations. The way you win cooperation is through good-humoured persuasion.**

It is actually difficult to imagine a more succinct and persuasive description of a PCSO's role than this, nor one in which the range of skills and qualities which a PCSO must have is so clearly and practically illustrated.

1.4.2.2 *Structure of the application form*

The application form is actually a booklet, bound in dark blue paper with lighter blue templates inside. It consists of five sections:

(1) **About you**
(2) **About your employment**
(3) **About your education and skills**

(4) **Competency assessment**

(5) **Declaration.**

Demonstrating all the competences

There is no presumption in section 2 that people cannot apply who have not worked (such as school leavers) but it is unlikely that all such candidates would have the life skills needed to be a PCSO. Candidates must be able to demonstrate potential for *all* the competences required of a PCSO, throughout the whole assessment process. That said, Thames Valley Police employed two 16-year-old PCSOs in 2007, commenting in the face of considerable media criticism that 'if you've got the skills, you can do the job'. One or two other police forces have employed 17-year-old PCSOs, but such occasions are rare. The majority of PCSOs are mature people with extensive life experience.[3]

1.4.3 Section1: about you

Personal information

The usual requirements for your full name, current postal address, and so on head this section, with the additional request for your National Insurance number (so make a note of it in advance). You must list all surnames (family names) by which you have been known because of the security and vetting checks that will be employed to ensure that you are (a) who you say you are, (b) that you have no serious criminal convictions (see below) and (c) that you are not associated with any criminal in such a way as to inhibit your proper function as a PCSO. You are asked to put down the name of the police force that you want to join; the recruitment process is handled nationally, so it is important that you know where you want to be located. Your **nationality** is also a factor, or rather, restrictions around your right to residence in the UK are factors. If you can live in the UK free of restrictions then you can apply to become a PCSO, so your nationality is not actually an issue on its own. That said, your **written and spoken English** must be of an acceptable standard (ESOL level 5 for example) so that you could function effectively as a PCSO in England and Wales. If you come from the Commonwealth or if you are a foreign national, you will have to supply proof that your **residence in the UK is unrestricted**—for example you would not be eligible if you are only allowed to reside here as a student or if your work permit is valid only for six months. Foreign nationals or Commonwealth citizens need to take passports with them if called for assessment.

1.4.3.1 *Have you been in trouble with the law?*

There follows a section on **convictions and cautions** and it is important that we discuss what this is about. You are asked if you have ever been convicted for any offence or if you have had a formal caution by the police for any offence, or if any court has ever 'bound you over'. This category includes traffic offences and any cautions you may have had as a juvenile, or any appearances before a court martial if you have served in the Armed Forces.

1.4.3.2 *Declaring convictions, cautions, fixed penalty notices, and so on*

Having a conviction or a caution does not mean that you are automatically debarred from becoming a PCSO. It will depend on the circumstances of the offence and the nature of the offence. If, for example, you had a caution ten years ago at the age of 17 for under-age drinking, it *probably* will not disbar you, provided that the offence was not aggravated (made worse) by criminal damage or assault, or some other offence. Speeding offences, fixed penalties, and fines for disorder may also be discounted or regarded with a tolerant eye after a sufficient time has elapsed without re-offending.[4] The really important point is that **you must declare on the application form any such convictions or cautions**. If you do not, your application will be rejected when any undeclared offences come to light—as they surely will. Equally, if there is a summons against you at the time of application or if you are facing any charge, you must declare it (as you must any 'spent convictions' under the **Rehabilitation of Offenders Act 1974**). Police records are extensively searched for applicants for the police family (in any capacity) and these may include details that you might have thought were no longer held, including 'spent' convictions. *Failure to disclose will lead automatically to your rejection as a candidate.* If in doubt, include the details and let the police decide whether they are relevant or not. Just to keep this in context, you should note that research in 2008 under the provisions of the Freedom of Information Act by Chris Huhne, Liberal Democrat Party's Home Affairs spokesperson, revealed that there are more than a thousand police officers serving in England and Wales who have a criminal record. 77 serving police officers appear to have convictions for violent offences and 96 have convictions for dishonesty; whilst 210 officers have been dismissed or required to resign in the years 2003 to 2008 as a result of other criminal convictions. One thousand police officers represent 0.7 of a percent of the police service.[5]

1.4.3.3 *Checks are also made on your family*

You should know that **the search doesn't stop with you**: there will be criminal record checks of members of your close family to find out if there are any criminal convictions or cautions lodged against any of them, as in Figure 1 below. The application booklet specifically asks you to tell your family that this will happen. Under the **Data Protection Act 1998**, *the police can't disclose to you the results of enquiries into a third person*—even if the person concerned is your partner or your child. The last point to be made is that if you have had a conviction for a serious offence, such as a crime of violence, or dishonesty, no matter when it was, you are unlikely to be accepted in any capacity in the police.

In summary, the process of declaration looks like this:

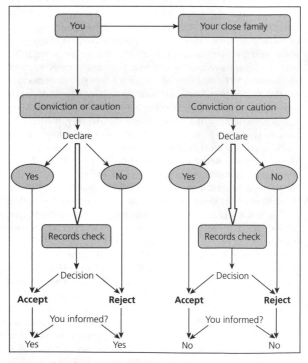

Figure 1: Flow diagram of declaration of convictions or cautions

1.4.3.4 *Other parts: health, business interests, finances*

The remainder of the sections to be completed concern your health (including days absent from work), your business interests, especially whether there might be a clash of interests between your new job as a PCSO and your partner's involvement in running a pub or a gaming house (gambling) for example, together with a summary of your financial position. This last is of interest. In recent years, with the availability of credit made easier, some people have got into considerable debt. By this we don't mean standard mortgages, student loans or other small-scale debts on credit cards or car finance, but really large debts such as the £374,000 gambling debt declared by one applicant in the North-East or the 27 credit cards owned by another PCSO applicant in southern England, the *average* debt on each of which was £16,857. This applicant's total debt in unsecured loans exceeded half a million pounds. Such indebtedness would almost certainly disbar you from acceptance as a PCSO, especially since the size of the debt might render you vulnerable to corrupt approaches by criminals. However, each case would be judged on its merits. Personal debt is likely to have increased as a result of the economic recession and this will be taken into account when applicants are assessed, but massive debts on the scale indicated above are nonetheless likely to disbar such candidates from acceptance as PCSOs.

1.4.3.5 *'Identifying particulars' of your family members*

The final part of section 1 about yourself is a full-page table requesting the full names, dates and places of birth, and addresses of all members of your immediate family. The **immediate or close family** includes:

- **Your mother**
- **Father**
- **Stepfather or stepmother**
- **Mother's or father's partner**
- **Brother(s) and sister(s)—full, half or step**
- **Your spouse or partner**
- **Your spouse's or partner's parents or step-parents**
- **Your children (over 10 years)**
- **Your partner's children (over 10 years)**
- **Any grandchildren or step-grandchildren (over the age of 10)**
- **Any other adults living at your address.**

If you are to have this information to hand when you fill in your application booklet, then it does mean that you have to prepare yourself in advance and pretty thoroughly. If you come from an extended family, it may take several days of enquiries to amass all the necessary details.[6] A last point on the financial side: if you have any outstanding **county court judgments** against you or if you have been registered **bankrupt** (and your debts in bankruptcy have not been discharged) your application is likely to be rejected. Credit references are examined, as are any court records around your solvency, but if debts have been discharged together with any county court judgments, you may be considered after three years.

1.4.4 Section 2: about your employment

This is the record of the jobs you have done, or service you have had if in HM Forces, over the last ten years, including any period of unemployment or part-time work as well as full-time employment. If you are currently serving in HM Forces, your application will only be considered if you are within 12 months of release or discharge. Incidentally, it will be up to your Chief Constable to decide if you remain on the Reserve List following discharge.

1.4.4.1 *Previous employment details*

What the police need to know about your employment is what sort of job it was and what position you held, who your employer was and the address of the organization or company for which you worked, and the period of your employment. You will also be asked to provide reasons why you left an employer. You will need to provide a contact name at the company or organization, so that the police can verify the details that you provide, and ascertain that your employment there was unblemished. The only other characteristic of this straightforward provision of detail is that the process works in reverse order; in other words you put your most recent or current employment first and work backwards from there.

1.4.4.2 *References: the importance of using people who know you well*

You will also be asked to provide contact details, including physical addresses, for two **referees**, together with the position held by the individual referee and an indication of whether the referee can be approached immediately or not. (Nothing sinister in delay: it would only be courtesy to ask someone if s/he would provide you with a reference.) Please note that **a reference is not a testimonial**, nor is it a mere record of work. It is a statement by someone who knew, or knows, you and who can attest to your attributes, skills, probity (honesty), and that you did indeed work in the role you described at the place referred to for the times stated. (If this intense desire to prove facts bothers you, you should think of another career choice. Attention to detail, and not taking statements on trust but seeking to corroborate them, are highly characteristic of police work.) One of your referees can be a 'character' referee if need be (if, for example, you have not worked anywhere long enough to have more than one referee), but it is preferable to provide two who can talk about you as an employee. This is important in respect of the way that the police will perceive you as a potential employee, of course. The health declaration in Part 1 is also relevant here, since a poor attendance record *might* indicate unreliability. Referees are usually asked to confirm your diligent attendance at work. Finally, you will be asked to enter details of any service with HM Forces or in any previous capacity with a police force (for example as a Special constable, a police cadet, or as a police staff employee). All this will be very familiar to those who have experience of applying for jobs in any sector. Do make a mental note to consider suitable referees— don't use someone who detested you, for example, nor the name of your best friend, who may not know you in a work environment. It is conventional to use a previous line manager, tutor, or commanding officer, but in addition, anyone who has known you in a professional or social capacity might do; such as your local charity organizer or sports club chairperson.

1.4.5 Section 3: about your education and skills

The difference between the education and skills is simple, despite what some academics will tell you: **educational qualifications** are usually about **knowledge**, like GCSE Geography, whilst **skills** are about what you can do, such as creating Powerpoint slideshows on a computer. First, you are asked for a list of the school or colleges, universities, or other institutions that you have attended in reverse date order (put the most recent first). Using the same principle, you are then asked to give your most recent educational qualifications first and then work backwards to your first (oldest). You will be asked for all of your qualifications, including **vocational** (such as NVQs) and **professional** (such as CIPD or FCA), with dates and details of any examinations taken or about to be taken, short courses, in-house training, or any other relevant educational attainment (such as Grade 6 in playing a musical instrument).

1.4.5.1 *Skills, membership of civic bodies, charities, local groups*

In the part of the application form which follows, you are asked to itemize your skills and to provide details of any voluntary or community activities in which you have been involved. Skills might include using a computer effectively (as noted above), or driving skills (you will be expected to be able to drive), cycling proficiency, and so on, together with any **membership of organizations** such as Guides or Scouts, church or faith groups, Army Cadets, Air Training Corps, Sea Cadets, the Duke of Edinburgh's Award Scheme, charities like Help the Aged or Shelter, or local community projects and such like, especially if you have had an organizational role or command role in any of these. If you have a **knowledge of languages**, then this should also be shown— not just your educational attainments such as GCSE German, but any periods of residence in the country and continuous learning, which would show that you have a grasp of idiom and contemporary speech, for example. It is clearly helpful for a PCSO to have some acquaintance with a language used by minority groups in the community and this can cover a wide range of languages from Urdu and Punjabi to Mandarin or Cantonese Chinese.

1.4.6 **Section 4: competency assessment**

We referred to this earlier. It is without doubt the most important part of your whole application because this will show to assessors whether or not you may have the potential to become an effective PCSO. Indeed, your performance here will determine whether or not you are invited to Part 2 of the recruitment process, the assessment sessions (see 1.3.1, above). So read the following with care— we are providing you with pointers and suggestions, not model answers. Start thinking about experiences you have had which will help to illustrate your competences.

1.4.6.1 *'Worked' examples*

You will be asked to give **three** detailed examples from your recent (say, last three years') experience. The assessors are looking for the kinds of behaviours that both experience and research have shown to be integral to the role of a PCSO. Such competences are obvious if you stop and think about it: for example, being able to persuade somebody to do something differently is a generic competence that you will use on a daily basis as a PCSO. It calls for tact, a persuasive tongue, an understanding of logic, and the need to appeal to people's sense of belonging to a group or community. *What is really central to success in answering these kinds of question is that you use very specific examples and explain clearly what part you personally played and how you managed yourself to change things or achieve a desired outcome.* If you are woolly or vague, you will be marked down and could fail altogether. Each of the three main questions has a series of prompt questions; make sure you answer these specifically as you go. Above all, use examples from your personal experience (at work, or from your social, domestic, or leisure life, or from your educational experience) which you found challenging or difficult and which show you to have had a bit of a struggle to get the result you wanted. The more challenging the circumstance you describe, and therefore the more difficult to get a 'good result', the higher it will be marked. Lastly, write clearly in fluent English, avoiding slang or jargon (specialized words) and use complete sentences. As you are reminded by the notes at the back of the application booklet:

> **Remember that this is a formal application for an important and responsible job.**

The section then goes on to ask you about your motivation (discussed at length in 1.2 above), what you think the job will entail, and what you have done already to prepare yourself for it (such as speaking to existing PCSOs or visiting your local police station, reading through the literature on the PCSO role, and so on). Enough of exhortation (*telling you what to do*); let's look at the kinds of question you will be asked.

1.4.6.2 *Situation 1: competence is assessed against the service which PCSOs give to the public through problem solving*

You are asked to:

> Recall a situation when you had to deal with someone who was unhappy with the service [s/he] had been given or the way [s/he] had been treated, and you helped [him or her] to resolve [the] problem.

1.4.6.3 *Showing what you did to solve someone's problem*

Remember that your example has to show *what you did, and how you personally contributed to solving the person's problem*. If you imagine that you may have been working in a shop when someone came to complain about something they bought which did not work, your prompt referring of the complainant to a supervisor is not a good illustration of your ability to solve problems. It would be far better in such an example to show what *you* did proactively to replace the damaged or broken object or that you obtained expert advice on the operation of the equipment and helped the complainant to understand what s/he should do to prevent the problem recurring. In acting like this, you are taking the lead in solving the problem and demonstrating your resourcefulness. Perhaps now you can see how the assessors will examine your examples carefully in order to find evidence of your potential competence as a PCSO. However, if you choose a 'service' example like a shop, do make sure that it entails more on your part than simply replacing a faulty bit of kit.

1.4.6.4 *Describing what you did*

As you develop your example of how you personally did some problem solving, you are asked to do specific things in order. These are:

- Briefly describe the situation, explaining why the complainant was unhappy.
- Tell us what you did and said to try to sort the problem out.
- When did you do these things?
- If you hadn't acted the way you did, what do you think the consequences for everyone involved would have been?
- How did you know that the person was happy with what you had done for him or her?

Using these guiding questions (if you're interested, they're technically known as '**prompts**') helps to structure a coherent and intelligible account of your problem-solving capabilities (and potential). Notice that the final pair of questions is actually quite searching in terms of what they ask you to do. The first effectively asks what would have happened if you hadn't taken responsibility for solving the problem, and invites you to project imaginatively the alternatives to your helpful action. Understanding what you need to do here will clearly impact on your role as a PCSO because it will show that you are aware of consequences to actions and, equally, consequences to you **not** doing something. The second (that is, the last) question is about **evaluation** of what you did. How do you know that the complainant was content with your attempt to solve the problem? You might cover both verbal and non-verbal (body language) responses such as a smile and the words 'thank you', but be careful not to exaggerate people's supposed gratefulness; complainants are often angry and may need to be calmed before matters can be resolved. How you dealt with that calming process (taking the sting out of confrontation) can often be an important part of your success in problem solving.

1.4.6.5 *What the examples are for*

We don't want to labour this: you should be able to see from the scenario and the prompts what sort of examples the assessors are looking for, and you should be experienced enough to be able to supply a good and complex example. We hope though that you've grasped the essence of the exercise: this approximates very closely to a PCSO's daily activities. One last point: we don't want you to think that somehow a PCSO is a superhero. Very few problems can be solved by a single person acting alone. It's perfectly acceptable to show, in your example, how you would make use of others, including the complainant once calmed, in your drive towards solving the problem. **The essential fact is that you were proactive, organized, and led the resolution**, whoever and whatever you called in to help.

1.4.6.6 *Situation 2: revolves around how a PCSO should show respect for the lifestyles of other people*

You are asked to:

> Think of an example of a situation when you have shown respect for someone who had an important part of his or her lifestyle that differed significantly from your own.

The booklet offers the example of someone with a deep-rooted moral or religious belief which you don't share, but which you can understand. The scenario setting also suggests that what is important in this example is **your understanding and sensitivity to difference** between you and this other person, and how you changed what you said or did to meet their needs.

1.4.6.7 *Think of a real clash of values*

We advise you not to think in narrow or limited ways about this problem, but choose an example where there genuinely could have been a clash or substantial difficulty between you and another person because of the differences between you, except that what you did prevented that from happening. Think of experiences you have had such as dealing with someone who is profoundly deaf. People with disabilities of this degree will tell you that, often, other people talk as though the deaf person wasn't there, speaking only to the carer or another companion. This is sometimes called the '*Does he take sugar?*' syndrome and it is profoundly careless of the deaf person's feelings. What you would need to show, if you used an example from your genuine experience of this kind, is how you used sign language or ensured that the deaf person could lip-read what you were saying (some people can cleverly use both sign language and speech together to do this), and that you took time to find out what the problem or difficulty was which the deaf person had and that, although *you* can hear, you showed sensitivity by your actions and speech to the other person's needs. Simple but telling things such as gently touching the person's forearm to attract attention, always speaking directly in the deaf person's line of sight (to your lips), and speaking more slowly and clearly than normal—but not patronizingly so—will demonstrate how you modified your behaviour to suit the person's need. Above all, you didn't simply bellow.

1.4.6.8 *Don't make unsupported assumptions about people*

You might argue that this example doesn't illustrate a genuine difference from you. It might be better if you asked a deaf person the same question and then you would find out more about the often-unthinking barriers which come between deaf people and others. Being deaf is simply a physical condition that impairs communication; it doesn't mean that communication can't happen, nor that the deaf person is stupid or unintelligible. The danger always is in unthinkingly making assumptions about other people.

The assessors offer four fairly straightforward prompts:

- Tell us how the situation arose.
- Tell us in detail what you did and said.
- What did you learn about the other person from this experience?
- How were you able to adapt what you did to suit the other person?

Remind yourself of the nature of race and diversity as we have set it out in a number of ways in this Handbook, by reading **NOS 1AA** at 4.4, and at 6.7 below.

1.4.6.9 *Respect for diversity is a key PCSO strength*

Your responsiveness to difference, the breadth of your understanding, and the imaginativeness of your solutions are all key factors in the role of PCSO. You cannot, of course, police only one part of a community; you must police all and this may mean accommodating yourself to considerable ranges of difference (think of the yawning gaps between teenage culture and that of people over 75).

1.4.6.10 *Choosing the appropriate example*

The same principles apply in answering this question, founded as it is upon respect for race and diversity, as applied in the problem-solving question with which we began. The same principles of evidencing your active and effective role in the examples you choose, the clarity with which you express yourself, and the fluency of your writing will all be elements which you should aim to display as well as you possibly can. *Don't pay lip service*: assessors will see straight through it. Try if you can to find a situation which you found difficult. If you solve a difficult problem, or even show how you mitigated (*made a bit better*) the worst effects of the problem, you are likely to gain more credit from the assessors than if you choose a simple example which was easily handled.

1.4.6.11 *Situation 3: acting without being told what to do and attempting to do the best possible job as a PCSO*

You are asked to:

> Tell us about a situation where you have acted without being told, gone beyond what was expected of you, and even gone further than others would have done.

'Going the extra mile'

Note that this is a two-pronged question: the first part is about your ability to **exercise individual initiative**—to do things which need doing without waiting to be told to do them—and the second part is how you **surpass the normal parameters for action** and how you have tried to attain a really excellent result; it's about going 'the extra mile'. Both are key elements in being a successful and effective PCSO and you need to follow the same careful planning here as you have done in the other two questions.

1.4.6.12 *Example where you gave the lead*

Choose a specific example which illustrates your leading role in acting (without being prompted) for the good of the community or on behalf of someone in the community, and how your persistence in getting the best result you could went further than others would have done: *you weren't content with just doing enough, you wouldn't settle for less than the best.* There may be plenty of examples from work—if a teacher, how you turned a disruptive class into a supportive and focused group of young people; if a librarian, how you not only helped someone to research making a will, but found them examples, recommended low-fee solicitors for consultation, and offered to go with the person if s/he was nervous or shy. This would be acting outside the standard parameters, without waiting for someone else to stimulate you to action. Or your example could come from the community, where you establish a site for a skate park (see Photograph 1 below), persuade the local or parish council to build the basic infrastructure there, and then you recruit a small army of volunteers to construct more

(Photograph by Helen Jacobs)

Photograph 1: Skateboard park and graffiti wall

sophisticated ramps and jumps, install lighting, and persuade the local media to cover the opening.

1.4.6.13 *Using prompts to keep focused*

What we have offered above are short but expandable examples that demonstrate in general terms what the assessors are looking for, but you need to be specific and detailed. The following are the prompts which the assessors have provided to help you structure your competence:

- **What was the situation and why did you feel the need to act?**
- **Exactly what did you do and say?**
- **If you had not acted as you did, what do you think the consequences for everyone would have been?**

1.4.6.14 *Define and describe in detail what you did*

You are familiar by now with these structures, and you should have a fair idea what the assessors are looking for. You need to put your actions and decisions in the forefront of the action, defining and describing in detail what it was that you did and said which demonstrates the competence. The final prompt is similar to that in Question 1 in that it encourages you to map what the consequences might have been if you had not acted. If you have something similar to our skateboard park example, it isn't enough for you to say that 'things would have stayed the same' because things don't. Tense situations invariably get worse; bored and disaffected youths get into trouble; streetlamps left broken and unrepaired continue to create hazards and to provide criminal opportunities in the darkness, and so on. The assessors expect you to be able to think through the course of events that would have developed if you had not acted: would someone have lost his/her life? Would someone have been put at risk? Might a vehicle have crashed? Could the community have split into factions and bred mistrust? Your alternative scenarios, which show that you understand the value of your intervention, need careful thought before you write anything down.

1.4.6.15 *Plan it first*

One last general point: it always helps to rough your ideas out on separate pieces of paper or on the computer screen before writing your 'fair copy' in the application booklet. Remember that there is no electronic or on-line version yet; so if you are not used to using pen and paper, or if you haven't done so since schooldays, do practise! Another advantage of drafting your thoughts first is that you are likely to make fewer mistakes and your handwriting will be neater and more legible, with fewer crossings-out. Think about the advice in the **Notes** at the back of the application booklet, which reads, in part:

> Write clearly and concisely. If we can't read it or understand it, we can't score it. Pay attention to your **spelling, handwriting, punctuation and grammar**. You are being assessed throughout this application form on your written skills. We also expect your examples to be focused, succinct [*brief and crisp*] and fluently written, as any police report or statement would need to be.

This is unequivocal (*crystal clear*), as is the instruction that **the application must be your own unaided work**. Since you should expect to be questioned during the assessment process on the answers you have given, it makes sense that you are the only author. Any evidence of **collusion** with another is an automatic fail anyway.

1.4.6.16 *Motivation and knowledge*

The final questions in the **Competency assessment**, as we noted above, concern **your motivation and your knowledge of the PCSO role**. We have already dealt with motivation in 1.2 above, and will not repeat the discussion here. Go back and re-read what we stated there. You need to be aware that the assessors' prompt for **Question 4** not only notes that '*we want to know why you want to be a PCSO*', but also what experience, skills, and abilities you have which you feel will make you suitable as a candidate PCSO. The final question, **Question 5**, is designed to find out how well informed you are about the work of a PCSO. [Read this Handbook and you will be superbly prepared!] Specifically, the assessors want you to tell them what tasks you expect to carry out if appointed, to demonstrate to them that you know what the job entails. Importantly, the assessors will explore with you if you have properly considered whether the job really is for you.

1.4.6.17 *The sorts of task a PCSO undertakes*

Helpfully, the *Guide* details some of the PCSO tasks, which we reproduce here:

What sort of things do PCSOs do?

- Go on highly visible uniformed foot patrols
- Support Community Beat Officers and Community Action Teams in solving local problems
- Make house visits to gather intelligence and offer public reassurance after minor crimes or anti-social behaviour
- Get involved with key people in the community, such as community, religious, and business leaders
- Work with *Community Watch, Neighbourhood Watch, Business Watch, Pub Watch, Farm Watch,* and *Horse Watch schemes*
- Protect crime scenes until police officers arrive
- Collect CCTV evidence
- Provide low-level crime prevention and personal safety advice
- Carry out low-level missing person enquiries
- Act as professional witnesses, attending court when needed
- Support crime prevention
- Engage with youths
- Interact with schools
- Support the Mobile Police Station
- Support Crime and Disorder Reduction Partnerships

Whilst this list is a helpful indicator of the range of a PCSO's activities, *it is not definitive* (it doesn't cover all PCSO activities) and you should not reproduce it wholesale and undigested in answer to **Question 5** (you'll get no marks if you do). Instead, think about these tasks and what they represent, and look at all aspects of the work of the PCSO, which of course we discuss at length in this Handbook. Make a list of activities, bearing in mind the National Occupational Standards, perhaps dividing your notes for convenience into:

- **Support for the police**
- **Support for the community**
- **Support of the NOS**
- **Support of local partnerships and other agencies**

then your answer to **Question 5** will be in your own words and will show that you have a very good grasp of the PCSO role.

1.4.6.18 *Can you do the job?*

Finally, you need to ask yourself, very honestly, whether you have the necessary qualities to be a PCSO and whether you can cope with all the problems, frustrations, situations, confrontations, and obstacles that you will meet on a daily basis. Helpfully, the *Guide* notes some of the 'right qualities to be a PCSO':

- a confident, level-headed, positive and mature manner
- the ability to deal with difficult people and situations
- to be sensitive but objective
- good communication and listening skills
- good team-working skills
- stamina for long periods of foot patrol
- skills to deal with all types of people, some of whom may be drunk, hostile or upset
- to be accurate when completing paperwork
- an appreciation of the confidential nature of police work.

Again, you will appreciate that this is not an exhaustive list of the qualities, some of which we looked at in 1.2 above, when we discussed motivation, and in 1.3 above, when we talked about what qualities police forces are looking for in their PCSOs. Remember the key skills of:

- **resilience**
- **effective communication**
- **respect for race and diversity**
- **personal responsibility**
- **team working**

all of which we looked at in 1.3 above when we examined the behavioural competences. (**Community and Customer Focus** is missing; this is because it is seen as something which you will develop as a competence once you are doing the job and implementing your local neighbourhood policing plan.)

1.4.7 Section 5: declaration

The final part of the application booklet, **Section 5**, is a **declaration (see Figure 2 below)** by you about a number of things, which you sign and date.

If you take on board the points we have developed with you here, and follow them in any interview situation, you will come across as a competent and effective person—which, as a PCSO, is precisely the image you want to convey.

The Declaration

I declare that all the statements I have made in this application are true tothe best of my knowledge and belief and that no relevant information hasbeen withheld.

I understand that:

- I must inform the Recruitment Office without delay of any change in mycircumstances;
- criminal conviction checks will be made against myself and my familymembers and I have informed them of this;
- financial checks will be undertaken to verify my financial status and allsuch information will be treated in confidence. I consent to these checksbeing made;
- formal disclosure of my Service Character Assessment (Armed Forces)will be sought and I consent to this;
- any offer of appointment will be subject to satisfactory references andvetting, a medical examination, continued good conduct and themaintenance of fitness;
- a member of a police force who has deliberately made any falsestatement or omitted information in connection with his or herappointment may subsequently be liable to misconduct proceedings;
- if I am appointed my fingerprints and a sample of my DNA will be takenand held on record for elimination purposes;
- successful candidates must serve wherever required to do so within theForce area;
- the Chief Officer retains the right to reject any application with-outgiving reasons and
- the information I have provided may be held on manual filing andcomputer systems as part of the recruitment process and may be sharedby other police forces.
- I am not and have never been a member of the British National Party orsimilar organisation whose aims, objectives or pronounce-ments maycontradict the duty to promote race equality.

....

Signature   Date

Figure 2: The Declaration

1.4.7.1 *Think about what the declaration entails*

Think about what you are signing up to here. There has been some critical public discussion about whether a specific political party should be mentioned as proscribed (*banned*) for members of the police family, or whether a simpler statement would be better, noting that any group espousing intolerance of others should not have police staff or police officers as members. The fact that the British National Party's views are repellent to many is not the point; it is the membership, public acceptance of, or the signing up to the aims of such organizations which is to be disavowed. But there is a simple test which we may apply to all this. Look again at the discussions about race and diversity at 1.3.1.2 and 1.3.4 above and you will understand that **nothing may modify your duty to respect race and diversity**. Outlawing membership of any party holding views which run counter to that duty is therefore irrelevant. No one signed up to respect race and diversity could consider membership of such an organization for a moment.

1.4.8 The assessment process

Your completed application booklet has now been carefully scrutinized and, as a result of your breadth of knowledge and understanding (provided in major part by this Handbook), you have impressed the initial assessors enough to receive an invitation to attend the assessment process. This section explains what is involved and offers you advice on how to prepare for the assessment and how to conduct yourself on the day.

1.4.8.1 *What and where and when*

The assessment process is run in regional assessment centres or sometimes, for larger forces, in force assessment centres and normally the national assessment takes place over five working days, usually a Monday to Friday. Candidates are assessed in syndicate groups of up to eight, usually with three syndicates in the morning and three in the afternoon sessions. This allows, evidently enough, for 48 candidates per day. Each of the sessions, morning and afternoon, lasts about three-and-a-half hours. Normally, morning syndicates begin at 08.30 and finish at 12.00, while afternoon sessions begin at 13.00 and finish at about 16.30 (get used to the twenty-four hour clock; all police forces use it all the time and so should you). A candidate will attend **one** session of three and a half hours. You will be informed about your results about three weeks (or 15 working days) after the final day of the assessment process. Therefore, if you were assessed on the Monday morning in the first syndicate, it might be 20 working days or four weeks before you hear how you got on. This is a tedious wait, but assessments have to be made judiciously and with care, so no parts of it can be rushed. Remember that much activity in terms of your assessment takes place after you have gone, with marking, cross-checking, research, moderation meetings between assessors and a quality assurance team ensuring that the processes are rigorous and fair.

1.4.9 Testing the competences and marking

We explained to you in 1.3 above what the police force that employs you will be looking for, and we spent some time examining the behavioural competences which underpinned the assessment. We noted to you that each of the competences is tested at least twice during the assessment process, both in written and in verbal (or 'oral' as the framework guidance erroneously insists) communication. To be successful, candidates must achieve at least:

50% of the overall marks and
50% in Respect for Race and Diversity and
50% in verbal ('oral') communication and
33% in written communication.

The assessment sessions for each syndicate consist of:

- a competence-based **interview**
- **two** competence-based written **tests**
- **two** competence-based interactive role-play **scenarios**.

1.4.9.1 *Preparing for the assessment process: Interview*

The obvious things that you have to do in advance of being interviewed are to think about your interview techniques, think how you would construct your answers to questions, and ensure that you have rehearsed with someone the examples you intend to use which demonstrate your competence and potential to be a PCSO. Your assessors are there to focus upon the job in hand—assessing you—not to gossip or pass the time of day. This means that you too have to be professional about the whole process, focused on what you need to do, and not diverted by other things (even by being nervous ...). The assessors are working from a script from which they do not deviate; this means that you have to concentrate as much as they do on what is being discussed. Watch things like talking for too long, wandering off the point, or getting sidetracked. If you don't give enough information, don't worry. The assessors can ask supplementary questions to draw out your knowledge and thoughts. Don't go to the other extreme either: avoid being monosyllabic, terse, or abrupt. Such attitudes can seem rude or aggressive. Steer a middle course between not giving enough information and giving too much. Practise with friends and family in explaining something simply and clearly—imagining that you are explaining something to someone who is not familiar with British society is a good exercise and discipline in this respect. **You cannot go wrong in your preparation if you think clearly and carefully about how you can show your abilities in each of the competences, using real-life examples which you can remember clearly and which had an effect on you.**

1.4.9.2 *Written exercises*

Whilst the content of what you are asked to write about is clearly very important to your success in these exercises, spelling and grammar are assessed as well. Currently, if you make *four or more* grammatical errors or *four or more* spelling mistakes you will fail the exercise.

Guidelines to help you in your written work

Keep it simple: more errors are caused by being over-complicated than any other factor

Writing is a formal activity: don't use the jargon words or slang that you employ in casual conversations

Every sentence has a *subject* **and a** *verb* (a word which names something and a word which does something, such as The *cat purrs* or *I write* notes). Each sentence begins with a capital letter and ends with a full stop.

Don't abbreviate words: you are not sending a text message, you are writing formally

It helps to **plan out what you are going to write** first, even if this is only in the form of a few scribbles. This helps you to remember to put material in a logical order and to ensure that you have missed nothing

Read over what you've written so that you can correct any inadvertent errors

Don't try to impress, ever, by using words which sound impactive and serious but which you do not understand; such things are *egregious*

1.4.9.3 *Why written skills matter*

In case you are wondering why so much emphasis is laid upon proper formal writing, presentation, and grammatical accuracy, it is because much of police work is in the form of formal records. It doesn't matter whether these are in your Pocket Notebook, or in a formal statement, or in a report, or in a plan, or in written submissions to partners: you will look inept, ill-educated, and slipshod if your writing is careless, strewn with errors, confused about the meanings of words, and badly spelled. This is particularly the case if your written work is produced in court or if it is widely copied outside the police force, such as a notice from you put up in a public place, or a plan that is put before a council meeting.

1.4.9.4 *The interactive exercises*

The two exercises concern scenarios (*little plays*) which are based in a fictional place (like the tasks around our imaginary **Tonchester** in Chapter 8). This is to give you a context in which you can make judgements and help you to understand or visualize what it is you have to do. The essence of the idea is to make the exercise practical rather than theoretical. Do read all the preparation material thoroughly before you go into the exercises, and make notes. When you go into the exercise scenario area, you will meet a role-player (an actor) who will play the part of one of the characters in the scenario, while you normally play the part of the PCSO. The role player will not step outside the part s/he is playing, so don't expect the actor to say that you are doing well, or whisper an aside such as '*Don't forget to say ...*'. You are expected to play your role seriously too, so if, for example, you are asked to play the part of a PCSO meeting a distraught lady in a shopping centre who has lost her small son aged four, you are not expected to laugh and joke but to act as you would if the scenario were a real one and you were really on duty. The role-player will be convincingly distraught, or angry, or distressed, or whatever else it is that is required by the scenario.

1.4.9.5 *Playing the part*

Listen carefully to what the role-player says to you. Respond appropriately to what you are being told. One last, but very important, point is that if you are awarded a D grade (fail) for Respect for Race and Diversity in either the written exercises or the interactive exercises, you may fail the entire process, irrespective of the grades you obtained in other parts of the assessment. If you think about this for a moment, you will see why, and we refer you again to the short discussion in the section on the Declaration (at 1.4.6 above). Respect for race and diversity is at the core of what you will do as a PCSO and to fail to attain this as a competence because of inappropriate behaviour or comments suggests that you will not make it as a PCSO either.

1.4.10 Medical, security, and references check

These are all straightforward matters, very much linked to you as an individual and we cannot see much point in discussing any of the factors in detail. We have in any case covered many of the elements earlier in this section. Here they are in brief:

1.4.10.1 *Medical*

You know that you must be:

> in good health, of sound constitution and able both mentally and physically to perform the duties of a PCSO once appointed.[7]

PCSOs, like all other members of the police family, are covered by the **Disability Discrimination Act 2003** and employers must make reasonable adjustments if a disability is declared. Disability is defined as *'a physical or mental impairment that has a substantial and long-term adverse effect on the ability to carry out normal day-to-day activities'*.[8] It is your responsibility to bring to the attention of your employer, or potential employer, any disability in order that reasonable adjustments may be made to accommodate you. All applicants will fill out a medical questionnaire and have a medical examination prior to appointment. You will have your eyes tested at the medical examination and there are restrictions around colour blindness and eye surgery which you need to read and understand (look at the notes at the back of the application booklet).

1.4.10.2 *Security*

There will be vetting checks on your background and that of your family, including the criminal records and financial checks which we discussed earlier. You may expect to undergo re-checks every five years or so, or whenever your circumstances change (such as moving in with a new partner, changes in your financial status, and so on). Because you will continue to have access, in the course of your duties, to confidential police information, including to criminal records databases, your security status is of continuous importance.

1.4.10.3 *References*

We have discussed this in relation to the application form and need not discuss it further now. Your referees may be approached at any time, depending on your indications, after receipt of the application form. References will have been taken before confirmation of a job offer.

The general point about this part of the recruitment process is that you will probably have been given a conditional offer of employment, which means that all other things being equal, you will soon be appointed as a PCSO. The 'other things being equal' are clearance of all conditions which might disbar you, but which emerge only after the specific medical and security checks, and what your referees have to say about you. Unlike medical and security checks, what your referee may say about you is not a reason on its own to disbar you. In other words, if one of your references asserts that you are dishonest and not to be trusted, we would expect independent evidence to corroborate what was said.

1.4.11 **Summary**

The comments and discussion in this section are no substitute for your careful reading and understanding of the guidance notes for prospective PCSOs, nor for your careful perusal of the application booklet, including the useful Notes at the back of the booklet. **We would strongly advise you to talk to serving PCSOs and police officers before you commit yourself** to a thorough and painstaking process. Your motivation and commitment must be strong and unwavering to see you through this process, which, after all, only gets you through the door. The key to success in applying to become a PCSO is **assiduous preparation, prior thought, and planning**—just like being a PCSO for real.

1.5 **Ethical Standards in Brief**

Ethics is about right behaviour. You are joining an organization that prides itself on the maintenance of professional standards of behaviour and integrity. It is time to explore what that means, since, if you become a PCSO, you will be expected to sign up to the codes of practice, ethical and professional standards, and your Force's internal standards.

1.5.1 The importance of ethical standards

We have already seen something of this in the discussions about behavioural competences (at 1.3.1 above, and 4.15.8 below), which we don't propose to repeat here. The point is that **there are acceptable behaviours and unacceptable behaviours**. These now need to be set in a wider context and used in a broader discussion with you about what ethical standards are and why they are important.

1.5.2 Defining ethics

A working definition of Ethics is as follows: **Ethics are the values and standards of behaviour by which individuals govern their conduct and organizations regulate their members and societies manage the actions of their citizens.**

1.5.3 Principles

Such principles as respect for others, honesty, integrity, fairness, and treating people equally, can all help to define ethical behaviour and will find their way into various codes of conduct to which organizations, particularly the police, are publicly committed. You are joining the police service, and there exists a framework for ethical behaviour in **Police Regulations**. These govern the activities of police officers in the discharge of their duties and whilst you, as a PCSO, are not subject to Police Regulations, your police colleagues are and this will impact upon you.

1.5.4 Ethical standards for police officers

Police (Conduct) Regulations 2004 set out the acceptable behaviours, attitudes, and conduct which are expected of police officers. This is a summary:

- Officers should respect confidentiality—they must not disclose confidential information unless authorized and they should not use confidential information for their personal benefit
- Police officers must act with fairness and impartiality in their dealings with the public and their colleagues
- Officers should avoid being 'improperly beholden' to any person or institution
- They should be open and truthful in their dealings
- They should discharge their duties with integrity

- They must obey all lawful orders
- Officers should oppose any improper behaviour, reporting it where appropriate
- Officers should treat members of the public and colleagues with courtesy and respect, avoiding abusive or derisive attitudes or behaviour
- Officers must avoid favouritism of an individual or group; all forms of harassment, victimization, or unreasonable discrimination; and overbearing conduct to a colleague, particularly to one junior in rank or service
- Officers must never knowingly use more force than is reasonable, nor should they abuse their authority
- Officers should be conscientious and diligent in the performance of their duties
- They should attend work promptly when rostered for duty
- Officers on duty must be sober
- Officers should always be well turned out, clean, and tidy
- Whether on or off duty, officers should not behave in a way which is likely to bring discredit upon the police service.[9]

1.5.4.1 *A flavour of ethical standards and 'right' behaviour*

The full details and all provisions of the Regulations are not reproduced here; indeed we have mainly provided a summary of the **Code of Conduct**, but it is enough, we hope, to give you a flavour of ethical standards. Some of these issues, and the words used to express them, should be familiar to you, especially concepts such as *'respect'*, *'courtesy'*, *'open'*, *'truthful'*, *'impartial'* which we encountered when examining the behavioural competences. Other phrases may be less familiar: *'improperly beholden'* is an example. This means that police officers should never be in a position where they have an obligation to someone which gets in the way of their duty. The idea that you owe anyone a favour has no place in policing. There are some interesting negatives too, such as not being overbearing (oppressive) because of one's authority, avoiding favouritism, and avoiding abuse of, or being derisive about, others.

1.5.4.2 *Smartness is part of the maintenance of standards*

We doubt that there is anything here which you and the public would not sign up to as **preferable behaviour**. There may be some eyebrows raised about the need to be 'well turned-out, clean, and tidy' in these more permissive and relaxed days, but in fact such punctiliousness has its place in policing, because a smart, groomed officer commands attention in ways that a dishevelled or untidy person would not. It is part of the image of the police officer and continues to be part of our expectation of behaviour. That is not the same as saying that the same regulations should apply to you the PCSO. The regulations have the force of law because they are enshrined in statute and therefore can apply only to sworn officers, not to you.

1.5.5 Other codes

What other possibilities are there to give guidance to PCSOs about proper behaviour and codes of conduct? There is a European Code of Police Ethics, published in 2001, which gives general guidance:

- The police help to safeguard the law
- The police depend upon the people for support
- Public confidence in the police is linked to the protection of rights and freedoms, especially those in the European Convention on Human Rights.

1.5.5.1 *Different images of the police: protectors or oppressors?*

These may seem obvious statements to us, but a brief glance at any of the police systems in any of the former Communist Bloc states, such as Estonia, Poland, Slovakia, or the former East Germany, will show that these were not their roles. The police in those countries, following the dominant Soviet model, sustained the ruling party (the Communist Politburo) in power through repression and intrusive surveillance of the individual. They did not police with the public's consent or support, and individual freedoms, such as the right to privacy or the right to a fair trial, were never protected or guaranteed by the police (quite the opposite). That said, although the **European Code of Police Ethics** gives general direction as to the relationship between the citizen and the police officer, there is no explicit guidance on behaviour or ethical standards expected of the PCSO.

1.5.5.2 *No codes of ethics for police staff*

The boundary line between the role of a sworn officer and anyone else is blurred, and growing less certain by the year (we discuss this in Chapters 3, 5, and 7 more extensively). However, there is no national standard for the conduct of any of these support roles. This doesn't mean that in your ordinary duty on a day-to-day basis you are going to be racked with complex moral dilemmas and the need to apply profound thinking about ethical positions. But you may feel that you want to be bound or guided by some principles similar to those that police officers have in their Regulations. Many people would feel more comfortable if there was a standard to which they were expected to adhere. In early March 2007, the Home Secretary, John Reid, produced a statement which contained *Common Values for the Police Service of England and Wales*, and which included a vision ('to protect and reassure the public') and a short statement of values based on 'a sense of service to the public'. But it is by no stretch of the imagination a Code of Ethics nor a proper and unambiguous Statement of Values. The values, indeed, are buried in the political 'text' (Reid, 2007). There is no evidence that this was taken to consultation with the police service, nor that there has been 'buy-in' from forces. And it is not specific to PCSOs. In December 2008, the Home Office's Police Leadership and Powers Unit, in association with ACPO and the NPIA, published a **Code of Professional Standards** for police officers, which consists of ten sections, each of which details acceptable standards of behaviour, attitude, and performance. These do not yet apply to police staff, and therefore not to PCSOs. If you are interested, you can find the detail at Home Office Crime Reduction and Community Safety Group, Police Leadership and Powers Unit; available from: <http://www.Code@homeoffice.gsi.gov.uk> accessed 6 August 2009.

Most police forces have an *internal* standards statement that governs the activities of all staff, not just sworn officers.

1.5.5.3 *Police standard*

Let us look briefly at extracts from one such example of a **Police Service Standard**, in use for *all* staff in a police force (we tell you which one at the end). The full document is too detailed to reproduce in its entirety, so we give you here a flavour of what it says:

> [This] Standard describes the quality of service that residents and visitors [...] can expect [...]; the new minimum standards for policing nationally – also known as 'the Policing Pledge' (see below at 1.5.6.2). The Pledge is [...] a commitment, not a guarantee, to do something.[...]
>
> **Police station visits:** we will aim to provide a safe and pleasant environment that offers useful information and includes somewhere private to discuss personal or sensitive matters.

- We aim to ensure that callers at police station front counters receive personal attention from a trained member of staff
- We will publish the opening hours of police stations, offices and front counters locally and on [the Force] website
- We will also provide a free direct telephone line outside our main police stations for use when […] front counters are closed

Partnership working: we recognise that to resolve long-term crime, disorder, and quality of life concerns in our communities we need to work with residents and businesses as well as other organisations […]. We will:

- Recognise and support partner agencies
- Ensure consistent representation and participation in partnership work
- Provide appropriately skilled staff to key partnership roles
- Reflect an understanding of, and commitment to, partnership working across the force

Complaints: We always welcome feedback; it helps us to improve our service. […] We undertake to investigate all complaints swiftly and fairly and provide the results of our investigation to the complainant. If the complaint relates to the conduct of a member of our staff and the [complainant] is dissatisfied with the outcome of our investigation, the Independent Police Complaints Commission (IPCC) should be contacted. […]

What the standard does

The Kent Police Service Standard, which we have greatly abridged above, is actually 20 pages long, and not only incorporates the national 'Policing Pledge' (see below), but amplifies and expands the provisions of the Pledge into a police commitment at local, BCU, and County levels. It makes a **contract of fair dealing** and ethical behaviour with the public (those who are 'policed'). It is a very public statement about **how officers and staff should behave and respond and therefore it constitutes a code of behaviour**, not just for police officers but for police staff as well.

Being accountable for your actions

There is something more; this 'contract' with the public is about **accountability**, and this is an ethical dimension which is not often discussed. To return to our example of the police forces in the old Warsaw Pact countries, which were largely repressive, answerable only to the ruling politburo, and extraordinarily inward-looking and suspicious of everyone; the idea of police forces being accountable for their actions is laughable. They answered only to brutal political power. The fact that our police forces publish the means by which the ordinary citizen can achieve redress to wrongs, injustices, unfair treatment, rudeness, incivility, or discrimination is profoundly ethical. What is more, it sustains the notion of the police as a public service product of society, rather than a force imposed by the unchallenged rulers of a tyrannical regime.

1.5.6 Who watches the watchers?

You might argue that this is all very well, but does it work? Are police officers and police staff really accountable for what they do? If they are, who or what makes them so? There are a number of mechanisms of which you should be aware, which hold the police (and anyone who works for the police, so including PCSOs) accountable for their actions. These are some of them:

- **The Independent Police Complaints Commission** (national)
- **The Force's Police Authority**
- **The Force's Professional Standards Department**—PSD (many PSDs now have the remit to investigate complaints and allegations against police staff as well as against police officers)
- **The Police Standards Unit** (national)
- **The National Police Improvement Agency** (generic agency but safeguarding standards of policing excellence among other things).

1.5.6.1 *Other checks and balances*

If you add to that the right of any individual to request information under the **Freedom of Information Act**—any individual can request action by a Chief Constable into complaints against the Force as a whole, not just individuals—and the right of any citizen to seek redress through the courts, the ultimate appeal court for which is the European Court of Human Rights, the opportunity for illegal or discriminatory police actions to remain unaccountable is small. We do not say it would not happen, but the dice are loaded against systematic oppression of an individual or group by the police, and quite right too. Finally, there are those within the Force itself who would stand up to, and report, any wrongdoing or unacceptable behaviour. Indeed, if you look at Chapter 4, this is one of the positive behaviours expected of a member of the police family and is in the behavioural competences. On this basis, we can confidently assert that **ethical behaviour is integral to policing** as we know it in England and Wales, as befits an occupation with ambitions to become a profession.

1.5.6.2 The Policing Pledge

Part of the government's desire that the police engage more with local communities, and as replacement of part of the performance measurement system, the **Policing Pledge**, introduced in late 2008, is designed to offer commitments to the local community of what it can expect from its police force. We saw above how in 2009 Kent Police has taken the Pledge and amplified it into a 'contract' of service provision for the people of Kent. Now it is time to look at the Pledge itself in more detail. It consists of ten commitments structured as shown below and with this preamble, shown in italics:

'The Police Service in England and Wales will support law abiding citizens and pursue criminals relentlessly to keep you and your neighbours safe from harm . We will:

1 Always treat you fairly with dignity and respect ensuring you have fair access to our services at a time that is reasonable and suitable for you

2 Provide you with information so you know who your dedicated Neighbourhood Policing Team is, where they are based, how to contact them and how to work with them

3 Ensure your Neighbourhood Policing Team and other police patrols are visible and on your patch at times when they will be most effective and when you tell us you most need them. We will ensure your team are [sic] not taken away from neighbourhood business, more than is absolutely necessary. They [the NPT] will spend at least 80% of their time visibly working in your neighbourhood, tackling your priorities. Staff turnover will be minimised.

4 Respond to every message directed to your Neighbourhood Policing Team within 24 hours and, where necessary, provide a more detailed response as soon as we can

5 Aim to answer 999 calls within 10 seconds, deploying to emergencies immediately, giving an estimated time of arrival, getting to you safely, as quickly as possible. In urban areas, we will aim to get to you within 15 minutes and in rural areas in 20 minutes

6 Answer all non-emergency calls promptly. If attendance is needed [we will] send a patrol, giving you an estimated time of arrival, and:

- If you are vulnerable or upset, aim to be with you within 60 minutes
- If you are calling about an issue that we have agreed with your community will be a neighbourhood priority [...] and attendance is required, we will aim to be with you within 60 minutes
- Alternatively, if appropriate, we will make an appointment to see you at a time that fits in with your life and within 48 hours
- If agreed that attendance is not necessary we will give you advice, answer your questions and/or put you in touch with someone who can help

7 Arrange regular public meetings to agree your priorities, at least once a month, giving you a chance to meet your local team with other members of your community. These will include opportunities such as surgeries, street briefings and mobile police station visits which will be arranged to meet local needs and requirements

8 Provide monthly updates on progress, and on local crime and policing issues. These will include the provision of crime maps, information on specific crimes and what happened to those brought to justice, details of what action we and our partners are taking to make your neighbourhood safer and information on how your force is performing

9 If you have been a victim of crime agree with you how often you would like to be kept informed of progress in your case and for how long. You have the right to be kept informed at least every month if you wish and for as long as is reasonable

10 Acknowledge any dissatisfaction with the service you have received within 24 hours of reporting it to us. To help us fully resolve the matter, discuss with you how it will be handled, give you an opportunity to talk in person to someone about your concerns and agree with you what will be done about them and how quickly

1.5.6.3 *Commentary*

There is little here that will not be familiar to a Neighbourhood Policing Team and the 'Pledge' echoes a great deal of what we have to say in this Handbook about interaction with and listening to neighbourhoods and communities. What is new is that police forces will now be assessed on how well they perform these ten tasks and the arbiters of the quality of the police service will be the communities themselves. This is a major departure from the gamut of quantitative and rather sterile performance measures which were largely imposed by the Home Office as a species of 'new public management' and which formed the basis of assessing police forces for the best part of fifteen years. The old performance measures were comprehensively discredited in police eyes because they did not capture some important interactions in policing, and because 'what gets measured gets done', their replacement with the Pledge is broadly, if cautiously, welcomed. A sceptic might remark at this point that this is all very well, but the sort of people who comment on police performance tend to be white, retired, articulate people who have time to think about such things and not those vulnerable or inarticulate people who are trying to struggle along with jobs, schools, children, and economic pressures. However, in defence of the Pledge, you should note that **victims of crime** will be canvassed for their opinions (more widely than previously) and that, for the first time, many of the measures by which 'an effective and efficient' police service will be judged are **qualitative**, and have to do with the perceptions of those whom the police serve, the 'law-abiding citizens' mentioned in the preamble.

1.5.6.4 *Listening to what people say*

How well this works, and what effect such deliberate parochialism will have upon the delivery of a police service to the public, is yet to be proved, but this is undoubtedly a start. It shows that the police *have* listened to what communities have had to say and that the police have taken on board what concerns and worries the local inhabitants—including things like being informed of the progress of cases. This has direct implications for the ways in which PCSOs do their job—because they will now be at the forefront of police performance and they will either contribute directly to the successful quality delivery of policing services or they will detract just as directly from the achievement of local satisfaction with the police in the same degree. No pressure then. Additionally, this will bring the attention of the whole police force on to its neighbourhood performance, and means that what you do as a member of your NPT is now among the most important things done by your force. At the same time that this brings pressure on you and upon the members of your NPT, so it is likely also to bring real change, real initiatives, and real support. But, just in case you thought the entire police service had become community minded and locally focused—perhaps to the exclusion of the bigger crime and public order picture—there is a caveat at the end of the Policing Pledge and it looks like this:

> We want to do our best for you but if we fail to meet our pledge we will always explain why it had not been possible on that occasion to deliver the high standards to which we aspire and [which] you deserve.

In a sense, this provides the 'cop-out' for not meeting local targets and provides an excuse to move NPTs elsewhere as occasion demands. But the local responses are important to police forces—especially to chief officers—and it is likely that the Pledge may, in time, become the basis of a genuine two-way commitment between police and community.[10] At present, it is aspirational and has yet to bed-in fully. The test will come as HMIC begins fully to inspect forces on the basis of local satisfaction with the service provided.

1.6 **Race and Diversity Issues in Brief**

1.6.1 **Why we repeat information on race and diversity**

We know that you will dip into this Handbook in different places, depending on your need at the time; you won't sit and read the Handbook though like a novel. Rather than risk your not knowing about the importance of **respect for race and diversity**, we have included it in key places, such as in the recruitment process earlier in this chapter, and in the behavioural competences in 4.15 below, or thinking about communities in 6.7 below. We shall continue to do this throughout the Handbook where it is relevant and where we think you need to be alerted to its importance.

1.6.2 **Policing a diverse community**

This time, though, we are going to look quickly at some of the main headlines concerning race and diversity and glance at the legislation and the obligation which all this places on you, the PCSO. You police a diverse community, with many different needs and viewpoints, and we discussed earlier (at 1.3 above) how that means that your duty obliges you to respect the points of view, customs, and practices of others. You have to provide the same high standard of service to everyone, regardless of their backgrounds, origins, beliefs, and personal or social circumstances. This is often shortened to calling your attitude 'an even-handed approach', where everyone is accorded the same impartial respect. That extends to the workplace as well, where you have every right to be treated with respect by your colleagues and to have a working atmosphere free from discrimination of any kind, harassment, bullying, or victimization. It follows that your attitudes, if you discriminate against people, or harass, bully, or victimize others, will not be tolerated. Remember, you may be the hedge or the only visible support which some people see between their beliefs and cultures and other people's prejudiced discrimination.

1.6.2.1 *Ethical behaviours and diversity*

We have just discussed, in 1.5 above, the sorts of things involved in ethical behaviour. Here is a quick summary of the sorts of ethical behaviour in your day-to-day exchanges with the public and with colleagues, which relate to race and diversity:

- Improve trust and confidence in policing among all members of the community, especially the vulnerable
- Always lead by your own unprejudiced, non-discriminating example
- Understand the value and strength of diversity, know why respect is important, and accept the rights of all to personal dignity
- Engage with local partnerships and agencies to enhance the sense of safe community
- Apply your powers sparingly, proportionately, and justifiably
- Aim for and achieve consistently high standards in the quality of your interventions with the community
- Be open-minded and flexible in responding to people's needs: don't stereotype them, or stereotype your responses.

This is not hard—thousands of police officers, PCSOs, and public sector workers do this all the time without evident difficulty. It is a mind-set, not a gymnastic contortion. There is no reason why you cannot do the same.

1.6.2.2 *Six diversity strands*

Each of the six 'strands' to diversity—**Race, Sexuality, Gender, Age, Disability, Religion and Belief**—is backed by legislation, making it unlawful to discriminate against people on any of these grounds. You should familiarize yourself with the provisions of the laws and Regulations supporting each of the strands, and note too that there are other laws, for example **the Public Order Act 1986,** or the **Crime and Disorder Act 1998,** which would support you if you were involved in dealing with racism. The major relevant laws and Regulations are:[11]

Race: Race Relations Act 1976 and the Race Relations (Amendment) Act 2000; Criminal Justice Act 1991 (stops and searches, section 95)

Sexuality: Sex Discrimination Acts 1975 and 1986; Gender Reassignment Regulations 1999, Gender Recognition Act 2005; Civil Partnership Act 2004

Gender: Sex Discrimination Acts 1975 and 1986; Equal Pay Act 1970 and 1984

Age: Age Discrimination Act 2006

Disability: Disability Discrimination Acts 1995 and 2005 (often referred to as the 'DDA' in police circles)

Religion and Belief: Employment Equality Religion or Belief Regulations 2003; Equality Act 2006

1.6.2.3 *Allport's scale*

In 1953, an American psychologist called Gordon Allport published a book called *The Nature of Prejudice* (now long out of

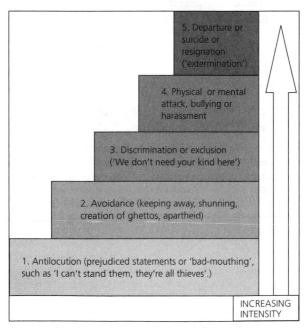

Figure 3: Adaptation of Allport's scale, 1953

print)[12] in which he described a rising scale of prejudicial treatment of people, based on his studies of the ways in which the Nazis treated the Jews in Germany. **Allport's scale**, as it is called, is a familiar model to use when discussing the ways in which discrimination can develop and intensify.

1.6.2.4 *Forms of discrimination*

We have had to substitute some of the steps, such as level 5 'extermination', where Allport clearly had the Holocaust and the Nazis' deliberate genocide of the Jews in mind, by saying that forcing someone out of a job, or making a family pack up and move away, would be the community equivalent. Remember, we are discussing all forms of discrimination not only racial discrimination. Allport's scale applies as much to prejudiced activity against old people (or young 'hoodies') or gays or Muslims or blind people, as it does to gender or race. It follows generally that a determined intervention at level 1 (**antilocution**), when you hear racist chanting or remarks about minority groups, may prevent escalation to any of the other levels. But prejudices, born of fear, envy, or bad experiences in the past, run very deep within society and inevitably you will encounter many instances of discrimination in the course of your work as a PCSO.

1.7 Physical Fitness and Standards

1.7.1 Why fitness and good physical standards are important

For those considering embarking on a career as a PCSO, one of the factors that needs to be considered is physical fitness. Many PCSOs are engaged on daily foot patrols that can often encompass anything up to 15 miles in distance travelled, and for those on cycle patrols this figure will be even higher. This figure will vary enormously from PCSO to PCSO, from one Basic Command Unit (BCU) to another, even from force to force. The sheer physicality of the job is something that needs to be taken into account when thinking of taking up community policing as a career. Nor is this just a random consideration. This Handbook explores the role of the PCSO in providing a highly visible patrol presence within a community, because it is this presence that is precisely a reassurance factor for the community. This reassurance is better evidenced when a PCSO is on foot or on a bicycle, because it allows the opportunity for the officer to stop and communicate with members of the public. Think how much harder it is to feel reassured by a police or liveried 'community team' car going past you, often at speed, as the anonymous and unreachable occupants move on to the latest in a series of calls.

1.7.2 Not an Olympic athlete

Many PCSOs will gain important community intelligence from such conversations and they will attest to the powerful effect that being seen to be approachable, unthreatening, and on foot or pushbike, has upon members of the community. Therefore, physical fitness is important in attaining and maintaining this role. What is important to stress at this stage is that a PCSO should approach the training and acquisition of knowledge responsibly and with an eagerness to learn (see 2.2 and 2.3 below). It also means, of course, that you are trained in the primary role of being a PCSO, not a detention officer, nor an investigating officer, nor an escort officer, each of which roles requires separate and different skills training, even if some overlap with yours.

1.7.3 Fitness tests vary, but the need to measure fitness is constant

The fitness tests on entry or at selection may vary from force to force in terms of the actual test and the exercises used, but the need for some means to assess physical standards is universal. The national recruitment process requires the new entrant to undergo a medical test and the job-related fitness test (JRFT) is a corollary of this. The officer safety training that you will undertake as part of your overall induction training will require that a basic fitness level be established and sustained. One of the most commonly used fitness tests involves two basic fitness requirements:

- **Dynamic strength**—this involves performing five seated chest pushes and five seated back pulls on a machine designed to measure your strength.
- **Endurance**—this involves running back and forth along a set length of track in a measured time-period, indicated with a series of bleeps, which become faster as the test goes on.

1.7.3.1 *Find out what your preferred police force requires in terms of fitness standards*

If you are thinking of applying for a PCSO job then you should look at the individual force requirements for further information on both the fitness tests and the performance indicators required, as well as the procedures should you fail the fitness test. It is worth mentioning that in many cases a failure at this stage will *not* result in your failing to get the PCSO job. You will have the chance to get yourself fit to retake the test, even whilst you are on your induction training course. There is, though, a requirement to pass the fitness test within an allotted period of time.

1.7.4 The 'honest reflection' test

Assuming that the thought of a fitness test, or of a daily foot patrol, or sessions of keep-fit in the gym, has not put you off applying to be a PCSO, then there is much that you can do to be in a position to pass the test first time. Much of this revolves around your honest assessment of your physical fitness and so this should be your first task—**ask yourself unflinchingly if you are fit enough to pass the test**. If the answer is yes, then all you have to do is to maintain your levels of fitness in preparation for the test. If your answer is an equally honest no, then you must look at ways of improving your fitness to optimize your chances of passing first time round. Methods will not simply include training or physical effort, you should look at basic principles in fitness and the nature of your **nutrition, diet, and lifestyle**. Consider the effect of that chocolate craving on Mondays or the few beers with your friends on a Saturday night. Are you eating lots of fried food? How many portions of vegetables and fruit do you have each day? Is it five or more? And are you exercising regularly, sleeping well, not stressed by other factors which may inhibit your fitness? Are you balancing your working life with home and leisure time? This Handbook will not (and should not) provide a 'how to get fit' guide, because there is already a wealth of information in any bookshop on that very subject. Using the standard test as shown in 1.7.3 above provides the areas that your fitness regime should concentrate on: **dynamic strength and endurance**. You should know that some forces are lobbying to use a lower standard of fitness for PCSOs, to match the physical demands of the PCSO patrol role rather than the more confrontational role of the police officer in obtaining compliance. At present, there is no national agreement on how to design a PCSO fitness test, nor any national fitness standard.

1.7.5 Staying fit

Passing the existing fitness test to become a PCSO is one thing, maintaining that fitness during your career is another. The daily patrols will help with that in part (you could wear a simple pedometer to 'clock' your daily patrol miles, for example), but looking at your overall fitness will help to ensure that your health is maintained in a holistic manner. Many police forces will have information on maintaining a healthy work–life balance as part of the internal information available to all staff. Various initiatives may be held in your Force throughout the year to improve staff fitness levels, not least because such initiatives help to reduce absenteeism through sickness. Many police stations also have gyms or corporate membership at private gyms, so that staff can maintain and improve their fitness levels.

1.8 **Chapter Summary**

This chapter has been all about your **entry** into the world of the police and the PCSO. We discussed your reasons for wanting to become a PCSO and examined different kinds of **motivation**. Then we looked at the corollary: what a police force is looking for in its recruits to the ranks of PCSOs. From there it was a short step to looking at the PCSO **application** booklet, the regional or large-force **assessment process**, and the **medical, security, and other standards** which you must meet. Then we examined **ethical issues** and how acceptable forms of behaviour must characterize your performance as a PCSO, before we made a quick résumé of **race and diversity** issues. We concluded with a short discussion about **physical fitness** and standards.

This chapter was designed for the aspirant PCSO, from thinking about police and community service as an occupation, through how to apply and the parameters and standards which you will be expected to meet, to what sorts of issues you need to think about, both before and after you join. None of it is easy. If it were easy, perhaps the role of PCSO would not be so challenging and so rewarding. Let us go on now to look at joining up and staying on. The world of policing and the PCSO awaits.

Notes

1 Correct at the time of going to press. The contents and description of the PCSO application pack may vary over time, but differences are likely to be slight in the short term.

2 Home Office, *Guide to becoming a Police Community Support Officer*, (ref 275499, Central Office of Information (COI), August 2006); close reference to this Guide and to the existing application booklet is

used extensively in this section. We are grateful to the Office of Public Service Information (opsi) for licence to quote from publications produced by HM Government.

3 See Justin Davenport's report on PCSOs in *The Daily Mail*, 24 February 2009, in which the Federation is referred to in this way:

'Police Federation officials are convinced that PCSOs are being recruited as cheap replacements for mainstream officers. They cost at least £10,000 a year less to employ than full-time regular officers. Glen Smyth, chairman of the Metropolitan Police Federation, said: "There used to be laws to stop children going into dangerous occupations such as down mines. Now kids are going on the beat. It is reminiscent of sending boys into the trenches of World War One. It is totally inappropriate for 16- and 17-year-olds to be PCSOs." '

4 There are quite complicated rules about spent convictions and cautions, to which, generally, common sense is applied. People *do* mature and grow up, living down stupid things they did when they were younger (even including the sober and upright authors of this Handbook ...), such as getting drunk or causing damage. That said, any conviction for serious crime, or involvement in any crime entailing the use of violence or dishonesty, is likely to result in rejection. We discuss this more fully in the text that follows and note it further in the Declaration section at 1.4.6 above.

5 For a full report on the number of police officers apparently with convictions for serious offences, see Sarah Bebbington's article 'Cops and Robbers', in Police Review, 20 March 2009, pp. 19–21.

6 If you want to research further into police policy on criminal convictions, visit <http://www.policecouldyou.co.uk> accessed February 2007.

7 Note 7, guidance notes in the application booklet (n 2 above) (Home Office, COI, August 2006).

8 Application booklet notes, taken from the definition in the Disability Discrimination Act.

9 Police (Conduct) Regulations 2004, Sch 1, reg 3, Code of Conduct, available at <http://www.opsi.gov.uk/si/si2004/20040645.htm> accessed January 2007; these have now been replaced by Police (Conduct) Regulations 2008, Schedule 3 (Statutory Instrument 2864) and are called 'Standards of Professional Behaviour', <http://www.opsi.gov.uk/si/si2008/plain/uksi_20082864_en_8>; accessed 5 August, 2009.

10 We are grateful to the Office of Public Service Information (opsi) for permission to reproduce the Policing Pledge, under Class Licence C2007000322. More information may be found at <http://www.homeoffice.gov.uk/documents/policing-pledge> accessed 11 May 2009.

11 Note also that the **Human Rights Act** 1988 legislates for protection of the individual, but of course the 'HRA' is not criminal law. All six diversity strands have been subsumed within one 'guardian' body, the **Commission for Equality and Human Rights**. It is probable that one general Act, embracing all six strands and incorporating the disparate legislation, will come into being by 2012, assuming that such issues remain at the forefront of this, or any other government's, priorities.

12 But see J Dovidio *et al* (eds), *On the Nature of Prejudice: fifty years after Allport* (Blackwell, 2005).

Chapter 2
Joining Up and Staying On

2.1 Impacts on PCSOs from the Start

This chapter looks at issues which will impact on you from the time that you join a police force and put on the PCSO uniform, covering the following areas: the nature of the PCSO uniform itself, what your training will probably include in the first few weeks, your 'rules of engagement' as a PCSO, and the calls in some quarters for PCSOs to have even more powers.

2.1.1 PCSO training and learning

We also look at your training and learning, focusing on the 'experiential learning cycle' (ELC). We follow this with a discussion about what needs to be done to establish policing as a profession and what your part in that could be, before briefly considering various professional qualification routes for police officers and for PCSOs.

2.1.1.1 'Designation' and its importance

We then glance at the nature of Designation and documents about this which you carry, before looking at what a typical tour of duty might entail, together with a discussion of PCSO duties and obligations. This is followed by a discussion about some hostility towards the PCSO concept from within policing itself, and we look at associated elements such as 'mission creep' and argue the need to keep PCSO work distinct from policing, even when neighbourhood management is shared between the two roles of police officer and PCSO. We examine carefully the first pieces of research into, and evaluation of, the PCSO role across the country.

2.1.1.2 *The courts system in England and Wales*

This leads us naturally enough to examine the outcome of the work you do in bringing offenders to justice, and we look at the courts system in England and Wales, examining the characteristics of the criminal justice system and what is entailed in both magistrates' courts and Crown Courts.

2.1.1.3 *Human rights and criminal justice*

This is followed by a short analysis of human rights and how these relate to your work as a PCSO, but also more generally in the way that human rights and the Human Rights Act 1998 impact on criminal justice. The chapter concludes with a summary of what we have examined and discussed. As usual, there are discussion points, points to note, and some tasks throughout the chapter to reinforce your learning and understanding.

2.2 Joining Up

2.2.1 Typical induction for a PCSO

We must emphasize at the outset of this section that what we describe and comment upon is a typical induction into a typical police force. There may be something like 43 minor variations on what we describe as typical, and the chances are that your own induction, whether several years ago or next month, may have had or will have differences. Please bear that in mind: we are not offering a template of how induction should be handled, but describing what we have seen to be pretty uniform practice across the police service of England and Wales. We have already examined in depth the recruitment process and talked about your fitness and physical standards in Chapter 1. Now is the time to discuss joining the police.

2.2.2 Starting as a PCSO

When you receive your letter of appointment as a PCSO, you will have contained within it your start date for training and instructions to 'parade' or to arrive in time for your uniform fitting. In late 2006, there was something of a minor scandal about the supply of uniform to some southern police forces, with a delay particularly in the provision of black trousers. Indeed, some forces reported that male PCSOs had been erroneously issued with skirts by the single supplier because there were no trousers available. There has been no shortfall since, and indeed, no agreement nationally on PCSO uniform (see below). The frustration expressed by forces and by PCSOs about this episode centred more on the sense of 'belonging' and identity which a uniform provides, than on any sense of incompleteness in not having the uniform issue in all its components. A shortfall in the availability of epaulettes would not have been so much of a problem, of course, but male PCSOs cannot patrol without trousers. Female officers can choose to wear skirts or trousers.

2.2.2.1 *Uniform*

You will see in 2.6 below (Designation) that the PCSO uniform is described in the designation by some forces and a distinction is made between Police CSOs and any other kind. Some rural community support officers, or those who patrol a country beat, may have green facings, green hat bands, and green-embroidered epaulettes to distinguish them from the royal blue colours associated with the standard PCSO uniform. Other CSOs may have the standard uniform which we itemize below, with the omission of the word 'police'. Some forces will not use the 'police' designation for fear of further confusing the separate identities of community support officers and police officers. The standard description is, as we have adopted throughout this Handbook, **Police** Community Support Officer; the distinction made by ACPO is entirely sensible: **PCSOs have the police prefix if their appointments are made by the Chief Constable,** under section 38 of the Police Reform Act 2002. If the officer is funded by a partnership or through non-police agencies, then the words 'Community Support Officer' or CSO suffice.[1]

2.2.2.2 *The uniform's components*

The PCSO uniform typically consists of:

- Police-type flat cap (male officers) or bowler (female officers) with a reflective hat band in royal blue or edged in royal blue (a lighter blue than that associated with police officers)
- Blue enamel hat or cap badge with 'Police Community Support Officer' (or sometimes 'Community Support Officer' only); sometimes with the Force badge

- Blue epaulettes embroidered with 'Police Community Support Officer' and the officer's number (or sometimes with 'Community Support Officer' only and the force number), sometimes with the Force badge

Because of the Welsh Language Act, all public authorities in Wales must produce a Welsh version of whatever they do, so PCSO is rendered as **SCCH—Swyddog Cefnogi Cymuned yr Heddlu**. Both English and Welsh versions are printed on blousons, high-visibility jackets, *Gore-Tex* (trade-marked description of the waterproof material) anoraks, epaulettes, cap badges and so on, much the same as is done for police (*Heddlu*) designations in Wales.

- White shirt with epaulettes and radio loops, though some forces have issued light-blue or grey shirts to distinguish them from those issued to police officers
- Blue or black tie (plain) with collar inserts
- Trousers (black heavy duty); plus all-weather or waterproof black trousers (see kit 'table' [at 2.2.2.3] below)
- Black leather belt
- Blue sweater (jumper or pullover) with an embroidered badge with 'Police Community Support Officer' (or sometimes 'Community Support Officer' only) and the Force badge
- Black *Gore-Tex* type anorak, with epaulettes, radio loops and a badge embroidered with the words 'Police Community Support'

Variations on a uniform theme

Some forces issue black 'blouson'-type jackets, embroidered or printed with the words 'Police Community Support Officer' and the Force badge. Many forces additionally issue high-visibility yellow tabards or 'gilets' to go over the uniform jacket or anorak, and nearly all forces will incorporate a reflective panel in the rear of the anorak or blouson which reads 'Police Community Support Officer' or 'Swyddog Cefnogi Cymuned yr Heddlu' (or sometimes 'Community Support Officer' only). There is also a suggestion that the 'collar and tie', or cravat, will disappear in time, to be replaced by a roll neck or similar. Even if this proposal is accepted by the police service at large, it will be some time before it is universal.

Document pouch

Note that the document pouch is similar to the type issued to traffic wardens or parking attendants, and is often used to hold fixed penalty notices or penalty notices for disorder (FPNs and PNDs), though increasingly, PCSOs are carrying their Pocket Note Books (PNB) in the document pouch rather than in the blouson or anorak top pocket, assuming that their uniform has such pockets. Police officers, too, increasingly find that the newer blouson is not as useful for housing the PNB as the old-style tunic with two chest pockets.

2.2.2.3 *Specifying equipment*

Many forces additionally specify the uniform and the amount of equipment issued to male and female officers respectively as we show in the table below.

Male PCSO issue	Female PCSO issue
1 × Anorak with lining	1 × Anorak with lining
1 × general service (GS) over-trousers	1 × general service over-trousers
1 × hard-wearing trousers	3 × skirt or trousers (choice of the individual officer) not usually issued AW trousers
2 × all-weather trousers	
7 × shirts white (but see 2.2.2.2 above)	7 × shirts white (but see 2.2.2.2. above)
1 × cap (police-type)	1 × bowler hat
1 × cap badge numerals	1 × hat badge numerals
2 × epaulettes	2 × epaulettes
1 × document pouch	1 × document pouch
1 × leather belt	1 × leather belt
2 × pullover (unlined)	2 × pullover (unlined)
2 × ties (clip-on type)	2 × cravat or clip-on tie
1 × gloves black leather	1 × gloves black leather
1 × woollen scarf	1 × woollen scarf
1 × 'Hi-Viz' over-jacket	1 × 'Hi-Viz' over-jacket

We are not making a gender point here; it is enough to note that female PCS officers have different headgear from their male colleagues, different trousers, and they can opt for a cravat rather than a tie, if they wish.

2.2.2.4 *Uniformity*

A report by NPIA into PCSOs in July 2008 (see 2.8.3.5 below) noted that there was no consensus for a national uniform for PCSOs and that to set a standard uniform for PCSOs was unrealistic and the potential cost implications would be prohibitive, but the report went on to recommend consistency of uniform, in particular a common approach and appearance:

- The uniform should be of good quality, fit for the duties performed, and ensure the health and safety of the wearer
- It must be distinct from that of a police officer
- It should identify the wearer as a 'Police Community Support Officer' or 'Community Support Officer'
- The uniform should identify the wearer as a member of the wider police force they belong to
- The PCSO identifying features should be nationally consistent:
  Plain blue hat band
  Plain blue epaulettes
  Plain blue tie

[adapted from NPIA's PCSO Review, July 2008, Recommendation 14, p. 19]

POINTS TO NOTE

It is a matter for individual forces whether footwear is issued or not, but in many forces, PCSOs have to supply their own black shoes or boots.

2.2.3 **PCSO training**

So there you are, fully equipped and ready to take on your first patrol duties, except that there is the small matter of training to be considered first. We cannot prescribe for you the training you will receive; not only will the content of your training vary from force to force, but its length and intensity will also be a matter for each individual force within the broad framework of **Knowledge, Understanding, Skills, Attitudes and Behaviours** (KUSAB). There is also variation in *when* you may receive particular training; some forces concentrate on 'core' training, others have a broader programme which includes some of the National Occupational Standards at the outset. The extent of this training is not prescribed, merely advised.

2.2.3.1 *Components of training*

However, there are elements of PCSO training which are almost certain to be covered in the first year. A list might include most of these elements that follow, which we have split into KUSAB headings for convenience of presentation [and to show you how important all parts of your learning are to your effectiveness as a PCSO]. The capital 'C' shown against some learning elements denotes that the element is considered as 'core' to the learning for a PCSO:

Knowledge

- Introduction to the National Occupational Standards: what they are, how you achieve them, and over what time-frame
- Police ranks C
- Police stations: locations, staffing, and how they function C
- Structure and organization of your police force C
- The criminal law, including law to define PCSO powers, sex offenders, RIPA, etc
- The criminal justice system; going to court, giving evidence
- Your powers (the standard powers and any powers specified by your force, such as powers to issue additional fixed penalty notices (FPNs), or to have the powers of a traffic warden, etc) C
- Professional qualifications
- Personal issues: welfare, shifts, pay, benefits, sickness, and counselling
- Criminal intelligence and how to report it
- Attending a crime scene C
- Gathering evidence; the 'continuity of evidence' C
- Making dynamic risk assessments
- Forensic evidence and scene-preservation C
- Sudden deaths
- Laws relating to property; 'lost and found'
- Pocket Note Book C
- Drugs and solvent abuse
- Missing persons and searches

Understanding

- Your powers C
- Learning opportunities provided by tutors, assessors, supervisors, and managers
- On-the-job assessment
- The criminal justice system; going to court, giving evidence
- Anti-social behaviour (including ABCs and ASBOs)[2] C
- Your status in law
- Criminal intelligence and how to report it C
- Attending a crime scene C
- Major incidents

- House-to-house enquiries
- Searches
- Pocket Note Book C
- Gathering evidence; the 'continuity of evidence' C
- How you learn
- Your community and how it works C
- Partnerships and how to develop them C
- Understanding victims' needs
- Missing persons
- Personal development (advancement, appraisal, moving on, or moving up)

Skills

- Safety awareness training (sometimes called by different names: 'personal safety programme', 'self-defence', 'aggression-handling', 'unarmed combat', 'empty-hand skills', and the like) C
- Chairing meetings
- Negotiating and persuading
- Running a public assembly meeting
- Dealing with disputes, arguments, and differences
- Fitness training C
- Making dynamic risk assessments
- Interviewing and questioning
- Communications C
- First aid training C
- Forensic evidence and scene-preservation C
- Writing and self-expression (including making entries in the Pocket Note Book)

Attitudes

- Human rights and the police C
- Race and diversity C
- How you respond to your community
- Ethical and professional standards
- Portfolios of evidence (SOLAP)
- Dealing with disputes, arguments, and differences
- Dealing with the vulnerable
- Partnerships and how to develop them
- Communication C

Behaviours

- Race and diversity C
- Relations with the community C
- How you respond to your community C
- Dealing with the vulnerable
- Communication C
- Working with colleagues
- Partnerships and how to develop them C

2.2.3.2 *Applied learning*

You don't need to be an Einstein to realize that many aspects of KUSAB inter-relate and overlap, which is why we have put some learning elements twice under different headings. **This has to do with possible differences between what you know and what you do**. For example, you may think that you understand all the elements around diversity, and genuinely believe that you are tolerant of others' points of view and non-judgemental in your approach. Yet your behaviour out on the street may signal something very different, if you patronize the elderly, dismiss their concerns, always plead the cause of the 'misunderstood young', and fail to preserve balance and fairness in your dealings with all members of the community. Another instance might be that you have learned and noted down what to do when you are first to arrive at a crime scene, but, in the heat or stress of the moment, you forget important matters such as a 'common approach path' (CAP); as a result, vital evidence is lost. In other words, there may be a gap between how you *think* you come across and how in fact you impact on others, or between what you know you should do and what you actually do.

2.2.4 Outcomes

Your trainers and tutors will properly emphasize that you will do a great deal of learning 'on the job'; that is, out on patrol and engaging with members of the community. This is when you will understand the value, for example, of a persuasive tongue and you will learn how your effectiveness may be enhanced by your knowledge. The outcome of a particular negotiation might confirm your (perhaps) newly acquired skills, whilst a public meeting in which the community starts to create a unified approach to its problems may testify to your skills as a chair of such activities. These are the outcomes of applying your learning, exemplifying that old military dictum that 'the battle is the pay-off' for all the hard work which went into preparation for, thinking about, and understanding the terrain in which to operate. (Incidentally, it should also be clear to you that many of the learning items and outcomes which we list above form the basis of this Handbook, and thus we try to contribute directly to your KUSAB as a PCSO.)

2.2.5 Concerns about 'mission creep'

We discuss in 2.8 below the possible hostility which you may encounter when you join, from colleagues within the police service. We do not seek to exaggerate this potentially negative reaction to you and to PCSOs in general, but we certainly should not ignore it either. The hostility is there and it is tangible and, inside the job at least, has much to do with impressions that PCSOs are blurring the distinctions between police support staff and police officer. The perception that, slowly and with deliberation, forces are giving PCSOs more of the traditional constable's role to perform, has been described as '**mission creep**'. The Association of Chief Police Officers (ACPO) acknowledges that this hostility exists, and that it was marked when PCSOs first began:

> The role of the PCSO in comparison to [sic] that of the police officer is still relatively new. It is clear that there is still some lack of understanding of the role of the PCSO. … It is imperative that all those in the police service are aware of the importance of the role, what the role actually entails [and] ensuring that there is no mission creep, nor abuse of authority.[3]

2.2.5.1 *Potential and actual confusions between PCSOs and police officers*

ACPO has asserted also[4] that the successful deployment of PCSOs in non-police roles had mitigated much of the initially negative response and that criticism of PCSOs is slowly ebbing. This may be true, though we continue to obtain evidence of the continued hostility to PCSOs in some quarters, and the Police Federation has remained implacably opposed.[5] What is painfully evident is that the distinction between the roles of police officer and PCSO must continue to be tightly and publicly distinguished. We should remind you at this point that ACPO has made very clear the distinction in practice between the role of a police officer and that of a PCSO. ACPO defined the 'preserve of sworn police officers' as:

- Whenever there is a clear likelihood that a confrontation will arise
- When there is scope for [the] exercise of a high degree of discretion
- Where police action is likely to lead to a higher than normal risk of harm to anyone
- Where there is a clear likelihood that police action will include any infringement of a person's human rights
- Where the incident is one which is likely to lead to significant further work.[6]

2.2.5.2 *Rules of Engagement*

In the British Army, and especially when 'policing' a hostile area, soldiers are issued with a yellow card on which are printed the rules under which they may open or return fire. These are called '**Rules of Engagement**' and the idea has been transferred to police practice by an imaginative ACPO team, which proffers the following as the PCSO version of the Rules of Engagement (you will note, of course, that there will be the inevitable minor variations from force to force):

[This framework governs all interventions, including the exercise of powers, and draws on risk assessments for the particular location where the PCSO or SCCH will patrol or be engaged.]

- There will be no expectation that PCSOs will be engaged in activities assessed as 'high risk'
- The decision by a PCSO to withdraw, observe and report is a valid tactical option and will be supported by the Force
- There is no positive duty for PCSOs to intervene: they are not police officers
- The PCSOs' main purpose is to support police officers by performing (primarily) observation and reporting activities
- PCSOs' actions will support the human rights of individuals according to PLAN guidance (or equivalents, such as JAPAN and SOCAP) to ensure that actions are proportionate, legal, authorized and necessary
- PCSOs are expected to use their judgement in determining what the benefits and risks are in any given situation

2.2.5.3 *Safe working*

We look at making **dynamic risk assessments** in greater detail in 5.7 below, but it is worth noting at this point in the Handbook that a **'safe working' flow diagram** has been developed by forces (notably Lincolnshire) for inclusion in the *ACPO Guidance* to forces, which was written originally in 2003, published in 2005, and updated in late 2006.[7]

2.2.6 Conclusions

We have examined several matters which relate directly to your entry into the PCSO ranks and to your deployment by

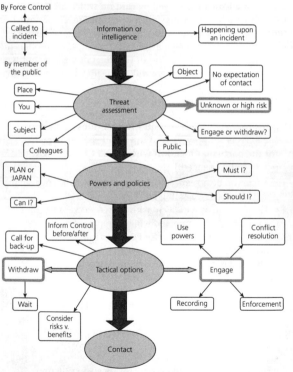

Figure 4: Safe working—risk-assessing PCSO work

(We are grateful to ACPO for permission to reproduce the flow diagram here, though we have

your police force. We have looked at the way you will dress and the close association between your uniform and that of a police officer, whilst noting that distinctions between the two are sustained, reasonably neatly. There is a distinction too between your uniform and that of CSOs in other partnerships or arrangements. We examined the probable content of your training, within KUSAB, and noted which elements may be denoted as 'core' and which might follow later. We looked at the 'Rules of Engagement' for PCSOs and at a flow-diagram which expressed graphically the complexities involved in intervention. These debates will not end with this discussion in the Handbook, but will probably continue to take place as long as there is a central confusion about what a PCSO is and how that is different from, or increasingly identical to, the role of a sworn police officer.

2.3 **Teaching and Learning**

As soon as you enrol as a PCSO you will receive training. To some extent the content of your training will reflect the number of powers designated to you by your force. You may be aware that there is now a standardized agreement on a common set of powers for all PCSOs in England and Wales (differences persist concerning powers to *arrest, detain, and report*), see our extensive discussion in Chapter 3. Forces still have the autonomy to add to those 'standard' powers if they wish, based on existing legislation. Increasing standardization, and a stronger emphasis perhaps on 'one size fits all PCSOs', may be ushered in through the introduction of the **Wider Policing Learning Development Programme** (the WPLDP), an NPIA learning programme that outlines the core elements of initial training for PCSOs, underpins the learning from the National Occupational Standards (NOS), and looks at continuous learning within the wider policing family. We touched on this briefly in 2.2 above, with our glance at lists of topics which PCSOs will have to know.

2.3.1 **Basic training components**

Typically your initial training is likely to last anything between three weeks and two months and will include a combination of classroom and supervised practical activity. In some forces you may be undertaking some training in common with trainee police officers. You will certainly learn about the **community** that you will support (including issues of diversity and human rights), **health and safety** (including your own personal safety), a number of **basic offences** (such as theft, assaults, and criminal damage), and your **powers**. You may also be given some instruction in interviewing and **statement taking**.

2.3.1.1 'Bespoke' training is preferable

This might involve the use of NPIA-designed learning materials (old police training materials, some of which appear to have been rather hastily adapted from existing police training manuals; there is nothing wrong with doing this except that the learning for PCSOs would be better, we think, if specifically designed or 'bespoke'). You could well receive follow-up training at later dates, particularly if your number of designated powers increases.

2.3.1.2 Controversy and good practice

Although the format and content of your training is largely a matter for your Force, the Home Office (2002) does recommend the following:

- That it is locally delivered.
- That your trainers are appropriately qualified to train, particularly in specialist areas such as health and safety.

There has been some controversy in the past concerning the appropriateness of PCSO training, some of which was fuelled by a *Daily Mirror* article by an undercover journalist in May 2005 (Sampson, 2005). The undercover reporter claimed that his four weeks' training left him unprepared for and 'terrified' of the role as a PCSO. However, at least some of his claims were refuted by the then-Commissioner of the MPS, Sir Ian Blair, and others (Blair, 2005). Other concerns on training were reported in the Home Office Research Study 'A national evaluation of Community Support Officers', particularly with regard to IT and use of radio training (Cooper et al, 2006; we examine this in more detail in chapter 4 below). Good practice was also identified by the Study, particularly in terms of PCSO trainees' induction into both their organization (specifically their BCU) and their local communities (Cooper *et al*, 2006).

2.4 **Teaching and Learning as a Trainee PCSO**

If you are in class with a number of other trainees, there is every chance that each of you has a different **preferred learning style**. Therefore, it is obviously a challenge to the training staff to accommodate each trainee PCSO with an appropriate learning activity best suited to his or her preferred learning style. A popular approach in training is that of 'facilitation' where trainers adopt styles and techniques to bring out (you may hear the phrase 'tease out') ideas and views from the group whilst at the same time reducing their own roles as conventional, didactic, 'stand at the front and talk' teachers.

A number of activities commonly employed by trainers are described below. They are used to engage all members of the group at least once during a session.

The whole class response (the 'boardblast')

The **'boardblast'** is a very popular teaching method used by police trainers. The tutor will invite responses from some or all of you which will be written down on a pen board ('whiteboard') or flip-chart, and then discussed in the whole group or in smaller 'syndicates'. The content of the boardblast will be assessed by the tutor and revisited at different stages of the lesson. This can often be a very effective method. A rather tedious variation on this is the **'sticky paper notes session'** where individuals or groups put their ideas, thoughts or reactions on small pieces of coloured semi-sticky paper and then collect and display such notes under various headings. Anyone who has ever endured management training will recognize this much over-used technique. Straight work from group to pen board or flip-chart is preferable because of its immediacy and engagement.

Case studies

Case studies involve a practical example of a community-related problem which will be given to you as an individual or a group activity. You will be invited to read the material and form conclusions about its content to show your understanding of the subject.

Demonstration

Demonstration can be used if the subject matter involves the use of the body in the psychomotor domain, such as personal safety training. The tutor will demonstrate how your body should move in order that you can repeat the activity afterwards.

Working in small groups

Small group work is a very common method in training. You will be invited to work in small groups and share ideas between the groups. For this approach to work well, it is very important that each member of the group is actively involved in the task and that nobody sits back allowing the rest to carry the main burden. It is important also that concentration is maintained on the task in hand, and that your mind does not wander to unconnected matters; this is important, but not easy to achieve (and see our comments on the 'sticky paper notes' sessions above).

Discussions led by trainers or tutors

Facilitated discussions are particularly useful for exploring attitudes and behaviours. Your trainers will encourage you to share your own thoughts with others in the 'safe learning environment' they expect to have established. You should be prepared to maintain confidentiality as you and your colleagues may disclose private and sensitive matters (you will certainly be reminded of this need on numerous occasions). From the discussion you will have the opportunity to draw your own conclusions. The discussion may be initiated by watching a video or DVD, or by reflecting on the presentation of a guest speaker, or by some of the topics we raise in this Handbook, designated as '**Discussion points**'. Finally, as a member of staff of a police organization, you should remember throughout discussions that you are probably under observation by your tutors. **Confidentiality does not protect you from disciplinary action against inappropriate language, attitudes, or behaviour**.

Presentations

Presentations are used for some topics. If the subject matter is appropriate for this form of delivery (for example an overview of a piece of legislation), or time is short, your trainers may well deliver a presentation, often using Microsoft 'PowerPoint' software. Throughout the presentation, you will be given the opportunity to ask questions and make notes. Your trainer might direct questions to you. Different trainers will have different approaches to delivering presentations which may or may not coincide with your learning style. For example, a trainer may use the technique of progressively revealing bullet points which, although they may keep your attention, can be irritating to some. Most trainers welcome feedback on matters such as this, possibly in the evaluation (sometimes called 'happy') sheets you might be asked to complete and submit.

Playing a part

Role plays are where you adopt or 'play' given roles in a certain situation. For example, one of you may act as a PCSO and the other a member of the public in a simulated scenario, such as you saw when we discussed the PCSO assessment process in Chapter 1. Role plays are normally used when you have gained sufficient knowledge and skills to make them meaningful (particularly in terms of the extent of your powers). One underlying principle in the role-play approach is that adult learners are able to draw upon previous experiences to enhance their learning. Just as significant for your learning as the role play itself, is the '**debrief**' that normally happens later (you could even be videoed to assist with this). In all cases the brief for the role play should be carefully explained to you at the outset. Note that, as we discuss in Chapter 4, with the exception of practising first aid, role plays and simulations cannot normally be used as evidence against achievement of the NOS.

2.4.1 The experiential learning cycle (ELC)

You have undoubtedly heard of the sayings, 'If at first you don't succeed, try, try again', or, 'We all learn by our mistakes'. Much of your learning will take place through your own experiences, and as adults we can actually teach ourselves, at least in part. How many times have you mentally said to yourself, 'I won't do that again!' or 'That didn't work! Is there another way?'

Task

Think of a situation you found yourself in recently, after which you decided to do something differently next time. Now relate those circumstances to the diagram below, starting with 'Experience' and moving through the diagram in a clockwise fashion.

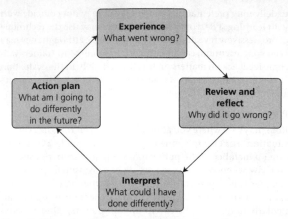

Figure 5: Adaptation of Kolb's experiential learning cycle

This diagram in the task above shows the *experiential learning cycle* (ELC) and has been adapted from the work of David Kolb (Kolb, 1984). Many of your trainers are likely to have used the model to inform the way in which they have structured and organized your taught sessions.

2.4.2 Stages of the cycle

The four stages to the cycle are as follows:

- **Experience** (called '*Concrete Experience*' in the Kolb original)
  This is direct experience, often through practical application. As a trainee PCSO, you will often want to know what the practical applications of the session will be. You may want to get 'hands on' as soon as possible. The trainer may provide 'hooks' for you to hang on to—for example by asking you 'to think of times in your own life when you have been subject to bullying or harassment'.
- **Review and reflect** ('*Reflection*')
  What does the experience mean to me? This stage is the beginning of understanding through review and reflection, or thinking about what has happened to you and how you felt about it. A request such as 'describe your feelings when you were bullied or harassed' may be made.

- **Interpret** (*'Abstract Conceptualization'*)
  This involves placing the experiences in some form of theoretical and more abstract framework. 'How might victims feel about this?'
- **Action plan** (*'Active Experimentation'*)
  This stage of action-planning focuses on how we take this learning forward and test it against reality. 'How do we act as a police service to support victims of harassment?'

2.4.3 Using the ELC in other training

The experiential learning cycle is also used by trainers during other forms of learning. For example, after a role play (see 4.12 below, **NOS 4G4**, *Administer First Aid*), the participants may be asked, among other things: 'What did not go quite so well? What was the outcome of that? What are you going to do differently in the future?'

2.4.3.1 *Styles of learning*

Many trainers are taught to link the learning cycle with **styles of learning**, for example by devising approaches for activist learners to help them through the interpret stage of the ELC. This is part of the 'facilitation' tradition in training that we described earlier.

Task

You are on uniformed patrol and accompanied by an experienced NOS assessor. You are deployed to a street where there are reports of a vociferous argument between two neighbours concerning the alleged dumping of an old sofa. You are made aware that uniformed police assistance has also been summoned. You attempt to calm the neighbours down, but the situation deteriorates, violence is threatened, and your more experienced colleague has to intervene. After the incident is dealt with, your assessor asks you a number of questions, such as: 'Were there any risks to you during the incident?' 'How did the neighbours respond to your intervention?' 'What might you have done differently?'

That night you consult your notes on strategies for defusing situations and the reasons why certain strategies might work but others not. The next day, presented with a similar situation, you think: 'Now what did I do wrong yesterday and what did it say in those notes I read? I'll try it like this today.'

Identify, in the above, each of the four stages of Kolb's ELC.

2.4.4 Tutoring, assessing, and mentoring

About 60% of trainee PCSOs are allocated a tutor or assessor after basic training (Cooper *et al*, 2006). As in many other aspects of training, whether you are allocated an assessor or a tutor or not will be down to local Force policy. If you are tutored, then the tutorship period will probably last less than two months after your basic training. Your tutor is likely to be either a police officer or a more experienced PCSO (some undertake a PCSO tutorship course before going on to become assessors or mentors). The role of the tutor or mentor (meaning 'trusted adviser') is to provide you with support, guidance, and advice in your first few months after your basic training.

Discussion point

What are the qualities which you would look for in a tutor or mentor?
Do you think that the roles are different?
Would there be a wide variation, do you think, between people's needs for tutoring or mentoring?
If so, what might they be?

2.5 Potential Professional Qualifications and Learning Routes

In this section, we want to examine possible options concerning the issues of professionalism, academic and vocational qualifications, and routes which may lead to other kinds of learning for the individual PCSO. We examine the potential for the *role* of PCSO in more detail at 7.8 below, but in this section, thinking about the possible development of your individual career as a PCSO, we need to consider what you might want to do and where you might want to go.

2.5.1 Policing as a profession

For many years, more than a century in fact, policing was considered a 'blue collar' job; that is, one which largely consisted of manual skills rather than intellectual or knowledge-based ones (though this perception was often at odds with the expectations of both theoretical and practical knowledge of the criminal law).

At all events, policing, certainly up to the Second World War, was not an occupation which regularly attracted graduates, nor was it widely seen as a 'white collar' (professional, technical, managerial) vocation. Indeed, with an unconscious irony, uniformed police officers physically wore blue shirts until the mid-1980s.

2.5.1.1 *The professions*

Historically, there were only four professions for 'gentlemen' (aristocrats did not engage in anything as low as work; they were perhaps the original managers):

- The armed forces[8]
- The law
- Medicine
- The Church.

Other professions

Accountancy, education, finance, engineering, and architecture joined the 'professions' during the course of the nineteenth century—admitting women as members in some professions more easily than others (teaching rather than medicine), but now there are many occupations which would regard themselves as professions, such as teaching, nursing, the civil service, publishing, and local government, just as there are many jobs which refer to themselves, somewhat obliquely, as 'industries', such as entertainment, leisure, and horse-racing.

Elements of a profession

There is general agreement among academic commentators, though not among all journalists, that there are certain preconditions for an occupation or trade to be thought of as a profession. Think, for a moment, of the regard in which the 'profession' of surgeon was held in, say, Nelson's time (1780–1805 roughly). This was when the skills involved in medicine and surgery were largely self-taught, or not really skills at all after all, how clever did you have to be to saw off a leg without hygiene or anaesthetic?—with the predictable outcome that 'doctors' were regarded as little more than 'sawbones', quacks, or liars, drunken and incompetent, little better than tooth pullers and barbers (often one and the same).[9] It was only from the mid to late nineteenth century, when gradual advances in medicine entailed a greater understanding of science, especially anatomy and physiology, and through the development of increasingly sophisticated medical techniques (including anaesthesia and more successful invasive surgery), that medicine changed from a more or less blood-stained body butchery to a highly regarded, technical, and sophisticated profession. Indeed, contemporary polls continue to put medical doctors at the top of lists of well-regarded professions, usually followed by nurses, the law (especially at the top end of barristers and judges), and teaching. See, for example, the BBC poll of 2002, which showed that doctors and nurses were the most respected of professionals.

2.5.2 Characteristics of a profession

It is generally accepted that **professions have a distinct, written, accessible, and sophisticated corpus (or body) of knowledge**. The knowledge requires effort and application, as well as intelligence, to master (think of detailed knowledge of commercial or patent law, or the physiological functions of the circulatory system, or the material stresses involved in bridge-building). It is possible, within a profession, to specialize in a detailed but limited—in the sense of self-contained—area of knowledge; consider:

- Tax advisers
- Investment brokers
- Geodesic structural engineers
- Divorce lawyers
- Consultants in geriatric medicine or rheumatology
- Experts in military ordnance (guns)
- Researchers in linguistics
- Human resource managers
- Curators of fine art in a museum
- Speech therapists
- Social workers specializing in hearing-impaired children
- Teachers of mathematics
- Designers of software for computers
- Engineers of electronic signalling systems.

These are only a few which we thought about for a couple of minutes from our own experience; we're sure you could think of more yourself:

Discussion point

Make your own list of about 10 specialisms within professions, ensuring that each of them has specialist knowledge which is written and accessible, and which practitioners have carefully studied, often for a long time before 'qualifying' as expert or specialist.

2.5.2.1 *Professions as exclusive bodies*

We could also note that **professions control themselves** and whom they admit to membership. For example, it is unlikely that you could study medicine with a view to becoming a brain surgeon with only a GCSE in media studies. The entrance qualifications to the medical profession usually require you to have knowledge of sciences, though it is possible that you might be accepted on a general medical programme with extensive and sophisticated **APEL** or Accredited Prior Education and Learning. Even then, your continuation towards the exclusive specialism of brain surgery would be conditional first on your successful performance in most of the main branches of medicine and secondly in showing some aptitude or leaning towards surgical skills (not just using a saw!). The same would be true of any comparable profession where the accumulation of knowledge has to be matched, generally, with application and practice.

2.5.2.2 *Professional standards*

It is likely that, when you apply to become a member of a profession, you would have to **sign up to the standards** which that profession's 'governing body' has established for all members. These include things like a competence-based approach to the work of the profession, so convicted fraudsters may find it hard to be accepted as financial advisers. Our point is only that professions largely regulate who can join them, and this tends to be on the basis of skills, ethics, and qualification.

2.5.2.3 *Self-regulation*

Most professions do not take kindly to external interference, and insist that they **regulate themselves** and their members' conduct. Members who do not conform to the profession's standards, or who act unethically, or who 'take pecuniary advantage' (steal from or defraud the profession) are often debarred from continuing membership, sometimes described as 'struck off', or deemed to be 'unlicensed'.

2.5.2.4 *Continuous professional development (CPD)*

Nearly all professions require members to keep up their skills and to adhere to what is called '**continuous professional development**' (CPD, which you will come across again at 4.2 below, when we discuss the National Occupational Standards for PCSOs). This is to ensure currency and to sustain members' capability. Would you want a financial adviser who worked only in pre-decimal currency, or a GP who hadn't shown any interest in the spread of 'avian flu'? There is a sense too in which **all professions demand a minimum acceptable standard of knowledge to qualify as a member**, with corresponding gradations of membership: the Chartered Management Institute is a case in point, where *Member* is the standard grade, followed by advanced standing with *Fellow*, and the highest recognition of skills, status, and practice in *Companion* (the same grades are used for membership of the Chartered Institute for Personnel and Development (CIPD), which is the oversight body and guardian of standards for HR professionals).

2.5.2.5 *Summary*

To sum up this short excursion into what constitutes a profession, we may say that:

- A profession entails extensive and sophisticated technical and examined knowledge, usually leading to a nationally recognized academic qualification, such as a degree or the passing of a professional, qualifying examination (for example that for Chartered Accountants)
- Membership qualification requires application to and understanding of the basis of the profession's corpus (body) of knowledge
- Membership is sustained by continued learning (or continuous professional development, CPD)
- Members are expected to behave within the law and ethically, or face sanctions, including the withdrawal of membership, by the profession's governing or disciplinary bodies
- There are gradations of membership, which depend on status, position, and the degree or extent of individual contribution to the profession
- Professions largely are autonomous, self-regulating, and highly sensitive to how they are publicly regarded. They dislike interference from outside, especially by politicians (think of the prickly independence of barristers and surgeons).

You may be able to think of other characteristics, but we believe that we have made the point sufficiently.

Discussion points

To return to our consideration of policing, in the light of what we have just discussed, can policing be regarded as a profession?
Does it matter if policing is or is not a profession?

2.5.3 Is policing a profession?

On the basis of what we have identified as the prevailing characteristics of a profession, **no**. But there are signs that policing is moving very deliberately towards the components of a profession, with the aim of being regarded as one.

> **Task**
>
> Can you list what those signs could be?

We would point to the following indicators (though our list is not exhaustive and you may be able to think of more):

- *Corpus of knowledge:* there is a considerable body of knowledge, for example the criminal law, but this exists independently of the police, not through or because of policing. There are some doctrinal areas of police-specific knowledge—investigating murder for example—but these are neither codified, nor widely accessible in written form, and therefore do not conform to our definition of a corpus of knowledge. Entrance to policing is not predicated on a nationally recognized academic or vocational qualification— indeed, the police entrance examination is mechanically based for those entering policing as constables—it is not a qualification for membership of a profession (nor, to be fair, was it ever designed to be). Other areas of theory and application with a specifically police flavour do exist, but are often more to do with procedure or practice (the 'how to?' of missing persons searches or dealing with a vulnerable adult, for example) rather than independent knowledge which exists objectively for any to access. Also, there is no recognized route by which the overall knowledge of policing may be advanced, such as through published research.
- That said, there are distinct and deliberate **moves to place policing on a professional footing.** The creation of the National Occupational Standards for police officers (and for PCSOs) is an instance of registering openly the competences specifically associated with policing *and no other occupation.* Skills for Justice, as the guardian of the NOS and, through its applied standard called **Skillsmark** (which assesses the learning provision by police organizations to its staff, and by others such as universities to police staff on behalf of police organizations), is developing a professional approach

to policing. This is underpinned by the **National Police Improvement Agency** (NPIA; the current CEO is Peter Neyroud, ex-Chief Constable of Thames Valley Police), within which is the **National Centre for Policing Excellence** (NCPE, part of the old Centrex, or national police training), which in turn develops police-specific knowledge or 'doctrine'. These signs all suggest that policing is now being conceived as having distinct and separate areas of knowledge, peculiar to and rooted within the 'business' of policing.

- Policing is increasingly subject to **political interference**— including the statutory control exercised centrally by the Home Secretary over policing as well as over individual police forces—and the interference of others (such as Liberty or the Independent Police Complaints Commission) in the regulation, ethical standards, and professional membership of a police force. Until policing has its own governing body, it can hardly be regarded as autonomous and self-regulating, which are characteristics of mature professions.

- *Policing in England and Wales is fragmented*; there are 43 separate 'home forces' and a number of ancillary forces such as the British Transport Police and the Ministry of Defence Police. It is increasingly unconvincing to assert that policing has a single voice, especially when central utterances (for example from the Policing Minister or from assorted Home Office officials) are often flatly and emphatically countered by, say, the Police Federation, Unison, the Superintendents' Association, or ACPO itself, as well as any one of a number of policing agencies which have separate 'voices'. (The police pay round in early 2006 was a good example, as was the unanimous rejection by Chief Constables of the Home Secretary's unconsulted proposal in December 2006 to transfer 400 police constables in support of the Immigration Service's backlog of deportations.)

- Individual police officers have undoubted **autonomy of action** and can exercise initiative in a wide variety of situations, and membership of the police is ordered hierarchically (by rank), so it would not be difficult to read across to stages or levels of membership of a profession. Membership of the police is limited to those regulars and Special Constables who hold a warrant from the Crown, though there are various levels of unofficial 'associate membership' through police staff, PCSOs, and the like.

- There is a sophisticated and extensive **code of ethics** in policing (see 1.5 above and 7.2 below, for extended discussion about ethics in police forces) and this is reinforced by Professional Standards Departments in every police force, as well as additional local standards which are individual to police forces (a *Police Standard*, for example, covers matters like the smart appearance of uniformed officers, courtesy, promptness, rapid and sustained follow-up to enquiries, and so on, which are all strictly behavioural; but we remind you to go back to the discussion in 1.5 above). There are discipline codes and **Police Regulations** which can be used as sanctions against police officers who derogate from the high standards expected of them. Such Regulations are enshrined in law, the guardians of which tend to be Police Federation officials and representatives; there is no corresponding set of regulations for police staff, though the latter may , in time, be subject to the **Standards of Professional Behaviour**, introduced in 2008–2009 as part of Police (Conduct) Regulations 2008, Schedule 3 (SI 2864), for all police officers.

- Policing is probably a **vocation**, though it could be argued that this decreases in proportion to the marginalization of policing as a factor in local communities. Where policing continues to have a positive local impact (for example through neighbourhood teams), there is a vocational flavour to the nature of policing and in the motivation of those who take part, but the desire to 'do good' is much less of a factor in recruitment than it used to be.[10] Also, policing is less likely to be seen as a life career for new entrants. We do not see people joining the police now and intending to stay for 30 or more years. Since the 1990s, new intakes seldom commit beyond ten years, and some go after five. Recruits increasingly see policing as an episode in a portfolio of employment, from which they move to other occupations or professions, including from public service to private enterprise and back again over a period of time (see 7.9 below). This is not to say that people will not stay 30 or more years in policing in the future, but if multiple points of entry become a reality (and in the teeth of opposition from the traditionalists), people are likely to go out of policing at some point after five years (at Sergeant or Inspector rank) and may come back ten or fifteen years later expecting to be superintendents. This may be modified by the economic recession to some degree, as it is unlikely that a flexible job market with easy options to move in and out of public service or private enterprise will be the norm for some years. Those in policing at the moment may well hold on to their jobs for the next few years for fear of the prospect of being unemployed.

2.5.3.1 *Is policing flexible enough for multiple entry?*

Whether policing will be sufficiently flexible to allow multiple entry is a moot point. Structures and attitudes in policing may not even be sufficiently professional to allow it twenty years from now, let alone ten. The fact that it is being discussed at all perhaps might augur well for the eventual professionalizing of the police, but professions are not created through a proliferation of governing bodies, nor through scarcity of resources. Professions become so when they become exclusively self-regulating, of high status, attractive but difficult to get into, and the focus of intelligent and able people's aspirations. The 34% to 37% of graduates who currently enrol in policing may be a welcome sight, but **we are still a long way from being a graduate profession**, and there is no prerequisite of subject in terms of the degree. We are however, some way from the police service stipulating the degree necessary to join the profession, although in 2009, this was the subject of lively debate in the pages of *Police Review*. That said, we must acknowledge that the Association of Chief Police Officers (ACPO), which requires formal entry recommendations, a learning programme, and appointment by a Police Authority to a chief officer position, is the closest that the police service comes to a professional body. That all but a handful of the current ACPO ranks have one or more university degrees suggests that policing—at least at this level — has the capability to be a 'graduate profession'.

2.5.3.2 *Where does the PCSO fit into this debate?*

Where does this leave the PCSO and what relevance does professional standing have for you and your role? As the police service itself is not yet structured in a way to allow easy transition into a profession (other than, perhaps, at the Command level), it is not likely that a new and evolving part of the organization such as PCSOs would be in a position to do so. The PCSO sits very much within the professional public police family, and may capitalize in time on any transition of the police from public service to a professional body. The PCSO cannot, it seems, be considered separately from the rest of public policing any more than police staff in general could be. **If or when the police as a whole become** a professional body, PCSOs will come too. We further discuss professionalism at work and briefly look at what that means to the role of the PCSO at 7.4 below.

2.5.3.3 *Qualifications routes for PCSOs*

Until policing becomes a profession on a par with medicine or engineering (and the transition could be some years away, if then), the question is what can the PCSO do to ensure that there is some kind of national recognition of, and qualification for, his or her role? The discussion centres, currently, somewhere between a **Higher Education** (HE) qualification route and a **National Vocational Qualification** (NVQ) route. The former requires some form of cooperative alliance with an HE institution, such as a university; the latter can be delivered through most police forces and almost any further education college locally, under licence from national bodies, such as City and Guilds. There are other options, not just these bi-polar choices, but we do not detect any appetite nationally for **modern apprenticeships** for PCSOs for example, nor for a 'baccalaureate' type of qualification route. Interestingly, the *Stadswacht*, the equivalent of PCSOs in The Netherlands (from whom the idea first came to Britain), are entered more or less automatically on a foundation degree programme. Only when they are judged capable of attaining a full 'honours' (higher) postgraduate qualification can they move from Stadswacht to fully fledged police officer. Thus the Netherlands has established, *de facto*, a graduate profession for its police officers, which might also explain the ease with which the Dutch police embrace the academic world as partners.

2.5.4 What does the PCSO need?

What is clearly needed for PCSOs is a national qualification linked to the attainment of competences through the National Occupational Standards (NOS, dealt with in detail in Chapter 4). There is at present no national acceptance of the need for or structure of any such award and it is left to individual police forces to devise, arrange, or commission their own. NPIA currently recommend that forces consider adopting an NVQ route for training of PCSOs. However, NPIA also suggests the Chartered Management Institute (CMI) 'Introductory Certificate in Neighbourhood Management' as an alternative (NPIA, 2008, p. 16).[11] We are unlikely to have a resolution of this incoherence for some years.

2.6 Designation

2.6.1 Carrying the 'Designation'

In something like the same way that a police officer carries a warrant card, you carry your PCSO Designation from your Chief Constable, the possession of which, whilst you are on duty and in uniform, gives you the legal right to exercise your PCSO powers.

2.6.2 No uniformity for the Designation

The manner of the Designation varies from police force to police force; there are no hard and fast rules as to what the document should look like. That said, common features should specify the powers which you have within the law and carry your Chief Constable's name and signature. Look at the example below:

DESIGNATION

(Sections 38 & 42 & Schedule 4, Police Reform Act 2002)

This is to certify that .... who is an employee of Gloucestershire Police Authority and is under my direction and control, is designated *POLICE COMMUNITY SUPPORT OFFICER with powers and duties set out in Paragraphs 1 (excludes 2(a) disorder) 2,3,5,6,7,8,9,10,11,12,13,14,15,16 of Part 1 (Paragraph 4 is currently suspended) of Schedule 4 to the Police Reform Act 2002.

Chief Constable *Timothy Brain.* Timothy Brain QPM BA PhD

Date ....

The Chief Constable may at any time by notice to the Police Community Support Officer modify or withdraw this Designation.

This Certificate of Designation is to be retained by the Police Community Support Officer. When producing this Designation upon request in accordance with s.42 of the Police Reform Act 2002 the Community Support Officer shall produce the Constabulary Identity Pass bearing a photograph of the holder.

A copy of this Certificate of Designation will be retained with the Police Community Support Officer's personal file.

If this Certificate is modified, withdrawn or replaced it shall be surrendered immediately to Gloucestershire Constabulary Personnel Department and retained within the Police Community Support Officer's personal file.

s.38(7)(a)

EXAMPLE

(Reproduced with the kind permission of Gloucestershire Police, and of Dr Tim Brain, QPM, Chief Constable)

Figure 6: Designation of a PCSO in Gloucestershire Police

2.6.2.1 *The meaning of the Designation*

Notice how the authority of the Chief Constable over PCSOs derives from the Police Reform Act 2002, which we look at in more detail in Chapter 3. The essential point is that the bearer of the Designation is under the 'direction and control' of the Chief Constable, and acting with his or her authority. This is supplemented by specifying which of the powers designated under the Police Reform Act 2002 are applied by the Chief Constable. In some forces, each of the powers is specified (see 3.2 below), and in others a summary of the powers is provided. In this instance, Gloucestershire Police gives a short summary of the references to Schedule 4 to the Police Reform Act 2002, but gives further and specific detail on an attached page. Since the agreement to grant 'standard powers' to PCSOs in 2006, such specifics on the Designation are largely redundant, and may soon disappear to be replaced by the standard powers list, or brief reference may be made to the existence of powers only. The Designation is not an identity document (that is supplied separately as a police staff identification, which, again, varies from police force to police force) and possession of the Designation paper simply confirms that a PCSO can exercise specified powers, in uniform and on duty. Production of the Designation (under section 42 of the Police Reform Act 2002) is likely only in circumstances where the PCSO's authority is challenged or questioned. Note that production of the Designation is 'upon request': it is not used like a warrant card.

2.6.2.2 *Distinction between PCSO and police officer*

Note too, that the Chief Constable of Gloucestershire Police is careful to comment that the PCSO who carries the Designation is 'an employee of Gloucestershire Police Authority' and not a police officer or officer of the Crown. We discuss this aspect of your employment further in Chapter 3, but essentially it means that PCSOs are support staff, employed by their Police Authority and not subject to the disciplined requirements of police regulations or sworn authority. In fact, police support staff, including PCSOs, are subject to and protected by employment legislation in ways that police officers are not. This is why the Chief Constable's 'direction and control' are specified. The Chief Constable does not employ you but he or she does have **operational command**, which means that he or she can tell you what to do, where to go, and how to discharge your duty in accordance with the operational priorities and directions established for your police force.

2.6.2.3 *Your authority*

In summary, then, the Designation sets out the legal authority and conditions under which you are deployed and specifies your powers. The Designation is signed by the Chief Constable of your Force and this is your legal entitlement to be a PCSO and exercise the powers of a PCSO whilst on duty. There are important differences in this from being a sworn police officer, which we might glance at briefly.

Discussion point

Can you enumerate the differences between a police officer and a PCSO in terms of powers and 'office'?

2.6.3 Differences between PCSOs and police officers

The differences are quite profound, and the greater extent of powers, the wide exercise of them, the use of discretion, and the ability to use force to ensure compliance means that a police officer's training, both in terms of physical training, skills for the job, and in knowledge of the law, is much more extensive and thorough than a PCSO's (about 23 months as against a maximum of seven weeks).

2.6.3.1 *The powers of 'the office of constable'*

A police officer is attested (or 'sworn') before a magistrate, whereupon the powers of **the office of constable** are conferred upon the individual officer, who may now act in the name of the Crown. S/he is issued with a warrant card which identifies the holder by name, photograph, and rank, and which is signed by the Chief Constable or Commissioner of his or her force. The warrant card is an important form of identification for a police officer, but s/he can continue to exercise his or her powers whether or not actually holding the card physically on his or her person. The powers of the office are available all the time, whether or not the police officer is on duty and whether or not the officer is in uniform. In practical terms, however, a police officer usually carries his or her warrant card at all times, and, of course, especially when on duty. Also, in practice, he or she is unlikely to have to exercise police powers in another Force or in another part of the country unless participating in a joint police operation of some kind, in which case arrangements for the inter-operability of powers will have been made (such as happened when English and Welsh officers assisted Scottish police forces at the G8 'Summit' at Gleneagles in July 2005).

2.6.3.2 PCSO Powers

All this is a far cry from being a PCSO. You can see that the powers for a PCSO are much more limited:

PCSO Powers and Jurisdiction

- Limited to the powers designated by a Chief Constable (irrespective of the 'standard powers')
- Operable only when on duty
- PCSOs must be in uniform
- PCSOs must carry their Designations
- In any law-enforcement or crime situation where police officers are present PCSOs are always subordinate to police officers in terms of powers and jurisdiction.

2.6.3.3 Another form of Designation

Let us look at another Designation by a Chief Constable of a PCSO, this time on the other side of the country, in Kent. The Designation for a Kent PCSO looks like this:

KENT POLICE COMMUNITY SUPPORT OFFICERS DESIGNATED POWERS
Kent Police Community Support Officers, having passed an accredited training course, are hereby designated under Part 4 of the Police Reform Act 2002, to exercise the following powers when on duty by the Chief Constable of Kent.
To issue Fixed Penalty Notices for dog fouling, littering and cycling on the footpath
Power to stop a pedal cyclist riding on a footpath
To issue Penalty Notices for Graffiti and Fly Posting
To request the name and address of a person acting in an anti-social manner
To request a person to stop drinking in a designated public area and to surrender open containers of alcohol
To confiscate alcohol from young persons

Figure 7: PCSO Designation—Kent Police

2 Joining Up and Staying On

To confiscate cigarettes and tobacco products from young people
To enter premises to save life or limb, or to prevent serious damage to property
To seize vehicles used to cause alarm and distress under section 59 of the Police Reform Act
To require removal of abandoned vehicles
To stop vehicles for the purpose of a road check where the road check is authorized by Police Superintendent under Section 4 Police & Criminal Evidence Act
To maintain and enforce a cordoned area under Section 36 Terrorism Act 2000
To stop and search vehicles and things carried by driver, passengers and items carried by persons in authorized area under Sections 44 and 45 Terrorism Act 2000
Signed: Michael Fuller QPM Chief Constable

KENT POLICE COMMUNITY SUPPORT OFFICERS POWERS TO REQUIRE NAME AND ADDRESS

Police Community Support Officers have the power to require the name and address of a person in the following circumstances:

Where a PCSO has reason to believe that a relevant offence has been committed.

A relevant offence includes:

- a relevant Fixed Penalty Offence (as listed above)
- an offence involving injury, alarm or distress, or an offence involving loss or damage to property (in respect of offences involving Thefts, Assaults, Criminal Damage or Harassment)

OR

- a reasonable belief that a person is or has been acting in anti-social manner

It is an offence to
- Assault, resist or wilfully obstruct designated PCSOs in the execution of their duty
- Fail to give your name to a designated PCSO when required to do so
- Impersonate a designated PCSO

APPROVED UNIFORM

The Chief Constable of Kent has approved the following uniform to be worn by Kent Police Community Support Officers:

Figure 7 *(continued)*

(Reproduced with the kind permission of Mike Fuller, QPM, Chief Constable)

Black trousers, white shirt, blue tie, blue epaulettes with approved Kent Police PCSO badge
Black jumper, black fleece and yellow reflective outer coat with approved Kent Police PCSO badge on the front and rear
Black cap for men and black bowler hat for women with approved Kent Police PCSO badge
Badge bearing Police Community Support Officer and Force number will be worn at all times
Community Partnership PCSOs will wear green ties, epaulettes, jumpers, fleece and coat with an approved Community Partnership PCSO badge

Figure 7 *(continued)*

2.6.3.4 *Differences in emphasis and detail*

This reproduction of the Kent Police Designation points up some subtle differences from the Gloucestershire example. The paper makes explicit the powers with which the Chief Constable designates patrol PCSOs in Kent's Neighbourhood Policing Teams, and specifies each of the powers, together with the necessary references to sections of the **Police Reform Act 2002, PACE 1984**, and the **Terrorism Act of 2000**. Then the Designation makes clear the compulsion powers which a PCSO has in respect of requiring a name and address and defines the related offences for which that power can be invoked. The offences of 'assault, resist or wilfully obstruct' and impersonation of a PCSO are also spelled out in the Designation, serving both to remind the individual PCSO what his or her powers are, and explaining a PCSO's powers to any enquirer.

2.6.3.5 *Function of the Designation*

Those of you about to enter service as PCSOs should now have an appreciation of how your Designation serves as the legitimation of your function, as well as being a handy form of reference for your legal powers. For those of you already with some service in, you may wish to note that Designations vary from force to force. It is worth comparing your Designation with others, since there may be elements in yours which could assist or clarify the Designation used in another force, and vice versa. For the foreseeable future, the Designation paper will continue to act in the 'standing' of a police warrant: it is simultaneously the PCSO's authority and the means of defining that authority.

Task

Compare your Designation with that of two of your neighbouring forces.

What points are there in common between Designations?

Are any of the differences worth importing to your Force? How would you go about that?

2.7 What Do You Do? Varieties of PCSO Deployment, Variations from Force to Force: A Typical Tour of Duty

The difficulty in producing a PCSO Handbook whose guidance and information apply across all police forces and circumstances is that some of the topics we cover will vary in emphasis, utility (whether it works), and popularity from force to force, from BCU to BCU, from neighbourhood team to neighbourhood team, and even from PCSO to PCSO. *None will vary more than what you actually do*. The strength of the PCSO role, of course, is that it adapts to the local community in which it is placed and, in terms of community engagement and problem solving (two of its chief functions), it takes its cues from the people in the community themselves. Therefore, a definitive guide to what you do on a daily basis is impossible to compile and could actually take you down a wrong path, especially if what you attempt (because you saw it here) is at odds with what your community wants and expects.

2.7.1 Generic and specialist roles

This section will look at some generic roles that would probably be included in a PCSO's daily duty, as well as looking briefly at some of the specialist *roles* that a PCSO could play. We are not providing a 'to-do list', rather we are suggesting a guide to some of the common areas of work undertaken by a PCSO. The NOS determine the standards you must attain to demonstrate competence, but the NOS don't tell you *what* to do or *how* to do it. We make some suggestions about what we know works, what we have tried ourselves, what we have observed, what has worked elsewhere as 'best practice' in policing, and what we have been informed about as having been effective and productive in other places. The way forward is for you to try out such ideas or suggestions in your own

---

area and then see if they are suitable for that neighbourhood or that community.

Discussion points

What work would you consider to be in the daily routine for a PCSO?

Make a note of the tasks you identify and see if they crop up in the following section or perhaps elsewhere in the Handbook. However, do not neglect or forget your own ideas because they could be really suitable for your BCU and worth trialling.

2.7.1.1 *What would be likely to occur on a 'standard' PCSO shift?*

Task

Using the table below identify which of the following tasks you think would occur on a 'standard' PCSO shift.

Task	Yes or No
Visible foot patrol	
Intelligence gathering	
Organizing a road safety event at a local school	
Community surgery at the local library	
Dealing with anti-social youths, or anti-social behaviour by any age group	
Issuing 'tickets' for littering	
Chairing a public meeting	
Attending a multi-agency meeting	
Seizing a mini-motorbike	
Taking part in a truancy sweep	
Manning a police cordon in the event of a terrorist incident	
Mediating in a neighbour dispute	
Meeting local business owners	
Directing traffic at the scene of an accident	
Administer first aid to a casualty	
Taking a statement from a victim of crime	

A varied day

As you know, of course, all the above are events that could occur in a shift and are ones that a PCSO could deal with at any time. The likelihood of them all occurring on the same day is remote unless you happen upon the shift from hell (though we envisage one such in the risk assessment section: see 5.7 below). This simple table demonstrates the wide variety of work within the PCSO remit but it is far from definitive and you will very probably have thought of more.

2.7.1.2 *Core purpose of a PCSO*

What we have shown you here is that there is a breadth and a 'complexity of exchange' within the PCSO role that is hard to replicate on a Handbook page or even in a sustained exercise. We do know, though, what is expected of you and what you may be called upon to do. The core **purpose** of a PCSO has been articulated well by ACPO:

> The fundamental role of the PCSO is to contribute to the policing of neighbourhoods, primarily through highly visible patrol with the purpose of reassuring the public, increasing orderliness in public places and being accessible to communities and partner agencies working at local level. The emphasis of this role, and the powers required to fulfil it, will vary from neighbourhood to neighbourhood and force to force.[12]

This description provides us with a handy basis from which to look at a typical PCSO day, as well as containing the useful caveat that the role does vary dependent on location, circumstances, and the composition of the community with which you engage. It will also vary according to your temperament, your inclinations, your strengths, and your sense of purpose. That said, and allowing for local variability and the peculiarity of circumstances applying at any particular time and place, the key themes in the ACPO Guidance are clear—**policing, reassurance, increasing orderliness**, and **accessibility**. These elements would therefore form the core of any PCSO day.

2.7.2 The four basic themes

We can take these four basic themes and begin to build a perspective on how they modulate and clarify the daily work of a PCSO.

2.7.2.1 *Policing*

In 1829, Sir Richard Mayne, one of the first Commissioners of the Metropolitan Police, provided a definition of policing that has stood the test of time even in today's more complex and fragmented world.

> The primary object of an efficient police is the prevention of crime: the next that of detection and punishment of offenders if crime is committed. To these ends all the efforts of police must be directed. The protection of life and property, the preservation of public tranquillity, and the absence of crime, will alone prove whether those efforts have been successful and whether the objects for which the police were appointed have been attained.[13]

This vision of what policing a community entailed and what should be the measure of success still has a resonance for PCSOs, as it does indeed for police officers. With the addition of the concept of **community engagement policing**, we can still look at 'protecting life and limb', maintaining 'tranquillity' (or 'keeping the peace'), and 'prevention of crime' as primary objectives for any PCSO, engaged with any community anywhere in the country. It is also of equal contemporary importance that the definition proffered by Mayne for success is the community judging the police on these issues. It is not only a key facet of neighbourhood policing and therefore a core part of your work, it also shows that the essence of policing has not changed, because the fundamentals of human nature have not changed. Sir Richard was a far-sighted man, but even he could not have foreseen how, in the 1980s and 1990s, the police would become divorced from the communities they were sworn to protect, and how it is through the 'reinvention' of the neighbourhood team concept, including introducing the PCSO, that the police now seek to recapture the lost ground. The Policing Pledge (see 1.5.6.2) and the police Standards of Professional Behaviour (see 1.5.6.4) are measures that attempt to contribute directly to re-engagement with communities, and try to re-establish trust between the police and the policed.

2.7.2.2 *Reassurance*

ACPO has identified reassuring the public as a crucial part of PCSO responsibilities and this has itself evolved from the **National Reassurance Policing Programme**, a project designed to assess the impact of neighbourhood policing within some selected test communities.

> Reassurance policing is a model of neighbourhood policing which
> seeks to improve public confidence in policing. It involves local com-
> munities in identifying priority crime and disorder issues in their neigh-
> bourhood, which they can then tackle together with the police and
> other public services and partners.[14]

Listening to what the community wants, in terms of its feelings of
safety, security, and reassurance, has become a key theme for successive governments, with special emphasis on the notion that all
public services, not just policing, should have a 'citizen focus'. As
we note elsewhere in this Handbook (for example at 6.5 below),
the annual publication of the **British Crime Survey** records
people's responses to crime and to what the police do. Consistently, over a number of years, such surveys have said in summary that **no matter what the crime statistics tell you about
falling crime or the decreasing likelihood of theft or robbery,
people judge the effectiveness of their police forces [in part at
least] by whether they can go out safely at night and whether
they can live in their communities without the constant fear
of being mugged, burgled, robbed, assaulted, or subjected to
anti-social or low-level criminal behaviour.** Taking the need
to reassure the public as a central strand of police work, it is very
much the neighbourhood teams, of which you are a part, which
will deliver on this reassurance. Being there and being seen, being
approachable and being effective, are thus very important components of what you do.

2.7.2.3 *Increasing orderliness*

In seeking to increase orderliness, or, as we noted briefly above, the
'keeping of the [Queen's] peace', the government has embarked
on an almost evangelical crusade against anti-social behaviour
in its many guises, particularly in the form of the 'hoodie'. This
'scary, faceless young male' character has been developed into
the current generation's stereotypical 'folk devil'[15] and is almost
omnipresent as a demonization of the threatening behaviour
of youth in media representations of anti-social behaviour. The
drive to eradicate, or at the very least to suppress, anti-social
behaviour has become a central theme of New Labour's law and
order agenda. Consider this extract from the then-Prime Minister
Tony Blair's foreword to the **Respect Action Plan**.

> It is not in my gift, or that of anyone in Central Government, to guar-
> antee good behaviour or to impose a set of common values about
> acceptable behaviour. But we will set out a framework of powers and

approaches to promote respect positively; bear down uncompromisingly on anti-social behaviour; tackle its causes; and offer leadership to local people and local services.[16]

2.7.2.4 *The law-and-order vote: political pressures*

This clearly impacts on the daily duties of the PCSO and it confirms the centrality of the PCSO in the government's claim to occupy the 'law-and-order high ground' in British politics. Using the law-and-order 'vote' for political ends is nothing new (it was central to Conservative Party manifestos for generations), and whether you believe the rhetoric from any political party is a matter for you, but you have to get used to the notion that what you do and how you affect your community may be seized on as evidence that government policies 'work' or that they don't. What is evident is that, political imperatives aside, the community of residents and commercial property owners in towns and villages overwhelmingly want to be able to go about their business safely, in orderly tranquillity, free from disorder, interference, or crime. Whilst some commentators on the police and policing tend to dismiss the importance of orderliness, it is a real enough aspiration for most people and a fundamental aspect of the reassurance agenda.

2.7.2.5 *Accessibility*

This role requirement extends to both the public and the partnership agencies with which the police work. The PCSO needs to be accessible on a practical level; that is, known to the public and available to consult on a regular basis, as well as on a perceptual level where the individual officer is amenable and open to new ideas or new opportunities. How accessible you are depends very much on what sort of person you are, as well as what sort of training you have. You will see in Chapter 4, where we look at the National Occupational Standards, that there are expectations about people in the community feeling confident about approaching you, and that you will be a focus for them in doing something about their problems. You are expected to be a good listener with a bent for practical resolutions (that doesn't mean, by the way, that you have to suffer fools gladly, but you do have to show 'imperturbable impartiality'). Your competence in this area (**NOS 1AA2:** *communicate with communities*) is judged on a recurrent basis, as those of you with service will acknowledge. This is part of the central 'toolbox' of your skills and effectiveness, whether working with hard-to-reach groups in the community, influencing partners and partner agencies to help you, or influencing your superiors to undertake a sustained policing operation to assist the community. It all begins with members of the community seeking access to you.

2.7.3 The PCSO's daily job

Your daily PCSO job will revolve around the four themes of:

- **Policing**
- **Reassurance**
- **Increasing orderliness**
- **Accessibility.**

You would most probably start your shift by accessing the latest briefings in regard to your BCU, such as intelligence reports, crime reports, operational activities, and so on (**policing**) and deal with any correspondence from the public or partner agencies (**reassurance, accessibility**). Having then left the station or office where you are based, visible patrolling will be a large part of your role as you walk, cycle, or drive around your patch (**reassurance**). In providing this high visibility you will be meeting residents, business owners, young people, schoolteachers, parents, and other members of the community as you make your way around. This will allow you to talk to people and give them the opportunity to talk to you (**accessibility**). You will conduct an Environmental Visual Audit (see, in particular, 4.5, 5.2, and 5.3 below, on '*signal crimes*'; this means, briefly, that you make careful note of what has happened or changed as you patrol), and that will allow you to identify problems within a community that need solving and highlight which partners would be best to work with to achieve this (**accessibility, policing, reassurance, increasing orderliness**).

You will deal with any relevant matter within your remit, such as calls from your Force Control Centre with regard to your BCU (**policing**) and deal with any spontaneous events that occur whilst you are out on patrol (**policing, reassurance, increasing orderliness**). Throughout the whole shift you will collate community intelligence that you discover or that comes your way and which can be reported in the appropriate manner on return to your station or office at the end of the shift (**policing**).

2.7.4 Variable tasks

Within the police forces of England and Wales there are many variations in PCSOs' tasking and we have already said that we cannot provide a comprehensive guide to all the permutations which may be devised or pieced together, as local circumstances, partners and funding dictate. In whatever way these tasks are constituted, and whatever the PCSOs' described roles in the community, at the core are the four themes. There is, though, a further permutation which builds on the core themes, and adds a specialism. Some PCSOs may have been allocated to 'specialist' positions because of the needs of their individual force or area. Such positions include:

- **Schools PCSOs**—based in a school, often joint-funded with that school and working with that school (this can be popular with PCSOs who want to work 'term-time only', but watch dictatorial head teachers who want you there all the time, acting as a super-caretaker). Your working day will almost exclusively concern young people and the problems which beset them, but your crime prevention and detection skills will not be neglected and you may become an invaluable source to the sworn police, for example in detecting or gaining intelligence on drugs dealers.
- **Family projects**—working with 'problem' families to ensure that low level anti-social behaviour does not escalate into full-blown criminality. This role can entail very close liaison with social services (indeed some have criticized this use of PCSOs as being 'social workers on the cheap'—sometimes you can't win), but in places it has proven most effective in 'straightening' someone who otherwise might have drifted into criminality.
- **Prisoner resettlement programmes**—this can involve working within **Multi-Agency Public Protection**

Arrangements (MAPPA), which deal with the complexities of staging the return from prison to communities of violent or sex offenders. In our experience, MAPPA tends to be highly specialist and the PCSO's role in it tends to the minor. You are much more likely to be partnering the Probation Service and Social Services in resettling those who have served prison sentences for non-violent crime such as theft, burglary, or deception.

- **Missing persons programmes**—our research shows that PCSOs have enjoyed the challenges of 'misper' work and have rapidly accumulated both specialist knowledge and credibility, but do not expect that, by playing this role, you will necessarily be involved in exciting murder investigations. Most of the time you will be involved in tracing runaways—which is valuable in its own right—or bringing family members back into contact with each other, with any potential for conflict modulated through you. It can be a long-haul job, with many people choosing to cover their traces when they opt to disappear, or those who wish to remain undiscovered to their families, which can be frustrating. On the other hand, there are huge psychological and professional rewards in finding unharmed a child who has strayed, or returning a vulnerable adult to the protection of the community.

- **Road Safety programmes**—these are primarily aimed at young people, and may involve coordination with cycling safety schemes and other established ways of raising safety awareness, but it may also have to do with schools' visits, work with local environmental groups, and liaising with your Force's roads-policing staff. The work can also entail raising road safety awareness among the frail and elderly, or among those with mental disorders who need gentle instruction in the safest places to cross the road or how to be visible at night.

2.7.5 What next?

What of the future? Where is the PCSO role going? We look at this in some detail at 7.6 and 7.8 below, but it seems that the opportunities for PCSOs over the coming years will grow to encompass further projects or specialist positions. Although the core role for most PCSOs will always be in neighbourhood policing on the street (which is where the 'reassured' community wants you to be), it is not difficult to propose where future challenges may arise. Perhaps new housing estates will have a dedicated PCSO working and living within that defined geographical community. Maybe the PCSO will become a fixture in the community with an office in the doctor's surgery or in the local library as a 'one-stop' community approach is adopted. There is a strong possibility that PCSOs could work in hospitals in a visible reassurance capacity (such as in Accident and Emergency departments) as well as assisting with other community and social problems that exist within hospitals. We will see more PCSOs 'embedded' in schools and having a patrol beat among the children and on the school premises; this is a specialist role that is certain to expand. Finally, though, the role of the PCSO will change and adapt largely because of the success of the work you do in your area, and will expand through the innovation, tolerance, and adaptability which you bring to the role. It is very much a case of **the job is what you do**.

2.8 **Pitfalls and Problems: Potential Hostility in the Job and How to Deal With It**

Hostility to PCSOs does exist, but not everywhere and not all the time. You may well be prepared, at least mentally, for displays of open or concealed hostility to you in the exercise of your function as a PCSO and in the discharge of your duty. You will assume that parts of the community will not welcome your presence, and those people who may previously have got away with anti-social behaviour may be actively hostile to you and to your neighbourhood team colleagues.

2.8.1 There can be hostility from those who don't understand your role

What you may be less prepared for is open or concealed hostility from among some of your 'police family' colleagues. Yet it exists, and we would be failing in our duty in writing this Handbook if we glossed over the fact that some police officers think that you are a threat to them, or think that, by some weird alchemy, you represent the end of policing as we know it (Gilbertson, 2007). *Why this has happened and what you can do about it are the themes for this section.* It may be that you never encounter, by look or action, the slightest resentment or hostility towards you and what you do. If so, congratulations and you can move on. If, however, you are one of the huge majority of PCSOs who has encountered precisely this, then read on.

> **Discussion points**
> Why would your colleagues feel hostility towards the PCSO role?
> What sort of threat do you pose to your police colleagues?

Don't expect to find much written about this hostility in your training notes: publicists for the PCSO concept will not allow themselves to be diverted by what they see as a 'bedding in' or adjustment between the two sides, and those who oppose the whole concept of the PCSO are warring on a different political plane from the humdrum everyday role of the PCSO.

2.8.2 The Police Federation's open hostility

The Police Federation has led criticism of the PCSO concept. Much of the commentary from the Federation, particularly over the potential and actual confusions of role between PCSO and police officer, has been reasoned and intelligent, but sometimes the language used by Federation leaders reflects the emotional aggression which is sometimes used 'on the ground' by police officers, such as calling PCSOs *'numties in yellow jackets'* when the concept was first introduced on the streets in 2002; whilst in 2006, the Federation chairman of the Metropolitan Police's constable branch board said this: '[there is] a growing army of community support staff who walk around like gaggles of lost shoppers [recruited to take the place of constables on the street]'. Paul Kelly, Chairman of the Police Federation in Manchester is reported as saying in 2007 that 'PCSOs [...] are a failed experiment' and calling for them to be 'done away with'.[17]

The Police Federation in London took out full-page advertisements in south-east London newspapers in late June 2006 in an attempt to influence public opinion about PCSOs and the perceived threat which they pose to traditional policing. Two pictures were shown in the advertisement, one of a police officer and one of a PCSO. Each picture was surrounded by a dotted border and the image of a pair of scissors. The Federation is reported as saying: 'real officers are being replaced by the new breed.'[18] Readers were invited to choose which they would 'cut out', a police officer or a PCSO.

2.8.2.1 *PCSOs: Policing on the cheap?*

The Federation's argument is essentially in defence of its members, police ranks from constable to chief inspector. Within that membership there is widespread unease that PCSOs *are* policing on the cheap; that the increase in the PCSO numbers threatens the recruitment of more police officers; and that there may be a withering of the need for fully-warranted police officers to perform core neighbourhood 'policing' tasks. However, what the Federation appears to miss, or ignore, is that there are fundamental changes afoot in the nature of policing which have very little to do with the role of PCSO or any other community support officer or rural warden. **It has everything to do with the rise and rise of 'private policing'** in which many of the functions of the traditional police are being contracted out to private companies, to security firms, or to people, more or less skilled, who undertake patrol, engage in prevention, and collect evidence for the prosecution of offenders. We go into this is much more detail in Chapter 7, particularly at 7.9 below, but the point we want to make here is that **policing in England and Wales is already in flux**, it is already changing in profound ways, and PCSOs are merely one among many manifestations of that change.

POINTS TO NOTE

Think about private policing, commercial security companies, 'gated communities', roads policing with the Department of Transport, 'immigration police' in the UK Border Agency, the Security Industries Authority, which licenses 'door stewards' among others, rural wardens, community support officers paid for from local authority funds, schools security officers, police staff, police authorities, and public/private investment schemes (PPIs). The wider police family can only expand.

2.8.2.2 *Unison, not the Police Federation, represents the PCSO*

This gives a context for some of the organized hostility that PCSOs have faced, and which they may continue to face, but of equal importance is the likely reaction to PCSOs 'on the ground', especially as they feature in Neighbourhood Policing Teams in increasing numbers. Perhaps what happens is that people distrust statements from politicians, both national and local, when the latter try to say what it is that PCSOs will do. Certainly the Police Federation was so disenchanted with the whole PCSO concept that, in June 2006, its members voted 'overwhelmingly' against a proposal to extend membership of the Federation beyond sworn officers.[19] The union which represents police staff, Unison, was swift to move into the vacuum and promptly offered membership to PCSOs. The response from PCSOs themselves was equally rapid, and by the late summer of 2006, Unison reported the formation of a PCSO National Working Group under its auspices.[20] For all that, in February 2007, PCSOs were being described contemptuously in print, as 'minimally-trained auxiliaries who, despite their best intentions, are not up to it' (Gilbertson (2007) 27).

2.8.3 How good are PCSOs? Public perception and public survey

Research carried out in West Yorkshire in 2004 suggested that PCSOs were a popular innovation within the community. The West Yorkshire study was a twin-site public opinion survey carried out by Adam Crawford, Deputy Director of the Centre for Criminal Justice Studies at the University of Leeds, and a team of his colleagues from the Centre. The results were published as *Patrolling with a purpose*.[21] Among the survey results analysed by Crawford's team, we might note the following:

- 69% of those surveyed perceived an increase in the number of officers patrolling the city centres
- 22% saw a community support officer more than once a day while 40% saw a community support officer at least once a day
- 96% of those who had encountered a community support officer reported high levels of satisfaction with how their problem had been dealt with
- 82% agreed that the presence of visible patrol personnel makes [the city centre] a more welcoming place to work, shop and visit.[22]

Interestingly, the report came to this conclusion:

[West Yorkshire Police] successfully shielded CSOs from the normal demands of policing, such as dashing from incident to incident and dealing with a backlog of incident enquiries, which have traditionally served to undermine locally-tied foot patrol. *Furthermore, community support officers have demonstrated that they can deliver effective patrols and engage with different communities without the need for the full range of powers vested in constables.* [Our italics.][23]

2.8.3.1 *Reassurance and impact on fear*

A detailed study of the effect of PCSO patrolling, in concert with a carefully developed neighbourhood policing plan, suggests that the impact on the community's sense of safety and security is out of proportion to the numbers involved. Additionally, there was a measurable effect on crime; the report suggests that in Leeds city centre, theft of vehicles fell by almost half, theft from a vehicle declined by a third, and tampering or interference with a vehicle fell by more than half. These are spectacular figures, even in a high crime-rate area, and the falls are confirmed by similar results in Bradford city centre, where theft from a vehicle fell by nearly a quarter, theft of vehicles was reduced by a quarter, and vehicle interference and tampering dropped by almost a quarter. The proportions are remarkably consistent, matched by the decline in personal robbery (down 47% in Leeds and down 46% in Bradford). That most reductions occurred in 'hot spot' areas suggests too that the PCSOs were appropriately deployed.

Discussion points

What does this tell you about the need for accurate targeting and focused deployment?
Are you surprised by the survey results?
Will they change the minds of your critics?

2.8.3.2 *PCSO survey in Kent*

At the other end of the country a year later, a similar survey of public opinion, conducted in Kent, came to very similar conclusions.[24] PCSOs tackle 'real crime', the public said, and are not simply a visible presence, reassuring though that is. Vehicle crime fell by a fifth in the 'control sites', which was more than double the rate in other areas where PCSOs were not deployed. There was a reduction in criminal damage three times that of the areas outside the control site. There was an increased perception of safety by residents, especially walking alone in the dark, or at home alone during the day and during the night. The Kent report goes on to note that PCSOs appeared to have little impact on reducing perceptions of

---

anti-social behaviour ('and may even have heightened the awareness of some types of anti-social behaviour'). For all that, two-thirds
(62%) of residents had contact with a PCSO and nearly 90% noted
that their expectations of PCSOs regarding community involvement had been fulfilled. Three-quarters of those surveyed (76%)
agreed that their PCSO represented 'good value for money'.[25]

2.8.3.3 *The first national evaluation of the PCSO*

In 2006, a national evaluation of the work of Community Support
Officers was published by the Home Office[26] and for the first time
gave us a picture of the effectiveness of PCSOs on a national scale.
The study was carried out by the Home Office between July 2004 and
June 2005. Among the survey's key aims was an attempt to provide a
'national profile' of PCSOs and their deployment, and to explore perceptions by the public of the PCSO role. The findings which emerged
were relatively straightforward and may be summarized thus:

- PCSOs were seen as more accessible than police officers.
  Members of the public were more likely to report things to
  PCSOs which they would not bother a police officer with. The
  public was more likely to pass information to PCSOs.
- The public valued the role of PCSO and there was strong
  evidence from two of the 'case study areas' [Merseyside,
  Sussex] that, where PCSOs were known in their communities,
  there was a perception that PCSOs had made a 'real impact' in
  their areas, 'especially in dealing with youth disorder'.
- More than 40% of PCSOs said that they joined as a stepping-
  stone to becoming a sworn police officer.
- The diversity of PCSOs, particularly in terms of ethnicity and
  age, has been a marked feature of the implementation.
- The survey found that there was no evidence that PCSOs were
  having a measurable impact on the level of recorded crime or
  incidents of anti-social behaviour in the areas where they were
  deployed.[27]

2.8.3.4 *Early results confirm the value of the PCSO*

Some of the conclusions are a little suspect, or may be predicated on
too little data. For instance, it is probably too early to say that PCSOs
have no effect on crime or anti-social behaviour in their localities;
though nationally, the evaluation appears to confirm some of the
findings in the Kent survey. It seems axiomatic that the presence
of PCSOs will have a deterrent effect on low level criminality and
on anti-social behaviour over time, as we saw illustrated quite

dramatically in the Force-level studies in West Yorkshire. The best comparators will be found when the role has more completely bedded into the community and results are quantified on a neighbourhood (and thence to a BCU) level. At present, the community is getting to know and accept its PCSOs and the PCSOs are getting to know and understand their communities. Any appreciable or measurable effect on national crime figures is probably still some distance away. Meanwhile, should we be content with the positive effect which PCSOs are having on public opinion?

By contrast, there have been a number of stories in the media which have criticised the so-called 'disengagement' role of PCSOs. One occurred on 3rd May 2007 when two Lancashire PCSOs turned up at a lake near Wigan after reports of a boy, Jordon Lyon, getting into difficulties in the water. The boy was nowhere to be seen and the two PCSOs did not enter the lake and dive to search for him, leaving this to a police officer who was trained to do so. The boy's body was later recovered. When the matter came before a coroner's inquest some months later, there was much media comment on the apparent supineness of the PCSO role. An Assistant Chief Constable from Lancashire Police, Dave Thompson, publicly defended the actions of the PCSOs, noting that they had not been trained to perform such rescues and that observing and reporting were valid tactical options. The public grumbling continued, and surfaced again with reports in November 2007 that two Metropolitan Police PCSOs did not go to the aid of a man being attacked by three girls. A female member of the public went to his help and she led the subsequent media criticism, in which the PCSO's were labelled as 'plastic policemen'. An internal enquiry was launched by the Metropolitan Police, but the outcome was not made public.[28]

2.8.3.5 *More recent evaluations of the PCSO*

An NPIA report into the effectiveness of PCSOs was published in July 2008, as part of an evaluation of the Neighbourhood Policing Programme.[29] We note from the NPIA report that 'neighbourhood policing can increase public confidence in policing, feelings of safety, and reduce crime and anti-social behaviour'; self-evidently, PCSOs have a major role to play in the delivery of such reassurance. The report identified that there was an element of PCSO 'role drift' in some forces where PCSOs were taken away from NPT duties and set to do other things, for some of which they had not been trained, and for others their duties played no part in public reassurance. To counter this tendency to treat PCSOs expediently, NPIA recommended that they should either be fully 'integrated into a Neighbourhood Policing Team (normally geographic but could be for a defined community of interest, for example, Safer Transport Teams [or located in schools]), or deployed directly to support Neighbourhood Policing Team[s] in their neighbourhoods'. The NPIA Report went on to recommend that PCSOs should spend the majority of their time within neighbourhoods and not be office/police station based and/or undertaking administrative roles. NPIA concluded that 'PCSOs in reality engage in activities that contribute to two outcomes, that of **effectiveness** (their contribution to improving reassurance, reducing anti-social behaviour, confidence and satisfaction), and **efficiency** (engaging in tasks that free up more expensive resources, [that is] fully sworn officers)'. [Adapted from NPIA's *PCSO Review*, July 2008, Chapter 3 'Review Findings', pp. 8–21, our additions in square brackets.]

Discussion points

What evidence do you have locally for the effectiveness of PCSOs in driving down crime?

What performance indicators on your BCU do you directly affect? How 'effective and efficient' do you think PCSOs are in their contribution to Neighbourhood Policing?

2.8.3.6 *Reponses to criticism of PCSOs*

What should you do if you encounter some or any of the criticisms which we have looked at above? There are a number of tactics which you can use. The most obvious is to ignore the sniping and carry on doing your job as well as you can. Another tactic is to ensure that *your* work is singled out for praise because you have indeed 'gone the extra mile'. Again, you can use feedback from the community to evidence your effectiveness (you will be collecting all of this to demonstrate that you continue to meet the Competences), ensuring that good news stories get as much prominence as the bad ones. You could use some of the statistics we have referred to, from West Yorkshire (2004), Kent (2005), the national evaluation study (2006), and the 2008 NPIA Review to prove that **the popularity and effectiveness of PCSOs is growing exponentially year by year**. Indeed a report by the Home Office into the work of PCSOs (see Mason and Dale, 2008, published at the same time as the NPIA PCSO Review in July 2008), agreed with the Association of Chief Police Officers' (ACPO) conclusion about a PCSO's primary role. The guidance states that 'the fundamental role of a PCSO is to contribute to neighbourhood policing, primarily through highly visible patrol in order to reassure the public, increase public order and be more accessible to communities and partner agencies at the local level'. Home Office findings confirm that PCSO activity corresponds well with ACPO guidance since PCSOs spend the majority of their time being highly visible within the community, dealing with minor offences and supporting front-line policing.[30]

Ultimately, it is by *your* effectiveness that you will prove the doubters wrong. You can probably empathize now with those first women police officers struggling to be taken seriously by their male colleagues. Then and subsequently, the female officers were patronized, belittled, ignored, or expected only to deal with lost children and female suspects. Seldom were they seen as police officers who could handle whatever was thrown at them. The same unthinking prejudice is founded on insecurity and a lack of understanding about what PCSOs do.

2.8.4 Weather the storm

The message we want to leave you with is a simple one: if you encounter hostility at work from your police colleagues, it is likely to be from ignorance of your role and its value. As long as you have the support of your neighbourhood colleagues, and the community you serve, you can safely ignore the sniping from the sidelines. Most NPTs staunchly support the work of their PCSO colleagues and would not be without them. The criticism will diminish in time. After all, the Police Federation finally admitted women to membership in 1948, only fifty years after female police officers began service. Maybe, by 2052 ...?

2.9 The Criminal Justice System in England and Wales: Magistrates' Courts, Crown Courts, and Coroners' Courts

You will almost certainly have visited a court to watch what happens as part of your initial training as a PCSO. You might have been able to visit a **Crown Court** (see below) where criminal trials take place, or a **coroner's court**, which is convened (usually) to determine how someone died, but it is more likely that you attended a **magistrates' court**. You may be familiar from your local paper or news broadcasts with the role of the magistrates' court (the fines and appearances there of local people fill many column inches in local newspapers, for example). The Crown Court deals with serious criminal cases, and will attract national media attention sometimes. We're going to discuss now how these courts and the appeals processes in criminal law make up the **criminal justice system** of England and Wales.

2.9.1 Magistrates' court

This is the lowest level of '**judicial process**' (meaning *the working of the law*) in England and Wales and the first court for any criminal proceedings. Magistrates are ordinary, worthy, local people who apply to become magistrates and who are given some minimal training in the law. At the end of this process and after 'sitting' in judgement for a time, they are appointed by the Lord Chancellor on behalf of the Crown and are then styled as **Justices of the Peace** or **JPs**. Such people are **lay magistrates**—they do not get paid—and usually work part-time as a civic duty. If you talk to magistrates you will often find that they are experienced, mature people who are as concerned about society and community as anyone else, and that they have a strong sense of communal duty, keen to 'put something back' into the society which nurtured them.

2.9.1.1 Unpaid magistrates

This is all very good and very laudable, and we can be proud that the amateur tradition which has persisted in our justice system for a thousand years is still going strong. But (and there has to be a but), the sorts of people who can become magistrates and devote time to hearing cases during the working day, are either those who have retired or those who do not have to work. A *very* small number of the current magistracy in England and Wales also have full-time jobs. It's possible to juggle any full or part-time job with the demands of sitting as a lay magistrate, but it isn't easy and not many do it.

> **Discussion points**
> Why should it matter that magistrates are drawn from those who don't work or who have retired?
> Shouldn't we be grateful that people want to do it at all?

2.9.1.2 *Some responses*

Of course, we should be grateful that ordinary people volunteer to give up their time to assist the community. This is not just a carping from the sidelines about people who can afford the time to sit as magistrates, but a concern about how representative they may be of the community. If the magistracy is drawn overwhelmingly from the white majority and professional occupations (which they are), what kind of handle will such people have on the tensions and problems of, for example, minority ethnic communities? How well will they understand the boredom of young people with nowhere to meet and nowhere to let off their exuberant energy? We are *not* saying that there is a permanent barrier of incomprehension between magistrates and those upon whom they sit in judgement, but we are saying that there is a danger that drawing magistrates from a rather restricted stratum of society may lead to their being unrepresentative.

2.9.1.3 *The importance of representing all sides of a community*

Why do we have the tradition of drawing magistrates and JPs from the community? Because society needs to protect itself against social predators, and the best way to ensure that its interests are served is to choose people from within the society or community to 'police' and control it. It is also the basis of 'common law' which we look at later. One of the first measures of self-protection which a community will impose is conformity with expected norms of behaviour. We explore this in more detail in Chapter 6, when we look at what a community is. To go back to the main point of this; it is surely better for a society that those charged with its protection should represent all parts of that society, than that it should merely default to those with time and inclination?

2.9.2 Stipendiary magistrates

There exists a kind of compromise between the points we have been making above and the higher courts, and that is the **stipendiary magistrate**, now more commonly called 'District Judge'. 'Stipendiary' means that the office holder receives a '*stipend*' or payment. In other words, the stipendiary magistrate (District Judge) is paid and is always a person trained in the law. The incumbent could have been either a solicitor or barrister, but his or her experience of practising law, for at least seven years, is a prerequisite. The stipendiary magistrate usually sits alone in judgement, whereas lay and unpaid magistrates usually sit in a panel or 'bench' of three, but there can be any combination between two and seven. Lay magistrates are always advised on matters of law by the **magistrates' clerk**, who is also a paid professional lawyer with at least five years' experience of practising law. In most magistrates' courts, the Clerk sits immediately in front of the bench of magistrates, and in some courts the Clerk will wear a black gown, even a little wig made of horsehair. It is worth noting that, as a professional lawyer, the stipendiary magistrate is likely to be even less representative of society at large than the lay magistracy, but the public appears to care less about the stipendiary District Judge, probably because s/he is paid and therefore a 'servant of the state', than about those who volunteer to become JPs and who cost us very little. It is a characteristic hypocrisy which underlies much to do with public justice.

2.9.2.1 *Role of magistrates*

Magistrates make judgements about guilt or innocence in **petty offences**. These are offences which, characteristically, attract fines or community service rather than imprisonment. This has recently caused controversy, because magistrates are concerned about what they see as increased police use of fines at the expense of the 'transparency of justice' in the magistrates' court. The use of out-of-court penalties by the police has increased markedly: across England and Wales in the twelve months to March 2008, only 724,179 of the 1.4 million offenders 'brought to justice' actually came before the courts. John Thornhill, chairman of the Magistrates' Association, commented: 'What is happening is that more than 50 per cent of offences never appear in court. That is a drop of 20 per cent over five years.' The police use of summary fines is reported to extend now to some forms of violent behaviour, but a proposal by the Justice Ministry in February 2009 to add a further 21 offences which were to be punishable by fines (including 'drunken and yobbish behaviour on trains') was withdrawn after strong protests from the magistracy.[31]

There are no juries in a magistrates' court, so the judgment is handed down from the 'bench'. Accused people can be defended in a magistrates' court, usually by a solicitor. However, it is entirely normal for the accused not to be represented by a lawyer. There is a high incidence of 'guilty' pleas in a magistrates' court. If you expect the clash of styles and approaches between defence and prosecution in a magistrates' court, familiar from many a hackneyed television or film drama, you will be sadly disappointed. Proceedings in the real world are often brisk, often low-key and undramatic, and most offences are dealt with **summarily**, that is, there and then without fuss. A developing area is to create a 'virtual' magistrates' court, where defendants will lose their right to have a courtroom hearing and physically to appear in court. Instead, video links between a police station and a magistrates' court are designed to speed up 'summary justice'. Young people, the mentally impaired, and any case involving more than one defendant, are excluded from the 'virtual hearing' process. A trial scheme was set up in 2009 and one case, involving a guilty plea to drink-driving, meant that the individual concerned was fined and banned from driving, merely hours after he was arrested. The process means that a person pleading guilty to an offence in future can be sentenced on the spot.[32]

2.9.2.2 *Uniformity of sentencing?*

A further controversy between magistrates and the Ministry of Justice began in February 2009, focused on part of the **Coroners and Justice Act** which was then being debated in Parliament. Magistrates were exercised about proposals for an augmented Sentencing Guidelines Council which imposes uniformity of sentencing of offenders. At present magistrates 'have regard to' sentencing guidelines, but are free to move outside them — and give their reasons when they do. In future, it is proposed that magistrates 'must follow' the guidelines, 'except where the interests of justice dictate otherwise'. Magistrates believe that this is an assault on their independence and have made representations to the Minstry of Justice, where officials denied that the intention of these words in the Bill was to curb the independence of the magistracy. If nothing else, the episode demonstrated that magistrates are neither supine nor passive and are perfectly capable of mobilizing public and press opinion in support of their independence.[33]

2.9.2.3 *'If it ain't broke ... '*

Our view is that, although sometimes the magistracy creaks at the seams, and although the magistrates themselves (and certainly the lay ones) ought to be drawn from a wider cross-section of the community, and although their judgments may reflect society's current prejudices rather than some dispassionate concept of the law; the system works pretty well and it is difficult to think of anything as effective to replace it. Certainly, *'people's courts'* as attempted in parts of eastern and middle Europe and in Africa have a Stalinist echo to them and no independent evaluation as to effectiveness; US-style *district courts* are expensive and entirely professional, so replicating the stipendiary principle; whilst in other parts of Europe and elsewhere the *'neighbourhood judiciary'* (an approximate term, covering the local systems in Germany, the Netherlands, Italy, Austria, and Denmark) is so very like our own magistracy as not to be a viable alternative. We know of no system so obviously superior that it could substitute for or replace our magistracy or 'lower court', and we are likely to have something very like the present system and process for many years to come. That's not to say that it should be above reform, though.

2.9.3 Referral to the Crown Court

The magistrates' court plays other very important roles that we have not yet considered. All criminal cases, however serious, must come first to the magistrates' court for assessment of the weight of evidence (we discuss evidence at 5.2 below). This is often called the '**preliminary hearing**' or '**committal hearing**'. What this means in practice is that the magistrates (lay or stipendiary District Judge) will consider the evidence of the serious crime and listen to what the police or the Crown Prosecution Service (CPS) lawyers and any defence lawyers have to say about the charges and about bail for the accused. The accused may 'reserve defence' against the charge at this stage, and make no statement or admission to the court.

2.9.3.1 *Bail*

The magistrate(s) will then refer, or 'commit', the case to be heard at the Crown Court, and make a determination about bail. The police will often oppose bail if they believe that the offender may offend again, or abscond (*run away*), or disappear. If their case is strong enough, the magistrates will remand the accused in custody. Alternatively, the magistrates may release the accused on bail or against a '**surety**' or bond of money. Occasionally this brings the amateur status of lay magistrates into sharp conflict with the police or CPS, where the former may be seen (in prosecution eyes) as too lenient or too trusting. Magistrates for their part sometimes regard the police or CPS as over-zealous about keeping people in prison while the case is prepared.

2.9.4 **Other roles for magistrates**

Some cases may take a year or more to come to trial; this can be a long time for a person to spend on remand in prison, given that no case against him or her has yet been proved. Each case is considered on its own merits: for example, it is unlikely that a person accused and charged with a crime of great violence would be granted bail, but a person charged with a theft might be. The magistrates will determine which course to take, and often decide at committal, when the accused has to be returned to court for checks on the case's progress. Before we leave magistrates, there are a couple of minor but police-relevant duties that magistrates perform, of which you should at least be aware. These are the **attestation** of a police constable (the administering of the oath or affirmation which a constable makes in order to receive full warranted powers) and the signing of some arrest or search **warrants**. This makes the entry to property, or searches, legally permissible. Such warrants are usually for specific persons, specific buildings or places and are valid for a specified time.

2.9.5 **'Habeas corpus'**

An arrested person, under the **Police and Criminal Evidence Act 1984** (PACE 84), must be charged and brought before a magistrate within 48 hours of his or her arrest (though the term may be varied by a senior police officer on short extension bases). This is the principle which you will often hear mentioned, called **habeas corpus**. This is Latin, meaning 'having or possessing the body'; in other words it is *producing to be seen the person charged*. It is a very old right of the accused, and goes back to mediaeval times. It was designed to prevent unlawful imprisonment, or stopping what we would now call 'detention without trial'. People who are not charged must be released (unless subject to the arcane terrorist holding powers of the Home Secretary, which are in dispute anyway). You should equally be aware that human rights legislation (the *right to a fair trial*) is also in effect here: **it is a serious business to arrest and detain another person**. That person's welfare is important to the courts. Those with powers of arrest must exercise those powers responsibly and in a proportionate and justified way. And that means you, when you exercise your (admittedly more limited) powers to detain—so the safeguard of **habeas corpus** isn't academic.

2.9.6 The importance of the magistracy

You can conclude from this brief survey of the magistracy that the functions of a magistrate are an important part of safeguarding the rights of the individual. Issues such as warrants and **habeas corpus** are designed to prevent abuse of powers by the police or anyone else (including you as a PCSO). Whilst some aspects of the magistracy may be in need of reform (some would argue, of urgent reform), the existence of a lower court to prevent abuse and to guard the liberties of the subject is reassuring. It might not be glamorous, but it is important to the proper and legal functioning of society. Now it is time to go to the theatre.

2.10 The Crown Court

Sometimes referred to (wrongly) by the old name of 'County Court'[34] and even sometimes as the much older '*Circuit Court*', the Crown Court is usually located on two or three sites throughout each county or shire. There will be at least one Crown Court in each major city. Although it is something of a joke to refer to the trappings of the Crown Court as 'theatre' (and we mean no disrespect), nonetheless there is something inherently dramatic in the Crown Court setting, which is so much more majestic (deliberately so) than the magistrates' courts: the judge, robed and throned above the court; the prosecution and defence lawyers in gowns and wigs; the dark, formal dress of the court officials; the presence of uniformed escorts to the accused; the appearance, in 'not guilty' pleas, of a jury of twelve men and women; the wood panelling of the court and royal coat of arms on the wall behind the judge; the solemnity and ceremony; the often old-fashioned language (including Latin) and the confrontation between prosecution and defence; the sometimes brutal, always probing, questions to witnesses and victims; the questioning of the accused; the tensions whilst the jury considers its verdict; these are all elements of high drama. Some critics argue that the absurd melodrama of seventeenth-century costumes and wigs has no part in a modern criminal justice process. Indeed, in some cases such as those involving child witnesses, judges and barristers can and do remove their wigs (see below). Nonetheless, the experience of appearing in a Crown Court is daunting for the average adult; it must be surreal to a child.[35] Yet this is the 'majesty of the law'.

2.10.1 Dressing up in costume?

We should not forget that the law and its process had its origins in the monarchy, and that the words 'Crown', 'Rex', or 'Regina' (King or Queen) in recorded case law and prosecutions, as well as the enactment of legislation, are still located in and part of the monarchical system. It also has a lot to do with the quintessential British love of pageantry and stylized drama. And, though other countries can be mildly mocking of such trappings, American judges wear black gowns, whilst judges in European courts usually wear black robes with characteristic high hats. We are not alone in retaining the pomp of justice, but perhaps we enjoy the spectacle and colour a little more than others. In September 2006, the Lord Chief Justice (Lord Philips of Worth Matravers) began a consultation exercise with the judiciary about the wearing of wigs and robes. It is expected that the horsehair wigs and gowns will become a thing of the past in commercial, family, and civil cases, though it is probable that the 'costumes' will be retained in criminal courts, at least for the foreseeable future. The Lord Chief Justice apparently favours 'a simple European-style robe and collar or foulard'.[36] At least part of the reason for the move away from wigs and gowns is that solicitors, who now represent some clients at Crown Court, are not permitted to wear wigs as barristers do, and the injustice of such deprivation evidently rankles with the solicitors. The outcome is likely to be that all wear wigs or none.

2.10.2 Functions of the Crown Courts

The Crown Court tries criminal cases. As noted above, such cases are always handled by a judge, who will have been appointed from within the legal profession (that is, usually having practised as a barrister or, more rarely, a solicitor). Judges begin as Recorders before progressing to 'Circuit' judges and then to High Court judges. Broadly, judges oversee proceedings in the Crown Court, usually giving considerable latitude to prosecution and defence lawyers, and direct the jury when law becomes complex or ambiguous. Judges sum up a criminal trial and, if a jury finds the defendant guilty, will pronounce sentence (how long the offender will be kept in prison). Judges are by no means unchallenged. Should the judge's summing up seem to have prejudiced the jury, the defence may appeal. The defence may also appeal against a sentence (though this can be fraught, because sentences can now be increased as well as decreased) or against some aspect of the trial which it perceives the judge to have mishandled. Appeals go formally to the Court of Appeal, and appeals from there go to the Supreme Court (opened in October 2009), where they are heard by the Law Lords. There is appeal beyond the Supreme Court to the European Criminal Court, which is very rarely invoked; it is also quite expensive to take a criminal appeal to Europe. Most parties in most cases are content with the decision of the Supreme Court; certainly in criminal trials. Unless there has been a gross abuse of a person's human rights, cases are not likely to prosper by referral to the European Court. That has to do with different criminal and penal codes in Europe from those followed in the UK (with small differences in Northern Ireland and Scotland).

2.10.2.1 *The adversarial criminal justice system*

The criminal justice system followed in the UK is usually called the 'adversarial' system. An 'adversary' is an opponent, and this reflects what happens, especially in criminal trials (but also in libel cases and in some defamation cases). The prosecution sets out to prove ('beyond reasonable doubt') that Person X committed the crime of which s/he stands accused. The prosecution case (determined as to viability not by the police but by the CPS) will use police and witness evidence to prove that the crime was committed, and that the person charged with the crime committed it. This will be opposed by Person X's defence team, if Person X has pleaded 'not guilty' to the charge. The defence team will do everything it can to show that Person X not only did not commit the crime, but could not have committed the crime, which was committed, indeed, by someone else, and that Person X was 500 miles away when the alleged crime allegedly happened. All this is part of the defence tactic to have the case dismissed, discredited, or made doubtful. The principle of 'beyond reasonable doubt' is precious in British law (though Scotland can return a jury verdict of 'not proven'), because the adversarial process is founded on the **presumption of innocence**. Indeed, critics of the adversarial system point to the deviousness of defence tactics in undermining a criminal prosecution. Sir David Phillips, former Chief Constable of Kent and a past President of ACPO, is reported to have said: 'The purpose of a trial is to find out the truth. But we no longer have trials about who did it—the trial is always about whether somebody broke the rules in trying to find out who did it.'[37]

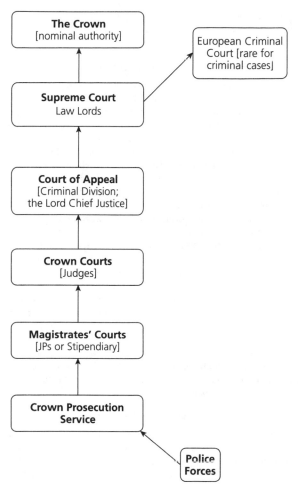

Figure 8: Simplified diagram of the criminal justice processes in England and Wales

In the USA, where the adversarial system is also used, the characterization of the defence is something like this: *deny the accused's involvement in anything. When you can, fault the charge; if you can't fault the charge, fault the evidence; if you can't fault the evidence, undermine the credibility of witnesses; if you can't undermine the witnesses, ridicule the process; if you can't ridicule the process, delay the trial, obscure the facts, and bewilder the jury.*

2.10.2.2 *Court procedures and appearances*

You will often hear people, particularly police officers, speaking bitterly about defence tactics and the 'artificial' tricks and ploys of a criminal justice system which is based on two sides slogging it out in court. You may even have to deal with witnesses who have been subject to such ploys. It's hard to remain impartial when you see people who have been confused, bewildered, bamboozled into contradicting themselves, or whose testimony is undermined by a resourceful (if unscrupulous) defence lawyer. However, you have to try to see this as business and nothing personal. This is not to say that the process is a game, far from it. It can be the most serious thing in the world to the family of an abused child, or to a woman accused of her partner's murder. However, since the CPS lawyers, criminal barristers, and defence counsel are doing this sort of thing all the time, they become so detached and objective that it can seem indeed a game to those who come for the first time, or who are emotionally traumatized by what has happened to them, watching the point-scoring or the unpleasantly deliberate attack on witness credibility or character. If you have to give evidence (see 5.2 and 7.5 below), you will yourself be subject to cross-examination by a defence lawyer in a Crown Court trial. In fact, come to that, you could have your evidence challenged in a magistrates' court by a retained lawyer for the defence, though this is less likely. We discuss this extensively in 7.5 below.

2.10.2.3 *Dealing with victims and witnesses*

We deal in more detail later on with how you should present yourself and your testimony in court (see 7.5 below); all we need to note at this point is that you must try to remember what it feels like when you first go to court. You will soon become familiar with the rituals and processes; you may even get to enjoy them over time. Those whom you are dealing with (witnesses, victims) may never have been in a court before in their lives. Remember that, and then explain, reassure, accompany, and listen: your help will be of great benefit to frightened or awestruck or inarticulate people, in the grip of a system and a process which they may not understand.

2.11 **Human Rights**

2.11.1 **The police role in supporting human rights**

The concept of human rights and the responsibilities of police officers in the preservation and maintenance of those rights runs throughout this Handbook. Tuition in human rights should certainly have formed part of your initial training as a PCSO. At this stage, it is perhaps worth noting that the recent legislation concerning human rights marked a significant change towards an emphasis on rights ('you shall') rather than the usual focus of the law on prohibition ('you shall not'). By this we mean that most laws, until recently, **defined what constitutes wrong-doing** and how law enforcers and the criminal justice system should respond to this wrong-doing. Human rights legislation by contrast stresses an individual's entitlement to expect certain fundamental rights as part of the social contract between the person and the State and other forms of authority. **The Human Rights Act 1998** is the prime example. It falls to public authorities such as the police (and by extension, to a PCSO as a member of that police service), to maintain the fundamental rights of all individuals who come into contact with that authority.

There are a number of NOS relevant to human rights and the PCSO, most notably the element **1AA.1** to '*foster people's rights and responsibilities*' (see Chapter 4).

2.11.2 **Origins of the concept of protecting human rights**

The roots of the Human Rights Act 1998 are to be found in a set of Articles containing rights, agreed by the **European Convention for the Protection of Human Rights and Fundamental Freedoms** (often referred to more briskly as 'the Convention' or in written form as the ECHR), which came into force in 1953 as part of the reconstruction of Europe after the Second World War, and was itself derived from the declaration of the United Nations of the principles of human freedom.

There are two main features of human rights legislation:

First, all new statute law must be compatible with the rights.

Secondly, an individual may take a public authority to a UK court if the authority has not acted in a manner compatible with the rights.

2.11.3 What are the rights?

These are normally described in terms of the 'Article number'.

Article number	Article title
2	Right to life
3	Prohibition of torture
4	Prohibition of slavery and forced labour
5	Right to liberty and security
6	Right to a fair trial
7	No punishment without law
8	Right to respect for private and family life
9	Freedom of thought, conscience, and religion
10	Freedom of expression
11	Freedom of assembly and association
12	Right to marry
14	Prohibition of discrimination
16	Restriction on the political activities of aliens
17	Prohibition of the abuse of rights
18	Limitation on use of restrictions on rights

(You may be wondering what has happened to Articles 1, 13, and 15. These refer merely to technical aspects of the adoption of the European Convention.)

2.11.4 The three types of Convention rights within the Act

There are three types of convention rights within the Human Rights Act 1998: absolute, limited, and qualified rights. We examine each in turn but this is only a summary.

2.11.4.1 *Absolute rights*

Within these rights, the interests of the community as a whole cannot restrict the rights of the individual in any way. They are 'absolute'.

Article number	Article title
2	Right to life
3	Prohibition of torture
4	Prohibition of slavery and forced labour
7	No punishment without law

2.11.4.2 *Limited rights*

These rights are not absolute because the articles are 'limited'.

Article number	Article title
5	Right to liberty and security
6	Right to a fair trial

An example of a limitation is in Article 5; the *right to liberty and security* does not apply if the detention is lawful as a result of six listed arrest situations and is carried out in the manner set down by law. One of these circumstances, for example, is when the arrest is made to ensure 'the detention of a minor by lawful order for the purpose of educational supervision or his lawful detention for the purpose of bringing him before the competent legal authority'.

Article 5 is of particular note for the PCSO. As we discuss in Chapter 3, you have powers to detain a person, using reasonable force if necessary, and for up to 30 minutes for one or more of a specified number of reasons.

2.11.4.3 *Qualified rights*

These rights contain circumstances in which interference with them by the public authority is permissible if it is in the public interest and can be qualified; for example to prevent disorder or crime, for public safety, or for national security.

Article number	Article title
8	Right to respect for private and family life
9	Freedom of thought, conscience, and religion
10	Freedom of expression
11	Freedom of assembly and association

However, a public authority (such as the police) may only interfere with one of these qualified rights under one of three circumstances:

- The interference is lawful and must form part of existing common or statute law (see 3.2 below) such as the power to stop and search
- The interference is made for one of the specifically listed permissible acts in the interests of the public so as to prevent disorder or crime for public safety
- The interference is necessary in a democratic society because the wider interests of the community as a whole often have to be balanced against the rights of an individual, but it must be proportionate, not excessive, heavy-handed, or over the top

2.11.4.4 *Applying the Human Rights Act to community and neighbourhood policing*

You may need to ask yourself the following questions in relation to any individual or group before you 'interfere' with their qualified rights:

- Are my actions **lawful**? Is there a common or statute law (such as the Police Reform Act 2002) to support my interference with a person's rights?
- Are my actions **permissible**? Am I permitted to interfere with a person's rights because it is in support of a duty such as the preventing of crime?
- Are my actions **necessary**? Do the needs of the many outweigh the needs of the few: in other words, must I take into account the interests of the community and balance one individual's rights against another's?
- Are my actions **proportionate**? Having considered everything, will my actions be excessive or could they be less intrusive and more in proportion to the outcome I need to achieve?

There are mnemonics to help you recall these principles, which we consider further in Chapters 3 and 4, such as PLAN (as Proportionate, Legal, Authorized, and Necessary), all of which express some elements of the points we make above.

2.11.4.5 *Task: Performance criteria*

A standard that you will need to achieve is **NOS 1AA.1**: to '*foster people's rights and responsibilities*'. (Note that **Skills for Justice** defines people '*to cover individuals, families, groups, communities* *and organisations. The people may be clients, colleagues or anyone else with whom you come into contact'*.)

This element has the following performance criteria (see Chapter 4):

(1) Recognize people's right to make their own decisions and acknowledge their responsibilities
(2) Interpret the meaning of rights and responsibilities consistent with existing legislative frameworks and organizational policy
(3) Provide information, which is up-to-date and takes account of the complexity of the decisions which people may need to make
(4) Give appropriate help to people who are unable to exercise their rights personally
(5) Acknowledge and provide appropriate support towards the resolution of tensions between rights and responsibilities
(6) Ensure the necessary records relating to the promotion of rights and responsibilities are accurate, legible, and complete
(7) Provide the necessary information to people who wish to make a complaint about an infringement of their rights.

How would you seek to meet criterion 4, to *'give appropriate help to people who are unable to exercise their rights personally'*? What evidence would satisfy the performance criterion for this?

2.11.4.6 *Human rights and the context of policing*

A final point we might make about the importance of human rights in the context of policing, and specifically in the context of your work as a PCSO, is that you should always uphold such rights, never gratuitously infringe them. Occasionally you must interfere with an individual's rights where these adversely affect the needs of the many in our communities. No one has any 'right' to make the lives of others miserable, nor to impose his or her 'anti-social' behaviour upon others. Whilst most democratic societies would accept Winston Churchill's dictum that **the price of freedom is eternal vigilance** (now a motto of the FBI in America), it does not mean that we should accept the stealthy erosion of our civil liberties in the name of convenience. You have a role to uphold the law, as do your police colleagues. You are often the last protection of the vulnerable or the last hope of the weak. The debate is yet to be properly aired in Britain of whether **the price of security is the erosion of liberty**. We look to human rights legislation to ensure that the balance is kept.

2.12 **Chapter Summary**

In this chapter, we have looked at matters which will affect you when you enter a police force as an employee and the subjects which will preoccupy you at the outset. In some cases, we have been very specific and detailed in order to show you what may be involved when you join up; in others we have been broader in approach because we cannot generalize for all PCSO experiences across all forces (and some of them are very different from others).

2.12.1 **Uniform**

We began with issues which you might encounter from day one, such as the uniform you will wear and the equipment with which you may be issued.

2.12.2 **Training**

Before you go out on the streets, you need to be trained, and we looked at the likely nature of your initial training and what your Force training programmes are likely to cover. This is by way of being a reference and preparation section because not all forces will train the same things in the same order; but we do think it is likely that you will cover the 'core' subjects and the National Occupational Standards which we outlined. We emphasized that the police approach to training is based on the **KUSAB** principles of **k**nowledge, **u**nderstanding, **s**kills, **a**ttitudes, and **b**ehaviours, and we explored how important it is that your experiences are reflected not only in what you learn *and* in what you know and understand, but also in how this affects your attitudes (to people and to situations) and what you actually do out on the ground.

2.12.3 **Ways of learning**

There followed two short technical sections covering how you learn, what you have to learn, and the varieties of learning, with the emphasis on the practical application of knowledge to what you do in your daily work. Then we looked briefly at the kinds of professional qualification which are on offer or in prospect for you as a PCSO, and we summarized the current debate on professionalizing the police and how this may affect the future of PCSOs as well. The service as a whole has not yet decided where in the longer time frame and how, in the greater scheme of things, a professional career path for PCSOs will be constructed.

2.12.4 Designation and what it means

This was followed by a discussion about Designation, and we looked at examples of Designation and the debate surrounding PCSO powers and general duties, before considering what a PCSO may expect to do after training, and what a typical tour of duty might look like. This led us to a controversy which persists concerning some hostility towards the PCSO from inside the service. We noted some of the critical things which have been said about PCSOs and concluded that the fault largely lies with the police service itself which steadfastly refuses to define, and thereby limit, the role of the PCSO against that of the police officer. The probability is that performance pressures are forcing the hands of some police forces that do not have the luxury of a well-resourced workforce. We looked carefully at some recent research work into the role of PCSOs and concluded that the public steadfastly thought that PCSOs were doing a good job, whatever some internal police critics may say.

2.12.5 Criminal justice and human rights

We then turned our attention to the broader areas of criminal justice in England and Wales, looking at the role and characteristics of the courts (magistrates' and Crown Courts). We briefly discussed the adversarial system and the context of law and lawmaking. The chapter concluded with a discussion about human rights deriving from the **European Convention on Human Rights**, and the impact of legislation and thinking on your everyday work and interaction with other people.

Notes

1 Though there has been talk of giving all PCSOs all available powers *de statu* (as of law) and excising the word 'Police' from the PCSO title. However, the first flush of enthusiasm for this, espoused by the Home Secretary in November 2008, has not surfaced again. It may be that other things have occupied the Home Secretary's attention—and her successor's—in the interim. There are no current plans in the Home Office to revive the issue, which has not been welcomed by Chief Constables.

2 ABCs are 'acceptable behaviour contracts' and ASBOs are 'anti-social behaviour orders'.

3 See ACPO, *Guidance on Police Community Support Officers* (2005) 25, paras 9.24 and 9.25.

4 See ACPO, *Guidance* (n 3 above). We are grateful to ACPO for permission to refer to and quote from this *Guidance*, and similarly to the revisions and draft guidance in ACPO's *PCSO Practitioners' Guide*, Version 1 (November 2006).

5 See eg the description by Jan Berry, the Federation Chairman (*sic*), in *Police Review*, 24 November 2006, in which she described PCSO powers as a 'dog's dinner' (ibid 6). On other occasions, PCSOs have been derided by Federation spokespersons as '*numties in yellow jackets*', '*traffic wardens lookalikes*', '*police-lite*', and '*half-cops*', none of which appears to shed light on the police/PCSO debate.

6 Introduction to ACPO, *PCSO Practitioners' Guide* (n 4 above) and referring to ACPO, *Guidance* (n 3 above) para 3.9.

7 *ACPO Guidance* (n 3 above) para 10.12 and Appendix J.

8 In the 18th and 19th centuries, much more than the amateur but gentlemanly muddle which was the Army (other than in the 'hard bits' of gunnery and engineering), the Navy was self-evidently a profession, requiring technical competences in seamanship, gunnery, navigation, logistics, victualling, navigation and so on. See NAM Rodger's superbly definitive history of the Royal Navy, *The Command of the Ocean, a Naval History of Britain 1649–1815* (Penguin, 2004).

9 See Rodger, *The Command of the Ocean* (n 8 above) Ch 31 (Administration 1793–1815) 487–8, for a description of naval surgeons.

10 This is from personal observation of recruitment of police officers nationally and in Kent over the last ten years, but we understand from many conversations with our counterparts in other forces, allied to more general information in human resource development about demographics and career planning, that this is certainly a national trend and may be as widespread in Europe and North America. There are several published and on-going studies of the impact of the ageing population and the 'inverted' pyramid of young people in employment, and we have no doubt that this, allied to a more general restlessness about 'career', is impacting on young people's choices of vocation, profession, inclination to enter public service or private industry, and so on. Thus far, the prolonged economic recession and stringencies in the UK do not seem to be moderating this trend. The impact on the police of these demographic, social, economic and professional changes is eminently suited to a separate study, but we do not know at this time whether one has been commissioned.

11 NPIA (2008) Neighbourhood Policing Programme NPIA *PCSO Review* [Online]; available at <http://www.npia.police.uk/en/docs/PCSO_Review_Final_Report.pdf> accessed September 2009.

12 ACPO, *Guidance* (see n 3 above) 2003, updated 2005, again in 2006.

13 Sir Richard Mayne 1829, quoted on <http://www.met.police.uk> accessed 17 October 2006.

14 R Tuffin, J Morris, and A Poole, 'The National Reassurance Policing Programme: a six-site evaluation', Home Office Research Study 296 (Findings 272) January 2006, 1.

15 For an exploration of this topic, see Stan Cohen's seminal work, *Folk Devils and Moral Panics* (3rd edn, Routledge, 2002).

16 T Blair (Prime Minister, 1997–2007), Foreword to the *Respect Action Plan*, Respect Task Force, January 2006, 1.

17 Reported in *Police*, June 2006, 30. Part of this section formed the basis of B Caless, 'Numties in Yellow Jackets', *Policing: a Journal of Policy and Practice*, Vol. 1, No. 2, August 2007, OUP.

18 Reported by BBC news on-line, 27 June 2006, at <http://news.bbc.co.uk/.1/hi/england/london/4505040.stm> accessed 29 June 2006.

19 Reported in *Police*, June 2006, 7.

20 Reported in *Police Staff* (the Unison magazine), Summer 2006, 4.

21 A Crawford, S Blackburn, S Lister, and P Shepherd, *Patrolling with a purpose: an evaluation of police community support officers in Leeds and Bradford city centres* (Centre for Criminal Justice Studies, University of Leeds, 2004). Crawford and Lister published an article, 'Patrol with a purpose', *Police Review*, 6 August 2004, 18–20, in which their research was quoted extensively.

22 Crawford and Lister, *Police Review* (n 21 above) 19.

23 ibid 19.

24 V Harrington, G Down, M Johnson, and C Upton, *Police Community Support Officers: An Evaluation of Round 2 in Kent, 2004/2005* (O&D, Kent Police, 2005).

25 ibid i, ii, and v.

26 C Cooper, J Anscombe, J Avenell, F McLean, and J Morris, 'A National Evaluation of Community Support Officers', Home Office Research Study No 297 (2006).

27 ibid, 'Key Points', 1.

28 See for example, *BBC News* 'PCSOs 'did not watch boy drown'', 28 September 2007, available from <http://bbc.co.uk/mpapps/pagetools/print/news.bbc.co.uk/1/hi/england/manchester/7007081.stm> and 'Community police officers stood by as grandmother rescued man attacked by three girls', *Daily Mail*, 5 November, 2007, available from <http://www.dailymail.co.uk/news/article-491645> accessed 28 May 2009.

29 In summary the Review focused on role, powers, selection, training and career development, supervision, uniform and protective equipment with some ancillary research on age and the volunteering scheme. The Review, fronted by Chief Constable Matt Baggott (ACPO lead for PCSOs), Bob Jones, Chair of the Association of Police Authorities (APA), and the Rt. Hon Tony McNulty, then Minister of State for security, counter-terrorism, crime and policing, was published by NPIA in July 2008. Details of the report are NPIA, Neighbourhood Policing Programme, *PCSO Review* (July 2008, National Police Improvement Agency, available from <http://www.npia.police.uk/en/docs/PCSO_Review_Final_Report.pdf> accessed 1 May 2009.

30 On 17 July 2008, the Home Office published a report on the activities undertaken by Police Community Support Officers (PCSOs) while on

active duty. The report summarizes findings from an Activity-Based Costing (ABC) analysis of PCSOs taken in 2006/07. See Mason, M and Dale, C, *Analysis of Police Community Support Officer (PCSO), Activity Based Costing (ABC) data: results from an initial review*, (July 2008), Home Office, available from <http://www.homeoffice.gov.uk/rds/pdfs08/horr08.pdf> accessed 1 May 2009.

31 See Gibb F, 'JPs win first round in battle over extension of on-the-spot fines,' *The Times*, 5 February 2009, available from <http://timesonline/tol/business/law/article4622156.ece> accessed 5 May, 2009.

32 See Gibb, F 'Straw goes to court to defend trial run of virtual hearings', *The Times*, 28 May 2009.

33 See Gurr, B 'En garde! Magistrates ready for battle over punishments', *The Times*, 26 February, 2009, also available in timesonline archive by date, see reference in n 31 above.

34 Civil cases proceed through county courts, not criminal ones.

35 We should note in fairness that, increasingly, children's evidence is given by video-link rather than by physical presence in a courtroom.

36 Frances Gibb, 'Judges to hang up gowns and wigs', *The Times*, 23 September 2006, 39.

37 Sir David Phillips, quoted in P Hitchens, *A Brief History of Crime: the decline of order, justice and liberty in England* (Atlantic Books, 2003) Ch 2, 41.

Chapter 3
Knowledge and Skills

3.1 **Introduction**

This chapter looks in detail at the knowledge you will need to have in order to carry out the range of PCSO duties. No one will expect you to be able to do everything straight away. Indeed, it is more important at this stage that you understand 'why?' rather than understand 'how?' 'How?' comes with practice and experience, 'why?' comes with knowledge and understanding. We concentrate most of our attention on a very substantial piece about your **General Duties and Powers**, covering each of the powers which may be designated by your Chief Constable to PCSOs. You must remember that not all Chief Constables confer all powers, not all the designated powers available will come to you (it will depend on what you do), and that, although there is agreement on what a PCSO's 'standard 20 powers' should be, there is still some controversy and debate surrounding the designation of other powers.[1] We will task you to go and find out what PCSOs' designated powers are in your force, and for the particular role you will be undertaking. Let's start with your legal status.

3.1.1 **Your legal status**

Your legal status derives from two sources: the first, as we have seen, is the Designation of powers from your Chief Constable (usually endorsed by your Police Authority whose employee you are—as distinct from a police officer who is a 'Crown servant'), and the second derives, ultimately at least, from the Police Reform Act 2002 (which we abbreviate as PRA02). We looked at Designation and what that entails in 2.6 above, so it is the second element, your status as derived from primary legislation, which we shall look at now.

3 Knowledge and Skills

3.1.1.1 *Police Reform Act provisions*

The Police Reform Act of 2002 was something of a 'catch-all' Act, which swept up a number of issues, ranging from the establishment of the Independent Police Complaints Commission (IPCC), the body which oversees and investigates complaints against the police in England and Wales, including the investigation of police shootings, through to clarification of the remit of the Ministry of Defence Police, notes on Metropolitan Police Authority housing, and the powers of the Secretary of State to make orders and regulations. Sandwiched in between all this is *Schedule 4*, dealing with Police Powers, of which a short part is to do with PCSOs (principally Chapter 1 and sections 48–61 of Chapter 2). This can be a little confusing for people coming to PRA02 for the first time and expecting to find some sort of specific statement about the status, definition, and remit for PCSOs. Such language is not there.

3.1.1.2 *Designation*

Let's start by looking at the relevant parts of Schedule 4, Chapter 1 on police powers. Section 38, subsection (1), notes that 'the chief officer of police of any police force may designate any person who a) is employed by the police authority maintaining that force and b) is under the direction and control of that chief officer, as an officer of one or more of the descriptions specified in subsection (2).'

Section 38, subsection (2), goes on to specify that:

… the description of officers are [*sic*] as follows—
a) community support officer
b) investigating officer
c) detention officer
d) escort officer.[2]

> **Discussion point**
> What seems to you to be significant about the power granted to the chief officer (Chief Constable or Commissioner) in subsection (1) of section 38?

Whilst these two sections enable a chief officer to designate you and your colleagues, they actually give that chief officer a great deal more latitude than simply investing you with the powers that we are going to examine in detail in 3.2 below.

3.1.1.3 *The importance of the Police Authority*

We noted briefly above that an important phrase in the Act is *'employed by the police authority'*, because all **police staff**[3] are employed by the Police Authority. Essentially, a police authority is a body composed from elected local, district, borough or unitary authority, or county, councillors. Independent members can put themselves forward for co-option or for direct election to the authority. In some police authorities, Justices of the Peace and magistrates serve on police authorities, as 'independents', by invitation or by ballot. Members of police authorities can also represent the spectrum of political opinion in a police force. Police authority members, numbering 17 in total, serve for a maximum of two periods of four years each, though there is a current debate about whether that should be extended. The role of the police authority is to oversee the efficient, effective, and economic work of the individual police force and, as far as is possible, to reflect the wishes and priorities of the communities which the force serves. That said, police authorities have no powers over operational police decisions, deployments, or what is or is not investigated, nor can the authority set more than the most general and strategic priorities for chief officers. But it would be a bold (or foolish) chief constable who ignored the express wishes of his or her police authority (which incidentally has the power, in consultation with the Home Office through HMIC, to appoint and appraise the performance of all chief officers).

3.1.1.4 *Doing your duty*

That said, the second part of subsection (1) contains an important statement about where authority lies and refers to 'any person who b) is under the direction and control of that chief officer'. What *'under the direction and control'* means in effect is that you are expected to perform to the expected professional standards for a PCSO (or indeed, to the professional standards of any member of the police staff: see 7.2 below). You will be expected to adhere to Force ethical norms and standards (such as we discuss on ethics and corruption, at 1.6 above and 7.2 below respectively), to carry out your duties diligently and with proper expertise and skill, and to conform to Force priorities and operational orders (rather than going off and doing what you feel like). You are expected to behave as one entrusted with a public office should behave: honourably, fairly, without discrimination (without prejudice), always demonstrating high levels of skill and knowledge. Also it means that once you are designated as a PCSO within your Force, the designations have legal status, and therefore so do you, as long as you are in uniform and on duty. Subsection (4) of section 38 of PRA02 specifies that:

> . . . 'a chief officer of police . . . shall not designate a person
> . . . unless [s/he] is satisfied that the person—
> (a) is a suitable person to carry out the function
> (b) is capable of effectively carrying out those functions and
> (c) has received adequate training in the carrying out of those functions and in the exercise and performance of the powers and duties to be conferred on [him or her] by virtue of the designation.

You may like to refer to 2.6 above, which looked at Designation in more detail.

3.1.1.5 *Definitions concerning the capability of a PCSO*

We think that a chief officer need not designate someone of whom s/he is not confident. '*Suitable*' means that someone who is a PCSO is expected to be a responsible citizen, to have a law-abiding profile, and not to have criminals of any kind as friends (instances have been known). '*Capable*' refers to having the required physical fitness and mental resilience to do the job properly. Default on either of these could lead in extreme cases to dismissal or, in less severe cases, to redeployment or withdrawal of designated powers. The important thing is that you have been adequately trained to do what is required of you. The training you receive has an implicit two-way contract. This requires the Force to make sure that you know what to do in most eventualities, and have the skills and knowledge to respond adequately in the few instances which cannot be foreseen or planned for, but also that you will approach the training and acquisition of knowledge responsibly and with an eagerness to learn (see 2.3 and 2.4 above). It also means, of course, that you are trained in the primary role of being a PCSO, not a detention officer, nor an investigating officer, nor an escort officer, each of which roles requires separate and different skills training, even if some overlap with yours.

3.1.1.6 *Derivation of your legal status as a PCSO*

We believe that it is really important for you to know from where you derive your legal status, how your powers are vested in statute, and to whom you are responsible. People may ask you where your powers in law come from (and we look at this in 3.2 below) so it would be well if you were conversant with the Act which gave birth to your role and which specified the powers which your Chief Constable or Commissioner has designated for it.

3.1.2 Criminal law in brief

Before you read (and learn) the next section (3.2 on PCSO powers), you should be aware of the 'headline' components of criminal law. In the summary table which follows, we introduce you to the basics.

The Law in England and Wales	Police Community Support Officers have **street and life skills, knowledge**, and the **powers** vested in them by Parliament to give PCSOs the legal status to carry out their duties.
• **Statute law** (modern) • **Common law** (ancient)	The law in England and Wales is split into two main areas, ancient and modern, or common law and statute law. **Statute law** includes Acts of Parliament that you may be familiar with, such as the Police Reform Act 2002 under which Police Community Support Officers were first introduced and given legal standing. **Common law** was not written down but was agreed by our ancestors as the expected behaviour of a civilized society, such as laws against theft or murder. Nearly all countries in Europe have 'common law', established by practice and custom, still in force.
• **Statute law** (primary and secondary legislation)	**Statute law** is legislation that is written down and provides the basis upon which the modern day legal system in England and Wales is founded. It consists of the creation of Parliamentary Acts (primary) and *subordinate* (secondary) legislation such as orders or regulations, for example in road signs and the offences committed if they are contravened.
Acts of Parliament (primary), eg • *Police Reform Act 2002:* which introduced PCSOs • *Road Traffic Act 1988:* most motoring offences	Government ministers take advice from professional public bodies such as the police and judges, as well as from surveys of public attitudes, as a result of which ministry officials are commissioned to begin the process of creating an Act of Parliament by drafting a *Bill* (an Act apart from its formal approval). The Bill is then put before both Houses of Parliament (Commons and Lords) for debate, modification, and acceptance (or defeat).

If accepted ('passed'), it is placed before the monarch to receive Royal Assent, at which stage it becomes an **Act of Parliament.** Examples include: the Police Reform Act 2002, under which the role of PCSO was created and the Road Traffic Act 1984, under which a PCSO has the power to stop a vehicle on a road.

• **Subordinate** (secondary) legislation, eg Statutory Instruments

This is secondary legislation but has no less importance than its parental Act of Parliament in terms of meeting a perceived need in society. **Subordinate legislation** allows changes to be made to existing legislation by government ministers without having to go through the full parliamentary procedure. An example of this kind of legislation is called a **Statutory instrument.**

• **Statutory instruments** (SI)

Legislation that regularly requires updating, such as codes of practice, penalties, and alterations, can be made in the form of Orders, Regulations and Rules. Examples include The Removal and Disposal of Vehicles Regulations 2002 SI (**Statutory instrument**) No 746, in which the Secretary of State, in exercise of the powers conferred upon him/her by sections 3 and 4 of the Refuse Disposal (Amenity) Act 1978, provided for the removal and disposal of vehicles.[4] This power in turn is used by the PCSO to act within the neighbourhood to arrange for abandoned or burnt-out vehicles to be taken away.

• **Local byelaws**

Within towns and cities, local authorities are empowered to make **byelaws** in their areas to deal with local problems such as restrictions on parking, and the use of recreational areas and other public places. Byelaws are enforceable in the areas designated for their use and do not extend to surrounding borough areas unless stated.

• **Common law** (ancient)

Before Parliament began to make enactments, the law in England and Wales was common to everyone. No new **Common law** is made these days but the laws remain in being, dealing with offences such as:
• Murder
• Manslaughter
• Perverting the course of justice.

Case law:
• Precedents set by decisions in court

Although Common Law is no longer made, 'precedents' are set through decisions by members of the judicial system such as judges. These are the result of legal arguments in court by the prosecution or defence counsels, or by appeals to higher judgement, and are written down as guidance to future court cases. These decisions are referred to as **case law.**

[*Note:* One such decision has a bearing on the evidence of identification of a suspect for which you must learn the mnemonic ADVOKATE (or **SOCRATES**[5]), as a result of the case of ***R v Turnbull* [1976] 3 All ER 549**. To decipher this legal 'coding', it is necessary to know that these abbreviations tell you where to find commentary on the case. It means that this case can be found in *Volume 3* of the *1976 All England Law Reports* on *page 549*. '*R*' is an abbreviation for '*Regina*' (the Crown as prosecutor, or '*Rex*' when the monarch is a King), '*v*' for '*versus*' (against), and *Turnbull* is the name of the defendant.]

The classification of offences:
• Summary
• Indictable offences:
  – Either Way
  – Indictable Only

Offences are classified according to their severity and impact on the community. Offences with less relative impact, such as those associated with minor aspects of road safety and public disorder, can only be dealt with at a magistrates' court and are referred to as **Summary offences.**
Another group of offences with a bigger impact can be tried either at a magistrates' court or a Crown Court (see 2.9 and 2.10 above), and are called **Either Way** offences, like theft. The third category of most serious offences can only be tried at a Crown Court and are referred to as **Indictable only** offences, as they are heard before a judge and jury. However, apart from classifications according to the location where offences are tried, there is another group heading required for a number of powers of investigation, such as arrest by a person other than a constable. This group includes *Either Way* and *Indictable only* offences and together they are called **Indictable offences.**

Criminal liability:
- Criminal act (*actus reus*)
- Guilty mind (*mens rea*)

To be found guilty of a criminal offence a suspect must not only carry out a **criminal act** (*actus reus*) but it must be also proved that the person did so with a **guilty mind** (*mens rea*). Evidence accumulated by an investigating officer will therefore include what the suspect was seen or heard to do by a witness in order to prove that the suspect committed an offence. In addition the suspect will be given an opportunity to explain his/her actions and what s/he was thinking at the time. The investigating officer, a police officer or a PCSO, will question the suspect on *points to prove* the offence.

The Police and Criminal Evidence Act 1984:
- *Codes of Practice* (protection of individuals' rights)

The judicial guidelines governing the treatment of suspects by an investigative authority (such as police officers or PCSOs) are contained in the **Police and Criminal Evidence Act 1984, Codes of Practice.**[6] The Codes themselves are not binding and therefore it is not a criminal offence if the Codes are breached. However, the consequences of not applying them may lead a court to decide that the evidence placed before it is inadmissible. There are eight main sections ranging from Code A, *the exercise of statutory powers of Stop and Search*, to Code H, *the detention of terrorism suspects*. The most important code for PCSOs is **Code C** which involves *the detention, treatment and questioning of persons,* for which strict guidelines must be followed.

Methods of disposal for a suspect:
- Punishment or education?
- Court hearing or no court hearing?

Many people would argue that the only way to stop a person committing another offence is to punish that person; others see a need to educate the offender, so that the offence is not repeated. Either recourse *should* lead to a change (reform) in the person and that is why both the courts and the investigative agencies of England and Wales have the power to apply penalties to people who break the law for minor offences. The aim is also to speed up the court processes. This may include a somewhat vexed area of debate around **discretion**; the decision to charge or not to charge, to report or not report, exercised by a police officer or a PCSO, in the execution of their duty. There are some areas, of course, where discretion cannot be exercised, such as in serious or violent crime.

Non-court appearance:
• **Fixed penalty notices**
• **Penalty notices for disorder**
• **Police cautions**
• **Conditional cautions**

The **fixed penalty notice** system allows people who commit less severe offences, such as traffic-related crimes, the opportunity to pay a fixed fine instead of going to court. The **penalty notices for disorder** scheme is similar and gives the opportunity to deal with people who have committed low-level public nuisance offences. Both schemes are designed to relieve the burden on administration and the courts, and both forms of notice may be issued under designated powers by a PCSO. A **police caution** is a formal warning given by a senior police officer to an adult who has admitted his/her guilt. A **conditional caution** may be given to an adult if the suspect agrees to comply with the conditions attached to it. Failure to comply with the conditions attached to any of the schemes will render the suspect liable to prosecution in court.

Non-court appearance (juveniles):
• **Reprimand**
• **Final warning**

A person under the age of 17 is referred to in law as a *juvenile*. A **reprimand** is a formal warning given to a juvenile by a police officer on admission of guilt of a first offence that is of a minor nature. A **final warning** is also a formal warning but in addition sets up a referral of the juvenile to the Youth Offending Team which can monitor the young person's future actions.

Court appearance:
• Written charge and requisition
• Charge
• Arrest warrant

If a decision is made to prosecute a suspect at court, criminal proceedings will be instituted by the issuing of a document called a **written charge**. At the same time a **requisition** will be issued which requires the person to appear before a magistrates' court to answer the **written charge**. These documents will then be served upon the person. For more serious offences, a suspect can be **charged** with an offence which is a formal written accusation informing the suspect that s/he is to face a court appearance. A **warrant** is a written authority issued by a magistrate or a judge authorizing the persons named on the warrant to carry out the arrest of a person in order to place him/her before a court.

Prosecution of offenders: • The Crown Prosecution Service	In order to promote fairness and impartiality and to relieve the burden of responsibility on police authorities, the prosecution of suspects in courts is dealt with on behalf of the Crown (the State) by a government legal agency called the **Crown Prosecution Service** or **CPS**. Its responsibility is to take a case once it has been investigated by one of the investigative authorities (which include PCSOs) and present the case to a court (magistrates' or Crown Courts) for a decision on whether or not a suspect is guilty. CPS lawyers are professionally qualified in the law like their defence team counterparts, but cannot command such high fees. The normal description of a CPS lawyer is one who acts '***pro bono publico***'—'for the public good' rather than private gain. Much the same may be said of many defence lawyers who appear under the legal aid scheme.

3.1.3 Summary

Although the law in England and Wales appears complicated and segmented, with a number of organizations holding different responsibilities, it is regarded throughout the world as one of the foremost examples of a criminal justice system. We may think sometimes that it creaks at the seams, that it is boringly nit-picking, and that it is both slow and ponderous, but the fairness and impartiality which should characterize any Criminal Justice System are perhaps more important than speed of resolution. The only alternative to the rule of law is anarchy, hence the strategic importance of the law as a hedge between society and tyranny, or order and chaos.

3.2 Powers and Duties of a PCSO

This section is long and very thorough, and it shows you all the implications behind using each of the powers which your Chief Constable may have designated you to have. Of course, you may not have some powers; but as we do not know which they are and how your own particular force parcels them out, and since your role and related powers may change, it's best to include all which you *could* have. We have omitted, however, those specialist powers that relate to an entirely separate function, such as that of being a traffic warden. We relate the exercise of your powers to practical examples, where possible. That is why it is important that you check carefully with your own force to ascertain which of the 53 possible powers and (incorporated with them) the 20 'standard' powers you have been designated to have. See also Chapter 8, where the **Tasks,** based in the fictional city of Tonchester, are set out to help you consolidate your learning.

3.2.1 Powers and duties in one section

We're sorry that this is so long; we think that you are unlikely to read it through in one go, but rather dip in when you want to check your references and your understanding of a particular power. It is best to have all the Powers and Duties here in one section, to avoid you spending ages thumbing through to find a particular power.

3.2.1.1 'Standard powers': attempts to bring order to the variations

Before we discuss the powers themselves, we need to set the scene and illustrate some of the factors involved in PCSO's powers. On the last day of August 2005, the Home Office published a consultation paper entitled *Standard Powers for Community Support Officers and a Framework for the Future Development of Powers*. The consultation period ran for eight weeks, closing near the end of October 2005. The purpose of this exercise was to address inconsistencies in the designation of PCSO powers as set out in Schedule 4 to the Police Reform Act 2002. As the Home Office succinctly put it, 'CSOs in different [police] forces can be designated with some of the available powers, all of the powers or occasionally none of the powers'.[7]

Agreeing on a standard set of powers

The consultation was to ascertain if key groups involved in the deployment of PCSOs (police forces, local authorities, Unison, Police Federation, ACPO, safety partnerships, crime and disorder reduction partnerships, and so on) could agree on a standard set of powers which could be adopted nationally and give, as a result, a core of recognized powers that all PCSOs might have.

3.2.1.2 *ACPO's response*

One of the more articulate responses came from the then-ACPO leader on PCSOs and Neighbourhood Policing Teams, Peter Davies, who noted that there must continue to be a distinction between what a PCSO does and what a police officer does, and that therefore the standard powers should reflect this. He went on to support the notion of a national set of minimum powers, but sounded a warning note that there was a danger of 'mission creep' if PCSOs were being asked more and more to take on roles traditionally ascribed to, or empowered through, police constables. ACPO itself deprecated this 'mission creep' (as did the Police Federation) because, they argued, PCSOs don't have the training to be able to do things that a warranted officer can do. Sensibly, Peter Davies made ACPO's position clear, when he said: 'The national set of powers must not include powers that are coercive or otherwise lead to a higher than normal risk of confrontation, of harm to persons, or of infringement of human rights.'[8]

Extensions of a PCSO's powers are counter-productive

ACPO and the Police Federation have shared a concern since the inception of PCSOs, that gradual (even surreptitious) extensions of PCSOs' powers would impinge on the proper role of a **warranted police officer** (that is, a police officer who has a constable's powers as granted under warrant). Not only would such extensions be subversive of a police officer's role, and indeed provide the 'policing on the cheap' gibe with some substance, but they would also run the risk of exposing the individual PCSO to a situation, especially a confrontational one, which s/he could not control and for which s/he was not trained. There seemed to be real and present dangers in confusing the two roles. We discussed this at length in 2.7 and 2.8 above.

3.2.2 Standardized powers for PCSOs

The following table sets out what the standard PCSO powers are and the legislation from which the powers derive.

Power	Legislation
Environmental Powers	
Issue fixed penalty notices (FPNs) for dog fouling.	Para 1(2)(c) of Schedule (Sch) 4 to *Police Reform Act 2002* (PRA02).
FPN for littering.	Para 1(2)(d) of Sch 4 to PRA02.

Power	Legislation
FPN for graffiti/fly-posting.	Para 1(2)(ca) of Sch 4 to PRA02, inserted by section 46 of the *Anti-Social Behaviour Act 2003* (ASBA03).
Remove abandoned vehicles.	Para 10 of Sch 4 to PRA02, and under regulations made in section 99 of *Traffic Regulation Act 1984*.

Transport powers

Power	Legislation
FPN for cycling on a pavement.	Para 1(2)(b) of Sch 4 to PRA02.
To stop cycles.	Para 11A of Sch 4 to PRA02, inserted by section 89(3) of ASBA03.
Stop vehicles for testing, escort abnormal loads, and carry out road checks.	Paras 11, 12, and 13 of Sch 4 to PRA02.
Require name and address for road traffic offences.	Para 3A of Sch 4 to PRA02, inserted by para 6 of Sch 8 to *Serious and Organised Crime and Police Act 2005* (SOCAP05).
Direct traffic and place traffic signs.	Para 11B of Sch 4 to PRA02, inserted by para 10 of Sch 8 to SOCAP05, and para 13A of Sch 4 to PRA02, inserted by para 11 of Sch 8 to SOCAP05.
Issue public notice for disorder (PND) for throwing fireworks, and trespassing and throwing stones on a railway.	Section 80 of *Explosives Act 1875* and sections 55 and 56 of *British Transport Commission Act 1949*.
Seize vehicles used to cause alarm.	Para 9 of Sch 4 to PRA02.

Alcohol and tobacco powers

Power	Legislation
Limited power to enter licensed premises.	Para 8A of Sch 4 to PRA02, inserted by para 9 of Sch 8 to SOCAP05.
Enforce certain licensing offences (including sale of alcohol to person who is drunk, sale to children, etc).	Para 2(6A) of Sch 4 to PRA02, inserted by paras 3(3) and 3(8) of Sch 8 to SOCAP05.
Require persons drinking in designated area to surrender alcohol.	Para 5 of Sch 4 to PRA02.
Require persons aged under 18 to surrender alcohol.	Para 6 of Sch 4 to PRA02.

3 Knowledge and Skills

Power	Legislation
Search for alcohol and tobacco (using 'reasonable belief').	Para 7A of Sch 4 to PRA02, inserted by para 8 of Sch 8 to SOCAP05.
To seize tobacco from a person aged under 16 (and dispose of it).	Para 7 of Sch 4 to PRA02.
Seize drugs and require name and address for possession of drugs.	Paras 7B and 7C of Sch 4 to PRA02, inserted by para 8 of Sch 8 to SOCAP05.
PNDs for sale of alcohol and consumption etc, all relating to persons under 18.	Sections 146(1), 150(1) and (2), and 151 all of *Licensing Act 2003* and section 12 of *Criminal Justice and Police Act 2001*.
Issue PND for drunk and disorderly behaviour and drunk in highway.	Section 91 of *Criminal Justice Act 1967* and section 12 of *Licensing Act 1872*.

Powers to tackle anti-social behaviour

Require name and address for anti-social behaviour.	Para 3 of Sch 4 to PRA02, inserted by para 3(10) of Sch 8 to SOCAP05.
Deal with begging.	Para 2(6)(ac) and 2(3B) of Sch 4 to PRA02 (see also paras 3(4), 3(5), 3(6), and 3(7) of Sch 8 to SOCAP05).
Disperse groups and remove persons under 16 to their place of residence.	Para 4A of Sch 4 to PRA02, inserted by section 33 of ASBA03.
Issue PND for breach of fireworks curfew, possession of cat 4 firework, possession of excessively loud firework, etc.	Fireworks Regulations 2004 under section 11 of *Fireworks Act* 2003.

Enforcement powers

Require name and address for relevant offences.	Para 1A of Sch 4 to PRA02, inserted by para 2 of Sch 8 to SOCAP05.
Issue FPN for truancy.	Para 1(2)(aa) of Sch 4 to PRA02, inserted by section 23 of ASBA03.
Detain (up to 30 minutes for person believed to have committed a relevant offence).	Para 2 of Sch 4 to PRA02, inserted by para 3(2) of Sch 8 to SOCAP05.
Enforce bye-laws.	Paras 1A(3), 2(3A), 2(6)(ad), 2(6B), 2(6C), 2(6D), 2(6E), and 2 (6F) of Sch 4 to PRA02; see paras 2, 3(4), 3(7), and 3(8) of Sch 8 to SOCAP05.

Power	Legislation
Photograph persons away from a police station.	Para 15ZA of Sch 4 to PRA02, inserted by para 12 of Sch 8 to SOCAP05.
Search detained persons for dangerous items or items … to assist escape.	Para 2A of Sch 4 to PRA02, inserted by para 4 of Sch 8 to SOCAP05.
Use reasonable force to prevent a detained person making off.	Para 4 of Sch 4 to PRA02.
Use reasonable force to transfer control of detained persons.	Paras 2(4A), 2(4B), 4(ZA), and 4(ZB) of Sch 4 to PRA02 (see paras 2, 3, and 4 of Sch 9 to SOCAP05).
Remove children in contravention of curfew notices to their place of residence.	Para 4B of Sch 4 to PRA02, inserted by section 33 of ASBA03.
[Persons] destroying or damaging property, causing alarm, harassment or distress.	Section 1(1) of *Criminal Damage Act 1971* and section 5 of *Public Order Act 1986*.
PND for wasting police time, giving false report, false alarm, etc.	Section 5 *Criminal Law Act 1967*, section 127(2) *Communications Act 2003*, and section 49 *Fire and Rescue Act 2004*.
Use reasonable force.	Section 38 of PRA02, but PCSO only has this power if a PC would have power to use reasonable force in same situation.
Security powers	
Enter and search any premises for purposes of 'saving life and limb' or preventing damage to property.	Para 8 of Sch 4 to PRA02.
Stop and search in authorized areas (powers under *Terrorism Act 2000*).	Para 15 of Sch 4 to PRA02.
Enforce cordoned areas (again under section 36 of *Terrorism Act 2000*).	Para 14 of Sch 4 to PRA02.

3.2.2.1 *A formidable list of powers*

Although it does not compare with a police officer's powers, or with the even greater powers of a customs officer, this is still a formidable list of up to 38 powers; for you may **detain**, **require**, **enter**, **seize**, **demand**, **dispose**, and **enforce** a lot of things. No wonder ACPO was getting concerned about any plans to extend PCSOs' coercive powers. It is one thing to have a range of powers, it is another to know when to use them and when to use your discretion, to know when to intervene and when to wait and watch. In the sections which follow, our principal aim is to help you in precisely these areas: What does the power mean? When do you use it? Why do you use it?

3.2.2.2 *Powers' layout*

Each of the powers is laid out in the same way. We give the power a context (when you might use it) and then analyse the power in two columns. The left-hand column describes the power and looks at elements in applying the power, such as 'points to prove'. The right-hand column gives the relevant law, statute, or bye-law from which the power originates. We hope that by presenting each power in tabulated form like this, it will be easier to look up and easier to absorb. However, there will still have to be some committing to memory on your part.

3.2.3 Power to issue fixed penalty notices for dog fouling on designated land

Context

The Environmental Health Department has commented on the excessive amount of dog faeces in one part of the city. It has been proposed that patrolling take place in the area to overcome the situation. The following powers and relevant legislation are available to a designated PCSO to deal with the problem:

If a designated PCSO has reason to believe that a person in charge of a dog has committed an offence of failing to remove any faeces as a result of the dog defecating on designated land, the PCSO has the power to require his or her name and address and issue a fixed penalty notice as an alternative to conviction.	*Empowering legislation* 1. **Power to issue fixed penalty notices for dog fouling**: para 1(2)(c) of Sch 4 to the Police Reform Act 2002.* [*To avoid lengthy repetition, we shall refer to Schedule 4 of the Police Reform Act 2002 from this point forward as **S4PRA02**, but will continue to use specific paragraph numbers.] *Primary legislation*

NB: Due to a repeal of legislation in 2005, no further land can be designated under this Act, but the offence can still be enforced on land previously designated.

1. **Power to require name and address:** para 1A(3) of S4PRA02.
2. **Power to issue fixed penalty notices in respect of dog fouling:** s 4 Dogs (Fouling of Land) Act 1996.

Points to consider to prove the offence

1. That the defecation took place on land that has been designated for the purposes of this Act by a local authority.
2. Evidence of defecation by the dog, obtained through observation by you or a witness, in which case the use of ADVOKATE (or **SOCRATES**) will support evidence of identification.
3. Failure of the person in charge of the dog to remove the faeces from the land. Exceptions:
   1. The person in charge of the dog has a reasonable excuse.
   2. The person is registered as blind.
   3. The owner, occupier, or authority of the land consents.
   4. The person subsequently places the faeces in a suitable receptacle nearby.

Offence

Dogs fouling on designated land: s 3 Dogs (Fouling of Land) Act 1996.

Mode of trial and penalty

Summary—fine not exceeding a level 3 fine.

Points to consider to prove the offence

1. That you were designated under para 1A of Sch 4 to the Police Reform Act 2002.
2. That you had reason to believe that the person had committed the offence of dogs fouling on designated land.
3. That you were in uniform and clearly made a requirement for the person's name and address because you had reason to believe s/he had committed an offence of dog fouling.
4. That you made a note of the description of the suspect.
5. That you use ADVOKATE (or **SOCRATES**) to evidence identification of the person.

Offence

Failing to give name and address when required: para 1A(5) of S4PRA02.
Mode of trial and penalty
Summary—level 3 fine.

See also **Power to issue fixed penalty notices in respect of offences under dog control orders**.

3.2.4 Power to issue fixed penalty notices in respect of offences under dog control orders

Context

The communities around your patrol area have voiced their unease about the number of dogs roaming the area in packs. You have been tasked to trace the owners of these dogs. The following powers and relevant legislation are available to a designated PCSO to deal with the problem:

If a designated PCSO has reason to believe that a person has committed a dog offence on any land for which a 'control of dogs' order has been made by a local authority, the PCSO has the power to require his or her name and address and issue him or her with a fixed penalty notice as an alternative to conviction.

Empowering legislation

1 **Power to issue fixed penalty notices in respect of offences under dog control orders:** para 1(2)(e) of S4PRA02.

Primary legislation

1. **Power to require name and address:** para 1A(3) of S4PRA02
2. **Power to issue fixed penalty notices in respect of offences under dog control orders:** s 59 of the Clean Neighbourhoods and Environment Act 2005. *

[*To avoid lengthy repetition, we shall refer to Clean Neighbourhoods and Environment Act 2005 from this point forward as **CNE05**.]

Points to consider to prove the offence:

1. That the defecation took place on land subject to a control order which is open to the air on at least one side '*and to which the public are entitled or permitted to have access (with or without payment)*'.
2. Evidence of defecation by the dog, eg through observation by you or a witness using ADVOKATE (or **SOCRATES**) to support evidence of identification.
3. Failure of the person in charge of the dog to remove the faeces from the land. Mitigating circumstances:
   • The person in charge of the dog has a reasonable excuse.

Offences relating to the control of dogs under a dog control order
Fouling of land by dogs and the removal of dog faeces.

Enabling legislation
Provision of a dog control order s 55 CNE05.

Refer to local authorities for local control order references.

- The person is registered as blind.
- The owner, occupier, or authority of the land consents.

4. The person subsequently places the faeces in a suitable receptacle nearby.

Points to consider to prove the offence

1. That the dog was not on a lead on land subject to a control order which is open to the air on at least one side '*and to which the public are entitled or permitted to have access (with or without payment)*'.

2. Evidence of the dog not wearing a lead, eg through observation by you or a witness using ADVOKATE (or **SOCRATES**) to support evidence of identification.

Offences relating to the control of dogs under a dog control order

The keeping of dogs on leads

Enabling legislation

Provision of a dog control order s 55 CNE05.

Refer to local authorities for local control order references.

Points to consider to prove the offence

1. That the dog was excluded from land subject to a control order which is open to the air on at least one side '*and to which the public [is] entitled or permitted to have access (with or without payment)*'.

2. Evidence that the dog was on the land, eg through observation by you or a witness using **SOCRATES** (or ADVOKATE) to support evidence of identification.

Offences relating to the control of dogs under a dog control order

The exclusion of dogs from land

Enabling legislation

Provision of a dog control order s 55 CNE05.

Refer to local authorities for local control order references.

Offences relating to the control of dogs under a dog control order

The number of dogs which a person may take on to any land

Enabling legislation

Provision of a dog control order s 55 CNE05.

Refer to local authorities for local control order references.

Points to consider to prove the offence:

1. That you were designated under para 1A of S4PRA02.
2. That you had reason to believe that the person had committed one or more of the offences relating to the control of dogs under a dog control order (see offences in the other column).
3. That you were in uniform and clearly made a request for the person's name and address because you had reason to believe s/he had committed an offence relating to the control of dogs under a dog control order.
4. That you made a note of the description of the suspect.
5. That you used **SOCRATES** (or ADVOKATE) to evidence identification of the person.

Offence

Failing to give name and address when required: para 1A(5) of S4PRA02.

Mode of trial and penalty

Summary—level 3 fine.

See also **Power to issue fixed penalty notices for dog fouling on designated land.**

3.2.5 Power to issue fixed penalty notices for littering

Context

From time to time towns face a mountain of litter around their streets. This sometimes coincides with local football matches or street celebrations of some kind. If excessive in amount, or left to accumulate, there could be health problems. You have been tasked to investigate the matter. The following powers and relevant legislation are available to a designated PCSO to deal with the problem:

If a designated PCSO has reason to believe that a person has committed an offence of littering, the PCSO has the power to require his or her name and address and issue him or her with a fixed penalty notice as an alternative to conviction.	*Empowering legislation* 1. **Power to issue fixed penalty notices for littering:** para 1(2)(d) of S4PRA02. *Primary legislation* 1. **Power to require name and address:** para 1A(3) of S4PRA02. 2. **Power to issue fixed penalty notices in respect of litter:** s 88 Environmental Protection Act 1990.
Points to consider to prove the offence 1. That the littering took place anywhere in the area of a principal litter authority (eg a local authority). 2. That the littering took place in an area which is open to the air (eg the entrance to a large shopping complex but not a telephone box with a gap at the bottom of the door). 3. That the littering took place in an area to which the public have access with or without payment (not privately owned). 4. That the person threw down, dropped, or deposited any litter on land or in water and left it.	*Offence* **Littering:** s 87 Environmental Protection Act 1990 *Method of disposal* Local authority fixed penalty notice. *Mode of trial and penalty* Summary—a fine not exceeding level 4. **NB: Although this is an offence for which a lower tier Penalty Notice for Disorder can be issued, a PCSO cannot issue a PND for this offence.**

5. That the littering took place without being authorized by law and without the consent of the owner.

- See **3.2.4** above: **Power to issue fixed penalty notices**, where the points to prove are itemized in respect of failing to give name and address when required.

Offence
Failing to give name and address when required: para 1A(5) of S4PRA02.

Mode of trial and penalty
Summary—level 3 fine.

3.2.6 Power to issue fixed penalty notices for graffiti and fly-posting

Context

For some time the area around local municipal housing in high-rise buildings has been the target of graffiti (see example below), petty vandalism, and anti-social behaviour. In an effort to overcome this problem, you have been tasked with patrolling the area. The following powers and relevant legislation are available to a designated PCSO to deal with the problem:

(Photograph by Bryn Caless)

Photograph 2: Graffiti on a wooden fence

---

3 Knowledge and Skills

If a designated PCSO has reason to believe that a person has committed an offence in connection with acts of graffiti and/or fly-posting, the PCSO has the power to require his or her name and address and to give a person a fixed penalty notice as an alternative to conviction.

NB: There are no specific offences of producing graffiti or fly-posting and therefore they are investigated and prosecuted using the following legislation.

Empowering legislation

1. **Power to issue penalty notices in respect of graffiti or fly-posting:** para 1(2)(ca) of S4PRA02.

Primary legislation

1. **Power to require name and address:** para 1A(3) of S4PRA02.
2. **Power to issue penalty notices in respect of graffiti or fly-posting:** s 43(1) of the Anti-Social Behaviour Act 2003.*

[*To avoid lengthy repetition, we shall refer to s 43(1) of the Anti-Social Behaviour Act 2003 from this point forward as **S43ASB03**.]

Points to consider to prove the offence

1. That the suspect did not have any lawful excuse to cause the damage, such as s/he had no reason to believe s/he had the owner's consent.
2. That the property was damaged, for example a wall was defaced by paint from a spray can, or
3. that the property was destroyed or damaged beyond repair.
4. That the property belonged to someone other than the suspect (it can be jointly owned).
5. That the suspect intended to damage or destroy the property and s/he meant to do it, or
6. that the suspect was reckless as to whether or not the property was damaged or destroyed; s/he took a risk in his or her actions.

Offence

Damaging property etc: s 1(1) Criminal Damage Act 1971.

Method of disposal

Penalty notice for disorder (upper tier)—under Criminal Justice and Police Act 2001 (see 5.2.8 and 5.2.9 below, on issuing PNDs).*

[*To avoid lengthy repetition, we shall refer to the Criminal Justice and Police Act 2001 from this point forward as **CJP01**.]

Mode of trial and penalty

- If the value of the damage is **below** £5,000:

  Summary—three months' imprisonment and/or a level 4 fine.

- If the value of the damage **exceeds** £5,000 then it becomes an EITHER WAY offence:

  Summary—six months' imprisonment and/or a fine.

  Indictment—ten years' imprisonment.

Points to consider to prove the offence

1. That the suspect did not have lawful authority or reasonable excuse.
2. That the suspect pulled down a traffic sign, milestone, or direction post, or
3. that the suspect obliterated a traffic sign, milestone, or direction post.
4. That the traffic sign, milestone, or direction post was placed on or over a highway.
5. That the traffic sign, milestone, or direction post was placed lawfully.

Offence

Pulls down or obliterates a traffic sign:
s 131(2) of the Highways Act 1980.

Method of disposal
Local authority fixed penalty s 43(1) ASB03

Mode of trial and penalty
Summary—level 3 fine.

Points to consider to prove the offence

1. That the suspect did not have the consent of the highway authority, or any authorization or reasonable excuse.
2. That the suspect painted, inscribed, or affixed any letter, sign, or other mark.
3. That the letter, sign, or other mark was left on the surface of any highway, tree, structure, or words on or in a highway.

Offence

Painting or affixing things on structures on the highway etc:
s 132(1) Highways Act 1980.

Method of disposal
Local authority fixed penalty S43ASB03.

Mode of trial and penalty
Summary—level 4 fine.

Points to consider to prove the offence

1. That the suspect did not have lawful authority or reasonable excuse.
2. That the suspect personally affixed or placed the poster if it was an advertisement.
3. That the posters were affixed within the Metropolitan Police Area.

Offence

Affixing posters: para 10 of s 54 of the Metropolitan Police Act 1839.

Method of disposal
Local authority fixed penalty S43ASB03.

Mode of trial
Summary.

---

4. That the posters were affixed
   without the consent of the
   owner or occupier.

Points to consider to prove the offence	*Offence*
1. That the suspect did not have lawful authority or reasonable excuse.	**Defacement of streets with slogans etc:** s 20(1) London County Council (General Powers) Act 1954.
2. That the suspect painted or inscribed slogans.	*Method of disposal* Local authority fixed penalty.
3. That the streets in London were defaced as a result of the suspect's actions.	*Mode of trial* Summary.

Points to consider to prove the offence	*Offence*
1. That the suspect did not have lawful authority or reasonable excuse.	**Displaying advertisement in contravention of regulations:** s 224(3) Town and Country Planning Act 1990.
2. That the suspect displayed an advertisement in contravention of planning regulations.	*Method of disposal* Local authority fixed penalty S43ASB03.
3. That the suspect did not have authority from the local planning authority.	*Mode of trial and penalty* Summary—level 3 fine.
4. That the suspect personally affixed or placed the advertisement.	

See **3.2.4** above: **Power to issue fixed penalty notices**, where the points to prove are itemized in respect of failing to give name and address when required.	*Offence* **Failing to give name and address when required by a PCSO:** para 1A(5) of S4PRA02.
	Mode of trial and penalty Summary—level 3 fine.
	NB: Once designated under paragraph 2 of S4PRA02, you have the power to detain a person for 30 minutes to await the arrival of a police officer, if the suspect fails to give his or her name and address or s/he gives a false one.

3.2.7 Power to remove vehicles which are illegally parked, causing an obstruction or danger, or broken down on a road

Context

As a result of three sets of road works taking place simultaneously in your town centre, a large traffic jam has been created on all routes. A number of vehicles appear to have been left by their owners in prominent but 'undedicated' places on the highway, adding to the general chaos. The following powers and relevant legislation are available to a designated PCSO to deal with the problem:

A designated PCSO may remove from a road vehicles which are illegally, obstructively, or dangerously parked, or broken down. The purpose of the power is to enable the PCSO to deal with obstructions which are a matter of **urgency** that would affect people using a road currently or in the future, thereby preventing situations such as large traffic jams.	*Empowering legislation* para 10 of S4PRA02. *Enabling legislation* s 99 of the Road Traffic Regulation Act 1984. *Primary legislation* Regs 3 and 4 of the Removal and Disposal of Vehicles Regulations 1986.* [*To avoid lengthy repetition, we shall refer to Removal and Disposal of Vehicles Regulations 1986 from this point forward as **RDVR86**.]
Points to consider That the vehicle **broke down** on a road, for example a vehicle with a seized engine which cannot be moved under its own power.	*Situation under which removal can take place* 1. **Broken down:** reg 3(1)(a) RDVR86.
Points to consider That the vehicle was permitted to remain at rest on a road in such a position, condition, or circumstance as to cause **obstruction** to persons using the road, such as a vehicle left unattended outside the exit to a building housing or utilizing emergency services vehicles.	*Situation under which removal can take place* 2. **Causing an obstruction:** reg 3(1)(a) RDVR86.

3 Knowledge and Skills

Points to consider	*Situation under which removal can take place*
That the vehicle was permitted to remain at rest on a road in such a position, condition, or circumstance as to cause **danger** to persons using the road, such as a vehicle or part of a vehicle left unattended at the side of a road without wheels or left with the chassis standing on piles of bricks.	3. **Causing a danger:** reg 3(1)(a) RDVR86.

Points to consider	*Situation under which removal can take place*
That the vehicle was permitted to remain at rest on a road in contravention of a **prohibition**, for example at rest in the area of a junction controlled by a stop sign.	4. **Illegally parked as a result of a prohibition:** reg 3(1)(b) RDVR86.

Points to consider	*Situation under which removal can take place*
That the vehicle was permitted to remain at rest on a road in contravention of a **restriction**, for example at rest in the area of white line hatchings near a traffic island or junction.	5. **Illegally parked as a result of a restriction**: reg 3(1)(b) RDVR8.

Points to consider	*Situation under which removal can take place*
That the vehicle **broke down** and remained at rest on a road in contravention of a **prohibition**, such as having broken down on a route designated for use by buses and pedal cycles only.	6. **Broken down and illegally parked as a result of a restriction**: reg 3(1)(b) RDVR86.

A designated PCSO may:	7. **Power to remove vehicle:** reg 4A RDVR86.
1. remove any vehicle in any of the circumstances described above or 2. 'arrange for its removal from that road	

- to a place which is not on that or any other road, or
- may move it or arrange for its removal to another position on that or another road'.

3.2.8 Power to stop cycles, power to issue fixed penalty notices for cycling on a footpath

Context

Elderly residents living near a local park have been complaining recently of young cyclists on footpaths being aggressive and dangerous. The following powers and relevant legislation are available to a designated PCSO to deal with the problem:

If a designated PCSO has reason to believe that a cyclist has committed an offence of riding a cycle on a footpath, the PCSO has the power to require the cyclist to stop the cycle, to require his/her name and address, and to give a person a fixed penalty notice for riding on a footway as an alternative to conviction.	*Empowering legislation* 1. **Power to stop cycles**: para 11A of S4PRA02. 2. **Power to issue fixed penalty notices for cycling on a footpath**: para 1(2)(b) of S4PRA02. *Primary legislation* 1. **Power to stop cycles:** s 163(2) Road Traffic Act 1988.* [*To avoid lengthy repetition, we shall refer to the Road Traffic Act 1988 from this point forward as **RTA88**.] 2. **Power to require name and address:** para 1A(3) of S4PRA02. 3. **Power to issue fixed penalty notices:** s 54 Road Traffic Offenders Act 1988.
Points to consider to prove the offence 1. That the person on the cycle is riding purposefully, for example in and out of pedestrians, or taking a short cut, or avoiding riding on the road or pushing the cycle.	*Offence* **Riding on a footway:** s 72 Highway Act 1835. *Mode of trial and penalty* Summary—level 2 fine.

2. That the area in which the cycle is being ridden is identifiable as a footpath.
3. The name and classification of the road that the footpath borders.
4. That you made a note of the description of the suspect.
5. That you used **SOCRATES** (or ADVOKATE) to evidence identification of the person.

Points to consider to prove the offence

1. All of the above.
2. That you were in uniform and clearly made a request for the cyclist to stop.
3. That you had reason to believe the cyclist was committing an offence of riding on a footpath.
4. That you made a note of the description of the cycle, rider, and direction of travel.
5. That you used **SOCRATES** (or ADVOKATE) to evidence identification of the rider.

Offence

Failing to stop a cycle: s 163(2) RTA88.

Mode of trial and penalty

Summary—level 3 fine.

Points to consider to prove the offence

See **3.2.4** above: **Power to issue fixed penalty notices**, where the points to prove are itemized in respect of failing to give name and address when required.

Offence

Failing to give name and address when required:

para 1A(5) of S4PRA02.

Mode of trial and penalty

Summary—level 3 fine.

3.2.9 Power to stop vehicles for testing

Context

There is an operation being planned which involves a multi-agency team to stop large goods vehicles near a local industrial estate. You have been tasked to take part in that road check. The following powers and relevant legislation are available to a designated PCSO to support such an event:

If designated, a PCSO in uniform has the power to require a motor vehicle to stop on a road for the purposes of being tested by an authorized examiner.	*Empowering legislation* **Power to stop vehicles for testing:** para 11 of S4PRA02.

This power is necessary because although authorized vehicle examiners such as employees of the Department of Transport have powers to test and inspect motor vehicles, they do not have powers to stop the vehicles on the road in the first place.

NB: Do not confuse this kind of 'road check' with a s 4 PACE 1984 'road check' for which you have additional powers to stop vehicles relating to indictable offences and escaped prisoners.

Points to consider when using the power

1. That you are in full uniform.
2. That the road is a highway or any other road to which the public has access.
3. That the vehicles you stop are motor vehicles, defined as mechanically-propelled vehicles intended or adapted for use on a road, such as a car or articulated lorry.
4. That the person on whose behalf you stopped the vehicle is an authorized examiner, such as *bona fide* employees of the Department of Transport.

Primary legislation
Power to stop vehicles for testing: s 163(2) RTA88.

3.2.10 Power to direct traffic and pedestrians for the purposes of escorting abnormal loads

Context

You receive a memo from your supervisor requesting your support in escorting an abnormal load through your town. The load itself is a complete operating theatre for a nearby private hospital. The slow transit will attract crowds of onlookers as well as causing traffic delay. The following powers and relevant legislation are available to a designated PCSO to deal with the process:

If designated, a PCSO has the power to regulate traffic and pedestrians in a road for the purposes of escorting a vehicle or trailer carrying a load of exceptional dimensions either to or from the relevant police area. If a driver or pedestrian fails to comply with the directions, a designated PCSO has the power to require their name and address.

Empowering legislation

1. **Power to direct traffic and pedestrians for the purposes of escorting abnormal loads:** para 12(1) of S4PRA02.
2. **Power to require name and address for road traffic offences:** para 3A of S4PRA02.

If the suspect fails to comply with the requirement or gives a name and address which the PCSO reasonably suspects to be false or inaccurate, the suspect commits an offence.

If the PCSO is further designated under paragraph 2, s/he may then detain the person and await the arrival of a police officer or request the suspect to accompany him/her to a police station (see 3.2.24 below).

If the PCSO is designated under paragraph 4, s/he may use reasonable force during the detention of the suspect (see 3.2.24 below).

Primary legislation

1. **Failing to give name and address when required by a PCSO:** para 3A(2) of S4PRA02.
2. **Whilst driving a motor vehicle, neglects or refuses to comply with traffic directions given by a PCSO:** s 35(1) or (2) RTA88.
3. **Whilst a pedestrian on foot, refuses to comply with traffic directions given by a PCSO:** s 37 RTA88.

Purpose under which the power to direct traffic and pedestrians for the purposes of escorting abnormal loads can be used:

• To escort a vehicle or trailer carrying a load of exceptional dimensions either to or from the relevant police area.

Power to direct traffic and pedestrians for the purposes of escorting abnormal loads: s 12(1) of S4PRA02.

- *To direct a vehicle to stop* whilst engaged in the regulation of traffic in a road, eg stopping other traffic at a junction to allow the abnormal load to continue its journey in the safest way.
- *To make a vehicle proceed in, or keep to, a particular line of traffic,* eg by directing vehicles to use the outside lane of a dual carriageway only in order to pass the abnormal load in the interests of road safety.
- *To direct pedestrians to stop,* eg by requesting pedestrians to wait at the kerbside of a road to allow the abnormal load to pass in the interests of road safety.

Points to consider to prove the offence

1. That you were acting in the lawful execution of your duty.
2. That you were directing traffic for the purposes of escorting a vehicle or trailer carrying a load of exceptional dimensions either to or from the relevant police area.
3. That you were engaged in the regulation of traffic in a road and gave an obvious direction to a vehicle to stop which was evident to the driver.

Offence

Whilst **driving** a motor vehicle, neglects or refuses to comply with traffic directions given by a PCSO: s 35(1) RTA88.

Mode of trial and penalty

Summary—A fine not exceeing level 3, discretionary disqualification and obligatory endorsement with three penalty points, if committed in respect of a motor vehicle.

4. That you were engaged in the regulation of traffic in a road and gave an obvious direction to a vehicle to proceed in, or keep to, a particular line of traffic, which was evident to the driver.
5. That you made a note of the description of the suspect.
6. That you used **SOCRATES** (or ADVOKATE) to evidence identification of the person.

Circumstances under which the power can be used

1. That all of the above were satisfied.
2. That you are designated under para 3A of S4PRA02.
3. That you informed the suspect you had reasonable cause to believe they had neglected or refused to comply with traffic directions.
4. That you request the name and address from the suspect.

Power to require the name and address of a *driver* who refuses to comply with a traffic direction from a PCSO who is for the time being directing traffic and pedestrians for the purposes of escorting abnormal loads: s 165(1) RTA88.

Points to consider to prove the offence

See **3.2.4** above: **Power to issue fixed penalty notices**, where the points to prove are itemized in respect of failing to give name and address when required.

Offence

Failing to give name and address when required by a PCSO: para 3A(2) of S4PRA02.

Mode of trial and penalty

Summary—level 3 fine.

See 3.2.24 below for details of your power to detain under PRA02.

Points to consider to prove the offence

1. That you were acting in the lawful execution of your duty.

Offence

Whilst a *pedestrian* on foot refuses to comply with traffic directions given by a PCSO: s 37 RTA88.

2. That you were directing traffic for the purposes of escorting a vehicle or trailer carrying a load of exceptional dimensions either to or from the relevant police area.
3. That you were engaged in the regulation of traffic in a road and gave an obvious direction to a pedestrian to stop which was evident to the person.

Circumstances under which the power can be used

1. That all of the above in relation to a pedestrian failing to comply with traffic directions were satisfied.
2. That you are designated under para 3A of S4PRA02.
3. That you informed the suspect you had reasonable cause to believe they had neglected or refused to comply with traffic directions.
4. That you requested the name and address from the suspect.

Power to require the name and address of a *pedestrian* who refuses to comply with a traffic direction from a PCSO, who is for the time being directing traffic and pedestrians, for the purposes of escorting abnormal loads: s 165(1) RTA88.

Points to consider to prove the offence

See **3.2.4** above: **Power to issue fixed penalty notices**, where the points to prove are itemized in respect of failing to give name and address when required.

Offence

Failing to give name and address when required by a PCSO: para 3A(2) of S4PRA02.

Mode of trial and penalty

Summary—level 3 fine.

See 3.2.24 below for details of your power to detain under PRA02.

3.2.11 Power to control traffic for purposes other than escorting a load of exceptional dimensions

Context

A power cut in the town renders the traffic lights' system completely out of action. You are tasked to support other members of the police family in carrying out traffic control to alleviate the problem, which has been made worse by highways repairs in process and recent very heavy rain. The following powers and relevant legislation are available to a designated PCSO to deal with the process:

If designated, a PCSO has the power to regulate traffic in a road and give directions to a person driving or propelling a vehicle, and to do so for the purposes of a traffic survey. Similarly, a PCSO has the power to regulate vehicular traffic in a road and give directions to a pedestrian. If a driver or pedestrian fails to comply with the directions, the PCSO has the power to require their name and address.

If the suspect fails to comply with the requirement, or gives a name and address which the PCSO reasonably suspects to be false or inaccurate, the suspect commits an offence.

If the PCSO is further designated under para 2, s/he may then detain the person and await the arrival of a police officer or request the suspect to accompany him/her to a police station (see 3.2.24 below).

If the PCSO is designated under paragraph 4, s/he may use reasonable force during the detention of the suspect (see 3.2.24 below).

Empowering legislation

1. **Power to control traffic for purposes other than escorting a load of exceptional dimensions:** para 11B of S4PRA02.
2. **Power to require name and address for road traffic offences:** para 3A of S4PRA02.

Primary legislation

1. **Failing to give name and address when required by a PCSO:** para 3A(2) of S4PRA02.
2. **Whilst driving a motor vehicle, neglects or refuses to comply with traffic directions given by a PCSO:** s 35(1) or (2) RTA88.
3. **Whilst a pedestrian on foot, refuses to comply with traffic directions given by a PCSO:** s 37 RTA88.

Purpose and circumstances under which the PCSO has the power to direct traffic

1. During the regulation of traffic in a road.
2. *To direct a vehicle to stop*, eg stopping traffic at a junction in the interest of promoting road safety.
3. *To make a vehicle proceed in, or keep to, a particular line of traffic*, eg by directing vehicles to use particular parts of a road to avoid obstructions perhaps.
4. To direct traffic in the above ways while a traffic survey of any description is being carried out on or in the vicinity of a road.

Power to direct traffic in a road and for the purposes of a traffic survey: para 11B(1) (1) of S4PRA02.

Purpose and circumstances under which the PCSO has the power to direct pedestrians

1. During the regulation of vehicular traffic in a road.
2. To direct pedestrians to stop proceeding along or across a carriageway, eg by requesting pedestrians to wait at the kerbside of a road in the interests of promoting road safety while vehicular traffic is beckoned on.

Power to direct a person on foot in a road: para 11B(1), (2) of S4PRA02.

Points to consider to prove the offence

1. That you were acting in the lawful execution of your duty.
2. That you were directing traffic in a road for the purposes of the regulation of traffic in the relevant police area.

Offence

Whilst *driving* a motor vehicle, neglects or refuses to comply with traffic directions given by a PCSO: s 35(1) or (2) RTA88.

Mode of trial and penalty

Summary—a fine not exceeding level 3, discretionary disqualification and obligatory endorsement with three penalty points, if committed in respect of a motor vehicle.

3. That you were engaged in the regulation of traffic in a road and gave an obvious direction to a vehicle to stop which was evident to the driver.
4. That you were engaged in the regulation of traffic in a road and gave an obvious direction to a vehicle to proceed in, or keep to, a particular line of traffic, which was evident to the driver.
5. That the driver refused to comply with your directions.
6. That you made a note of the description of the suspect.
7. That you used **SOCRATES** (or ADVOKATE) to evidence identification of the person.

Circumstances under which the power can be used

1. That all of the above were satisfied.
2. That you are designated under para 3A of S4PRA02.
3. That you informed the suspect you had reasonable cause to believe they had neglected or refused to comply with traffic directions.
4. That you request the name and address from the suspect.

Power to require the name and address of a *driver* who refuses to comply with a traffic direction from a PCSO who is for the time being directing traffic: s 165(1) RTA88.

Points to consider to prove the offence

See **3.2.4** above: **Power to issue fixed penalty notices**, where the points to prove are itemized in respect of failing to give name and address when required.

Offence

Failing to give name and address when required by a PCSO: para 3A(2) of S4PRA02.

Mode of trial and penalty
Summary—level 3 fine.
See 3.2.24 below for details of your power to detain under PRA02.

Points to consider to prove the offence	*Offence*
1. That you were acting in the lawful execution of your duty.	**Whilst a *pedestrian* on foot, refuses to comply with traffic directions given by a PCSO:** s 37 RTA88.
2. That you were directing vehicular traffic in a road in the relevant police area.	
3. That you gave an obvious direction to a pedestrian to stop proceeding along or across the carriageway which was evident to the person.	
4. That the person did not stop and refused to comply with your directions.	
5. That you made a note of the description of the suspect.	
6. That you used **SOCRATES** (or ADVOKATE) to evidence identification of the person.	

Circumstances under which the power can be used	**Power to require the name and address of a *pedestrian* who**
1. That all of the above in relation to a pedestrian failing to comply with traffic directions were satisfied.	**refuses to comply with a traffic direction from a PCSO who is for the time being directing traffic and pedestrians:** s 165(1) RTA88.
2. That you are designated under para 3A of S4PRA02.	
3. That you informed the suspect you had reasonable cause to believe they had neglected or refused to comply with your traffic directions.	
4. That you request the name and address from the suspect.	

Points to consider to prove the offence	*Offence*
See **3.2.4** above: **Power to issue fixed penalty notices**, where the points to prove are itemized in respect of failing to give name and address when required.	**Failing to give name and address when required by a PCSO:** para 3A(2) of S4PRA02.
	Mode of trial and penalty
	Summary—level 3 fine.
	See 3.2.24 below for details of your power to detain under PRA02.

3.2.12 Power to carry out a road check under section 4 of the Police and Criminal Evidence Act 1984

Context

Whilst being transported from a remand prison, a prisoner has escaped from custody. This occurred when the detention van pulled in to the local magistrates' court. Under section 4 of the Police and Criminal Evidence Act 1984, road checks have been authorized by your Superintendent (Operations) to search for the missing prisoner and/or to obtain witness accounts of his escape. You have been tasked to take part in one of the road checks. The following powers and relevant legislation are available to a designated PCSO to deal with the problem:

If designated, a PCSO has the power in the relevant police area to carry out a road check under s 4 of the Police and Criminal Evidence Act 1984 which has been authorized by a senior police officer to locate a witness or suspect in connection with an indictable offence, or a person unlawfully at large. For the purposes of carrying out such a road check, the PCSO also has the power to stop vehicles on a road.	*Empowering legislation* **Power to carry out a road check under s 4 Police and Criminal Evidence Act 1984:** para 13 of S4PRA02.* [*To avoid lengthy repetition, we shall refer to the Police and Criminal Evidence Act 1984 from this point forward as **PACE84**.]
Points to consider when using the power 1. That the s 4 Police and Criminal Evidence Act 1984 road check has been authorized by a police officer of the rank of superintendent or above except in an urgent case. 2. That the vehicles are stopped for the purposes of ascertaining if they are carrying:	*Enabling legislation* **Power to carry out a road check:** s 4 PACE84.

(a) a person who has committed
an indictable offence other
than a road traffic offence or
a vehicle excise offence;
(b) a person who is a witness to
such an offence;
(c) a person intending to commit
such an offence; OR
(d) a person who is unlawfully
at large, such as an escaped
prisoner from HMP.

*Points to consider to prove the
offence*
1. That you are in uniform.
2. That you are carrying out a s 4
Police and Criminal Evidence Act
1984 road check.
3. That you gave an obvious
direction to a mechanically
propelled vehicle to stop which
was evident to the driver.
4. That the mechanically propelled
vehicle was being driven on a
road.

Enabling legislation
**Power to stop a mechanically
propelled vehicle:** s 163(1) RTA88.

*Points to consider to prove the
offence*
1. All of the above.
2. That the driver refused to comply
with your directions.
3. That you made a note of the
description of the suspect and
vehicle.
4. That you used **SOCRATES**
(or ADVOKATE) to evidence
identification of the person.

Offence
**Failing to stop a mechanically
propelled vehicle on being
required to do so:** s 163(3) RTA88.

Mode of trial and penalty
Summary—a fine not exceeding
level 3.

3.2.13 Power to place traffic signs

Context

You have been requested to provide some assistance in your town centre as a result of a serious road traffic collision. There is a need to divert traffic away from the site of the collision without impeding the flow into and out of the town. As always with such events, traffic is also slowed by those wanting to see what has happened (the morbidly curious). The following powers and relevant legislation are available to a designated PCSO to deal with the situation:

If designated, a PCSO has the power to place temporary traffic signs on a road during emergency incidents such as the scene of a road traffic crash or other abnormal road policing incident. If a driver fails to comply with a traffic sign placed by a PCSO, s/he commits an offence.	*Empowering legislation* 1. **Power to place traffic signs**: para 13A(1) of S4PRA02. 2. **Drivers to comply with traffic directions**: para 13A(2) of S4PRA02. *Primary legislation* 1. **Placing on a road or any structure, a traffic sign:** s 67(1) Road Traffic Regulation Act 1984.* [*To avoid lengthy repetition, we shall refer to the Road Traffic Regulation Act 1984 from this point forward as **RTR84**.] 2. **Failing to comply with traffic signs placed by a PCSO:** s 36 RTA88.
Circumstances under which the power to place temporary traffic signs on a road can be used 1. Signs which can be placed are those which include 'object or device (whether fixed or portable) for conveying to traffic on roads or any specified class of traffic, warnings, information, requirements, restrictions or prohibitions of any description'.	**Placing on a road or any structure, a traffic sign:** s 67(1) RTR84. **Meaning of traffic sign which can be placed:** s 64(1) RTR84.

2. Signs to be placed on a road or any structure on a road.
3. Signs to be placed in consequence of extraordinary circumstances.
4. Purpose of placing signs to include indications of prohibitions, restrictions, or requirements relating to vehicular traffic.
5. Placing of signs must be necessary or useful to prevent or alleviate congestion or obstruction of traffic, or danger to or from traffic.
6. Includes directions given by signs at the site of a traffic survey.
7. Signs to be placed for a maximum of seven days.

Points to consider to prove the offence

1. That the traffic sign was of the prescribed size colour and type.
2. That you were on duty, in uniform, the sign was lawfully placed on or near a road, and you made a note in your PNB of the time and location of the sign placing.
3. That a person driving or propelling a vehicle failed to comply with the indication of the sign.
4. That a note was made of the description of the driver and details obtained of the vehicle.
5. That **SOCRATES** (or ADVOKATE) was used to evidence identification of the driver.

Offence

Failing to comply with traffic signs placed by a PCSO: s 36 RTA88.

Mode of trial and penalty

Summary—a fine not exceeding level 3, discretionary disqualification, and obligatory endorsement with 3 penalty points.

NB: S 36 RTA88 is not listed as an offence for which you can require name and address under para 3A of S4PRA02.

3.2.14 Trespassing on railway property

Context

One of your PCSO supervisors has been informed by the regional railway company that it is experiencing problems with trespassers on the railway line. Apparently, what the trespassers like to do is come down a steep bank, hop over the 'live' and other rails, and scramble up the opposite bank, to get to a supermarket. This short cut saves about ten minutes, locals say. The following powers and relevant legislation are available to a designated PCSO to deal with the problem:

If designated, a PCSO has the power to issue a penalty notice for disorder to any person who trespasses on railway property as long as s/he fulfils the criteria for issuing a PND (see 5.2.8 below for issuing criteria).	*Empowering legislation* 1. **Power to issue penalty notices for disorder for trespassing on railway property:** para 1(2)(a) of S4PRA02. 2. **Power to require name and address:** para 1A(3) of S4PRA02. *Primary legislation* **Trespassing on railway property:** s 55(1) British Transport Commission Act 1949.

Points to consider to prove the offence
 	
 1. That the person was trespassing on any:
   • railway lines,
   • sidings, tunnels,
   • embankment cutting or similar work connected to a Railway Board, or any other Railway Board lands in dangerous proximity to
   • railway lines,
   • any other works, or
   • electrical equipment connected to the working of the railway.
 2. That a public warning to persons not to trespass on the railway existed in the form of a clearly exhibited notice or sign sited at the railway station closest to the incident.
	Offence
	
	 Trespassing on railway property s 55(1) British Transport Commission Act 1949.
	
	 Method of disposal
	
	 Penalty notice for disorder (lower tier)—under CJP01
	
	 (See 5.2.8 and 5.2.9 on issuing PNDs.)
	
	 Mode of trial and penalty
	
	 Summary—a fine not exceeding level 3.

3. That you made a note of the
   description of the suspect.
4. That you used **SOCRATES**
   (or ADVOKATE) to evidence
   identification of the person.

Points to consider to prove the offence	*Offence*
See **3.2.4** above: **Power to issue fixed penalty notices**, where the points to prove are itemized in respect of failing to give name and address when required.	**Failing to give name and address when required by a PCSO:** para 1A(5) of S4PRA02
	Mode of trial and penalty
	Summary—level 3 fine.
	See 3.2.24 below for details of your power to detain under PRA02.

3.2.15 Throwing stones or objects at railway equipment

Context

Your PCSO supervisor has been informed by the regional railway company that it is experiencing problems with objects being thrown on to the main railway line. It seems that people have been congregating on a bridge over the railway and objects thrown have included furniture and a supermarket trolley as well as large rocks and heavy pieces of wood. It is evidently not accidental damage, and British Transport Police has requested assistance from your Force. The following powers and relevant legislation are available to a designated PCSO to deal with the problem:

If designated, a PCSO has the power to issue a penalty notice for disorder to any person who throws stones or objects at railway property as long as the offence (and offender) fulfils the criteria for issuing a PND.	*Empowering legislation*
	1. **Power to issue penalty notices for disorder for throwing stones or objects at railway equipment**: para 1(2)(a) of S4PRA02.
	2. **Power to require name and address**: para 1A(3) of S4PRA02.
	Primary legislation
	Throwing stones or objects at railway equipment: s 56(1) British Transport Commission Act 1949.

Points to consider to prove the offence

1. That the person unlawfully:
   - threw,
   - caused to fall,
   - caused to strike at, against, into or upon, any
   - engine,
   - tender,
   - motor carriage, or
   - truck

   used upon or any works or equipment upon any railway or siding connected to a Railway Board.
2. That the projectile was a stone or other object.
3. That the object was likely to cause damage or injury to persons or property.
4. That you made a note of the description of the suspect.
5. That you used **SOCRATES** (or ADVOKATE) to evidence identification of the person.

Offence

Throwing stones or objects at railway equipment: s 56(1) British Transport Commission Act 1949.

Method of disposal

Penalty notice for disorder (lower tier)—under CJP01

(See 5.2.8 and 5.2.9 below on issuing PNDs.)

Mode of trial and penalty

Summary—a fine not exceeding level 3.

Points to consider to prove the offence

See **3.2.4** above: **Power to issue fixed penalty notices**, where the points to prove are itemized in respect of failing to give name and address when required.

Offence

Failing to give name and address when required by a PCSO: para 1A(5) of S4PRA02.

Mode of trial and penalty

Summary—level 3 fine.
See 3.2.24 below for details of your power to detain under PRA02.

3.2.16 Power to seize vehicles used to cause alarm

Context

The area around a local estate has recently been the target for people gathering to watch displays of stunt car driving by young car drivers. In addition, off-road motorcycles are being pushed or towed to a local park and ridden around the area without silencers, consequently making a lot of noise and becoming a nuisance to people in the locality. You have been tasked to find out who is involved and to put a stop to it. The following powers and relevant legislation are available to a designated PCSO to deal with both problems:

A designated PCSO has the power to stop and seize a vehicle which s/he has reason to believe is being used in a manner which contravenes s 3 or 34 of the Road Traffic Act 1988 (careless and inconsiderate driving and prohibition of off-road driving/riding) under s 59 of the Police Reform Act 2002.

Empowering legislation

Power to seize vehicles used to cause alarm: para 9 of S4PRA02.

Primary legislation

1. **Power to stop and seize a vehicle:** s 59 PRA02.
2. **Careless and inconsiderate driving/riding:** s 3 RTA88.
3. **Prohibition of off-road driving/riding:** s 34 RTA88.

Points to consider before using the power

1. That the motor vehicle is being or has been used on any occasion in a manner which:
   - contravenes s 3 or 34 of the Road Traffic Act 1988 (careless and inconsiderate driving and prohibition of off-road driving, see below); and
2. that the motor vehicle is being used or has been used in a manner which is causing, or is likely to cause or has caused:
   - alarm, distress, or annoyance to members of the public;
3. that you warn the person driving that you will seize the vehicle if its use is continued or repeated; and
4. it appears to you the use of the vehicle has been continued or repeated.

Circumstances under which a warning is not required

1. It is impracticable to give a warning;

Power

Power to stop and seize a vehicle: s 59 PRA02.

2. you have already given a warning in respect of any use of that motor vehicle or of another motor vehicle by that person or any other person on the same occasion; or
3. you have reasonable grounds to believe the driver has been given a previous warning in the past 12 months.

Your powers

1. To order the person driving it to stop the vehicle if it is moving.
2. To seize and remove the motor vehicle.
3. In order to exercise the powers above, to enter any premises (not a dwelling) on which you have reasonable grounds for believing the motor vehicle to be, only when in the company, and under the supervision of, a constable.

Points to consider to prove the offence

1. That a person is driving a mechanically propelled vehicle (any vehicle powered by mechanical means).
2. The vehicle is being driven on a road or other public place.
3. The vehicle is being driven:
   • without due care and attention, or
   • without reasonable consideration for other persons using the road or public place.

Offence
Careless and inconsiderate driving: s 3 RTA88.

Points to consider to prove the offence

1. That a person is driving a mechanically propelled vehicle (MPV) without lawful authority:

Offence
Prohibition of off-road driving/ riding: s 34 RTA88.

- on to or upon any common land, moorland, or land of any other description, not being land forming part of a road, or
- on any road being a footpath, bridleway, or restricted byway (unless previously it was shown on a map as a road or for obtaining access to land using an MPV).

2. That the MPV was not driven on land for the purposes of parking within 15 yards of a road.
3. That the MPV was not driven on land for the purposes of dealing with an emergency.

Points to consider to prove the offence

1. That you had reasonable grounds for believing that a motor vehicle has been driven carelessly or without consideration or in prohibition of off-road driving/riding on any occasion.
2. That you gave an obvious direction to a mechanically propelled vehicle to stop which was evident to the driver/rider.
3. That the driver refused to comply with your directions.
4. That you made a note of the description of the suspect and vehicle.
5. That you used **SOCRATES** (or ADVOKATE) to evidence identification of the person.

Offence

Failing to stop the vehicle at the request of a PCSO: s 59(6) PRA02.

NB: s 59(6) of the PRA02 is not listed as an offence for which you can require name and address (viz: under para 3A of S4PRA02).

3.2.17 Limited power to enter and search premises to investigate licensing offences

Context

Following reports, and indeed some CCTV coverage, of under-age drinking in your town centre, you are beginning to suspect that one or two off-licences in and around the shopping area are knowingly or unknowingly selling alcohol to young persons. It could be that the shop staff are not asking for proof of identity, or that an adult is buying the alcohol, or that the shops don't care to whom they sell. The matter needs quiet investigation. If you envisage any problems in going into the premises to investigate matters, the following powers are available to a designated PCSO to deal with the problem:

If designated, a PCSO has a limited power to enter and search licensed premises for the purposes of investigating relevant licensing offences. PCSOs may not enter clubs (members-only clubs, NOT nightclubs) and must enter all premises with a constable unless the premises are licensed for the sale of alcohol off the premises.

Empowering legislation

Limited power to enter and search premises to investigate licensing offences: para 8A of S4PRA02.

Primary legislation

Power to enter and search premises to investigate licensing offences: s 180 Licensing Act 2003.[*]

[*To avoid lengthy repetition, we shall refer to the Licensing Act 2003 from this point forward as **L03**.]

Circumstances under which the power can be used

1. Premises that are entered and searched include 'any place and includes a vehicle, vessel or moveable structure'.
2. That one or more of the following licensing offences are being committed on those premises:
   • sale of alcohol to a person who is drunk,

Empowering legislation

Limited power to enter and search premises to investigate licensing offences: para 8A of S4PRA02.

Primary legislation

Power to enter and search premises to investigate licensing offences: s 180 L03.

- obtaining alcohol for a person who is drunk,
- sale of alcohol to a child,
- purchase of alcohol by or on behalf of a child,
- consumption or allowing consumption of alcohol by a child,
- delivering alcohol to a child (see later sections on these offences).

3. That the premises are not 'club' premises (members-only clubs, NOT nightclubs).
4. That you are in the company of a police constable UNLESS you reasonably believe the premises holds an off-licence only, in which case you can enter by yourself.
5. That you use reasonable force only in exercising this power (see 3.2.24 below on reasonable force).

3.2.18 Power to require a person who is consuming alcohol in a designated place to stop drinking and to surrender the alcohol and its containers to a PCSO

Context

Your town or borough council recently 'designated' your town centre for the purposes of stopping the consumption of alcohol in public places. The problem of drinking there continues, however, and you have been tasked to monitor the situation and deal with any incidents. The following powers and relevant legislation are available to a designated PCSO to deal with the problem:

A designated PCSO has the power to require a person whom s/he believes is or has been consuming, or intends to consume alcohol in a designated public place, not to consume that alcohol and to surrender any alcohol or container for alcohol. If the person fails to comply with either of the requirements placed upon them, s/he commits an offence. The PCSO also has the power to dispose of the alcohol surrendered.

If the PCSO is further designated under para 7A(2) and the suspect fails to surrender his/her alcohol and/or container, the PCSO has the power to search the suspect.

If the person fails to consent to being searched without reasonable excuse, s/he commits an offence and the PCSO may make a requirement for the suspect's name and address.

If the suspect fails to comply with the requirement or gives a name and address which the PCSO reasonably suspects to be false or inaccurate, the suspect commits an offence.

If the PCSO is further designated under para 2, s/he may then detain the person and await the arrival of a police officer or request the suspect to accompany the PCSO to the police station (see 3.2.24 below).

If the PCSO is designated under paragraph 4, s/he may use reasonable force during the detention of the suspect (see 3.2.24 below).

Empowering legislation

1. **Power to require persons drinking in a designated public place to surrender alcohol:** para 5 of S4PRA02.
2. **Power to issue penalty notices for disorder to persons drinking alcohol in a designated public place:** para 1(2)(a) of S4PRA02.
3. **Power to require name and address:** para 1A(3) of S4PRA02.
4. **Power to search for alcohol:** para 7A of S4PRA02.

Primary legislation

Power to require a person consuming alcohol in a designated public place to stop drinking and to surrender the alcohol to the PCSO: s 12 CJP01.

Points to consider before using your powers

1. That the area is designated.
2. That you believe the person:
   - is, or
   - has been consuming, or
   - intends to consume
   alcohol in the designated place.

Your powers

1. To require the person not to consume anything which is, or which you reasonably believe to be, alcohol.
2. To require the surrender of anything in the person's possession which is, or which you reasonably believe to be, alcohol or a container for alcohol (sealed or unsealed).
3. To dispose of anything surrendered to you in such manner as you consider appropriate (see your local policy for details).

Circumstances under which you can search

1. That all the circumstances surrounding your power to seize alcohol from a person were satisfied.
2. That the person from whom you wanted to seize the alcohol/container had failed to surrender it to you.
3. That you reasonably believed s/he had alcohol/containers in his/her possession.

Circumstances surrounding the search

1. That you only search to the extent that is reasonably required to find the alcohol/containers.

Primary legislation

Power to require a person consuming alcohol in a designated public place to stop drinking and to surrender the alcohol: s 12 CJP01.

Power to search for alcohol/ containers: para 7A(2) of S4PRA02.

2. That you cannot require a person to remove any of his or her clothing in public other than an outer coat, jacket or gloves.
3. That, when you find what you are looking for, you can seize and dispose of it (see your local policy for disposal).

Requirement to give name and address

That you may require the person's name and address if s/he fails to consent to being searched.

Requirement to give name and address: para 7A(7) of S4PRA02.

See 3.2.24 below for details of your power to detain under PRA02.

Points to consider to prove the offence

That, before you carried out the search, you informed the person that, without reasonable excuse, failing to consent to being searched is an offence.

Offence

A person who without reasonable excuse fails to consent to being searched is guilty of an offence: para 7A(5) of S4PRA02.

Penalty and mode of trial

Summary—fine not exceeding level 3.

Points to consider to prove the offence

1. That you are designated under para 5 of S4PRA02.
2. That, at the time you made the requirement, you informed the person concerned that, without reasonable excuse, failing to comply with your requirement was an offence.
3. That the person continued to drink what you believed to be alcohol after you required him or her to stop; and/or
4. that the person failed to surrender anything in his/her possession which you reasonably believed to be alcohol or a container for alcohol.

Offence

Failing to comply with a requirement to stop drinking or surrender alcohol: s 12(4) CJP01.

Method of disposal

Penalty notice for disorder (lower tier)—under CJP01.

(See 5.2.8 and 5.2.9 below on issuing PNDs.)

Mode of trial and penalty

Summary—a fine not exceeding level 2.

5. That the person did not have a reasonable excuse for not complying with your requirements.
6. That you have evidence of sight, hearing, or smell to support your belief of the consumption or possession of alcohol.
7. That you made a note of the description of the suspect.
8. That you used **SOCRATES** (or ADVOKATE) to evidence identification of the person.

Points to consider to prove the offence	*Offence*
See **3.2.4** above: **Power to issue fixed penalty notices**, where the points to prove are itemized in respect of failing to give name and address when required.	**Failing to give name and address when required by a PCSO:** para 1A(5) of S4PRA02.
	Mode of trial and penalty
	Summary—level 3 fine.
	See 3.2.24 below for details of your power to detain under PRA02.

3.2.19 Power to require a person who is under 18 (and/or a person who supplies alcohol to a person under 18) to surrender the alcohol and its containers to a PCSO

Context

The town centre has been hit by a spate of underage drinking. The problem is exacerbated because adults over 18 appear to be buying and supplying alcohol to the young people. Understandably, the off-licences and pubs deny serving alcohol to persons under 18, but the evidence is very clear that children as young as 14 or 15 are consuming alcohol in and around the area. You have been requested to monitor the situation and deal with the problems. The following powers and relevant legislation are available to a designated PCSO to deal with the matter:

A designated PCSO has the power to require a person who s/he reasonably suspects to be under 18, or to be a person who is or has been supplying alcohol to another person under 18, to surrender any alcohol in his/her possession and to give his/her name and address.

The PCSO also has the power to require such a person to surrender sealed containers of alcohol if the PCSO has reason to believe that the person is or has been consuming, or intends to consume, alcohol. The power continues with the authority to dispose of the alcohol that is surrendered.

If the PCSO is further designated under para 7A(2) and the suspect fails to surrender his/her alcohol and/or container, the PCSO has the power to search the suspect.

If the suspect refuses to be searched, the PCSO may make a request for the suspect's name and address.

If the suspect fails to comply with the request, or gives a name and address which the PCSO reasonably suspects to be false or inaccurate, the suspect commits an offence.

If the PCSO is further designated under para 2, he/she may then detain the person and await the arrival of a police officer or request the suspect to accompany the PCSO to the police station (see 3.2.24 below).

If the PCSO is designated under para 4, he/she may use reasonable force during the detention of the suspect (see 3.2.24 below).

Empowering legislation
The power to require a person who is under 18 (and/or a person who supplies alcohol to a person under 18) to surrender the alcohol and its containers to a PCSO: para 1 of S4PRA02 and s 1 Confiscation of Alcohol (Young Persons) Act 1997.*

[*To avoid lengthy repetition, we shall refer to the Confiscation of Alcohol (Young Persons) Act 1997 from this point forward as **CAYP97**.]

Primary legislation
The power to require a person who is under 18 (and/or a person who supplies alcohol to a person under 18) to surrender the alcohol and its containers to a PCSO: s 1 CAYP97.

Points to consider before using your powers

1. That the person is in a relevant place, eg:
   - any public place (accessible on payment or otherwise),
   - not on licensed premises,
   - any place which is not a public place to which the person has unlawfully gained access, such as gate-crashing at a private party.

2. That you reasonably suspect the person is in possession of alcohol and that either:
   - s/he is under 18, or
   - s/he intends the alcohol to be consumed by a person under 18 in a relevant place, eg an adult supplying an under-18 with alcohol, or
   - s/he is or has been recently in the company of a person under-18 who has consumed alcohol in a relevant place, eg an adult who has recently accompanied an under-18-year-old who has alcohol.

Your powers

1. To require the surrender of **anything** in the person's possession (the under-18-year-old and/or the person accompanying/supplying the under-18-year-old) which is, or which you reasonably believe to be:
   - alcohol, or
   - a container for alcohol (sealed or unsealed).

Primary legislation

The power to require a person who is under 18 (and/or a person who supplies alcohol to a person under 18) to surrender the alcohol and its containers to a PCSO: s 1 CAYP97.

2. To require the person under 18 or the person accompanying/supplying the person under 18 to state their name and address.

3. To dispose of anything surrendered to you in such manner as you consider appropriate (see your local policy for details).

Circumstances under which you can search

4. That all the circumstances surrounding your power to seize alcohol from a person were satisfied.

5. That the person from whom you wanted to seize the alcohol/container had failed to surrender it to you.

6. That you reasonably believed s/he had alcohol/container in his/her possession.

Circumstances surrounding the search

1. That you only search to the extent that is reasonably required to find the alcohol/containers.

2. That you cannot require a person to remove any of his or her clothing in public other than an outer coat, jacket, or gloves.

3. That, when you find what you are looking for, you can seize and dispose of it (see your local policy for disposal).

Requirement to give name and address

That you may require the person's name and address if s/he fails to consent to being searched.

Power to search for alcohol/containers: para 7A(2) of S4PRA02.

Requirement to give name and address: para 7A(7) of S4PRA02. See 3.2.24 below for details of your power to detain under PRA02.

Points to consider to prove the offence
That, before you carried out the search, you informed the person that failing without reasonable excuse to consent to being searched is an offence.

A person who without reasonable excuse fails to consent to being searched is guilty of an offence: para 7A(5) of S4PRA02.

Penalty and mode of trial
Summary—fine not exceeding level 3.

Points to consider to prove the offence
1. That, at the time you made the requirement, you informed the person concerned of your suspicion and that failing without reasonable excuse to comply with your requirement was an offence.
2. That the person failed to surrender anything in his/her possession which you reasonably believed to be alcohol or a container for alcohol.
3. That the person failed to state his/her name and address.
4. That the person did not have a reasonable excuse for not complying with your requirements.
5. That you have evidence of sight, hearing, or smell to support your belief of the possession of alcohol.
6. That you made a note of the description of the suspect.
7. That you used **SOCRATES** (or ADVOKATE) to evidence identification of the person.

Offence

Failing to comply with a requirement to surrender alcohol or state name and address: s 1(3) CAYP97.

Mode of trial and penalty
Summary—a fine not exceeding level 2.

3.2.20 Power to search and seize tobacco from a person aged under 16 years

Context

In response to expressions of concern about schoolchildren smoking, it has been decided to carry out patrols in the areas around secondary schools to combat the practice. You carry out a visual scan and see plenty of evidence from discarded butts and cigarette packets that covert smoking is going on. The following powers and relevant legislation are available to a designated PCSO to deal with the problem:

A designated PCSO has the power to seize tobacco in the possession of a person apparently under 16 years and dispose of it.

If the PCSO is further designated under para 7A(2) and if the suspect fails to surrender his or her tobacco, and the PCSO reasonably believes that the suspect has it in his/her possession, the PCSO has the power to search the suspect.

If the person fails to consent to being searched without reasonable excuse, s/he commits an offence and the PCSO may make a request for the suspect's name and address.

If the suspect fails to comply with the request, or gives a name and address which the PCSO reasonably suspects to be false or inaccurate, the suspect commits an offence.

If the PCSO is further designated under para 2, s/he may then detain the person and await the arrival of a police officer or request the suspect to accompany them to the police station (see 3.2.24 below).

If the PCSO is designated under para 4, s/he may use reasonable force during the detention of the suspect (see section 3.2.24 below).

Empowering legislation

1. **Power to seize tobacco from a person aged under 16 years:** para 7 of S4PRA02.
2. **Power to search for tobacco:** para 7A of S4PRA02.

Primary legislation

Power to seize tobacco from a person aged under 16 years: s 7(3) Children and Young Persons Act 1933.

Points to consider before using your power

1. That you were in uniform.
2. That the objective was to seize tobacco or cigarette papers.
3. That the person was apparently under the age of 16.
4. That the person was smoking.
5. That the person was in a street or public place.

Your powers

1. To seize tobacco or cigarette papers.
2. To dispose of the tobacco or cigarette papers in a manner prescribed by the police authority (refer to your Force's policy).

Power to seize tobacco from a person aged under 16 years: s 7(3) Children and Young Persons Act 1933.

Circumstances under which you can search

1. That all the circumstances surrounding your power to seize tobacco from a person under 16 years were satisfied.
2. That the person from whom you wanted to seize the tobacco had failed to surrender it to you.
3. That you reasonably believed s/he had the tobacco in his/her possession.

Power to search for tobacco: para 7A(3) of S4PRA02.

Circumstances surrounding the search

4. That you only search to the extent that is reasonably required to find the tobacco.
5. That you cannot require a person to remove any of his or her clothing in public other than an outer coat, jacket, or gloves.
6. That, when you find what you are looking for, you can seize and dispose of it (see your local Force policy for disposal).

Requirement to give name and address	**Requirement to give name and address:** para 7A(7) of S4PRA02.
That you may require the person's name and address if s/he fails to consent to being searched.	See 3.2.24 below for details of your power to detain under PRA02.

Points to consider to prove the offence	*Offence*
1. That, before you carried out the search, you informed the person that failing without reasonable excuse to consent to being searched is an offence.	**A person who without reasonable excuse fails to consent to being searched is guilty of an offence:** para 7A(5) of S4PRA02.
2. That you made a note of the description of the suspect.	*Penalty and mode of trial*
3. That you used **SOCRATES** (or ADVOKATE) to evidence identification of the person.	Summary—fine not exceeding level 3.

Remember: You need to make a dynamic risk assessment (Chapter 5) on whether any seizure (alcohol, cigarettes, drugs) will exacerbate a situation—by provoking hostility or resistance, for example.

3.2.21 Power to seize drugs and require name and address for possession of drugs

Context

You have been involved in searches of people carrying alcohol in the town centre, but you have realized that you may come across other things, like controlled drugs, when carrying out the searches. The following powers and relevant legislation are available to a designated PCSO to deal with the problem:

A designated PCSO has the power to seize obviously-placed drugs or concealed drugs found when searching for alcohol, tobacco, or dangerous items. Until a constable	*Empowering legislation*
	Power to seize drugs and require name and address for possession of drugs: para 7B and 7C of S4PRA02.

instructs him/her what to do with the drugs, the PCSO must retain them. If the PCSO finds drugs in a person's possession or has reason to believe that a person is in possession of drugs then the PCSO may require that person's name and address. An appropriately designated PCSO may detain a person on failure to comply with the requirement.

Circumstances under which you may seize and retain the drugs	**Power to seize drugs:** para 7B(1) and (2) S4PRA02.

1. That you are designated under para 7B and 7C of S4PRA02.
2. That you find a controlled drug in a person's possession.
3. That the drugs were found whether or not you were using your powers to search for alcohol, tobacco, or dangerous items.
4. That you reasonably believe the person is in unlawful possession of the drugs.

Circumstances under which the requirement to furnish name and address can be made	**Requirement for name and address to be given on request:** para 7B(3) S4PRA02.

1. That you find controlled drugs on the person; or
2. that you reasonably believe the person in is possession of a controlled drug.
3. That you reasonably believe it is unlawful for the person to be in possession of the drugs.

Points to consider to prove the offence

1. That you found a controlled drug in a person's possession.
2. The circumstances under which the drugs were found, whether or not you were using your powers to search for alcohol, tobacco, or dangerous items; or
3. that you reasonably believed the person was in possession of a controlled drug.
4. That you reasonably believed the person was in unlawful possession of the drugs.
5. That you requested the person's name and address.
6. That the person refused to give you their name and address.
7. That you made a note of the description of the suspect.
8. That you used **SOCRATES** (or ADVOKATE) to evidence identification of the person.

Offence

Failing to comply with a requirement for name and address: para 7B(5) S4PRA02.

Mode of trial and penalty

Summary—A fine not exceeding level 3.

See 3.2.24 below for details of your power to detain under PRA02.

Responsibilities

1. Inform the person from whom the drugs were seized where enquiries about the recovery of the drugs can be made if the person maintains s/he was in lawful possession of them.
2. Request the assistance of a police officer and comply with the instructions from the constable as to the method of disposal for the drugs.

Responsibilities of the PCSO once drugs have been found: para 7B(4) of S4PRA02.

3.2.22 Power to enforce 'relevant licensing offences' and similar offences

Context

Following complaints of aggression, drinking in the city centre, and vandalism by youths, as well as allegations of drunkenly-abusive behaviour by groups of girls from local schools in the area, it has been decided to investigate how pupils under 18 are obtaining their alcohol and to deal with the drink problem in general.

Suppose that you have been assigned the task of 'cleaning up' the town centre and of finding out how and from where the young people are obtaining alcohol. The following powers and relevant legislation are available to a designated PCSO to deal with the problem:

A designated PCSO has the power to enforce 'relevant licensing offences'. Where these offences apply to *members' clubs*, such as working men's clubs which are licensed, they cease to be 'relevant licensing offences'. A designated PCSO can also issue a PND to a person who has committed other 'relevant fixed penalty offences' which are alcohol-related.

A designated PCSO may require the name and address from a suspect, but even a designated PCSO under para 2 of Sch 4 to the Police Reform Act 2002 may not detain for those 'relevant licensing offences' which are most likely to be committed by licensees.

Useful definitions for this section

'Relevant premises' means:

1. licensed premises (pubs, off-licences);
2. premises in respect of which there is a club premises' certificate (members' clubs); and
3. premises which may be used for a permitted temporary activity (occasions such as wedding receptions on non-licensed premises).

NB: For information on issuing a PND in relation to these offences, please refer to 5.2.8 below.

Empowering legislation

1. **Power to enforce 'relevant licensing offences':** para 2(6A) of S4PRA02.
2. **Power to require name and address:** para 1A(3) of S4PRA02.
3. **Power to issue penalty notices for disorder:** para 1(2)(a) of S4PRA02.

Primary legislation

'Relevant licensing offences'

1. **Selling or attempting to sell alcohol to a person who is drunk (PND):** s 141 para 2(6A) of S4PRA02, s 146(1) LO3.
2. **Purchasing alcohol by a child (not PND):** s 149(1)(a) LO3 **Purchasing alcohol on behalf of a child (not PND):** s 149(3)(a) LO3.
3. **Purchasing alcohol on behalf of a child for consumption on relevant premises (not PND):** s 149(4)(a) LO3. **Consuming alcohol by a person under 18 years (PND):** s 150(1) LO3.
4. **Allowing a child under 18 years to consume alcohol (PND):** s 150(2) LO3 **Sending a child to obtain alcohol (not PND):** s 152(1) LO3.

'Relevant fixed penalty offences' by their virtue of being PND offences:

5. **Delivering alcohol to a person under 18 years or allowing such delivery (PND):** s151 LO3.

6. **Drunk and disorderly behaviour (PND):** s 91 Criminal Justice Act 1967.

7. **Drunk in the highway (PND):** s 12 Licensing Act 1872.

Points to consider to prove the offence

1. That the offence took place on
   - licensed premises, such as pubs, off-licences, or
   - premises which may be used for a permitted temporary activity (occasions such as wedding receptions on non-licensed premises).
2. That the suspect was:
   - any person who works at the premises, or
   - the holder of the licence or a designated premises supervisor on licensed premises, or
   - the premises user of a permitted temporary activity.
3. That the suspect sold or attempted to sell alcohol to a person who was drunk; or
4. that the suspect allowed alcohol to be sold to such a person.

Offence

Selling or attempting to sell alcohol to a person who is drunk (PND): s 141(1) LO3.

NB: If designated under para 2 of S4PRA02 a PCSO cannot detain a person who has committed this offence on licensed premises if his or her name and address cannot be obtained.

Mode of trial and penalty

Summary—a fine not exceeding level 3.

Points to consider to prove the offence

1. That the offence took place on 'relevant premises' (see above).
2. That the suspect (any person) knowingly:
   - obtained, or
   - attempted to obtain alcohol.
3. That the alcohol was for consumption on those premises.

Offence

Obtaining alcohol for a person who is drunk (not PND): s 142(1) LO3.

Mode of trial and penalty

Summary—a fine not exceeding level 3.

4. That the person for whom the alcohol was intended was drunk.

Points to consider to prove the offence

That the suspect (any person) sold alcohol to an individual under 18 anywhere.

Defences

1. The suspect believed the individual was 18 or over.
2. The suspect took all reasonable steps by asking for evidence of age and the evidence would have convinced a reasonable person.
3. Nobody could have reasonably suspected as a result of the individual's appearance that s/he was under 18.
4. The suspect exercised all due diligence to avoid committing the offence.

Offence

Selling alcohol to a person under 18 years (PND): s 146(1) LO3.

NB: If designated under para 2 of S4PRA02, a PCSO cannot detain a person who has committed this offence on licensed premises if his/her name and address cannot be obtained.

Mode of trial and penalty

Summary—a fine not exceeding level 5.

Points to consider to prove the offence

1. That the suspect is under 18 years.
2. That the suspect buys or attempts to buy alcohol.
3. That the suspect did not buy or attempt to buy at the request of a police officer or weights and measures inspector.

Offence

Purchasing alcohol by a child (not PND): s 149(1)(a) LO3.

Mode of trial and penalty

Summary—a fine not exceeding level 3.

Points to consider to prove the offence

1. That the suspect:
   • bought, or
   • attempted to buy alcohol.
2. That the alcohol was bought or attempted to be bought on behalf of an individual under 18.

Offence

Purchasing alcohol on behalf of a child (PND): s 149(3)(a) LO3.

Mode of trial and penalty

Summary—a fine not exceeding level 5.

Points to consider to prove the offence	Offence
1. That the suspect: • bought, or • attempted to buy alcohol. 2. That the alcohol was bought or attempted to be bought on 'relevant premises' (see above). 3. That the alcohol was bought for consumption by a person aged under 18.	**Purchasing alcohol on behalf of a child for consumption on certain premises (not PND):** s 149(4)(a) LO3. *Mode of trial and penalty* Summary—a fine not exceeding level 5.

Points to consider to prove the offence	Offence
1. That the suspect was under 18. 2. That the suspect consumed alcohol. 3. That the alcohol was consumed on 'relevant premises' (see above).	**Consuming alcohol by a person under 18 years (PND):** s 150(1) LO3. *Mode of trial and penalty* Summary—a fine not exceeding level 3.

Points to consider to prove the offence	Offence
1. That the suspect worked at the premises in a position that can authorize the prevention of such consumption. 2. That the suspect allowed the consumption of alcohol on 'relevant premises' (see above). 3. That a person under 18 consumed the alcohol. 4. That the person consuming the alcohol was not 16 or 17 and drinking beer, wine, or cider at a table meal and in company with a person aged 18 or over.	**Allowing a child under 18 years to consume alcohol (PND):** s 150(2) LO3. **NB:** If designated under para 2 of S4PRA02, a PCSO cannot detain a person who has committed this offence on licensed premises if his or her name and address cannot be obtained. *Mode of trial and penalty* Summary—a fine not exceeding level 5.

Points to consider to prove the offence	Offence
1. That the suspect knowingly sent a person under 18 to obtain alcohol. 2. That the alcohol was sold or to be sold on 'relevant premises' (see above).	**Sending a child to obtain alcohol (not PND):** s 152(1) LO3. *Mode of trial and penalty* Summary—a fine not exceeding level 5.

3. That the alcohol was to be consumed off the premises.

4. That the alcohol, if not obtained from 'relevant premises', was obtained from any other premises from which it was delivered in the course of sale or supply.

5. That the person under 18 does not work at the 'relevant premises' delivering alcohol.

6. That the person under 18 was not sent by a police officer or weights and measures inspector.

Points to consider to prove the offence

1. That the suspect worked on 'relevant premises' (see above), paid or unpaid.

2. That the suspect knowingly delivered alcohol sold on the premises.

3. That the suspect delivered to a person under 18; or

4. that the suspect worked in a position on 'relevant premises' that could prevent such a delivery but still allowed somebody else to make the delivery.

5. That the delivery was not meant for an adult who had lawfully purchased the alcohol.

6. That the person under 18 did not work at the 'relevant premises' involving the delivery of alcohol.

7. That the alcohol is not sold or supplied for consumption on the 'relevant premises'.

Offence

Delivering alcohol to a person under 18 years or allowing such delivery (PND): s 151 LO3.

Mode of trial and penalty

Summary—a fine not exceeding level 5.

Points to consider to prove the offence

1. That the suspect was drunk.
2. That the suspect behaved in a disorderly manner.
3. That the place where the person was drunk, was a public place.

Offence

Drunk and disorderly behaviour (PND): s 91 Criminal Justice Act 1967.

Mode of trial and penalty

Summary—a fine not exceeding level 3.

Points to consider to prove the offence

1. That the suspect was found drunk.
2. That the suspect was on:
   • 'any highway, or
   • other public place,
   • whether a building or not, or
   • on any licensed premises'; or
3. that the suspect was 'drunk while in charge on any highway or other public place, of any
   • carriage,
   • horse,
   • cattle, or
   • steam engine'; or
4. that the suspect was 'drunk when in possession of any loaded firearms'.

Offence

Drunk in the highway (PND): s 12 Licensing Act 1872.

Mode of trial and penalty

For points to consider 1 and 2:
Summary—Fine not exceeding level 1.
For points to consider 3 and 4:
Summary—one month's imprisonment or a fine not exceeding level 1.

Points to consider to prove the offence

See **3.2.4** above: **Power to issue fixed penalty notices**, where the points to prove are itemized in respect of failing to give name and address when required.

Offence

Failing to give name and address when required by a PCSO: para 1A(5) of S4PRA02.

Mode of trial and penalty

Summary—level 3 fine.
See 3.2.24 below for details of your power to detain under PRA02.
The power to detain, whether designated or not, cannot be used for offences 1, 3, and 7 (on pp 203–4).

3.2.23 Power to require name and address from a person who has committed a 'relevant offence', a 'relevant licensing offence', or who has offended against a 'relevant byelaw'

Context

Your town is suffering a spate of offences for which penalty notices for disorder can be issued. It is also subject to a litany of complaints relating to girls from local schools who are being supplied with and who are consuming alcohol in the town's shopping complex. To appease local residents, the Chief Constable and Town Council have agreed on a number of new byelaws. You are concerned that during the investigation of any of these offences, the suspect might fail to give you his/her name and address. The following powers and relevant legislation are available to a designated PCSO to deal with the problem:

A PCSO who is designated under para 1A of S4PRA02 has the power to require the name and address of a person that has committed a 'relevant offence', a 'relevant licensing offence', or a 'relevant byelaw'. Such a designation can specify any number of 'relevant offences', 'relevant licensing offences', or 'relevant byelaws' and does not have to specify them all.

If the suspect fails to comply with the requirement, or gives a name and address which the PCSO reasonably suspects to be false or inaccurate, the suspect commits an offence.

If the PCSO is further designated under para 2, he/she may then detain the person and await the arrival of a police officer or request the suspect to accompany the PCSO to the police station (see 3.2.24).

If the PCSO is designated under para 4, he/she may use reasonable force during the detention of the suspect (see 3.2.24 below).

Empowering legislation

Power to require name and address from a person who has committed a 'relevant offence', 'relevant licensing offence', or offended against 'relevant byelaw': para 1A of S4PRA02.

Primary legislation

Failing to give name and address when required by a PCSO: para 1A(5) of S4PRA02.

Circumstances under which the power can be used

1. That you are designated under para 1A of S4PRA02.
2. That you had reason to believe that the person had committed a 'relevant offence', a 'relevant licensing offence', or offended against a 'relevant byelaw'.
3. That you required the person to give you his or her name and address.
4. That the place in which you made the requirement in relation to a 'relevant byelaw' was one to which the byelaw related.

Power to require name and address: para 1A of S4PRA02.

Definition of 'relevant offence'

Any offence which is:

1. An offence for which a fixed penalty notice can be issued and includes:
   • Penalty notices for disorder, eg drunk and disorderly behaviour (see 3.2.22 above),
   • Fixed penalty notices for truancy (see 3.2.28 below),
   • Fixed penalty notices for riding a cycle on a footpath (see 3.2.8 above),
   • Fixed penalty notices for dog fouling (see 3.2.3 above),
   • Fixed penalty notices for graffiti or fly-posting (see 3.2.6 above),
   • Fixed penalty notices for litter (see 3.2.5 above),
   • Fixed penalty notices for offences under dog control orders (see 3.2.4 above).

Legislation that defines a 'relevant offence': para 2(6) of S4PRA02.

2. An offence of knowingly contravening a direction given to disperse groups and remove persons under 16 to their place of residence (see 3.2.33 below).
3. An offence committed in a specified park.
4. An offence relating to begging (see 3.2.35 below).
5. An offence which is a 'relevant byelaw' (see 3.2.27 below).
6. An offence which appears to you to have caused:
   • 'injury alarm or distress to any other person, or
   • the loss of, or any damage to, any other person's property'.

Definition of 'relevant licensing offence'
Any of the following offences under the Licensing Act 2003, which are:
1. Selling or attempting to sell alcohol to a person who is drunk (PND), **s 141**.
2. Obtaining alcohol for a person who is drunk (not PND), **s 142**.
3. Selling alcohol to a person under 18 years (PND), **s 146(1)**.
4. Purchasing alcohol by a child (not PND), **s 149(1)(a)**.
5. Purchasing alcohol on behalf of a child (not PND), **s 149(3)(a)**.
6. Purchasing alcohol on behalf of a child for consumption on relevant premises (not PND), **s 149(4)(a)**.
7. Consuming alcohol by a person under 18 years (PND), **s 150(1)**.
8. Allowing a child under 18 years to consume alcohol (PND), **s 150(2)**.
9. Sending a child to obtain alcohol (not PND), **s 152(1)**.
   (see 3.2.22 above for details of the above offences).

Legislation that defines a 'relevant licensing offence': para 2(6A) of S4PRA02.

Definition of a 'relevant byelaw'

1. A byelaw included in a list of byelaws which have been made by a relevant body such as:
   - a county council,
   - a district council,
   - a parish council,
   - a London Borough Council, and
   - the chief constable of the police force for the area has agreed its inclusion in the list.
2. The list of 'relevant byelaws' must be published for the benefit of the general public.
3. The list may be amended by agreement with the chief constable and the relevant body, but the alterations must be published.
4. The agreement can also be made between the Secretary of State and the local chief constable (see 3.2.27 below regarding your powers to enforce 'relevant byelaws').

Legislation that defines a 'relevant byelaw': para 2(6B)–(6F) of S4PRA02.

Points to consider to prove the offence

- See **3.2.4** above: **Power to issue fixed penalty notices**, where the points to prove are itemized in respect of failing to give name and address when required.

Offence

Failing to give name and address when required by a PCSO: para 1A(5) of S4PRA02.

Mode of trial and penalty
Summary—level 3 fine.
See 3.2.24 below for details of your power to detain under PRA02.

3.2.24 Power to detain and use reasonable force to prevent a person making off or to transfer control of a detained person

Context

Recently, whilst dealing with members of 'problem families', you have encountered a growing boldness among the suspects, even an open hostility to you and your function, and you have found it increasingly difficult to obtain their names and addresses. The following are the powers and relevant legislation available to a designated PCSO to deal with the problem:

Power to detain

A PCSO who is designated under para 2 of Sch 4 to the Police Reform Act 2002 has the power to detain a suspect who fails to furnish his or her name and address, or gives incorrect details, under the following circumstances:

1. When a PCSO is designated under para 1 and requests the name or address of a person who is suspected of committing a 'relevant offence' (see 3.2.23 above), except some 'relevant licensing offences' (see 3.2.22 above, and below).
2. When a PCSO is designated under para 3 and requests the name or address of a person who is believed to be acting, or to have been acting, in an anti-social manner (see 3.2.32 below).
3. When a PCSO is designated under para 3A and requests the name or address of a person who is believed to have committed a listed road traffic offence (see 3.2.10 and 3.2.11 above).
4. When a PCSO is designated under para 7 and the suspect does not consent to being searched for alcohol or tobacco (see 3.2.20 above).
5. When a PCSO is designated under para 7 and the PCSO reasonably believes the person to be in possession of a controlled drug (see 3.2.21 above).

Empowering legislation

1. **Power to detain:** para 2 of S4PRA02.
2. **Power to use reasonable force to prevent a detained person making off:** para 4 of S4PRA02.

Primary legislation

Making off from a PCSO: para 2(5) of S4PRA02.

NB: If designated under para 2A, a PCSO also has the power to search detained persons for dangerous items or items that could be used to assist escape (see 3.2.25 below).

A PCSO who is designated under para 2 of Sch 4 to the Police Reform Act 2002 also has the power to detain a suspect in the following circumstance:

When a PCSO is designated under para 1, s/he believes a suspect is committing an offence relating to begging and the suspect fails to stop the activity on request (see 3.2.35 below).

Under the above circumstances, the PSCO has the power to detain the suspect for up to 30 minutes whilst awaiting the arrival of a police officer, or to request the suspect to accompany him/her to a police station if the suspect elects to do so. If during either period the suspect makes off, s/he will have committed a further offence.

In relation to byelaws you have any power a police officer has under a 'relevant byelaw' to remove a person from a place to which that 'relevant byelaw' refers (see 3.2.27 below).

Power to use reasonable force

A PCSO who is designated under para 4 has the power to use reasonable force under the following circumstances:

1. To prevent the suspect under detention from making off from him/her whilst waiting for the **arrival of a police officer.**
2. To prevent the suspect under detention from making off from him/her until s/he has **transferred control** of the suspect to a police officer.
3. To prevent the suspect under detention from making off from him/her whilst s/he **accompanies the suspect to a police station.**

4. To prevent the suspect under detention from making off from him/her while s/he accompanies the suspect to a police station until s/he has **transferred control of the suspect to a custody officer.**

5. To prevent the suspect from making off (or escaping) and to keep control in relation to using his/her powers to:
   - disperse groups and remove persons under 16 to their place of residence (see 3.2.33 below);
   - remove children in contravention of curfew notices to their place of residence (see 3.2.34 below).

Circumstances under which the power can be used

Power to detain: para 2(3) of S4PRA02.

1. That you are designated under the relevant paragraph of Sch 4 to the Reform Act 2002 to apply the power or investigate the offence (see applicable sections).
2. That you are designated under para 2 of Sch 4 to the Reform Act 2002 to detain.
3. That you had reason to believe that the suspect had committed an offence.
4. That you required the suspect to give you his/her name and address.
5. That the place in which you made the requirement in relation to a 'relevant byelaw' was one to which the byelaw related (see 3.2.27 below).
6. That the suspect failed to comply with your requirement; or
7. that you had reasonable grounds for suspecting that the suspect had given you a false or inaccurate name and address.

8. That the 'relevant licensing offence' was not one of the following committed on licensed premises:
   - **selling or attempting to sell alcohol to a person who is drunk**
   - **selling alcohol to a person under 18 years**
   - **allowing a child under 18 years to consume alcohol** (see 3.2.22 above).

Circumstances surrounding the requirement to remain with you until the arrival of a police officer

1. That all of the above have been satisfied.
2. That you request the suspect to wait with you for a period not exceeding 30 minutes for the arrival of a police officer or to accompany you to a police station.

Circumstances under which you can use reasonable force 1. That you are designated under para 4 of Sch 4 to the Reform Act 2002. 2. That you had required the suspect to wait with you for a period not exceeding 30 minutes for the arrival of a police officer. 3. That the person did not comply with your requirement.	**Power to use reasonable force to prevent a detained person making off while waiting for a police officer:** para 4 of S4PRA02.
Your responsibilities to remain with the suspect and to transfer control That, having made the request for the suspect to remain with you for 30 minutes to await the arrival of a police officer, you are under a duty to remain with the suspect until you have transferred control of the suspect to the police officer.	**Responsibility to remain with the suspect under detention while waiting to transfer control to a police officer:** para 2(4A) of S4PRA02.

Circumstances under which you can use reasonable force	**Power to use reasonable force to carry out your responsibilities to remain with the suspect and transfer control to a police officer:** para 4ZB of S4PRA02.
1. That you are designated under para 47B of Sch 4 to the Reform Act 2002.	
2. That, having made the request for the suspect to remain with you for 30 minutes to await the arrival of a police officer, you are under a duty to remain with the suspect until you have transferred control of the suspect to the police officer.	
3. That the suspect did not comply with your requirements to remain with you until you could transfer control.	

Circumstances surrounding the request to accompany you to the police station and the election of the suspect to do so	**Request to the suspect under detention to accompany you to the police station:** para 2(4) of S4PRA02.
1. That the circumstances under which to use the power to detain were satisfied.	
2. That you requested the suspect to accompany you to a police station in the relevant area.	
3. That the suspect elected to do so.	

Circumstances under which you can use reasonable force	**Power to use reasonable force to prevent a detained person making off while accompanying you to the police station:** para 4 of S4PRA02.
1. That you are designated under para 4 of Sch 4 to the Reform Act 2002.	
2. That you requested the suspect to accompany you to a police station in the relevant area.	
3. That the suspect elected to do so.	
4. That the suspect did not comply with your requirements to remain with you.	

Your responsibilities to remain with the suspect and transfer control	**Your responsibilities to remain with the suspect under detention whilst accompanying you to the police station to transfer control:** para 2(4B) of S4PRA02.
1. That, while you took the suspect to a police station, you:	
• remained with the suspect until control was transferred to the custody officer,	

- treated the suspect as being in your lawful custody until your control was transferred,
- were under a duty to prevent the suspect from escaping and to assist to keep him/her under control all the while you were at or in the vicinity of a police station whilst transferring or having transferred control to the custody officer.

Circumstances under which you can use reasonable force

1. That you are designated under para 4ZB of Sch 4 to the Reform Act 2002.
2. That you took the suspect to a police station.
3. That you were carrying out your duties until lawful control was transferred.
4. That the suspect did not comply with your requirements.

Power to use reasonable force to carry out your responsibilities to remain with the suspect and transfer control to the custody officer: para 4ZB of S4PRA02.

Points to consider to prove the offence

1. That your reasons for detention were lawful.
2. That the suspect made off whilst subject to a requirement of waiting with you for 30 minutes, or
3. that the suspect made off while accompanying you to a police station, or
4. that the suspect failed to comply with your responsibilities to transfer control to a police officer, or
5. that the suspect failed to comply with your responsibilities to transfer control to a custody officer.
6. That you made a note of the description of the suspect.
7. That you used **SOCRATES** (or ADVOKATE) to evidence identification of the person.

Offence

Making off having been detained by a PCSO: para 2(5) of S4PRA02.

Mode of trial and penalty

Summary—a fine not exceeding level 3.

NB: For the power to detain in relation to offences connected with begging and use of reasonable force, see 3.2.35 below.

For the power to use reasonable force in relation to dispersing groups and removing young persons, see 3.2.33 and 3.2.34 below.

3.2.25 Power to search detained persons for dangerous items or items that could be used to assist escape

Context

There has been a sharp increase in the number of people in your BCU area who carry offensive weapons and you are concerned that, should the need arise to detain a person until a police officer arrived, you might run the risk of significant harm from a suspect determined to get away from you. The following powers and relevant legislation are available to a designated PCSO to deal with the problem:

A designated PCSO has the same power as a police officer in relation to a person who has been detained at a place other than a police station, to search that person for any item which may present a danger to him/herself or others or assist his/her escape from lawful custody. Having found any such item, the PCSO may seize and retain the item.	Empowering legislation **Power to search detained persons for dangerous items or items that could be used to assist escape:** para 2A of S4PRA02. *Primary legislation* **Searching a person who has been arrested at a place other than a police station:** s 32(1) PACE84.
Circumstances under which you can search 1. That you are designated under Para 2 of S4PRA02. 2. That the person had committed a 'relevant offence' or an offence connected with begging. 3. That you had required the person's name and address and s/he had not complied or given false details or had failed to stop his or her activity in relation to begging. 4. That you had required the person to wait with you for 30 minutes for the arrival of a police officer.	**Power to search detained persons for dangerous items or items that could be used to assist escape:** para 2A of S4PRA02.

5. That you had detained the person at a place other than a police station.
6. That you had reasonable grounds for believing the detained person might present a danger to him/herself or others.
7. That you had reasonable grounds for believing the detained person had anything which he/she might use to assist him/her to escape from lawful custody.

Circumstances surrounding the power to seize

1. That you had reasonable grounds for believing that the person being searched might use the item(s) you found to cause injury to him/herself or any other person.
2. That you had reasonable grounds for believing that the person being searched might use the item(s) you found to escape from lawful custody.
3. That you seized and retained anything you found on exercising your power other than an item subject to legal privilege, for example, a letter from the person to his/her legal representative.

Responsibilities after the search

1. That, having seized or retained anything, you:
   • tell the person from whom the items were seized where s/he can make enquiries about the recovery of the objects,
   • request the assistance of a police officer and comply with the instructions from the constable as to the method of disposal for the seized item.

NB: Again, as we warned with your powers to effect seizures of alcohol, tobacco, and drugs, you should make a dynamic risk assessment (see Chapter 5) before searching under this power, since your action, or intended action, *could* provoke violent resistance.

3.2.26 Power to photograph persons away from a police station

Context

The Intelligence Unit for your BCU has produced a report that people in the area who have been issued with penalty notices for disorder may well be liable to arrest for other offences. In order that these people can be properly identified, you have been instructed to photograph the recipient whenever you issue a PND. The following powers and relevant legislation are available to a designated PCSO to deal with the situation:

A designated PCSO has the power to photograph a person away from a police station who has been: • arrested, • required to wait by a PCSO for the arrival of a police officer, • issued with a PND or FPN for a 'relevant offence', and to require the removal of any item or substance from the face of the person being photographed, or, on refusal, to remove the item or substance him/herself.	*Empowering legislation* **Power to photograph persons away from a police station:** para 15ZA of S4PRA02. *Primary legislation* **Power to photograph persons away from a police station:** s 64A(1A) PACE84.
Circumstances under which the power can be used: 1. That the photography takes place elsewhere than at a police station. 2. That the person taking the photograph is a police officer or designated person, such as a PCSO. 3. That the photography takes place with the person's consent; or	*Primary legislation* **Power to photograph persons away from a police station:** s 64A(1A) PACE84.

4. that the photography takes place without consent which was withheld or impracticable to obtain.
5. That the person being photographed has been:
   - arrested by a police officer or designated person,
   - arrested by a person other than a police officer and then taken into custody by a police officer or designated person,
   - required to wait by a PCSO for the arrival of a police officer,
   - issued with a PND or a FPN for a road traffic offence by a constable,
   - issued with a penalty notice by a PCSO (see sections in this chapter for relevant offences),
   - issued with a penalty notice by an accredited person (a person outside the police 'family', such as a Trading Standards Officer).

Circumstances surrounding the requirement to remove coverings

1. That the person proposing to take the photograph may require the person to be photographed to remove:
   - any item or any substance,
   - worn on or over,
   - the whole or any part of,
   - the face or head, and
2. that, if the requirement is not complied with, the person proposing to take the photograph may remove the item or substance him/herself.

Purpose for which the photograph is taken

The use by, or disclosure for any purpose related to:

- 'the prevention or detection of crime,
- the investigation of an offence,
- the conduct of the prosecution,
- the enforcement of a sentence'.

Having taken the photograph, it can be retained but cannot be used or disclosed except for a related purpose.

3.2.27 Power to enforce byelaws

Context

To tackle a number of minor anti-social activities, your town/ borough council and your chief constable have agreed to a number of byelaws in the area becoming 'relevant byelaws'. The following powers and relevant legislation are available to a designated PCSO to enforce such byelaws:

A designated PCSO has the power to investigate offences committed under relevant byelaws. From a list of byelaws, a 'relevant byelaw' is one that has been agreed between a chief constable and a relevant byelaw-making body.

Such byelaws are 'relevant offences' for the purposes of a PCSO requiring the name and address of a suspect during the investigation and for asking the suspect to remain until a police officer arrives (see sections on power to require name and address and power to detain).

Failure to provide a name and address, having been required to do so, is an offence.

Empowering legislation

Power to enforce byelaws: paras 1A(3), 2(3A), 2(6)(ad), 2(6B), 2(6C), 2(6D), 2(6E), 2(6F) of S4PRA02.

Primary legislation

Failing to give name and address when required by a PCSO: para 1A(5) of S4PRA02.

If designated under para 2, a PCSO can also enforce a byelaw by removing a person from a place if a constable would also have the power to enforce a byelaw in that way.

Circumstances under which the power can be used

Power to require name and address: para 1A(3), of S4PRA02.

1. That you are designated under para 1A of S4PRA02.
2. That you had reason to believe that the person had committed an offence against a 'relevant byelaw'.
3. That you requested the person to give you his or her name and address.
4. That the place in which you made the request in relation to a 'relevant byelaw' was one to which the byelaw related.

Points to consider to prove the offence

Offence

- See **3.2.4** above: **Power to issue fixed penalty notices**, where the points to prove are itemized in respect of failing to give name and address when required.

Failing to give name and address when required by a PCSO: para 1A(5) of S4PRA02.

Mode of trial and penalty

Summary—level 3 fine.
See 3.2.24 above for details of your power to detain under PRA02.

Circumstances under which the power can be used

Power to remove a person from a place: para 2(3A) S4PRA02.

1. That you are designated under para 2 of S4PRA02, and
2. that you are designated under para 1A of S4PRA02 (power to require name and address).
3. That, in the first instance, a constable has the power under the relevant byelaw to remove a person from a place.

Definition of a 'relevant byelaw' as a 'relevant offence' In para 2 S4PRA02 a 'relevant offence' means any offence which is an offence under a 'relevant byelaw'.	**Legislation that defines a 'relevant byelaw' as a 'relevant offence':** para 2(6)(ad) of S4PRA02.

Definition of a 'relevant byelaw'
1. A byelaw included in a list of byelaws which have been made by a relevant body such as:
  • a county council,
  • a district council,
  • a parish council,
  • a London Borough Council, and
  • the chief constable of the police force for the area has agreed its inclusion in the list.
2. The list of 'relevant byelaws' must be published for the benefit of the general public.
3. The list may be amended by agreement with the chief constable and the relevant body, but the alterations must be published.
4. The agreement can also be made between the Secretary of State and the local chief constable.
	Legislation that defines a 'relevant byelaw': para 2(6B)–(6F) of S4PRA02.

3.2.28 Power to issue fixed penalty notices for truancy

Context

In an effort to alleviate the problems faced by the communities in local residential areas, particularly their fear of rowdiness from disaffected and bored youths in the area, you have been tasked with investigating which youths are playing truant from school. The following powers and relevant legislation are available to a designated PCSO to deal with the problem:

A designated PCSO has the power to issue an FPN to the parent of a child of compulsory school age who is registered and fails to attend school on a regular basis; this is a 'relevant offence'. The parent escapes conviction if the penalty is paid in accordance with the notice.

A PCSO who is designated under paragraph 1A of S4PRA02 has the power to require the name and address of a person who has committed a 'relevant offence'. If the suspect fails to comply with the requirement, or gives a name and address which the PCSO reasonably suspects to be false or inaccurate, the suspect commits an offence.

If the PCSO is further designated under para 2, s/he may then detain the person and await the arrival of a police officer or request the suspect to accompany the PCSO to the police station (see 3.2.24 above).

If the PCSO is designated under para 4, s/he may use reasonable force during the detention of the suspect (see 3.2.24 above).

Empowering legislation

1. **Power to issue fixed penalty notices for truancy**: para 1(2)(aa) of S4PRA02.

2. **Power to require name and address:** para 1A of S4PRA02.

Enabling legislation

Penalty notice issue: s 444A Education Act 1996.*

[*To avoid lengthy repetition, we shall refer to the Education Act 1996 from this point forward as **E96**.]

Primary legislation

1. **Failure to attend school regularly**: s 444A E96.

2. **Failing to give name and address when required by a PCSO**: para 1A(5) of S4PRA02.

Points to consider to prove the offence

1. The offence took place in England.
2. The child was of compulsory school age, 5–16 years.
3. The child was a registered pupil at a school.
4. The child failed to attend on a regular basis, or
5. the child was a boarder at a school and was absent in any part of the school terms except when sick or because of an unavoidable cause.

Offence

Failure to attend school regularly: s 444A E96.

Method of disposal

Penalty notice—under The Education (Penalty Notices) (England) Regulations 2004

Mode of trial and penalty

Summary—a fine not exceeding level 3.

Circumstances under which the child will not be taken to have failed to attend school on a regular basis where the child is not a boarder.

- S/he was on leave.
- S/he was sick.
- S/he was observing a religious event.

When the parent can prove (not applicable if the child has no fixed abode):

- the school is not in walking distance (for under 8 years: 2 miles, for over 8 years: 3 miles),
- no suitable transport arrangements have been made, or
- no boarding accommodation has been arranged, or
- no other place at a school was made available by the local authority.

When the parent can prove (applicable if the child has no fixed abode):

- his or her employment requires him or her to travel from place to place,
- the child has attended school as regularly as the work allowed,
- the child is 6 or over and has attended on at least 200 occasions in the last 12 months.

Points to consider to prove the offence

- See **3.2.4** above: **Power to issue fixed penalty notices**, where the points to prove are itemized in respect of failing to give name and address when required.

Offence

Failing to give name and address when required by a PCSO: para 1A(5) of S4PRA02.

Mode of trial and penalty

Summary—level 3 fine.

See 3.2.24 above for details of your power to detain under PRA02.

3.2.28.1 *Power to remove truants and excluded pupils*

A designated PCSO has the power to take pupils of compulsory school age back to their school or to other premises selected by the local authority if the pupils are found in a public place and believed to be truanting. The power also extends to children and young persons of compulsory school age who have been excluded, have not been admitted to another school and cannot justify being in a public place.

Empowering legislation

1. **Power to remove truants and excluded pupils and return them to school or designated premises:** para 4C of S4PRA02

Primary legislation

2. **Power to remove truants and excluded pupils and return them to school or designated premises:** s 16 of the Crime and Disorder Act 1998

Circumstances under which the power can be used

1. That you are designated under para 4C of S4PRA02.

2. That the local authority has, for the purposes of removing children and young persons of compulsory school age, designated premises to which they can be removed, and

3. That the local authority has notified the chief officer of police for that area of that designation.

4. That the power can only be used:

    a. in an area specified in a direction given by a police officer of or above the rank of superintendent, and

    b. during a specified time period.

5. That you find in a public place, in a specified area and time, a child or young person who you have reasonable cause to believe:

    a. is of compulsory school age, and

    b. is absent from school without lawful authority.

If all the above are satisfied, you can remove the child or young person to designated premises, or to the school from which s/he is absent.

6. That you find in a public place, in a specified area and time during school hours, a child or young person who you have reasonable cause to believe:

    a. is of compulsory school age,

    b. has been excluded from a relevant school on disciplinary grounds, either permanently or for a specific time,

    c. has not been admitted to another school, and

    d. cannot reasonably justify being in a public place.

If all the above are satisfied, you can remove the child or young person to designated premises.

Designated premises are not defined by the Crime and Disorder Act but will include premises selected by your local authority

Lawful authority means sickness, unavoidable cause, permitted leave or a day set apart for religious observance.

Relevant school means an institution providing primary, secondary or combined education, but does not include the further or higher education sector.

School hours means any time during a school session or a break between school sessions.

3.2.29 Offences connected to malicious, false, and diversionary activities

- Wasting police time or giving a false report
- Sending annoying or offensive messages via a network
- Making false fire alarms

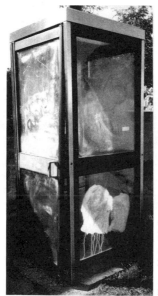

(Photograph by Bryn Caless)

Photograph 3: Vandalized telephone box CN

3 Knowledge and Skills

Context

To avoid detection and prosecution, a small number of people in your patrol area have begun diversionary tactics, so that police resources are sent to false incidents, whilst in other parts of the town real damage is being caused. In addition, the Fire and Rescue Service has been receiving a number of hoax calls. Your Intelligence Unit suspects that a group of bored youths are responsible, but there is a fear that this may escalate to more serious levels of crime unless stopped. You have been tasked, along with your colleagues, with finding out who has been making the hoax calls. The following powers and relevant legislation are available to a designated PCSO to deal with the problem of wasting police time:

A designated PCSO has the power to issue penalty notices for disorder. Three of the offences for which a PND can be issued are:

1. Causing wasteful employment of the police.
2. Sending annoying or offensive messages via a network.
3. Making false fire alarms.

Having been designated under para 1 of S4PRA02 to issue PNDs, the PCSO has the power also to require the name and address of the suspect. Failure to comply is a separate offence.

If the PCSO is further designated under para 1 of Sch 4, s/he can detain the person if s/he does not prove his or her name and address, or it is incorrect (see section 3.2.24 above).

If the PCSO is further designated under para 2, s/he may then detain the person and await the arrival of a police officer or request the suspect to accompany the PCSO to the police station (see 3.2.24 above).

Empowering legislation

1. **Power to issue fixed penalty notices:** para 1 of S4PRA02.
2. **Power to require name and address:** para 1A of S4PRA02.

Primary legislation

1. **Causing wasteful employment of the police:** s 5(2) Criminal Law Act 1967.
2. **Sending annoying or offensive messages via a network:** s 127 Communications Act 2003.
3. **Making false alarms:** s 49 Fire and Rescue Services Act 2004 (England only); s 31 Fire Services Act 1947 (Wales only).
4. **Failing to give name and address when required by a PCSO:** para 1A(5) of S4PRA02.

If the PCSO is designated under para 4, s/he may use reasonable force during the detention of the suspect (see 3.2.24 above).

Points to consider to prove the offence

1. That the suspect caused any wasteful employment of the police.
2. That the suspect knowingly made a false report tending to show that an offence had been committed; or
3. that the suspect knowingly made a false report to give rise to apprehension for the safety of any persons or property; or
4. that the suspect knowingly made a false report tending to show that s/he had information material to any police enquiry.

Offence

Causing wasteful employment of the police: s 5(2) Criminal Law Act 1967.

Method of disposal

Penalty notice for disorder (upper tier)—under CJP01. See 5.2.8 and 5.2.9 below on issuing PNDs.

Mode of trial and penalty

Summary—6 months' imprisonment and/or a fine not exceeding level 4.

Points to consider to prove the offence

1. That the suspect sent or caused a message or other matter to be sent by means of public electronic communications which was:
   - grossly offensive, or
   - indecent, or
   - obscene, or
   - of a menacing character, or
2. that the suspect for the purpose of causing annoyance, inconvenience, or needless anxiety to another:
   - sent a false message via a public electronic communications network, or
   - caused such a message to be sent, or

Offence

Sending annoying or offensive messages via a network s 127 Communications Act 2003.

Method of disposal

Penalty Notice for Disorder (upper tier)—under CJP01. See 5.2.8 and 5.2.9 below, on issuing PNDs.

Mode of trial and penalty

Summary—6 months' imprisonment and/or a fine not exceeding level 5.

- persistently made use of a public electronic communications network, and
- that it was not done in the course of providing a television service under the Broadcasting Act 1990.

Points to consider to prove the offence	*Offence*
1. That the suspect knowingly:	**Making false alarms:** s 49 Fire and Rescue Services Act 2004 (England only); s 31 Fire Services Act 1947 (Wales only).
• gives, or	
• causes to be given	
a false alarm of fire to a person acting on behalf of a fire and rescue authority.	*Method of disposal* Penalty notice for disorder (upper tier)—under CJP01. See 5.2.8 and 5.2.9 below on issuing PNDs.
	Mode of trial and penalty Summary—3 months' imprisonment and/or a fine not exceeding level 4.

Points to consider to prove the offence	*Offence*
See **3.2.4** above: **Power to issue fixed penalty notices**, where the Points to Prove are itemized in respect of failing to give name and address when required.	**Failing to give name and address when required by a PCSO:** para 1A(5) of S4PRA02.
	Mode of trial and penalty Summary—level 3 fine. See 3.2.24 above for details of your power to detain under PRA02.

3.2.30 Power to enter and search any premises to save life and limb or prevent serious damage to property

Context

Whilst you are on duty near your local football club car park on a very hot summer day, you are informed by a member of the public that a child had been left in a locked vehicle and appeared a few minutes ago to be in great distress. When you arrive at the vehicle, the child is motionless on the back seat and may have become unconscious, because she does not respond to your calling and tapping on the window glass. Faced with the urgent need to break

into a locked and alarmed vehicle, the following powers are available
to a designated PCSO to deal with the problem:

A designated PSCO has the same
power as a police officer to enter and
search any premises in the relevant
police area for the purpose of saving
life or limb or preventing serious
damage to life and property **(but
remember Risk Analysis, and do
not yourself become a casualty
through misplaced enthusiasm to
be heroic. See 5.6 below).**

Empowering legislation

**Power to enter and search any
premises to save life and limb
or prevent serious damage to
property:** para 8 of S4PRA02.

Primary legislation

**Power to enter and search any
premises to save life and limb
or prevent serious damage to
property:** s 17(1)(e) PACE84.

*Circumstances under which the power
can be used*

1. That you are designated under para
   8 of S4PRA02.
2. That you entered and searched any
   premises in the relevant police area
   for the sole purpose of saving life or
   limb or preventing serious damage
   to life and property.
3. That the premises were any place
   including any:
   • vehicle,
   • vessel,
   • aircraft,
   • tent, or
   • moveable structure.
4. That you only searched to the extent
   that is reasonably required for the
   purpose of saving life and limb or
   preventing serious damage and no
   further.

**Power to enter and search any
premises to save life and limb
or prevent serious damage to
property:** s 17(1)(e) PACE84.

3.2.31 Power to stop and search persons and vehicles to prevent terrorism and the power to maintain a cordon area during a terrorist investigation

Photograph 4: Police cordon

Context

The security threat level has been raised owing to increased terrorist activity nationally, especially in London and Birmingham, and a house on the outskirts of your BCU, which is suspected of being used by a terrorist group, has been cordoned off as a possible crime scene. Your Chief Constable has signed an authorization to stop and search (which is to be confirmed or amended by the Home Secretary or other Minister of State within 48 hours). You have been tasked to support this initiative by carrying out stops and searches and maintaining the cordoned area. The following powers and relevant legislation are available to a designated PCSO to deal with the situation:

A designated PCSO in an authorized area has the power to stop and search persons and vehicles to prevent terrorism activity but only whilst in the company and under the supervision of a police officer.

A designated PCSO has the power to maintain the cordoned area under terrorist investigation.

Empowering legislation

1. **Power to stop and search persons and vehicles to prevent terrorism activity:** para 15 of S4PRA02.
2. **Power to maintain a cordon area during a terrorist investigation:** para 14 of S4PRA02.

Primary legislation

1. **Power to stop and search persons and vehicles to prevent terrorism activity:** para 15 of S4PRA02.
2. **Power to maintain a cordon area during a terrorist investigation:** s 36 of the Terrorism Act 2000.*

[*To avoid lengthy repetition, we shall refer to the Terrorism Act 2000 from this point forward as **T00**.]

Circumstances under which the power to stop and search can be used

1. That you are designated under para 15 of S4PRA02.
2. That an authorization under s 44 of the Terrorism Act 2000 exists.
3. That you are in the company and under the supervision of a police officer.
4. That the only purpose of the search is to find articles of a kind which could be used in connection with terrorism.
5. That the search can be carried out whether or not you have grounds for suspecting the presence of articles of that kind.

Power to stop and search persons and vehicles to prevent terrorism activity: s 44 T00.

6. That you stop and search vehicles including anything
   - **in** the vehicle,
   - **on** the vehicle,
   - **carried** by the driver,
   - **carried** by any passenger of the vehicle.
7. That you search anything carried by a pedestrian.
8. That you seize and retain anything discovered in the course of your search or the search made by a police officer.
9. That your powers **do not** extend to searching drivers of the vehicles or their passengers, pedestrians, or people in general.

Points to consider to prove the offence

1. That you are designated under para 15 of S4PRA02.
2. That an authorization under s 44 of the Terrorist Act 2000 exists.
3. That you are in the company and under the supervision of a police officer.
4. That the suspect failed to stop a vehicle when you requested him or her to do so; or
5. that the suspect wilfully obstructed you whilst you searched anything:
   - **in** the vehicle,
   - **on** the vehicle,
   - **carried** by the driver,
   - **carried** by the passenger of the vehicle,
   - **carried** by a pedestrian.
6. That you made a note of the description of the suspect.

Offence

Failing to stop a vehicle or wilfully obstructing a PCSO in the exercise of powers to stop and search under s 44(1) and (2) T00: s 47 T00.

NB: The consent of the Director of Public Prosecutions (DPP) is required before proceedings for an offence against this section are instituted.

Mode of trial and penalty

Summary—3 months' imprisonment and/or a fine not exceeding level 5.

7. That you used **SOCRATES** (or ADVOKATE) to evidence identification of the person.

Circumstances under which the power to maintain a cordon can be used

Power to maintain a cordon area during a terrorist investigation: s 36 T00.

1. That you are designated under para 14 of S4PRA02.
2. That the cordon area has been designated for the purposes of a terrorist investigation.
3. That you may:
   '(a) order a person in a cordoned area to leave it immediately;
   (b) order a person immediately to leave premises which are wholly or partly in or adjacent to a cordoned area;
   (c) order the driver or person in charge of a vehicle in a cordoned area to move it from the area immediately;
   (d) arrange for the removal of a vehicle from a cordoned area;
   (e) arrange for the movement of a vehicle within a cordoned area;
   (f) prohibit or restrict access to a cordoned area by pedestrians or vehicles'.

Points to consider to prove the offence

Offence

Failing to comply with an order, prohibition or restriction imposed by a CSO in the area of cordon: s 36(2) T00.

1. That you are designated under para 14 of S4PRA02.
2. That the cordon area has been designated for the purposes of a terrorist investigation.
3. That a person had failed to comply with one of your requirements above.
4. That the person did not have a reasonable excuse for failing to comply with your requirements.

NB: This is not a 'relevant offence' for the purposes of para 1 of S4PRA02 when using your powers to require a suspect's name and address.

5. That you made a note of the description of the suspect.	*Mode of trial and penalty* Summary—3 months'
6. That you used **SOCRATES** (or ADVOKATE) to evidence identification of the person.	imprisonment and/or a fine not exceeding level 4.

3.2.32 Power to require name and address for anti-social behaviour

Context

Whilst on patrol, you witness some low level anti-social behaviour by children which was rowdy and disruptive, but which did not amount to committing a specific offence. You therefore decide to obtain the names and addresses of the individuals involved, with a view to meeting parents to explain to them that the young people involved could be on the verge of getting into trouble. The following powers and relevant legislation are available to a designated PCSO to deal with the problem:

A designated PCSO under para 3 of S4PRA02 has the same power as a police officer under s 50 PRA02 to require any person s/he believes to have been acting in an anti-social way to give his or her name and address.

If the suspect fails to comply with the requirement or gives a name and address which the PCSO reasonably suspects to be false or inaccurate, the suspect commits an offence.

If the PCSO is designated under para 2, s/he may then detain the person and await the arrival of a police officer or request the suspect to accompany the PCSO to the police station (see 3.2.24 above).

Empowering legislation

Power to require name and address for anti-social behaviour: para 3 of S4PRA02.

Primary legislation

1. **Power to require name and address for anti-social behaviour:** s 50 PRA02.
2. **Failing to give name and address when required by a PCSO:** para 1A(5) of S4PRA02.

If the PCSO is designated under para 4, s/he may use reasonable force during the detention of the suspect (see 3.2.24 above).

Circumstances under which the power can be used

1. That you are designated under para 3.
2. That you are in uniform.
3. That you have reason to believe that the person:
   • was acting previously, or
   • is acting at the time
   in an anti-social manner (causing or 'likely to cause harassment, alarm or distress to one or more persons not of the same household as [him/herself]'.
4. That you required the person to give you his/her name and address.

Power to require name and address for anti-social behaviour: para 3(1) of S4PRA02.

Points to consider to prove the offence:

• See **3.2.4** above: **Power to issue fixed penalty notices**, where the points to prove are itemized in respect of failing to give name and address when required.
• If you are designated under para 4, you may use reasonable force during the detention of the suspect (see 3.2.24 above).

Offence

Failing to give name and address when required by a PCSO: para 1A(5) of S4PRA02.

Mode of trial and penalty

Summary—level 3 fine.

See 3.2.24 above for details of your power to detain under PRA02.

3.2.33 Power to disperse groups and remove persons under 16 to their places of residence

Context

After a protracted period of graffiti writing, petty vandalism, and anti-social behaviour around the town, your BCU commander, with the consent of the town council, has made an authorization in that area for the dispersal of groups and the removal of persons under 16 to their places of residence. The following powers and relevant legislation are available to a designated PCSO to deal with the situation:

A PCSO's power to disperse groups and remove persons under 16 to their places of residence cannot be used without two designations: first, a written authorization made by a senior police officer, with the consent of the local authority, to designate an area in which the power can be used and, secondly, the PCSO must be designated under para 4A.

Where the PCSO is further designated under para 4ZB, s/he may use reasonable force to prevent members of the dispersed groups and removed persons from making off, and to keep them under control.

Empowering legislation
1. **Power to disperse groups and remove persons under 16 to their places of residence:** para 4A of S4PRA02.
2. **Power to use reasonable force to disperse groups and remove persons under 16 to their place of residence:** para 4ZB of S4PRA02.

Primary legislation
Power to disperse groups and remove persons under 16 to their place of residence: s 30 ASB03.

Circumstances under which the power to disperse groups can be used
1. That a written authorization designating an area has been made by an officer of at least the rank of superintendent.
2. That you are designated under para 4A of S4PRA02.
3. That you are in uniform.
4. That there was a group of two or more persons in any public place in the designated area.
5. That you had reasonable grounds for believing that the presence or behaviour of that group:
   • has resulted, or
   • is likely to result in any members of the public being:
   • intimidated,

Power to disperse groups: s 30(1) ASB03.

- harassed,
- alarmed, or
- distressed,

in which case you can then give one or more of the following directions to the members of the group:

1. To disperse either immediately or by such time as you specify and in a way you specify.
2. To leave the designated area or any part of it, either immediately or by such time as you specify and in such way as you specify (**only applies to members of the group whose place of residence is not within the designated area**).
3. To prohibit their return to the designated area or any part of it for a period you specify (not exceeding 24 hours) from when the direction was given (**only applies to members of the group whose place of residence is not within the designated area**).

Your power to disperse does NOT extend to any members of any groups who are taking part in a lawful trade dispute or a lawful procession.

Circumstances under which the power to remove persons under 16 to their places of residence can be used

1. That a written authorization designating an area has been made by an officer of at least the rank of superintendent.

Power to remove persons under 16 to their place of residence: s 30(6) ASB03.

2. That you are designated under para 4A of S4PRA02.
3. That you are in uniform.
4. That the time is between 2100 hrs and 0600 hrs.
5. That you find a person in any public place in the designated area who you have reasonable grounds for believing:
   - is under the age of 16, and
   - is not under the effective control of a parent or a responsible person aged 18 or over.
6. That you **do not** have reasonable grounds for believing that the person would be likely to suffer significant harm if removed to his or her place of residence.

Only if all of the above are satisfied can you remove the person to his/her place of residence.

Circumstances under which you can use reasonable force

- That you are designated under para 4ZB of S4PRA02.
- That all of the above circumstances relating to the power to use reasonable force to disperse groups and removal of persons under 16 to their places of residence were satisfied.
- That the member of the group or person under 16 made off from you or you were unable to keep him/her under control.

Power to use reasonable force to disperse groups and remove persons under 16 to their places of residence: para 4ZB of S4PRA02.

Refer to 3.2.24 above for further details regarding reasonable force.

3.2.34 Power to remove children in contravention of child curfew notices to their places of residence

Context

As a result of your work with other members of the police family, a number of young people have been placed under curfew in your BCU area. You have had information that some, though not all, of these young people are contravening the curfew and you must now intervene. The following powers and relevant legislation are available to a designated PCSO to deal with the problem:

A designated PCSO has the power under para 4B to remove children in contravention of child curfew notices to ttheir places of residence. The purpose of the curfew notices made by a chief officer of police or a local authority is to prevent children under 16 from being in areas without a responsible adult. The areas, hours, and ages of the children to whom the curfew relates will be dictated by the curfew notice.

Where the PCSO is further designated under para 4ZB, s/he may use reasonable force to prevent the removed persons from making off and to keep them under control.

Empowering legislation

1. **Power to remove children in contravention of child curfew notices to their place of residence:** para 4B(1) of S4PRA02.
2. **Power to use reasonable force to disperse groups and remove persons under 16 to their places of residence:** para 4ZB of S4PRA02.

Primary legislation

Power to remove children in contravention of child curfew notices to their place of residence: s 15(1) Crime and Disorder Act 1998.

Circumstances under which the power to remove children can be used

1. That a local authority or a chief officer of police has made a local child curfew scheme which has been confirmed by the Secretary of State and suitably advertised.

Power to remove children in contravention of child curfew notices to their places of residence: s 15(1) Crime and Disorder Act 1998.

2. That the notice specifies the curfew hours, the ages of the children to be banned, and the relevant public place.
3. That you are designated under para 4B of S4PRA02.
4. That you have reasonable cause to believe the child is in contravention of a ban imposed by a curfew notice by way of age, time, and locality.
5. That you **do not** have reasonable cause to believe that the person would be likely to suffer significant harm, if removed to his or her place of residence.

Only if all of the above are satisfied can you remove the child to its place of residence.

Circumstances under which you can use reasonable force

1. That you are designated under para 4ZB of S4PRA02.
2. That all of the above circumstances relating to the power to remove children in contravention of child curfew notices to their places of residence were satisfied.
3. That the child you were removing made off from you or you were unable to keep him/her under control.

Power to use reasonable force to disperse groups and remove persons under 16 to their place of residence: para 4ZB of S4PRA02.

Refer to 3.2.24 above for further details regarding reasonable force.

3.2.35 Powers and legislation to deal with begging and associated offences

Context

Your police station has received a number of complaints about people begging, soliciting donations, and importuning passers-by outside local shops. You have been tasked to investigate these complaints and, if there is a genuine problem, to deal with it. The following powers and relevant legislation are available to a designated CSO to deal with the problem:

A designated PCSO under para 1 has the power to deal with any person who is begging or asking for charitable donations and then require his or her name and address.

In addition, a PCSO who is designated under para 2 has the power to detain a person who is committing an offence associated with begging and, after requesting the suspect to stop, which is then refused, can detain the person to await the arrival of a police officer.

If the PCSO is designated under para 4ZA, s/he has the further power to use reasonable force to impose a requirement on the suspect to remain with him/her whilst awaiting the arrival of a police officer and to keep control of him/her until the custody of the suspect is transferred.

See also 3.2.24 above, Power to detain and use reasonable force to prevent a person making off or to transfer control of a detained person.

See also section 3.2.25 above, Power to search detained persons for dangerous items or items that could be used to assist escape.

Empowering legislation
1. **Power to detain when dealing with begging:** para 2(3B) PRA02.
2. **Making begging offences 'relevant offences':** para 2(6) (a–c) PRA02.
3. **Power to require name and address:** para 1A of S4PRA02.
4. **Power to use reasonable force:** para 4ZA of S4PR02.

Primary legislation
1. **Begging or asking for charitable donations:** s 3 Vagrancy Act 1824.
2. **Obtaining donations under false or fraudulent pretences:** s 4 Vagrancy Act 1824.
3. **Failing to give name and address when required by a PCSO:** para 1A(5) of S4PRA02.
4. **Making off from a PCSO:** para 2(5) of S4PRA02.

Points to consider to prove the offence	**Begging or asking for charitable donations**:
1. That you found the suspect begging for charitable donations in any of the below named places; or	s 3 Vagrancy Act 1824.
2. that you found the suspect procuring or encouraging any child or children to beg for charitable donations in any:	*Mode of trial and penalty* Summary—a fine not exceeding level 3.
• public place,	
• street,	
• highway,	
• court, or passage.	

Points to consider to prove the offence	**Obtaining donations under false or fraudulent pretences:**
1. That the suspect showed a wound or deformity in order to obtain donations; or	s 4 Vagrancy Act 1824.
2. that the suspect endeavoured 'to obtain donations of any kind under any false or fraudulent pretences'.	*Mode of trial and penalty* Summary—a fine not exceeding level 3.

Circumstances under which the power can be used	**Power to detain when dealing with begging (if designated):**
1. That you are designated under para 2.	para 2(3B) PRA02.
2. That you reasonably suspected a person to be committing an offence relating to begging.	
3. That you required the suspect to stop whatever s/he was doing and to wait with you for a period not exceeding 30 minutes for the arrival of a police officer.	

See 3.2.25 above, Power to search detained persons for dangerous items or items that could be used to assist escape.	**Power to search detained persons for dangerous items (if designated):** para 2A PRA02.

See 3.2.24 above, Power to detain and use reasonable force to prevent a person making off or to transfer control of a detained person.	**Power to use reasonable force to prevent a detained person making off (if designated):** para 4 of S4PRA02.
See 3.2.24 above, Power to detain and use reasonable force to prevent a person making off or to transfer control of a detained person.	Offence **Making off having been detained by a PCSO:** para 2(5) of S4PRA02.
Points to consider to prove the offence • See **3.2.4** above: **Power to issue fixed penalty notices,** where the points to prove are itemized in respect of failing to give name and address when required.	Offence **Failing to give name and address when required by a PCSO:** para 1A(5) of S4PRA02. *Mode of trial and penalty* Summary—level 3 fine.

3.2.36 Powers and legislation to deal with the unlawful supply, possession, and misuse of fireworks

• Throwing fireworks in a public place
• Unlawful possession of a category 4 firework
• Unlawful possession by a person under 18 of an adult firework
• Breach of a fireworks curfew (night hours)
• Supplying excessively loud fireworks

Context
Every year around October and November, and sometimes at Christmas and New Year celebrations, your town suffers from incidents involving the mishandling of fireworks. Some incidents have involved throwing lighted fireworks at people or putting lighted fireworks in pillar boxes or litter bins. Not only is this dangerous, but it is making residents very fearful of going out. Your BCU Commander has ordered that this year there will be a thorough crack-down on people who misuse fireworks throughout the period. The following powers and relevant legislation are available to a designated PCSO to deal with such problems:

A designated PCSO has the power to issue a PND to a person who has committed an offence of:

- Throwing fireworks.
- Unlawful possession of a category 4 firework.
- Unlawful possession by a person under 18 of an adult firework.
- Breach of a fireworks curfew.
- Supplying excessively loud fireworks.

Such a PCSO can then request a name and address from the suspect, who commits a further offence if he/she fails to comply with the request or gives false or inaccurate details.

A PCSO who is designated under para 2 of Sch 4 to the Police Reform Act 2002 also has the power to detain a suspect who failed to comply with your request for his/her name and address.

A PCSO who is designated under para 4 has the power to use reasonable force on the suspect to remain with him/her whilst awaiting the arrival of a police officer and to keep control until the custody of the suspect is transferred.

See also 3.2.24 above, Power to detain and use reasonable force to prevent a person making off or to transfer control of a detained person.

See also 3.2.25 above, Power to search detained persons for dangerous items or items that could be used to assist escape.

Empowering legislation

1. **Power to issue fixed penalty notices:** para 1 of S4PRA02.
2. **Power to require name and address:** para 1A of S4PRA02.
3. **Power to detain:** para 2 of S4PRA02.
4. **Power to search a detained person:** para 2A S4PRA02.
5. **Power to use reasonable force:** para 4 of S4PRA02.

Primary legislation

1. **Throwing fireworks in a public place:** s 80 Explosives Act 1875.
2. **Unlawful possession of a category 4 firework (reg 5 FR04):** s 11 Fireworks Act 2003.*

[*To avoid lengthy repetition, we shall refer to the Fireworks Act 2003 from this point forward as **F03**.]

3. **Unlawful possession by a person under 18 of an adult firework (reg 4 FR04):** s 11 F03.*

[*To avoid lengthy repetition, we shall refer to the Fireworks Regulations 2004 from this point forward as **FR04**.]

4. **Breach of a fireworks curfew (night hours) (reg 7 FR04):** s 11 F03.
5. **Supplying excessively loud fireworks (reg 8 FR04):** s 11 F03.

Points to consider to prove the offence

1. That you are designated under para 1 of Sch 4 to the Police Reform Act 2002 to issue PNDs.
2. That the person:
   - threw,
   - cast,
   - fired
   any firework
   - in, or
   - onto
   any
   - highway,
   - street,
   - thoroughfare, or
   - public place.

Offence

Throwing fireworks in a public place: s 80 of the Explosives Act 1875.

Method of disposal

Penalty notice for disorder (upper tier)—under CJP01.
See 5.2.8 and 5.2.9 below, on issuing PNDs.

Mode of trial and penalty

Summary—a fine not exceeding level 5.

Points to consider to prove the offence

1. That the person had possession of a category 4 firework.
2. That the person was not a person who is employed by, or in business as:
   - a professional organizer of firework displays,
   - operator of firework displays,
   - firework manufacturer,
   - firework supplier,
   - local authority organizer of firework displays,
   - entertainments' special effects organizer,
   - Government organizer of firework displays,
   - Armed Services organizer of firework displays or pyrotechnics (such as for military tattoos)

and who possesses the firework in question for the purposes of his/her employment or business.

Offence

Possession of a category 4 firework (reg 5 FR04)): s 11 F03.

Method of disposal

Penalty notice for disorder (upper tier)—under CJP01.
See 5.2.8 and 5.2.9 below on issuing PNDs.

Mode of trial and penalty

Summary—6 months' imprisonment and/or a fine not exceeding level 5.

Points to consider to prove the offence	Offence
1. That the person was under 18. 2. That the person possessed an adult firework. 3. That the person was in a public place.	**Possession by a person under 18 of an adult firework (reg 4 FR04):** s 11 F03. *Method of disposal* Penalty notice for disorder (upper tier)—under CJP01. See 5.2.8 and 5.2.9 below on issuing PNDs. *Mode of trial and penalty* Summary—6 months' imprisonment and/or a fine not exceeding level 5.
Points to consider to prove the offence 1. That the person used an adult firework during 'night hours' (see below for definition). 2. That the period was not a 'permitted firework night' (see definition below). 3. That the person was not a local authority employee putting on a local authority or commemorative firework display.	*Offence* **Breach of a fireworks curfew (reg 7 FR04):** s 11 F03. *Method of disposal* Penalty notice for disorder (upper tier)—under CJP01. See 5.2.8 and 5.2.9 below on issuing PNDs. *Mode of trial and penalty* Summary—6 months' imprisonment and/or a fine not exceeding level 5.
Points to consider to prove the offence That the person: • supplied, • offered, or • agreed to supply any category 3 firework exceeding 120 decibels.	*Offence* **Supplying excessively loud fireworks (reg 8 FR04):** s 11 F03. *Method of disposal* Penalty notice for disorder (upper tier)—under CJP01. See 5.2.8 & 5.2.9 above on issuing PNDs. *Mode of trial and penalty* Summary—6 months' imprisonment and/or a fine not exceeding level 5.
'Any device intended for use as a form of entertainment which contains, or otherwise incorporates, explosive and/or pyrotechnic composition, which burns and/or explodes to produce a visual and/or audible effect.'	**'Firework':** Fireworks (Safety) Regulations 1997.

A display firework that can be used by the general public but only at larger displays where the audience gets no closer than 25 metres and the debris is not scattered beyond 20 metres.	**'Category 3 firework':** FR04
A professional firework that cannot possibly be sold to the general public because of its size and potential power and requires a specialist to be in possession of it.	**'Category 4 firework':** FR04
Any firework that does not comply with part 2 of British Standard 7114 (tested for safety, explosive strengths, etc) 'except for a cap, cracker snap, novelty match, party popper, serpent, sparkler or throwdown'.	**'Adult firework':** FR04
'… includes any place to which at the material time the public have or are permitted access, whether on payment or otherwise'.	**'Public place':** FR04
Starts at 2300 hrs and ends at 0700 hrs the next day.	**'Night hours':** FR04
'(a) beginning at 11 pm on the first day of the Chinese New Year and ending at 1 am the following day; (b) beginning at 11 pm on 5th November and ending at 12 am the following day; (c) beginning at 11 pm on the day of Diwali and ending at 1 am the following day; or (d) beginning at 11 pm on 31st December and ending at 1 am the following day.'	**'Permitted fireworks night':** FR04

Points to consider to prove the offence	*Offence*
• See **3.2.4** above: **Power to issue fixed penalty notices,** where the points to prove are itemized in respect of failing to give name and address when required.	**Failing to give name and address when required by a PCSO:** para 1A(5) of S4PRA02.
	Mode of trial and penalty
	Summary—level 3 fine.
	See 3.2.24 above for details of your power to detain under PRA02.
	See also 3.2.24 above, Power to detain and use reasonable force to prevent a person making off or to transfer control of a detained person.
	See also 3.2.25 above, Power to search detained persons for dangerous items or items that could be used to assist escape.

3.2.37 Powers and legislation to deal with threatening, abusive, or insulting behaviour likely to cause harassment, alarm, or distress

Context

It seems that the most of your duty time is being spent patrolling a local municipal housing complex. The area has been 'designated' for the purposes of dispersing groups and removing young persons to their places of residence. It is also an area under a **child curfew notice**, but the local residents still feel intimidated and are too scared to leave their homes except in groups in daylight. The following powers and relevant legislation are available to a designated PCSO to deal with the problem:

	Empowering legislation
A designated PCSO has the power to issue a PND to a person who has committed an offence of using threatening, abusive, or insulting behaviour likely to cause harassment, alarm, or distress.	1. **Power to issue fixed penalty notices:** para 1 of S4PRA02.
	2. **Power to require name and address:** para 1A of S4PRA02.
	3. **Power to detain:** para 2 of S4PRA02.

Such a PCSO can then require a name and address from the suspect who commits a further offence if s/he fails to comply with the requirements or gives false or inaccurate details.

A PCSO who is designated under para 2 of Sch 4 to the Police Reform Act 2002 also has the power to detain a suspect who fails to comply with the PCSO's request for his/her name and address.

A PCSO who is designated under para 4 has the power to use reasonable force on the suspect, to remain with him/her whilst awaiting the arrival of a police officer, and to keep control until the custody of the suspect is transferred.

See also 3.2.24 above, Power to detain and use reasonable force to prevent a person making off or to transfer control of a detained person.

See also 3.2.25 above, Power to search detained persons for dangerous items or items that could be used to assist escape.

4. **Power to search a detained person:** para 2A of S4PRA02.
5. **Power to use reasonable force:** para 4 of S4PRA02.

Primary legislation
Using threatening, abusive or insulting behaviour likely to cause harassment, alarm or distress: s 5 Public Order Act 1986.

Points to consider to prove the offence
1. That you are designated under para 1 of S4PRA02 to issue PNDs.
2. That the person used any of the following conduct:
   - threatening, or
   - abusive, or
   - insulting words or behaviour, or
   - disorderly behaviour.

Offence
Using threatening, abusive or insulting behaviour likely to cause harassment, alarm or distress: s 5 Public Order Act 1986.

Method of disposal
Penalty notice for disorder (upper tier)—under CJP01.

See 5.2.8 and 5.2.9 above on issuing PNDs..

Mode of trial and penalty
Summary—a fine not exceeding level 3.

---

3 Knowledge and Skills

3. That the person displayed any of the following conduct:
   - threatening, or
   - abusive, or
   - insulting writing, signs, or other visual representation.
4. That the person took part in any of the above conduct in the hearing or sight of a person who was likely to be caused:
   - harassment,
   - alarm, or
   - distress.
5. That the conduct could be seen or heard in public (even if the conduct took place in private).
6. That the suspect intended his/her conduct to be:
   - threatening,
   - abusive, or
   - insulting, or
   - disorderly.
7. That the suspect is aware that his/her conduct is:
   - threatening,
   - abusive, or
   - insulting, or
   - disorderly.

Points to consider to prove the offence

- See **3.2.4** above: **Power to issue fixed penalty notices,** where the points to prove are itemized in respect of failing to give name and address when required.

Offence

Failing to give name and address when required by a PCSO: para 1A(5) of S4PRA02.

Mode of trial and penalty

Summary—level 3 fine. See 3.2.24 above for details of your power to detain under PRA02.

3.2.38 Power of arrest for persons other than a constable under section 24A of the Police and Criminal Evidence Act 1984

Whether or not you are designated to detain a person under paragraph 2 of the Police Reform Act 2002, you—and any other citizen in England and Wales—have a power to **arrest** any person who is committing or has committed an **indictable offence** (see 3.1.2 above). The power of 'the citizen's arrest' is based on a number of conditions being met, none greater than the necessity for the offence for which the arrest is being made, being an indictable offence.

3.2.38.1 *Powers of arrest*

To help you understand the power of arrest, there follows a description of the component parts in paragraphs. The power is available to every citizen other than a police constable. It is, for example, the power to arrest that store detectives use to detain a person they suspect of shoplifting. This power of arrest, therefore, includes you. It does not mean you have to use it. This Handbook recognizes the sometimes ambiguous framework under which you work and your association with the community which you support, but the power to arrest is there should you require it. The term 'arrest without warrant' still exists in modern day legislation to differentiate between warrants of arrest issued by courts and powers of arrest for which no warrant is required:

(1) The power can be used to arrest a person who is in the act of committing an **indictable offence.** This means that the person making the arrest can see the suspect carrying out the crime there and then. Look ahead to the incident, in '**Evidence**', involving the graffiti artist incident in 5.2 below. Here you walked into the 'Precinct' and saw the graffiti artist at work with spray cans. The suspect was therefore committing the offence.

(2) Another opportunity to use the power is when somebody other than a constable has reasonable grounds for suspecting a person to be committing an **indictable offence.** We have already discussed in other sections that 'reasonable grounds' are subjective. Going back to the incident in the 'Precinct', let's say you had been given a description by a witness of a person spraying a shop front and you went inside and saw a person of the same description standing with a spray can in his/her hand next to a wall with fresh paint on it. As the suspect was not in the process of spraying

right at that moment but may have been about to start spraying again, you would have 'reasonable' grounds for suspecting the person to be committing the offence.

(3) An indictable offence is an offence that can be tried **either way**, either in a magistrates' court or in a Crown Court, such as theft. An offence that can be tried on indictment only in a Crown Court and nowhere else, is a serious or major crime, such as manslaughter or murder. These classifications of offences are together known as 'indictable offences'. You will know the classification of an offence by looking at each of the offences you have the power to deal with. Here the mode of trial and penalty will be listed. Obviously, those offences listed as summary can only be tried in a magistrates' court and are therefore not indictable offences.

Indictable offences 'in the past'

(4) In the first two situations above, in which you would be entitled to use the power of arrest, the suspect was committing an indictable offence and the situations referred to something happening at the present time. The power can also be used when an indictable offence has been committed in the past. An example of this would be if you were given a description by a witness of a person spraying a shop front and you went inside and saw a person of the same description walking away from a wall with fresh paint on it. The suspect would no longer be **committing** the offence, but the offence would have been **committed**.

'Completion of the offence'

(5) A suspect in England and Wales is innocent until proven guilty. Some legislation makes reference to a person being 'guilty' of committing an offence. This way of writing is simply trying to say 'a person who has just arrived at the end of completing the offence'. This power of arrest is one of those pieces of legislation. An example would be if you had received a description from the witness, and then you had gone inside the 'Precinct' and seen the suspect standing next to the paint on the wall, having just completed the damage and throwing the can into the rubbish bin; you would arrest 'at the end of completing the offence'.

Grounds for suspicion of guilt

(6) In the past, when an indictable offence had been committed, there was a fourth situation in which the power of arrest

could be used. This is when the person making the arrest has reasonable grounds for **suspecting** another to be guilty of the offence. This is the most tenuous of the four situations under which the power of arrest can be used. Using the 'Precinct' example again, having received the description given by the witness, you go inside, see the graffiti on the wall of the shop and see a person walking away from it who fitted the description given by the witness. The witness's description, if sufficiently distinctive, gives you grounds for 'suspecting' the offender.

'Reasonable grounds' and 'believing an arrest is necessary'

(7) Having considered the situations under which the power can be used, we are now going to consider the **conditions which have to be met as far as circumstances are concerned**. (Therefore, without either of the following two circumstances ((8) and (9)) being present, the power cannot be used.)

(8) The person making the arrest must have *reasonable grounds for believing that the arrest is necessary*. The reasons that make the arrest necessary are listed in points (12) to (15) below. If the arrest is not necessary for one of these reasons, along with the circumstances dictating that it is not reasonably practicable for a constable to make it, the power of arrest cannot be used.

(9) In addition to meeting the requirements of having reasonable grounds for *believing that the arrest is necessary*, it must appear to the person making the arrest that *it is not reasonably practicable for a police constable to make it instead*. The person making the arrest must therefore not only believe it is necessary for one or more of the reasons listed below, but, for example, because of the length of time it might take a police officer to arrive, the person must make the arrest there and then.

Necessity

(10) To meet the *necessity* criterion, the person making the arrest must believe the suspect is going to carry out one or more of **four** activities which must be prevented. If the person making the arrest does not have reasonable grounds for believing that the arrest is necessary to prevent the suspect from carrying out one or more of these four activities, then the arrest cannot take place.

Prevention of injury to self or others

(11) The *first* of the four reasons is to prevent the suspect from causing physical injury to himself/herself or any other person. An example of this would be if the suspect was in possession of an article which s/he could use upon him/herself or on any other person, including the person making the arrest.

Preventing the suspect from suffering injury

(12) The *second* of the reasons is to prevent the suspect from suffering physical injury. An example of this would be if the suspect was surrounded by a group of people who were intent upon causing the suspect harm owing to the crime s/he had allegedly committed (a common instance when people find out where a convicted paedophile is living).

Preventing loss or damage

(13) The *third* of the reasons is to prevent the suspect from causing loss of or damage to property. An example of this would be if the suspect was in possession of proceeds from the crime s/he had committed and was about to throw them away into a place from where they could not be recovered.

Preventing the suspect from 'making off'

(14) The *fourth* and final reason is to prevent the suspect making off before a constable can assume responsibility for him/her. An example of this would be if the suspect was not complying with the request to remain until a police officer arrived or s/he appeared to be about to make off.

We will look now at requirements placed upon you by the Police and Criminal Evidence Act 1984 Codes of Practice and your own designated powers.

3.2.39 Recording of encounters with the public not governed by statutory powers

Whenever you stop and ask members of the public to account for their behaviour, actions, presence or for their possession of a particular item and they are in a public place, you are required to make a record of that interaction and offer the person a receipt in return. It does not involve searching and it is not a power – it is only a requirement to record a certain kind of encounter. This process has become known as **'Stop and Account'** and is a requirement placed

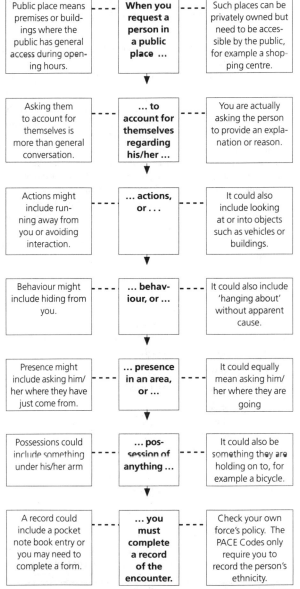

Public place means premises or buildings where the public has general access during opening hours. - - - **When you request a person in a public place ...** - - - Such places can be privately owned but need to be accessible by the public, for example a shopping centre.

Asking them to account for themselves is more than general conversation. - - - **... to account for themselves regarding his/her ...** - - - You are actually asking the person to provide an explanation or reason.

Actions might include running away from you or avoiding interaction. - - - **... actions, or ...** - - - It could also include looking at or into objects such as vehicles or buildings.

Behaviour might include hiding from you. - - - **... behaviour, or ...** - - - It could also include 'hanging about' without apparent cause.

Presence might include asking him/her where they have just come from. - - - **... presence in an area, or ...** - - - It could equally mean asking him/her where they are going

Possessions could include something under his/her arm - - - **... possession of anything ...** - - - It could also be something they are holding on to, for example a bicycle.

A record could include a pocket note book entry or you may need to complete a form. - - - **... you must complete a record of the encounter.** - - - Check your own force's policy. The PACE Codes only require you to record the person's ethnicity.

upon you by the Police and Criminal Evidence (PACE) Act 1984 Codes of Practice. Code A paragraph 4.12 states:

You must both:

- inform the person of their entitlement to a receipt of the encounter; and
- make a record of the person's self-defined ethnic background at the same time .

If you provide the person with a receipt, your name must be included on the receipt you give to the person you have encountered. However, you are not empowered to require the person to provide his/her own personal details.

If s/he refuses to give his/her self-defined ethnic background, you should instead record your own observed description of his/her ethnic background. If s/he gives you what appears to be an obviously wrong answer to the self-defined ethnic background, you should record both his/her original response and the incorrect version which the person provided. You should also record your own perception of the ethnic background of every person stopped.

3.2.39.1 Exceptions

You must make a record at the time of the encounter unless it is out of the question to do so (for example in serious public order situations or when you have to leave the scene urgently). If you do not make a record at the time, you must do so as soon as practicable afterwards (Code A para 4.1).

Other exceptions

You do not have to complete a form if you are either:

- in general conversation;
- giving directions;
- looking for witnesses;
- seeking general information;
- questioning people in order to establish the background to incidents which have required you to become involved;
- issuing a person with a Penalty Notice for Disorder (PND).

3.2.39.2 Request for a receipt for non-recordable encounters

If a person requests a receipt but the encounter or chance meeting does not satisfy the conditions to make it recordable (see PACE

1984, Code A, paras 4.12 and 4.19) you should still provide him/
her with a receipt. Nevertheless, make sure that you record on
it that the encounter did not meet the criteria to make the stop
recordable in terms of Code A, para 4.12.

If the encounter or chance meeting does not meet the conditions to make it recordable and if you reasonably believe that
the purpose of the request is to deliberately frustrate or delay
legitimate police activity, you can refuse to issue the receipt. An
example might be if you are being talked to (or shouted at) in a
public order situation by an individual or group of people who
are trying to distract you from your duty. As long as you have
not initiated or engaged in contact with the person about his/her
individual circumstances (such as why the person is there, what
s/he is doing, where s/he has been or is going), then there is no
need to issue a receipt.

3.2.39.3 *Summary of what to do after speaking with a member of the public*

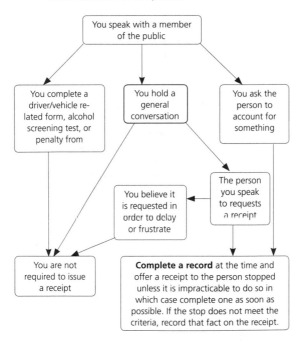

3.3 **Checking Your Own Designated Powers**

3.3.1 The law

Under the Police and Justice Bill 2006, signed into law as the **Police and Justice Act 2006**[9] in November 2006 and enacted from April 2007, PCSOs have standard powers, which we looked at in 3.2 above. Having now taken you through the powers and duties of a PCSO and noting that we will consider **evidence** in the same sort of detail in 5.2 below, there is an on-going task upon you to ascertain with what specific powers you have been designated by your Chief Constable. However, part of this may become academic. In the Police and Justice Act (PJA06), section 5 of Part 1 (**Standard powers and duties of community support officers**, amending section 38 of the Police Reform Act 2002, includes the following:

(1) In section 38 of the Police Reform Act 2002 (c.30) (police powers for police authority employees), after subsection (5) there is inserted—

'(5A) A person designated under this section as a community support officer shall also have the standard powers and duties of a community support officer (see section 38A(2)0).'

As we noted in the beginning of 3.2 above, the government consulted closely with ACPO (among others) in the formulation of PCSO standard duties and powers, in an attempt to impose (or perhaps to encourage) a national consistency in what PCSOs were being asked to do. What the PJA06 does, in the subsection we have quoted above, is to enshrine those standard powers in legislation. In other words, it seems to us, as soon as you are designated a Police Community Support Officer by your Chief Constable, you acquire the range of standard powers, *whether your role requires the range or not.*

3.3.2 Are your powers automatic now that they are standardized?

This is quite a departure, if our interpretation is correct, from the original status quo, which was that a PCSO would be designated by the Chief Constable according to the powers s/he needed to carry out the role to which s/he was allotted. This may seem like an undue focus on meanings and interpretations, but both the authorization and the legislation surrounding PCSOs are apt to be a bit woolly and imprecise, so it is important in this context for you to know what you can and cannot do. So too, when our emphasis in this Handbook is as much upon what you can do as a PCSO *without invoking your powers*, the automatic acquisition of powers when you put on the uniform and are given the Designation letter, can appear both arbitrary and contradictory.

3.3.2.1 *The reassurance of possessing the powers*

It has been argued, however, that just as a police officer has a range of powers which s/he doesn't always need to use, so a PCSO needs the reassurance of possession of the powers, even though not be called upon to use them in the normal run of duty. The powers are there in case they are needed.

> **Discussion point**
> Do you think that you need the standard powers, or would a set of specific powers tailored to the role you do, be preferable?

3.3.2.2 *Adequate training is a necessity*

There is of course a corollary to the standard provision of powers to a PCSO. This is that a Chief Constable must 'ensure that the person [the PCSO] receives adequate training in the exercise and performance of the additional powers and duties' (PJA06, PJB references Part 1, section 5(6)).

As a result, the standard training programme for PCSOs has expanded from the original three-and-a-half weeks or so to nearly seven weeks (some forces train over eight weeks, including longer modules on personal safety), to ensure that the standard powers are covered adequately before the PCSO is deployed. You can best judge whether or not the training you have received, or are receiving, or are about to receive, is 'adequate', but, as we showed in Chapter 2, and go on to show in Chapter 4 at some length, if your training is based on the attainment of the National Occupational Standards (NOS) and the core behaviours, and you carefully study the laws and powers above, you cannot go far wrong. We discuss briefly, in Chapter 7, whether these skills and competences can be taken further into a recognized national qualification or professional certification.

3.3.2.3 *Note what your own powers are in your PDP (SOLAP)*

As we have noted, there are potentially 53 distinct powers with which a PCSO could be designated, though some of them relate only to the dual function of 'Traffic Warden who is also a PCSO' (and not the other way around). Your **task**, at the end of this very brief section, is to establish in your Personal Development Portfolio (PDP), the powers with which you as an individual have been designated, and to record the nature of the training related to those powers. This will vary, evidently, from force to force, as well as from PCSO to PCSO, and so we cannot posit any standard answer to the task which will fit all circumstances (see footnote 1 below).

3.4 **Chapter Summary**

We will not conventionally summarize the contents of this chapter, which is largely geared to the referential, because we think you will use it piecemeal, dipping in and out of it when you need to check something. But we want to leave you with one important thought: **your powers are a means to an end, not an end in themselves**. Be careful how you use your powers, remembering that proportionality and necessity should guide your choice.

Notes

1 Matters have not clarified since the first edition of this Handbook was published in late 2007.

During the consultation phase of the NPIA *PCSO Review* (2008), both the Police Federation and the PCSO Staff Union Unison wanted all 53 powers to be assigned to PCSOs 'to ensure national standardisation'. Local Authorities, for their part, wanted to see powers which could impact on local issues such as 'enforcement of environmental & parking offences, but did not want [...] to add to PCSOs' administrative burdens or remove them from the streets'. The NPIA Report went on to say:

'Some forces have designated their PCSOs with all 53 powers available whilst others adopt a more selective approach. What is clear from research carried out by the Neighbourhood Policing Programme is that the majority of powers issued are seldom used, particularly when large numbers of powers are designated. There is also variation between forces regarding those powers outside the Police Reform Act 2002 that are allocated to PCSOs. Many forces have designated PCSOs as Traffic Wardens and as such [they] have a number of additional powers and a considerable amount of their enforcement activity utilises these powers.'

See NPIA, *Neighbourhood Policing Programme, PCSO Review*, (Ju
National Police Improvement Agency, available from <htt
npia.police.uk/en/docs/PCSO_Review_Final_Report.pdf>   acc........
1 May 2009, 11–12.

2 Police Reform Act 2002 (The Stationery Office (TSO)) pp 39–40.

3 Also called support staff, they were once known, dismissively and inac-
curately, as 'civilians', as though police officers were somehow members of the armed forces (the only meaningful distinction between
civilian and anyone else). Indeed, PRA02 itself continues to refer to
non-warranted staff in police forces as 'civilians', though the term had
dropped from common parlance by 2001.

4 See <http://www.opsi.gov.uk/SI/si2002/20020746.htm> accessed May
2007.

5 **ADVOKATE** stands for: **A** Amount of time under observation,
D Distance between witness and suspect, **V** Visibility at the time,
O Obstructions to view, **K** Known or seen before by the witness, **A** Any
reason to remember suspect (if only seen occasionally and not well
known), **T** Time lapse between observation and subsequent identification to the police or to the PCSO, **E** Error or material discrepancy
between the description given to the police or to a PCSO and the actual
appearance of the accused.

   This is actually not a very clever mnemonic (the 'word' is based
on a gross misspelling; the first 'A' should really be 'T' for 'time', not
'amount'; the second 'A' standing for 'any' rather than 'R' for 'remember', for example). Although this has currency in the police—principally through familiarity—we have devised a mnemonic which,
naturally, we prefer.

   Ours is **SOCRATES**, which stands for: **S** Suspect descriptors,
O Observation by witness, **C** Clarity of the witness' observation,
R Reason to remember the suspect, **A** Appearance of the suspect,
T Time elapsed between observation and identification, **E** Errors of
fact or mistakes, **S** Space (how much distance between witness and
suspect). Not as familiar, but at least our mnemonic letters stand for
something, and the word SOCRATES exists as a proper noun.

6 The 1984 Police and Criminal Evidence Act (PACE) is due for reform
and modification. A group comprising lawyers, police, the judiciary
and Home Office officials has been scrutinizing the existing provisions
of the Act for some time and are expected to report towards the end of
2009. The subsequent amended legislation may go before Parliament
in 2010, becoming law by the end of that year or early in 2011. The
intervention of a General Election may mean that this timetable is set
back by a year or two.

7 Home Office, 'Summary of Responses to the Consultation Document
"Standard Powers for Community Support Officers and a Framework
for the Future Development of Powers"' (2006) 2.

8 P Davies, *The ACPO Response to Consultation Paper on Standard Powers
for Police* [sic] *Community Support Officers and a Framework for the Future
Development of Powers* (ACPO, 2006) para. 1.1.5.

9 Police and Justice Bill (HL Bill 104) (TSO, 2006).

Chapter 4

The National Occupational Standards and Behavioural Competences

4.1 Introduction

This chapter looks in detail at what skills standards and competences you need when working as a PCSO. Most of you will undergo, or have already undergone, in-Force structured training based on the **National Occupational Standards** (NOS) as well as assessment based on behavioural competences. Specific skills training for PCSOs embraces the NOS and the behavioural competences. You are expected to keep an evidence portfolio (SOLAP) of your steady advancement towards competence, and attaining that competence, in each NOS.

4.1.1 This chapter is a reference guide, not a 'crib'

All this may sound a bit daunting and achievement may seem a very long way ahead, but this chapter guides you through what is needed and what you must learn, with plenty of practical examples and self-knowledge tests as usual. **However, we must sound one warning**: whilst we are very willing to guide and advise you through the NOS and the core behavioural competences, all the elements of which go into assessing you as competent and sufficiently skilled to perform your job well, what we cannot do is provide you with 'crib' answers. You must think, consider, assess, and record your own experiences in your **Student Officer Learning and Assessment Portfolio** (SOLAP) upon which your assessment will be based. Suppose that you are working through **Unit 2A1** in the NOS (*'Gather and submit information that has the potential to support policing objectives'*). In the chapter that follows, we will explain what you need to do to evidence your abilities in this

Standard and give some practical examples, but the first of the 'performance criteria' is

> Identify opportunities within your area of responsibility to gather information which is relevant to, and has the potential to support, organisational and policing objectives.[1]

In other words, the assessment of *your* ability to reach this Standard is to be based on what *you* identify, in *your* beat or patrol or neighbourhood team, contributing to *your* Force objectives. Additionally, it will be assessed by *your* tutors, or police officer supervisors, or team supervisors, or sergeants, or whatever oversight system your Force uses.

4.2 NOS and Associated Assessment Criteria

The National Occupational Standards are owned and developed by **Skills for Justice** (often rendered in the shorthand form of **SfJ**, though sometimes as S4J), which is the 'Sector Skills Council' for the 'Justice Sector'. This may not mean much to you at the moment, but you need to know that SfJ developed from National Training Organizations (NTOs) which used to exist as a kind of professional 'standards keeper' in many parts of the Service and Manufacturing industries. Successive surveys of 'skills at work' identified inconsistent attainment of necessary skills, patchy appraisal processes, unfair or subjective assessment of skills in some areas, and a general lack of rigour about the sorts of skills standards which people should be exhibiting in the performance of their roles.

4.2.1 NOS may change or reduce

Readers should note that, at the time of writing (mid 2009), there was much active discussion in the police about reducing the standard NOS for a police officer from 22 Standards to 9 or 10, and that, correspondingly, the existing 11 NOS for PCSOs came under similar scrutiny and comment. The consensus appears to be that the number of PCSO NOS may reduce from 11 to 5, but it is not at all certain what is to stay and what is to go, and what will be amalgamated as a kind of composite NOS.

The discussions have been in process now for a couple of years and we have seen nothing to suggest that change is imminent. This means that the NOS, as presented here, have currency in full and are continuing to be fully assessed for competence in the field.

4.2.2 How the NOS developed

The NTOs emerged from this consensus on standards, but each NTO was aligned only to its particular 'niche' until combinations of 'skills sectors' began to coalesce in the late 1990s. By 2004, our own sector, Justice, had merged the Police Skills and Standards Organisation, the Custodial Care NTO, and the Community Justice NTO, each with their separate suites of occupational standards, into one: **Skills for Justice**. From 2004 to 2006, SfJ has produced, in consultation with expert practitioners, the National Occupational Standards for PCSOs, which are broadly based on the competences expected of a police patrol, or 'beat', officer.

4.2.2.1 *The NOS will change again*

As we noted in the box above, we should not suppose that all NOS will remain fixed. In essence we will probably retain the core assessments, even if they are reduced, but the NOS and associated assessment criteria are evolving and developing all the time, and they will 'mutate' to ensure that the developing needs of PCSOs, and the communities they serve, are met in the occupational standards. And this makes sense; until 2001, PCSOs did not exist. It would be odd indeed if the needs and standards of a newly-developing body within the extended police family did not change over time. This is particularly the case if PCSO NOS advance or retreat in line with changes to policing occupational standards; in other words, it seems likely that if police NOS are consolidated and reduced, the PCSO NOS will be too. It would be a bold prophet who attempts to predict what skills will be needed in technology in 20 years' time. The point of all this is to say that, whilst we can tell you what NOS are needed now, you should not assume that these are fixed and invariable. Things will change as being a PCSO will change, and the NOS need to keep in step.

4.2.2.2 *What the NOS consist of*

Organizationally, the set-up as currently practised looks like this:

- **1A1:** Legal powers
- **1AA:** Equality, diversity and rights
- **1A2:** Communicate with communities
- **4G2:** Reducing the risks to health and safety
- **2A1:** Gathering information to support policing objectives
- **1B9:** Anti-social behaviour
- **4G4:** Administer first aid
- **2C4:** Minimize and deal with abusive and aggressive behaviour

2C2: Contribute to initial response to incidents
Contribute to planned policing operations
2J2: Present information in court
4C1: Develop one's own knowledge and practice

4.2.3 What do NOS do?

National Occupational Standards describe competent performance in terms of an individual's work; defining what needs to be achieved rather than what needs to be done.[2] This means, simply, that you do not pass or fail NOS, you either achieve the competence or you are not yet competent. This makes the NOS very flexible in terms of what you have to demonstrate or evidence about competence to your assessor. Further, the NOS can help you as an individual, and your Force as an organization, to face current challenges by ensuring that you (and the organization) have the necessary knowledge, understanding, and skills (refer to KUSAB at 2.2.3.1 above). What is more, a PCSO in West Midlands Police will be judged on the same independent and objective criteria through NOS as will a PCSO in Dyfed–Powys *Heddlu* (police). This gives a common performance benchmark across all forces in England and Wales.

4.2.3.1 *How are NOS organized?*

The whole set of NOS for an 'occupational group', in your case the PCSO, is called a **suite**. The suite is divided into individual **units** which group together the outcomes required to demonstrate competence. The whole unit then becomes a statement of that competence. It sounds complex but is not; indeed when you look at each of the NOS as we set them out later on, simplicity is actually key to understanding what is required. Each unit contains:

A **unit summary** This is not part of the standard, but it does give you a context and suggests how the unit is applied in your daily work, specifying some of the activities involved.

An example might be **Unit 2C2:** *Prepare for, and participate in, planned policing operations*, where part of the unit summary is:

This unit is about contributing to planned policing operations. The unit applies to all types of pre-planned policing operations such as crowd control, football matches and galas and the use of ANPR (automatic number plate readers) …

Elements Units are divided into **elements**. Typically there are about four in each unit, but this can vary from a single element to five. An element contains both '**performance criteria**' and '**range**'.

An example is **Unit 2C4**: *Minimize and deal with aggressive and abusive behaviour*, where there are two elements:

Element 2C4.1 Help to prevent aggressive and abusive behaviour

Element 2C4.2 Deal with aggressive and abusive behaviour

A caveat is added which says that all performance criteria must be evidenced from **direct performance** (in other words, simulation is not acceptable in this unit).

Performance Criteria* These describe what you need to demonstrate your competence. Please note that these are not merely lists of tasks to do, nor are the criteria a simple chronology of how to achieve competence.

*Just for the record, 'criteria' is plural. The singular is 'criterion'.

As an example, we can look at **Unit 2J2**: *Present evidence in court and at other hearings*, where performance criteria are specified. This is the first:

1. Consider [what is needed at court or at the hearing] and ensure that you are in possession of the appropriate notes and materials.

To record this, each of the performance criteria might be entered in a template which has an 'achieved' box and a reference with date to show when the competence was attained.

Range This defines the different circumstances in which you perform your role, and indicates how many examples are needed.

An example may be drawn from **Unit 4G2**: *Ensure that your own actions reduce risks to health and safety*, in which the **range** includes workplace policies to cover:

A The use of safe working methods and equipment

B The safe use of hazardous substances

C Smoking, eating, drinking, and drugs

D What to do in the event of an emergency

E Personal presentation

From this you can see that a single instance is never going to prove your competence. It is rather a range of activities across a spectrum that provides the necessary evidence.

Knowledge and Understanding You will remember these as the first two parts of KUSAB (see 2.2.3.1 above). In Chapter 3 we talked about the 'why?' of your powers as the vital bit about understanding. We said then that the 'how?' (skills) part would come later. Both 'how' and 'why' combine now in this part of each NOS to give assessors the opportunity to assess that **you know how to do something and you know why you should do it**. This includes the requirement that you know and understand relevant facts, opinions, theories, and principles in the particular Standard.

We may take an illustrative example from **Unit 4G4:** *Administer first aid*, in which the requirement to 'know and understand' covers:

1 Limitations and risks in applying first aid to others
2 How to detect an obstructed airway and methods of clearing obstruction
3 How to check for signs of life and for life-threatening conditions
4 Methods of CPR* and how to use [the techniques] appropriately
5 How to manage an unconscious casualty and the main causes of unconsciousness
6 Precautions to be taken when performing CPR*
7 Different types of wounds and their treatment
8 Methods for controlling bleeding
9 Signs and symptoms of shock
10 Recognition and treatment of sprains, strains, and fractures
11 Main safety considerations when dealing with burns or scalds
12 How to recognize and assess the severity and extent of injuries
13 Appropriate treatments for hypothermia, frostbite, heatstroke, and heat exhaustion
14 How to recognize and respond to local dangers and risks when dealing with casualties

*Cardio-pulmonary resuscitation.

We have quoted this list at its full length so that you can grasp the range of competences that you need to show, emphasizing once again that to achieve each NOS you have to show competence in *all* the elements listed. It is not enough to treat a scald, you must also know and understand how to do all the other things, including how to resuscitate someone, recognize and treat shock, control bleeding, and so on, through all 14 requirements for evidence of knowledge and understanding.

Evidence Requirements This describes what you need to prove, or demonstrate that you have achieved, the required competence in this particular unit or range.

This is the totality of the Unit, because if you can produce the proof (evidence) that you are competent, you can then move on to another aspect of learning. As an example, let us look at the some of the requirements for attaining competence in **Unit 1A1:** *Use police actions in a fair and justified way.* [Our additions are in square brackets.]

This unit focuses on the use of legal powers in a fair and justified way. It is a general unit and applies across the use of all legal powers (statutory, non-statutory) and procedures. This could include, for example, detention of suspects (common law).

You **must** be able to apply principles of reasonable suspicion or belief within the limits of your designated powers and role. Objective facts and information **must** support the use of reasonable suspicion or belief.

You must also be able to demonstrate the use of your legal powers proportionately and fairly. This means that you must show that you used legitimate, necessary and lawful actions in dealing with a situation. Such actions must be 'non-arbitrary' [objective, justified and intelligence-led] and 'fair' [without prejudice, bias or presupposition].

There are three elements:

1A1.1   Apply principles of reasonable suspicion or belief
1A1.2   Use legal powers proportionately
1A1.3   Use legal powers fairly

[The guidance goes on to note that the performance criteria for *each element must be demonstrated on at least three separate occasions* and makes other comments on evidencing range statements.]
Simulation is not allowed for any performance evidence within this unit.

Assembling your evidence of competence

This gives an indication of the way in which evidence must be assembled, and you will note the parameters that have been set on how evidence is to be presented. You will see further examples of this once we get into the detail of meeting the NOS later on.

You will need to approach the business of demonstrating your competence in a logical, structured, and deliberate manner. Your portfolio of written and attested evidence must reflect this organized approach; practise now getting your evidence requirements together in a clear presentation.

4.2.3.2 *The wider application of competences*

Individual units may serve to specify the performance standard needed to complete a particular task or they may be grouped together to define competent performance in a role. Your BCU Commander has a suite of Units to define his or her competences just as you do. They may be different in outcomes and levels of competence, but the essence is the same in both cases. Indeed, nearly all roles in the police service, including many of those for police staff, are now defined by NOS and core behavioural competences. They are used to assess for recruitment, selection, and promotion, and are used too as the basis of a **Personal Development Review** (PDR, what used to be called an 'appraisal') to ascertain development needs. The important point about all of this is that NOS now underpin everything we do in terms of objectively assessing whether or not we can do a particular job or role, and, by extrapolation, to help others decide whether an individual may have the potential to perform competently.

> **Discussion points**
>
> In our judgement, your competence, assessed across a range of standards, is more important than your powers, though not all will agree with us. Do you?

4.2.3.3 *Assessment*

You will be assessed, not just during your training, or during your probation, but throughout your career with the police. Why? Well, skills abrade, or wear away. Your recall of what to do may get a bit rusty if you are not performing the task on a daily basis. A line manager (supervisor or direct manager) will assess your performance against a range of tasks which will be underpinned by NOS, and the core behavioural competences, and may decide in discussion with you that you need a refresher, or an opportunity to demonstrate competence in areas where you are not currently tested but which are parts of your role. This isn't something done *to* you passively, but with your agreement and (we hope) enthusiastic participation. The technical name for this, which you will come across often, is

continuous professional development or 'CPD'. It can also be described as keeping all your competences sharp.

4.2.3.4 *How is assessment made?*

So, how are you assessed? There are several ways in which assessment may be made, and it is always helpful to discuss with your assessor which you prefer and which you are most comfortable with. That said, your assessor will want to see the full range of assessments used, even when making allowances for your 'preferred learning and experiencing style' (refresh your memory of this by referring to 2.4 above). The following are the standard assessment methodologies which you can expect to experience.

4.2.3.5 *Observation of your work activity*

This relates to the assessor observing you as you carry out your usual duties and assessing your competence against one or more of the relevant units that make up the PCSO suite of NOS. You will record the fact that you were observed for a particular task or performance criterion, and you will do it on a 'record of achievement' form, see below. The assessor who observed you will also sign the form, but that need not mean that you have attained the necessary competence, only that you were observed. The assessor may well decide that you need to try again or try something different. It will make sense for you to record that as well, so that you can demonstrate (or evidence) your improvement.

4.2.3.6 *Observation of 'products'*

This method entails the assessor looking at the end product of an activity or task. Most of the time, an assessor will not have needed to observe you doing the work which led to the end product; it is enough that you have achieved the end product, and the assessor will be able to judge whether or not you are competent. An example might be in drawing up an action plan for agreement with members of the community about graffiti. The assessor need not sit through the consultation period with community members (though that might be productive in assessing your other competences), nor observe you through the period when you were hunched over your keyboard or staring into space hoping for inspiration. The action plan itself may be enough to demonstrate that the end product entailed all the consultation and thinking time. Or it may not: the assessor may send you back to try again if the action plan does not show you to be competent in this task. You may have missed some important aspects of planning (such as identifying the perpetrators) which puts your competence in doubt. Note too that the assessor may ask you questions to confirm your understanding and to ensure that you did the task without help. These are called '**ADQs**' (Assessor-Directed Questions) and may be used to evidence your competence or your need for further development. Many of the criteria in many of the units will entail ADQs as a matter of routine. The evidence form, a copy of which you put in your portfolio once completed by your assessor, might look like the example in Figure 9:

NOS Unit	Performance
Unit 1A2: Communicate effectively with members of communities [PCSO 00122 MATTHEWS]	Criteria 1A2

Range Statement
A: neighbourhoods
B: communities of interest
C: communities of identity
Evidence needed that the PCSO has communicated effectively with members of at least TWO of the communities

Circumstances of the assessment:
PCSO Matthews was ill during the previous on-site observation. Despite the good work reports from parts of the community, I wished to test Matthews' knowledge of community tensions and to examine what has been initiated to resolve the tensions.

List of questions and student officer's response:
Q: What would you say are the principal sources of tension in this community?
A: The biggest source of tension is between the elderly residents in and around the Common and the pupils at Chesterton School: the complaints always centre on the kids being noisy and smoking outside the school, in the little hollow by Grace Way. The kids can't be seen from the school if they congregate there, but the residents can see them.
Q: Any other sources of tension?
A: There are some difficulties being experienced by the small Asian community which tends to be located around Filton Way and Morgan's Street; there have been some racist graffiti and last year there was an incident with a firework being stuffed through a letterbox, but there has been nothing recent. The Community Liaison Officer is happy with things at present. I spoke with her on my last shift on Monday 09th September at Tonchester Police Station. My notes of the conversation are in my PNB.
Assessor's note: PNB entry seen and approved. HGW

Figure 9: Sample of typical form of record of assessor-directed questions (ADQs) and student officer's answers

---

Q: What procedure would you adopt to deal with the smoking?
A: I have powers under Schedule 4 of the Police Reform Act 2002 to deal with underage smoking. Specifically, under paragraph 7, I can seize tobacco and under 7A I can search for tobacco, if I have a reasonable belief that the offenders are under 16. Additionally, under section 7(3) of the Children and Young Persons' Act 1933 I can seize tobacco from under 16s. I would have no hesitation in using any of these powers if I had reason to believe that the smokers from the school were under age, but in fact they're nearly all years 12 and 13 using Grace Way. I have spoken to them, and they say that the principal complainant is a woman who is virulently anti-smoking. This is Mrs Mellitt, who lost her husband to smoking-related diseases. I've spoken to her and she agreed that she has been the one leading the complaints. She has said that she will leave the problem to me to solve, provided that I'm not soft on the kids. I've drawn up an action plan in consultation with Chesterton School and the Residents' Action Council has also approved it. The plan is at folio 197 in my PDP, and copy-filed in my SOLAP.

Note by assessor: I have seen and approved the detailed action plan at folio 197. HGW

I now believe that this officer has demonstrated competence in performance criteria 1 and 2 of this unit. HGW

Copy provided to student on 18th September 2009 HGW

Assessor's Signature: ....…............................. Date: 16/09/09
Hans Wellertoch
PC 11287

PCSO's signature and number: ....…............. Date: 18/09/2009
PCSO 00122
Jo Matthews

Figure 9 (continued)

4.2.3.7 *Testimony*

Just as a witness statement in a court of law carries a certain weight, so in your SOLAP portfolio of evidence of your competence, a witness testimony is important. **The testimony is a written statement confirming that you have carried out a particular task or activity competently.** It must be completed by someone who knows the subject thoroughly. As you would expect, there is a form or template for witness testimony, a typical example of which we reproduce below. The person providing the testimony should look at the unit that you are working towards, and state clearly what s/he has seen you do. The person writing the testimony does not have to be an assessor, but must have specialist knowledge about the particular subject. Testimony is a useful source of evidence of your competence, since your assessor cannot be expected to observe everything you do. Note though, that in most forces, you cannot use a fellow PCSO as a witness to provide testimony. One person may witness a number of sources of evidence, and could put them all on the same form. The witness must sign the testimony.

4.2.3.8 *Content of the testimony*

We cannot prescribe what a witness should say about you in evidence but you should be aware that assessors will be looking for **balance** in the testimony, **accuracy, evidence** that the witness knew what s/he was talking about, **honesty** (you can't be expected to get everything right, and an assessor would be suspicious of someone who did), and **relevance**. Practical examples will help the evidential process and the testimony should be collected at or around the time of the action or task. It may not always be possible to get a contemporaneous (*at the time*) account as testimony, but going back six months later is unlikely to persuade your assessor of the testimony's timeliness. In this example, there is general competence, but an identified need for more practice in directing traffic, which the Police Sergeant Supervisor has picked up and noted, and which PCSO Matthews has arranged to be re-tested.

4.2.3.9 *Student officer's explanation of a process*

You might be asked by your assessor to describe how you carried out a particular action or task, or you may be invited to describe what you would do in a given set of circumstances. This method is often used to assess your knowledge (for example of the police caution or about one of your powers) or those parts of the range that might be difficult to evidence at the time. For example, your assessor might ask you to explain what procedures are involved in reporting a 'suspicious' or sudden death. It isn't always possible to produce a body on demand, so the assessor may resort to your explanation of what you would do in the circumstances. The evidence of your competence may be recorded on an ADQ form as shown in Figure 10, or as a separate entry. Either way, the evidence needs to be referenced carefully.

4.2.3.10 *Written questions*

The assessor may give you some questions in written form and invite you to write your answers; either there and then, or at your leisure. Be warned that the assessor will follow up the written questions with verbal questions when you submit the evidence: this is to ensure that

Witness Name: Jerry Bradley, Department of Transport Principal Officer, Vehicle Safety Checks Unit	PCSO 00122 Matthews J.
Reference Number WT/ 66/3/10 **Date Completed: 6th April 2010**	Other references NOS 4G2, 2C2 & 4C1

Testimony

[Note that the testimony can best be provided by a 'competent person' who has been present and who has witnessed your performance. Only if the witness is familiar with NOS standards and the performance criteria should s/he comment on whether the standard of competence required was demonstrated.]

On 30th March, from 1005 hrs until 1335 hrs, I superintended TIR vehicle safety checks on the A552 by-pass interchange with Tonchester City, supported by PC 11712 Royston and PCSO 00122 Matthews. Both officers were properly clad, properly equipped, and performed their duties with full recognition of the health and safety requirements and cognizant of the dangers inherent in stopping TIR vehicle drivers. (It was indeed fortunate that PCSO Matthews was able to speak some Italian since one of the drivers whom we stopped for defective load fastenings spoke no English. PCSO Matthews was able to explain what we were doing and secured the driver's full cooperation.) During the course of the vehicle check exercise, the weather worsened and it was PCSO Matthews who produced extra hazard warnings and parked the police vehicles appropriately to give drivers clear notice of the checks, with warning lights in operation. PCSO Matthews did not need to be instructed in doing this, and it is my judgement that the necessary competence to apply this NOS unit already exists; as evidence I point to the work undertaken by PCSO Matthews in terms of 4G2: 'ensure your own actions reduce risks to health and safety'. However, PCSO Matthews needs to rehearse the confidence of gestures designed to direct drivers into the assessment bays; at times the gestures looked tentative.

Signed (Witness)

.... Jerry Bradley, DOT Principal Safety Officer
Date 6th April 2010

Signed (Student Officer)

.... Jo Matthews PCSO 00122
Date 6th April 2010

Signed (Assessor or supervisor)

.... Khalid Trione Salim PS 9675
[note need to develop confident hand gestures for directing traffic]
Date 6th April 2010

Note by PCSO 00122 Matthews: this testimony to be filed in SOLAP at serial 225: observation by assessor of my traffic direction was arranged for Monday 19 April 2010 at 0855 (Albany Street, junction with Common Road) JBM

Figure 10: Typical example of a witness testimony form (not prescribed)

you understood what you were doing and that the written answers were your own, unaided, work. The method could be used on any of the performance criteria, but it is likely that the assessor will use the written question to test your knowledge of a process. As before, the evidence of your reply should be filed as evidence in your assessment portfolio (SOLAP), and it would help if the assessor signs the answer to show that s/he has seen and read what you have said. Unlike the ADQs, when it is the assessor's responsibility to write up the question and answer, *written answers are your responsibility.* Don't separate the answer from the question: this will look inefficient in your portfolio and may lead to such confusion that the written answer is disregarded and you will have to do the whole thing all over again.

4.2.3.11 *Projects*

These are helpful, practical ways in which a range of competences can be evidenced. The important points are that you agree the scope of the project with your assessor, its length, and when it needs to be assessed. Do not embark on an ambitious project to hit as many competences as you can or you may find yourself bogged down in detail, casting about frantically for additional range material, and running out of time to get testimony or assessor evidence. **Make sure instead that the project is small, self-contained, short in duration and able to be done by one person:** you.

An example of a project: creating a skateboard park

A sample project that meets these requirements might be to scope the cost, siting, and contents of a skateboard park on common land near a problem estate. You would need to talk to members of the community (witness testimony); ascertain what land is available (councils, borough departments, agencies, partnerships); ascertain costs of the land (Land Registry, estate agencies); identify sources of finance (local businesses, local charities, local youth groups, fund-raising activities); and purchase of equipment (local youth who will use it, other such projects, suppliers). If you undertook to do all this, you would hit a number of competences simultaneously and your performance criteria would be well evidenced. If you could get your assessor to observe you doing some of it as well, you'd end up with a useful range of evidence in your portfolio and you would have been doing your job properly too.

4.2.3.12 *Simulation and role play*

SfJ is rightly sceptical of too much role play or simulation: you do not get to be an effective PCSO by living only in a classroom or acting out scenes away from the real world. Correspondingly, there are few occasions when simulation or enactment will suffice for the NOS evidence. As you work through the NOS you will see which criteria permit simulation or enactment (role play) and which do not.

Some limited simulations are important: in first aid for example

The major area where role play and simulation *is* justified is in Unit 4G4, *Administer First Aid*, of course, because you cannot rely on simultaneous nose-bleeds or a similar series of neatly-fractured limbs, to demonstrate your cool competence. SfJ recognizes that the likelihood of your being involved in a major accident during assessment, where your first aid skills can be observed in real time, is pretty remote, even across a number of months; hence the allowance of simulation. Don't expect the same latitude over Unit 2C4: *Minimize and deal with aggressive and abusive behaviour*. There, you will be expected to do it for real.

4.2.3.13 *What happens once your competence has been assessed?*

If you are assessed as competent, the assessor signs off the relevant evidence and helps you plan for your next assessment, or any outstanding work still to be completed.

What to do if you are assessed as 'not yet competent'

If you are assessed as 'not yet competent', your assessor may ask you questions to cover gaps, or plan another opportunity for you to collect sufficient evidence, or set a date to review what you need to complete the evidence. You will be given reasonable time to amass what is needed, and it is important that you see the assessor as an objective support to you, and you should make sure that you tap into his or her expertise and experience in assessing PCSOs.

4.3 The National Occupational Standards in Detail

4.3.1 NOS 1A1: Legal powers

This section within your NOS framework looks at your legal powers and divides the use of them into three distinct sections:

- Applying principles of reasonable suspicion or belief.
- Using legal powers proportionately.
- Using legal powers fairly.

4.3.1.1 *Apply principles of reasonable suspicion or belief*

The first section within this NOS, **1A1.1**, entitled *Apply principles of reasonable suspicion or belief*, is divided into six sections, and has various range criteria. The first of these is: 'Carry out necessary checks of **information** and sources before acting on reasonable suspicion or belief'. Think about how many situations you will find yourself in where you need to check information prior to an action and what checks you could do in advance of action to ascertain the necessary information.

Discussion point

What information sources might you use to obtain information prior to an action?

Suggested answers might include the use of PNC, local police databases, colleagues, supervisors, CCTV, local residents, and so on.

Plenty of evidence in your daily duty

It therefore follows that you should be able to find plenty of evidence on an almost daily basis, especially when you consider there are three range statements: **history, events**, and **description**.

Example

Consider the following situation: you are on patrol in your area when a call comes over your radio informing you of a complaint that a car has been doing handbrake turns in a supermarket car park. Information identifying the make and colour of the car has been provided. You attend and there is a car matching that description but it is stationary. There are two people inside. You ask the control room to repeat the description of the vehicle (**description**). You speak to the CCTV operator of the car park and find out what occurred (**events**). Only then do you speak to the people in the vehicle and obtain their details. You use this new information to get a PNC check done on the vehicle and its occupants to see if there is any relevant information held—are they known? (**history**). All of this is done to ensure any subsequent actions are based on reasonable suspicion or belief. Had you challenged the car's occupants without having done some checking first, you might have got the wrong people entirely.

> Think how many red Toyotas there are, or blue Fords. Unless you have the registration plate of the vehicle in advance, you have to proceed carefully. Even with the registration, there is no immediate objective evidence that these were the culprits who had been driving without due care and attention in the car park. The CCTV and eyewitnesses will supply that information to you, and help to clinch the identity of the offender(s).

4.3.1.2 *Legal powers and procedures*

The next range criterion is: 'Exercise **legal powers**, which rely on reasonable suspicion or belief, fairly and without bias'. The range statements identified are **legal powers** and **procedures**. Therefore, when, for example, dealing with a group of under-age drinkers in a park, you are able to establish their ages and confiscate their open cans of alcohol, you are using your prescribed **legal powers** (refer to 3.2 above if you are uncertain from where these powers derive). Following local guidance (**procedures**), you tip away the alcohol from the open containers. You have obtained the evidence needed for completion of this performance criterion and the evidence would be entered in your PNB.

4.3.1.3 *Using information: history, events, and descriptions*

The third performance criterion for **1A1.1** states: 'Ensure that the use of reasonable suspicion or belief is supported by objective facts and **information**'. The range statements are again **history, events**, and **descriptions**.

Task

Take the following example, which could be used to evidence this performance criterion, and identify where the range statements could be located.

You are aware of criminal damage occurring in your area where stones have broken the street lighting and there have been reports of youths in the area with a catapult. A description of these youths has been provided. Whilst on patrol you encounter a group of youths and, whilst talking to them, you notice one has a catapult sticking out of a back pocket. Out of the hearing of the group, you speak to a colleague back at the station who confirms that these youths are similar to the ones reported by members of the public. You take their details for use in an intelligence report.

You should have identified the range statements as follows:

You are aware of criminal damage occurring in your area where stones have broken the street lighting and there have been reports of youths in the area with a catapult (**history**). A description of these youths has been provided. Whilst on patrol you encounter a group of youths and, whilst talking to them, you notice one has a catapult in a back pocket (**events**). Out of the hearing of the group, you speak to a colleague back at the station who confirms that these youths are similar to the ones reported by members of the public (**descriptions**). You take their details for use in an intelligence report.

4.3.1.4 *Applying the principles*

The next performance criterion states that you must: 'Apply principles of reasonable suspicion or belief in accordance with legislation and current policy'. There are no range statements identified and therefore this is quite a straightforward criterion to evidence. Consider the situation where you have to deal with underage drinkers. Let us suppose that they had no open cans or bottles and denied drinking, merely saying they had bought the alcohol for their parents and were walking home with it. Whilst talking to them, you smell alcohol. You decide to confiscate the unopened cans and inform the youths that the alcohol will be placed in 'found property' at the police station, should their parents wish to collect it. You have then applied 'reasonable suspicion' to the situation and used legislation and procedure to deal with the event. This will all be evidenced by PNB entries and 'found property' documentation.

4.3.1.5 *Dealing with people ethically: respect for human rights*

The next performance criterion requires you to: 'Deal with individuals in an ethical manner, recognizing their needs with respect to human rights and diversity'. This should not prove a difficult section to evidence because we hope that you would treat everyone in accordance with these principles. Your professionalism and adherence to Force policies would ensure this, as would your own intrinsic personal ethics. Therefore an example of dealing with a homeless person begging for money to acquire accommodation, might entail you enforcing local byelaws about begging, but also demonstrating that you show compassion and respect for the person who is begging (bearing in mind our caveats about beggars in the section on your powers in 3.2 above), perhaps through contacting a local housing or homeless shelter charity. Because this criterion could be one of the first you achieve, it would be counter-productive to produce a huge list of possibilities for inclusion. You will have plenty of opportunities to evidence your competence here, from very early in your deployment.

4.3.1.6 *Recording information*

The final performance criterion in **1A1.1** is: 'Record all **information** on which reasonable suspicion or belief is based correctly and within the required time'. The familiar range statements of **history, events**, and **descriptions** are used to define the nature of the evidence. Again, it will not be difficult for you to evidence this particular criterion because it could apply to any information submitted within the context of your role. Therefore, submitting any intelligence report within the required time limits of your individual Force would constitute evidence.

4.3.2 **Use legal powers proportionately**

The next element within Unit 1A1 is **1A1.2** *Use legal powers proportionately*. The first criterion is: 'Consider all options available before using **legal powers**'. This comes with two range statements **legal powers** and **procedures**. If you exercise any legal powers or procedures, you should do so only after considering other options available. We believe that this is something that should be second nature to a professional PCSO. The 'default' recourse to legal powers in all cases would make your community engagement role much more difficult and quickly alienate some parts of the community from talking to you. You are not a police officer, remember, and exercise of powers should be a last, not a first, resort.

Acquiring evidence for your portfolio in this performance criterion should be easy. If you issue a fixed penalty notice for littering (**legal powers**), then you would do so only after having asked the person to pick the litter up. The 'ticket' is only issued because the person refused to comply. Similarly if there is a local operation to deal with the dangers of cars parking on double yellow lines outside schools (**procedures**), you would first ask the offending driver to move before having recourse to other compliance measures.

4.3.2.1 *Using legal powers and procedures*

The next criterion requires you to: 'Balance the severity of the effect of using **legal powers** with the benefit being sought'. Again, this criterion comes with the range statements **legal powers** and **procedures**.

Example

Consider the situation where, on a Friday, you come across two youths in school uniform drinking cider in a public park at 1100 hrs. You know from police intelligence that there has been trouble in this park with anti-social behaviour and criminal damage, allegedly involving people from this school. You confiscate their alcohol (**legal powers**) and, in accordance with a policy arranged with the school, you take the youths home, informing the parents and the school that you have done so (**procedures**).

How do you justify balancing this severity of action with the benefit being sought?

A model response

Our suggestion is that you would say that by taking this action you have prevented the possibility of further problems occurring, such as public drunkenness and possibly criminal damage. You could also argue that, having encountered underage drinking, you could not ignore it and you had a duty of care to the youths to ensure that they got home safely. On the other hand, it might have been better to take the youths to school first, and then ascertain if their parents were at home. Since so many parents work, it is likely, even probable, that there might be no one at home in either family. If that were the case, the youths may be safer at school than at home alone. You will have to exercise your best judgement in such matters.

4.3.2.2 *Using the least power compatible with requirement*

This criterion states: 'Use the least restrictive legal powers that can be reasonably expected to achieve the legitimate lawful aim'. The same range statements apply as the previous criteria in this element.

You could use the same scenario as in 4.3.2.1 above, and evidence this criterion because the actions taken were the least restrictive available, merely the confiscation of the alcohol and the taking of the youths home or back to school. There was no recourse to requiring a name and address for anti-social behaviour or seeking police assistance to look at possible involvement with criminal damage. What was done resolved the situation (achieved the legitimate legal aim) with the minimum of fuss. Don't forget that you can use one situation or event to evidence any number of criteria, not least because this reduces the workload for you.

4.3.2.3 *Dealing ethically and respecting human rights*

This criterion requires you to: 'Deal with individuals in an ethical manner, recognising their needs with respect to diversity and human rights'. See 4.3.1.5 above.

4.3.2.4 *Keeping it in proportion*

Under this criterion you are required to: 'Use legitimate, necessary and lawful **legal powers** in dealing with a situation'. The two range statements are **legal powers** and **procedures**.

When you consider PLAN, as you should with any action, then it becomes apparent that this criterion is relevant to the *proportionate, legal, authorized, and necessary* components, and so evidencing this part of the portfolio should be straightforward. It should coincide with any exercise of powers or procedures you undertake. Arranging for the removal of an abandoned vehicle causing an obstruction would fall under the **legal powers** auspices, because the action is lawful, legitimate, and necessary to avoid a possible accident. It would also fall under **procedures** because there would be a Force or local authority protocol or policy detailing how this removal would be arranged.

4.3.2.5 *Using powers fairly*

This criterion requires you to: 'Ensure that **legal powers (i)** are directed in a **non-arbitrary (ii)** and fair way'. The range statements have four aspects—**legal powers and procedures; only aimed at those responsible; having minimum effect on those not responsible; and being non-discriminatory.**

Example

You are on patrol and have been briefed about the nuisance use of 'mini motorbikes' in your area, which have been causing alarm and distress to local residents. You are asked to provide information to any people seen with, but not using, mini motorbikes, about the potential ramifications for illegal use of the bikes as part of an overall area publicity campaign. During your patrol, you hear mini motorbikes being used in a field where you know the landowner has not provided permission for such activity. When you arrive, you see one bike being ridden whilst others are not in use and their owners are watching the one rider. After all the necessary checks, you issue the one identified rider with a Section 59 warning and provide the others with the information about what could happen if they use their bikes in such a manner.

How can this scenario be used to evidence the entire criterion outlined in 4.3.2.5 within your portfolio?

A model response

We suggest that your answer might be structured like this:

After all the necessary checks, you issue the one identified rider with a Section 59 warning (**legal powers** and **only aimed at those responsible**) and provide the others with the information about what could happen if they use their bikes in such a manner (**legal powers procedures; having minimum effect on those not responsible; non-discriminatory**).

4.3.2.6 *Recording your actions*

This criterion states that you should: 'Record any **legal powers** correctly and within the required time'. In the scenario outlined in 4.3.2.5 above, you gave the Section 59 warning (**legal powers**). You now record this act in accordance with the time constraints and also submit intelligence reports detailing those who were advised as to the proper use of mini motorbikes (**procedures**).

> **Discussion point**
>
> You could use the scenario to evidence the entire criterion. Go back through each part and see how this could be achieved.

4.3.3 Using legal powers fairly

The final part of Unit 1A1 is Element **1A1.3**, *Use legal power fairly*, and this has nine distinct parts, each with its own range statements (bracketed), as detailed here:

1. Use **legal powers** fairly and without bias, acting on reliable and objective information and observation (**legal powers** and **procedures**)
2. Use **legal powers** in accordance with current legislation, policies and procedures (**legal powers** and **procedures**)
3. Inform the **subject i)** clearly of the reason for the use of **ii) legal powers** (**suspect, witness, informant, victim,** and **legal powers** and **procedures**)
4. Check that the **subject i)** understands the reasons for the use of **ii) legal powers** (**suspect, witness, informant, victim,** and **legal powers** and **procedures**)
5. Question the **subject i)** about the circumstances that gave rise to suspicion and the use of **ii) legal powers** in accordance with legislation and current policy (**suspect, witness, informant, victim,** and **legal powers** and **procedures**)

6. Keep others appropriately informed of the use of **legal powers** (**legal powers** and **procedures**)
7. Deal with individuals in an ethical manner, recognising their needs with respect to diversity and human rights
8. Record the use of **legal powers** correctly and within the time required (**legal powers** and **procedures**)
9. Report the use of **legal powers i)** to the **relevant authority ii)** (**legal powers** and **procedures, internal** and **external**)

If ever you feel like abandoning all the NOS, remember that this one criterion, with all nine parts, can be evidenced in respect of one event. That makes the completion of the SOLAP more manageable and enables you to chart your progress effectively. So keep trying!

Example

Consider the following event and try to place **all** nine elements of 1A1.3 and **all** the range statements.

You are on patrol in a park, which has recently been designated as a 'dispersal area' (that is, an area where people are not allowed to congregate) because of problems with gatherings of youths engaging in anti-social behaviour and causing criminal damage. You receive a phone call at 1530 hrs from the park manager that he has seen some youths in school uniform who are congregating in the area. Whilst en route you receive a radio message from your Force Control Room that a person walking by the group asked them to move on, knowing of the dispersal order, and in return received some verbal abuse.

Upon reaching the group you explain the complaints to the youths, who are good-natured and amenable. You ask what the youths are doing and explain why the dispersal area exists and where it is, showing them the signs displayed in the park, and explain why the dispersal order was made in the first place. You inform the youths that you are not saying that they are responsible for anything bad but the dispersal area order applies to all. The group explains that there is nowhere else to go. You ask them what facilities they would like to have and engage in a dialogue about how this might be achieved. The group then leaves the area.

Following their dispersal, you inform the Force Control Room of what occurred, with the details, which you also enter in your PNB. You then speak to the park manager about what occurred and thank him or her for the information and explain what has happened and why.

You also speak to the person who apparently had originally asked the group to move on, ask the person for his or her version of events, and explain what had occurred and why the group was dispersed.

Upon return to your station you submit an intelligence report to the anti-social behaviour officer in charge of the dispersal area. You then arrange to speak to the school so that teachers can inform their pupils about the dispersal area in an effort to avoid a repetition of the day's events. You might think about planning to create a place in the area where young people can safely congregate.

A model response

We suggest that your answer might include the following:

The group then leaves the area. **(1 legal powers and procedures; 2 legal powers and procedures; 3 suspect, legal powers and procedures; 4 suspect, legal powers and procedures; 5 suspect, legal powers and procedures; 7).** Following their dispersal, you inform the Force Control Room of what occurred, with the details, **(6 legal powers and procedures)** which you also enter in your PNB **(8 legal powers/procedures)**. You then speak to the park manager about what occurred, thank him or her for the information, and explain what has happened and why **(3 informant, legal powers and procedures; 4 informant, legal powers and procedures; 5 informant, legal powers and procedures; 7).**

4.3.3.1 *Further necessary actions*

You also speak to the person who apparently had originally asked the group to move on, ask the person for his or her version of events, and explain what had occurred and why the group was dispersed **(3 witness/victim, legal powers and procedures; 4 witness/victim, legal powers and procedures; 5 witness/victim, legal powers and procedures; 7).** Upon return to your station you submit an intelligence report **(8 legal powers/procedures)** to the anti-social behaviour officer in charge of the dispersal area **(9 legal powers and procedures, internal)**. You then arrange to speak to the school so that they can inform their pupils of the dispersal area **(9 legal powers and procedures, external)** in an effort to avoid a repetition of the day's events.

4.3.3.2 *Summary of working through the NOS 1A1*

We have now completed **Unit 1A1** in some detail and we hope that this has shown you that the NOS are not difficult to complete. Indeed, judicious exploitation of the events you encounter on a standard, everyday patrol can make the completion of your SOLAP straightforward and much more user friendly, as well as ensuring that it becomes part of your overall learning experience. This reflective philosophy forms the basis for the completion of all the other units as well. Just remember to think about what you might need to evidence at the start of your patrol and record it as you go.

4.4 **NOS 1AA: Equality, Diversity, and Rights**

We now move on to the next unit within the PCSO NOS framework—**Unit 1AA**, *Equality, diversity and rights*. This is very similar to the previous unit, in that it should be easy to evidence as it is a 'golden thread' running throughout all your work as a PCSO.

4.4.1 **Unit 1AA.1: Foster people's rights and responsibilities**

The first three performance criteria could be completed using separate incidents/events, but in terms of completing the NOS portfolio it makes sense, both practically and evidentially, to use one event or situation to evidence several criteria:

1) Recognize a person's right to make [his/her] own decisions and acknowledge [his/her] responsibilities
2) Interpret the meaning of rights and responsibilities consistently with existing legislative framework and organizational policy
3) Provide **information**, which is up to date and takes account of the complexity of the decision which people might need to make

The third criterion comes with two range statements, **written** and **unwritten**.

Example

Imagine a resident in your area speaking to you about an instance of domestic violence, but asking that it not be reported because s/he fears this would escalate the problem. The first part of the unit has been accounted for because you are allowing that individual to make his or her own decisions. If you then decide that this knowledge needs to be made known, for example to your BCU's Domestic Violence Unit because you want expert advice, then this would be used to evidence the second part

---

(making sure, as usual, that all entries in the portfolio respect the need for anonymity, confidentiality, and *sub judice* rules). An intelligence report could be submitted detailing the information given, which expresses the person's desire not to make this official and detailing his or her fears to explain why s/he wants this. This would cover the **written** range statement. Providing the person with the details of a drop-in surgery for domestic violence, or telling him or her of charities and organizations that could offer help and support, would cover the **unwritten** part.

Don't forget: domestic violence is not solely 'partner on partner', it can include abuse of children or of elderly relatives by carers.

4.4.1.1 *Appropriate help*

The next performance criterion within this unit is: 'Give **appropriate help** to people who are unable to exercise their rights personally'. This has two range statements attached—(a) speaking on behalf of the person when s/he is not able to do so, and (b) seeking support from someone else to help in the exercise of rights.

Discussion points

Why might some people be unable to exercise their rights personally?

What benefits and/or problems could arise from helping people to exercise their rights?

Example

Take the situation of a refugee family living in your area who do not speak fluent English and who have no contact with other people from their country of origin to assist them. They might have a problem with their housing and nervously approach you at your community surgery. If you then speak to the housing association/local authority/landlord on their behalf, you are meeting this criterion along with range statement (a). If you put the family in touch with a refugee help group or community group that has access to an interpreter for their particular language or dialect, you are meeting range statement (b).

4.4.1.2 *Support, record, inform*

The next three criteria can also be bracketed together as a further illustration of the evidential value, within the context of the NOS portfolio, of events that you deal with:

5) Acknowledge and provide **appropriate support** towards the resolution of **tensions** between rights and responsibilities

6) Ensure that the necessary records relating to the promotion of rights and responsibilities are accurate, legible, and complete

7) Provide the necessary information to people who wish to make a complaint about an infringement of their rights

Criterion 5 comes with four range statements, the first two relating to the **appropriate support** portion. These are (a) **direct challenges to the people concerned** and (b) **help sought from others towards a resolution.** The two relating to the **tensions** aspect are (c) **within people** and (d) **between people.**

Task

Using the following example, place the performance criteria and the range statements so that they can be used as evidence within your NOS portfolio.

Example

At a community surgery, a couple approach you who are having problems with their neighbour over the issue of a replacement fence. They claim that the fence is the responsibility of their neighbour and is shown on their property deeds as such. This fence is in poor repair and the neighbour's dog is forever getting through and fouling their garden. They state that when they speak to their neighbours they receive abuse. The couple have resorted to chucking the dog mess back over the fence because they are fed up with this situation.

You advise the couple that throwing the mess back over the fence merely exacerbates the situation and explain that this is a civil issue and that they need to speak to a solicitor. You also advise them to contact the Environmental Health Agency, or that part of their local council that deals with environmental health issues, and offer to find out if there are mediation services available to help resolve these tensions. You make full notes in your PNR throughout

---

A model response

We suggest that your answer might include the following points:

You advise the couple that throwing the mess back over the fence merely exacerbates the situation (**5(a) direct challenges to the people concerned, 5(c) tensions within people**) and explain that this is a civil issue and that they need to speak to a solicitor (**7**).

You also advise them to contact Environmental Health and offer to find out if there are mediation services available to help resolve these tensions (**5(b) help sought from other towards a resolution, 5(d) between people**); you might intervene directly with the neighbours themselves in respect of the alleged abuse (**5, 7**). You make full notes in your PNB throughout (**6**).

4.4.2 Unit 1AA.2: Foster equality and diversity of people

This unit has five performance criteria:

1) Show consistency with people's expressed beliefs and views and acknowledge the benefits of **diversity**
2) Promote anti-discriminatory practice in ways which are consistent with legislative frameworks and organizational policy
3) Take **appropriate action** to minimize the impact of discrimination and oppression on people
4) Promote equality and diversity and seek advice and guidance when difficulties arise
5) Record information which is consistent with the promotion of equality and diversity

Criterion 1 has two range statements attached—(a) **individual and social characteristics**, (b) **values and beliefs**. There are also two range statements for part 3—(a) **challenge the source of discrimination**, (b) **seek the support of others to challenge discrimination**. See also 1.5 above, and 6.6 and 6.7 below.

Task

Rather than provide you with an example to illustrate the practicality of these issues, this time we want you to do some research on your own (some, but not all, of the answers are within this Handbook):

(a) What are the six strands of diversity?
(b) What legislation applies to each of these strands?
(c) Within your own police Force, identify the policies relating to each of these strands and where they can be found.
(d) Consider what agencies/support groups exist within your community for each of the six strands of diversity.
(e) Look at what anti-discriminatory activities are taking place in your area and consider what role you could play in promoting and upholding these.

Undertaking this within your community and within your police Force, on your own or with other colleagues, will then provide you with all the tools and information for the successful completion of this unit, and help to ensure your professional commitment to the principles of embracing diversity and promoting it wherever you are and whatever you do.

4.4.3 Unit 1AA.3: Maintain the confidentiality of information

The first performance criterion is: 'Show that **information stored** in, and retrieved from, recording system is consistent with the requirements of legislation and organizational policy'. There are two range statements attached, (a) **electronically** and (b) **in writing**.

This can be achieved by ensuring that you work within the auspices of the **Data Protection Act 1998** and the **Freedom of Information Act 2000**, in both of which you should have received training whilst on your PCSO induction course.

> **Task**
> Make sure that you are aware of the appropriate Force policies in your area pertaining to confidentiality of information.

4.4.3.1 *Maintain records*

The second criterion within this unit is: 'Maintain records, which are accurate and legible and contain only the information necessary for the record's purpose'.

This is, once again, an easy criterion to evidence since you maintain records in relation to your community engagement activities. You submit intelligence reports ($5 \times 5 \times 5$) (a reference for intelligence reports; see *Glossary*) on a weekly basis (perhaps even daily depending on the area you patrol), and your supervisor often checks these, particularly while you are new to the role. An intelligence analyst will also check these reports to ensure that they are suitable. Any problems with **legibility**, **accuracy**, or **unwanted information** will therefore be picked up during these checks. When you have a series of reports that have passed this internal quality control, you have the evidence for this criterion which your assessor will accept.

4.4.3.2 *Disclosure of information, taking precautions, sharing and handling*

The remaining criteria for this unit are:

3) Disclose information only to those who have *the right and need to know* once proof of identity has been obtained
4) Take **appropriate precautions** when **communicating** confidential or sensitive information to those who have *the right and need to know* it
5) Share information with others, in a clear and appropriate manner
6) Securely handle and store confidential records in the correct place
   [Our italics.]

Some range statements apply to 4 above: when taking **appropriate precautions** consider (a) **others who might overhear or oversee the information** and those (b) **who might access** the information. The **communicating** of this information applies when it is in any format—(a) **electronic**, (b) **in writing**, (c) **oral**.

Task

Look again at **Task 1 (at 4.4.1.2** above) regarding the neighbour dispute.

In what ways could we evidence the final four criteria of Unit **1AA.3**?

A model response

Our suggested answer to this task is that, when dealing with this neighbour dispute, you will have to speak to both parties. When doing so, you need to make sure that you do not allow the other party to see documentation relating to the others (**4 take appropriate precautions, others who might oversee the information, in writing**), and be careful what you say and where you say it (**4 take appropriate precautions, others who might overhear the information, oral**). If you provide an e-mail address for contact, ensure that you reply singly to each party to avoid the error of inadvertently supplying information to the other (**electronic**).

If you bring in a mediator to help with this dispute, ensure that the person is appropriate for this role (**3**), and share with the person the appropriate information (**5**). Ensure that all records are kept confidential in accordance with your Force policy and national legislation (**6**).

4.4.3.3 *Summary of NOS 1AA1*

You now have the tools to complete another section of your NOS portfolio and you might want to look at the information you have accumulated to see where it could be used to evidence further criteria.

4.5 **Unit 1AA2: Communicate Effectively with Members of Communities**

If there were one unit in the entire PCSO NOS portfolio that encompassed the rationale for being a PCSO, it would be Unit 1AA2. This sits at the heart of the PCSO experience and should *never* prove to be a difficult one for you to complete and evidence. The very concept of neighbourhood policing or community engagement is what brought the PCSO into being. It is possible that this unit could be evidenced from one event but it is far more likely that you will gather evidence over an extended period, utilizing experiences that occur as your involvement in the community follows an organic pattern of engagement.

4.5.1 **Performance criteria for 1AA2**

These are the performance criteria for Unit 1AA2:

1) Develop and maintain effective channels of communication with individuals in the **communities** within your local area
2) Deal with individuals in an ethical manner, recognizing their needs with respect to diversity and human rights
3) Ask individuals for advice and information when you are not sure how their religion and other aspects of their identity might affect police practice or behaviour
4) Make yourself accessible to individuals by your manner, work style, and the way in which you respond to enquiries
5) Give individuals the opportunity to check their understanding of information you provide
6) Encourage individuals to ask questions and give them appropriate, accurate information in response
7) Monitor the understanding of individuals and modify your own way of communicating to improve understanding

There are three range statements for the **communities** aspect of criterion one—(a) **neighbourhoods**, (b) **communities of interest**, (c) **communities of identity**.

Discussion points

What do you understand to be the difference between neighbourhoods, 'communities of interest', and 'communities of identity'?

Are these definitions fixed for all communities?

What difference in approach by a PCSO may be needed in recognizing these differences between community types?

Task

Within your own geographical patrol area, can you distinguish between neighbourhoods, 'communities of interest' and 'communities of identity'? What contacts do you, or the Neighbourhood Policing Team, have within each of these communities? If there are recognizable gaps in your knowledge about any of the communities that exist in your area, how can you gain a better understanding?.

This could be one of the first tasks you seek to complete when new to your BCU area. It does not have to be solely for your portfolio but should form the basis for engaging with your area in all its diversity. Because of the number of possible permutations involved in this Task, we do not provide a definitive answer to it. Instead, we'll try to show you how you would differentiate between the categories, by developing our own example (below). There are no tricks to completing this element. Since you do not have to complete the portfolio in a linear fashion, you can add evidence as it accumulates. In other words, you should decide when and what to evidence.

Example

You are working in an area in which a Sikh 'gurdwara' (place of worship) has recently opened. Within the local community, there have been some concerns over the difficulties in parking at certain times, apparently because of the services or events that are being conducted at the gurdwara.

You arrange to meet the local residents' association to talk to them about the situation and the problems that they perceive are being caused (**1 (a) neighbourhoods**). Many of the businesses on the street opposite the gurdwara have also raised the issue of parking and so you arrange to

---

meet the local business association (**1 (b) communities of interest**). Before attending these meetings, you speak to the BCU police community liaison officer (CLO) and ask for details about the gurdwara and the person responsible for running it. Armed with this information, you arrange to meet the 'granthi' (reader of the Sikh services) and the committee responsible for overseeing the gurdwara (**1 (c) communities of identity**).

You also meet with the Sikh community representatives and introduce yourself, explaining your role and the part you can play in community engagement within the whole neighbourhood (**2**). You outline the problems the wider community has raised in relation to parking and seek clarification on which days services are held, what future important events may be planned, and other information concerning use of the gurdwara and any likely impact on the larger community (**3**).

Based on the information you obtain, you report to the various meetings and establish a regular meeting schedule with the residents' association, the businesses and the gurdwara (**4**). These meetings become part of your routine and develop into regular consultations where people can raise specific concerns about community issues (**5, 6, and 7**). Such meetings also allow you to engage fully with the community and establish links between groups. In turn, this allows you to develop systems for communication and dialogue to ensure that you link in with the community completely, not just with 'single issue' groups limited by their identity or interest.

Task

Look again at this scenario. What other NOS units could be evidenced in respect of this situation?

A model response

Our answer would be to include:

Unit 1AA: *Equality, diversity and rights*
Unit 2A1: *Gathering information to support policing objectives*
Unit 4C1: *Develop one's own knowledge and practice*

This is not a definitive answer but we mention it because it shows how the completion of the portfolio can be made easier by linking units in respect of one event or incident.

Commentary

What this Unit shows is the need for the PCSO to be proactive in seeking to engage with differing groups within his/her area. There is no advantage in waiting for these diverse elements to seek you out; it would be more beneficial for all concerned if you make the initial contact. This could ensure that relations start on a positive footing. If you identify communities that you know little about, then the onus is on you to ensure that you build up your knowledge to an appropriate level. This allows engagement to occur on a level that potentially benefits all. As with the gurdwara example (for which, of course, you could substitute any special interest group), you can then develop systems of communication so that these positive relations can be sustained. You might also try to get various groups together so that discussion of community issues need not be confined to geographical areas or communities of interest and identity, but could be used for the benefit of wider society.

4.5.2 Proactivity: taking yourself to the community

This is not something that you can make happen overnight and you will need to work on it as a central part of your role. Fostering better relations between the police and various groups, as well as between the groups themselves, could have important consequences for policing that area. Being proactive in taking yourself to the community, rather than waiting for an event to throw you together, may be another way in which we can distinguish between a PCSO and a police officer.

4.6 Unit 4G2: Ensure that Your Own Actions Reduce Risks to Health and Safety

This unit has two distinct elements, which seek to identify and reduce the health and safety risks that exist in your workplace or within your role. Read what we say in 5.7 below about **dynamic risk assessment** so that you are familiar with both the process and the reasons for doing it. Several of the elements in this NOS will be particular to your own individual workplace and the role you will be expected to perform in your area, and so this section needs to be general rather than specific. As with the other NOS sections, it is about highlighting potential avenues for exploration rather than providing actual events.

Discussion points

What health and safety training were you given on your PCSO training course, or since?

Do you have access to handouts, booklets, advice sheets, or course notes that may help you to complete this unit?

Were you informed of the main legislation in relation to health and safety?

If the answer to any of these questions is no, try to find out which legislation is applicable in your workplace (a good place to start this research would be the website of the Health and Safety Executive at <http://www.hse.gov.uk>)

4.6.1 Hazards and risks in the workplace

The first element of this unit is **4G2.1**, *Identify the hazards and evaluate the risks in your workplace*. This is divided, for ease of understanding, into seven distinct performance criteria; but, as always, they do not have to be evidenced individually. It may be that one event can be used to evidence several simultaneously:

1) Correctly name and locate the person(s) responsible for health and safety in the workplace
2) Identify which workplace policies are relevant to your working practices
3) Identify those working practices in any part of your job role, which could harm you or other people
4) Identify those aspects of the workplace, which could harm you or other people
5) Evaluate which of the potentially harmful working practices and the potentially harmful aspects of the workplace are those with the highest **risk** to you or to others
6) Report those hazards which present a high **risk** to the persons responsible for health and safety in the workplace
7) Deal with hazards with low **risks** in accordance with workplace policies and legal requirements

The last three criteria have five range statements attached to them—(a) **use and maintenance of machinery and equipment,** (b) **working practices which do not conform to established policies,** (c) **unsafe behaviour,** (d) **accidental breakages and spillages,** and (e) **environmental factors.**

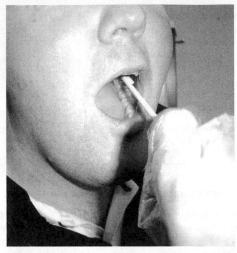

(Photograph by David Morgan)

Photograph 5: DNA swabbing

4.6.1.1 *Evidencing your responses to risk*

The first four criteria could be evidenced within your initial period on station or BCU. It may be that you receive a welcome pack or a structured introduction which could identify most of these points, such as who the nominated health and safety representative is (**1**), or how to access your Force policy on health and safety (**2**). Given that your 'workplace' includes your patrol area and community, these too can be taken into account when completing this section. If a formal risk assessment (see 5.7 below) has been completed, then this could serve as substantive evidence for your portfolio (SOLAP) because it would identify potential risks for the PCSO role (**3**) as well as physical or environmental risks in the area itself (**4**). If your arrival in your BCU does not include a structured induction, then you could still meet the performance criteria by finding out for yourself the answers to the questions, remembering of course to commit the answers to some form of evidential trail. You could also use an ADQ format to relate to each of the four aspects.

4.6.1.2 *The remaining criteria to evidence your responses to risk and hazard*

The final three criteria, along with the five range statements, require a substantive approach by you so that they can be evidenced fully.

Perhaps the best way to achieve this is to look at the range statements and identify ways to evidence them. They can then be 'bolted on' to one of the remaining three criteria.

Task

Identify within the PCSO role, or within the wider policing or community context, potential evidence for these range statements:

(a) **Use and maintenance of machinery and equipment**
(b) **Working practices which do not conform to established policies**
(c) **Unsafe behaviour**
(d) **Accidental breakages and spillages**
(e) **Environmental factors**.

A model response

Our suggested answers to this rather complex task would include the following:

(a) **Use and maintenance of machinery and equipment**—using a police vehicle; using a mountain bike as part of your role; operating mobile CCTV equipment; operating computers.
(b) **Working practices which do not conform to established policies**—working at night in a poorly lit area.
(c) **Unsafe behaviour**—incidents where the behaviour of others has led you to call for police assistance.
(d) **Accidental breakages and spillages**—photocopier toner; chemicals; fuel on the road after an accident; blood and broken glass.
(e) **Environmental factors**—specific hazards in your area, such as rivers, ponds; heights; unsafe buildings; building sites, derelict areas and poorly lit areas.

Conclusions about responses to risk and hazard

Therefore, if you were asked to operate any equipment and you then read the health and safety instructions pertaining to the equipment, you would satisfy criterion **5** and range statement (**a**). Calling for assistance when confronted with a potentially dangerous situation, such as a group of underage drinkers refusing to hand over their alcohol, would satisfy criterion **6** and range statement (**c**). If you were on the scene of a road traffic collision, noticed that there was fuel on the road, and arranged for it be cleaned off or hosed down, you would have evidence of criterion **7** and range statements (**d**) and (**e**).

In all of these situations, you would need evidence to show that the criteria had been met before ticking them off your portfolio checklist.

4.6.2 Reducing the risks to health and safety

The second element of this unit is **4G2.2**, *Reduce the risks to Health and Safety in your workplace*, in which the onus on you switches from merely identifying risks to actually reducing them. This element has eight criteria:

1) Carry out your working practices in accordance with legal requirements
2) Follow the most recent **workplace policies** for your job role
3) Rectify those health and safety risks within your capability and the scope of your job responsibilities
4) Pass on any suggestions for reducing risks to health and safety within your job role to the responsible persons
5) Ensure that your personal conduct in the workplace does not endanger the health and safety of you or other people
6) Follow the **workplace policies** and suppliers' or manufacturers' instructions for the safe use of equipment, materials, and products
7) Report any differences between **workplace policies** and suppliers' or manufacturers' instructions as appropriate
8) Ensure that your personal presentation at work
   • ensures the health and safety of you and others
   • meets any legal duties
   • is in accordance with **workplace policies**

4.6.2.1 *The criteria in detail*

The four criteria in which workplace policies are identified, 2, 6, 7 and 8, have five range statements attached—(a) **the use of safe working methods and equipment**, (b) **the safe use of hazardous substances**, (c) **smoking, eating, drinking, and drugs**, (d) **what to do in the event of an emergency**, and (e) **personal presentation**.

Your evidence must show how you reduced risk to health and safety

In order to evidence these criteria and range statements, the emphasis is on showing how you reduce the risks to health and safety and so these actions by you need to be clearly identified in the evidence provided. For example, in making sure that your day-to-day activity is in conjunction with your risk assessment, you can evidence criterion **1** and if you encounter a situation in which the risk assessment needs to be updated, you are satisfying criterion **4**. The evidence may be in the form of a report that you wrote and submitted, copied to your portfolio (SOLAP).

Examples of how you amass evidence

In the previous unit, we used the example of calling for police assistance in a situation that had gone beyond your personal ability to control. This example would also serve to evidence criterion **3**, because the PCSO role is clearly defined as non-confrontational and therefore dealing with non-compliance would necessitate police assistance. If you could also show that your behaviour in this situation was calculated to *avoid* confrontation, for example you showed politeness and respect, you were non-judgemental and so forth, then criterion **5** could also be included.

4.6.2.2 *The remaining four criteria*

This leaves four remaining criteria and the range statements to complete before the unit can be evidenced.

Task

Use the following statements to identify which remaining criteria and range statements they could evidence (our suggestions are in bold after the statement).

(i) As a PCSO, you always go on patrol wearing your personally issued and fitted stab vest in conjunction with your Force's policy. [**Criterion 8, range statements (a) and (e)**]

(ii) A member of the public reports that there is a fire in a building nearby. You immediately use your radio to seek fire brigade assistance. Upon reaching the building, you use the correct fire extinguisher having read the instructions. [**Criteria 2 and 6, range statements (b) and (d)**]

(iii) You find a hypodermic syringe in a children's play area. You cannot leave it there and so pick it up safely and arrange for its disposal at a nearby doctor's surgery. [**Criteria 2 and 6, range statement (b) and (c)**]

(iv) When using your police-issued mountain bike, you request a load vest rather than a belt because it is proving difficult to cycle with a belt. [**Criterion 7, range statement (a) and possibly (e)**]

These are by no means the only evidential interpretations of the scenarios and you may feasibly have a different set of answers. These too can be used for NOS completion, provided always, of course, that they can be evidenced.

4.6.3 Linking health and safety with other NOS

This section has looked at the health and safety aspects in isolation but you will be able to evidence them in conjunction with an incident or event that has already been used for another NOS.

Task

Go back through the NOS sections covered thus far and use the scenarios to identify where health and safety criteria could also be evidenced.

We won't provide answers to this task on this occasion because it should now be self-evident that most tasks that you will be required to undertake have a health and safety element to them. We urge you not to use them merely to tick off a section of your NOS portfolio; rather you should make sure that dynamic risk assessment becomes an integral part of your daily activity.

4.7 Unit 2A1: Gather and Submit Information that has the Potential to Support Policing Objectives

This unit should not prove difficult to evidence since it involves competence in one of the key aspects of the PCSO role: gathering and disseminating community intelligence. The expression, often over-used but still appropriate, is that *the PCSO is the Police Force's 'eyes and ears'*. The PCSO is more than that, particularly in terms of engaging with a community and problem-solving within that community; however, it is still the case that, by being available to people, and representing, paradoxically, a non-threatening (even a 'quasi-official') police presence, you will become party to some very worthwhile community intelligence. This unit also requires you to be familiar with the fundamentals of the **National Intelligence Model** (NIM) which underpins this whole objective, and which is discussed in 4.8 below.

4.7.1 **Performance criteria for 2A1**

This unit has nine performance criteria:

1) Identify opportunities within your area of responsibility to gather **information**, which is relevant to, and has the potential to support, organizational and policing objectives
2) Use appropriate ethical and lawful methods to gather **information**, obtaining any necessary authorizations before doing so
3) Conduct an initial evaluation and risk assessment in respect of the **information** and take any necessary immediate action
4) Record **information** accurately using the appropriate systems and protocols
5) Deal with individuals in an ethical manner, recognizing their needs with respect to race, diversity, and human rights
6) Maintain the security, integrity, and confidentiality of the **information** and source during the gathering, handling, recording, and storage of the **information**
7) Ascertain whether the provenance of the **information** is known and record it accurately in the correct manner
8) Apply the correct grading to the **information** using recognized methods
9) Submit the **information** promptly and in an appropriate format to the appropriate person or department using recognized methods of submission

All the above criteria, with the exception of 5, come with two range statements regarding the source of the information— (a) **directly received** and (b) **indirectly received**.

Discussion points

What is the difference between information directly received and that which is indirectly received?

Under what circumstances might you obtain these types of information?

What consideration would you give to these two distinct forms of information gathering?

How might they be handled differently?

Example

Let us consider the situation in which a PCSO is working in his or her community and has organized a fortnightly drop-in surgery at the local library. (**Performance Criteria 1 and 2** have been achieved because the surgery has been identified as a means of garnering community intelligence and it has been authorized.)

During this surgery a member of the public comes in and reports that an individual, whom she names, is spraying racist graffiti on the walls of the local mosque. The person rather anxiously says that she does not want to provide a formal statement because she is fearful of potential reprisals and intimidation from the people involved. The PCSO writes down the information provided in the **PNB** (**4**). He/she asks the person how she knows that the information is correct and she comments that, when looking out of her window, she saw the graffitist spraying the words (**7**—establishes the provenance of the information). The **PCSO** has the address of the witness and knows that her house indeed faces the mosque (**3**—evaluating the information to see if it could be correct). The **PCSO** explains that this information will need to be passed on to the police intelligence team and allows the person to read the **PNB** entries to ensure that they are accurate. The **PCSO** explains that the intelligence will include the caveat that the person wants to remain anonymous and does not want to make a formal statement (**5 and 6**). On returning to the police station, the **PCSO** completes an intelligence report before finishing the shift because s/he recognizes the importance of the information received. S/he grades the information appropriately, based on knowledge of the person who provided the information, and ensures that this is copied to the relevant officers (**8 and 9**). This would be an example of **directly received** information.

If the information had been passed on about a third party witnessing the same event, who wanted anonymity but felt you should know the details, then this could be **indirectly received** information. This would be graded differently to take into account that this is *hearsay* (see also our discussion at 7.5.1 below).

Discussion points

What is *hearsay*?

How does this differ from the intelligence received in the first scenario (that is, directly and verbatim from the witness)?

Is it still valuable intelligence?

Check in the **Police and Criminal Justice Act 2006**, where hearsay receives some legal sanction.

4.7.1.1 *Links with the National Intelligence Model (NIM)*

As we noted at the outset of this NOS, the unit needs to be read in conjunction with 4.8 below, which goes into more detail about gathering intelligence, assessing it, and the use of the National Intelligence Model. The **NOS** also requires you to make sure that you know the correct intelligence reporting procedures for your Force. It will become evident to you within a couple of weeks of working in your community, what varied forms of community intelligence you will be party to. That is why we say that evidencing this unit should not be difficult for you.

Contributing to the intelligence 'picture'

The key point to remember with intelligence is that you might think you are submitting a trivial piece of information, but to the intelligence analyst working on the bigger picture, it may be the final piece needed to make sense of a situation. You will soon receive feedback as to the usefulness or otherwise of the intelligence you submit.

4.8 An Aside—the National Intelligence Model (NIM): Intelligence-gathering and Intelligence-led Policing

What is intelligence and what has it to do with policing? This section steps away from the National Occupational Standards for a moment, to discuss what is meant by **intelligence**, the **NIM**, and **intelligence-led policing.** We feel that it is important to include this explanation and commentary, because you will come across many references to the subject, both written and verbal, in the course of your work; and you may well be tasked to obtain local intelligence with an assumption that you know what is wanted and how you should obtain it.

4.8.1 Is your police force intelligence-led?

A word of warning first, perhaps. You may well be a member of a police force which has never fully embraced intelligence-led policing. Equally, you may have joined a Force in which intelligence-led policing is alive and well. Again, you may be in a police force which is struggling to accommodate a number of policing models, from intelligence-led policing through problem-orientated policing to neighbourhood reassurance or community-focused policing (we discuss all these briefly at 7.6 below). These models are not necessarily incompatible, but may have different emphases, depending sometimes on the 'mission' articulated by your Chief Constable, sometimes through the priorities established by the Police Authority, or, sometimes, as a result of the kinds of crime which dominate the BCU or Force. In this section, our focus is exclusively on the role and function of intelligence about crime and criminals.[3] Some commentators on intelligence in policing can obscure rather than clarify the issues, giving rise to comments like this: 'Intelligence-led policing has been defined as the gathering of information designed for action' (Grieve in Harfield et al, 2008:4). Yes, quite. But so is a train time-table. Resounding clichés of this kind do not take us very far forward, and instead we might construct for ourselves some idea of what 'criminal intelligence' is about.

4.8.2 Defining intelligence and knowledge

Let us begin by trying to build a straightforward definition: *what distinguishes ordinary information from intelligence, when it is about crime?*

4.8.2.1 *The nature of information*

You will be used to accessing all sorts of sources of information, from reference books to searches on the internet. You rightly expect most information to be freely available; you would expect to be able to find out a fair bit about the police force you have joined or are contemplating joining, for example, and to be able to find out what is involved in becoming a police officer. However, information about crimes and criminals is not normally easy to obtain in advance of the commission of a crime. Using Chapter 8's fictional Tonchester setting as an example, it is fair to say that few criminals announce to the world at large, let alone to the police, that they will carry out muggings for I-Pods and 'Blackberries' in The High in Tonchester on Friday afternoon between 1515 and 1625 hrs, or that they will announce that a group of armed robbers will hold up the Tonford Mutual Building Society at the corner of Bumble Close and Pasture Walk on Monday 22nd at 1106 hrs. Those criminals who do signal their crimes in advance may do it vaguely, getting tanked up on 'alcopops' in advance of a fist fight on a Saturday night, for example; or indirectly, the loner who has no 'previous' for sex offences; or in a way which does not come to the previous attention of the police, such as a muttered threat of violence in a pub or club.

4.8.3 Need to know

Criminals actually spend a lot of time preventing information about their activities from leaking out. They often apply strictly the principle of '*need to know*' far more rigorously than most police forces, in our experience, by not confiding any details of planned criminal activity to anyone not directly implicated in the planned crime (we touch on this briefly at 7.3.3.2 below). This often extends even to immediate family members and long-established friends.

4.8.3.1 *Careless talk can get you nicked*

Criminals know that loose talk, or wagging tongues, will eventually find an appreciative audience at the local police station, and unpleasant surprises in the form of arrests *in flagrante* (at the scene of the crime in commission of the criminal act) await those who do not keep their plans to themselves.

4.8.3.2 *Intelligence about crimes and criminals*

This may suggest to you that **criminal intelligence** (*information about what is planned or intended in terms of crime*) is hard to come by. It is. But that doesn't mean that it is impossible to obtain or that it is hopeless trying to penetrate the intentions of known 'lifestyle' criminals. The information may not be complete, in fact it seldom is, but indications here and suggestions there, linked with some definite facts somewhere else (such as may be obtained from covert surveillance, see below), might add up to a positive indication that a crime is planned. So this may help us to build the first part of a definition when we say that:

> Criminal Intelligence is information obtained about criminal intentions, which criminals do not want known.

Key questions in criminal intelligence

In other words, criminal intelligence can be '*secret*' in the sense that a criminal does not want to let it be known. The key questions will be: What is going to happen? When will it happen? Where will it happen? Who will be involved? What will they do?

Who or what is the victim or target? How do the criminals expect to get away with the crime? How long has this been in the planning? What is the expectation of profit? (If the crime has already happened, valuable intelligence can be indicators or information about who did it and why—this is particularly applied to stranger violence, such as rape, murder, or assault.) Sir David Phillips, pioneer of intelligence-led policing in UK policing, describes this sort of information as 'a distillate of meaning' (Harfield et al, 2008:89).

4.8.4 Crime types

You can see that we are mostly assuming that the crime in prospect is **acquisitive**, that is, a crime which makes money, such as theft, robbery, embezzlement, defrauding, deceiving, illegal importing, drugs smuggling, or people trafficking; the commission of the offence is intended to make a profit for the criminals. This is not always the case, of course. Some criminal intelligence can be about **violence**, the activities of gangs to eliminate rivals, pithily described by the police as '*bad on bad*'; about the **discouragement of others**, rife among rival brothel-keepers and pimps in the sex trade, for example; or about **maintenance of position**, where no one is allowed to come in on an established criminal's 'patch', for instance. We can therefore add a little more to our developing definition:

> **Operations to disrupt criminal actions, or mounting an operation after a crime has been committed to expose the offenders, using covert methods and based on intelligence, is called intelligence-led policing.**

We mean by this that, because the criminal will not willingly give up the secret information about what he or she plans, or has already done, in the commission of a crime, police forces have to devise ways in which the information—partial or incomplete, as we have said—is to be obtained. It is worth noting that 'intelligence-led policing' as a concept is slowly giving way to a more general term: **knowledge-based policing**, which makes use of *all* sources of information about crime and criminals, including that which is openly and publicly available. However, we are here concerned with obtaining special criminal information which is held secretly by others. We will look briefly at some of methods of obtaining this information below. In the interim, there is another important principle about intelligence which we need to discuss.

4.8.5 Assessing intelligence

Weighing and evaluating the intelligence, giving it a context, linking it with other known intelligence, adding in facts such as the replacement of items, the previous history of known offences and offenders (the '*modus operandi*' or characteristic, 'signature', activity, of the criminal), together with analysis of things like 'hot spots' and 'hot victims', where similar crimes are geographically or socially concentrated, leads to **assessed intelligence**. Intelligence which is not assessed is often of limited value, or is bitty and fragmented, or is simply misleading. This is why the intelligence assessment activity is sometimes compared to completing a jigsaw: the fitting together of apparently unrelated pieces of information is a skilled activity undertaken by a trained analytical researcher, often not a police officer.

4.8.5.1 *Completing our definition of criminal intelligence*

So, when in the NOS we talked about you submitting an intelligence report on something you learned, it is important to distinguish that piece of the jigsaw from the larger picture.[4] The final part of our definition might now look like this:

> **Intelligence which is assessed and evaluated has value; it is the basis for police operations.**

In other words, all the contexts, additions, other snippets, and analysed facts are brought together and an assessment is made. This is where your bit of reporting finds its context. What we can now offer, in effect, is a working definition of the practical use to which intelligence is put in a policing context (edited for style and content):

> **Criminal intelligence is secret information obtained covertly about crimes and criminals, which is sanitized, assessed, and evaluated in order to mount police operations to disrupt, frustrate, or bring to justice, those involved.**

This isn't the official, approved intelligence-led definition, it is our own, but it shows you the difference between 'ordinary' information and intelligence, it describes what is involved in building an intelligence picture about crime and criminality, and it shows you the value of intelligence in how '*the battle is the pay-off*' when a police operation is mounted successfully. You may not have the complete picture as a PCSO (indeed, you may only have a very small part) but at least you can see how the operation in which you are involved was conceived and developed.

4.8.6 Examining the National Intelligence Model (NIM)

We now need to look at the model which lies behind most intelligence-led policing. It is the **National Intelligence Model** (NIM), of which Figure 11 is an example :

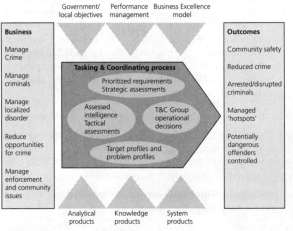

Figure 11: Simplified diagram of the National Intelligence Model

It is important to note that most police forces use the NIM (all officially have the model) but sometimes the way in which it is used varies from force to force. Given that what we are going to describe may not be exactly what happens in your Force, please note that we will be discussing the **typical use of the NIM** rather than force-specific use.

4.8.6.1 *Interpreting the NIM*

You 'read' the model from left to right. Note that the primary determinants are **managing crime, criminals and disorder** of all kinds, together with crime reduction and community issues (which includes enforcement, such as curfew orders and summonses). The outcomes are controls on these things, i.e. **reduced crime, controlled criminality** (including through arrest and disruption) **and disorder, controlled offenders** (particularly the potentially dangerous) and **managed hotspots**.

Tasking and coordinating

In the middle is the engine of the Tasking and Coordinating Process, the T&C, which in turn is affected by government and local **objectives** and targets—as we discussed earlier— management of police **performance**, and the use of the business excellence model. The T&C Group uses **analytical products** (your 5x5x5 report, assessed and evaluated and put with other pieces of the jigsaw); **knowledge products** which include what we know about the type of crime, the place where it happens, the victims of the crime, and the MO of prolific or repeat offenders; and **system products**, which include Force and national criminal databases and intelligence 'traces', criminal records, past crimes, hotspots, and so on.

Strategic and tactical intelligence, plus profiles

These lead to **strategic assessments**—determining what is important in the longer term, and **tactical assessments**—determining what we are going to do about the problem now. Finally, the Tasking and Coordinating (T&C) process, bringing together all the **intelligence and knowledge resources** within the context of the assessments, produces **profiles of the targets** for operations together with **profiles of the problems** faced by the BCU.

4.8.6.2 *Practical example of the use of the NIM*

This may all seem a bit abstract and theoretical, so let us populate and describe the whole process using a real-life example.

(Photograph by Bryn Caless)

Photograph 6: Wrecked car

Example

Your town has been plagued by volume crime (**Government objective**) involving thefts from vehicles, mostly private cars, but also thefts of tools from vans and some quite brazen thefts from lorries and larger vans outside transport cafes ('**hotspots**') or when parked on the dual carriageway lay-bys (**crime, criminals and disorder**). Local opinion is fuelled by criticism in the district newspapers and by a vociferous campaign led by highly-vocal local councillors. They have pressured the BCU Commander, who in turn has asked the T&C Group to come up with solutions (**local objectives**). You were told by a local resident that at least three local youths had been seen to be suddenly 'in the money', wearing expensive clothes, flashing banknotes, and living well beyond their normal unemployment benefit. Another person, a parent concerned that the three youths were exercising a bad influence on her daughter, suggested to you that the youths were stealing from cars and passing the stolen items to Billy Parker, a dealer and would-be antiques trader who organizes weekly boot-fairs in the summer months at the back of the market near the river (**knowledge and analytical products**).

You pass this information to your BCU Intelligence Unit as a 5x5x5 report (remembering to put a sanitized copy in your portfolio ...) and think no more about it. Meanwhile, your snippet, with the names of the suspects, joins other intelligence (**assessed intelligence**) to form an intelligence package, which is then presented to the T&C Group at its weekly meeting (**prioritized requirements**). The requirement then is made of BCU source handlers to get more information, and you are also tasked to go and get more detail from the original sources of information. You do this and submit another 5x5x5, but you are still unaware of the general interest which this has generated. The **assessed intelligence** is added to what the BCU knows about volume crime thefts from motor vehicles and a number of names are added to the list of possible suspects (**knowledge products**). Billy Parker, who has a criminal record for theft and minor drugs-dealing (**system products**), is placed under surveillance. The T&C Group, chaired this time by the BCU Commander, authorizes a covert operation to monitor Parker closely (**T&C Group operational decision**). He is caught in possession of stolen goods, arrested, and charged. Some of those on the list of suspects are arrested and questioned. (One agrees to become an informant and we deal with her later.) The focus of the police operation is against Parker and the route for the stolen items to be turned into cash (**managed hotspots**).

From this, the police learn about Henry Wood, an apparently respectable property dealer who lives in a large detached house in the smart residential area of town, and who seems to act as a conduit for Parker's 'fencing' of the stolen items, but Wood is selective: only the best quality items are accepted by him for sale elsewhere. Intelligence suggests that he is commissioning some thefts 'to order', which means that Wood lets it be known what he wants to be stolen and then waits for it to materialize. This intelligence is added to other traces and a new operation is ordered, this time with Wood as the focus (**business excellence model, disrupted criminals**).

The outcome a few weeks later is that Parker pleads guilty, is sentenced to 18 months, and the youths are given community orders of varying lengths (**outcomes: potentially dangerous offenders controlled, reduced crime, controlled criminality, community safety**). Press and media coverage is generally complimentary and the BCU Commander looks happier than for some time (**performance management**). Eventually, the plaudits find their way to you too, and you remember to let your original sources of information know the outcome.

4.8.6.3 *The use of intelligence to disrupt crime is open-ended*

This example has shown you the NIM process from start to finish, but we have made it deliberately open-ended. We wanted to suggest to you that linkages such as those between Parker and Wood often occur in criminal investigations, and a man like Wood, outwardly conventional and law-abiding, might never have come to notice had it not been for the spate of vehicle-related thefts bringing pressure to bear on local priorities in crime fighting. He was the end of one part of the investigation, and the beginning of another. Your information also played its part, so we hope that you're feeling pleased with yourself.

Criticisms of the NIM

You should not suppose that we accept the NIM as some sort of Holy Grail of criminal intelligence. It is not. Indeed, some commentators have drawn attention to potential pitfalls, such as this from Clive Harfield: 'The greatest vulnerability of the NIM is its exposure to the possibility that the processes could be followed and the various tick-boxes achieved without intelligence-led policing actually happening' (Harfield et al, 2008:2). This describes a mechanistic approach to criminal intelligence which defeats the whole purpose and point of painstakingly acquiring usable information in a criminal context. It has actually happened in police forces across England and Wales, and in some has tainted the notion of intelligence-led policing. Be aware then that some of your colleagues may be sceptical of the NIM's efficacy, if it has not been properly utilized in the past.

Task

To keep you sharp, take the following crime types and apply the NIM process to them in a simulated T&C Group played by you and your colleagues (refer to the map of Tonchester in Chapter 8):

- **Muggings of students from the FE College in Anchor Way for MP3-type players**
- **Apparent targeting by thieves of electrical goods stores in Albermarle Street**
- **A series of handbag snatches in the Victoria Centre**
- **A rise in violent assaults using knives in the 'clubbers' district' of Pennsylvania Street and Underwood Lane**

Can you think what these criminal incidents might have in common?

A model response

These incidents seem to us to be of a type which would generate much local unease, build pressure on the BCU Commander, and lead to media coverage, with possible criticism and unwelcome headlines. Three of the incidents involve violence, and this may make people feel unsafe. The fourth incident, targeting the electrical stores, is more marginal, but the store owners will certainly put your local force under some pressure to deliver counter-measures. The item which will get the most coverage is likely to be the handbag snatches in the 'safe' environment of the Victoria Centre, with plenty of visual imagery of distressed shoppers and angry residents. In other words, the element that all the criminal incidents have in common is that your BCU (and hence you) will come under pressure to deliver an outcome which (a) controls the crime and (b) makes the community feel safer.

4.8.7 Other aspects of intelligence and crime: criminals, informants, and source handlers

We have some more parts of the intelligence scene to cover before we return to the NOS, but you may well be asking at this point why we are spending a fair bit of time and space on one aspect of policing, rather than covering, say, community focused policing as well. Our answer to this is in two parts: first, the thrust of this entire Handbook is about community policing and your role, as a PCSO, in the neighbourhood police team concept, so a few pages on intelligence-led policing is not disproportionate; secondly, we have commented throughout the NOS discussions on your role as local 'eyes and ears'.

Giving you the proper context for intelligence, and its undoubted contribution, among other things, to a reduction in crime, seems to us a sensible course of action. It gives a rationale for you to pass on what you learn locally and shows you how operations (in which you may play an active part) are conceived, developed, and mounted in your BCU. Reasons enough, we suggest, to turn now to look at **informants** and **source handlers**. One caveat: these are hugely complex areas of modern policing and we can only skim the surface. Look for more detail in the Bibliography but better yet, go to your local Intelligence Unit and talk to the people there about what they do.

4.8.7.1 *Informants*

The police and other law-enforcement agencies usually call an informant a **CHIS**, which stands for Covert Human Intelligence Source. Criminals give informants less neutral names such as 'nark', 'snout', and 'grass'. Because informants, or CHIS, give information about crimes and criminals, it follows that they are themselves usually involved in, or party to, criminal activities. Most of the time, ordinary people don't come across criminal information of high and immediate value; the police rely instead on 'participating informants' (sources of information who are themselves involved in crime) to give intelligence of operational use. This is not to downplay the value of intelligence from the community, because this can often be very useful in building a picture of criminal activity and the prevalence of crimes.

4.8.7.2 *RIPA 2000 (the Regulation of Investigatory Powers Act)—governing the use of informants*

The real distinction is that criminals will know more about crimes in prospect than members of the public; it is therefore the former upon whom the police must concentrate. The police use of informants is governed by the **Regulation of Investigatory Powers Act 2000**, known colloquially as '**RIPA**', which lays down procedural rules for recruitment of CHIS, their 'handling' and use, and their reward. There are especially stringent rules for the use of juvenile informants (for obvious reasons; the opportunity to exploit a young person unfairly is high). When the police identify a suitable informant (or have one volunteer his or her services to the police), there has to be **authorization** from the Force, usually through a designated superintendent, before an approach or recruitment is made. Such authorization normally lasts a year and may be inspected by a nationally appointed **surveillance commissioner** who will determine whether the case is properly justified and run. Some forces have their own internal scrutiny of CHIS and CHIS handling through an Operational Security Officer (**OPSY**).

4.8.7.3 *RIPA governs covert relationships*

This may seem a bit rarefied to you, since as a PCSO you will not be employed in the handling of CHIS. However, you need to know that RIPA governs covert relationships to obtain criminal intelligence and that you cannot cultivate anyone as a CHIS on your patch without authority. This does not mean that people can't tell you things, of course. It means that you can't recruit a criminal informant to work for you for money without going through the proper procedures. You are far more likely to find that you receive 'lifestyle' intelligence about criminals living on your patch or snippets about who is up to what and when. All this is worth reporting, but it is only subject to RIPA procedures if you cultivate someone deliberately to provide you with criminal intelligence. Such people do exist, of course, and it is just about feasible that you might get a volunteer. If you do, don't be tempted to run the CHIS yourself. You don't have the extensive training involved in being a professional source handler[5] and you would be falling foul of RIPA in any case. Make sure that you report any approach, and you could then be instrumental in setting up a first contact between volunteer and potential police handler. Don't get too excited though; there is often a considerable gap between the first tentative shufflings of contact and the engagement of a paid informant.

4.8.7.4 *You may contribute intelligence but you don't need to know the bigger picture*

Another point to make is that, even if a contact made by you is developed into a CHIS, you are not likely to know much about it. You don't have any **need to know**, do you? Unless something really drastic happens (such as the urgent need for exfiltration of a CHIS because of a life-threatening situation), you will be kept out of the developing intelligence picture and the relationship will be handled exclusively within the intelligence unit in your BCU, or rarely, for sources with especially good or very sensitive access, from a central team at Headquarters.

'Sanitizing' intelligence

The intelligence obtained from a CHIS is passed to the BCU's Research and Development Unit, which combines the report with other pieces of intelligence (like a snippet which you have provided) and the report will be **sanitized**. This means that any feature which might identify the source(s) of the intelligence is removed. The essence of the intelligence is not changed or modified; only its context or circumstances are disguised. The resultant report will also be assessed. As we saw earlier, this means that the intelligence will be given meaning, and the access, reliability, and provenance of the source will be designated (through the 5x5x5 system of evaluation).

4.8.7.5 *The intelligence 'package'*

The resultant combination of the sanitized intelligence, analysis, assessment, and evaluation makes up an **intelligence package** which, as we have seen, is presented to a T&C Group. Thus, we have essentially come full circle: secret criminal intelligence is gathered, reported, assessed, analysed, sanitized, combined with other information, given a context and an evaluation, is presented to an operational planning group, and helps to determine policing operations against crime and criminality. We could express the intelligence 'cycle' in a *'virtuous circle'* diagram as shown in Figure 12 below.

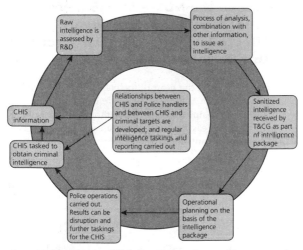

Figure 12: The 'virtuous circle' of intelligence, from tasking to operation

Want to know more?

We are about to return you to consideration of the National Occupational Standards following our aside into the shadowy world of criminal intelligence. For those of you who are interested in exploring this murky subject a little further, good texts include: Kleiven, M 'Where's the intelligence in the NIM?' (2007, International Journal of Police Science and Management, Vol.9, No.3), P Hanvey, *Identifying, Recruiting and Handling Informants* Home Office Police Research Group, Special Interest Paper Series 5 (1985); and T John and M Maguire, 'Rolling out the National Intelligence Model: Key Challenges' in K Bullock and N Tilley (eds), *Crime Reduction and Problem-Oriented Policing* (Willan, 2003). A good general text is Tim Newburn's Handbook of Policing (Willan, 2003), in which Nick Tilley's essay 'Community Policing, problem-oriented policing and intelligence-led policing' is outstanding. There is also the quirky *Handbook of Intelligent Policing; Consilience, Crime Control and Community Safety,* edited by Harfield, C., MacVean, A., Grieve, J., and Phillips, Sir D (2008, Oxford University Press).

4.9 Back to the NOS—Unit 1B9: Provide Initial Support to Individuals Affected by Offending Behaviour or Anti-Social Behaviour

This NOS unit goes to the heart of the public perception of the justification of the PCSO role. It therefore has significance far beyond the mere completion of a NOS, although this should be one that is relatively easy to evidence because you will spend a lot of time dealing with anti-social behaviour.

Discussion points
What is anti-social behaviour?
What form could it take?.

4.9.1 The origin of the PCSO role is in countering or dealing with anti-social behaviour

This facet of the PCSO role is also very much one which the government had in mind when it responded to public pressure to create the role. Think back to the recruitment campaign of 2006 and you will see that tackling anti-social behaviour was very prominent in the literature and in the images of PCSOs which were promulgated in the advertisements. It could also be that when you arrived on your BCU, this too was accompanied by a media push and among all the fanfare about you and what you were going to do, there would have been much about dealing with nuisance behaviour.

4.9.2 NOS 1B9: Looking in detail at dealing with anti-social behaviour

This Unit is divided into two **elements**:

Element 1B9.1: Provide initial support to individuals affected by offending behaviour or anti-social behaviour.

Element 1B9.2: Assess with individuals their needs and wishes regarding further support.

We will look at each element in terms of the performance criteria and range statements and consider one example of how the elements could be evidenced. This example, or pointer, will use youth nuisance as the initial anti-social behaviour factor but it is important to recognize that **anti-social behaviour is not the sole preserve of young people**. This though is the 'spin' that provokes the majority of media coverage, where repetition often combines the two factors, youths and anti-social behaviour, in the public perception of the problem.

Discussion points

Why do the media focus on anti-social behaviour in respect of youths only?
To what extent do you perceive this to be a link?
Are we less tolerant of different patterns of behaviour today?

4.9.3 Giving support to affected individuals

The first element is **1B9.1**, *Provide initial support to individuals affected by offending behaviour or anti-social behaviour.*

It has nine **performance criteria**:

1) Communicate with individuals in a manner and at a level and pace, which is consistent with [what you know of] their preferred form of communication, manner of expression, and personal beliefs and preferences

2) Encourage individuals to communicate [with you] through [your use of] appropriate body language, position, tone of voice, and active listening

3) Explain clearly the [Force]'s confidentiality policy, [noting] who will have access to information provided by individuals, [and] how information will be recorded and stored

4) Encourage individuals to express their own views about their immediate needs

5) Give initial **support** in a manner appropriate to individuals' immediate needs and your role

6) Seek advice and support from an appropriate person as soon as possible, if you are unable to meet individual's needs or are unsure about the action that you should take

7) Explain clearly to individuals the range of services available from your [Force]

8) Provide individuals with clear and accurate details of how to contact you and your [Force], and other agencies that may be able to assist

9) Make accurate, legible, and complete records of the individuals' immediate needs and the initial support provided, in accordance with [Force] policy on the recording of information

NB: the generic performance criteria refer to 'organization' rather than Force; and the whole is a little oddly expressed, probably because it is a direct 'lift' from weakly-written police guidance. We have tried to clarify the meaning of each criterion by adding words, where appropriate, in square brackets.

Performance criterion 5 has four range statements attached to the **support** element—(a) **information**, (b) **practical assistance**, (c) **empathy, reassurance, and understanding**, and (d) **safety and protection**.

4.9.3.1 *Elderly neighbours feeling intimidated by youths—an extended example*

Let us consider the following example and suggest where the performance criteria and range statements could be evidenced.

Example

You receive a call from a local resident who states that her elderly neighbours living on a social housing estate are fed up with the local children kicking a football into the neighbours' back garden and then running in and out, uninvited, to collect it. You are given a contact number for the couple and ring them to offer advice and support. They tell you that they are concerned about you coming round to see them, because it may lead to intimidation if the youths believe they are 'grassing them up' to the police. You therefore arrange to meet them at a surgery you run at the local library (**1**).

When you meet the couple you explain who you are and what you can do in relation to the problems they may be experiencing (**3**), as well as allowing them to explain how they feel about the situation (**2** and **4**). You tell them that you need to take notes about the information provided but that the notes are for internal use only (**9**). Having been apprised of the situation, you provide the necessary support in these circumstances and provide reassurance that the situation will be dealt with (**5 (c)**). You ask the couple to keep an 'events diary' so that they can log all the incidents that occur and the times and descriptions of those involved (**5 (a)**). In response to their concerns about their garden you explain about the local crime reduction initiatives (**7**) and arrange for locks to be fitted to their gates and a free alarm fixed to the shed (**5 (b)** and **(d)**). At the end of the meeting, you provide the couple with your contact details and explain the situations in which they should contact you direct (**8**). After the meeting, you make an appointment to see the local housing department to inform them about the relatively minor anti-social behaviour and invite officials to consider a joint problem-solving approach, particularly in relation to tenancy agreements (**6**).

Discussion points

What other NOS could this example be used to evidence?
What other advice could have been given and what other agencies could have been consulted?

4.9.4 **Helping people with support**

The second element in this unit is **1B9.2**, *Assess with individuals their needs and wishes regarding further support*. It also contains nine performance criteria:

4 The National Occupational Standards

1) Encourage individuals to express their own views and feelings about their needs
2) Gather information from individuals about their needs in a manner which is sensitive to their situation and feelings
3) Enable individuals to explore fully the nature and extent of their needs
4) Help individuals to identify for themselves which of their needs are priorities and to explore what would help to address them
5) Explain clearly to individuals the range of **support and other services** available from your [Force] and other agencies that may be able to provide relevant services
6) Encourage individuals to express their own wishes and preferences about how their needs should be met
7) Discuss and agree with individuals their **need for further support**
8) Seek advice and support from an appropriate person if you are unsure about the action you should take
9) Make accurate, legible, and complete records of individuals' needs and wishes, agreements reached with them, and the resulting action taken, in accordance with organizational policy on the recording of information

Criterion 5 comes with six range statements relating to **support and other services**—(a) **information**, (b) **practical assistance**, (c) **counselling and emotional support**, (d) **safety and protection**, (e) **medical help**, and (f) **help with media attention**.

Criterion 7 has four range statements associated with **need for further support**—(a) **no further support needed**, (b) **providing support directly to individuals**, (c) **seeking information and support from other agencies on individuals' behalf**, and (d) **individuals seeking support from other agencies**.

4.9.4.1 *Problems with a neighbour—another example:*

If we now choose a different example, we can show you how some of the second element aspects could be evidenced.

Example

You receive a call from a local family who are having problems with a neighbour, which has resulted in a very difficult atmosphere between the two households. You arrange a meeting to see the family at a neutral venue, so that they are not seen by their neighbour to be speaking to a police representative (**2**). At the meeting, you encourage the family members to provide all the details they see as being relevant (**1**), as you seek to

---

gain an understanding of their view of the situation (**3**). You explain to the family that you will be taking notes, but go on to say that the notes are confidential and they can read what you have written if they wish (**9**).

The family explains that this whole episode started with their complaint to their neighbour about the noise levels coming from his house late at night, especially at weekends. The family explain that, following their complaints, the neighbour has made a point of increasing the noise, has verbally abused them, and has started to throw his rubbish into their garden. They are now fearful about leaving their house and this has started to affect them; particularly their younger children who have trouble sleeping. You ask the family to identify which of these problems they feel needs to be addressed first and they tell you that it is the noise that bothers them the most (**4**). You also ask the family for suggestions as to how they feel this could be best achieved (**6**). During the meeting, you speak by phone to a contact at the environmental health office about options so that the advice you give can be authoritative and specialized (**8**). You provide the family with the contact details of the local environmental health officer, explaining what services are provided in relation to noise abatement and neighbour disputes (**5 (a)**) and tell them that you are willing to arrange for the officer to meet them at one of your surgeries, thus sustaining anonymity and confidentiality (**7 (c)**). You encourage the family to keep an incident diary of the events and also provide them with details of a local victim-support scheme that could help with the family's emotional problems resulting from this dispute (**5 (c)**), and explain that the family would need to seek a referral from a GP for this (**7 (d)**). You provide the family with your direct contact details (**5 (b)**) and explain in what circumstances they should contact you and in what circumstances they should contact 999 direct (**5 (d)** and **7 (b)**).

Discussion points

How could the remaining range statements be brought into this little case study?

What other factors would need to be considered if criterion 5, range statements (e) medical help and (f) help with media attention were applicable?

4.9.5 Links to other NOS

This NOS unit sits at the centre of the PCSO experience. **1B9** also has links to other NOS units and so there is the potential for lots of evidence building, but it should not be approached solely within this narrow scope. Look again at the performance criteria and consider the impact that successful implementation of each of these areas would have on victims of anti-social behaviour. The

PCSO is listening, encouraging, reassuring, supporting, providing practical help, liaising with other agencies, implementing, leading, suggesting, discussing, assessing, and so on.

4.10 An Aside—the 'Golden Hour' of Scene Preservation and the 'Continuity of Evidence'

The term 'golden hour' is in frequent use among police officers and you will often hear it applied to the immediate aftermath of a crime scene or to the first report of an incident. **It means that the time immediately after first police arrival at a crime scene or incident is of vital importance for the preservation of evidence.**

Traces of physical evidence may still be very fresh (footprints and fingerprints, for example) and people's recall of events may be clear and focused. Sometimes, poor management of a crime scene can mean that evidence is lost or obliterated (for example by rain washing away bloodstains), that material can be carelessly imported into a crime scene from outside, and that slight traces (such as when the offender leaned against a parked car nearby) may be lost for ever, because they were never properly noted in the first place.

4.10.1 *First officer attending*

You are often going to be the first officer attending (*FOA*) a crime scene, because you are the one on patrol to whom members of the public will come to say that something somewhere is not quite right. It may be that no one has seen the occupants of No 42 for a week, or it may be that a neighbour reports hearing screams, or someone may report a broken window or forced door. There is an expectation of, and an obligation on, you that you will get right the police response and any subsequent investigation, because you did the correct things in the correct sequence at the outset. That makes this section of enormous value to your credibility, so learn it well.

Let us look at a case study of how **not** to manage a crime scene.

4.10.2 First on the scene

Consider the following: you are on routine patrol when an agitated postal worker tells you that there is something wrong at a house around the corner. You accompany this person to the premises, a semi-detached house with a longish drive which has shrubs on either side. The postal worker shows you that when she attempted to put letters through the box, she met an obstruction. When she stooped and looked through the letter box, she could see someone slumped on the floor in the hall and what looked like blood on the stair carpet behind. What do you do?

Case Study

You are a solidly built person, and so you shoulder-charge the door which, at the third attempt, gives way and splinters around the lock. The door crashes inwards, dislodging whoever was behind it. You are just in time to catch an expiration from the slumped body, which is now, of course, a corpse. In the hallway it looks as though there is blood everywhere, because some of it is sticking to your shoes, but, pausing only to check for signs of life on the body behind (now actually under) the front door, you rush upstairs to check if there is anyone else in the house. There is no one in any of the bedrooms but someone has evidently been sick in the bathroom. Feeling slightly green, you use the shower head to flush away the debris from the side of the bath before resuming your search. Coming downstairs at speed, you slip and cannon into the postal worker who had come nervously over the threshold and was standing at the foot of the stairs, and the pair of you end up in a welter of arms and legs in the front room, where you notice that there is glass all over the floor. You ask the postal worker to sweep it up (mindful of the health and safety of others) while you search the remaining rooms downstairs. Pausing only to use the downstairs loo (well, it has been quite a day in one way or another), you open the back door and check the back patio. Only a few muddy footprints there, probably from the children playing outside. Back in the kitchen, you notice that there is a knife missing from the large wooden rack and you walk back to the front door to look at the body. Sure enough, there is the knife sticking out of the dead person's chest. You pull it out to check that it is in fact the missing knife. (It's OK, you were wearing gloves.) Now is the time to let Force Control know what is happening, so you phone in, using the phone conveniently located in the hall, to let them know, in some excitement, that you've come across your first suspicious death. 'Why is it suspicious?' you are asked. 'Because of the corpse and the blood', you reply. 'How do you know it's blood?' asks Control. 'It's red, still wet and sticky', you reply drawing your thumb across a splash on the wall above your head. 'Someone will be with you in about twenty minutes,' says Control, 'meanwhile, get the place cordoned off.' Not having any tape, you use a ball of string from the kitchen to close off the front drive to the house and wait for reinforcements (pausing to let the postal worker out of the cordon; she walks away with a cheery wave). You fish out your PNB while you are waiting, and chat amiably with some of the neighbours.

4.10.2.1 *Outcomes*

You might be lucky enough only to be sent for retraining after this, but the greater likelihood is that you and the police will be parting company in short order. You have done nearly everything wrong that you could do, and you have not done what you should have done.

> **Task**
> Consider and list what you did wrong in the scenario, and explain what you should have done.

A model and comprehensive response

Our answer is long and complex, for reasons which will quickly become apparent. Although we have greatly exaggerated the errors in this scenario, none of the individual actions which we itemize is particularly uncommon. Even experienced police officers can make a mess of a crime scene if they don't think before they act. In the list which follows, we have put the **identifiable error in the left-hand column** and the **proper course of action** (which you should have followed) **in the right-hand column**. We hope that you agree with our divisions, but by all means use any disputes as a discussion point with your colleagues.

Errors	Remedies
Breaking down the door—the splintering and bits of door have now been added to the crime scene inside, contaminating it (and you).	Find another route in which will not wreck the crime scene within.
'Expiration' from the (now) corpse—perhaps literally the last gasp. Although you have an absolute duty to preserve life and limb, that does not include crashing through doors on top of people. Of course, saving life takes precedence over any other consideration, but that doesn't give you licence to wreck the place.	It is possible that the victim was still alive. Having found another route into the building which did not compromise the victim, you might have been in a position to render first aid in a life-saving measure. Unlikely, but possible.
Blood in the hall sticking to your shoes	You should not have entered the crime scene without some form of protection: in your rush to enter, you should not

Errors	Remedies
	neglect to put on surgical gloves. You should have been aware of the possibility that the blood could be infected and you should have taken precautions for your own safety. You don't know at this stage whether all the blood is from the same source (it might be that of the victim and assailant mixed together).
Body under the door—irrevocably contaminating the crime scene (who knows what you have obliterated by causing the heavy front door to crash on the corpse, and who knows what you have imported from outside?).	Had you come by a different, non-invasive or non-contaminating route, you might have been able to check the victim for signs of life without treading blood everywhere. You might have spotted the knife earlier too.
Rush upstairs—actually better to check the ground floor first.	You don't rush anywhere at a crime scene, you proceed steadily and methodically. You should be thinking too about a common approach path (CAP) to avoid any cross-contamination.
Flushing away the vomit—(by the way, you are still spreading bloody footprints everywhere).	Body fluids can be a bit off-putting but you should **never** destroy potential evidence in this way. You don't know whose vomit it is (it might be the assailant's) and at this stage, you don't know if it will help the forensic investigation or not. Preserve it and note it, are the key actions for you.
Coming downstairs at speed	See above; don't rush anywhere on a crime scene.
Crashing into the postal worker	The postal worker should not have been there (an additional potential contaminant) especially since she is unlikely to have received crime training or be used to rather gory scenes of crime. You should prevent anyone else coming into the crime scene until colleagues arrive (the exceptions are paramedics to save life, or Fire and Rescue to extinguish a blaze or make safe).

Errors	Remedies
	Had you not been rushing and had the postal worker not been present, there would have been no accident.
Gross contamination of the crime scene—caused by falling on the postal worker and rolling over the glass in the front room.	In addition to what we have said above, actually coming into contact with another (ungowned and unprotected) person on the scene will merely intensify the contamination of the scene. The glass in the front or sitting room might indicate a point of entry or the scene of a struggle. Either way, rolling in it doesn't help, and will, of course, smear or obliterate any forensic traces on the glass surfaces and wreck any 'pattern of fall' of the glass fragments.
You ask the postal worker to sweep up the glass—thereby destroying any potential evidence completely.	Leave things as they are. If broken glass is a health hazard, draw it to the attention of those who join you, but the scene must *not* be touched or altered in any way until a Crime Scene Investigator (CSI) has completed his or her work.
Using the downstairs toilet	How do you know that this is not a site for the recovery of evidence? You should not touch or *use* anything in a crime scene.
Ignoring the muddy footprints outside	How do you know that they belong to children? They might be relevant to the crime scene, and you should assume that they are and take steps to preserve them, such as covering them with a box or positioning a chair above them. If the weather is cold, don't worry but if it is wet you must do what you can to try to preserve the prints until a CSI can get a cast of them. Take care as you go outside: you'll need a CAP there too.
Walking about the ground floor	You should stick to one CAP. The CSI will do the forensic examination of the rooms, not you. You should merely note the missing knife from the kitchen in your PNB and draw it to the attention of the CSI when s/he arrives.

Errors	Remedies
Taking the knife out of the body	**Never** touch anything which might be the murder weapon and especially do not remove it from where it was first found. The fact that you have gloves on is irrelevant: *you should not touch anything in a way which might damage potential evidence.*
Letting Control know	You should have done this before you entered the premises, and you should have been keeping them up to date throughout.
Dialogue with Control … using the phone in the hall	If the dialogue is as reported, then Control staff may gain redeployment along with you. More importantly, you should not use a telephone within the crime scene premises, for the same reasons of contamination which apply to not using other things on the premises. If you do not have a Force radio, you should have a 'job' mobile. If none of these things, get to a landline outside the crime scene or use someone else's mobile phone until someone with a radio arrives.
Drawing your thumb across the blood	The fact that you know the blood is still wet and sticky means that you have touched it. **Don't**. Never smear a blood stain in this way—especially as it is a high blood splash (above your head). Analysing 'blood spatter' is an important forensic technique because it gives an indication of the force used and the point of attack, among other things.
Cordoning	No harm in using string if you don't have cordon tape, but probably better not to use it—especially as you had to take it from the house. If you don't have cordon tape about your person, wait until it arrives in the kit carried in a police car. Meanwhile, closing external doors and preventing immediate access to the crime scene is more effective than trying to make a physical barrier (you'll only have to remove the string when the CSI and other officers come anyway).

Errors	Remedies
Letting the postal worker go	You should be taking evidence statements and recording the personal particulars of any witnesses in your PNB. For all you know to the contrary at this stage, the postal worker might have done the deed, and at the very least she is a material witness who can describe—partially—the crime scene before you blundered into it.
Chatting amiably with the neighbours	Fine if you are on a conventional patrol to engage with the community in this friendly way, but you are at the scene of a murder, and you should be taking statements, questioning the neighbours about anything they may have seen or heard, and taking down their personal particulars in your PNB. *Being professional is what this is all about*, and you are utterly amateur in the left-hand column; properly competent in this column.

4.10.2.2 *Locard's 'principle of exchange'*

A pioneer in forensic science, Edmond Locard (1877–1966), believed that material from a crime scene would be on the suspect, and material from the suspect would be at the crime scene. This is often rendered as **'every contact leaves a trace'**. It is a principle rather than a scientific law, but you need to know that in forensic investigation, *'transfer' is used as a demonstration of contact*; practically putting Locard's Principle in reverse. Such contacts include **'traces'** (paint, hairs, fibres, blood), **'impressions'** (fingerprints, footprints, tools, keyboards), and **'intangible data'** (such as that on computer hard drives, disk, or mobile phone data). This in turn raises the question of 'uniqueness'.

Things we use develop unique characteristics

We are familiar with the concept that each of us has individual fingerprints or that our DNA profiles are unique (except those of twins), but much other forensic investigation is based on a similar notion that things acquire uniqueness (or 'individualization') through use. The keyboard used to type these words will have different 'impressions' from those on your keyboard, because of the way that my fingers hit individual keys and because the keyboard is in my house and not in yours. The untested implication behind all this is that no two things can be identical (except at the particulate, molecular, or atomic level). That means that paint flakes from your car found against the shattered tree in someone's front garden raise the likelihood that your car hit the garden owner's tree (proving that you were driving the car at the time is more difficult, but you see the point).

'Leaps of faith' in forensic science

Scientists describe belief in the Locard principle of exchange and in the principle of the uniqueness of things as '*leaps of faith*' because they cannot be disproven scientifically, but that debate has not yet reached the criminal justice system, and is therefore unlike to delay us in the assumption that forensic evidence is often compelling.

4.10.3 The 'golden hour'

We began by calling the period when a crime scene is discovered and support is summoned as the 'golden hour', noting its importance in the preservation of evidence. It is unlikely actually to be an hour unless the crime scene is in some remote place which is difficult to access, such as a mountainside or deep in a forest.

4.10.3.1 *Locating resources and coordinating support*

Your early reporting of a possible crime to your Force Control is very important, because the allocation of resources calls for appropriate judgement and understanding of all the available facts. Otherwise, you might be supported by a dog team when what you really need is an armed response unit. So too, there might be need for coordination of other services and contributors (such as Transco for a gas leak, heavy building equipment from civil engineers for a collapsed road, commercial, RAF, or other police force helicopters for wide area searching, and so on). You can't do that, it has to be coordinated by the BCU Command or by Headquarters—especially in the invocation of *military aid to the civil power* (MACP), when anything from a unit of Royal Engineers with bridging equipment, to specialist Arctic-trained soldiers may be needed for a specific operation. The rule is therefore to **keep Control informed**.

4.10.3.2 *Dos and don'ts at a crime scene*

So, what should you do, and what should you not do, at a crime scene when you are the FOA? You saw with our scenario that rushing in and blundering about is likely to be counter-productive. **Your first duty is to preserve life and limb**, so you have to enter the crime scene itself if there is the remotest possibility that you could intervene to save someone's life. Even if there is evidently a dead body at the scene, it is not for you to decide whether life is extinct or not. A CSI of our acquaintance once tried to argue that life was extinct because the 'body' was a skeleton, but even this was deemed rather to be the province of a 'suitably qualified medical person'. **Your second duty is to preserve evidence**. You should, in order, do the following:

- Ensure safety for you, anyone in the area, and anyone following you into the scene.
- Check the building or area for anyone vulnerable (remember that children can squeeze into very small spaces).
- Make a note of anything material which you see (possible murder or assault weapon, marks on a polished surface, broken windows, signs of forced entry).
- Make a sketch in your PNB of what is where, including the position of any body or victim, extensive bloodstains, and so on.
- Establish a **common approach path** (CAP) which does not impinge on any visible physical evidence (but be prepared for the CSI to change it if s/he thinks it necessary to do so).
- Talk to and record the particulars of any witnesses or people in the vicinity who might have information of use to an investigation.
- Secure the approach to the crime scene, with cordon tape to mark the 'exclusion zone' if you can, or by using your authority if not, perhaps by closing doors and gates leading to the scene. Remember not to attach cordon tape to any potential source of material evidence, nor to anything which may have to be moved (such as a car or gate).
- Recce for, and report, a suitable **RV** (meeting) point for the support which is on its way. That RV should be big enough to accommodate vehicles and enable them to turn around, and should be far enough from the crime scene to avoid contamination. In an urban setting, a pub car park or public car park may be suitable. If not, move the cordon outwards (it can always be tightened afterwards). In a rural setting, the nearest large area of hard-standing (such as a farmyard) may be suitable. Try to avoid fields unless absolutely necessary: in heavy rain such places rapidly become quagmires. Finally, where you can, try to make the CAP on firm ground, not

grass or earth, as this will minimize the likelihood of cross-contamination.

- If you can, make further notes in your PNB about what you are doing and why—this will be relevant if matters come to court and for your duty statement, though we accept that you are likely to be pushed for time. Write up your notebook as soon as you can thereafter and certainly before you go off duty.

- On a related topic, you will need to note in your PNB to whom you handed control of the crime scene and when, in order to preserve the continuity of evidence, and so that the Force can ensure that there is an auditable trail from your arrival to the closure of the crime scene.

4.11 Unit 2C4: Minimize and Deal With Aggressive and Abusive Behaviour

This is another unit that has genuinely wider significance for the PCSO role and the context of community engagement in which it resides. This unit looks at aggressive and abusive behaviour and considers how to prevent it, as well as dealing with it. It would be naive to think that you will not encounter such behaviour on the streets wherever you work. The potential for members of the public to react negatively to you or your actions exists whether you work in a socially and economically deprived inner city or in a leafy, affluent suburb. Therefore, this unit has some very real learning potential because it helps to demonstrate ways in which you may seek to lessen abuse or aggression.

Discussion points

Where in your community do you see potential for aggressive or abusive behaviour to occur?

What actions can you take to prevent this behaviour?

Can such actions be anticipated?

4.11.1 Dealing with aggression and abuse

During your training for the PCSO role, you would have been given advice about and practice in dealing with situations involving aggression and abuse. These form the backbone of your response to such circumstances and can be used within the NOS unit to demonstrate a successful completion of the criteria.

> **Task**
>
> What elements of your training could be utilized when dealing with a member of the public who is abusive or aggressive?

These are the tools and skills you would use to deal with hostility:

- **Officer Safety Training**—you will have been taught techniques to protect yourself from assault, as well as ways to disengage from dangerous situations. We hope you refresh these skills regularly.
- **Personal Protective Equipment**—such as your stab-proof vest.
- **Radio training**—how to call for assistance quickly and what information is crucial when making the call.
- **Patrol techniques**—knowing where you are at any time, knowledge of the area and some of the problems that could occur.
- **Communication techniques**—how to talk to people and, just as importantly, to listen to them. You could use 'Betari's Box' as a reminder of how to communicate with people:

- **Disengagement**—it could be appropriate for you to remove yourself from that situation if you feel that your health and safety is being threatened.
- **Mediation techniques**—you may feel confident enough to attempt to resolve the issue by discovering the root causes of the aggression or abuse.

If there are any aspects of this answer that you are not conversant with, you should research them so that they can become part of your overall PCSO toolkit. You should also look again at **Rules of Engagement** in Chapter 2 and at 5.4 below, on dealing with aggression.

4.11.2 **NOS 2C4 in detail**

This NOS unit is divided into two elements and these are the performance criteria for the first part, **Element 2C4.1**, *Help to prevent aggressive and abusive behaviour*:

1) **Communicate** with **people** in a way that: a) shows respect for them, their property and their rights; b) is appropriate to them; c) is free from discrimination and oppressive behaviour
2) Explain clearly what your role is and what you have to do
3) Explain clearly what is expected of them
4) Plan how you will leave a situation if there is a risk of abusive and aggressive behaviour
5) Remain alert to, and minimize, actions or words that could trigger abusive and aggressive behaviour

The first criterion has some range statements attached. For **communicate,** there are three aspects—(a) **language and speech**, (b) **actions, gestures and body language,** (c) **space and position**. Then for **people** there are four aspects—(a) **adult**, (b) **young person**, (c) **male**, and (d) **female**.

4.11.2.1 *One event could evidence all, or it may take several*

Completing this particular element could take just one event or it could be a combination of several, depending on which provides the best evidence to demonstrate its completion. The following example shows how an event could provide evidence for criterion and range statements.

Example

Whilst on patrol in your area you come across two boys who are smoking. You know them both and know that they are both 14 years of age. You speak to both of them in a manner that is appropriate and respectful (**1 communicate (a) and (b); people (b) and (c)**) and explain that you know them to be under age and will therefore be confiscating their cigarettes (**2**). They reply abusively and state that they will not hand over the cigarettes. You explain that should they not do so, you would have to take the matter further but at this stage you do not want to escalate the issue. You remain calm throughout, using conciliatory language (**5**). You explain what the law entails and that the pair has no option but to hand over the cigarettes (**3**). They do so reluctantly and having taken their details, you continue on your patrol. A short while later one of the mothers of the boys confronts you and as she approaches, she starts shouting and swearing at you. You take note of where you are should

---

you need to call for assistance as well as looking at other health and safety factors (**4**). You ask the lady to calm down and explain what is causing her to be so upset, and remain at a suitable distance in case her aggression reignites (**1 communicate (c)**). She states that her son has informed her that he was not smoking and should not have had his name taken. You calmly explain to her what had occurred and what powers you have in relation to this topic (**1 people (a)** and **(d)**). Having heard the whole story, she realizes that perhaps her son has not given her the full story, and walks away.

This is merely illustrative of how this element could be evidenced. You will encounter numerous situations where you could demonstrate how your behaviour and your professional manner can defuse potentially difficult situations. That is not to say you will encounter aggression and abuse on a daily basis; rather it is an acknowledgement that in any situation it is your manner, your speech, and your actions that might determine how that incident will unfold.

4.11.3 Dealing with actual events of aggressive or abusive behaviour

The second element in this unit is 2C4.2, *Deal with aggressive and abusive behaviour*, and as you can see, it is different from the first element in that it is looking at actual events of aggressive or abusive behaviour. The performance criteria determine what your role is when dealing with such incidents.

1) Recognize when a situation is leading to aggressive and abusive behaviour
2) Take constructive action to defuse aggressive and abusive behaviour that will not make the situation worse and which is consistent with your organization's policies and procedures, and your legal responsibilities
3) Point out to the **people** concerned the likely consequences of their aggressive and abusive behaviour
4) Act in a way that is likely to promote calmness and reassurance
5) Physically break away from and leave situations, if it is necessary to do so, in a way that minimizes the risk of injury to yourself and others
6) Promptly and accurately, report what has happened and complete all the necessary records

Criterion 3 has range statements related to the **people** aspect—(a) **adult**, (b) **young person**, (c) **male**, and (d) **female**.

Task

Look back at the powers section of this Handbook (3.2 above). Look at each power and consider where situations related to the enforcement of these powers could lead to or provoke aggressive or abusive behaviour.

Discussion points

Where might this sort of behaviour be associated with the exercise of your powers?

What other factors may be involved that could increase aggression or abuse?

In what ways could you achieve criterion 4 (*act in a way that is likely to promote calmness and reassurance*)?

What behaviours could you exhibit that would exacerbate, not resolve, the situation?

4.11.3.1 *An argument in the street—another example*

If we look at another example, we can identify where the performance criteria and range statements could be evidenced. Consider what other forms of action could have been taken to deal with the aggressive and abusive behaviour on display in this situation.

Example

Whilst on patrol you are alerted by a member of the public to an argument that is taking place in the next street. As you round the corner, you see an adult male apparently arguing with a young female, aged about ten. As you near you can hear that the adult is accusing the girl of breaking the wing mirror on his car. The male is using abusive language to the girl and you can see that another male is coming towards them also using abusive language (**1**). The second male is shouting that he is the father of the girl and is threatening the first male for verbally abusing his daughter. As you come closer to the argument, you use your radio to alert Control to the possibility of needing assistance (**6**) and provide the appropriate location and details.

You intervene in the argument by announcing your presence and asking for calm so that you can listen to all sides and attempt to mediate in the dispute (**2**). You explain to all parties that the issue will not be resolved unless some calm is restored and ask that all abusive language stop as it merely makes things worse. You also explain that there could be possible public order offences if the aggression on display gets out of hand (**3 (a), (b), (c) and (d)**). Throughout this whole confrontation, your body language is positive and you use language designed to reduce tensions and not apportion blame (**4**).

Just when you think the possibility of violence has been averted, the car owner announces that he is going home to get a hammer and 'do the mirrors' of the other male's car. You immediately call for assistance, break away from the situation (**5**), and advise the other parties to go home until the situation has been dealt with.

Discussion points
Did you think of any other potential actions in this situation?
How would they have influenced the performance criteria?

4.11.4 Some considerations about evidencing this NOS

This NOS unit has the potential to be a difficult one to evidence and it should be stressed that if you repeatedly encounter aggressive or hostile situations, you need to inform your supervisor. This serves a dual purpose; it ensures that any risk assessments for your 'beat' are kept up to date, and it may be that your Force has a 'near miss' policy where incidents such as these are reported. It also helps you if you talk through such situations with an officer (your supervisor) who has more experience of dealing with such things and who should be able to offer practical advice for dealing with any future experiences. This is a point that goes beyond merely evidencing your portfolio, making sure that you engage in reflective learning so that your knowledge is expanded in a very real way.

4.12 Unit 4G4: Administer First Aid

As we have noted above a couple of times, this is the only NOS which can be achieved fully through simulation. It would be somewhat remiss of the authorities to allow PCSOs to wander the streets waiting for accidents to happen, or to go 'ambulance chasing', so that they could use the casualties to evidence their NOS portfolios. The sight of a group of PCSOs queuing to assess a casualty with their folders at the ready might be something that would send out the wrong signals to the public.
Professional training in first aid is a must. In order to achieve completion of this unit, you will need to attend a professionally

managed first aid course, which covers the four units detailed below. If it is not part of your induction training, you should book yourself on a course as soon as possible. We noted earlier that St John Ambulance run frequent courses in basic first aid, as do some Health Trusts (using paramedics) and Primary Health Care centres. **Don't rely on a book:** first aid is something you have to practise with a 'casualty' in a proper, structured, learning environment (hence we do not try to teach first aid in this Handbook).

4.12.1 **NOS 4G4 in detail**

This unit is divided into four elements:

Element **4G4.1:** Respond to the needs of casualties with minor injuries

1) Check the area for danger and respond accordingly
2) Ask the casualty for the history and symptoms of the injury
3) Assess the casualty and establish the nature and extent of the injury
4) Apply first aid treatment appropriate to the type and severity of the injury
5) Call for additional help as appropriate
6) Inform the casualty of action taken and sources of further help

Element **4G4.2:** Respond to the needs of casualties with major injuries

1) Assess the extent and severity of the casualty's injuries
2) Place the casualty in an appropriate position of rest to maximize blood flow to vital organs
3) Protect the casualty from heat or cold
4) Comply with hygiene procedures and avoid infection
5) Control bleeding by applying direct or indirect pressure and appropriate dressings or bandages
6) Check for, and where possible maintain, circulation beyond bandaging
7) Immobilize and support injuries in line with current practice
8) Call for additional help promptly

Element **4G4.3:** Respond to the needs of unconscious casualties

1) Check the area for danger and take the appropriate action
2) Check casualty's level of consciousness and breathing
3) Assess the casualty and establish the nature and extent of any injury

4) Check for presence of any life-threatening conditions
5) Move the casualty to the recovery position in accordance with current practice
6) Call for help promptly
7) Monitor the casualty's condition and note any changes

Element **4G4.4:** Perform cardio-pulmonary resuscitation (CPR)

1) Check for danger and take the appropriate action
2) Open the casualty's airway by head tilt and chin lift, and position the casualty correctly for ventilation
3) Check for breathing and remove any obstructions from the mouth
4) Apply CPR at the correct rate, depth, and ratio
5) Apply chest compressions in the correct position and at the correct rate
6) Demonstrate that you recheck for circulation
7) Call for additional help promptly

4.12.2 Making sure that the training fits the requirement for competence

When you attend a first aid course or refresher, it would be prudent to have a list of these performance criteria to hand, to be sure that the course covers the necessary evidential points. If a skill or learning area were to be omitted (though this would be most unlikely), you could prepare an ADQ and answer the questions to the assessor's satisfaction. What is crucial is that this unit is not merely seen as an NOS exercise, because one day the knowledge gained could be crucial in dealing with a casualty or even saving someone's life. Whether it's bandaging a grazed knee or applying CPR, your actions need to be decisive, prompt, and necessary. *Remember that because you are wearing a uniform, the public will expect you to know what you are doing* and that your intervention 'to save life or limb' is not an option: you must do this as part of your essential duty.

4.12.3 What *must* be in the training?

It is not for us to prescribe what you learn, and your Force will have its own policy on first aid and the competence of its staff, but you cannot go far wrong if you really thoroughly learn:

• how to deal with hygiene and prevention/barriers to infection methods

- how to apply CPR and give mouth-to-mouth resuscitation
- how to deal with injuries such as fractures
- how to deal with wounds and bleeding
- how to make a casualty comfortable and safe
- calling for appropriate help.

4.12.3.1 *Practice*

Practice may make you competent, but it will not make you perfect. Any paramedic or nurse will tell you that unused first aid skills degenerate over time, and, for example, where once you knew how to deal effectively with a casualty with a fractured leg, the procedure for immobilizing the affected limb may get a bit rusty if you don't practise. Your Force will probably provide refresher first aid programmes every year or so, but if this is not provided for you, you will have to ensure that you keep your skills polished.

4.12.4 Always double check with a health professional after you have administered first aid

Incompetent first aid is worse than no first aid at all; and you could be liable to proceedings in law by the affected person (injured party) if you make a major blunder. This is why we urge you that, even when you have administered first aid, you still call for a paramedic to check the casualty, or you take the casualty to a doctor's surgery or to a hospital's Accident and Emergency Department. You may not be able to assess internal bleeding, or diagnose trauma. Make sure that the casualty sees practitioners who can do these things. And write up your PNB at the first opportunity; litigation or a criminal investigation may follow the initial accident.

4.13 Going to Court—Unit 2J2: Present Information in Court and at Other Hearings

Now we come to a unit that you may not be able to evidence immediately. It concerns giving evidence or presenting information at a court or in another form of hearing. There are ways of evidencing this unit other than attending court as a witness, and these will be discussed here. You should also look at 7.5 below, on going to court.

> **Discussion points**
>
> What other hearings could a PCSO attend to give evidence or present information?
>
> How would these formats differ from the court setting and how would this affect the information given?

4.13.1 NOS 2J2 in detail—preparing for court

This unit is divided into two distinct elements and the first is **2J2.1**, *Prepare for court or other hearings*:

1) Respond promptly to any warnings, citations or notifications received from courts or other hearings
2) Provide any information requested by the court or hearing accurately and expeditiously
3) Ensure the availability of exhibits within your area of responsibility, taking steps to ensure their continuity and integrity at all times
4) Consider your evidence in advance of the hearing and ensure that you are in possession of the appropriate notes and materials
5) Confirm that the relevant **victims and witnesses** are attending, and report any problems or difficulties promptly to the appropriate person or organization, in accordance with legislation and policy
6) Liaise with the relevant **victims and witnesses**, and take all reasonable steps within your authority to ensure their safety and welfare, in accordance with legislation and policy
7) Liaise with representatives of the prosecuting authorities as required
8) Deal with individuals in an ethical manner, recognising their needs with respect to race, diversity, and human rights

Criteria 5 and 6 are accompanied by the same four range statements relating to **victims and witnesses**—(a) **vulnerable**, (b) **intimidated**, (c) **significant**, and (d) **other**.

4.13.2 NOS 2J2 in detail—presenting evidence

The second element in the unit is **2J2.2**, *Present evidence to court or other hearings*:

1) Present yourself at the venue in a timely manner and in possession of all the necessary exhibits and documents

2) Ensure your appearance and behaviour conform to acceptable professional standards at all times
3) Liaise with victims, witnesses, and defendants in accordance with current policy and legislation
4) Deliver your evidence and respond to questions in an **appropriate manner** with due regard to the rules of evidence and the procedures of the venue
5) Provide oral evidence that is consistent with any written materials provided by you as part of the case
6) Respond to all directions of the court or hearing promptly and appropriately
7) Report any breaches of court procedure or protocol that come to your attention promptly to the relevant authority

Criterion 4 has four range statements attached to **appropriate manner**—(a) **truthfully**, (b) **objectively**, (c) **clearly**, and (d) **concisely**.

4.13.3 Likely evidencing problems—think laterally

Given the difficulties in obtaining the evidence to meet these criteria, this unit requires some lateral thinking on your part. You could use ADQs based on the criteria themselves, work through them, and then copy them as part of your portfolio, but would this accurately reflect any learning on your part?

> **Discussion points**
> How could you obtain experience of court procedures or hearings?
> What other learning could follow from obtaining these experiences?

Simulations of court appearances. It could be that your Force runs a simulated court exercise that provides an opportunity to experience the format of giving evidence. These 'moot court' exercises could then be used to format the ADQs that, in turn, you use to evidence this unit. They would also provide an opportunity to look at the other aspects of learning that could originate with this exercise, such as the importance of good PNB note taking, or the need for clarity in written reports.

4.13.3.1 *Visit a court*

If there are no such exercises available, then arrange to visit your local court as a member of the public. You can witness the court procedures and use the experience to highlight the criteria referred to in the NOS. This would also serve to prepare you for the physical layout of the court, where people sit, how people are addressed (see 7.5 below, where we explain much of this). As a learning experience, it also helps to build confidence because when you come to give evidence later, you are not stepping into the unknown.

4.14 Concluding the Discussion of NOS

This concludes our discussion of the National Occupational Standards and how they will apply to you as you seek to obtain, or sustain, your competence as a PCSO. Now it is time to turn our attention to the core behavioural skills which must accompany your knowledge skills, and to look in detail at what is required of you in your external dealings with colleagues and the public alike.

4.15 Core Behaviours

Now it is time to focus on what is needed from a PCSO in terms of behaviour.

Behaviour Area	Behaviour	PCSO Role
Working with others	Respect for diversity	A
	Team working	C
	Community and customer focus	C
	Effective communication	C
Achieving results	Personal responsibility	B
	Resilience	B

The PCSO Behavioural Standards: modified from Skills for Justice comparative data 2006.

You should remind yourself of the various references to behaviour, ethics, professional standards, and diversity throughout the Handbook, but most importantly, you should read **1.5**, **1.6**, **4.4.2** above and **6.7** and **7.2** below.

4.15.1 **How behaviours are measured and assessed**

Each behavioural area has a description of preferred behaviour and what your Force can expect from you. This description is followed by sets of **positive indicators** which show where the individual will attain competence in the behavioural standard. There is a corresponding set of **negative indicators** that demonstrate how an individual does not meet the required level of competence. Just as for the NOS, this is not a question of pass or fail: an individual officer is either competent or has yet to attain competence.

4.15.1.1 *Take the respect for diversity agenda seriously*

In **respect for diversity** any demonstration of prejudiced or discriminatory behaviour (either towards colleagues or towards members of the public) is very likely to result in dismissal. The police service cannot afford to have its officers and staff at any grade showing intolerance for diversity, or not respecting the vulnerable in society whom we are pledged to protect. So be warned: the police service takes these matters very seriously indeed, and that means that you have to show that you accept and demonstrate the standards of required behaviour. It is not enough not to show discrimination—you should show that you will stand up for minority rights and champion those who are victims of disrespectful behaviour.

4.15.2 **Respect for race and diversity**

Your police force has a statutory duty in law, through the **Race Relations Act 1976** and the **Race Relations (Amendment) Act 2000**, to:

- eliminate unlawful racial discrimination
- promote equality of opportunity
- promote good relations between people of different racial groups.

Additional legislation makes it **illegal to discriminate** on the grounds of **gender**, **religion or belief**, **disability**, **age**, or **sexual orientation**. Taking all these elements of diversity together with race, produces the six strands which together we call '*Diversity and Race Equality*'. We are concerned here with behaviours which demonstrate your competence across all six strands.

4.15.2.1 *Positive indicators*

The **positive indicators** are that you:

- See issues from other people's viewpoints (empathy)
- Are polite, tolerant, and patient when dealing with people, treating them with respect and dignity
- Respect the needs of everyone involved when sorting out disagreements
- Show understanding of and sensitivity to people's problems, vulnerabilities, and needs
- Deal with diversity issues and give positive, practical support to staff who might feel vulnerable
- Make people feel valued by listening to and supporting their needs and interests
- Use language in an appropriate way and you are sensitive to the way in which it can affect people
- Identify and respect other people's values within the law
- Acknowledge and respect a broad range of social and cultural customs and beliefs
- Respect confidentiality, wherever appropriate
- Can deliver difficult messages
- Challenge attitudes and behaviours which are abusive, aggressive, and discriminatory

Adapted from Skills for Justice, *Core Behaviours* (2003).

Commentary

This is a deliberately challenging set of behaviours to ensure that you can approach members of the community in an open spirit of enquiry. This can sometimes be hard, especially if, ironically, a member of a minority group shows intolerance or a lack of respect towards another (a black person expressing homophobic attitudes, for example). An early lesson you may have to learn is that membership of a minority group does not grant 'saintliness': there can be as much intolerance within such groups as there is in society as a whole.

That doesn't excuse the behaviour, of course. But gay people can be intolerant of transgender people, women can be contemptuous of the deaf, old people can stereotype those from minority ethnic communities, and so on, in endless permutations. The point is that you don't show any discrimination or prejudice towards any. You should also be alert to such behaviours in the workplace. Sadly, there are plenty of examples of prejudice and bigotry within the police service, from biased stop and search operations, through the investigation into the death of Stephen Lawrence (1993), the *The Secret Policeman* TV exposé of police training in 2003, and the apparent racist behaviour of two London (Metropolitan Police) PCSOs in 2007 which culminated in the resignation of both.[6]

This may mean that you have to challenge attitudes expressed by your colleagues; and that you will not be deflected by comments such as 'this is political correctness gone mad'. Sensitivity to others and the celebration, rather than the fear, of difference are not matters of convention or custom, or of wanting to appear to embrace modern attitudes. It goes much deeper than that: *it is to do with the fundamental respect which you grant to another human being who may be different from you, expecting similar and reciprocal respect for your views in turn.*

4.15.2.2 *A workplace example*

Let's look at a workplace case study which captures some of the positive indicators which we itemized above.

Case Study

You have just finished a long patrol, you have written up your PNB notes, your feet ache, and you are looking forward to going home, having a bath, and an early night. As you come out of the locker room, one of your female colleagues, Jane, approaches you and asks if she can have a word in private. Surprised and slightly mystified, you agree. In a quiet corner, she tells you that she is deeply unhappy and, as a result of your patient questioning, she tells you that a male colleague, Tim, whom you know and like, has been making unwanted advances to her, and that this is making her frightened and unhappy. She says that she approached you because you always seem so positive and outgoing, whilst she is shy and a bit mousey. She knows that you have a friendly relationship with Tim and hopes that you will speak for her. She says that she doesn't want to make an issue of it: she simply wants the unwanted behaviour to stop. It has got worse very recently because Tim has started to text her at all hours of the day with sexually provocative messages. You think longingly of the bath and bed, but struggle to your feet and go off to talk to him.

4.15.2.3 *Getting the message across is not easy*

Well, what would you say? Would you confront Tim straight on, saying '*Leave Jane alone, you sexist bastard!*', or would you come to the subject in a roundabout way? The second is preferable. People confronted with direct aggression often respond with equal aggression, and all you will get is a shouting match composed of three parts incomprehension and one part anger (Betari's box). It is better to use the less direct approach, but there are no half measures here. You can't approach the subject so obliquely with Tim that he doesn't understand what you are saying, nor should you take so long to get to the point that he actually thinks you are talking about something quite different. What you have to do is make sure that he gets the message.

Focusing on the outcome

What is the message? That Jane doesn't want his advances. They have to stop, as does the texting. The consequence of continuing is quite serious; he could face disciplinary action and, if he persists, dismissal. That stick should be kept in the bag for the moment and you should concentrate on telling Tim that it must stop now. He will be hurt. He may say: *'But she gave me every encouragement! She kept smiling at me and nodding when I told her she was pretty.'* You may have to explain how people can misread cues and signs, and that what may appear to mean one thing in body language, may be different if you actually talk to the person concerned.

4.15.2.4 *Monitor the situation—this may not be the end of it*

With luck, that will be the end of it, especially if you have shown the sympathy and understanding towards Tim that he deserves. However, it might not be. Whilst the unwelcome attentions may end, you need to watch that spite and vindictiveness do not replace admiration (as can happen all too easily). Make sure, over the intervening weeks and months, that Tim does not seize opportunities to put Jane down, in front of colleagues or in public. Watch too that Jane doesn't typify him to others as a chauvinist who treats women badly. For a while, you may hold the ring; it's not comfortable, but you can't avoid the responsibility.

4.15.2.5 *Negative indicators*

Now let's look at the **negative indicators**, where you:

- Do not consider other people's feelings
- Do not encourage people to talk about personal issues
- Criticize people without considering their feelings and motivation

- Make situations worse with inappropriate remarks, language, or behaviour
- Are thoughtless and tactless when dealing with people
- Are dismissive and impatient with people
- Do not respect confidentiality
- Unnecessarily emphasize power and control in situations where this is not appropriate
- Intimidate others in an aggressive and overpowering way
- Use humour inappropriately
- Show bias and prejudice when dealing with people.

Adapted from Skills for Justice, *Core Behaviours* (2003).

4.15.2.6 *Negative outcomes from negative behaviours*

It's important to realize that the negative indicators are not simply the polar opposites of the positives. There are indications here of a genuine streak of cruelty and indifference to others which, if manifested in a PCSO, go against the grain of what the job is about. If we were to continue with our example, the following might be the outcome if you show negative behaviours towards Jane or Tim.

Alternative case study

Jane: '… I wondered, um, if you'd speak to him for me. I'm a bit shy and … and … he's started texting me now and …' (She starts to cry.)

You: 'Oh for God's sake! What am I? Your nursemaid? You're a grown woman and you should be able to deal with it on your own! It's so typical of you! You're a mouse all the time with other people; mousey in class, mousey out on patrol, mousey with the public! You're useless, you. Do you know what they call you behind your back? Minnie! If you think I'm going to tell Tim that you don't want him to text you, you've another think coming! So stop snivelling and pull yourself together! I'm off.'

(Exit in towering rage. Jane sobs.)

An unhelpful response . . .

Not helpful and supportive really, is it? All the inappropriate language is here, together with threats, intimidation, contempt, and lack of empathy. Jane may be a bit of a fragile person, perhaps not even cut out to be a PCSO, but your contempt for her is overpowering—and who are you to tell her she's no good? Indeed, it's doubtful that she would have any way back from here, and you have made the situation infinitely worse with your inappropriate humour and caustic sarcasm. If this genuinely was your reaction to such a situation, it would in fact be you who ought to go, not Jane. But human beings are infinitely variable and we're sure that you would never react in reality as your negative self has done in this example.

4.15.3 *Team working*

Although you have independence, you often work alone, and you have a sturdy self-reliance, doing your job properly actually relies a great deal on team work and getting on well with others. This core behaviour, graded at a 'C', tends to emphasize the importance of team working with colleagues but, given the nature of your job as a PCSO, we think it should be extended to cover those partnerships and liaisons which you develop within the community and in which you are the catalyst or cement, either driving on or binding together the team effort (or both). The general description notes that you will:

> **Develop strong working relationships inside and outside the team to achieve common goals** [and that you will] **break down barriers between groups and involve others in discussions and decisions.** [In doing this you will] **work effectively as a team member and help to build relationships within the team, actively helping and supporting others to achieve team goals.**

Adapted from Skills for Justice, *Core Behaviours* (2003); our additions are shown in square brackets.

4.15.3.1 *You are part of a team*

At the centre of this is a recognition by you that you cannot do the job effectively if you act on your own. You need others to help; each playing a different part. With that in mind, the core behaviour identifies these **positive indicators**, specifying that you:

- Understand your own role in a team
- Actively take part in team tasks
- Are open and approachable
- Make time to get to know people
- Cooperate with and support other people
- Offer to help others
- Ask for and accept help yourself when it is needed
- Develop mutual trust and confidence in others
- Willingly take on unpopular or routine tasks
- Contribute to team objectives no matter what the direct personal benefit may be

- Acknowledge that there is often a need to be a member of more than one team.

Adapted from Skills for Justice, *Core Behaviours* (2003).

Commentary

In your working life you are a member of the larger policing 'family' and identify with your Force. On a local level, you are a member of your BCU and immediately a member of your Neighbourhood Policing Team. You are a member of the team on duty at that time on that day. When you are in the context of your community, the team membership starts to grow through specific local partnerships to attain limited local goals, through larger engagement with different parts of the community, through to your actions on behalf of the whole community and the groups at that level within which you play a part, and back eventually to the local policing aims for the whole BCU. The team structures shift and move about; new people come and old colleagues and partners go. Within that flux and movement, your role in the teams will shift too, but essentially you will be the positive, supportive person with time to listen and time to get to know the other members of whichever teams you are in at that time.

4.15.3.2 *Negative indicators*

What if you don't act positively as a member of a team? The **negative indicators** suggest that you:

- Don't volunteer to help other team members
- Are only interested in taking part in high-profile and interesting activities
- Take credit for successes without recognizing the contribution of others
- Work to your own agenda rather than contributing to team performance
- Allow small exclusive groups of people to develop
- Play one person off against another
- Restrict and control what information is shared
- Do not let others say what they think
- Do not offer advice or get advice from others
- Show little interest in working jointly with other groups to meet the goals of everyone involved
- Do not discourage conflict within the team or organization.

Adapted from Skills for Justice, *Core Behaviours* (2003).

Commentary

We all know people like this, don't we? They play havoc with the team ethos because they are selfish and careless of the needs of others. They take on work only if it is interesting and if it brings them to the attention of those whom they wish to influence. They encourage schisms in the team, often siding with one and then another to create a clique or 'inner group'. They deliberately isolate those in the team who 'don't belong' in some way. This has no place in the adult world of policing and certainly no room at all in the world of the PCSO. Aside from being such a disruptive influence within your own policing team, if you tried these tactics with the community or the partnerships in which you need to be effective, you would fail rapidly and spectacularly.

In your assessment, in your SOLAP, and in your annual PDR, your function as a 'positive team player' will be constantly appraised because it is one of the most important skills you can have.

4.15.4 Community and customer focus

This core behaviour, graded as a 'C', is fundamental to the work of a PCSO and covers what the customer (member of the community) wants, and how you can provide a high-quality service tailored to meet those, sometimes poorly-articulated, needs. It is about *being* the reassurance and living the message of support to the community which you serve.

4.15.4.1 *Positive indicators in community and customer focus*

The **positive behaviours** are straightforward and will not be a surprise. It is expected that you should:

- Present an appropriate image to the public and to the partner organizations with whom you have dealings
- Support strategies that aim to build bridges into the community and reflect the needs of that community
- Focus on the customer in all activities
- Try to sort out customers' problems as quickly as possible
- Apologize for mistakes and sort them out as quickly as you can
- Respond quickly to customer requests
- Manage customer expectations
- Keep customers updated on progress
- Balance customer needs with organizational needs.

Adapted from Skills for Justice, *Core Behaviours* (2003).

Commentary

It should not surprise you that these positive indicators were imported wholesale from police core behaviours and sometimes the adjustments to fit the PCSO are less well-polished than they could be. This is a case in point, but the essence of the message conveyed by the positive indicators is nonetheless clear-cut.

This is about responding to need as well as you can. It is about listening to what the community wants and needs and then trying to help the community to get it. It is very much about managing expectations too: you have to keep people's feet firmly on the ground. Things happen relatively slowly, everyone has a part to play and has to work together to make things happen. Your community customers can't expect you to do it all. But it is also about acknowledging when things go wrong and taking the blame quickly and good-humouredly, if the fault is yours. The police service has a tendency at times to become a *'blame culture'*. Try not to let that happen to you; it is corrosive of good relationships and wastes too much time looking for scapegoats, or hiding behind an organizational facade, instead of readily admitting that you were wrong, that you've learned from it, and now can move on. An intelligent PCSO will also know when to take the blame for a mistake not of his or her making, but where acceptance of a spurious fault will break a log-jam of attitudes and posturing.

4.15.4.2 *Negative indicators*

What are the corollaries of getting the positive behaviours wrong? The **negative indicators** are not simple polar opposites, but are systemic failures based on a lack of professionalism, where you:

- Are not customer-focused and do not consider individual needs
- Don't tell customers what is going on
- Present an unprofessional image to customers
- Only see a situation from your own view, not from a customer's
- Show little interest in the customer, only dealing with the immediate problem
- Do not respond to the needs of the local community
- Focus on organizational issues rather than customer needs
- Do not make the most of opportunities to talk to people in the community
- Are slow to respond to customers' requests
- Fail to check that customers' needs have been met.

Adapted from Skills for Justice, *Core Behaviours* (2003).

Commentary

It would probably be true to say that failure in any one of these areas would seriously impair your ability to do your job as a PCSO, but what is worse is that the short-term unfocused actions which the negative indicators suggest will inhibit any chance of long-term strategic planning within the community. We all accept that you can't get everything right immediately and that some solutions to community problems will take time, but if you do not respond to the needs of the local community, or you focus on organizational issues rather than customer needs (process rather than progress), you will not be doing your job properly. No one will expect you to get it right all the time, but there is a general expectation that you will get it right most of the time and that you will amend matters when they do go astray. Your motivation to do that comes from showing great, not little, interest in the needs of the local community.

4.15.5 Effective communication

Listening skills and being able to put ideas forward simply and effectively are keys to good communication and these are essential factors in your proper functioning as a PCSO. This core behaviour, graded at 'C', expects that you will be able to communicate ideas and information effectively.

4.15.5.1 *Positive indicators*

The **positive indicators** associated with effective communication are that you:

- Deal with issues directly
- Clearly communicate your needs and instructions
- Clearly communicate decisions and the reasons for those decisions
- Communicate face-to-face wherever and whenever possible and appropriate
- Speak with authority and confidence
- Adapt your communication style to meet the needs of your audience
- Manage group discussion effectively
- Summarize what has been said in discussions so that people can understand what went on and what has been agreed

- Support arguments and recommendations effectively in writing
- Produce well-structured reports and written summaries.

Adapted from Skills for Justice, *Core Behaviours* (2003).

Commentary

There's quite a lot in here which is worth unpicking. Changing your communication style to suit your audience does not mean that you have to learn to speak like a 15-year-old. It does mean though, that when you speak to young people what you say should be less formal and a bit 'slangier' than if you were talking at a meeting of crime reduction partners, led by officials from the borough or local council. It means suiting what you say to the people to whom you are saying it. The same applies to written work. A notice pinned up in a village hall or community centre does not have to be as formally written or structured as a report to your BCU Commander. The point about face-to-face communication is an important one: people derive a heavy percentage of meaning from the way that you say things and how you look. This can outweigh what you actually say and can be very important to observers in confirming or sustaining your local credibility and truthfulness.

4.15.5.2 *An example of direct communication*

Suppose that a project you had pursued enthusiastically locally (such as a crèche or an office to use for drop-in 'surgeries') collapsed from lack of funding. You would be more likely to rally the community around you to return to the issue and try again, if you tell them what happened directly and let them see how much on their side you were. Simply leaving a note about it somewhere, however prominent, would not have the same impact.

4.15.5.3 *Negative indicators*

The **negative indicators** tend to focus on poor communication, to which we would add that you should guard against talking too much, and focus strongly on your listening skills, if you are to avoid negative or counter-productive communication. Specifically, you send the wrong messages when you:

- Are hesitant, nervous, or uncertain when speaking
- Speak without thinking what you are going to say
- Use inappropriate language or jargon
- Speak in a roundabout or rambling fashion

- Do not consider the audience to whom you are speaking
- Avoid answering difficult questions
- Don't give full information without having to have it dragged out of you
- Write in an unstructured way
- Use poor spelling, punctuation, and grammar
- Assume that others understand but don't check to find out if they do
- Don't listen or interrupt inappropriately.

Adapted from Skills for Justice, *Core Behaviours* (2003).

Commentary

We tend to forget if we are ourselves confident speakers and/or writers what an ordeal it is for some shy or inarticulate people to stand up and say something in front of others (equally there are some others who will never shut up), *but the negative indicators are all about you putting barriers in the way of encouraging dialogue.* Part of getting the community to trust you may consist of your giving the community a collective voice which it did not think it had. You may find yourself being a spokesperson for the community you serve—particularly to professional partners who have the power to grant or withhold something the community needs. You might find yourself taking up cudgels on behalf of a community which finds it very difficult to speak to local politicians or council officials.

4.15.6 Personal responsibility

This is about taking responsibility for making things happen and getting results, and will involve your motivation, commitment, and conscientiousness as a PCSO, as well as how much you can persist or persevere in the face of opposition.

4.15.6.1 *Positive indicators*

The **positive indicators** would demonstrate that you:

- Take personal responsibility for your actions
- Take on tasks without having to be asked
- Use your initiative
- Take action to resolve problems and carry out your responsibilities
- Keep your promises and do not let your colleagues down
- Take pride in your own work

- Are conscientious about completing work on time
- Follow things through to a satisfactory conclusion
- Show enthusiasm for your role
- Focus on a task, even if it is routine
- Improve your job-related knowledge and keep it up to date
- Are open, honest, and genuine, standing up for what is right.

Adapted from Skills for Justice, *Core Behaviours* (2003).

Commentary

This behaviour is about how you approach your job and how professional your attitude to your work is. It is tempting sometimes to go through the motions, put in an appearance, but not take problems very seriously (especially if you have seen them before); in fact, to have an approach to work which is jaded and lackadaisical. Those temptations, however human they are, will destroy your credibility. The positive indicators above are the intangible things which people respond to. If you show yourself to be engaged and involved, people will be fired by your enthusiasm and will want to help—especially if they can see the chance of something tangible emerging at the end. Don't forget that, a lot of the time, you may be trying to engage with community members who believe that they have been overlooked, that their voices are not being heard, and that no one cares.

4.15.6.2 *Negative indicators*

What is the other side of the coin? We've indicated some of the polar **negatives** above, but here are the **indicators** of inadequacy and failure, where you:

- Pass responsibility upwards, inappropriately
- Are not bothered about letting others down
- Don't deal with issues, hoping they will go away
- Blame others rather than admitting mistakes or looking for help
- Are unwilling to take on responsibility
- Put in the minimum effort which just gets you by
- Show a negative and disruptive attitude
- Show little energy or enthusiasm for work
- Express a cynical attitude towards the Force and the job
- Give up easily when faced with problems

- Fail to recognize weaknesses and development needs in yourself
- Make little or no attempt to develop yourself or keep up to date with developments.

Adapted from Skills for Justice, *Core Behaviours* (2003).

Commentary

We all know people like this, and sometimes when we're tired or very frustrated, we can slip into these negative behaviours ourselves. We've made a point all the way through this Handbook about you being a '*people person*' and the sort who will not take no for an answer. Faced with these negatives, you would lose all focus on what makes the job important. You will also have forgotten, if these behaviours are typical, why you joined the police in the first place and what difference you have been trying to make. If these attitudes persist, your supervisor will intervene, and the negativity will be shown in your appraisal.

It may be that you need a change, or a rest (classically, these symptoms appear after repeated stress). It may be that you need another kind of work altogether.

4.15.7 Resilience

This final core behaviour, carrying a '**B**' grading, deals with how you withstand frustrations, disappointments, and difficulties. It is about how you deal with negatives and how you stand up to things which would daunt a person of lesser self-belief. On the contrary, you show persistence, you are not cast down when things go wrong, you are dogged in your pursuit of goals, and you stay buoyant when others are preparing to pack it all in.

4.15.7.1 *Positive indicators*

The **positive indicators** suggest that you:

- Are reliable in a crisis; you remain calm and think clearly
- Can sort out conflict, and deal calmly and with restraint in the face of hostility or provocation
- Respond to challenges rationally, unswayed by inappropriate emotionalism (you're not a 'drama queen' or 'king')
- Deal with difficult emotional issues and move on
- Manage conflicting pressures and tensions
- Maintain your professional integrity and an ethical stance when confronted with pressure from others

- Cope with ambiguity and deal with uncertainty and frustration
- Resist pressure to make quick decisions when full consideration is called for
- Remain focused and in control
- Make and carry through decisions even if unpopular, difficult, or controversial
- Stand firmly by a position when it is right to do so.

Adapted from Skills for Justice, *Core Behaviours* (2003).

Commentary

These are slightly unworldly prescriptions for the perfect behaviour of the ideal PCSO, and if someone exhibited all these characteristics all the time we would think him or her slightly inhuman; nonetheless it is expected that you will show all of them some or most of the time. It's almost bland to say 'deal with emotional issues and move on'; because, whilst that is the adult and rational thing to do, sometimes we revert emotionally to being children and wanting comfort. It can take a long time, for example, to get over a failed relationship or unreciprocated love. What the positive indicator more specifically refers to, of course, is that as a PCSO you should not let yourself get carried away with feelings if something goes wrong, but use it as a learning experience for next time. That's perfectly valid, but there is an automaton-like assumption about the imperturbability of the PCSO which may make you seem a little remote if this is your habitual demeanour. That said, your habitual calm and immovability in a crisis will have the effect of calming others at a time when emotions can be counter-productive.

4.15.7.2 *Negative indicators*

The **negative indicators** suggest that you:

- Get easily upset, frustrated, and annoyed
- Panic and get agitated when problems crop up
- Walk away from confrontation when it would be more appropriate to get involved
- Need constant reassurance, support, and supervision
- Use inappropriate physical force
- Get too emotionally involved in situations
- React inappropriately with rude or abusive people

- Deal with situations aggressively
- Complain and whinge about problems instead of dealing with them
- Give in when under pressure
- Worry about making mistakes and avoid difficult decisions whenever possible.

Adapted from Skills for Justice, *Core Behaviours* (2003).

Commentary

You may detect that this has a 'policey' whiff about it, and it is, of course, a direct import from police behavioural values which perhaps need some additional modifying for PCSOs. Let's look at the issue of *walking away from a confrontation*. Because you have not had a police officer's training in handling confrontation, and because you don't have police powers, it is **entirely justifiable** that you walk away from situations where your safety could be compromised. That said, there are plenty of occasions when you may have to confront poor or negative behaviour without there being any threat of violence, such as name-calling or the exhibition of bullying attitudes by others. You should certainly stand your ground in such an event. You are unlikely to use inappropriate physical force or deal with situations aggressively, because you will already know that such an approach can be counterproductive: remember the Rules of Engagement (2.2.5.2 above)? Remember though that you may find yourself the target of criticism from the media if you do not intervene in a situation where public emotions or ill-informed expectations think you should, such as an assault. The incident with the drowned boy in Wigan in May 2007 is one such example, whilst another alleged incident also occurred in 2007 when a woman claimed that two PCSOs stood by whilst an elderly man was mugged by three girls (see 2.8.3.4 above).[7]

4.15.8 Thoughts about core behaviours and what they mean

A final word about core behaviours. Don't rush to evidence the positives in your behaviours; these will be observed in your actions by your assessors and supervisors throughout your appraisal period, and your competence will develop over time, building on the strengths which were identified in you when you were accepted at national selection and by your Force. The assessor or supervisor will speak to you directly if there is a problem, then and there, because there is no sense in waiting to do so at a formal appraisal period which may be weeks or months away. The idea is to get you to address the behavioural shortfall without delay. Don't be afraid of making mistakes. Your resilience will ensure that you can bear your failures with good humour, and thereby you will remain human and improvable, like the rest of us.

4.16 **Chapter Summary**

This chapter, long and detailed as it is, has been about the way that you do your job. In the first place we defined the competences which you are expected to reach, looking at the NOS which you complete during your first year or so in the job. Then we examined the core behaviours, both the resolute and positive behaviours we expect to see if you are to be a success as a PCSO, and the negative side which prevents you from doing your job properly.

Notes

1 We are most grateful to Skills for Justice, the Skills Sector Council which owns and develops the NOS and Competences in the Justice sector, for permission to quote extensively from the NOS and other SfJ publications. This is from 2A1.1(1).

2 Parts of this commentary are adapted from descriptors in C Naseby, *Consultation Guidance for the Justice Sector* (SfJ, 2006).

3 If you want to read more about policing models, there is a very good discussion by RI Mawby in T Newburn, *Handbook of Policing* (Willan, 2003) Part I, Ch 2, 15–36.

4 Indeed, it must also be distinguished from evidence which could be admitted in a court of law; the standard of proof for such evidence is infinitely beyond that for establishing, in a police force, the probability of intelligence being true or not. Intelligence, both in its gathering and in its interpretation, is an art not a science, and it is as prone to error and inaccuracy as any other human endeavour. Remember 'weapons of mass destruction' in Iraq?

5 Usually detective officers who have undergone intensive training programmes and testing over weeks and months. The skills to be a good source handler are not common, and will include the ability to keep quiet when questioned by those with 'no need to know'.

6 Allegedly, the two (white) PCSOs operated some sort of racist 'apartheid' in transport to patrol beats in Westminster, with white PCSOs in one van and PCSOs from ethnic minorities in another. The allegations were never openly investigated and made public, but the two officers concerned resigned and the MPS carried out a review.

The Commissioner, Sir Paul Stephenson, commented that there were 'pockets of stupidity and bigotry' remaining in the police. See Davenport, J, 'Met is rocked by "apartheid" row', 24 February 2009, *London Evening Standard*, and Gill, C and Andrews, A, 'Scotland Yard accused of "apartheid" by Asian officer who claims PCSOs 'had one van for white officers, another for blacks''', *Daily Mail*, 25 February, 2009, available, respectively, from <http://www.thisislondon.co.uk/standard/article23651080>-details, and <http://www.dailymail.co.uk/news/article-1153923>, both accessed on 28 May 2009.

7 See <http://news.bbc.co.uk/go/pr/fr/-/1/hi/uk/7007041.stm>, accessed 28 September 2007, on the drowning incident and for the second an article entitled 'Community police officers stood by as grandmother rescued man attacked by three girls', available from <http://www.dailymail.co.uk/news/article-491645>, both re-accessed on 25 May 2009.

Chapter 5

Close Encounters

5.1 Introduction—Setting the Scene

In this chapter, we look at those elements involved in your day-to-day job of meeting and dealing with people. These encounters can require from you responses which develop from, or are complementary to, the Powers and the Competences which we examined in Chapters 3 and 4 respectively. We shall look at the nature of **evidence** and the importance of using your Pocket Note Book (PNB), and then look at areas of **negotiation** and **persuasion** in a PCSO's work (in other words, being effective and having an impact without resorting always to compulsion through the exercise of powers). We go on to look carefully at ways in which tense or angry situations can be **defused** and temperatures lowered. This is followed by an analysis of **aggression** and how you can deal with situations which become, or threaten to become, hostile and angry. We discuss your **safety awareness** training which is vital to your continued well-being and effectiveness as a PCSO. The chapter concludes with a detailed look at the process of making **dynamic risk assessments** and the part played by health and safety in your evolving role. It would help you if now you familiarized yourself with the map of Tonchester at the opening of Chapter 8 because we shall refer to our fictional town to illustrate points.

5.2 Evidence

5.2.1 The Pocket Note Book (PNB)

The importance of your PNB cannot be overemphasized. It is akin to your life support mechanism whilst on duty. Use it properly and the PNB will become a friend, an ally and a necessity if you are to follow the policy guidelines of your Force. Ignore it and the

PNB will rise like the Devil from wherever you keep it, accusing you of neglect and a lack of professionalism. The way you use your PNB will say a lot about you as an officer; others will think so too and will want to examine your recording standard from time to time. Note what it is for: **the primary function of the PNB is that of evidence gathering during your investigation of offences and recording the duties you carry out**. To maintain your integrity and that of the living document, you must employ a number of processes:

- At the start of each duty, write the day, date, month, and year in block capitals and underline them

	01
MONDAY 14TH JANUARY 2008	

- Write down your call sign, your period of duty, and the name of the area you are patrolling as the very first entry at the start of each new day

> Call sign–TT01, Duty–0800–1600, Patrol area–town centre. ————————————————

- Use the 24-hour clock to note down in the left-hand margin the times of your PNB entries

0745	

- Write down the location of the briefing you receive at the start of each day and/or the location from where you commenced your duty

0745	On duty in Police Station. Received daily briefing from Sgt TAGGART. ————————

- Write down details of tasks you are given by supervisors and/or control rooms, and intelligence you receive from briefing and members of the public

0750	Received taskings: Patrol the shopping areas—spray
	cans being used to paint graffiti on the walls and
	windows of the shops———

- Make your entries in a chronological sequence

| 0800 | Commenced foot patrol walking from police station to |
| | the shopping area. ——— |

- For the purposes of demonstrating a logical sequence with no breaks, your entries should be timed and the location in which you make them noted (continuity of evidence)

0855	North pavement 15 yards east of the south ———
	entrance to the shopping area—stopped by a———
	member of the public.———

- Your objective should be to make entries at the same time as they happen, noting down what you see, hear, touch, taste, and smell (the physical senses produce *evidence*). If it is not possible do so (because you are administering first aid, for example), then make your entries as soon as practicable afterwards and give a reason in your PNB for the delay

0900	Observe male spraying the wall of 'Buy One Get One
	Free' with a spray can on the western side of the
	walkway approx. 15 yards south of the exit to Daniell
	St.———

- When you ask a question of a person you are interviewing regarding an offence, or a witness about an incident, note down their replies *verbatim* (word for word) and in direct speech

5 Close Encounters

PCSO 0901	"Excuse me, my name is PCSO Matthews and I have just seen you spraying this wall with a spray can".
Suspect	"What are you doing here? You lot never come round here. What if I am? It's my tag, nobody's ever stopped me before. I'm quite proud of it actually, do you like it? Do you want me to put me tag on your nice white shirt?...only joking!"

- Make a note of the description of suspects that you investigate and, although it is your own PNB to make entries in as you see fit, make your writing legible so that, if necessary, other investigators and courts can read what you have written

	Description of suspect: white male, 20 years, stocky build, a mass of dark bushy hair, round face, wearing glasses, clean shaven, approx. 5'8'' tall with a scar over the left eye.

- Write down the full names, addresses, and dates of birth of victims, suspects, and witnesses and write all surnames in block capitals

PCSO	"Please tell me your full name, date of birth, and address."
Suspect	"Yeah, it's Toni STALYBRIDGE, born 06/04/88, address 24, Morgan St, Tonchester, Tonford."

- Make a note of the description and identifying features of property that forms part of your evidence

> *The graffiti were approx 33cm wide and 20cm tall.*
> *There were three symbols in total, all in the colour*
> *'British Racing Green'. There were no other painting*
> *marks on what was otherwise a clean wall made of*
> *bricks and mortar measuring 2x1m below the front*
> *window of the shop. When I arrived the symbols were*
> *still wet to the touch and I could clearly smell the*
> *odour of cellulose paint.————————————*

- Only write a single line of writing between each line on the page in your PNB and do not be tempted to make additional notes in any other part of the book. The only exception to this is when you make a drawing, in which case use the whole page

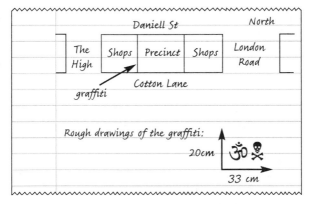

- Do **NOT** leave spaces in between words that could possibly be used to add words later. If you do leave spaces, then—draw— lines—in—between so that gaps cannot be filled. This is to ensure that your integrity is not called into question later on suspicion of adding evidence after the incident. Therefore, make sure you write on every line and page of the PNB

> The Precinct is a shopping area between ———
> Daniell St in the north east and Cotton Lane in the
> south, bordered east and west by The High and ——
> London Road. ————————————

- If you accidentally turn over two pages at once, then draw a diagonal line across the blank pages and write 'omitted in error' across them

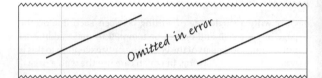

- Do not overwrite, erase, or obliterate errors. If you make a mistake, cross it out with a single line so that it can still be read, initial your error and then continue with what you want to write immediately afterwards

> There were no other people around at the time, and
> none of the shops in the area was ~~closed~~ open JBM
> PCSO1 ————————————

- Last few PNB tips:

1	Always use black ink to make your entries so that the PNB can be copied successfully. ————
2	Do not write on scraps of paper as a substitute for your PNB whilst on duty, always use your PNB ——
3	The PNB remains the property of your Force and, as it contains vital evidence, you must look after it very well indeed. ————————

The rules surrounding the use of the pocket note books have been successfully summarized in police circles in the past by the mnemonic **NO ELBOWS(S)**, see Glossary. Statements must always be written in direct speech.

		01
	NO ELBOWS	
E	Erasures. ———————	
L	Leaves torn out or Lines missed. ———	
B	Blank spaces. ———————	
O	Overwriting. ———————	
W	Writing between the lines. ———	
S	Spare pages. ———————	

5.2.2 Record, retain, and reveal

A very important rule of evidence is that at all stages of an investigation all investigators of crimes (including PCSOs) have a responsibility to **record** and **retain** material which has some bearing on the offence under investigation (referred to as **relevant** material), even if it is not subsequently used by the prosecution. It is **relevant** whether it applies to the defence or to the prosecution case. As an investigator, you have the responsibility to **record** and **retain relevant** material relating to both sides.

5.2.2.1 *The consequence of not recording*

The consequence of *not* recording relevant material is that the Crown Prosecution Service (CPS) cannot share the material with the legal representatives of the suspect. This lack of **disclosure** could provide the defence with support for any argument made to the court that the accused has no case to answer or that the accused should be found not guilty, because the legal process was flawed.

5.2.2.2 *Make records in a durable form*

It is particularly important therefore, as far as witnesses or potential witnesses are concerned, that you make a record of their personal details in a durable form, in your case in your PNB, as soon as you make contact with them. Just as important is the need to record an outline of their evidence if you are not going to take statements from them straight away (see below). If these steps are not taken, the prosecution case could be weakened. The importance of disclosure (even of things not done) arose from the case of *R v Heggart and Heggart* (November 2000 Court of Appeal). In this case, potential witnesses were located by police investigators but no statements of evidence were obtained from them.

5.2.2.3 *Back to the example*

Let's go back to what had happened with the graffitist. About ten minutes earlier, you were on patrol in the Precinct when you were stopped by a member of the public who gave you information about a man with a spray can. (Remember, even if the witness subsequently does not make a statement of evidence, you must record an outline of what s/he had to say in a durable form and your PNB will be the best place for that.)

0855	North pavement 15 yards east of the south entrance to the shopping area—stopped by a member of the public.
Witness	"Excuse me, I have just walked through the area and I have seen a bloke spray painting the wall outside a shop called 'Buy One Get One Free'".
PCSO	"Please give me a description of this person."
Witness	"Well, he's white, around 20 years old, stocky build, and his hair is a right mess 'cos it is a mass of dark bushy hair, round face, wearing glasses, clean shaven, approx. 5'8'' tall, wearing a black top with a hood and some of those baggy jeans and dirty white trainers."
PCSO	"What exactly did you see him do?"
Witness	"As I walked past, he was spraying a symbol on the wall outside the shop, it looked foreign to me. He was using a spray can, must have got it from the car superstore because it's the same colour as my old car, 'British Racing Green'. It's even metallic. The spray can he was using ran out and he threw it in a rubbish bin nearby. Here it is, you take it."
PCSO	"Please may I have your name and address as I may want to take a statement from you at a later stage?"
Witness	"Pat OLDFIELD, born 09/09/70, 221B, Baker St, Tonchester, Tonford; telephone 37510. I can't stop, I'm late for work, but I do think I've seen the guy before somewhere."

5.2.2.4 *Recording the details of witnesses is vital*

The necessity for you to record the details of witnesses and an out-line of their evidence applies to all investigations. It is important to note therefore that these rules apply even if you find yourself in the middle of an incident for which you are not the 'officer in the case'. An example might be when police officers are dealing with an assault, a robbery, or any other crime which might attract a crowd. You walk around the corner on a routine patrol and there you see a number of potential witnesses. First of all, you should make a PNB entry of the time and location you find yourself in, and then, if witnesses come forward to you, make sure you record their details and an outline of their evidence.

Disclosure

Lastly, having obtained any **relevant** material, you must **reveal** the entries in your PNB to the CPS in the case above if the suspect is going to plead not guilty, and to the officer in the case for all other investiga-tions. This can be done by submitting photocopies of your PNB.

5.2.3 **Evidence of identification—'Turnbull' principles**

You remember from Chapter 3 on the law in England and Wales what **case law** is and how it affects the investigative process. In Chapter 3 we referred to a major example of case law: *R v Turnbull* [1976] 3 All ER 549 which relates to the identification of suspects. As a result of this case, the evidence of any witness, including you, which involves observation of a suspect, must be gathered using the recommendations which were set as a precedent.

5.2.3.1 *Mnemonics to remember the importance of the case*

'Turnbull', as it has come to be known, has a memory tool to help you remember its component parts. This is the mnemonic *ADVOKATE*. As you will recall from Note 5 of Chapter 3 and from the Glossary, the authors of this Handbook prefer the more mean-ingful mnemonic **SOCRATES** to ADVOKATE, but the latter has a currency born of familiarity rather than accuracy. The principles are the same in either case though; it is about *awareness of your observation and recording of identification details*.

5.2.3.2 *Think of 'Turnbull' whenever you gather evidence*

Every time you gather evidence about a person which results from your observation of them you must use every applicable aspect of

5 Close Encounters

S(aw) 0900		Observed male spraying the wall of a shop with a spray can on the western side of the walkway approx. 15 yards south of the exit to Daniell St.
O(bserve)	A	I had the suspect under observation for 30 seconds. It was this amount of time as I looked at my watch when I first saw the suspect and again when I made contact with him.
C(larity)	D	The distance between me and the suspect was approx. 25 metres. I know this because when I started to walk towards the suspect I counted 25 steps.
	V	I could clearly see the suspect as the Precinct has a glass roof and the sun was shining through.
R(eason)	O	There were no obstructions between me and the suspect, there were no shoppers at the time because the shops were shut.
	K	I have not seen the suspect before nor did I know his identity.
A(ppearance)	A	I remembered the suspect easily because he had a mass of dark bushy hair.
T(time lapse)	T	There was no time lapse between me seeing the suspect and finally introducing myself as I had him under constant observation for 30 seconds.
E(rrors)	E	I made one and only recording of the description of the
S(pace)		suspect as there was no break.

'Turnbull' relevant to the incident/offence and make a note of it. Later, if you are required to make a statement of that evidence for a court case, you will be required to repeat the process and write down what you saw meeting the requirements of ADVOKATE/ **SOCRATES**. Be aware of the fact that you could lose sight of the suspect at any time and therefore take the earliest opportunity to write down a description.

5.2.3.3 *'Turnbull' in our example*

Let's return to our example of the graffiti artist inside the shopping area. At your first point of contact, you observed the suspect using the spray can on the wall. Now let's apply **SOCRATES**/ADVOKATE to that incident. To help you meet the requirements of 'Turnbull', you may wish to write **SOCRATES** or ADVOKATE in the margin of your PNB (see top of page 376):

5.2.4 Unsolicited comments by suspects (PACE Code C 11)

As a PCSO you will be required to investigate offences for which you have been designated (see 3.2 above, on powers). This section describes what you should do if the suspect you are investigating makes a comment before s/he has been cautioned or arrested, as what s/he says may contain information of evidential value. Comments which are made outside the framework of an interview are called '**unsolicited**' (voluntary) comments and the PACE Codes of Practice dictate a course of action to follow if such comments are to be documented. They are divided into two groups: **significant statements** and **relevant comments**.

5.2.4.1 *Significant statements and relevant comments*

Any comment made by the suspect at any time in your presence which contains significant information about the suspect's personal involvement in the offence and, in particular, an admission of guilt, is a **significant statement** (Code C 11.4A). Anything that the suspect says at any time which includes anything which might be relevant to the offence (Code C 11.13 and Note 11E) is a **relevant comment**.

5.2.4.2 *Illustration from our extended example*

As an example, think back to the previous section on Pocket Note Books when we introduced a suspect who was spraying graffiti on the wall of a shop in the shopping area. At the time you noted in your PNB the following conversation (see top of page 378):

PCSO 0901	"Excuse me, my name is PCSO Matthews, and I seen just seen you spraying this wall with a spray can."
Suspect	"What are you doing here? You lot never come round here. What if I am? It's my tag, nobody's ever stopped me before. I'm quite proud of it actually, do you like it? Do you want me to put me tag on your nice white shirt?...only joking!"

Significant statement

These comments were made voluntarily by the suspect about his involvement in the offence; they were an admission of guilt and therefore this was a significant statement.

Relevant comment

If the suspect had said, 'If you had been five minutes earlier there would have been two of us, but you are too late', the comment would have been relevant to the offence and therefore a relevant comment.

5.2.4.3 Recording unsolicited comments (Code C Note 11E)

- Having written down any such comment into your PNB, note the time it was made and sign the entry using your usual signature:

0901	The above statement was made in my presence and hearing by the suspect. Jo MATTHEWS PCSO

- Show the PNB entry to the suspect when it is practicable and ask him or her to read it over and decide whether or not s/he agrees that it is a true record of what s/he said:

PCSO	"Please read this entry. Do you agree it is a true record of what you said?" I handed my pocket book to the suspect to read.
Suspect	"Yes, I did say that."

- If s/he agrees, ask him or her to sign your PNB at the end of the following statement (Code C Note 11E):

PCSO	"Please sign the following statement, 'I agree that this is a correct record of what was said.'" Toni STALYBRIDGE

- If s/he **disagrees**, record in your PNB the extent of the disagreement:

PCSO	"Please read this entry, do you agree it is a true record of what you said?" I handed my pocket book to the suspect to read.
Suspect	"No, I just said it was someone else."

- Ask the suspect to read over the note you made on the content of the disagreement:

PCSO	"I have made a note of your disagreement. Please read it over and sign that I have done so correctly." I handed my pocket book to the suspect to read.

- Ask him or her to sign that the disagreement has been recorded correctly:

PCSO	"Please sign the following statement, 'I agree that the above comment accurately reflects my disagreement about what I said earlier.'" Toni STALYBRIDGE

- Any refusal to sign should also be recorded and signed by anyone else who heard the comments (See Code C Note 11E):

PCSO	"I offered my PNB to the suspect to read and sign but he refused."

5.2.4.4 Record anything which a suspect says at any time

By the very nature of your employment, you may well find your-self involved at the start of many types of investigations simply by being in the right place at the right time. **It is essential therefore** that you record anything any suspect says at any time and follow the Code of Practice accordingly.

5.2.5 Cautions

Proving the **guilty actions** (*actus reus*) and the **guilty mind** *(mens rea)* of the suspect at the time s/he carried out an offence (see 3.1.2 above), will require you to ask the suspect one or more questions. This constitutes an interview and is defined as the *'questioning of a person regarding* [his or her] *involvement in a criminal offence'* which must be carried out under caution (PACE Code C 11.1A). A suspect is given a caution forewarning him or her of the consequences of his or her actions should s/he decide to say anything, and the possible cost to his or her defence if s/he chooses not to say anything at this point, but later relies on things which s/he ought to have said at interview.

5.2.5.1 *Landmarks in the investigation—triggers for the caution*

The caution is given to a suspect at major landmarks throughout an investigation and it is at these locations that its wording differs depending on when the caution is administered.

- When a suspect is first suspected of committing an offence without being arrested, s/he is cautioned before being interviewed. Similarly, the caution will be administered just after the individual has been arrested and before s/he is interviewed at a police station. The words *'when questioned'* are said in this caution.
- When the investigation is completed and the suspect is charged, the suspect is cautioned to give him/her the last opportunity to say anything before the court appearance. The word *'now'* is said in this caution.

5.2.5.2 *The three parts to a caution*

The three parts to a caution are as follows:

1. *'You do not have to say anything*
2. *but it may harm your defence if you do not mention*

   (a) *'when questioned'*

   OR

   (b) *'now'*

   something which you later rely on in court.
3. *Anything you do say may be given in evidence.'*

5.2.6 Exhibits as evidence

To prove the existence of a material article seized in the course of an investigation, it is presented to a court as an **exhibit**. Examples of such items in the graffiti artist story would include the spray can of paint the suspect was using to spray the wall and, subsequently, any Closed Circuit Television (CCTV) recordings of the incident.

5.2.6.1 Reference tags

The first person who takes possession of the item after the commencement of the investigation (other than the suspect) is the person to whom the item is referenced; therefore the article receives a reference tag which is usually the person's initials and a sequential number. Everybody who later refers to that exhibit then uses the unique reference number derived from the person who first took possession of it, like this:

(1) A witness called **Pat OLDFIELD** sees a suspect using a spray can to paint graffiti on a wall. The suspect throws the spray can into a rubbish bin nearby and starts using a second spray can.

(2) The witness recovers the first spray can from the rubbish bin and gives it to **PCSO Jo MATTHEWS**. This spray can therefore has the reference number **PO/1** because it is the witness who first takes possession of it.

(3) **PCSO Jo MATTHEWS** then interviews the suspect and takes possession of the second spray can. This spray can receives the reference **JBM/1**.

(4) Both spray cans are taken to a shop owner to be identified. **PCSO Jo MATTHEWS** will refer to both exhibits as **PO/1** and **JBM/1** in his/her duty statement.

(5) The shop owner will refer to the identification of both spray cans and sign both labels of exhibits **PO/1** and **JBM/1**.

(6) In his/her statement the witness makes reference to handing the spray can that s/he found in the rubbish bin to **PCSO MATTHEWS**.

5.2.7 Closed Circuit Television evidence and the need to record, reveal, and retain

One of the products of modern technology in the fight against crime is town centre and retail CCTV camera and recording equipment. The recording of millions of images, including thousands of incidents up and down the country, has given courts the opportunity to prove or disprove accusations by both the prosecution and defence. Local knowledge of your area will help you to know which places are covered by CCTV and which areas are not.

5.2.7.1 *Relevant material*

Previously we outlined what is **relevant** material and how it affects an investigation. If you think that CCTV may have captured an incident that you are investigating, then you must view the tape recording to find out if it contains **relevant** material in connection with:

- The offence being investigated.
- Any person under investigation.
- The circumstances in which the offence took place.

If you consider the contents of the tape contain nothing of relevance, you should make a summary of the content of the recording, note it in your PNB, and reveal to the CPS that you have viewed the tape. If in doubt, always seize the tape.

5.2.8 Penalty notices for disorder under sections 1 to 11 of the Criminal Justice and Police Act 2001: objectives of the system

The penalty notices for disorder (PND) scheme provides you with a speedy and efficient way of dealing with minor anti-social offences. It carries a crime prevention message and is a simpler way to administer justice. There are two tiers of penalty: an upper one attracting a fine of £80 and a lower one of £50 (see 3.2 above).

5.2.8.1 *Legislation*

Community Support Officers are empowered under the PRA2002 to issue PNDs to persons aged 16 or over who have committed a penalty offence (see 3.2 above for the list of offences). By accepting the notice and paying the penalty, the recipient is no longer obliged to go to court. However, having been issued with the notice, the recipient then has two choices. S/he can either pay the penalty or choose to go to court, but s/he must make this decision within 21 days of the issue of the notice, otherwise s/he may be fined one-and-a-half times the original penalty.

5.2.8.2 *Circumstances in which notices can be issued*

To be in a position to issue a notice, you must have reason to believe that the person has committed an offence for which a PND can be issued and you must have gathered enough **evidence** to prove the offence (remember 3.2 above, 'Powers and duties of a PCSO', where we showed you the points to prove evidentially in applying the law). The incident itself must be of a simple kind and one that would benefit from being dealt with using the PND scheme. The suspect must be able to comprehend what is happening to him or her, such as having a reasonable understanding of English, or not being too drunk and incapable, and s/he must be amenable and cooperate fully. If the person is suspected of committing two or more related offences in addition to the one being considered, then a PND cannot be issued. The recipient must be aged 16 or over, and you must be satisfied with the validity of his/her age, identity, and address. Where a person aged 16 or over commits a penalty offence with a person under 16, a penalty notice cannot be issued to either person.

5.2.8.3 *Contents of the penalty notice for disorder*

There are two versions of the ticket. The English language version is a four-sheet document in six parts and the Welsh language version a five-sheet document in six parts; less the title sheet, these are:[1]

Part 1 Recipient copy		(Welsh language
Part 2 Payment slip		Sheet 2)
Part 2a Instructions		
Part 3 Hearing request slip		
Part 4 Central Ticket Office (CTO) copy	Sheet 2	(Welsh language Sheet 3)
Part 5 Hearing request (HR) copy	Sheet 3	(Welsh language Sheet 4)
Part 6a Details of recipient	Sheet 4	(Welsh language
Part 6b Statement of witness		Sheet 5)

5.2.8.4 *Process model for the issue of a PND*

Figure 14 (below) shows you the processes involved in the various stages of issuing a PND. Follow the 'flow' to see when you should issue a PND and when you should take other, alternative or lesser, actions.

5.2.9 Fixed penalty notices in respect of road policing

The fixed penalty notice (FPN) system for road policing offences was introduced in the 1980s and has therefore been established for much longer than the penalty notices for disorder (PND) scheme which we have just examined. The FPN scheme has similar objectives relating to time saving, speedier justice, and lessening the load on the courts. The scheme gives you the opportunity to issue a FPN (see Figures 13 and 14) to any person whom you have reason to believe is committing or has committed a fixed penalty offence (see 3.2 above for the lists of offences).

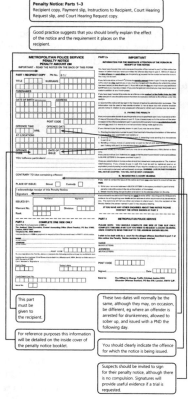

Figure 13: Penalty Notice forms

Penalty Notice: Parts 4 and 5
Central Ticket Office copy and Court Hearing Request copy.

This copy will be retained by the CTO for processing purposes

This copy will be retained by the Central Ticket Office (CTO) and provided to the court along with copies of parts 6a and 6b in the event that a hearing is requested.

METROPOLITAN POLICE SERVICE
PENALTY NOTICE
PENALTY AMOUNT £80

PART 4 CTO COPY   PN No. 0 1 /
TITLE   SURNAME
FORENAMES
DATE OF BIRTH (dd/mm/yy)   ADDRESS
POST CODE
OFFENCE TIME   OFFENCE DATE   HRS.
AT (LOCATION)
OFFENCE CODE   DATE OF ISSUE
YOU (offence particulars)
CONTRARY TO (Act containing offence)
PLACE OF ISSUE: Street   Custody
I acknowledge receipt of this Penalty Notice
Signature
ISSUED BY: Surname   Signature
Warrant No.   Division
Rank

MUST BE COMPLETED
ADDITIONAL DETAILS OF RECIPIENT
Gender: M   F   IC Code   SD Code
Occupation
3rd Party Witness Statement: Particulars Obtained?   Y   N
CRIS No.
Local Authority Code   Quality Check
A/S No.
Custody (PK) No.

METROPOLITAN POLICE SERVICE
PENALTY NOTICE
PENALTY AMOUNT £80

PART 5 COURT COPY   PN No. 0 1 /
(repeat fields as above)

The IC code box can be used to record the suspect's perceived ethnicity.

The suspect's ethnicity should be recorded using 16 + 1 self-defined ethnicity.

You should complete the person in custody number if your suspect is either held in custody and/or interviewed in custody.

If a third party witness offers a statement, this should be recorded in your notebook. You should tick this box and enter your notebook number. Third party details should be recorded in part 6a (see below).

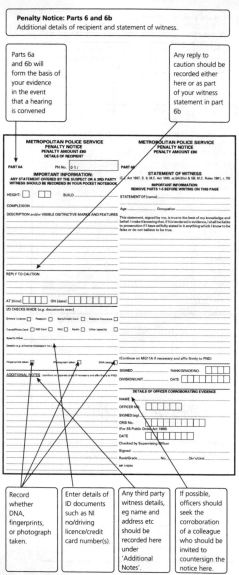

Penalty Notice: Parts 6 and 6b
Additional details of recipient and statement of witness.

Parts 6a and 6b will form the basis of your evidence in the event that a hearing is convened

Any reply to caution should be recorded either here or as part of your witness statement in part 6b

Record whether DNA, fingerprints, or photograph taken.

Enter details of ID documents such as NI no/driving licence/credit card number(s).

Any third party witness details, eg name and address etc should be recorded here under 'Additional Notes'.

If possible, officers should seek the corroboration of a colleague who should be invited to countersign the notice here.

Figure13 (continued)

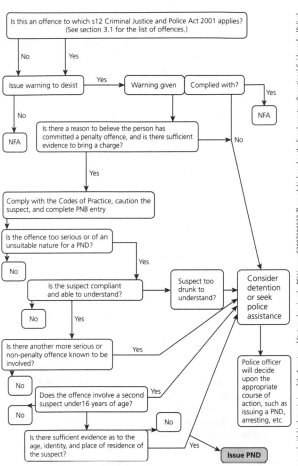

Figure 14: Process model for the issuing of a PND by a PCSO

5.2.9.1 *Types of fixed penalty notice you can issue*

Non-endorsable (No penalty points can be added to a driving licence)

1 **Moving vehicle/cycle**—Offender seen: this FPN is issued to drivers/riders, including those aged 16 and 17, who are seen at the time of an alleged offence. The fixed penalty gives the named

driver/rider 28 days in which to pay the fixed penalty or to request a court hearing. If no payment or hearing request is received within the specified period, a fine is registered automatically against the driver/rider. The fine will be registered at the offender's local magistrates' court and the fine amount is calculated as the fixed penalty amount (currently £30 for the majority of non-endorsable offences, see Figure 15) + 50%.

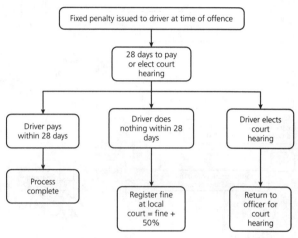

Figure 15: Non-endorsable fixed penalty procedure—driver seen[2]

2 Stationary vehicle—Parking/Driver not seen: This is the standard 'parking ticket', whereby an FPN is attached to a vehicle suspected of involvement in an alleged offence. On his or her return to the vehicle, the driver is then given 28 days in which to pay the fixed penalty or to request a court hearing. If, within 28 days, no hearing request or penalty payment is received, a Notice to Owner (NTO) is sent to the registered owner/keeper of the vehicle involved in the offence from the Central Ticket Office. The owner/keeper of the vehicle is then liable for the offence and must pay the penalty or request a court hearing within a further period of 28 days.

Action on receipt of the Notice To Owner (NTO)

On getting the NTO, the recipient also has the opportunity at that stage to state s/he was not the owner/keeper of the vehicle at the time of the offence, or that it was being driven by another person, or on hire (see Figure 16). As an alternative, s/he can return a request for a court hearing from the person using the vehicle at the time, signed by the driver. If no response is received, a fine registration is issued against the recipient of the notice and registered at the offender's local magistrates' court. The fine registration is calculated as the fixed penalty amount (currently £30 for the majority of non-endorsable offences) + 50%.[3]

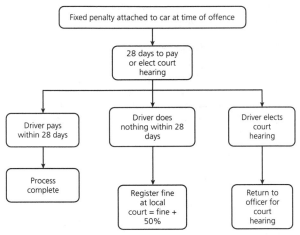

Figure 16: Non-endorsable fixed penalty procedure—driver not seen

PNB entries

Although there is no requirement to duplicate **all** the information noted on an FPN in a PNB, the following should be noted in the PNB every time:

- Time of issue
- Ticket reference number
- Vehicle registration number (if applicable)
- Offender's name.

5.2.9.2 *Entries in the PNB when issuing an FPN*

If there is not enough space on the FPN for a particular piece of evidence, then it should be noted down in the PNB. However, remember that the issuing of the FPN might not be the end of the process, nor necessarily an alternative to following the PACE Codes of Practice in relation to the treatment of a person under investigation. Therefore, always adhere to the Codes during the cautioning, interviewing, and reporting of the suspect.

Spoiled tickets

If, for any reason, a ticket is spoilt, as a result of an accident or inclement weather, for example, then mark all three copies accordingly and forward them through a supervisor to the Central Ticket/Processing Office for cancellation.

5.2.9.3 *Content of the non-endorsable fixed penalty ticket*

Non-endorsable fixed penalty tickets are supplied in a booklet form, encased in a card cover. Each booklet (at the time of writing) contains ten notices. Printed on the front cover of the booklet is the notice type, the offences applicable to the type of notice, and codes and other information necessary for its completion.

Each ticket consists of three parts:

Part 1—Police copy
Part 2—Offender's copy
Part 3—Clerk's copy

5.2.9.4 *Fixed penalty notice information*

Most information that you will need for the completion of an FPN can be found on the cover of the booklet. However, should you want further information, the Police National Legal Database (PNLD) provides a database of fixed penalty law, offence wording, and coding. All Police Forces in England and Wales subscribe to this system and any further questions you have in relation to the scheme can be answered by accessing PNLD through *Blackstone's Police Operational Handbook, Police National Legal Database*, I Bridges (ed) (Oxford University Press, 2006). For further reading see Home Office, *The Revised Guidance on the Operation of the Fixed Penalty System for Offences in Respect of a Vehicle*, April 2006, available at <http://police.homeoffice.gov.uk/news-and-publications/pub-lication/operational-policing/HO_00395_GFinalVersion.pdf? view=Binary>.

5.2.10 **The duty statement**

For the purposes of presenting evidence before a court, any witness, including those in the police 'family', writes down his or her evidence in the form of a **statement**. This form is 11th in a series of approximately 20 forms contained in a prosecution document called the **Manual of Guidance**, used to build case files. It is therefore referred to as an 'MG11'. It is also referred to as a 'section nine statement' because under Section 9 of the **Magistrates' Court Act 1980**, a person's evidence can be read out in court from such a statement if s/he has not been called as a witness.

5.2.10.1 *The duty statement in detail*

Based upon the incident with the graffiti artist, here is the duty statement applicable to that incident, assuming that the suspect had requested a court hearing or had pleaded not guilty. It has been designed in sections to help you understand the requirements for making a duty statement. (Some of what follows is adapted from an unpublished document '*A Guide to Form MG11, General Rules for Completion*' by Kent Police, reproduced by kind permission of the Chief Constable.)

The unique reference number (URN) at the top of the first page on the right will be generated by your own Criminal Justice Department or office.

- Always include your full name with your surname in capitals. If you usually write in capitals, then *underline* your surname.
- Always give your occupation as a Police Community Support Officer and add your collar/badge/PCSO number.

MG 11

RESTRICTED (when complete)

WITNESS STATEMENT
(CJ Act 1967, s.9; MC Act 1980, ss5A(3) (a) and 5B;
MC Rules 1981, r.70)

URN

Statement of: *Jo Britton MATTHEWS*

Age if under 18: *Over 18* (if over 18 insert 'over 18')
Occupation: *Police Community Support Officer 001022*

- Always complete the 'number of pages' section on completion of the statement.

- Always sign the declaration and take very seriously the content of the warning each time you make a statement.
- Always date the statement. Retain each statement you make subsequently which relates to the same investigation and reveal them to the CPS. Never destroy previously completed statements.

This statement (consisting of   4   page(s) each signed by me) is true to the best of my knowledge and belief and I make it knowing that, if it is tendered in evidence, I shall be liable to prosecution if I have wilfully stated anything in it, which I know to be false, or do not believe to be true.

Signature: *Jo Matthews PCSO1*   Date: *14th January 2008*

Starting the statement

Always begin all statements with the **time, day, date, location, PCSO status** (foot patrol or mobile patrol), and details of any other **persons present** (normally other colleagues). Always use the 24-hour clock when making reference to timings to lessen confusion. Do not use the phrase '*At approximately … hours …*', it should be either '*At*' or '*Approximately*' but as a PCSO, you should be specific and use '*At … hours …*'.

If your evidence has been visually recorded, the box must be ticked accordingly. Do not start your statement with the words '*I am the above named person …* '. It is not necessary to include your name, title, number, or station at the start of the main body of text as this is clearly displayed in the first box. Always write statements in chronological order.

Tick if witness evidence is visually recorded ☐
(supply witness details on rear)

At 0855 hours on Monday 14th January 2008 I was on foot patrol in uniform on the north pavement of Cotton Lane, 15 yards east of the south entrance to the Precinct, Tonchester. There I saw a member of the public who identified herself to me as Pat OLDFIELD

Always record relevant conversation in 'direct speech' (what the person actually said).

> Mrs OLDFIELD said to me "Excuse me, I have just walked through the Precinct and seen a bloke spray painting the wall outside a shop called 'Buy One Get One Free'." I said to Mrs OLDFIELD, "Please give me a description of this person." She replied "Well, he's white, around 20 years old, stocky build, and his hair is a right mess 'cos it is a mass of dark bushy hair, round face, wearing glasses, clean shaven, approx. 5'8"tall, wearing a black top with a hood and some of those baggy jeans and dirty white trainers." I asked, "What exactly did you see him do?" Mrs OLDFIELD replied, "As I walked past, he was spraying a symbol on the wall outside the shop, it looked foreign to me. He was using a spray can, must have got it from the car superstore 'cos it's the same colour as my old car, 'British Racing Green', it's even metallic. The spray can he was using ran out and he threw it in a rubbish bin nearby. Here it is, you take it." I then took possession of a "British Racing Green" spray can from Mrs OLDFIELD, exhibit labelled and marked PO/1.

Precision in evidence

Use your senses to evidence what it is that you saw, smelled, touched, tasted, or heard. Be definite. Instead of saying 'I noticed', say 'I saw'. If you are unsure of a detail, then say so, as this will inform the reader that you have at least considered the point even if you are unable to give succinct details. Set the scene so that the reader can form a mental picture of the layout of the area.

> At 0900 hours the same day I entered the Precinct via the south entrance. The Precinct is a shopping area between Daniell Street in the north-east and Cotton Lane in the south, bordered east and west by The High and London Road. As I entered the Precinct, I saw a white male, 20 years, stocky build, a mass of dark bushy hair, round face, wearing glasses, clean shaven, approx. 5'8" tall spraying the wall of "Buy One Get One Free" with a spray can on the western side of the walkway approx. 15 yards south of the exit to Daniell Street.

Always include the identification points, highlighted by the case of 'Turnbull'. Fully describe how it was you were able (or unable) to see the suspect so clearly.

> I had the suspect under observation for 30 seconds. It was this amount of time as I looked at my watch when I first saw the suspect and again when I made contact with him. The distance between me and the suspect was approx. 25 metres. I know this because when I started to walk towards the suspect I counted 25 steps. I could clearly see the suspect as the Precinct has a glass roof and the sun was shining through. There were no obstructions between me and the suspect; there were no shoppers at the time, as the shops were shut. I have not seen the suspect before nor did I know his identity. I remembered the suspect easily because he had a mass of dark bushy hair. There was no time lapse between me seeing the suspect and finally introducing myself, as I had him under constant observation for 30 seconds. I made the one and only recording of the description of the suspect as there was no break.

When setting out your statement, make use of paragraphs, but do not leave a blank line in between. You do not need to 'rule off' an incomplete line as you would do in your PNB.

> I walked up to the suspect and could clearly see that he had
> a scar over the left eye. I said to him, "Excuse me, my name
> is PCSO Jo MATTHEWS, and I have just seen you spraying
> this wall with a spray can." The suspect replied, "What are
> you doing here? You lot never come round here. What if I
> am? It's my tag, nobody's ever stopped me before. I'm quite
> proud of it actually, do you like it? Do you want to me to
> put me tag on your nice white shirt?...only joking!"

Always use proper grammar and sentence construction. Avoid
abbreviations and the use of police jargon. Write in plain English,
so that everyone can understand what you mean (see Chapter 1).

Surnames/family names should be written in CAPITALS. (If you
habitually write entirely in capitals, then *underline* names.) This
applies to all names written in a statement to avoid ambiguity and
misunderstanding by the reader.

> The suspect identified himself to me as Toni STALYBRIDGE,
> born 06/04/88, address 24, Morgan Street, Tonchester. I
> could clearly see the graffiti which were 33cm wide and
> 20cm tall on the outside of the "Buy One Get One Free" shop.
> There were three symbols in total, all in "British Racing
> Green". There were no other painting marks on what was
> otherwise a clean wall made of bricks and mortar measuring
> 2 metres in length and 1 metre in height, below the front
> window of the shop. When I arrived, the sprayed symbols
> were still wet and I could clearly smell the odour of cellulose
> paint.

There is no requirement to record the caution in full. However,
replies after caution should be recorded in direct speech.

> I said to STALYBRIDGE "It is an offence to damage the wall
> of this shop with paint from a spray can." I cautioned him
> and he replied, "Yeah go on, get it over and done with." At
> 0902 hours the same day, I had said to STALYBRIDGE,
> "Earlier, when I first walked up to you outside this shop,
> you said to me, 'What are you doing here? You lot never
> come round here. What if I am? It's my tag, nobody's ever
> stopped me before. I'm quite proud of it actually, do you like
> it? Do you want to me to put me tag on your nice white
> shirt?...Only joking!' STALYBRIDGE replied, "Yeah it's true,
> I did say all that."

Ensure that you correctly spell the names of places and people. Consider the effect on your credibility in court if important evidence, such as a location or a person's name, is spelled wrongly.

Take pride and care in the completion of your statement to avoid errors. Any errors you do make in the text should be corrected by striking through with ~~one line~~. This should then be initialled in the margin. You **must never** overwrite a mistake or use correction fluid.

Always write in black ink.

Pages should be held together by use of a paper clip and not stapled.

> I then said to STALYBRIDGE "I am reporting you and you
> may be prosecuted for the offence of causing criminal
> damage." I cautioned him and he replied, "Yeah, I
> understand, you've got a job to do." At 0910 hours the same
> day, the interview was terminated. STALYBRIDGE read the
> record of the interview and signed my pocket note book as
> correct. At 0915 hours the same day, I attended the security
> room at the Precinct. There I saw a person who identified
> herself to me as Gamme Ubelele NANATANGA. At that time
> I took possession of a CCTV video tape from Ms NANATANGA
> exhibit labelled and marked GUN/1.

After the last word of the statement and at the bottom of the first and subsequent pages, sign your name (including your PCSO number).

There is no need for anybody to witness your signature (this is for witness statements only).

Signature *Jo Matthews PCSO1*
Signature witnessed by

At the top of each subsequent page print your name.

Continuation of Statement of: *Jo Britton MATTHEWS*

In the top right hand corner of each page write the page number.

Page No 2 Of *X*

Other details identifying you which you need to consider

Do not put your home address or home telephone number on the rear of an MG11 because of the potential consequences if a defendant obtained these details. Record your Force address in the 'Home address' section in CAPITAL letters. Endorse the 'Home telephone number' section as 'N/A'.

Include the telephone number of your police station in the 'Work telephone number' section. The 'Preferred means of contact ...' section should be endorsed as 'N/A'. Delete 'Male/Female' as appropriate. Include your 'Date and place of birth'. Complete the 'Former name' section if you have one or endorse as 'N/A'. Your 'height' must be included. The 'Identity Code' section must be completed with your ethnic appearance code. The 'Dates of witness availability' section does not have to be completed. Your statement should be accompanied by a completed MG10 which records your availability.

Witness contact details

Home address: *c/o TONCHESTER CENTRAL POLICE STATION,*
             HIGH STREET, TONCHESTER, TONFORD

                                                      Postcode: *TO1 9TF*

Home telephone No: *N/A*   Work telephone No: *01 1212999*

Mobile/Pager No: *N/A*   E-mail address: *PCSO01@999.co.uk*

Preferred means of contact: *N/A*

~~Male~~/Female (delete as applicable)

Date and place of birth: *25.04.1980*

Former name: *N/A*   Height: *5ft 8ins*   Ethnicity Code: *W1*

Dates of witness non-availability: *N/A*

The Victim Personal Statement does not apply to you (unless
you are a victim) when you are making a duty statement. It
applies to a witness.

The '*Statement taken by …* ' section should be endorsed as 'N/A'.
This is for you when you take a statement from a witness. The
time and location of statement completion should be recorded
in your PNB.

Statement taken by (print name): *N/A*   Station:

Time and place statement taken:

All this may seem complicated, but with practice it will become
a straightforward exercise. Don't let it become routine and **always
take seriously the making of a duty statement**.

5.3 **The Upside—Winning through Negotiation and Persuasion**

Having looked at the powers designated to the PCSO role at some
length, and having recognized that not all of them will be in your
arsenal, you could be forgiven for thinking about your role only
in terms of how you may compel people to do things. However, as
we have suggested earlier, the PCSO role is not merely the sum of
all its power parts. We do not doubt that you need powers and the

designation of them by your Chief Constable should be appropriate and proportionate (remember the PLAN or JAPAN principles?). However, the exercise of power, or requiring someone to do something because you have the power to require it, is not the whole story. It isn't even half of it.

5.3.1 What is your role?

It therefore follows that other skills must come into play and these skills are actually the bedrock of the PCSO role. Consider the title of the role itself. Which do you represent, the police or the community? Do you support the police in the community, or support (interpret) the community to the police? The truth is that both of these will exist at the same time. PCSOs can be the conduit between the police and the community, and convey the concerns of the community to the police , thus having a foot in both camps.

Discussion points

What do you think you might be able to do about people being afraid to leave the security of their residences at night?

A model response

One evident solution which we hope you would consider is that targeted patrols during this time in the evening will provide a visible presence for the public. Has it solved the problem or has the reassurance generated by the visible patrols been registered by the community as a success? You may not need to deal with anything tangible on the streets during the evening, but the mere fact of your being there, and being seen to be there, will reassure some residents (especially the elderly), who may feel able to venture out if you are about. It's sobering to think that some people are so frightened to be a visible part of their communities, so scared of what might happen to them, that simply the sight of you in uniform in the neighbourhood will allay many of those fears.

5.3.2 PCSO as a problem solver

If we take this problem/challenge further we can expand on the concept of winning through negotiation and persuasion and develop the idea of the **PCSO as a problem solver**. Michael Stevens, in his book *How to be a Better Problem Solver*, defines problem solving as 'transforming one set of circumstances into another, preferred state.'[4]

You will know that 'problem solving' underpins many of the NOS and competences upon which a PCSO is judged, so this capability requires your full attention. In a very real sense, it will become something at which you become well-practised if your PCSO role sits within Neighbourhood Policing Teams, but you need to bring a critical, not to say sceptical, eye to bear upon what problem solving entails. If we look at the PCSO within the current parameters of 'citizen-focused' policing, within the idea of actively engaging with the community, and within 'Neighbourhood Policing Teams', then perhaps the best judges of the preferred state are the people who live within that community. This may sound perfectly logical to you but in terms of traditional policing it is a radical departure from the prevailing and rather paternalistic idea that 'we are the police and therefore we know best'.

5.3.2.1 *Dealing with non-policing problems*

Let's take this further and consider the notion that some people in Tonchester (see Chapter 8.3; the letter from the BCU Commander) are scared to go out even during the day unless in escorted groups. Obviously, we have very few details at this stage but whatever has been happening does not necessarily constitute a traditional policing problem. If no criminal offences have been committed, then within the parameters of coercive policing (that is, the exercise of designated powers) nothing can be done. This is a problem largely of perception on the part of the residents but, as the PCSO assigned to this area, your role allows you to go deeper in the quest for a solution.

Discussion points

What role should you now play?
How deep should you go?
What outcome is wanted?

A model response

You will have the time, the inclination (one hopes), and the responsibility to work on behalf of the community to try to get rid of this apparent climate of fear and help the community at large to 'regain the streets'. By speaking with the residents, by liaising with partnership agencies, and by transcending traditional divisions of responsibility, you may get to the root causes of the problem. One of the recurrent problems in any community, but especially communities of municipal or 'council' housing, is that there can be *'designed-in crime'*. What do you think this means?

5.3.2.2 *'Designed-in' crime*

You may be more familiar with the idea of 'designing out' crime; where architects and planners work with communities to ensure that there is good lighting, that there are no walkways or underpasses suitable for a mugging or an ambush of any kind, that there is CCTV live-monitored at key junctions, that there is a presence of adults at specific times, that the community takes on and holds the responsibility for the safe movement of its residents. The mirror negative, designed-in crime, might be an issue about inadequate lighting, or about malfunctioning lifts in multistorey buildings; it could be about graffiti, obscenities scrawled on bus-stops, the lack of CCTV, or lack of live monitoring of its passive product, the absence of police patrols; kids hanging about in groups because there is nowhere to go and nothing to do, where the discovery of used needles engenders the fear of drugs dealing and drugs taking, where there are reports of assaults, where windows are broken and not repaired, where cars are abandoned or 'torched', where families indulge in gross anti-social behaviour and go unchecked; in short it could be anything which gives the community genuine concern. Parts of the physical structure (the housing and hard landscaping, for example) of where the community lives may intensify that concern.

Working in the interests of the community is also working in the interests of law and order

But you will have spoken to the community and listened to what these concerns are. From that point on, you will be working in the interests of the community and more importantly with a legitimacy invested in you by the community because you have listened. What's more, you will also be working in the interests of the police because you are dealing with community issues in a positive manner. In this case the duality of the role is a positive. It won't matter that you now have a foot in each camp, because you will be the link between the two groups; you will be the interpreter of the police to the community and the conduit from the community to the police.

5.3.2.3 *Possible outcomes*

It might be through your liaison that better lighting is installed; that shrubbery is cut back; that CCTV cameras are manned and live-monitored; that adults take responsibility for their children; that somewhere is made, created, begged, or borrowed for the youth to go, and where the community can rediscover a spirit or sense of belonging which should have united it in common civic purpose. The difference is that you have been the catalyst, you have helped it to happen.

5.3.3 **The picture is complex and multilayered**

We appreciate that the examples we have talked about above might be seen as oversimplified because any such consultation with the community has to take place over a period of time, and will ebb and flow in terms of enthusiasm, commitment, or scepticism from both the community and the police. You may find that different members of the community have different roles to play, you may equally find that some members of the community cordially detest other members of it, and you may have to act as referee on occasions. Indeed, your availability to concentrate on the specifics of the challenge is also a factor. You won't be dealing with one problem at a time and then moving on to the next, only when the first is solved. You will be handling many tasks at the same time, some moving towards maturity, some only just being articulated.

Example

Suppose that part of the neighbourhood includes families of asylum seekers, who feel alienated and unwelcome, and who have not been integrated with any community. You may want to start reaching out to them and engaging with them, but at the same time you may have to work with people in the neighbourhood, important opinion formers some of them, who may be unremittingly hostile to asylum families.

5.3.4 **Different options to consider**

Whilst there is no magic formula to success there are certain aspects within this organic process of community consultation that could help you. These are wholly adaptable to local situations and may directly help you to engage with differing groups within

your community. One of the key constraints in community policing is the fact that no community is homogeneous and therefore a
'one size fits all' approach is not likely to succeed and risks further
alienating segments of the community. By utilizing **a variety** of
consultative methods, you stand a better chance of reaching out
to more members of the community. Always remember, though,
that your job is to bring them together and to extract, if possible,
some sort of working compromise. It isn't for you to do all on your
own, so you will need to be tough-minded, able to delegate, and
thick-skinned about making people do things.

5.3.4.1 *Public meetings*

Public meetings are a traditional means of imparting knowledge
or seeking approval but such meetings can also be used as discussion chambers designed to find out what the community wants
from its police force. Consultation with the community needs to
be seen as part of a process rather than an end in itself. It is not
enough just to say 'well, we had a meeting' if nothing comes of it.
Don't be tempted to hold meetings for meetings' sake—nothing
is so likely to give the illusion of progress with no substance.

5.3.4.2 *Surgeries*

Rather than seeking a mass audience, a 'surgery' allows individuals to come forward with problems or concerns; surgeries can also
elicit intelligence about the community. They can be held in a
variety of locations, which allow for best face-to-face contact with
the community. Good venues are libraries, health centres, leisure
centres, school halls, and so on. The point is that, regularly, people can air their concerns to you on a private basis; sometimes
simply talking to you is therapy enough for them. In the larger
picture, though, you will want to do something in response to
what you are told.

5.3.4.3 *Questionnaires*

Questionnaires can be used at either a macro or micro level and,
importantly, can be used on one-issue subjects or in terms of a
general 'forum'. They allow for people who cannot (or who will
not) attend meetings or surgeries to have a voice, as well as providing for quantitative and qualitative evaluation of any schemes
or initiatives undertaken. Be warned though; questionnaires have
to be crystal-clear in what they are seeking. The questions must be
unambiguous, thoughtfully designed, and not too long (or people
will toss them away; not to mention the cost of reprographics).

Get some advice from your Force business information unit, which will ensure that your questions are properly framed and that you can quantify the results. Alternatively, you could go for a cheap and cheerful option of writing, say, five questions on an A4 sheet and pinning it up in a community centre or an appropriate notice board, inviting people to write to or e-mail you with their thoughts.

5.3.4.4 *Mobile police stations*

Many areas have mobile police stations or trailers that are used at fairs, fêtes, and gatherings to publicize such initiatives as community safety. These can also be used for community consultation and can be parked literally on the community's doorstep. Promotional material and free gifts, such as purse chains (to prevent them being snatched) or shed alarms (in an area where garden tools are frequently stolen), can be used to draw in an audience which can then also be consulted on more general community issues and concerns.

Community engagement

Once again it is about the multitasking essence of community engagement, because even if the recipient of the purse chain or shed alarm does not want to be consulted by you about anything at all, then at the very least you may have prevented a purse snatch or the theft of a mower. Being seen as an approachable character, your unthreatening presence in a trailer devoted to security, may be all the invitation some people need to engage with you more deeply. The opportunity to talk to you is what is important.

5.3.5 **Permanence**

What is important to bear in mind is that once you have started the community engagement process, you have let loose a genie from the bottle. Community expectations will grow with each success or new initiative. Part of the (often voiced) public apprehension about the PCSO role is that people are anxious that it is merely the latest in a long line of much-heralded and then quickly-forgotten police or government initiatives (remember 'zero tolerance'?). There will be apprehension that, good as you are, you'll be gone tomorrow and that, even if the PCSO concept itself survives, there will be a new face every year or so. This unsettles people, particularly the elderly, who find that adjusting to change can be a source of acute worry.

5.3.5.1 *Back to the old days?*

We guarantee that you will have people come and talk to you about their memories of the days of the good old bobby on the beat and how he (it's always a he) dealt with rowdy youth by 'clipping them round the ear'. At its most basic and superficial, the PCSO does resemble this role and you can't blame people for thinking that you yourself are a throwback to the good old days. Those good old days are as much a myth as any other form of nostalgia: people could leave their front doors open because they didn't have much worth stealing, and community knowledge, and its sanctions, was strong. Nonetheless, domestic and sexual violence were seldom reported and abuse of children was largely unreported. It was not all golden in the 1950s.[5]

5.3.5.2 *Becoming a familiar face*

To be positive, as you walk your patrol beat, or engage with your particular remit in the community, you will begin to know people by name, begin to know who is in which family, who works where, which car belongs to which house, who goes to what school and information like this is crucial to your role. You will also be the person people talk to about the problems that they perceive in the community. You will be quickly identified as 'the person in the know'. This allows you to publicize the initiatives you have started in your area but it also means that for every community there will be an infinite number of potential problems which individuals will expect you to solve. It therefore follows that consultation alone is not enough. What must occur in tandem with consultation is a process whereby the problems are ranked in terms of what needs to be done in what order. Once again who better to choose than the members of the community themselves, the very people who live day-to-day with these problems and their consequences? Once again, it is a signal departure from traditional policing, if you encourage the community to help you set your priorities rather than using a remote national policing plan or a slightly less remote Force policing plan.

5.3.6 Choice is about managing expectation

At this point it is important to note that the community does not have complete freedom to decide how it is policed. A community cannot decide that it is not bothered this month by street robberies and therefore has no interest in solutions and actions which might benefit others. It cannot ask the police to ignore criminal offences. Rather, what we are talking about is giving communities a say in how policing is achieved and this is where the PCSO needs to become a skilled diplomat, utilizing skills in negotiating and persuasion to assist the process and to ensure that it does not become unrealistic or unrepresentative. The National Community Forum, in a report in 2006, discussed the importance and also the complexity of this:

> While choice can be empowering, unless it is handled carefully, it could exacerbate inequalities. Providing options is not sufficient to allow choice to empower people in deprived communities—there needs to be support to enable people to make use of the choices that are on offer.[6]

5.3.6.1 *Public meetings as benchmarks for action*

A public meeting designed to find out community priorities can be taken as a benchmark for action. What is interesting is that this type of meeting tends to highlight what are thought of as low-level nuisances, rather than criminal problems. Numerous studies, collated in a 2005 Home Office Development and Practice Report, have shown that environmental factors will feature heavily in terms of community concerns:

> Community members tend to show the most concern over the physical and social fabric of their own neighbourhood. Therefore, they may be most readily motivated to participate in responses to these problems. Neighbourhood regeneration schemes can be very successful as a precursor to greater community confidence and participation.[7]

Regeneration issues

These regeneration issues often surround matters such as graffiti, rubbish, litter, dog mess, etc. They are not the most glamorous of problems to solve and some critics have argued that they are not ones for the police to be solving at all, yet if we ask the community for their concerns, we cannot then censor or ignore the outcomes of that consultation. **We need to be wary of the imposed solution from the 'we know best' patronage; it is based on hubris (pride) and territoriality, which does not bring with it a lasting answer to social decay.**

5.3.6.2 *Plans determined by community consultation*

Consulting the community and then negotiating a plan of what can be done together provides the PCSO with a strong local grounding for action. Whilst the end result could be a coercive use of powers on offenders, the path towards it has been aided by community engagement. The knowledge and skills developed by PCSOs in their locality will be vital to the success of any initiative. How could those residents afraid to leave their homes get greater reassurance? Better street lighting, targeted patrols, closure of alleyways? If the residents feel safer in walking around both in daylight and at night, then the initiative will be a success, but what has been achieved could be far greater than this one outcome. The process will have engendered a greater regard for the police and the partners they have worked with to get these results. Therefore, the expectations for action with the next problem and with the one after that, will be higher still and the process will begin anew. On all subsequent occasions, there is a platform to build upon. The bad news about all this is that if you are good at winning through negotiation and persuasion, you'll be expected to do it again and again.

5.4 **Defusing Situations**

We have discussed at some length the 'upside' to the PCSO role and the skills needed to sustain the community engagement process, and we have highlighted some of the skills needed to start this particular ball rolling. However, you will also encounter situations where members of the community are not so amenable to this process and you will find occasions where you are required to defuse situations. The next section (5.5) will look specifically at dealing with aggression, whilst we will look now at non-aggressive situations which nonetheless need calming or defusing of tension. What is common to both situations is that the paramount factor is your own safety. **You are not a warranted Police Officer with the training, skills, or equipment to deal with open aggression.** Walking away and seeking suitable assistance is an entirely viable option and you should be conscious of the **Rules of Engagement** (see 2.2.5.2 above).

Discussion points

Where do the expectations for a PCSO to act to resolve a dispute come from?

What feelings might you have in walking away from a dispute?

5.4.1 Dispute between neighbours—an extended example

What difference could it make when you have to try to defuse a situation where the dispute is between individuals rather than between groups? Consider the following extended example involving two neighbours living in the residential part of town. You are in the area one sunny spring afternoon on a routine patrol when your attention is drawn by people shouting angrily. You turn the corner and come across two middle-aged men in their front gardens bellowing at one another. As you approach, you gather that most of the discussion involves *leylandii* hedges and car parking. Several other people have stopped to watch and the curtains are twitching in a few of the nearby houses.

Discussion points

At this stage, what are you thinking about?

Does this potential neighbour dispute have anything to do with you as a PCSO?

What differences might there be in resolving this angry quarrel as opposed to the shopping centre 'youth v. age' dispute which we discussed earlier?

5.4.1.1 *Sorting out disputes and spats*

We hope that you will be turning these matters over in your mind as you make your way towards the arguing neighbours (assuming of course, that your decision was not to turn around and walk back the way you came). As a uniformed representative of the community, people will expect you to intervene and sort out this dispute, but these expectations do not mean that you have to become embroiled with every spontaneous argument you happen across. As you approach this neighbourly spat, you should be undertaking a dynamic risk assessment to see whether there are any factors that may preclude you from intervening. Has either party a weapon to hand? Are specific and violent threats being made? Is this dispute actually in serious danger of escalation? If you feel that things are getting out of hand, you would be right to radio for back-up so that trained police officers with their greater powers, more comprehensive training, and more sophisticated equipment can take control of any escalation in the quarrel, whilst you remain at a distance and observe/record the situation.

5.4.1.2 *Seek information to strengthen your working actions*

You are seeking to obtain information prior to problem solving so that you are working from a position of **informed strength**, which allows you to establish the independence which is crucial to seeking an effective and binding resolution. You must remain Solomon-like in your actions and judgements so that both parties feel that you are objective and fair. This is tricky to do because it is only natural that you might already have formed an opinion as to who is right and who is wrong.

5.4.1.3 *Detailed bickering*

Following your initial intervention in the neighbour dispute, you have obtained the following information: Mr Drake at number 43 believes that his neighbour Mr Peacock of number 45 has been deliberately parking his car across the driveway to number 43, which has prevented Drake from accessing his own driveway. Countering this, Peacock asserts that this has all arisen because he has complained about the Drake's *cupressus leylandii* hedge at the rear of the property, which has drastically reduced the light to Peacock's rear garden. Both parties have been bickering for some time about these issues, but Peacock suggests that it has escalated recently because he threatened to go to a solicitor about Drake's hedge. Peacock also admits to deliberately winding up his neighbour by sometimes parking across Drake's driveway. You have also spoken to the neighbours on either side of the disputants who tell you that the tension between the two households has been palpable over the last couple of weeks and they fear that it could go further if nothing is done.

Discussion points

What strategies would you adopt in dealing with the issue?

Consider what other agencies could be involved in helping to solve this problem.

How would you characterize your role as a PCSO in settling this dispute?

5.4.1.4 *Early and decisive intervention may defuse potential dangers*

No one pretends that this is easy: you're dealing with imperfect, fault-ridden human beings, with all the variations in mood, tone, understanding, desire, and socialization that living in a community of similar beings will produce. You have to try your best to prevent things spiralling out of control, and your role is always going to be more effective if you intervene decisively and early, rather than waiting until one of the parties produces a shotgun. *This is a key point for us to make* because the PCSO cannot simply move from dispute to dispute putting out each fire in isolation without making sure that the fires do not reignite at a later date (especially when you may not be nearby with an extinguisher).

Managing disputes and achieving solutions are key indicators of your role as a PCSO, and of your relevance to the community.

Successful management of these problems will help to give you a meaningful role in the community and with each new situation/dispute you will gain more skills, understand what works and what doesn't, develop better and more practical strategies, and grow in confidence in your own abilities to take on the next problem you meet. Not only that, but as you resolve disputes successfully, word will get around and, in future, people may come to you directly and ask for your arbitration. That *would* be a useful community skill.

5.5 **Dealing with Aggression**

We can encounter aggression from others towards us in almost every aspect of our daily lives, irrespective of whether we wear uniforms or not, or whether we are engaged in law enforcement and keeping the peace, or not. This is not to say that we live in a particularly violent society—certainly compared with other parts of the world, the USA for instance, parts of Africa, or the Far East, the UK is largely peaceable—nor are we more violent now than we have been in the past. **Our history is violent.** The mid-eighteenth century, for example, was a time of considerable lawlessness, with *highwaymen* and *footpads* (the names to describe those, respectively outside or inside the cities, who used violence to effect robbery), and gangs of armed young men, called *Mohucks*,[8] roamed London, waylaying and assaulting passers-by and vandalizing property. Ordinary people routinely carried weapons, including firearms. Indeed, the rise in crimes of violence and the threat of mob rule were prime justifications used to introduce the Metropolitan 'new' Police, nearly a century later in 1830, following Sir Robert Peel's Bill of 1829. Other instances abound: after each of the World Wars in the last century, not surprisingly, there was an upsurge in violence, especially domestic violence and murder. This last was largely caused by men returning from service abroad, particularly, to find that wives or sweethearts had been unfaithful.[9] The recourse, for men trained in legalized aggression, was to violence, often fatally.

5.5.1 The myth of the 'golden age'

Nonetheless, though it has never been proven that the times we live in are more violent than those which have gone before, there is a widespread belief that there was a golden age, in and around the 1950s and early 1960s, when authority was respected, police officers admired, and you could leave your door open all day without being burgled.[10] Like any fantasy, this one is based in unreality and hedged about with wish fulfilment: police officers have hardly ever been loved (respected maybe, for a period in the 1860s–90s), there has *never* been a time when crime did not exist. The regret for the passing of 'respect' for age and seniority has much to do with a nostalgia for an unquestioning obedience to authority. That said, the chances are that as an ordinary citizen you will encounter at least one instance of verbal aggression in a year. As a PCSO on duty and in uniform, you will encounter five instances of verbal aggression and up to three instances of physical aggression, ranging from pushing and shoving to assault, in the course of a year.[11]

5.5.1.1 *Violence is endemic*

What this preamble suggests is that violence in our daily lives is nothing new and, despite the sensationalist parts of the media, not especially prevalent, at least at the serious end. The whole of the UK, Scotland and Northern Ireland included, has fewer murders in an average year (about 900 homicides) than Johannesburg (topping 4,300 in 2005–06). What may be new, or at least characteristic of the age in which we live, is that multiple reporting of violence is much more likely to happen, and this may well skew our perceptions, making aggression seem more prevalent than it is. That can apply to the whole of crime and anti-social behaviour, where people feel less safe in their streets, towns, and communities, especially at night, than the level of recorded crime suggests that they should. Perception, then, is not the same as cold fact.

Indeed, the perception of social disorder was one of the reasons for the introduction of the PCSO in the first place. This takes us back to our beginning: aggressive behaviour is all around us. We may even have learned to live with it as private citizens, and take it as a fact of modern life.

5.5.2 What makes someone act aggressively?

We can do no more in a handbook of this size than skim over the surface of human behaviour and psychology, but there are usually some recurrent triggers, or catalysts, which we can say with some certainty, provoke an aggressive response. Some of these are:

- **Frustration**
- **Inarticulacy**
- **Anger**
- **Defensiveness** or defence tactics
- **Desire to escape** the consequences of an action
- **Under the influence** of alcohol or drugs
- **Guilt; being caught out**
- **Fear** (especially of some stereotype).

5.5.2.1 *Responding emotionally*

You can see that most of these are emotions or feelings, and that is usually what aggression is: *an emotional response to a situation*, especially and particularly when an individual or group is backed into a corner from which there seems to be no way out except by fighting. We could define aggression in such a context as an '**attack on another, usually but not necessarily, as a response to opposition**'.[12] Let's examine the various indicators noted above; always remembering that aggression does not have to entail physical assault.

The nature of aggression

Aggression can be any demonstration of anger up to and including assault. It is likely, though, that physical assault may be preceded by posturing and aggressive language. Very few of us, other than quite rare **sociopaths** (*people who have no feeling for, or recognition of, social norms or behaviours*), will launch unprovoked attacks on another person without giving some indication that the attack is coming. Sometimes, the range of angry emotions can be linked, almost becoming a series. Suppose someone falls over on a slippery pavement and cracks his or her head and, on rising, finds some people laughing at his or her misfortune. (This laughter response is quite common. It has a long German descriptive name: *Schadenfreude*, meaning something like *gloating at someone else's hurt*.) The person may feel angry or embarrassed or plain silly for having fallen over. Of itself, the laughter is not likely to provoke aggression. But it might if accompanied with some sort of stereotyping, such as saying 'Stupid woman! Can't even stand up straight!', or 'Look at that; I always said Asians couldn't carry their booze ... ', 'That young idiot's pissed again ... Typical!' These racist, 'ageist', or chauvinist comments may act like fuel on a fire, and provoke aggression out of sheer frustration.

5.5.2.2 *Bottling up one's feelings*

Alternatively, the person might simmer in silence, because s/he can't think of a smart remark back, or cannot express how s/he is feeling. This inability to express oneself, or *inarticulacy*, is a common reason for frustration to turn to physical aggression (indeed, it can be part of the reason for domestic violence). Confronted sometimes with verbal aggression, such as shouted obscenities or homophobic chanting, individuals on the receiving end will respond with physical aggression—often the very response which the provoker wants, of course. Other instances of aggressive behaviour may arise because people are unable to put their anger into words, cannot express the turmoil of emotions within them, or do not find verbal aggression sufficient to expel the 'anger pressures' which they feel. It is a fact, of course, that those who are abused often go on to become abusers themselves; similarly, those who have learned aggressive behaviour at home or in school, may go on to use it themselves when adults.

5.5.2.3 *'It's always someone else's fault'—defensive responses*

Anger is a prevalent emotion; we meet it all the time but perhaps it is most common in responses to criticism. Some astute individuals, such as Anne Robinson or Simon Cowell, utilize their acid tongues and (often scripted) rudeness to others as a saleable product on television or other media. Most of us can identify with the sort of defensive emotions which criticism may evoke. We seek to excuse, deflect, or to put the blame on others for what are often our own shortcomings and inadequacies. One of the authors of this Handbook can recall distinctly, when at school, the attempt by well-meaning educationalists to protect students from the stigma of failure in examinations by instituting the category of 'incorrectly entered'. The idea of this euphemism was not only to avoid using the word 'fail', but to suggest that the blame for below-par performance was in fact the teacher's, for putting the student into the examination in the first place. And how such gentle deceit plays to our egos! Failure is not our fault; it's the teacher's, the doctor's, the police officer's, the probation officer's, the PCSO's; it's the fault of the system, of society's greed, it's the result of the class divide, it's any politician; **what it really, really isn't, is me**.

5.5.2.4 *Aggressive responses when guilty*

Scapegoats are always to hand if we want someone else to take the blame, and this defensiveness will often characterize responses to a PCSO intervening to enforce a law or regulation. You should be prepared for abuse and open hostility if you intervene to suggest to someone that he or she should pick up the litter s/he has just dropped. Guilt, and being caught out, can as easily provoke aggressive reactions as anger or frustration. None of us escapes such temptations to blame others, or, if there is no one else handy, to blame the law officer who has called us to account. All police officers have heard, at some time or other, the comment:

> Haven't you people got anything better to do than to pick on poor motorists/drinkers/football fans/parents/young people/students/protesters/foxhunters/party-goers ...?
> Why aren't you out catching real criminals?

When desires are opposed ...

You will certainly hear something similar if you intervene with young people whom you suspect of smoking or drinking under age. This takes us back to the original definition of aggression with which we began: aggression arises when wills or desires are **opposed**. Think of a toddler in a tantrum. Think how much scarier is an adult in a similar, thwarted, uncontrollable rage.

5.5.2.5 *Alcohol-fuelled violence*

People who have taken too much alcohol or illegal drugs can have personality changes of a marked kind. Alcohol can increase combativeness, anger, aggression, and it can heighten emotional responses, precisely because the normal social inhibitions have been loosened. The same artificial confidence which betrays us into thinking that we can drive brilliantly, or 'pull' someone to whom we are attracted, extends into other matters of one's prowess, such that intervention by others, especially the officially disapproving, may provoke sudden bursts of physical aggression. Fortunately, the signs are often there for you to see well in advance of any attack, and usually the alcohol makes it more difficult for the boozer to be pinpoint accurate in an assault. We dwelt on your options in these cases in 3.2 above, when examining specific powers. We noted then that you must anticipate aggression if you stop people drinking (in a designated place) and take and dispose of their alcohol. There is an ever-present need for you to assess risks dynamically in any situation where your actions might provoke an aggressive response.

5.5.2.6 *Drugs*

With drugs, the situation is similar, but reactions can be more aggressive. Drugs intensify perceptions (both of pleasure and of pain) for short periods—that is part of their dangerous seductiveness of course—but also, as the intensity subsides or begins to lose sharpness, so reaction sets in which often includes very powerful aggression. Add to this the fact that many drug takers are also criminals, who commit crimes to get money to feed the habit, and you may well find that a drug user may become very aggressive, not just to get away from you and the authority you represent, but also because he or she cannot bear the thought of being locked up and away from the next dosage or fix. You represent a tangible danger to the drug addict's habit, and as such, you are a legitimate target for attack. This is the convoluted reasoning which an addict may use to justify an attack on you or others. The effect is the same whatever the cause of the aggression: you are in uniform and in the firing line.

5.5.2.7 *The anger may turn on you because you're there*

The emotions of **guilt** (at being caught out at something) and **fear** are often similar in effect. Police officers will tell you that occasionally, kerb-crawlers seeking to set up a liaison with a prostitute can be very aggressive when challenged by someone in authority. There could be any number of reasons for this aggressive response, but principal among them are likely to be the fear of publicity, allied to guilt about what the kerb-crawler's partner might say if the whole episode came out. The same might apply to someone detected in homophobic or racist abuse (both crimes, of course). If people think that they can't get away with what they have done, and particularly if you have intervened and confronted them in the act, the guilt can be intense, and they can unload that guilt on you in short order: *you* are the killjoy, the Gestapo, the 'thought police', the fascist, the pig who has spoiled the fun; no harm was meant, some people can't take a joke, no lasting damage done, but you have to come along and interfere. This and much more is likely to be directed at you if you take action and provoke guilt in the offender. It is a form of defensiveness but it is more the fear of the consequence of being caught which provokes the aggression, not just the seeking of a way to escape.

5.5.3 What should you do if you become the target of aggression?

So far, we have talked about how and why people become aggressive and how your role within the community might well provoke aggression from those whom you detect doing wrong, breaking the law, being anti-social, or simply too drunk or drugged to care. Now it is time to consider what you should do when you become the target for aggression. The golden 'rule of *dis*engagement' for PCSOs is:

When in danger of assault, withdraw.

You should call for assistance and observe from a distance. Yet a situation may arise where you cannot avoid a confrontation. Populist commentators on body language (or non-verbal communication, as it is sometimes called) suggest that a Caucasian person's complexion may indicate whether or not an attack is imminent. The 'people watchers' tell us that if a person's face is white and sallow, then an attack may take place at any minute. If, on the other hand, the person's face is red and suffused, the anger has passed its peak and a physical attack, whilst still possible, is less likely.[13] On the other hand, the pale person could be sick and the florid person merely suffering from high blood pressure. Don't be misled by such 'pop' commentary.

5.5.3.1 *Modelling aggressive responses*

There has to be a *context* in which the aggression has arisen (see Figure 17)(we noted earlier that only fairly rare sociopaths attack without warning) and we can express that context in a diagram like this:

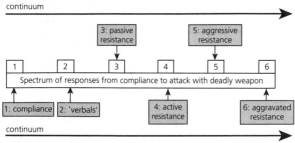

Figure 17: Aggression response spectrum

The intensification of aggressive responses

What this shows is that, in conventional aggression displays, there is a movement from compliant to really aggressive. That movement can be very swift and may not be linear (in other words, it won't necessarily pass through the stages shown, but jump across stages, depending on what is perceived as the level of provocation). What it *should* give you is time in which to respond and time to think.

5.5.3.2 *Response tactics*

You must look for *exit spots*, where you can get away from the aggressor, and visibly create space between you and the aggressor. The recommended distance is two metres (this is an approximation to two arms' lengths; the aggressor's and yours: you must keep the potential assailant 'at arm's length' if you can). Any attempt to shorten that distance must entail a step forward by the aggressor—which can then be matched by a step back by you, thus sustaining the distance. This should be accompanied by short commands, shouted by you, such as *'Back!'*, *'Stay back!'*, *'Step back!'* Keep your hands in sight, above your waist, and outstretched, palms towards the aggressor. This is not simply a pacific or 'calm down' stance; it is so that if the assailant suddenly produces a blade and slashes at you, your arms and wrists will take the impact rather than your face or vital organs.

5.5.3.3 *Think first, then react*

Of course, it's easy for us to write what you should do from the quiet of a study or workroom: it's quite another to react 'properly' and in textbook fashion, when you are alone in a tense situation, when it might be dark or raining, when you may be surrounded by menacing figures, and when your throat is dry and your heart pumping. We know; we've been there too. But if you can think about the *principles* of what we are describing, if you can give thought to how you might react and what the options are (even how not to get into the situation in the first place), and if you can rehearse with yourself (or better, with a trusted colleague) what you might be able to do, you stand a better chance of getting away unhurt than if you do not do these things.

5.5.3.4 *Advance the 'weak' leg*

Some other tips, garnered from years of 'front-line policing' and officer safety training. You have got a 'strong' leg or hand; in 85% to 90% of people, this is the right leg and right arm. You may also see it referred to as the 'dominant' leg or hand. It is the hand you do most things with, and the leg which takes the brunt of leaning, standing, starting to walk, and so on. **Always stand at an angle to a potential aggressor, on your weak leg.** (Why? because if you are pushed, struck, or if you are rushed, your weight will go back on to your stronger leg and enable you to resist more effectively.)

5.5.3.5 *Look for escape routes*

Don't get yourself backed up to a wall, and **never** with your back to a shop window (you may end up going through it), because you are closing off escape or withdrawal routes. This is nothing to do with heroism or being powerful or tough; it has to do with your survival in a situation not of your seeking and, we hope, not of your making. You must constantly seek ways to back away from the confrontation, or defuse the emotions and aggression that are being displayed. Some of the aggression signs will be **posturing**. You've seen birds or animals in 'fighting display' in which every aggressive sign is flaunted, short of actual combat. Some people do the same in attempts to convince you that he (usually, but it can be female of course) is a dangerous and frightening adversary. It's your judgement whether you think the person is blustering or whether s/he really does intend you harm, but be sure before you respond. Remember how lame it will sound in court when you have to say that you *thought* you were going to be attacked and that is why you fractured the complainant's skull. Conversely, it will be no consolation to your family if you end up in hospital because you misjudged your assailant's aggression signals.

5.5.3.6 *Remember Betari's Box*

You should also remember **Betari's Box**, (see Figure 18) which we have already seen, where your attitude and actions can impact on the actions and attitudes of another, sometimes adversely. In other words, aggression often provokes aggression. You should not fall into the trap of necessarily meeting like with like:

Figure 18: Betari's Box

5.5.4 **Flight, fight, or freeze: the chemical 'cocktail'**

We have talked about options in this context, but the essential option when all else is said and done is **flight, fight, or freeze**. This is the shorthand phrase for the action of a chemical 'cocktail' in your body. Strong emotions, such as fear, anger and extreme stress (such as you will experience in any potentially serious and aggressive confrontation) may trigger this chemical cocktail or combination:

- **Adrenaline** is the pre-eminent *fight or flight* chemical which increases your heart rate, increases the oxygen supply to your lungs, and pumps glucose into your blood for immediate energy.
- Another chemical is **dopamine**, which, with a similar substance called **norephrine**, gives you exhilaration, or the confidence to act, by speeding up nerve impulses in the brain; its effect is commonly described as 'clearing the mind'.
- **Nor-adrenaline** is a hormone which 'calls' blood from your hands, feet and face into the major organs, such as heart and lungs, to give you a burst of emergency energy.[14]
- Another hormone chemical is **cortisol**, which may reduce the effect of shock, temporarily, so that a person is not necessarily incapacitated, although injured.
- Finally, there are **endorphins**, which are a kind of painkiller manufactured by your body at moments of extreme stress. (It's also the 'feel good' factor from strenuous exercise, and why we feel good after going to the gym.)

If you put all these chemicals together, you have a heady mixture which can act upon your body in a very short time frame—faster even than alcohol. There is a school of thought which says that, just as the body can feel deprived if normal exercise programmes are suspended for any reason, so someone habitually aggressive enjoys the 'high' of chemical responses which his or her aggression produces. We do not know whether this is the case or not, though it seems plausible; the idea of someone becoming habituated to violence and being turned on by it, is genuinely scary.

5.5.4.1 *'Let down'*

The effect of these chemicals is short-lived (enough merely to satisfy the flight or the fight) and you can be left feeling exhausted, drained, and a bit flabby, once the chemical balance is restored. Actors, who commonly experience this 'cocktail' of chemicals before a demanding performance, call the aftermath the 'let down' period, and there is no doubting how deflated you feel afterwards. The common 'freeze' response at the first sign of aggression is one which you will consciously have to overcome. Paralysis or inaction is not an option for you: 'flight or fight' are the horns of this particular dilemma.

5.5.4.2 *Instinct is not always the best response*

We have laboured the point a little, perhaps, that you need to be able to train yourself to think in stressful situations, but if you do not do so, you have to rely only on instinct to get you through, which isn't always enough. In fact, instinct can betray you into acting first and thinking afterwards, with horrendous consequences if you get it wrong. There are stories, for example, of people lashing out at a sudden noise only to find that the source of the noise is a frightened child or animal. You have to be **counter-intuitive**; this comes with practice and experience, and we discuss it further in the section on risk assessment (at 5.7 below). What we can do to help you in this thinking phase, is to fix a **conflict model** in your head. We have devised the 'hand-off' model, as in Figure 19:

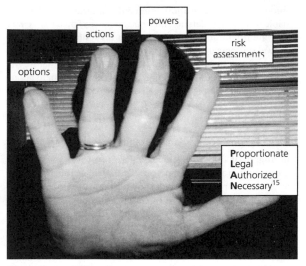

Figure 19: Hand-off conflict management model

5.5.4.3 *Explaining the hand-off conflict model*

Let's start with your thumb, because the PLAN principles are those which ensure that you do not contravene a person's human rights. What you do has to be **proportionate** to the circumstances in which you find yourself. In the cold calm of a courtroom you might have to justify what you did in the heat of the stressful moment. Your actions must have been **legal** and **authorized**, so that you acted properly within your designated powers and authority. Again, a failure or shortfall here may result in some discomfort for you in court. Your actions must be **necessary**. The test will be whether there was any other option open to you short of meeting force with force. The law says that you can use 'reasonable force', as we saw in 3.2.24 above. But the law does not define 'reasonable'.

A case where 'reasonable force' was tested in court

There was a case in 1999 of Norfolk farmer, Anthony Edward Martin, firing a shotgun at night-time intruders into his farmhouse.[16] As the result of the shotgun discharges, one of the intruders was killed and another injured. The farmer pleaded reasonable force in self-defence, but this was not accepted (there was also some doubt about the accuracy of his testimony). He was tried and sentenced to a prison term for murder, later reduced to five years for manslaughter, and he served three years before his release. The case occasioned some controversy and debate about self-protection and the protection of property. The fact remains that you might do what you think is reasonable, but the courts may take a very different view.

5.5.4.4 *Actions, options, powers, and risk assessment*

The fingers of our model hand tell you to think about your **actions**, which include what you *shouldn't* do as much as what you should. For example, you shouldn't make a bad situation worse by antagonizing an offender with moralistic finger-wagging. Such actions are an invitation to retaliation. You must consider what **options** you have got in any potential conflict or confrontation: have you enough information to move away at this point and renew your enquiry or investigation under better circumstances later? Can you call in support from police officer colleagues? How long will it take them to get to you? Can you talk down this escalating situation with a bit of humour and self-deprecation? Consider your **powers**: do they cover this eventuality? Have you a tailor-made power to use in this case? Do you know your powers well enough to invoke the particular one you want to apply here? Is the use of power appropriate in this instance, or might a quiet word be more effective? Finally, you must **assess the risk** in a fluid, developing (or dynamic) way, as matters unfold:

- Is it worth pursuing this enquiry right now if it is going to cause this person to lose face in front of his friends? Wouldn't it be preferable to return to the topic later, when he is alone?
- Is there a physical risk to you if you follow those youths down this dark alleyway?
- Can you be serious in wanting to pursue someone on to a railway line?

5.6 **Safety Training and Awareness**

We have looked at ways in which you can try to take the sting out of a confrontation in 5.4 above ('Defusing situations') and how you could respond when confronted with aggression in 5.5 above, but some of the difficulties or fraught situations which you will encounter during your time as a PCSO may have nothing to do with people behaving badly or unpleasantly. In the section which follows this one (5.7), we look at how an understanding of health and safety at work, as well as the ability to make risk assessments, will help you to perform properly in any crisis. Before that, in this short section, we look at your safety and that of others, your awareness of things going wrong around you, and the sorts of training which you might expect your Force to provide. We can't prescribe what your Force will give you in safety training, and this may vary according to how the individual Force assesses risks and problems. Please bear in mind, then, that what follows is based on what we think is 'typical' or 'average' in safety and awareness training, not what is mandatory.

5.6.1 **An example of sudden crisis**

Let's plunge you into a crisis at the outset of your foot patrol. In uniform, you are walking with due diligence and at the regulation pace, when you hear a tremendous crashing sound, a rumble, then what sounds like breaking glass, and you see what looks like a large cloud of dust or smoke rising up from an area to your right where building work has been going on. You sprint to the scene, calling Control as you go. When you arrive, you see that a network of scaffolding has apparently collapsed and part of the wall of a house has crashed down with it.

What are your action priorities?

5.6.1.1 *Judge each emergency on its merits*

No right or wrong answers here (though running away is not a good option), because much of what is needed will be dictated by the situation. For example, are builders or scaffolders injured by the fall, or are they rising from the dust and rubble, perfectly all right except for a cloud of profanity? Is anyone else injured (perhaps house occupants, or those underneath at the time)? Your first and unchangeable priority will always be '**the preservation of life and limb**', for which you can enter any building or site and render any necessary aid or help to ensure that lives are saved. We said earlier that this Handbook is not a first aid manual, and we cannot contribute specifically to your learning of first aid, but we can say that your first duty would be to anyone injured. *What should you do?*

- Assess the injury
- Render appropriate first aid (including resuscitation)
- Call for help
- Prevent further danger.

5.6.1.2 *Extending the example*

By this time, others should have responded to what has happened: passers-by, other work people on the site, people living nearby, your colleagues, and other members of the emergency services. However, before they actually make it through the entrance to the site, you notice that there is an obstacle in the way: a large portable cement mixer has fallen on its side after being struck by a scaffolding pole and it will prevent vehicles such as ambulances from getting on to the site. You run to the spot and start tugging at the industrial-sized mixer. *What safety aspects should you be aware of?*

5.6.1.3 *Risk assessment*

The danger here is that you may hurt yourself taking on a 'manual lifting' task for which you are either:

- untrained, or
- physically not capable.

When in doubt, don't. Get some assistance, or better still, leave it to those on the site who are used to handling such equipment. For all you know, there is more wet cement inside the mixer, making it even heavier. Lifting things which are too heavy or bulky for you, or not knowing how to lift, could cause you severe injury, such as a back injury, hernia, or rupture. You would be more usefully employed in coordinating the efforts of those on site who are trained or experienced in moving heavy machinery. Indeed, such coordination could clear a larger area for the reception of emergency vehicles than you could manage on your own, as well as asserting your control of the situation.

5.6.2 Buildings do collapse

You might argue that such a building collapse is a pretty unlikely scenario; well, there was a spectacular collapse of this sort in the Midlands in 2005 in which a number of building workers died and others on the site were severely injured. It happened without warning. In August 2006, again without warning, the whole upper facing (a kind of heavy plaster rendering) of a supermarket in Kent collapsed into the street below. Fortunately, the accident occurred very early on a Sunday morning and no one was injured, but this sort of thing *does* happen and it happens on someone's patrol. It might be yours. At Folkestone, in Kent, on Saturday 28 April 2007, a minor earth tremor damaged buildings and (miraculously) caused only minor injuries to people; but no one foresaw it happening.

5.6.3 Think about your and others' safety

As we commented above, we can't second-guess what your Force training policies will follow in terms of personal safety training and awareness, but they may include discussing or simulating scenarios of the kind outlined above, or they may consist of giving you the information and then testing your responses at real incidents. Either way, you need to give long and hard consideration to questions of safety, *yours and others'*, as we have noted in the preceding sections. Remember too that it is an **NOS** (4G2).

5.7 Risk Assessment

Unless you sit inside a sealed room, insulated against the world and impossibly padded against contact with anything or any-one from the outside, you will encounter risk. We meet risks all day and every day in our working lives, travel, relaxation, in our leisure, even in our sleep. It can be a deliberate courting of danger for thrills, like the Extreme Sports devotees, heli-skiers, or those who parachute from dam walls, and of course, bungee jumpers, or it can be the gentle and mild (apparently negligible) risk at the other end of the spectrum such as flower-arranging, embroidery, or sticking stamps in an album.

5.7.1 **Actions have consequences**

Whatever we do has some kind of consequence, and sometimes what we don't do has consequences too. The risks from the physically dangerous activities, like rugby or judo, are obvious enough, but stamp-collecting? Research has shown that some stamp glues can cause anaphylactic shock in susceptible people (like some people's responses to a bee-sting),[17] so self-adhesive stamps are evidently a boon. Embroiderers often stick needles in themselves (usually thighs or fingers) by accident, and flower-arrangers, despite their in-built gentility, wield secateurs, scissors, knives, saws, pruning hooks, pliers, and other cutting implements when arranging their often thorny and spiky materials. Bizarrely, though, most injuries to flower-arrangers are caused by top-heavy arrangements falling on them.

5.7.2 **Avoiding hazards**

Most of the time, our coping mechanisms are so automatic that we don't notice that we take avoiding action. We see an obstruction on the pavement and step into the gutter to walk around it. We register that there are icy steps on the way to the shopping centre and so step carefully and with smaller steps. We know that the cupboard in the bathroom is wonky and have evolved special techniques to balance things in it.

5.7.2.1 *Task—recognizing risk*

As an exercise in recognizing risk, try to put the following into order, with the commonest risk at the top and the least likely risk at the bottom (the order given here is entirely random):

- Catching a disease from a dog
- Spearing your foot with a garden fork
- Getting an electric shock
- Being hit by lightning
- Drowning while fishing
- Burning your finger
- Eating something which disagrees with you
- Being bitten by a snake
- Having part of a building collapse on you
- Being involved in a road traffic collision
- Falling off a chair at work
- Being hit by something falling from an aircraft

- Slipping in the bathroom
- Lifting something too heavy for you
- Pulling a muscle during exercise
- Singeing your eyebrows when lighting a barbecue
- Meeting an alien from outer space
- Sticking a finger in your own eye
- Falling downstairs (while sober)
- Choking whilst eating
- Falling down a hole at road works
- Breaking a bone.

Our commentary, and the correct order, is at 5.8.1 below.

5.7.2.2 *Not trusting your instincts*

As a PCSO, you will have to be **counter-intuitive** about some risks. As we have noted before, this means that you should not always do what comes naturally; indeed you should deliberately avoid any kind of 'automatic' compensatory behaviour when you confront a risk. So, if you go past a house, smell burning, see smoke, and hear someone cry 'Help!' from an upper window, do you plunge straight in and rescue whoever it is? If you see that someone has slipped on an icy pavement, do you skid blithely to his or her rescue? Are you an inveterate plunger into flood waters to pull out drowning infants? Do you lift the car back bodily on to the hoist when it has dropped on someone? Do you stop runaway horses in your sleep?

5.7.2.3 *There are dangers in instinctive reactions*

Seriously, if you charge into a burning building, or try to lift something really heavy, or go into dangerous currents, you are not only unlikely to effect the rescue you hope for, but you are very likely yourself to be a casualty. Throwing a rope to someone in difficulties in water could be more effective than diving in to save them. Remember the case of Jordon Lyon who drowned in a lake in Wigan in 2007, which we looked at briefly at 2.8.3.4 above. Calling for expert help (from organizations like the Fire and Rescue Service) is probably better than going into a burning building on your own. It may not always be the case, and of course, these things are governed by their own circumstances, but the very least you can do, when facing a problem like this, is to make a **risk assessment**. What do we mean by a risk assessment? It means making sure, as far as you can do so, that no one will get hurt, or become ill, as a result of an action. Another way of looking at it is that:

$$risk = hazard \times likelihood$$

where **hazard** is the potential for harm, **likelihood** the chances of it happening, and **risk** the severity of the danger caused by the other two factors. (Incidentally, this is not a mathematical formula, rather a model to explain the components.)

5.7.2.4 *Life is about judgements of risk*

To spend your life trying to avoid risks is impossible and a bit pointless. After all, if the pilot of the jet aircraft two miles up has a fit and falls unconscious, you're not going to be able to avoid the plane coming down on your head by thinking positively, or wearing a helmet (or even sheltering indoors). To act in this way, to try to protect yourself from all possible permutations of harm, is called being **risk-averse**. Inaction carries its own risks, since passivity may make circumstances worse than they need to be. But we are concerned with a positive approach to risk. The best PCSOs and police officers are those who ask '*what is the risk?*' and then '*what can we do about it?*' At its simplest, answering those questions is making a risk assessment.

5.7.3 **Kinds of risk**

There are three kinds of risk assessment: **generic**, **specific**, and **dynamic**. Let's look briefly at the first two of these. A **generic** risk is one which exists in general terms for similar tasks. Think of the generic risks for stopping moving vehicles in a roadside check, or dealing with a drunken person. A **specific** risk is, as the name suggests, something which happens in a specific operation or activity. Here the generic assessment needs to be added to, or *augmented*, in order to include those specific and significant factors unique to the work activity. What you have to do here is to think in advance about what is proposed and decide what the hazards are, and how you will overcome them, or diminish them, in your planning. Usually the specific risk assessment is formally documented and may be included in your Force task briefing.

5.7.3.1 *Dynamic risk assessment*

Dynamic risk assessment is applicable to you in your everyday work (and it's not that different from the sorts of decisions you make each day in your leisure time). To assess risk, you make an individual judgement, based on your knowledge of the general or generic standard and past practical experience, so that you can act as safely as possible. As we saw earlier, in your professional life your desire to act quickly must sometimes be modified by counter-intuitive thinking. Dynamic risk assessments are made at the time, there and then. There is no time to write it down and discuss it, so the way you approach risk dynamically will say a lot about you as a person, especially when others look to you for a lead, as they will in any crisis. Suppose you come first on a scene where someone has fallen over and suffered deep cuts. Bystanders and the idly curious will expect you to render first aid and to know how to stop bleeding.

5.7.3.2 *Again, think before you act*

Before you rush in to mop up the blood, you must make a dynamic risk assessment of the hazards: do you have surgical gloves so that you can avoid blood-borne contaminants? If not—what alternatives are there? Are the cuts life-threatening? (For example, has the person slipped and been gashed by a broken bottle so that there is arterial bleeding?) Do you need to call an ambulance, because the person may also be in shock? What about the original hazard? Might other people slip and fall if that is not dealt with promptly? Can you see what caused the fall in the first place? Are there other injuries? Shouldn't you keep the crowd back so that you can properly render first aid? When it's all over, what should you do to prevent any ongoing contamination to yourself?

5.7.3.3 *Always double-check injuries with health professionals*

Incidentally, it is a good standard rule to suggest that any victim of an accident be taken, or go, to be checked by medical experts, either at a GP's surgery or at a Hospital A&E. No paramedic will ever mind being called to something apparently trivial, but there have been examples where there were hidden injuries not revealed on first examination. You may render *first* aid in such a situation (people will certainly expect you to) but remember that there may be a need for *second*, even *third* aid, each requiring progressively more medically expert treatment. The questions which you ask yourself in the paragraph above may appear to you to have slowed down the process of going to someone's aid. They have, but only very slightly. **As you grow in experience, you will find yourself making dynamic risk assessments as you approach any crisis, and by the time you arrive, you will have assessed and made all the necessary**

decisions. That is why you will appear calm in such situations, and why you will make the right choices. Others may panic; with your dynamic risk assessment already made, you can take control.

5.7.3.4 *Training in making risk assessments*

Just as you should be trained in first aid, so you should be trained in making risk assessments; equally, just as first aid can be simplified to a few key principles, so can dynamic risk assessment. The standard way of presenting *what needs to be done* is through the mnemonic **SPRAIN**, thus:

S	**Situation**	What am I dealing with? What is going on?
P	**Plan**	What am I going to do? How will I do it?
R	**Risks**	What might get me or someone else injured or put in danger?
A	**Alternatives**	Are there other ways to do this?
I		
N	***IN*crease safety**	How do I reduce the risks and yet do what I have to, making it safer for all involved?

This is a shorthand method of thinking things through, and can be applied to any situation where risk has to be assessed and catered for. Let's look at workplace situations, occasions when you will have to *make dynamic risk assessments on the job*. What sort of problems might you face? To make it easier to remember, we've devised another mnemonic, **BEWARE**:

B	Biological (or chemical) dangers
E	Exposure to Fire
W	Weather conditions
A	Assault or Asphyxiation
R	Radiological contamination
E	Effort and physical exertion

Making it work

If you link **BEWARE** with **SPRAIN** you will be able to make effective dynamic risk assessments in the course of your daily work. We should emphasize that you will not encounter all of the following at the same time nor on the same shift. But, to give the authors of this Handbook an imaginative challenge, we've tried to invent a scenario that's not too far-fetched, but which incorporates all of the **BEWARE** dangers itemized above. We invite you to **SPRAIN** the following event.

5.7.4 Case study—the dynamic risk assessment patrol

Look at the map of Tonchester at the beginning of Chapter 8. This sets your scenario and shows you where you are patrolling on this particular shift. Now read on ...

5.7.4.1 *It was an ordinary day—the road traffic collision*

Your patrol route takes you along Pennsylvania Street and then right into Common Road. It is 0830 hrs on a Friday morning as you pass the hospital. You are en route to the castle ruins where there has apparently been some vandalism. You hear an ambulance approaching along Common Road (two tones and lights) behind you and then the sound of a crash, smashing glass, screams, and an impact. You turn and see the ambulance on its side, door open, a stretcher apparently containing a patient on the road, a paramedic lying nearby and not moving, a dazed paramedic driver, bleeding from a head wound and half out of the cab, another vehicle overturned and smoking, another injured person, panic-stricken pedestrians on the pavement nearby, and a line of halted vehicles in both directions. What are your first priorities and preliminary risk assessments?

5.7.4.2 *First officer attending (FOA)*

You are first officer on the scene. As you move quickly towards the scene, report the collision, asking for urgent back-up and medical personnel to the scene. You will certainly need the Fire and Rescue Service as well (to open crumpled vehicles and extinguish any fires). *Your priorities must be to contain and control the scene and, most importantly, to preserve life.* As you go towards the injured, you might summon help from the drivers of the two stationary vehicles closest to the scene in each direction, and request them to redirect traffic (you must get rid of the bottleneck to allow emergency vehicles access), but of course, only ask them if they look capable. Get someone else to go to the hospital and get immediate help. In other words, until your colleagues and expert help arrives, *use what you've got at the scene*, and keep talking to Force Control.

5.7.4.3 *Save life and limb*

At the collision scene, attend the injured, concentrating on signs of life. The patient who is on the stretcher might be seriously ill; it seems certain that the prone paramedic may be, but you also need to check the driver of the ambulance. If not seriously hurt, he or she can help you to give first and urgent aid to the injured. If you judge that the driver is also seriously hurt, you need to decide what has to be done first: the rough guide, depending on circumstances, would be:

- **Secure from further danger**
- **Signs of life**
- **CPR (cardio-pulmonary resuscitation)** if injured person not breathing
- **Put into recovery position** (but not if there are obviously fractured limbs)
- **Get help fast.**

5.7.4.4 *Bad weather and road-rage*

Did we tell you that it is snowing hard? (Sorry, it must have slipped our minds!) The weather conditions are simply awful, and you may need to assess the risks of exposure if people are left lying on the snowy street. Meanwhile, rush hour traffic is building in front of and behind you, and there is a lot of hooting and shouting. One of the people whom you asked to help you direct traffic appears to be threatened by an aggressive driver who is demanding to get through the blockage to his office in Spruce Street. You can see this person's red face and bunched fists even through the heavy flakes of falling snow, from where you are kneeling beside the cold and injured patient. Also, rolling along the ground beside you in the grimy slush is half of a broken glass container from which a greenish vapour is rising lazily. Part of the label bears a red skull-and-crossbones and the letters HAZCHEM.

5.7.4.5 *Infection and radiation*

Meanwhile, the ambulance driver has recovered sufficiently to assist with the injured, and tells you that the patient on the stretcher is in acute trauma from liver failure and may have

Hepatitis B. She should not be touched without surgical gloves. As an afterthought he asks you if you have seen a small package in the road. You have not. Why?

'It's part of a radio-active isotope we were taking back to the hospital X-ray department', he said, trying to staunch his own copious bleeding, *'We were actually on our way back when we were sent off to get this patient as well.'*

The driver goes on to say that the lead-lined box in which the isotope was being carried has broken open in the crash and the isotope itself must have fallen out somewhere nearby.

5.7.4.6 *Burning cars and fights*

As you hear the welcome sound of colleagues arriving in numbers and the first doctors and nurses running over from the hospital, you are able to straighten up and turn your attention to containing the scene. You ease your aching back just as the overturned car just across the carriageway from you bursts into flames, and a thick oily black smoke begins to uncoil across the road, reducing visibility (already bad because of the heavy snowfall). You can see an individual still in the vehicle, struggling with the door. You are choking in the dense smoke, which is also a hazard to the hospital nearby. As you register this, you also notice out of the corner of your eye that there is a group of struggling and shouting people by the line of stationary vehicles and, as you watch, one person is struck and falls to the ground ...

5.7.4.7 *The shift from hell*

We grant you that the totality of this scenario is not very likely, but we wanted to see if we could devise a situation which covered all the **BEWARE** elements. (Mind you, after a shift like that, you'd probably want to curl up with your blanket and thumb and shut the world out for a bit.) However, most of the individual components of the case study are not at all unlikely, and could form part of the fabric of everyday hazard (we concede the radioactive isotope ...).

Making risk assessments and prioritizing your actions

The point we are trying to make in the midst of all this mayhem in Tonchester, is that **you not only have to make risk assessments as you go into a fluid situation, but you have to prioritize the order in which you will deal with them.** Fortunately, the preservation of life is the single most important priority anywhere and at any time, so there's no debate about that. But how and in what order you deal with other factors will be a matter for your judgement and common sense. So **Beware the Sprain**; it may stand between you and chaos, between you doing the right thing and doing the instinctive thing.

Discussion points

No right answers for this, but, in learning groups, go back to each of the instances in the case study above, and, using **BEWARE**, work out how you would assess each hazard and what your priority order of actions should be. Note too, in your discussion, that the cause of the RTC may be of interest to the police, especially if a criminal prosecution is possible. Witness statements and interviews may be your next tasks at the scene, where the police have taken over, and have dealt with the fist fight. Don't forget that you are a witness too, and will have to make a duty statement.

5.7.4.8 *Think about potential risk whenever you confront possible dangers and hazards*

As you get used to making dynamic risk assessments at work, you will need to refresh your memory less and less, but always remember that the process should never be automatic; always think carefully about situations before you get into them, and remember that your safety training in dealing with angry people is simply another form of dynamic (on the spot) risk assessment.

5.8 **Chapter Summary**

This chapter has been about the knowledge and skills which you need to help you become an effective and efficient PCSO. What you know and **what you do with what you know marks you out as a professional** and it is about understanding the 'why?' of what you do. We have shown you the great importance of evidence and how you use it, and how vital the proper maintenance of your pocket note book can be to justice outcomes.

The emphasis on enforcement (the exercise of powers), despite the infelicities of national advertising campaigns, is actually only part of a **PCSO's** work, and often a small part. Far more time and effort is spent in finding solutions to community problems and we looked at your role in negotiating and persuading, to bring people together to solve such problems, and how you can be the ready catalyst for change and improvement. We noted that more effort should be expended in defusing difficult confrontations or conflicts than in trying to control people's aggression, but we acknowledged that, as an authority figure, you would inevitably encounter hostility. We gave you tactical advice and ideas, based on our experience, of how to deal with such situations as they develop. Safety training, responses to crises and accidents, counter-intuition, and risk assessment are all factors which you must consider, deliberately and consciously, in your efficient, professional approach to your daily duties.

A last thought: despite the fact that your PDP (SOLAP) will be checked for evidence that you have reached the requisite standards in knowledge and skills, and despite the natural emphasis within the force on assessing your performance against some kind of template measure, it is in fact your performance in the community which really matters. Only if you can help to solve problems which bedevil or blight a community, if you can deal with people's concerns, if you can respond appropriately to anti-social behaviour, if you use your powers when you have to, and use a persuasive tongue when you don't, will any of these skills and this repository of knowledge be of the slightest practical use.

5.8.1 Prioritizing risks and hazards

To finish the chapter, look again at those risks in 5.7 above, and the order of their frequency. This was only for fun, but there is a genuine risk involved in some of the activities mentioned.

Starting at the top of the list with the most frequent:

(1) **Pulling a muscle during exercise**—commonest of all accidents and the most easily prevented. Nearly all muscle strains are caused through ineffective warming up before exercise or, equally important, 'warming down' or cooling after exercise. Stretching routines in both cases avoid sudden rips and tears to both muscle and tendon which take time to heal.

(2) **Breaking a bone**—this is one of the commonest of all accidents, and it is estimated that one in three of us will break (fracture) a bone at some time in our lives. The most at-risk groups are the very young (children aged 2 to 14); young men aged 18 to 24, perhaps because they are vulnerable to, or espousers of, macho cultures, contact sports, drinking,

and posturing; and the elderly (aged 70 to 85) because of factors like osteoporosis (brittle bones) and growing frailty.

(3) **Slipping in the bathroom**—a very common accident, a dangerous combination of moisture, shiny surfaces, and bare flesh. Most require a trip to Accident and Emergency (A&E), or the GP's surgery.

(4) **Falling off a chair**—again, surprisingly common and thought to account for more than 40% of back strains and impact injuries to the spine. Sadly, you are as likely to fall off a chair at home as at work; apparently it has to do with tipping the standard chair back on to two legs.

(5) **Singeing your eyebrows**—caused nowadays by people using petrol or benzene-based propellants to light or hurry along their barbecues. (This accident has remained remarkably constant, because it used to be a common feature among those who smoked.) Every year, sadly, there are fatalities among those who indulge this form of barbecuing lunacy. The petrol/benzene vaporizes when heated. If you're really lucky, it will only be your eyebrows which suffer.

(6) **Being involved in a road traffic collision**—not quite as common as accidents in the home (of all kinds), but a significant cause of serious injury and death to thousands of road users every year. Even minor accidents can be expensive, take a lot of time, and result in a reduced no-claims bonus. Half of all road users may expect a road traffic collision (rtc) during any 10 to 15 years of driving. Who is principally at risk? No prizes for saying young men (aged 18 to 25), often fuelled by alcohol, bravado, or speed.

(7) **Lifting something too heavy**—linked with poor lifting postures and lack of technique, this is a common hazard and one easily avoided with a little training and care. Hernias and permanently-damaged backs are too often the outcome of lifting something beyond your manual handling capability.

(8) **Getting an electric shock**—this is increasing as households have more and more electrical/electronic equipment. The most frequent causes are frayed wiring, faulty plugs, or cramming too many plugs into one outlet socket (also a common cause of house fires). In gardens, mowing over the electrical cable is still a favourite Sunday exercise for many householders.

(9) **Eating something which disagrees with you**—this, with **choking whilst eating**, is becoming more frequent as a hazard. Dieticians and doctors seem to agree that it is because we:

(a) eat too quickly,

(b) eat without looking (perhaps because we're watching TV?), and

(c) store food poorly, and is linked, in the latter case, with a lack of understanding of basic food hygiene.

(10) **Sticking a finger in your own eye**—this is more common than **burning your own finger** (though only just) and may be related to putting on make-up or inserting contact lenses. Loss of sight in one eye is surprisingly on the rise. It does not appear to be related to other forms of self-inflicted wound, like shaving your nose, swallowing your electric toothbrush head, or drinking aftershave by mistake … Burning your finger usually arises not through smoking or trying to light the fire with a short match, but testing whether a gas burner or electric hob is on.

(11) **Falling downstairs (while sober)**—we don't have the statistics for people who fall downstairs while drunk, though it is sometimes argued that injury in such instances is less likely because of the relaxation of the drunk. Taking a header down the stairs while sober is, amazingly, on the rise, but the Royal Society for the Prevention of Accidents (RoSPA) and others seem at a loss to account for why this should be.

(12) **Spearing your foot with a garden fork**—garden accidents are also on the increase (and may be linked with the Olympic sports of Standing on a Rake, Running the Mower over Your Feet, and Being Blinded by Bamboo Sticks). Sticking yourself with a fork is the commonest cause of blood-poisoning among gardeners, apparently.

(13) **Catching a disease from a dog**—apparently caused by allowing a dog to lick you and then ingesting its saliva. Given what other things dogs like to lick, that this is a hazard should not be surprising (but you would think a nation of animal lovers would know enough to avoid gratuitous infection of this kind).

(14) **Being bitten by a snake/being struck by lightning/ falling down a hole at road works**—of a muchness as far as rarity goes; all of these are pretty unlikely unless you happen to be trekking in a rainforest, playing golf at considerable height during a thunderstorm, or walking drunkenly home at night on an unlit motorway: but they do happen. See our update note on injuries from biting, below.

(15) **Having part of a building collapse on you**—not very frequent, really, but there are some fatalities every year in the UK; mostly because of children playing on building sites, or poor heath and safety practice in some unregulated parts of the construction industry.

(16) **Drowning while fishing**—bank and river fishing (as opposed to sea fishing) is still the most popular pastime in Britain, but common risks involve hooks or fishing equipment. Some bank fishermen do fall in (stretching too far to show the size of a catch perhaps?), but the usual instance of this rare hazard is waders filling with water, and river fishermen being pulled under the water as a result.

(17) **Being hit by something falling from an aircraft**—no fun if it happens, but, despite the exponential increase in air traffic, such occurrences are extremely rare.

(18) **Meeting an alien from outer space**—no prizes for putting this as the least likely hazard, but reflect: 3 million Americans believe that they have been abducted by aliens in spaceships…

Some additional evidence of how people make heavy weather of risk, published early in 2009, is worth a quick glance:

'2,614 people were admitted to hospital in 2007–2008 after a bite or sting from a non-venomous insect, more than triple the number of a decade ago. Hornets claimed a further 810 victims—up 15 per cent on 2006–07. Spiders were responsible for 18 hospital admissions, and snakes and lizards a further 49. Other biters—such as rats (21), fish (28) and crocodiles (1)—also did their bit. Our growing fondness for exotic plants may be to blame for the 244 cases caused by contact with 'plant thorns and sharp leaves', up 30 per cent on 1998–99.

Of the 4,283 people who ended up in hospital after a fall [from] ice-skates, skis, rollerskates and skateboards, 166 were over the age of 60, with 24 older than 75. A possible over-enthusiasm among the older generation also led to 61 pensioners being admitted after 'falls involving playground equipment'. Forces of nature also added to national ill-health, with 44 victims of lightning, 15 of volcanic eruption, 10 suffering from the after-effects of being caught in an avalanche, and 18 from a 'cataclysmic storm'. Hot drinks caused considerable discomfort with 1,722 hospital visits, a steady rise over the past 10 years. A further 629 people went to hospital after scalds from the hot tap.'[18]

[adapted from Sam Lister: 'NHS admissions: bizarre mishaps that put patients in hospital', *The Times*, 26 February 26, 2009]

(*Other sources for the list of accidents and emergencies include:* the Royal Society for the Prevention of Accidents (RoSPA), domestic reports in *The Times*, Bill Bryson (the travel writer), the Health and Safety Executive, the Society of Actuaries' risk register, and Chicken Licken.)

Notes

1 Criminal Justice and Police Act (s 1–11), Penalty Notices for Disorder, Police Operational Guidance, March 2005.

2 Home Office, 'The Revised Guidance on the Operation of the Fixed Penalty System for Offences in Respect of a Vehicle' (April 2006).

3 It is worth remarking at this point that one of the Magistracy's concerns about the whole penalty system as operated by the police and PCSOs is, in addition to removing the transparency of the legal process, half of those fined do not pay: 'The use of out-of-court penalties has mushroomed: across England and Wales in the 12 months to March [2008], only 724,179 of the 1.4 million offenders 'brought to justice' actually came before the courts. There are also practical problems. Nearly 50 per cent of the tickets are unpaid. The offender must go to court as a fine defaulter, attending a hearing that cannot revisit the original offence.' Source: Frances Gibbs, *The Times*' Legal Editor, two articles published on 5 May 2009, 'On-the-spot fines mean justice is not seen to be done, say critics' and 'JPs win first round in battle over extension of on-the-spot fines', available from <http://timesonline/tol/business/law/article4622156.ece>, accessed 5 May 2009

4 M Stevens, *How to be a Better Problem Solver* (Kogan Page, 1996) 9.

5 C Emsley, *Hard Men: Violence in England since 1750* (Hambledon, 2005) especially Ch 2, 'Garotters, Gangsters and Perverts'.

6 J Morris, 'Removing the barriers to community participation', National Community Forum, 2006, 14.

7 S Forrest, A Myhill, and N Tilley, 'Practical lessons for involving the community in crime and disorder problem solving', Home Office Development and Practice Report 43 (2005) 16.

8 Named after the allegedly violent and anarchic Mohican tribe, as then perceived.

9 See eg J Gardiner, *Wartime Britain 1939–1945* (Headline, 2004) especially Ch 4, 'He's in the Army, Mrs Jones', 76–101

10 Though the cynics among us might say that that was because very few people had material possessions worth stealing; a metal clothes mangle was hardly a covetable item. '**CRAVED**' reminds us what items are 'stealable', that is attractive to a thief or burglar. The mnemonic is: Concealable, Removable, Available, Enjoyable and Disposable; see R Clarke, 'Hot Products: Understandings, Anticipating and Reducing Demand for Stolen Goods', Police Research Series Paper 112, Home Office and TSO (1999).

11 See extensive references in the Bibliography, and Clive Emsley's very readable *Hard Men* (n 5 above); the *British Crime Survey* 2006; and BBC Radio 4, 'The Violence Files', January 1995 and 'Violent Britain', November 2000. Two other good texts are G O'Neill's, *The Good Old Days: crime, murder and mayhem in Victorian London* (Viking, 2006) and F Linnane, *London's Underworld* (Robson Books, 2004).

12 J Drever, *A Dictionary of Psychology* (Penguin, 1952).

13 See eg D Morris, *People Watching* (Vintage, 2002) especially 'Autonomic Signals', 248–9, where this common theory is aired.

14 It may be the action of *nor-adrenaline* which produces the 'anger pallor' discussed above. Blood returning to the face when anger is passing may explain the flushed look of one whose anger has peaked—but don't bet on it.

15 Also known by the mnemonic **SCALP**, where S is **subsidiarity**, C is **controlled**, A is **appropriate**, L is **legal** and P is **proportionate**; but the meanings of most of these mnemonics, which come and go in fashions, are the same.

16 The case of Tony Martin was widely reported at the time. See eg <http://www.lawtel.com/~2e65779feb234974b9bf3689b5778460~/content/display.asp?ID> accessed December 2006.

17 Causing breathing difficulties, extreme allergic reactions, and sometimes rapid death.

18 Source: NHS: *Accident and Emergency Attendances in England* (Experimental Statistics), 2007–08, (opsi, January 2009).

Chapter 6

Community Focus

6.1 Introduction

In this chapter, we are going to examine your principal area of work; the community. It is here that you carry out your patrols, here that you respond to and speak with members of the community as well as with groups within that community, and here, when necessary, that you enforce behaviour in the community.

6.1.1 What is a community?

We begin by trying to describe what a community is, or, more strictly, what communities are, because we all belong simultaneously to numbers of communities. They are not just the people who live where we do. Following this, we analyse the make-up of different communities and how we respond to them. Then we look at success and failure factors in communities.

6.1.1.1 *Components of community*

We examine next some of the elements of community, such as how communities are socially organized, what constraints there are on behaviour, what the social taboos (curbs and conditions) are, and how behaviour is restricted. These are all aspects of community which you need to understand and respond to, in order to do your work effectively. This is followed by a complementary discussion about factors which encourage a sense of community and factors which inhibit that sense of community.

6.1.1.2 *Community and the fear of crime*

This leads us to a parallel discussion of the fear of crime, as evidenced in successive annual British Crime Surveys, and what causes social unease, as well as looking at how communities deal with those fears. We discuss the concept of 'signal crimes' which enhance our understanding of the fear of crime.

6.1.1.3 *Working with partners: relations with ethnic and diverse communities*

This takes us logically to a consideration of partnerships and the kinds of alliances, liaisons, and cooperative working which typify the PCSO's approach to problems within the community. We go on to look at the PCSO in relation to ethnic and diverse communities.

6.1.1.4 *Policing models, consensual and compliant policing, citizen focus*

The chapter concludes with a brief survey of policing models and how the PCSO fits, or does not fit, into prevalent modelling. We then discuss the larger issues of the tensions between **consensual** and **compliant** policing (service or force?), before suggesting that a depiction of the future of neighbourhood policing might entail some citizen ownership. There are the usual notes, discussion points, tasks, and points to note throughout.

6.2 **What a Community Can Be**

We often hear the word 'community' used as part of phrases such as 'the gay community', 'the academic community', and 'the business community'. Anecdotally at least, the use of the word 'community' seems to have grown in recent years, perhaps usurping the previous dominance of the elastic noun 'society'. This perhaps reflects, in turn, a perception that society/community is now more pluralistic (some would say, more fragmented) than before, although there is always the danger here of the myth of the 'golden age' of a homogeneous society located somewhere in the 1950s (see 5.5.1 above and 6.2.1.6 below). The widespread use of the word in many different contexts suggests that there is now a prevailing view that *rather than just a single community we have instead a series of interlocking and overlapping ones*. But as Myhill (2006, 6) notes:

> Community is a notoriously slippery concept, and many definitions exist in academic literature and elsewhere ...

and we should perhaps be cautious in assuming a shared understanding of the meaning of the term. Andy Myhill directly echoes Nick Tilley's comment (2003, 315) that:

> the term 'community' itself is notoriously slippery. It often seems to imply shared norms, values and ways of life. Groups with these attributes need not be geographically defined, of course. In practice, the community of community policing most often does amount to 'neighbourhood' …[1]

That said, we do try a definition of our own on you a little later, precisely to achieve a '*shared understanding of the meaning of the term*' with you.

6.2.1 Characteristics of a community

Essentially, communities are collections of individuals with something in common, shown through forms of interaction and common ties between those individuals. Examples you might think about include communities that embrace a single ethnicity, or others that share roughly the same set of values. Note the characteristic that there needs to be evidence of some kind of interaction, and a feeling of 'belonging'. The strength of our 'sense of belonging' to our communities will vary, in part as a consequence of the perceptions of others. For example, members of visible ethnic minority communities may feel a common tie more than, say, the business community. In some cases we may wish *not* to belong to certain communities and may even deny that we do so. For example, some people who live on the borders of public housing estates may prefer not to be grouped alongside members of that community.

6.2.1.1 There will be a range of views about PCSOs in any community

It is probably the case that you will not find unanimity of opinion or shared values among all members of the same community. Views about PCSOs, for example, are likely to stretch across the full spectrum from approval to disapproval as much in one community as in another. However, this is not to say that there are not variations between different communities in, for example, their levels of anxiety concerning anti-social behaviour and crime (see Chapter 5) but these do not normally form defining factors.

6.2.1.2 *Towards a descriptive definition*

Try this as a description of 'community', even if we cannot fully propose it, perhaps, as a dictionary definition:

> A community can be a number of people with some shared iden-
> tity, including geographic, as a group of people who live or work in
> close proximity to each other. But community is more than this; it can
> encompass shared values, shared outlooks, shared concerns, shared
> origins or ethnicity, even shared beliefs. What makes a community is
> a sense of belonging to it—both being a contributor to the values of
> the community and in drawing strength from what the community
> gives back to you. In a real sense, it is about fundamental identity and
> meaning for many people.[2]

The senses of **sharing** and **belonging** are profound emotions as
well as strong concepts, which we need to look at in greater depth
because they go to the heart of what you do as a PCSO. It is the
sense of identity, of belonging somewhere, which gives a community its coherence and which also defines it. You need to know
what it is if you are to encourage its development.

6.2.1.3 *Is the 'community' real?*

But how many of us would recognize these descriptions of a community? How many of us have a geographically distinct and defined
sense of space outside where we live? How many of us, particularly
in urban locations, have no sense of who our neighbours are? How
do we explain the neglect of elderly people who have died alone
and whose bodies remain undiscovered for weeks? How else can
we explain the systematic abuse of a child which goes unreported?
How else can we account for the repeated cycle of domestic violence that never comes to the attention of the police? Why is there
a tendency to wait for 'them' (usually the police or some other form
of authority) to solve problems rather than 'us'? Isn't it true that
many of us have a better relationship with work colleagues than we
do with the people who live next door?

Discussion point

Think about the community in which you are physically located.
Could people die undiscovered in your street?
Could children or vulnerable people be abused and no one know?
Why?
Compare experiences with your colleagues and draw up a list of the
factors which (a) make a community a positive shared experience and
(b) a negative isolated experience.

6.2.1.4 *The community as 'home' or home as the location of the self*

The community in which we are physically located for the most part, which we usually designate as 'home', is the place where we feel most comfortable and most relaxed. But it can also be paradoxically where we can experience most fear or most vulnerability, because this 'home' is where our loved ones are located, where we enjoy our material possessions, where we keep the things which, if not intrinsically valuable, have most significance and 'value' for us. It is the place where we sleep, trusting in locks and other forms of physical security as well as the police, to keep us safe and unharmed.

Our own space is our security against encroachment

We invest such physical places with our personalities and dreams and we tend to think of them as inviolable (they *cannot be touched*). So, when these places are threatened, or seen to be at risk from prowlers, burglars, or vandals causing criminal damage, we may believe that our whole social fabric, our entire edifice of trust and security, is at risk. This directly contributes to personal anxiety and to the belief that, somehow, the 'community' (whatever it is) has let us down. Our trust in our surroundings has been violated. We begin to fear crime and criminals.

6.2.1.5 *This place has gone to the dogs*

This sense of the security of place, which is very deep-seated in the human psyche, may radiate outwards to embrace those who live alongside us, or it may not. Any PCSO who has spent time on a patrol beat will tell you that one recurrent and standard conversation which they have, usually but not exclusively with the elderly, concerns **the degeneration of the area, the fact that people don't know each other any more and that it has become a place where neighbours keep themselves to themselves.** This perception of the deterioration of social 'glue', which used to hold us together in a community, is very widespread.

It is not just the old and frail who fear crime and social decay

Worry about an apparent deterioration in social 'glue' is not confined to the very old, or to the housebound and frail, but may equally apply to the single parent, the mother with children under school age, or the commuter who works many miles away for long periods during the week. All may seem to live *external* lives of fragile isolation. Many rely on family networks, or networks of friends, to supply the internal and emotional contact which living in a community normally provides. Others remain lonely and untouched by human interaction. Others take solace in the internet to create a 'virtual community'. Some people will tell you that they no longer intervene or remonstrate when they see anti-social behaviour because they are afraid of the torrent of abuse which this can unleash. Or they do not speak out when they hear a child cry or a woman sobbing because 'it is nothing to do with them'. Or they are too busy with their own lives to spend time interfering in other people's business. Or they have their friends and their family, thank you, and don't need anyone else, especially not those people down the road.

6.2.1.6 *Are we nostalgic for a mythical past?*

What has happened to society to produce this apparent fracture between what we assume to have been a warm, friendly community state where everyone cared about each other, and this anxious, cold, isolated, and uncommunicative modern reality? Is it true that we need to rediscover a sense of the group identity and a clear image of our place in the social structure in order to belong properly? Is the perception true that community has changed for the worse? Or is it variously a product of being old, poor, socially disadvantaged, or out of work? Was there ever a golden past in which most people could be trusted, where social roles and responsibilities were clearly defined, and where 'people knew their place'? Or is it, as some commentators claim (Hitchens, 2003), a world invented by film and television which never existed in reality? Is this lost, mourned, community as much a myth as the myth of the golden age of policing with PC George Dixon?

6.2.1.7 *Mobility inhibits us from belonging*

You may gather from the sheer number of questions above that we don't pretend to have the answers. The description of a community which we offered above suggested that belonging to or **identifying with a community was a reciprocal process; what you got out of it largely depended on what you put in**. The strength of the sense of identity may therefore stem from permanence, from long-term commitment, from continued residence and roots.

6.2.1.8 *Much of modern life is restless and impermanent*

Yet most of us do not live such settled, immobile lives unless we are sick, disabled, housebound, or very frail. Most of us move to where our work takes us, move to secure better prospects, move to a bigger house, or a better area, or a bigger garden, or an easier commute, move to get a better school for the children, move to care for an elderly relative, move to secure a different lifestyle, move because we don't like being in one place for too long, move because the grass is going to be greener somewhere else, or move because being 'nomadic' is part of contemporary life. Because of this mobility, we do not always know our present locality well, and the dilemma intensifies in an economic recession as we may have to move to find work but may find it hard to sell one house and buy another, or the threat of unemployment places house ownership or rental in jeopardy.

6.2.2 Community described by demography and other factors

A community may be described (rather than defined) in terms of its demography, location, and interests or combinations of these, as illustrated below.

Aspect	[Examples]
Demography	*Age* (as in the community of 'elderly people')
	Gender
	Ethnicity (a descriptor like 'the Afro-Caribbean community')
	Nationality ('the Turkish community in North London', 'the international community')
	Social class (eg 'the working class community')
Location	*Place* ('a Tonchester council estate', a 'virtual community' on the internet, a 'gated community')
Interest	*Interest or pressure groups* (such as a faith association, the local branch of Animal Aid, a sports 'supporters' association)

Your police force will have analysts who are able to produce maps, diagrams, tables, and charts describing the demographic and geographical nature of the communities that you support. Often these maps and diagrams are produced using a computer-based *Geographical Information System* (GIS). Try to access these to learn about different local 'communities' and how they overlap.

Your force might even have produced a 'Neighbourhood Profile' according to NPIA guidelines. This will include not only the demographic characteristics of a neighbourhood but also information about its infrastructure (both physical and human) and the fear of crime (see 6.5 below).

6.2.2.1 *Finding out about your communities*

Even if you are deployed as a PCSO to a particular location on a semi-permanent basis (for example to a town centre) you will still find yourself interacting with a number of communities, ranging from communities which share a common origin or ethnicity through to local communities of business people. We have chosen as a real example the Gipsy Hill ward within the London Borough of Lambeth.

6.2.2.2 *Gipsy Hill ward: a case study*

What can we discover about the demography of the Gipsy Hill ward? (A good starting point for this or any other real location is the government website of the Office for National Statistics to be found at <http://www.statistics.gov.uk>.) Consider, for example, the ethnicity statistics from the Gipsy Hill ward (based on the 2001 Census) and compare this respectively with the rest of Lambeth, with London as a whole, and then with the whole of England.

Ethnicity	Gipsy Hill	Lambeth	London	England
	%	%	%	%
White: British	54.5	49.6	59.8	87.0
White: Irish	3.5	3.3	3.1	1.3
White: Other White	6.5	9.6	8.3	2.7
Mixed: White and Black Caribbean	3.1	2.0	1.0	0.5
Mixed: White and Black African	0.7	0.8	0.5	0.2
Mixed: White and Asian	0.7	0.8	0.8	0.4
Mixed: Other Mixed	1.1	1.2	0.9	0.3
Asian or Asian British: Indian	1.8	2.0	6.1	2.1
Asian or Asian British: Pakistani	0.6	1.0	2.0	1.4

Ethnicity	Gipsy Hill	Lambeth	London	England
	%	%	%	%
Asian or Asian British: Bangladeshi	0.4	0.8	2.1	0.6
Asian or Asian British: Other Asian	0.5	0.8	1.9	0.5
Black or Black British: Caribbean	14.5	12.1	4.8	1.1
Black or Black British: African	8.2	11.6	5.3	1.0
Black or Black British: Other Black	2.5	2.1	0.8	0.2
Chinese or Other Ethnic Group: Chinese	0.8	1.3	1.1	0.4
Chinese or Other Ethnic Group: Other Ethnic Group	0.7	1.2	1.6	0.4

Adapted from data at the National Statistics website <http://www.statistics.gov.uk> accessed August 2009.
Crown copyright material is reproduced with the permission of the Controller of TSO.

6.2.2.3 *From particular to general*

We can see in terms of ethnicity that Gipsy Hill is a multicultural area, but it shows some interesting variations from Lambeth and from London as a whole. For example, the Black Caribbean population is the second biggest after the white British percentage and Black Caribbean is the largest minority ethnic community. These are local variations which directly determine the nature of the community and which help to define the relationships between its parts: the Asian or Asian British: Pakistani groupings are less than half the national average in Gipsy Hill; the white British population in Gipsy Hill is much smaller than that for the whole country. Similar analyses can be made in terms of age, numbers of dependent children, occupation, employment, crime, and so on. These statistics will give some indication of the range of communities you are likely to encounter, but remember that data may sometimes hide significant local variations, and also that generalizations on the basis of data alone may lead to **stereotypical assumptions**. For example, it does not follow that a community with a broad ethnic mix necessarily suffers from racial tensions, high unemployment, or crime.

6.2.2.4 Researching your communities

You can undertake much research using the internet and libraries to discover more about the communities in your area. For example, which associations are active in your area? Is there a *Facebook* or *Twitter* devoted to the town? Where are the local schools? Which buses run where? What sporting/leisure facilities are there and where are the sports grounds? Who has been leading campaigns or voicing concerns about the community? In libraries or online, you will find back numbers of local newspapers. Read a selection for the past year: this will give you a unique insight into what is preoccupying your community and may help you to identify those who are prominent opinion-formers or spokespersons for the community (look at 6.5 below, for example, under 'signal crimes', to read about Mrs Meldrew and her letter to the local press, which sparked strong police involvement in her problems). Your Force or BCU media advisers may also alert you to local sensitivities, for example what happened the last time the BCU Commander attended a public meeting on your 'patch'. Don't forget that members of your Police Authority (most of whom will be elected councillors or JPs) may well be located in or near your communities and may have valuable insights into what concerns local people and what the various pressure groups in the neighbourhood might be. Equally, local people may be using district or borough councillors to represent them to the BCU Commander or higher.

6.2.2.5 Know who is where and when

You will obviously learn more, in certain respects, about the communities that you support through your direct day-to-day contact with them, for example through regular patrol of a town centre. However, bear in mind that research has shown (see Waddington, 2004, for example) that the **'available' population** (that is, the people you are likely to encounter on the streets) is not necessarily the same as the **resident population** (those who live in the area), and particularly so in terms of demography. This is because some will be at school, many will be at work, often some distance away, and some will not be on the streets unless transported by others, such as the sick, the immobile or house bound, and the very old or very young. To gain a genuine understanding of the 'mix' of your community, it will be necessary to encounter members from it at different times of day and different days of the week. A 'dormitory' suburb, for example, where many commute

to work in a nearby city perhaps, may double its 'available population' on Saturdays and Sundays.

Task

1. Draw up a profile of the communities that you support, in terms of basic demography (age, gender, ethnicity etc)
2. Next, find the locations of:
   - Playgroups, pre-school groups, schools, colleges, and universities
   - Churches, mosques, etc
   - Community centres, Citizens' Advice Bureaux, etc
   - Sports Centres, Exercise Clubs, etc
   - Cinemas, clubs etc
   - Tourist attractions, museums, and heritage sites
   - Libraries, cultural centres, and drinking clubs
   - GP surgeries, medical centres and practices, and NHS clinics
   - Council offices, Department for Work and Pensions (DWP) office, Social Services, and Environmental Department
   - Public and municipal housing, estates
   - Bridges, tunnels, underpasses, alleyways
   - Railway and underground stations
   - Parks and other green spaces
   - Sports grounds, fitness centres, and gymnasia
   - Cemeteries and crematoria
   - Public amenities such as recycling centres
   - Public toilets
   - Relevant *Facebook* and *Twitter* Internet sites
3. Find out who are the:
   - Local councillors and other elected representatives (**think:** your Police Authority representatives might be able to help here)
   - Council officers and permanent staff
   - Community leaders, opinion formers, leaders of sporting organizations such as football or rugby or cricket teams
   - Representatives of voluntary organizations such as Age Concern, the Scout Association, The Women's Institute, The British Legion, and so on
   - Local head teachers, principals, lecturers and teachers
   - Managers of local supermarkets and other retail outlets

6.2.2.6 *Where to look*

There are numerous sources for this kind of information.
We suggest that the National Census website <http://www.
statistics.gov.uk/census/default.asp>, accessed May 2009, is a good

starting point. Indeed, the internet will provide you with much of the relevant information. Another good starting point for information about an area is the website UpMyStreet, <http://www.upmystreet.com/> accessed May 2009.

6.3 Social Organization, Disorganization, and Social Capital

Social organization refers to the tendency for groups of people to organize themselves in some way and form relationships with one another. Examples of the public manifestation of social organization include the existence of schools, colleges, religious groups, voluntary organizations, and, of course, families. You probably listed some of the visible evidence of social organization in your area in your response to the second part of the task we suggested above. The existence of social organization will be an important aspect of your work as a PCSO. There is also the wider concept of 'citizenship' (which features on the national curriculum for schoolchildren) and voluntary work (such as 'Cruse' bereavement care) undertaken by individuals within a community.

6.3.1 Social disorganization

On the other hand, **social disorganization** refers to the sense in which some communities have lost the sense of being part of a whole and have instead become fragmented and no longer appear to 'buy in' to the same values as some other communities. There is a tendency, at least among political and social commentators, to perceive a greater level of social disorganization and a reduction in the sense of a 'community'. However, this is not necessarily the case. Certainly there appears to be less participation than before in traditional civic activities (such as voting at elections), but it is also clear that in some other forms of community participation (such as the 'Freecycle' phenomenon on the internet, see <http://www.freecycle.org/> accessed August 2009, or access to allotments), there has been an increase. We may be dealing here with perceptions or changes in perspective rather than objective fact (as we discussed above); and some perceptions may be influenced by media reporting on the decay of the community and barriers to social responsibility which make much of the daily diet of news.

6.3.1.1 *Social disorganization: links to crime and disorder?*

Nonetheless, there are frequently attempts to **link the existence of social disorganization with the prevalence of crime and disorder**, much originating with the seminal work of the 1940s US sociologists Clifford Shaw and Henry McKay (see Bottoms and Wiles, in Maguire, 2002). Areas (particularly within cities) with high measures of social disorganization, such as the rapid turnover of a resident population, tend to experience higher levels of certain forms of crime and disorder, although the relationship is by no means simple and sometimes isn't there at all. It is perfectly possible to have two adjoining residential areas in a city, with similar levels of measures of social disorganization, but with very different rates of recorded crime and disorder (for example see Bottoms *et al*, 1989). Beware of those who may generalize massively about the transience of population in a particular area leading to a growth in criminal activity. Conversely, you may note those communities where efforts to stabilize the population 'turnover' have led to improvements in the general quality of life.

6.3.1.2 *Social capital*

The idea of 'capital' implies some kind of savings that we can utilize, or a reservoir that we can draw from. '**Social capital**' refers to the resources (networks, institutions, and individuals) that many of us draw upon from those around us—for example our neighbours, friends, work colleagues, and family—in order to sustain and develop ourselves through mutual cooperation and trust. *Social capital is often associated with the development of communities* (see 6.2.1.2 above) as the source of the 'glue' that sticks them together and assists individuals within those groups to make progress.

6.3.1.3 *Bonding, bridging, and linking social capital*

Social capital may be thought of as being subdivided in turn into **bonding**, **bridging**, and **linking** social capital (see Hall, 2005):

Social capital	[Examples]
Bonding	Strong 'horizontal' bonds within kinship groups that increase cohesiveness, such as bonding between members who share the same ethnic group in a community
Bridging	Weaker 'horizontal' bridging ties with other groups and networks beyond kinship, for example with work colleagues from a different ethnic group
Linking	'Vertical' links with other levels of the 'pecking order' like knowing the Chair of the local PTA of your child's school

We might summarize this notion by saying that *bonding social capital is deemed to be good for 'getting by' but bridging and linking capital is necessary for 'getting on'.*

6.3.1.4 *What does it matter?*

Why should social capital matter to the PCSO? Some observers have claimed that problems may occur in multicultural areas when bonding social capital 'drowns out' bridging social capital and leads to antagonism between ethnic groups (Easton, 2006, quoting Trevor Phillips). Social capital is also inextricably linked with social exclusion: the argument is that individuals are excluded precisely because they lack access to forms of social capital. More positively, communities which have greater resources of bridging and bonding capital are possibly better able to mobilize resources to improve the economic and social circumstances of those communities.

> **Task**
> Think of ways in which a PCSO can help to increase the social capital in a local community.

6.3.1.5 *Increasing 'social capital'*

An influential text on social capital is *Bowling Alone: The Collapse and Revival of American Community* by Robert Putnam (2001) (see Bibliography for this and other references).

Possible ways in which PCSOs could support an increase in **social capital** in their communities include:

- Increasing awareness among the local communities concerning '*Who's who*?'—not just in terms of formal authority and professional figures but also the name of the person who delivers the post. Undertaking the task we offered above will help you with this.
- When presented with problems and issues by members of local communities, suggesting ways in which they could become involved, for example by participation in school PTAs or by taking part in Neighbourhood Watch schemes.
- Helping local people to articulate their particular concerns, on both the community and personal levels. Do they know the name and contact details of their ward councillors? Do they know about the existence of Credit Unions?
- Contributing to local forms of information distribution, for example newsletters, electronic notice boards, etc (but check local Force policy first).

6.4 Factors which Encourage a Sense of Community

When we use the phrase 'sense of community' we are often referring to the extent, or otherwise, to which people identify with, and are concerned about, other people in their immediate vicinity. Note that our emphasis here is on **communities defined by location** rather than by *interest* or *demography* (see 6.2.2 above). This reflects the day-to-day reality of the work of the PCSO, concerned as it often is with particular areas of our villages, towns, and cities.

6.4.1 Historical examples of supposed 'community spirit'

There have been a number of occasions in the past where the sense of community ('community spirit') has apparently been so strong, and so widespread, as to enter public consciousness. Notable examples include Londoners' reaction to the Blitz during the Second World War and the actions of New Yorkers immediately following '9/11', the terrorist attack on the Twin Towers on 11 September 2001. However, these periods of heightened sense of community were relatively short-lived and some writers (particularly in the case of the Blitz) have even questioned the very existence of such a communal identity, at least in terms of popular mythology. Rather we are concerned here with the less tangible and more pervasive sense of place and community.

6.4.1.1 *Sense of community*

What factors would seem to encourage a sense of community? We offer the following as possibilities:

Sense of community	[Examples]
Belonging	The community has a name ('the North Down Road community'), newsletters from local groups, decorations inside and outside houses during religious festivals
Ownership	Attention paid to maintenance of buildings and shared spaces, Neighbourhood Watch schemes, abandoned vehicles are quickly reported
Participation	Volunteering, taking active part in recycling schemes, allotments-uk.com, local community groups ('Mothers and Toddlers'), local *Facebook* groups
Leadership	Individuals willing to accompany neighbours to make a case to the local council, 'spokespeople' appearing in the local media, visible and active local councillors
Mutuality	'Time banking' (reciprocal support such as the giving of lifts, gardening, DIY jobs),* mutual respect and tolerance between users of a local amenity
Rootedness	People living in a community for a significant length of time, often represented by a visible wide age distribution (the elderly, children)
Ties	Visible use of local tradespeople, neighbours lending tools, expertise

* This also has the added benefit of increasing **bridging social capital**; see Sayfang (2005) and 6.3.1.3 above.

6.4.1.2 *Exploiting community spirit*

What can you do, as a PCSO, to exploit or make use of the sense of community? We have commented throughout this Handbook that you will have to urge, persuade, cajole, wheedle, and otherwise pressure people to start thinking and acting like a community if they do not do so already, in order to achieve anything permanent or worthwhile in the community you serve. Part of that is knowing what a community is, but your overall strategy within your neighbourhood policing team will be to make use of those elements of 'community spirit' which you can identify and which welcome an approach from you.

6.4.1.3 *Analyse the community*

The first element, we would suggest, is to **analyse the groups** which we have categorized in the table above, and note which of them in your community you can approach or enlist immediately. Others may take longer and may require you to think through different inducements to help you or different ways in which you can persuade them to join in. Never underestimate the appeal of a 'bandwagon' because your activities to foster and encourage a sense of community identity and team spirit will develop a momentum of their own, and some organizations will come on board with you simply to be seen to do so.

6.4.1.4 *Allocate tasks*

The second element is in terms of the **allocation of work**. We suggest that you draw up a list of tasks in conjunction with the table of participants, or determinants of community spirit. That way you can ensure that, for every new recruit to your cause, whatever it may be (and we've looked at a number in the course of these pages) there is a real and defined task that they can take on. This will have the added benefit of ensuring that those who join you do so from a genuine sense of purpose. Those along just for the ride will look dismayed when you ask them to do something. Don't be afraid to nag.

6.5 **Fear of Crime—Fear Born of Social Unease?**

There is a general acceptance that the fear of crime has increased in the last decade or so, despite the fact that most forms of recorded crime have shown a decrease in the same period (although see Farrall and Gadd, 2004, for a critique). As Walker *et al* (2006, 34) note, 'despite the total number of crimes estimated by the BCS [British Crime Survey] falling over recent years, comparatively high proportions of people continue to believe crime has risen across the country as a whole and in their local area'.

It would also appear that members of particular communities are more likely to believe that both national and local crime has risen significantly when compared to others and also that they are likely to worry more about crime. The **British Crime Survey** for 2007/8 suggests that the following demographic factors are significant in people's concerns:

- **Gender**: Women are more likely than men to feel that burglary and violent crime has risen
- **Age**: Young people worry more about violence and car crime (although men and women in the 65 to 74 age group are most likely to perceive that there has been a significant increase in crime overall)
- **Ethnicity**: People from non-white ethnic groups are more likely to be concerned about crime than those from white groups
- **Location:** Those living in urban areas are more likely to worry about crime that those who live in rural areas.
- **Accommodation:** Those living in the social rented sector are more likely to worry about crime than those who rented privately or owned their own homes
- **Newspapers:** Readers of the 'red top' (tabloid) newspapers are more likely to worry about crime than those who read the 'broadsheets' or 'quality press'.

[source: Kershaw *et al* (2008) p 126 and Table 5/06.

6.5.1 Fear is not necessarily linked to being a victim

It is important to note that those who feel most worried about crime or who perceive crime to be increasing, are not necessarily those who are actually the most likely to become victims of recorded crime. Having said this, it could be argued that the fear of crime alone is a form of harm to an individual. It is also the case that, for those in our communities who fear crime the most, the implications of crime can be profound. To put this another way, an elderly person's statistically 'irrational' fears about crime are in fact quite rational if the effect of crime on such a person is factored in. Think of this as some kind of calculation: **the risk may be low but the negative consequences are very high** (for example in terms of recovery from an injury) and so overall the outcome might be significant for the individual concerned.

6.5.1.1 *Fear is perception of the threat*

This has important implications for the PCSO. Part of the 'reassurance agenda' that gave rise to the creation of the PCSO in the first place is concerned with perceptions as much as reality. These perceptions may be affected by actions and forms of anti-social behaviour and minor disorder which are not of themselves criminal offences but which nonetheless influence an individual's sense of well-being and security. Perceptions may also be affected by the views of family and friends and media reports. Indeed, some people's persistent fear of crime may be influenced by the success or otherwise of local police interventions. Those who have had a poor encounter with the police, particularly one in which their fears and worries were not seen to be taken seriously, are more likely to feel that the police are ineffective or incompetent. The fear of crime cannot be separated from other aspects of an individual's perception of the 'quality of life' of their communities such as the education their children receive, the housing stock in their area, and the cleanliness or otherwise of their neighbourhood, together with anxieties about continued employment, credit rating and debt.. The economic recession which began in mid 2008 has entailed a rise in acquisitive crime. Home Office data published in April 2009 indicated a 4% increase in the number of domestic burglaries since September 2008 and there has been a rise of 25% in personal theft over the same period. Yet overall crime fell by 4% (to 1.1 million recorded offences) in the last three months of 2008 compared with the same period in 2007. It seems that people's fears of knife crime, theft, burglary and robbery are not mollified by the overall decrease in recorded crime. [3]

6.5.2 **Fear of crime: the importance of 'signal crimes'**

One of the features we have explored in relation to the role of the PCSO is that some of the problems brought to you by members of the public or delegated to you will not seem like policing issues. We have touched upon these seemingly low-level, often environmentally focused, problems in previous chapters but it is important to understand why these particular issues are perceived by the public to be important in their communities. **It is directly relevant to the public's fear of crime and the way that this contributes to social unease.**

(Photograph by Bryn Caless)

Photograph 7: Graffiti on gates

Task

Consider this list of community-based problems. Put these problems in order of importance with 1 for the most important and 10 for the least important.

- Mini motorbikes on the pavements
- Post office closure
- Litter
- Graffiti
- Alcohol and drugs debris in the park
- Vandalism
- Abandoned cars
- Broken street lighting
- Unlit alleyways
- Lack of a bus route into town.

There is no right or wrong in this; each, in its time, has headed a list of priorities in a community. You may feel that some of these task items are not policing problems and therefore not applicable to a PCSO. Is the issue of broken street lighting a matter for police concern? What about litter? Is there really a policing element in the closure of the post office or the lack of a bus route into town? This is where the concept of **signal crimes** can prove useful to the PCSO and provides a good framework for the PCSO to start an exploration of his or her community's perceptions about crime.

6.5.2.1 *What is a signal crime?*

The term was coined by Dr Martin Innes and a team at the University of Surrey, working closely with Surrey Police, in 2001–02, and subsequently it has proved influential in neighbourhood policing because it allows the police to view certain crimes or disorders from the perspective of the community, that is, to see them through the community's eyes:

> The key idea of a Signal Crimes Perspective is that some crime and disorder incidents function as warning signals to people about the distribution of risks to their security in everyday life. Some crime and disorder behaviours matter more than others in shaping the public's collective perceptions of risk.[4]

Discussion points

Think about the community in which you live. What events would cause you to reappraise risk perception in your own neighbourhood? (Discount any major crimes such as murder or rape and think instead about the so-called minor crimes or disorders.)

Would these affect your idea of safety?

Would your perception of how secure your neighbourhood is, be influenced by any of these issues?

Crime signals lead to perceptions of other ills

Once spotted, these signals can lead to a heightened awareness and the perception that there are other examples in the neighbourhood, from littering to threats of anti-social behaviour. These perceptions may be affected by forms of minor disorder which are not *per se* criminal offences but none the less influence an individual's sense of well-being and security. Perceptions may also be affected by the views of family and friends and media reports. Nor can the fear of crime be separated from other aspects of an individual's perception of the 'quality of life' of their communities, such as the education their children receive, the housing stock in their area, or the cleanliness or otherwise of their neighbourhood.

6.5.2.2 *Broken Windows theory*

Linked with social disorganization arguments is the so-called '**Broken Windows**' theory made popular through the work of James Wilson and George Kelling in the USA. It could be argued that 'Broken Windows' theory has also been influential in the UK context, particularly in terms of past government thinking. We summarize the theory in the table below.

Stage	[Examples]
Relatively minor evidence of perceived criminal or anti-social behaviour	A single broken window (perhaps accidental) in a building, left unrepaired
Greater feeling that a community is vulnerable and 'law and order is breaking down'	More windows are broken in the same building, deliberately
A breakdown in forms of social cohesion that normally militate against crime and disorder	People are less willing to frequent the area close to the buildings
More serious forms of crime 'move in' to occupy the vacuum	Drug dealers begin to operate, muggers move in, organized criminals exploit the opportunities now available

Discussion points

How convinced are you by the 'Broken Windows' theory?

If the theory is correct, what are the implications for the PCSO?

6.5.2.3 *Criticism of the theory*

There has been significant criticism of 'Broken Windows' theory, largely because of the lack of supporting empirical evidence—that is, it has not been shown that the low-level problems identified by the theory by necessity lead to the more serious outcomes claimed; one element does not entail another. Despite this, 'Broken Windows' retains its attraction to some policy makers (particularly in the USA) and is often coupled with '*Zero Tolerance*' approaches to policing (see a brief discussion in 6.8 of this below).[5]

And if 'Broken Windows theory' is valid?

If the theory *is* valid then the implications for the PCSO are obviously to assist in facilitating the repair of the 'Broken Window' as soon as possible. For example, if the first stage is broken street lighting, then this will require coordination with the relevant county, borough, or district council highways department.

6.5.2.4 *Signal crime and signal disorder*

To look at this in more detail, we can identify three parts that make up a **signal crime/signal disorder**:

- The **expression**—the incident that makes a person concerned
- The **content**—how the person makes sense of the incident, particularly in the context of feeling at risk or being vulnerable
- The **effect**—what changes in the person because of the incident? For example, does it affect behaviour or how he or she feels?

We select as an example an elderly resident in a town such as Tonchester (see Chapter 8 and 6.5.2.8 below), Mrs Veronica Meldrew, who sees groups of disaffected youths congregating daily in the passage outside her house, engaging in rowdy behaviour and minor acts of vandalism. She might say, '*I see these kids outside my house every evening*' (the **expression**). '*They make me feel unsafe because they are always misbehaving*' (the **content**). '*I don't leave my house at night and keep my curtains closed*' (the **effect**).

6.5.2.5 *Police responses likely to be low key—residents' fear will increase*

Would the police respond to this sort of incident? Their resources are stretched and they have to prioritize depending on the seriousness of the situation. In this instance no criminal acts have been committed and therefore the police will concentrate on other incidents where a criminal offence *has* occurred. This then reinforces the resident's perceptions about her safety, as well as reducing her confidence in the police. This perception Mrs Meldrew then shares with her family, friends, and acquaintances, in turn affecting *their* perceptions about the risk posed by the youths in the passageway. The unease that she feels, and her perceptions of her safety, spread out like ripples on a pond, causing concern and anxiety to a larger part of the community. This unease is what the British Crime Survey records, and, as we commented earlier, the unease or anxiety can often be *despite* the reality of crime investigation and 'good' Force measurements.

6.5.2.6 *Actions to tackle perceptions of risk*

What is needed is action to tackle these perceptions of risk to increase public confidence and to improve relationships with the community. The problem may not strictly be a policing one but the fallout from inactivity from any agency will often end up at the police's door. Mrs Meldrew's perception is that the youths are engaging in anti-social behaviour and to her that is a police matter and therefore she expects a police response.

Discussion points

Consider the attitude of this particular resident—is she correct in expecting a police response?

Are there any other 'grey areas' where the police are often expected to deal with a problem that may not be strictly within their remit?

What should the police response be in such situations?

What is your role as a PCSO in dealing with these tricky situations?

6.5.2.7 *Control signals*

The signal crime approach goes further in its analysis of the perception of risk within the community and asserts that, as well as an **expression**, a **content**, and an **effect**, there is also a **control signal** which can work towards reducing the fear factor. *The control signal is an authority response to the particular problem that seeks a solution.* This does not have to come solely from the police but could encompass things like the installation of CCTV, the erecting of fencing, an improvement in street lighting, and so on. Therefore the approach provides an opportunity to make things better for the community and accordingly it is not simply a negative proposition. This was identified in a national evaluation of a government initiative, **The New Deal for Communities**:

> The advantage of the signal crime approach is its focus on those factors that are disproportionately generative of insecurity. Once the cause of the problem is understood, one can begin to effectively act against them … Tactics and strategies can be designed and implemented at the local level … (and) can have a disproportionate impact on the causes of insecurity, increase public trust and confidence in the police and thereby provide greater reassurance to residents over their safety. Signal crime theory is a method for problem identification in which issues and problems that cause most concern to residents can be targeted … [6]

6.5.2.8 *Mrs Meldrew's letter*

Mrs Meldrew has written to her local paper, *The Tonchester Herald* (see Chapter 8), about her predicament and her letter is reproduced below.

Dear Sir

I am an 83-year-old widow who has lived in Tonchester all her life and things are now so bad I cannot leave my house in the evening. Gangs of hooligans are outside my house every night and the language they use is terrible. I have to close my curtains at 5 o'clock every evening because I feel scared.

I have called the police but if they turn up, it is often several hours after I call them and the hooligans have gone. I cannot remember the last time I saw a police officer walking down the street.

Tonchester is not now the town that I grew up in and I worry about the world my grandchildren will inherit. The hooligans are winning and nobody is doing anything about it.

Yours in disgust

V Meldrew (Mrs)

6, Pickle's Passage
Tonchester

Task

Following the publication of the letter you are tasked by the neighbourhood teams' Inspector to investigate this issue. The Inspector tells you that this task has come directly from the BCU Commander who has asked to be kept personally informed of the progress in this matter.

What steps will you take to investigate and resolve this matter?

6.5.2.9 *Perceptions of risk*

We don't seek to be prescriptive in supplying a 'model' answer, but it is evident that this matter revolves around Mrs Meldrew's perception of the risk to her safety and her fears need to be taken into consideration when planning a response. Furthermore, the response has to be one that *sustains* a solution and does not merely attain one. A one-off initiative is no good and will be recognized by the public as merely a knee-jerk reaction to negative publicity. Therefore we make suggestions below that seek to achieve a long-term approach, but our suggestions are by no means exhaustive nor are they guaranteed to succeed:

- Mrs Meldrew states in her letter that she has previously called the police and that no action was taken. There will be a record of these calls and these need to be looked at, to establish what occurred and if any intelligence is available that may help your investigation.

- A visit to speak to Mrs Meldrew would be appropriate to gain further details of the problems she is facing. It might be worthwhile considering having a senior officer also attending to apologize for the problems she is facing and to reassure her that we are taking her complaint seriously.
- Visible patrols of the Passage (Pickle's Passage—see map, Figure 23 at 8.2 below) and the surrounding areas from Daniell Street in the north to Mandela Avenue in the south, in the evening. This will provide reassurance to the community that the perceived problem has been acknowledged and dealt with.
- Use these patrols to talk to other members of the community to find out what they think about the problem.
- Intelligence gathering of the details of the congregating youths (NB: it may be that there is no problem or that the problem has been exaggerated).
- Speak to the gathering youths and find out why they are in that area and why they happen to congregate in this one place. It is important to recognize that no criminal act is committed by youths congregating to speak to their friends. It is the behaviour as a result of this that may be an issue. 'Demonizing' the youths will only fuel their resentment of authority in general and the police in particular. The youths are as legitimate a part of the community as Mrs Meldrew.
- If you witness rowdy behaviour, then it may be appropriate to intervene and inform the youths that such behaviour will not be tolerated. This early intervention may disperse the group or quieten them down. It shows the public that you are there to make a difference.
- Work with youth groups and/or schools to find alternative spaces for the youths to meet.
- Look at physical security enhancements: CCTV, alley gates, improved street lighting, and so on.

Task

Think about failing to act on Mrs Meldrew's complaint to the press. To whom would this send out a message about the Tonchester police and what do you think will be the kind of publicity generated?

A model response

Our suggested answers would include:
- The youths themselves, who could feel that they now have a licence to act with impunity
- Mrs Meldrew
- Her neighbours and other residents of Pickle's Passage
- The readers of *The Tonchester Herald* if the newspaper did a follow-up story or if Mrs Meldrew submitted a further letter
- Possible lead story for other media, such as local television and radio, leading to greater public exposure and criticism of the police
- The public at large who might be encouraged by the 'band wagon' effect to write in themselves with criticisms of the local police, leading, iteratively, to renewed media pressure.

6.5.2.10 *The roles of the media*

It is essential that the communication aspect of the signal crimes process be managed effectively. This then focuses attention on media handling because it is in the full glare of the media that these signal crimes and the responses to them are carried out. The (fictional) newspaper mentioned above, in common with every other local newspaper, would carry these stories as will the other media outlets, TV, radio, internet blogs, and so on. The alternative scenario, of a positive police response and a proactive intervention by the PCSO, is akin to the effect recognized in the **New Deal for Communities** evaluation we quoted earlier:

> Publicity and communication are recurrent themes …
>
> The strategy here is that 'good news stories' act as a confidence-building measure in the local area and communicate some of the positive gains made in reducing crime … The pre-emptive use of communication may assert more control over these perceptions, perhaps leaving less to the imagination of the recipients.[7]

6.5.3 A media strategy

The PCSO needs to make sure that initiatives and successes are trumpeted and the wider community is aware of the steps being taken in neighbourhood policing. Each police station or BCU will have a media liaison officer who will be a handy contact for ensuring that these good news stories are put into the public domain. Such stories can demonstrate reassurance policing or accentuate positive initiatives like youth clubs; but the positive spin ensures that the community hears some good news. Initiatives like these act as control signals in the fight against the fear of crime. Episodes with visual impact could also be placed in the Force web-pages, where the media may also pick them up.

6.5.3.1 *Selling the 'good news' message*

All media outlets should be exploited to send the 'good news' message and one of the things you can do in your own area is to explore avenues you can use to communicate. It is also important to explore the demographics of your area to ensure that the media used are appropriate. There tends to be an assumption that everyone has access to the internet but this may not be true. Therefore use a variety of communication outlets to ensure you have targeted as wide a segment of the community as possible. Remember that pictures always help: don't forget positive images in this planning context.

6.5.3.2 *Making an environmental visual audit*

What we will now explore is how you can identify signal crimes/ disorders within your community and how these can then be used to inform and shape your work within that neighbourhood. The key tool for this is the Environmental Visual Audit (EVA) or as it sometimes known *a structured 'patch' walk*. The EVA is a way of looking at your designated community and identifying any signal crimes that exist within it. Essentially you walk around the neighbourhood and log all the problems that you can see.

Task

What signal crimes/disorders can you think of that may be seen in a neighbourhood? Have a look around your own neighbourhood to see if you can identify any.

A model response

Our suggested answers might include the following (but the list is not exhaustive):

- Litter/rubbish strewn around
- Graffiti—racist/offensive?
- Vandalism
- Broken windows/fences

- Derelict houses
- Furniture in the garden
- Drug paraphernalia
- Abandoned vehicles
- Prostitution—cards in the phone boxes, used condoms, 'cruising' cars
- Large groups of youths hanging about
- Dog mess
- Stray animals
- Broken street lighting—absence of lighting
- Alcohol debris.

The items listed are not necessarily indicative of a fear of crime within a community, but they do provide examples of things that give people a sense of unease. By identifying these in an EVA, you will provide a list of problems to solve in conjunction with other partnership agencies.

Discussion point

Looking at our suggested answers to the Task above, what agencies could you identify that would be useful in helping to solve these problems?

6.5.3.3 *Partners in an EVA*

Partnership agencies could be invited on an EVA so that they can have an input, which would then build into a joint problem-solving approach. This works well where there is an agency that has a responsibility for a large part of the community, such as a local authority or housing association. It could also be useful to take a member of the community or a community representative on an EVA (day or night), so that they can identify problems you may not see or which you have missed. This therefore allows you to access the 'eyes and ears' of a community so that the signal crimes identified as being the ones that cause most unease, will be the ones dealt with first. This may build a sense of ownership within the community because people's views are seen as an integral part of the process. The EVA will provide a snapshot of the community, which can then be used to inform your work patterns. If the EVA is repeated at regular intervals then the progress made within that community in dealing with signal crimes and disorders could be easily charted, as well as allowing for new problems to be identified. In the course of time, this could become an excellent qualitative measure of the impact of PCSOs.

6.5.3.4 *The wider value of an EVA*

The EVA works particularly well with environmental signal crimes such as littering, fly tipping, abandoned vehicles, not clearing up dog mess, or graffiti, because these tend to be highly visible problems which can often be resolved quite quickly. The litter can be picked up, the abandoned cars removed and crushed, the walls cleaned, the graffitists and fly tippers prosecuted, and these actions will have a symbolic significance within the community. The fact that the police are acting, in conjunction with other agencies, to tackle neighbourhood issues, will demonstrate to the community that you are listening to their concerns and reversing the 'broken window' state of neighbourhood deterioration. The EVA will fit well into the community engagement process because it can be used at public meetings where the community is asked which of its problems it wants to be tackled first.

6.6 Partnerships

In this and preceding chapters, we have explored many functions within the PCSO role and have looked at the community-based focus that is vital for the role to succeed. The idea of the PCSO as a **conduit** between the community and the police has also been touched upon.

> Conduit—a means of transmission or
> communication.

This description suggests a genuine metaphor for the role of the PCSO. There is a transmission of ideas between the community and the police through the PCSO. The PCSO facilitates communication that works both ways and to the potential benefit of both sides: the police receive important community based intelligence; the community correspondingly has the ear of the police in dealing with its perceived problems (which may not be crimes and which may not normally attract police attention).

6.6.1 Partnerships enter the mix

This image of the PCSO as a channel between two distinct groups is not one-dimensional or monolithic. Equally important are the partnership agencies with which the PCSO works on a daily basis.

The nature of police and community partnerships with other locally-based agencies and local government departments is important to the success of any civic enterprise which the PCSO, on behalf of the police, may seek to develop. The PCSO is firmly at the centre of this neighbourhood policing/community/agencies approach.

6.6.1.1 *How do partnerships work?*

To demonstrate the importance of the partnership approach to resolving community issues, consider the following:

> You are a PCSO working on an urban estate (mixed housing, both social and private) and at the heart of this community is a park that is the focal point for many of the problems brought to you at your regular community surgery. You receive complaints about matters such as litter, dog fouling, underage drinking, congregation of youths, criminal damage of the play park equipment, graffiti spraying, and so on. The residents complain to you that the park has become unsafe at night and that adults can feel intimidated by the youths who congregate there. Parents tell you that they have seen broken bottles on the children's play area, and there have been other reports of used hypodermic needles being found. The local children add that they cannot play football there because of the dog fouling and that there is only play equipment for younger children.

Task

Consider which agencies you would contact to deal with these issues.

A model response

We don't think that there is a right or wrong response to this task, but we suggest that you ought to consider the following possibilities:

- **Park authorities**—is there a park keeper or green spaces warden who can help with this issue? Does the park authority have a retained gardening company who could help identify issues within the park? Who is responsible for the maintenance and who is responsible for the provision of the play equipment?

- **Local authority**—who can help with removing the graffiti? Is the same department responsible for the litter collections within the park? Is there an issue with the lighting that could make the park better lit at night?
- **Housing association**—if offenders can be identified and linked to a particular residence, can their anti-social behaviour be linked to their tenancy agreements? Is there a designated housing officer for this area? Do the residents have an association that could provide such information, as well as reassurance visits? What do residents want to see in the park? What would the community regard as success?
- **Education**—there are potential issues to do with alcohol and drugs and so schools visits to highlight the long-term issues of both problems may help.
- **Health**—as above, but to include comment or publicity or both about the dangers of used hypodermic needles.
- **Youth services**—are there outreach workers who could speak to the youths who congregate there to understand the issues? What do they want to see in the park: a skate park, a teen shelter, bike tracks?
- **Dog warden**—is the issue of fouling to do with irresponsible owners or stray dogs? How often does the dog warden patrol? Is the area known for strays? (Residents can help with information here.) Can the dogs be identified and then linked to owners? You, as the PCSO, would want to include the park on your patrol, and perhaps put up notices warning of the Fixed Penalty offences for dog-fouling. Is there a facility to dispose of bagged dog mess? Is it emptied frequently?
- **Charities**—is there funding available to help put some equipment into the park? Is there room for things like skateboard areas, or facilities for playing sport?
- **Local businesses**—can they help with funding/sponsoring some of the projects? Point out the advantages of 'virtuous' publicity and the inclusion of their logos on equipment or facilities.
- **Police**—enforcement is needed on the issues of drinking, drugs, anti-social behaviour, criminal damage, graffiti, etc.
- **Parents**—it is necessary to inform them about their children when the latter transgress, as well as providing access to support services to stop some of the low-level problems escalating further.
- **The community itself**—showing how the residents of the estate and the park users can help with these issues by setting

up meetings, establishing surgeries, and collating information, as well as lobbying local councils, council officials, and media organizations. By doing these things the community has a voice on the issues and can strongly influence outcomes.

6.6.1.2 *Joined-up and coordinated approaches to problems*

This is by no means a guarantee of success. In any approach to resolving these issues, an agency on its own could only scratch away at one aspect of a pretty complex issue. A *joined-up partnership approach* is integral to dealing with problems in the round, particularly since the boundaries of organizational responsibility are so blurred. It would be easy to forget, in the complication of organizational accountability and negotiated responsibility, that **the real problem is encouraging the community to take ownership of its problems**. Part of your PCSO role will be to help to coordinate agency responses and to ensure that the needs of people living by the park, or wanting to use it as a recreation and leisure facility, are met. If you don't attempt a coordinated, joined-up partnership approach from the outset, it will be very hard to impose such a structure halfway through, and a project might drag on for far longer than it needed to.

6.6.1.3 *The Crime and Disorder Reduction Partnership (CDRP)*

An organizational approach to solving issues within the community has been given formal structure through **Crime and Disorder Reduction Partnerships** (CDRPs, known as *Community Safety Partnerships* in Wales), established in the **Crime and Disorder Act 1998**, and later amended by the **Police Reform Act 2002**. This provides a statutory framework for the 'joined-up partnership' approach and made the following authorities responsible for seeking a coordinated approach to community issues:

- **The police**
- **Local authorities**
- **Fire authorities**
- **Police authorities**
- **Primary care trusts** (England)
- **Local health boards** (Wales).

Colin Rogers, in his study of Crime Reduction Partnerships, provides a useful explanation of the rationale for cooperation:

Working together, these responsible authorities are required to carry out an audit to identify crime and disorder and problems of drugs misuse in their area, and to develop strategies that deal effectively with them. Partner organisations are required to work in cooperation with local education and probation authorities, and to invite the cooperation of a range of local private, voluntary, and other public and community groups, including the community itself.[8]

Discussion point

What do you think the advantages and disadvantages of this approach could be?

6.6.1.4 *What CDRPs should deliver*

The Government has indicated what it expects CDRPs to provide through partnerships or to develop through taking the lead in delivering a series of priorities which are shown in the *National Community Safety Plan 2008–2011*:

- Make communities safer (characterised by the government as: 'continuing to build on the significant reductions in crime achieved over recent years, fewer people will be victims of crime, especially the most serious crimes—violent, drug and alcohol-related crime—and the public will be protected from the most harmful offenders').

- Play a leading role in the development of the Safer and Stronger Communities block of Local Area Agreements and manage subsequent delivery, ensuring targets set by the CDRP are reflected in the LAA, working jointly with Local Criminal Justice Boards (LCJBs) and Reducing Reoffending Partnership Boards to develop effective local responses to tackling serious sexual offences, including the provision of effective victim care pathways to minimize harm and action to improve the investigation and prosecution of serious sexual offences.

- Reduce the most serious violence, including tackling serious sexual offences and domestic violence: identification of and early intervention with victims and perpetrators of domestic violence, to prevent escalation, including (in many areas) through implementation of Multi-Agency Risk Assessment Conferences (MARACs).

- Continue to make progress on **serious acquisitive crime** through a focus on the issues of greatest priority in each locality and the most harmful offenders. **Serious acquisitive**

crime includes burglary (including aggravated burglary), robbery (both of personal and business property), and theft of and from a vehicle (including aggravated vehicle taking). The Government expects all areas to be able to make further reductions in these crimes. A key principle is that partnerships should have flexibility to tackle local priorities, including management with neighbourhood policing to ensure a joined-up response to local concerns; developing local partnerships, such as Safer Schools Partnerships, to deliver solutions in response to specific issues, as appropriate.

- Tackle the crime, disorder and anti-social behaviour issues of greatest importance in each locality, increasing public confidence in the local agencies involved in dealing with these issues.
- CDRP to hold at least one public meeting per year to engage the community in tackling crime and working closely with the police on the delivery of neighbourhood policing as a key mechanism for understanding the priorities of the community and for responding to local concerns. [9]

[adapted and compressed from Home Office, *National Community Safety Plan 2008–2011*, (2008, Crown Copyright), also available from <http://www.homeoffice.gov.uk/national-policing-plan/national-community-safety-0811> accessed August 2009]; see also HMG's *Cutting Crime: A New Partnership 2008–2011*, July 2007, Crown copyright.

6.6.2 Research into community partnerships

In his work on *Community Engagement in Policing* (2006), Andy Myhill researched the literature around this topic and reached some interesting conclusions about some of the challenges relating to the partnership aspect of community engagement, which have profound implications for the work of the PCSO:

- Communities may not initially have the willingness to engage with the police, particularly in areas where there is a history of poor relations. This can be sometimes interpreted [...] as apathy. The police need to **foster trust and confidence** in these communities prior to attempting to secure community participation.
- Communities may not have the capacity to participate effectively in policing. Evidence suggests existing community networks are important to sustaining participation. The police

will have to work with partner agencies to help **build capacity** in communities.

- Communities need to be **trained and educated** about their role in policing. If citizens are being encouraged to participate actively, the nature and scope of their role needs to be clearly defined.
- The police must **provide communities with good quality information** about crime in their local area on a real-time basis if they are to participate effectively in policing.
- The police must value the input and contribution of the public if partnerships are to be successful. Information flow must be two-way. The police need to **provide communities with feedback** on how their contribution is being used. If action is taken, this should be publicized. If action is not taken, the reasons for this should be explained.
- **Effective multi- and inter-agency working** is crucial for community engagement on wider community safety issues. This is particularly so in relation to environmental/quality of life issues.[10]

Discussion point

Looking at each of Myhill's points, how can the PCSO help in overcoming these challenges?

6.6.3 Foster trust and confidence

One of the key responsibilities of the PCSO role within this engagement approach is to gain the trust and confidence of the community in which PCSOs work. Part of this derives from the visibility of the PCSO within the community and this was one of the findings of the National Reassurance Policing Project (NRPP). As communities become used to this new presence in their midst, they are more likely to engage with the whole neighbourhood management process. However, visibility and walking around are not enough on their own, since trust and confidence do not emerge purely from an osmotic process based merely on presence. The need to be present in the community on a regular basis forms part of this but trust also relies on three key factors—**reliability**, **sincerity**, and **competence**.[11]

6.6.4 **Building capacity**

One of the key objectives for any PCSO is to help provide opportunities for the community to participate in local problem-solving initiatives in an effort to move the community towards taking ownership of these problems. This requires more than just goodwill and the confidence of the residents involved. It involves utilizing the capacity within that community to band and bond together to tackle problems as well as involving the partnership agencies. One could argue, of course, that it is the job of the 'authorities' to provide help irrespective of whether the community itself is a cohesive force, but issues are better tackled when there is a will to **build capacity**. Building capacity may be difficult where there is a need to establish a shared identity first.

6.6.4.1 *Training and education*

Communities sometimes need to be encouraged to participate in local initiatives and the residents 'educated' about their potential role in helping to shape the partnership approach to policing. This needs to be done sensitively. The PCSO, having built up a degree of trust and confidence with community members, is ideally placed to help with this process in an empathetic and responsive manner. The PCSO should be in tune with the community's concerns and should have identified the leading players in the community who are in the best position to help with any initiative. By utilizing the structures that a PCSO has put into place, surgeries, public meetings, 'talking walls', and so on, the 'education' is better seen as part of a **continuous engagement** process which seeks to lead out from the community the abilities to solve problems, rather than impose solutions from outside. Ensuring that the community has basic skills, such as how to write a formal letter to a councillor, or how to set up a media campaign, involves skills training. Many people are eager to acquire skills (as opposed to knowledge) and it is probable that there will be some residents who want to know how to do things. The PCSO can act as a facilitator in such cases, putting people in touch and helping to secure the right community outcomes.

6.6.4.2 *Provide information and feedback*

One of the key initiatives used by Neighbourhood Management Teams across the UK is **PACT—Partners and Communities Together**. This is interpreted and implemented in many different ways by the police forces and agencies involved, so we can offer a description only of the generic process. The predominant approach is through the constructive use of 'surgeries' and public meetings. Used correctly, a public (PACT) meeting can **foster trust and confidence**; it can help to **build capacity** within a community; it allows for the **training and education** of a community; and it can help with **effective multi-agency work**.

Discussion points

What PACT initiatives are there on your BCU?

How can you get involved in its delivery?

6.6.4.3 *Community meetings*

The desire of a community to come together to discuss its problems can be facilitated by a PCSO to great effect by establishing community 'surgeries'. These could be held at schools, or in community centres, village halls, libraries, and so on—anywhere where there is a local authority-owned venue. This provides the residents with the opportunity to speak to their local PCSOs, or other members of the extended policing family, about their concerns and issues. Surgeries often take the form of a 'drop-in', staffed at specific times for anyone in the community to visit. At the same time, surgeries or surgery venues can be used to provide information about crime reduction initiatives or other policing projects. 'Surgeries' can be taken physically to a community using a mobile police station so that the surgeries are not necessarily fixed in a geographical sense. This will enable the PCSO to reach out to different sections of the community, particularly in scattered 'beats'.

Discussion points

What problems could arise with community surgeries?

Where could you hold one on your 'patch'?

Do they have to be regular?

Are there costs involved?

Why might some people be reluctant to visit a mobile police station rather than, say, a local library?

6.6.4.4 *The value of public meetings*

Don't forget that public meetings provide an opportunity for you to introduce members of the community to the partners and partnership agencies to resolve the community's difficulties mutually. This gives each of the participants a chance to meet, engage, and understand each other, with you acting as facilitator. Remember though that there are people who go to meetings and do nothing else. You mustn't let public meetings become a substitute for doing things and planning actions. You may have to be the catalyst to make other things happen.

POINTS TO NOTE

There are four key areas to consider when organizing a public meeting:

- The **venue**—what factors need to be considered in choosing a venue?
- The **rules**—what rules should be in place for a public meeting?
- The **agenda**—does a meeting need one?
- The **chairperson**—who should chair a public meeting and what qualities should they possess?

A model response

Born of many years of engagement in public meetings, our suggestions in answer to the questions we have just posed are these:

- **Venue**—location, accessibility, adequate seating, neutral (does the building convey ownership of the issue to the community?), disabled facilities, refreshments available, cost, time of meeting, adequate parking, adequate lighting
- **Rules**—no heckling, adherence to the agenda and to timings, courtesy at all points, no shouting, one speaker at a time
- **Agenda**—provides the structure to a meeting, provides a written framework for the meeting, provides audience with the format
- **Chairperson**—disciplined, experienced, empathetic listener, moves the meeting on, adheres to agenda, well respected, community figure.

POINTS TO NOTE

For further information on organizing a public meeting, have a look at the following website:

<http://www.bbc.co.uk/newswatch/ukfs/hi/newsid_4750000/ newsid_4758500/47585>, accessed August 2009

6.6.4.5 *PACT at public meetings*

The PACT process uses the meeting as a form of community dialogue and seeks to find the issues that are of concern in that community. The meeting often discusses these issues so that priorities can be put forward to the PACT Panel as objectives. It is on this basis that the **partners and communities** move forward together in solving the community's issues and concerns. The idea is that *by engaging everyone, partners, PCSO, and the community from the ground up*, the community priorities will emerge.

Task

A PACT Panel usually consists of leading community figures and partnership agencies—who do you think should compose such a panel?

A model response

Our answers, again, are by no means prescriptive but we think that the following may be key players often found on a PACT Panel:

Police representatives, housing officer, Neighbourhood Watch coordinator, faith leader(s), local business proprietors (or collective groups like the *Lions* or Chamber of Commerce), local councillors, parish councillors, residents' association members, representatives of local charities, school governors, head teachers, local authority officers, local citizens who have some prominent voice in the community.

You may be able to think of more. You should certainly be considering who, in your patch, should be approached to participate in a PACT panel: remember that it needn't be the same people each time. The composition of PACT panels should reflect the issues under consideration.

6.6.4.6 *Effective multi-agency work*

The final factor is that of effective multi-agency approaches and again the PCSO can be crucial to this activity at a community level. PCSOs can often deal with issues before they escalate into wider problems simply by having access to the agencies that can deal with that problem best; such as informing the local clean-up team from the council about fresh graffiti so that the team can remove the nuisance swiftly. This relies on the PCSO having a good knowledge of the partnership agencies available and making sure that this information is maintained in a readily available format. Direct numbers for key personnel (crucial to avoid the maze of bureaucracy that often surrounds getting hold of the right person) can be maintained on a **Key Individual Network** (KIN) or a contact list. This can then be made available to others to ensure a consistency of approach, as well as continuity should you move from your 'patch' or leave the job.

POINTS TO NOTE

Do you have a **KIN** (Key Individual Network)? If not, is your contact list available to others and kept up to date?

6.6.4.7 *Proper partnerships are hard to achieve and need lots of work*

The KIN approach is adequate for the daily PCSO routine of dealing with issues before they escalate but, at the strategic level, effective partnerships can be difficult to achieve. Gilling[12] has identified the following factors as being crucial to establishing good partnership protocols:

- All partners having a **shared purpose**
- **Leadership** is needed to drive the process on
- An appropriate **structure** is required
- Appropriate **resources** are needed
- Appropriate **time** needs to be allocated to the process
- **Durability** is needed to provide the necessary consistency and continuity.

Even with this in place, being able to sustain an effective partnership can still require constant effort, tact, patience, and resilience:

> ... it is the very diverse make-up of many of the agencies that constitute partnerships [which] can be problematic. Attention is drawn to the inter-organisational conflict and differential power relationships that can occur. Partnerships, especially within the field of crime control and criminal justice, by their nature, draw together diverse organisations with very different cultures, ideologies, and traditions that pursue distinct aims through divergent structures, strategies and practices. Deep structural conflicts exist between the parties that sit down together in partnerships. Criminal justice agencies have very different priorities and interests, as do other public sector organisations, voluntary bodies, the commercial sector, and local community groups.[13]

This is not intended to make you despair of ever finding an answer through the partnership approach, rather it is needed to show you how to ground the process in reality. By recognizing the limitations of such alliances and interdepartmental politics, PCSOs need be under no illusion about the magnitude of the task:

> The provision of Neighbourhood Policing and other related initiatives is most impactive, and has the most sustainable effects, when it finds ways to augment a community's informal social control resources. The police are not the ultimate guarantors of neighbourhood order and security. They are a standby institution that can intervene when social order that is ordinarily maintained by the norms, rules and conventions of everyday interactions in neighbourhoods has been breached or threatened. Thus, formal social control needs to be construed as part of the solution, rather than the solution in and of itself.[14]

6.7 Ethnic and Diverse Minority Communities

We have examined a number of aspects of community engagement in this chapter but we now turn to the issue of policing ethnic and diverse minority communities. This is a crucial area of policing as a whole (which we discuss in some detail in both 1.6 and in 4.4 above) but it has real resonance in the community sphere in which you work and for the role that you perform. One might be tempted to suppose that, after the **Macpherson Inquiry** (the 1999 report into the 1993 murder of Stephen Lawrence), the national picture in respect of race and diversity is slowly improving, but the deaths of Anthony Walker in 2005 and David Morley in 2004, in suspected homophobic attacks, suggest that there is a long way to go, both in the wider police family and in society as a whole, before we achieve genuine tolerance and respect for diverse minority communities. Controversies in the last few years have included the Catholic Church's adoption agency's refusal (subsequently moderated) to allow gay couples to adopt its orphans and the Channel 4 television show *Big Brother* being riven with accusations of racism. Issues of race and diversity often exist under the surface of things, needing only an appropriate occasion for them to emerge. A prominent example in 2009 centred on HRH the Prince of Wales' use of the word 'golliwog' as, he claimed, an affectionate nickname for an Asian polo-playing acquaintance.

6.7.1 'Hard to reach'

One phrase that you will often hear in relation to ethnic and diverse minority communities is 'hard to reach' groups (sometimes referred to as 'hard to hear' groups). These groups have assumed a symbolic significance in the pursuit of diverse policing. They are considered to be the groups that might require differing approaches or present a challenge in terms of attempting to involve these groups in the engagement process.

Task

What do you think is a *hard to reach* group?
Write down a list of examples. Discuss with your colleagues what their experiences are of encounters with such groups.

A model response

It is impossible to present a definitive list of 'hard to reach' groups because perceptions of what 'hard to reach' means will vary considerably. There may be additional groups that provide purely local or regional examples, such as some traveller or 'New Age' communities. A 'sample' list of hard to reach groups was provided in a Home Office Development and Practice Report of 2005. Compare what you produced in answer to the task above with the following:

- Ethnic minority groups
- Gay and lesbian groups
- Children and young people, especially those at risk
- Disabled people
- Sex workers
- Victims of crime
- Homeless people
- Drug users
- The mentally disordered
- Rural/farming communities
- Older people
- Single mothers
- Poor and acutely economically-deprived people
- Illiterate people (about 13% of the adult population, lest you think them invisible)
- Domestic violence victims
- Non-English speakers
- Those suspicious of the police

- Refugees
- Travellers
- Some faith communities
- Transient populations (for example the travelling community).[15]

Discussion points

Were many of these groups on your list?

How many of these groups are represented where you work?

Did some of the groups mentioned surprise you?

6.7.1.1 'Hard to reach' may be stereotyping

One aspect of the debate on community engagement that is often overlooked but which needs to be considered by practitioners within the community policing environment is the term 'hard to reach' itself. There is a possibility that people within communities that are designated with this term could find it patronizing or even offensive. It could be used as a term to stigmatize groups as being different, rather than one used to emphasize inclusion. By labelling, are we seeking to impose sanitized cultural norms on to a much more variable picture? Alternatively, it could be that using the phrase 'hard to reach' somehow implies that these minority groups are outside the norm and possibly reluctant to engage in processes with which the majority are happy to conform:

> The wide range of different meanings and applications of the term 'hard to reach' brings into question its utility as a term. It is clear that there are a number of population sub-groups that have traditionally been under-represented (or not represented at all) within formal consultation processes with the police and other official institutions. It is also clear that there exist [*sic*] a range of different groups that have traditionally had difficult relations with the police … However, few of these groups are hard to reach in any fundamental physical sense. It seems fair to say that there are a number of groups who have at least some elements in common in terms of their difficulties with the police. But in many cases 'hard to reach' actually means 'hard to engage with on a positive level'.[16]

6.7.1.2 Beware of the stereotype

We might also note that treating these groups as having some sort of homogeneous identity fails to convey the complexity of the wide range or spectrum of individuals and preoccupations within any

---

single group. There are black people who are happy to engage with the police, just as there are among representatives from any of the groups labelled as 'hard to reach'. Correspondingly, there are people in the larger population groups who will have nothing to do with the police at any price. Remember the dangers we emphasized earlier (in 1.6 above, for example) of '**ethnocentricity**'; the temptation to view everything unvaryingly from your own fixed individual cultural viewpoint, when in fact there are many, equally valid, viewpoints and positions. This is why it is called diversity, after all.

6.7.2 The PCSO has a positive role to play in the community

We have stated throughout this Handbook our belief that the PCSO has a positive role to play in working with all diverse minority communities. This belief is not merely based on conjecture or unfounded theories; rather it is the natural result of the work the PCSO was intended to do. Your work is grounded in implementing 'managed neighbourhood policing', which entails sustained efforts to provide community engagement through genuine consultation. As part of what we have called a **conduit** to a partnership approach, your work with and for minority communities can also be included. The PCSO provides a highly visible presence to deter crime and anti-social behaviour, as well as supplying reassurance to the community.

> **Task**
> What other roles can you identify that PCSOs might bring to the communities in which they work?

6.7.2.1 *Knowing the community ...*

Other dimensions which the PCSO brings to the neighbourhood management equation are local knowledge and expertise, which will have been built up through hard work, positive interaction with members of all communities, and efforts to foster trust and confidence within the neighbourhood (all part of the engagement and partnership approach).

6.7.2.2 *... and its background*

It is important to know some background to the minority communities you are working with, in the same way that research is crucial in any problem-solving approach. Do you consider that your knowledge of diverse communities is enough to answer these questions?

Task

Answer the following questions:

(1) What is a Sikh temple called?

(2) To the nearest million, how many people in the UK are defined as disabled under the Disability Discrimination Act?

(3) What are Gammon, Shelta, and Cant?

(4) What meat do Hindus abstain from eating?

(5) What are the five basic duties for followers of Islam?

(6) Where is Kosovo?

(7) What is homophobia?

(8) What are Ashkenazi and Sephardi(m)?

(9) What is gender dysphoria?

(10) Name any language spoken within the UK-based Chinese community.

A model response

We suggest that these might be the answers which you may have researched (but did you *remember*?).

(1) A *Gurdwara*

(2) 10 million (figure from the Disability Rights Commission <http://www.direct.gov.uk/en/DisabledPeople/DG_10023362> accessed 29 October 2009

(3) They are languages spoken by the traveller community

(4) Beef—the cow is considered to be sacred

(5) **Shahadah**—declaration of one's faith; **Salah**—five compulsory daily prayers; **Zakah**—tithing of money to charity; **Sawm**—fasting during Ramadan; **Hajj**—the pilgrimage to Mecca (if you can afford it)

(6) South-West Europe (think Adriatic Sea) bordered by Serbia, Montenegro, Albania, Macedonia, and Bulgaria

(7) A fear, dislike, or prejudice directed towards lesbian, gay, or bisexual people, or a fear, dislike, or prejudice directed towards their perceived lifestyles, cultures, or characteristics

(8) Ashkenazi—Jewish people originating from Central and Eastern Europe; Sephardi or Sephardi(m)—Jewish people originating from Spain, North Africa, or Arabic (Middle East) regions

(9) 'Gender dysphoria' is the accepted term for **transgender**. Remember this is about gender identity not sexuality

(10) Mandarin, Cantonese, Hakka.

6.7.2.3 *The immutability of the PCSO role from community to community*

Putting this task in here was not to show off our knowledge or to highlight some possible gaps in your detailed understanding of diverse minority issues, rather it was to show that *it can be difficult for anyone to be aware of all issues across all minority communities.* You are not expected to be an expert on the communities that you work with, but you are expected to provide neighbourhood policing to all groups within your area of work and to ensure that they are part of the overall engagement process. **The role of the PCSO does not alter from community to community.** However, you should be aware of the particular issues within those communities which you specifically support, and ensure that you are being responsive to their diverse needs. Remember to ask if you don't know, and never to be too proud to seek help. Most communities will courteously explain themselves to you (if a trifle wearily sometimes). If you show a genuine interest, this will also galvanize the interest of those members of the groups who talk to you.

No one expects PCSOs to be complete experts across the board, but the communities will expect PCSOs to try to master the basics. A report in 2000 noted the fact that in the London borough of Hackney, 95 different languages and dialects were spoken.[17] This would represent a stringent test for any agency, not just the police, but even with such an extreme example of diversity, the problems of comprehension and engagement are not insurmountable, and there are resources are available to help with such a challenge:

- **Diversity training**—this should have formed part of your PCSO Induction course and covered the main areas for your role. It will have involved discussion of the issues facing many communities in England and Wales, as well as wider issues relating to discrimination and equality.
- **Cultural awareness booklets**—some police forces produce for their staff cultural awareness books that identify key points in relation to diverse communities. These can be an invaluable source of information and have practical uses: for example there may be a section on the protocols of entering places of worship. Accessing this information could prevent you causing offence through ignorance.
- **Community Liaison Officers**—most police forces will have dedicated Community Liaison Officers, often part of the

Neighbourhood Policing Team, whose job is to promote better community relations. They will be a good source of information about communities and can help you to identify key people within your neighbourhood with whom you should make contact.

- **Other agencies/support groups**—within your area there may be support groups dedicated to particular groups that offer help and advice to that community. Again, they can be accessed to provide information about a community: researching this mine of information would be a good first task on your arrival in a new BCU or 'beat'.

- **Police support groups**—within your Force there will be support groups available to police officers and police staff based on the diversity strands (race, sexual orientation, gender, disability, religion—maybe not age) and these can also offer support in making contact with community groups. Are you aware of the existence of these groups within your Force? Are there representatives in your BCU or your local police station?

- **Communities themselves**—as a PCSO, part of your role is to go and speak to people in the community, so you would be sensible to extend the same approach to the diverse communities represented in your neighbourhood, such as elderly groups (identified as one of the 'hard to reach' groups). Perhaps too, going to events organized for that community would be a good chance to get your face known and to speak to people about the issues facing them and to ask them what they want from neighbourhood policing. It also affords you the opportunity to ask about areas you are unsure of concerning that particular group. If invited into a mosque, you can ask what the culture and traditions demand if you are unsure. This in itself will demonstrate a willingness to learn and you will be respected for your politeness.

- **You**—you are a resource because you can gain the knowledge of a community, either through your own research (try online as well as this Handbook), or by speaking to people within that community. We talked about the PCSO being a conduit for the partnership approach but also the PCSO can be a channel or route for improved community relations. You can achieve much in terms of raising people's diversity awareness through your own example.

Task

Looking at these sources of information/knowledge, how many have you utilized in your work so far?

Are there others, not on our list, that you can identify from your community?

6.7.3 **Not all groups will welcome you**

The PCSO has a proactive, outward-reaching role in seeking to involve diverse communities in the neighbourhood process which involves getting out there and making contact and dealing with the issues raised in the same way as with any other group. But it does come with a caveat. Not all groups will be responsive to approaches from the police and so your work will deal with local issues and problems rather than trying to eradicate entire social ills or change deep-seated discriminatory behaviour. Improved community relations will not happen overnight nor will relationships be established through one isolated contact, however well meaning and informed:

> Although universal popular approval for the police can never be a realistic aim of police–community relations policies, improved dialogue with marginalised groups may provide the opportunities for addressing aspects of policing that exacerbate adversarial relationships. At a minimum, it should enhance the possibility of achieving some workable compromises.[18]

This is not meant to put you off making the effort but rather making sure that your expectations are realistic. Improvements can, and will, occur, but **they take time**. Professor 'Tank' Waddington has discussed, in *Police Review*, research from the USA by Wesley Skogan, which concluded that **it didn't matter what the police did, they would receive little credit for it from the community**. If true (and the research is partial and US-focused), it is a depressing negative.[19] In fact, of course, the public's attitudes to the police cannot be simplistically attributed to the PCSO without more convincing and local surveys.

6.8 **Consensual or Cooperative, 'Service' or 'Force'? Kinds of Policing and the Match with the PCSO Role**

In some ways, this paragraph title is deliberately provocative: is policing about making people do things or is it about helping people who need support and protection? Is the police a *service* or is it a *force*? This debate is taking place currently in policing and it is proper that you should be aware of and able to contribute to it. It is not about achieving a simplistic compromise so that sometimes you help and support the citizen and sometimes you put bad people away. **It is about fundamentally what society wants its police system to be.** Think of contemporary political slogans on policing and society (we are *not* making a party political point):

Political slogans on policing and society

- Tough on crime; tough on the causes of crime
- ASBOs are working
- Hug a hoodie
- The Respect Agenda
- Building Communities; Fighting Crime
- Visible policing
- Recapture the streets
- More bobbies on the beat
- No more broken windows
- Safer streets initiative
- Community focus
- Citizen-centred

6.8.1 The latest initiative?

'Sound bites' like these turn crime reduction, community responses to disorder, and the work of the police in investigating crime and anti-social behaviour, into slogans or glib phrases; simplifying issues at the same time as suggesting that they are easily resolved. This over-simplification occurs in all the major political parties, irrespective of whether the slogan-makers are in office or not. The issues of law and order are vote winners, and we would be remiss to ignore that this *is* a party led debate, though the differences between political parties in terms of their respective approaches to law and order or criminal justice issues are not as big as they would have you believe, nor as distinct as the slogans themselves might suggest. Nevertheless, there is a debate about which model of policing best fits what the government of the day wishes to deliver. At the time of writing, the keynote is **'citizen focus'** where the needs of the people are placed at the centre of public services' responses. This in turn has led the police into asking themselves whether policing is something which they do to the citizen or whether it is something which has the citizen as the 'customer' or recipient of something called 'police services'.

6.8.1.1 *Different kinds of policing*

The debate has embraced different kinds of policing, each of which held centre stage in police thinking for a period. In summary these are:

> **Different kinds of policing**
>
> **Community policing**—first developed by Robert Trojanowicz in the USA, focuses on how police have become 'detached' from community and concentrates on community beat officers to reassure the local community.
>
> **Problem-oriented (sic) policing**—developed by Herman Goldstein in the USA, proposed that police needed to deal with social issues as well as crime, strongly interventionist on broad front of neighbourhood problems, because crime was a manifestation of social deprivation.
>
> **Intelligence-led policing**—developed by Sir David Phillips, argues that crime and criminality is where police attention should be centred and dealing with criminal intelligence at all levels will bring about reductions in crime, using National Intelligence Model (NIM) to 'business process' the policing function. Increasingly, this is referred to as 'knowledge-based policing', and is not a model as such, but is or should be generic to policing. See Harfield et al (2008).

6.8.1.2 *Each of the models has merit, but not monopoly*

There are other models, the so-called **'zero tolerance'** approach to policing for example, but the essential point for you to take on board is that **none of these models has a monopoly on the 'truth' of policing**. There is a place for knowledge-based policing (arguably at Level 2 (Force-wide) or Level 3 (nationwide or international) policing), but it probably is not at local or BCU level, where concentration on crimes and criminality can lead to neglect of what the community most fears. That said, 'intelligence' on what is happening in the neighbourhood, who is doing what and where, is standard information

which can inform 'intelligent policing'. Similarly, community policing cannot seem to deal effectively with crimes committed above the
purely parochial, such as drugs imports, whilst 'problem-oriented'
policing perhaps tries to make too much of the police officer as 'social
worker', dealing with conditions and social ills quite outside the law
and order remit, even to the extent of making the local police officer
responsible for doing something about housing and education. Each
of these models was seen at the time as *the* panacea, the definitive
answer to the rising tide of crime and disorder, but of course, each
supplied only part of the truth, not the whole of it.

6.8.1.3 *A synthesis model?*

It may be that we need some kind of **synthesis**, or bringing
together, of some of these models to produce a more inclusive
and more widely applicable single model of what policing the
community should be. There are arguments in the press and in
academic writing alike to the effect that the Serious and Organised
Crime Agency (SOCA) can *only* use the intelligence-led policing
model, and that the Respect and Neighbourhood Policing agenda,
including the work of PCSOs, can *only* work through an application
of the community policing model. These things may just about be
true in part; although it sounds to us more as though the facts are
being bent to fit the theory rather than the other way round. We
think that there is another description which avoids the rigidity
of the monopolistic theories and concentrates instead upon the
reality of what is needed on the ground. Look at Figure 20 below.

6.8.1.4 *This is a process or 'flux' depiction*

We could call Figure 20 the 'Neighbourhood Policing Model' and
engage in endless polemic about whether it captures every detail
of every requirement involving policing, and then promulgate
it as the latest panacea for policing, but that is not our aim. In
reproducing this model (or more accurately, *depiction*) of the
detectable and probable changes in policing, what we want to
draw attention to is the **process or flux which is driving policing
from the cold medium of compliance to the warm medium of**
'active citizen engagement', and it reinforces a point which we
have made a number of times in this Handbook: policing is not
something where the police themselves always know what is best.
There are occasions when the citizen should have a say in how s/he
is policed, what is done or not done by the police, and when there
is a deliberate distance interposed from the stereotypical assertion
that 'we are the police and we know what is good for you'.

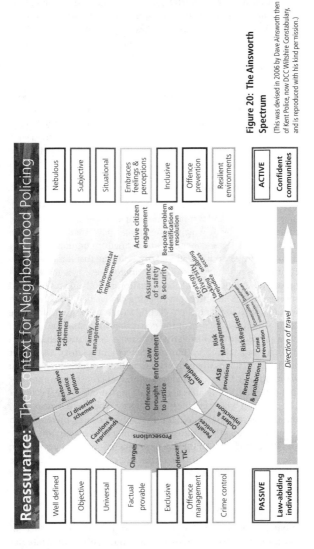

Figure 20: The Ainsworth Spectrum

(This was devised in 2006 by Dave Ainsworth then of Kent Police, now DCC Wiltshire Constabulary, and is reproduced with his kind permission.)

6.8.1.5 *Working on the left*

Look back at the Ainsworth Spectrum and note the two columns which flank the diagram. That on the left defines the nature of **compliance**: including criminal law; well-defined actions which entail restrictive orders and injunctions, ASBOs, penalty notices, offences taken into consideration, restorative justice, and offenders brought to justice. This is objective, universal, familiar, and of a part with the history of police as enforcing the obedience of citizens to the law. It is a world full of facts and definitions, all about managing offences and controlling crime. What it requires as its outcome is passive, law-abiding individuals, who are punished if they do not conform. In this mode, the police are concerned with the application of the law and the conformity of the individual to the law, not with freedoms and flexibilities of choice.

6.8.1.6 *Turning right*

By contrast, the right-hand column is looser, less well-defined, more subjective, and is more about empathy, perceptions, feelings, the 'soft stuff' with which police forces have traditionally been impatient. Yet, it is also inclusive and focused on communities rather than individuals; it is situational (that is to say that it is about how circumstances modify decisions or approaches); it is more about prevention of offences and about environments being resilient and strong; and it is an active state, making change happen rather than waiting for change and then reacting to it. It will require a massive cultural shift on the part of the police and the rest of the criminal justice system to move from the spectrum of **Law Enforcement** (the darker colours) to the **Assurance of Safety and Security** (the lighter colours). Yet, surely, where most communities and individuals would want to be is in the citizen-focused right side of the spectrum and not in the harsher, less flexible, and penalizing left side of the spectrum? The clever bit will be establishing a process whereby the movement can take place from left to right. In reality, of course, there will be a requirement to go back into enforcement if the leaders of the police and the government of the day find, or perceive, that the transition from enforcement to assurance is not reducing crime. Ironically, the right-hand side is about getting rid of the **fear of crime**: something which the left side has signally failed to do.

6.8.1.7 *Citizen-focused policing?*

What the Ainsworth Spectrum shows is that factors such as **dynamic risk assessment** (see 5.7.3.1 above), **diversity strategies** (see 1.6 and 6.7 above) and **crime prevention** (Chapters 4 and 5 *passim*), can influence the outcome as well as the nature of policing. If, as we have consistently argued here, **the salvation of any community is the community's own united response to the threats which face it**, facilitated by the Neighbourhood Policing Team, then the model proposes precisely that the community takes back ownership of how it is policed and decides, to a degree, what form that policing takes. This represents quite a culture shock for many police officers and police forces where the proposal has yet to take hold. We shall return to the debate from a different angle in 7.9 below, when we look at the future of policing, but in the interim consider the following:

Discussion points

Discuss with your colleagues where you think your police force is in terms of the **Ainsworth Spectrum** and how any transition will be managed from the 'cold' medium to the 'warm' one.

Do you think that this is the logical future of policing? If not, what is? How will this model, focused as it is upon what the citizen wants, deal with, say, crimes of violence, knife crime, outbreaks of lawlessness, or 'postcode' gang violence, such as we have seen in some English cities in the last few years?

6.9 **Chapter Summary**

This chapter has been about the fundamental focus of the PCSO's job: the **community**. It is the community which dictates the complexity of your role and which will pose you the problems which you have to resolve. It is the community which you are pledged to support and the community which needs your help. Yet communities are difficult to define, and each of us belongs simultaneously to several communities: where we live; where we work; and where we relax.

6.9.1 **Components of a community**

We tried to analyse **the dynamics of a community** and how it is organized, what unites it, and what divides it. We discussed with you what lies behind the often-surveyed **fear of crime**, and looked in some detail at the nature of **signal crimes** as indicators of social unease, and we noted that acquisitive crime increases in times of economic hardship.

6.9.2 Partnerships, communication, and allied matters

We followed this with a discussion about **partnerships** and how important they are in helping you to do your job, for you assuredly cannot do it without them, and we looked at the nature of **ethnic and diverse communities** and the challenges which these pose to your effective performance. We ended by talking through with you the debate issues around whether the police are coercive and an enforcer of **compliance**, or whether the police are moving steadily towards a new inclusive and **citizen-focused** role, in which the community has a positive and clear say in how it should be policed.

References

A Bottoms, R Mawby, and P Xanthos, 'A tale of two estates' in D Downes, (ed), *Crime & the City* (Macmillan, 1989)

A Bottoms and P Wiles, 'Environmental Criminology' in M Maguire (ed), *The Oxford Handbook of Criminology* (OUP, 2002) Ch 18

M Easton, *Does diversity make us happy?* available from <http://news.bbc.co.uk/1/hi/programmes/happiness_formula/5012478.stm> accessed January 2007

S Farrall and D Gadd, 'Evaluating Crime Fears: A Research Note on a Pilot Study to Improve the Measurement of the "Fear of Crime" as a Performance Indicator' (2004) 10(4) *Evaluation* 493–502

C Hall, 'Social capital: introductory user guide', ESDS, Government Office for National Statistics (2005)

Harfield, C, MacVean, A, Grieve, J, and Phillips, Sir D (eds), *The Handbook of Intelligent Policing* (Oxford University Press, 2008)

HMG, Cutting Crime: A New Partnership 2008-2011, July 2007, Crown copyright

M Innes, 'Crime as a Signal, Crime as a Memory' (2004) 1(2) *Journal for Crime, Conflict and the Media* 15–22

_____ 'What's your problem? Signal crimes and citizen-focused problem solving' (2005) 4(2) *Criminology & Public Policy* 187–200

C Kershaw, S Nicholas, and A Walker (eds), *Crime in England and Wales 2007/08 Findings from the British Crime Survey and police recorded crime,* Home Office Statistical Bulletin 07/08 London: Home Office

A Myhill, *Community engagement in policing: lessons from the literature* from <http://www.crimereduction.gov.uk/policing18.htm> accessed January 2007

PAJ Waddington, K Stenson, and D Don, 'In Proportion: Race, and Police Stop and Search' (2004) 44 *British Journal of Criminology* 889–914

A Walker, C Kershaw, and S Nicholas, 'Crime in England and Wales 2005/06', Home Office Statistical Bulletin, (2006)

Notes

1 See N Tilley, 'Community policing, problem-oriented policing and intelligence-led policing' in T Newburn (ed), *Handbook of Policing*, (Willan, 2003) Ch 13, 311–39.

2 This constitutes our best attempt to encompass all the various definitions and descriptions of community which we have researched and investigated. We do not claim that what we offer is definitive but it's better than anything else we've seen.

3 See Ford, R 'As if times weren't hard enough: a sharp increase in burglary, theft and robbery,' *The Times*, 24 April 24 2009, p 14 and Home Office, *British Crime Survey*, Quarterly Update, April 2009.

4 M Innes, N Fielding, and S Langan, 'Signal Crimes and Control Signs: Towards an Evidence-Based Conceptual Framework for Reassurance Policing', a report for Surrey Police, University of Surrey (2002).

5 If you want to read Kelling and Wilson's original 1982 article on 'Broken Windows' it is available at <http://www.theatlantic.com /doc/ prem/198203/broken-windows>, accessed August 2009.

6 K Christmann, M Rogerson, and D Walters, 'New Deal for Communities: The National Evaluation', Research Report 14. 'Fear of Crime and Insecurity in New Deal Communities Partnerships', Sheffield Hallam University (July 2003) 12.

7 Christmann *et al* (n 6 above) 12–13.

8 C Rogers, *Crime Reduction Partnerships* (OUP, 2006) 12.

9 See Home Office, *National Community Safety Plan 2008–2011*, (2008, Crown Copyright) available from <http://www.homeoffice.gov.uk/ national-policing-plan/national-community-safety-0811>, accessed 12 May 2009.

10 A Myhill, 'Community Engagement in Policing. Lessons from the Literature', Home Office Report (2006) 47, available at http://www. crimereduction.gov.uk/policing18.htm>, accessed February 2007.

11 R Solomon and F Flores, *Building Trust in Business, Politics, Relationships and Life* (OUP, 2003)

12 D Gilling, 'Partnership and Crime Prevention' in N Tilley (ed), *Handbook of Crime Prevention and Community Safety* (Willan, 2005).

13 Rogers (n 8 above).

14 Innes *et al* (n 4 above) 54.

15 S Forrest, A Myhill, and N Tilley, 'Practical Lessons for Involving the Community in Crime and Disorder Problem-Solving', Home Office Development and Practice Report 43 (2005) 4.

16 T Jones and T Newburn, 'Widening Access: Improving Police Relations with Hard to Reach Groups', Police Research Series Paper 138 (2001).

17 B Spencer and M Hough, 'Policing Diversity: Lessons from Lambeth', Policing and Reducing Crime Unit Paper 121 (2000).

18 J Foster, T Newburn, and A Sauhami, 'Assessing the Impact of the Stephen Lawrence Enquiry', Home Office Research Study 294 (2005) 57.

19 See PAJ Waddington, 'Turning the tide of police criticism', *Police Review*, 26 January 2007, 14–15. The research by Wesley Skogan is 'Asymmetry in the impact of encounters with police' (2006) 16 *Policing and Society* 99–126.

Chapter 7
Standards and Futures

7.1 Introduction

In this chapter, we look at matters concerning standards for you as
a PCSO, within the policing context. We look at the work of your
Force Professional Standards Department (PSD), before examining the incidence of corruption in the police and what 'the dark
side' entails, especially in comparison with the ethical standards
you are expected to uphold in a public office.

7.1.1 What does 'professional' mean?

We also briefly examine what we think is meant by being a professional in policing, before discussing what you ought to do when
you go to court and, for those of you new to the business, we
describe what being called to give evidence is like.

7.1.2 The 'mixed economy' of policing

We then take what we consider to be an intelligent and sober look
ahead to ascertain where we believe that policing and PCSOs are
going, always with the proviso that the unexpected may happen.
We suggest what the future of the extended police family may be,
and we model the 'mixed economy' of policing, and well as looking at the developing phenomenon of 'private policing'.

7.1.3 Supervision and advancement

How PCSOs are to be supervised is still somewhat controversial, but we look at the nature of supervision and what it means
for individual police forces. We anticipate the time when your
increased experience and seniority as a PCSO will lead naturally
to a supervisory position. We then look at the likely development

of PCSO roles and routes, including those which have been suggested to 'convert' PCSOs into police officers.

7.1.4 Futures

We conclude the chapter with a hard and unsentimental look at policing in the future and where we think criminal justice is going in England and Wales. As usual, we test, tease, provoke, and reflect with you on your learning throughout this chapter.

7.2 Professional Standards

We discussed the nature of the standards expected of you as a PCSO at some length in Chapter 1 (at 1.5 and 1.7 above) and again in Chapter 2. The reason for raising the subject again at this point is to look at a different aspect. Having joined the police, you have become a public servant. This brings with it obligations to behave in certain ways 'in public office', which we first looked at in our discussion of police ethics (1.5 above). In the next section (7.3) we examine corruption in the police, describing it as 'the dark matter' of the ethical debate. This is not a rehash of the discussion about ethics; it is more about what is expected of you in your role and the activities of the **Professional Standards Department** in your Force if things go wrong.

7.2.1 Codes of conduct remain parochial

There continues to be some ambiguity about the type and nature of the professional standards for PCSOs, a discomfort which we share, because there is such imprecision about the ethical and professional standards for the role. On the one hand, you are expected to be part of the law-enforcement element of policing, but the greatest percentage of your working time will be spent in dealing with non-crime issues. You will be expected to conduct yourself with the highest propriety, fairness, and honesty, giving equal treatment to all, and yet there is no published national standard of professional (PCSO) practice, or code of public service behaviour, to which you are expected to conform and whose provisions you are expected to observe. You are not a police officer and not quite police staff support. There's a sort of 'no man's land' around the role of the PCSO which needs to be occupied or yielded, to prevent the ambiguity from spreading.

7.2.1.1 *There is no specific Charter or ethical standard for PCSOs*

The sworn police have their codes enshrined in **Police Regulations**, which have the force and solemnity of statute. In 2008, the Code of Professional Standards was introduced, which we noted briefly in Chapter 1.5 above. However, there appear to be no national plans currently to extend the ten provisions in the Code of Professional Standards to PCSOs or to the rest of police staff, although this could be done quite easily. This means that there are no published regulations for PCSOs, and yet any local code governing the behaviour of police staff doesn't completely apply to PCSOs either. The Nolan Committee on standards in public life[1] did not concern itself with promulgating a general standard of professionalism which could be applied to the role of PCSO or anyone else in a police staff role.

Now that police staff across England and Wales (and in Scotland and Northern Ireland too) are taking more and more 'front line' roles, where there is daily interaction with the public, the need for a Charter setting out how such staff will conduct themselves becomes ever more pressing. At the time of writing, there is no indication whatever from the NPIA, the Criminal Justice Inspectorate, or ACPO that such a Charter or Code of Conduct for police staff and PCSOs is even at a discussion phase. In March 2007, John Reid, then the Home Secretary, produced a statement of '*Common Values for the Police Service of England and Wales*' as we have noted *passim* throughout this Handbook. None of his comments applies specifically to PCSOs and the statement of Common Values does not constitute a code of ethics for PCSOs or for any other police staff. Indeed, we gather that the police were not consulted upon the *Common Values* document before it was published. It has not been adopted by the police service; the Code of Professional Standards displaces any further need for any Home Secretary to venture into the world of ethics, relishably ironic though that might be, and despite the lack of national guidelines for any in the police service other than warranted officers.

Discussion point

Why do you think that sworn police officers have conduct regulations and the police staff who support them do not?

7.2.1.2 *There is no national public standard of values or conduct for PCSOs or police staff, as there is for police officers*

The question in the discussion point is not quite fair. Police support staff, who include PCSOs, **do** have generic ethical and professional standards, which we have already discussed elsewhere in this Handbook (at 1.5.5.2 above). Support staff in a police force, whether detention officers or Directors of IT, are expected to conform to expectations of integrity, honesty, fairness, equal treatment for all, respect, and so on. That said, there is **no national public standard** to which support staff are expected to sign up, and nothing that equates to the police officers' Code of Professional Standards is available to the PCSO nationally. There is nothing to stop local forces deciding to use the Code as the basis for preferred behaviour by *all* its staff, but the Code may not have the same status in 'civilian' disciplinary matters as it does for police officers.

7.2.2 Professional standards departments

In every police force, there will be a **Professional Standards Department** (PSD) which used to be known as **Complaints and Discipline**. This is a body composed largely of police officers, many of them detectives, who do specific jobs. What are these jobs?

As you might expect, details of the organization of PSDs vary from force to force, but most of them will be constituted like this:

Complaints and discipline	Investigation
Police investigators	Police investigators (occasionally with police staff investigators)
Legal services	
Media advisers	
Administration and finance	Security adviser(s)
Freedom of Information responses, data protection issues, vetting for posts	Specialist surveillance staff
	Specialist technical staff
Force standards, discipline, Police Regulations	Case preparation; liaison with CPS

7.2.2.1 *Investigation of complaints and corruption*

As you can see, there is a dual role for PSDs: one side is to investigate **complaints** against members of the police force, and any serious infractions (breaking the rules) of **discipline**; the other is to **investigate** corruption or criminality among police officers and police staff. The complaints and discipline side can range from the trivial to the major, whilst the investigation side deals only with the major. There is no such thing as trivial corruption, as we shall see in the next section. Whilst we do not suppose for a moment that readers of this Handbook would find themselves under investigation for corruption, you will excuse us for not going into detail. It is hard enough detecting corruption and criminality in the world at large. Doing it within a police force and investigating the actions of officers or police staff who may have detailed knowledge of techniques of surveillance and so on, is very hard indeed. So we will leave the investigation part of Professional Standards to one side (though we shall return to it in brief in 7.3.3.3 below) and look instead at the part of PSD which will concern you.

7.2.2.2 *Responses to you: complaints*

It is inevitable that, in your daily interactions with the public, there will be occasional friction. There may be times when, try as you might, someone cannot accept that s/he has done something wrong and that you are remonstrating, however gently, with him or her about behaviour. Equally, there may be times when you might get your responses spectacularly wrong, by being heavy handed, over-zealous, or too proscriptive of the behaviour of others. Parents will often refuse to accept that their children could possibly have done anything wrong or mischievous. 'Litterers' may not accept that they have dropped packages or food carelessly; they may even deny that the litter is theirs. There is often an aggressive response, as we noted in 5.5 above, from those who have been caught out, whether cycling on a footpath or drinking under age. In addition, people may have exaggeratedly high expectations of what you can do (or what they think you can do), and may feel disappointed and let down when you cannot deliver; stereotypically for example, the unease elderly people feel when they see groups of young people 'hanging about'. You may not want to penalize the young people in the way the elderly might wish; even 'moving on' groups of people who have done nothing wrong may give rise to complaint. Some of this will be down to how well you manage expectations, but you cannot expect to please everyone.

7.2.2.3 *Formal complaints from the public*

This can translate itself into a complaint about your conduct. Such complaints are sometimes justified, especially if you have been unfair, a bit officious about enforcement, or you have not treated people with respect. At other times such complaints will be malicious, because the offender wants to get back at you for catching him or her out. Rarely, the complainant will be a 'serial litigant': the sort who complains about everything and who goes to law or to the discipline process on the slightest pretext. Your legal department will know who such people are and how best to deal with them. **It is the job of the Professional Standards Department to find out if the complaint is justified or not.** If it is justified, the outcome is sometimes financial compensation for the complainant, hence the need for the involvement of finance advisers and staff on the complaints side. If it is not justified, there is no further recourse other than an unblemished record for you and a note in PSD of the outcome. It is most unlikely that you will be able to counter-sue the complainant.

POINTS TO NOTE

There are further outcomes if the complaint against you is justified or upheld. What do you think these outcomes may be?

7.2.2.4 *Outcomes*

The additional outcomes, other than the payment of compensation to the aggrieved party, may range from the relatively minor, such as written 'advice' to you to mend your ways and behave differently in the future, to a major discipline enquiry leading to a hearing of your conduct in front of a chief officer. The worst outcomes of all might be that you are dismissed from the force and face criminal charges.

7.2.2.5 *An example of the disciplinary investigation process*

There is a spectrum of discipline, from treating the experience as a learning point right through to criminal trial, in which the complaint and discipline side of PSD is involved. In the case of police staff, this may involve expert human resources input as well as the investigation of your conduct by police officers. See the example below.

Example: Operation Worst-Case Scenario

You are on patrol in the town centre when you see a group of youngish boys drinking from lager cans in the entrance to the pedestrian mall. On your approach, two or three run away. The remainder, about seven or eight in number, eye your approach and decide to brazen it out. Some of them are evidently intoxicated. Having opened the conversation by telling the group that drinking in this area is not allowed, you are met with abuse. You tell the group that you think they are underage drinkers and that you are going to seize their containers of alcohol. Three or four of the group hand over their cans, more or less sullenly. You pour the contents down the gutter and turn back to the remainder of the group. One boy, bigger than the rest, and much bigger than you, jostles you and elbows you in the face when you try to take his can. You grasp his arm and push back. The boy slips, falls, and bangs his head hard on the edge of a bench. He lies still, eyes closed, bleeding from a scalp wound. The other boys scatter.

You render first aid and summon support, including an ambulance. You ensure that the boy is looked after at the Accident and Emergency Department of the local hospital and identify the boy so that his parents can be informed. He recovers and is not badly hurt. You write up your account in your PNB and talk it through with your supervisor. Apparently, photographs were taken of the incident on a spectator's mobile phone and the police have asked for this as evidence.

The next thing you know, you are suspended from duty and a person from PSD has come to see you to say that the boy and his parents have made complaints about you, alleging excessive force, assault and harassment. An investigation has been ordered and in due course you will be interviewed under caution. You are referred to your local Unison branch office to obtain support and representation.

7.2.2.6 *Burdens of proof in the investigation*

We've called this a 'worst-case scenario' and in many ways it is; but it is actually all too common, and variations on the theme of 'excessive force' will be routinely investigated by PSD, whether into police officers or police staff. The process is different for police officers, who are served with a '*Regulation 9*' notice informing them of the PSD's investigation. This is often accompanied by physical movement from the police station where the officer is based to another place, or by suspension of the officer, pending the investigation.

PCSOs face 'civilian' investigation (not under Police Regulations)

In the case of police staff, the disciplines under Police Regulations do not apply. You are subject to a 'civilian' investigation code (which *may* entail transfer or suspension, depending on what you are alleged to have done). Before you think that the 'civilian investigation' is a better option, be warned. The burdens of proof in the investigation of wrongdoing or indiscipline by police staff are *'on the balance of probabilities'*, not *'beyond reasonable doubt'*, which is the standard of proof at court. This may mean that the complainant will not have to prove the complaint beyond the fact that what is alleged 'probably happened', which is a much lower standard of proof, obviously.

7.2.2.7 *Investigation of alleged misconduct*

The other faintly scary aspect to all this is that you will be investigated, almost certainly, by police officers (rarely by police staff investigators) whom you do not know. The whole process may also take quite a long time: it is not unknown, for example, for an investigation into alleged misconduct to last nine months or a year. The person complained of, in this case you, may be the last to be interviewed. This might mean that you do not work with the community for a long time and will be interviewed only towards the end of that time. It is hard to sustain your morale all the while, especially since you will not necessarily be informed about the progress of the case against you. We hasten to add that this is only in the most extreme of cases, and you will have meetings with advisers in the interim (legal counsel may be provided by Unison in very serious cases). One of the perennial complaints against PSDs is the length of time they take to investigate complaints, but, in their defence, the allegations have to be investigated meticulously and impartially, so that there can be no additional complaint of 'whitewash'. That said, PSDs can be overcautious and sluggish. You will only be suspended from duty if the allegation against you is very serious; otherwise you will be transferred or given a different role. Sometimes, you will be left *in situ*. Whatever the interim measures, the investigation into the complaint against you will be going on quietly in the background.

7.2.2.8 *The IPCC*

Sometimes really serious complaints (such as the lethal discharge of a weapon by a firearms officer, or a death in custody) may result in an investigation by the **Independent Police Complaints**

Commission (IPCC), a statutory body which, as the name suggests, independently investigates allegations of wrongdoing by the police. In our case study, the IPCC is not invoked and the complaint from the parents and boy against you is handled internally. We know of no occasion when the IPCC has investigated a case against PCSOs and consequently we do not know yet whether the IPCC 'writ' extends this far.

> **Discussion point**
> Your turn: what do you think that the outcome of the investigation into your actions will be?

How the case may turn out

It could go either way. The allegation against you is serious: you struck the boy, it is alleged, and occasioned actual bodily harm. The case outcome might depend on the recovery of the photographs or film on the bystander's mobile phone and also upon the testimony of witnesses—including the boys who saw it all happen.

Our model response

Our reading of this investigation (and we don't know what other complaints the PSD turned up about you) would be that you were innocent of assault, and that all you did was resist an attack launched by the drunken complainant. However, we would advise you that you blundered into the situation rather, and it might have been better in retrospect if you had called for back-up once it was evident that some of the drinkers were aggressively intoxicated. Remember the **Rules of Engagement** (see 2.2.5.2 above)? It's a fine judgement though, and you could well come out of the investigation without a single blemish.

7.2.3 Complaints are part of the territory

Experienced police officers will tell you that you are most unlikely to go through your police career without a complaint against you. Indeed, you would be unlikely to go for a year without complaint from someone that you were oppressive, heavy-handed, interfering, or incompetent, or that you exceeded your authority. Whenever you have some sort of confrontation with a member of the public, remember to note it in your PNB. If the Professional Standards Department (PSD) is called in to investigate a complaint against you, your meticulous PNB entries and records of what happened could make the difference between a '*balance of probability*' guilty charge and your exoneration from blame. As we will note to you in the section below about going to court, the role of the questioner is professional, not personal. In PSDs, the same is true: this is business, it is not personal. Whilst most of the Force may regard the PSD with some reserve, the officers in the department have a job to do. They are posted in and out as they are in any other part of the Force and they bring to the role the same professionalism, detachment, and 'imperturbable courtesy' which we hope you bring to yours.

Task
Get to know your Force PSD.

Some PSDs undertake close contacts with the rest of their Forces through open sessions, publicity about Force standards, and training inputs. Others remain professionally aloof, but that doesn't mean that staff in PSDs won't talk to you about what they do. Just don't expect detail about cases.

Above all, expect that, however ethically, straightforwardly, and honestly you behave in the course of your career as a PCSO, there will be complaints about you at some time. It comes with the territory.

7.3 'Dark Matter'—Police Corruption

This is not an extended essay on the nature of police corruption; there are other sources which you can consult for that.[2] Rather, this section looks briefly at the incidence of corruption and discusses what it is that makes people act corruptly. We conclude with advice about what you should do if you encounter corruption.

7.3.1 Defining our terms

At its simplest, **corruption in the police is about taking illegal advantage of your public office to your advantage or to someone else's advantage**. You are not supposed to do it; you know that you are not and yet you go ahead and do it, probably believing that you will not be caught. Technically, there are three specific offences (in ascending order of seriousness):

> **Corruption—offences**
> **Non-feasance**: not doing what you should
> **Misfeasance**: doing what you should not
> **Malfeasance**: the commission of indictable crimes

7.3.1.1 *Non-feasance*

Non-feasance can be understood as 'turning a blind eye' to something going on which you ought to intervene to stop, but you do not. Unless you are actually observed not to have properly performed your duty, you could get away with this once or twice (after all, the guilty party or perpetrator whom you're letting go is not going to complain). The defence is often that '*I was exercising my discretion*', which will only go so far. Conniving at wrongdoing is not the role of a PCSO. The decision whether or not to intervene with some high-spirited revellers is part of the PCSO's legitimate exercise of judgement. You need to know the difference between the two.

7.3.1.2 *Misfeasance*

Misfeasance is both less excusable and more obvious. Suppose you stop someone cycling on a footpath and, while chatting to the cyclist, you ask for her identity. She passes you some identification tucked in which is a £20 note. There is apparently an inducement to let her go, unpunished. This is bribery. If you pocket the £20 without further comment and walk away, you have committed **misfeasance in a public office** (the technical charge you will face), though increasingly 'misconduct in a public office' is being used as a 'catch-all' offence.[3] You run a huge risk in doing so. First of all, the would-be corrupter can identify you from your Force number or name badge, and this could render you liable to blackmail at a later date. Or you could have misinterpreted the woman's action, whereupon she could promptly accuse you of theft. Finally, and worst of all, this could have been an **integrity test**, where you were deliberately subject to temptation to see what you would do. If the cyclist then reveals herself as a police officer and arrests you, you have only yourself to blame.

7.3.1.3 *Malfeasance*

Malfeasance is worst of all three offences because it involves the actual committing of crimes. You are in a position of trust, in a public office, and to commit a crime is to betray everything that you stand for in that office. Sadly, this doesn't stop some police officers or police staff from being tempted to try. A standard example would be to do someone a favour, such as looking up details of someone else on the Police National Computer (PNC) or accessing your Force criminal intelligence database on someone else's behalf. It could begin innocently. There was a recent case in which a woman PCSO looked up her daughter's new partner to see if he had a record of violence. Eventually she went on to check on the progress of a criminal investigation into a friend of hers, to whom she passed the information. (She was dismissed from her Force and found guilty at court of a criminal offence.) For more detail, see Nicholls *et al*, *Corruption and Misuse of Public Office* (OUP, 2006).

The range of crimes and misdemeanours

What sorts of crimes and misdemeanours do PCSOs, police staff, and police officers get themselves involved in? Here is a sample:

- Falsifying evidence
- Illegal access to databases
- 'Framing' someone for a crime s/he did not commit
- Passing information to criminals (perverting the course of justice)
- Seizing loose cash in a house search
- Reselling seized drugs
- Having a relationship with a known criminal
- 'Pimping' for prostitutes.

Not all corrupt officers and staff will commit all or any of these, but research into the incidence of corruption among police officers and police staff suggests that these are the likeliest routes.[4]

7.3.2 How prevalent is corruption?

The best estimate of bodies such as the ACPO Counter-Corruption Advisory Group and Sir Paul (now Lord) Condon, when Commissioner of the Metropolitan Police, was that **considerably less than 1% of all staff are corrupt**.[5] This may seem very few, given the temptations and opportunities inherent in the police function, but even this suggests that throughout England and Wales there may be several hundred corrupt or potentially corrupt police officers, PCSOs, and police staff. If true, that is still a lot of corruption, especially since perpetrators have an effect out of all proportion to their number.

A model response

There is no right or wrong answer to the discussion as far as the future is concerned, but it is certain that, in the past, corrupt officers and staff have:

- Protected other corrupt officers and staff
- Impeded investigations
- Taken money from criminals
- Perverted the course of justice
- Passed valuable intelligence on policing operations to criminals (often to the targets of the policing operations)
- Allowed criminals to escape justice
- Abused the trust of their office
- Brought the police into disrepute.

Additionally, but less tangibly, a corruption culture may encourage others to become corrupt who might otherwise not take the risk. **The effect of corruption is corrosive and disproportionate**; all those involved in investigating corruption note that some of the grubbiness rubs off on them; the reputation of the police force is damaged and the trust of your community may be forfeited. Even when cases come to trial, the reluctance of juries to believe that law officers could be corrupt is endearing but frustrating to those who have tried to bring offenders to justice.

7.3.2.1 *Why?*

The biggest question of all is what makes a police officer, a PCSO, or another member of police staff corrupt? What thoughts and feelings must someone have to turn his or her back on all that s/he had previously upheld, and risk it all for what may be a minor gain? One example we came across involved a senior police officer who had been made President of his Force Social and Sports Club. He stole £2,000 from the Club's funds, was found out, confessed, was prosecuted, found guilty, and received a two-year prison sentence. While he served his time in jail, his wife divorced him, taking the house as settlement, and his police pension was reduced. He lost his job, much of his funding for retirement, his home, and his family, and all for £2,000 which he didn't have long enough to spend anyway. In the cold light of day, you feel, he would never have been tempted. Why did he do it then? What happened to distort his judgement?

Task

Think about this problem yourself and try to work out why people, particularly those in the police service, should become corrupt. Make a list of possible motivations and then compare them with ours.

7.3.2.2 *Some possible answers to the question 'why?'*

Our list below is not exhaustive, but it is the product of considerable experience in this field and our wide survey of corruption cases:

What makes someone corrupt?

Temptation + opportunity in nine out of ten cases, because the opportunity to commit an illegal act is combined with the attractiveness of the act itself, such as peeling some £50 notes from a roll used to pay off a drugs shipment. The guilty are not likely to complain, and who was to know how much was there in the first place? The dealers go to prison, and you have some cash in your back pocket: a win–win for the police and for you (provided the CCTV didn't capture your action).

There are other motivations, born of strong human emotions which can link with **temptation** and **opportunity** to create a heady cocktail in which common sense is suppressed and the risk of getting caught is ignored:

- Resentment at being passed over for promotion and envy of those younger in service than you, passing you by
- Sense of self-worth which is not matched by the Force's view of you
- Belief that you have not been adequately rewarded
- Dislike of the criticism in your appraisal, and a feeling that people are out to get you, and so they put you down, bending the truth about you
- Belief that you are facing dangers and pressures which your superiors could not handle.
- Belief that you know better than those who give you orders

- Thinking that crime actually pays quite handsomely, and frustration that criminals thrive and prosper
- Conviction that the criminal justice system is corrupt, so no reason for you to miss out
- Other people do it and get away with it
- Need to fund an extravagant lifestyle
- Intense desire to prove your cleverness when others don't think of you as clever.

There are many more such bundles of motivations, almost all of which have to do with inferiority and resentment. We are not psychologists and do not pretend to have a definitive answer to human motivations of greed and envy, but the recurrent features of corruption in a public office (and this includes other parts of the public service, such as local government, teaching, the law, the judiciary, and Parliament itself, as the various revelations about MPs' expenses made clear in 2009) clearly embrace these perceptions of inadequacy. See Ivkovic (2005) or MacLagen (2003) for further analyses.

7.3.3 Corruption is not easy to counter

Knowing, or thinking you know, what contributes to making people corrupt is one thing. Stopping it happening, or detecting when it has happened, are different things entirely.

> **Task**
> What difficulties would characterize an investigation into a corrupt police officer or PCSO?

7.3.3.1 *Dealing with insiders*

The problem is that such people are on the **'inside'**. They are likely to be experienced and long-serving and they will know how to look for surveillance, or to detect attempts to intercept communications. They may have friends who are involved in or on the margins of the investigation itself, the surveillance, or the interception operation, or they may learn what is happening through gossip or unguarded talk in the police station. The police generally trust each other and have no inhibitions generally in sharing information about operations, targets, and investigations. A corrupt officer's apparently innocent interest in the latest operations and orders might mask an attempt to access information to see if he or she, or criminal friends, have been targeted. When the Metropolitan Police mounted a prolonged investigation into corruption in the London force during 1998–2001, the entire operation had to be conducted by the 'Ghost Squad' in the strictest secrecy. The situation for PCSOs is no different because they are as likely as police officers to want to know what is happening and will want to be told what is planned. The same frankness and trust among colleagues could be as easily abused in the PCSO as it has been among police officers and other police staff.

7.3.3.2 *What counter actions are proven to reduce the opportunity for corruption?*

We cannot hope to eliminate greed, envy, or malice from the individual officer, but we can make it much harder for corruption to flourish, reducing opportunity whenever possible. Here are some tried and tested measures to counter corruption:

- Close-up and personal **supervision** prevents the 'maverick' approach to policing and makes it more difficult for corrupt officers to meet criminals alone (see 7.7 below)
- Scrutiny of **patterns of contact** between known criminals and members of the police force
- Using the **need to know** principle more effectively: if you are not directly involved in the police operation or investigation, you don't need to know the details and people should not tell you them
- Monitoring **tenure**, which is the length of time you serve in one place or in one role, and ensuring that this is not excessive, because it may lead to undue familiarity with resident criminals
- **Intelligence** on the corrupt activity (often from criminals themselves)
- **Vetting** people for posts and renewing checks regularly
- Having **audit trails** within information systems and criminal databases to see who is accessing what, when, and why
- Using **integrity testing** without notice
- Using the 'onion skin' principle to **protect information**, by setting many barriers, each light and flexible in itself, between the information and the merely curious
- Alerting or '**sensitizing**' people to the dangers of corruption (without exaggerating the problem) and ensuring that they know what to do if they come across suspicious activity.

7.3.3.3 *What you should do if you suspect corruption*

Let's expand that last bullet point a little more, because it will serve as guidance to you to know what to do if you come across activity or incidents which seem to you to have a whiff of corruption about them. The responsibility for the investigation of corrupt officers in most forces rests with the Professional Standards Department, whom we have just met in 7.2 above. Arrangements in some of the Metropolitan Forces are different, but they are well publicized and your supervisor should be able to advise you directly. Whom do you trust? Well, 99% of your colleagues, for a start, though you may feel that corruption isn't something you want to talk openly about and you may worry that you might choose the wrong person to confide in. You may feel that you want professional advice from the outset (see below).

7.3.3.4 *To whom do you talk about your concerns?*

You may feel that the activity you have witnessed and become concerned about (such as unexplained payments, the mysterious receipt of sealed packages, the disappearance of cash, suddenly and suspiciously well-off colleagues, unwarranted numbers of mobile phones, unexplained disappearances during patrol, a refusal to engage in small talk, over-keen interest in impending operations, and so on) is something you want advice on privately. If you cannot approach your supervisor (either because s/he is too close to the problem, or s/he is part of the problem), then our advice to you is to **trust your PSD** and go to someone there and talk over your concerns. Your Force may even have arrangements to do this anonymously by telephoning a particular number. Don't feel inhibited about taking this route and above all *don't feel guilty.* You might be nipping corruption in the bud; you might be exposing deep and covert dishonesty; you might be saving the Force's good name (which is of direct importance to the way you do your job); you might be helping to uncover a crime. Aren't these among the reasons why you joined? **You have no obligation whatever to protect a corrupt or venal colleague.**

7.3.3.5 *Don't hold back: tell someone*

If however, you feel that, after consideration, you can't talk to your supervisor, or to Professional Standards, seek a confidential meeting with a Chief Officer and explain your concerns. **Don't sit on the information.** Don't keep it to yourself. You may be assured that matters will not rest once you have brought it to attention.

7.3.3.6 *Keep it in context*

A final thought: corruption is not widespread and you still belong to an ethical organization with high principles. The huge, the utterly overwhelming, majority of your colleagues are honest and decent: that's something to be proud of.

7.4 **Being a Professional**

The nature of being a professional in the police family is a central theme in this Handbook. Earlier we discussed the meaning of a 'profession'. At this stage we examine what being a professional means in your everyday duties.

7.4.1 The meanings of 'professional'

You will often hear the word professional used in a wide variety of situations and contexts encountered by the PCSO. Examples include the need to maintain 'professional standards', to adopt a 'professional attitude' to your work, and so on. But what does being professional actually mean in these contexts?

We offer below a table of possible professional qualities together with a brief explanation and an example from the day-to-day work of the PCSO. The table is not meant to be exhaustive; no doubt you could add further qualities.

Professional quality	Explanation	Examples
Impartiality	Dealing with those around you fairly and without favour and based upon objective criteria	In a complaint about anti-social behaviour, examining all sides of the argument; meeting the requirements of the PCSO Core Behaviour Area *Respect and Diversity*
Integrity	Honesty, trustworthiness, respect for confidentiality	Not sharing confidential, sensitive, or personal information gained whilst undertaking your job with your family or friends

Professional quality	Explanation	Examples
Autonomy	Appropriate exercise of decision making, discretion	Able to provide a rationale for the non-issuing of an FPN
Self-development	Maintaining skills and knowledge	Keeping up-to-date on local Force policies
Responsibility	The duties on you; the expectations of others	'Whistle-blowing' to a supervisor on inappropriate behaviour of colleagues
Authority	The personal and legal 'right' that you have to control others	Your demeanour and body language; your understanding of the powers designated to you
Diligence	Conscientious and persevering; paying attention	Proper and timely completion of documentation
Capability	Ability to perform the tasks and responsibilities expected of you	Not drinking alcohol excessively the evening before a duty shift; not over-stretching yourself to the point of illness
Leadership	Setting an example, exercising influence over others	Attending a community meeting 'out of hours'

7.5 **Going to Court**

This is the end result of police work: the bringing of offenders to justice. It may not always be *your* end result, since your work is as much about prevention and negotiation as it is about enforcement. Yet there will be times when you have to go to court. Look back at our discussion in 2.9 above, when we described the courts structure in England and Wales and the processes involved in considering criminal cases. You ought to have visited *at least* one court (**youth court**, **magistrates' court**, **coroner's court**, or **Crown Court**) during your initial training. We hope that you have been back since those initial visits, so that you have a sense of how courts conduct their business and what goes on. You should note that Police **NOS 2J2**, *Present evidence in court and at other hearings*, has a direct relevance to your competence here.

Discussion points

What does go on?

Who does what?

What is likely to result in your going to court?

What will you do when you get there?

7.5.1 **What courts do**

The courts convene to '**hear**' (*try*) criminal cases or to impose fines for anti-social behaviour. The **magistrates' court** hears the lower charges and imposes fines, remand, or prison, according to the seriousness of the case. You will remember that magistrates' courts also decide if there is enough evidence in a serious 'charge' to warrant referral to the **Crown Court**. The circumstances surrounding the death of a person from other than natural causes will be heard in a **coroner's court**, while some youth offenders may be put on trial at a **youth court**. Crown Courts hear serious charges such as murder, rape, and assault.

7.5.1.1 *When you go to court*

You are likely to have to go to court to give evidence if, for example, you are asked to testify against a persistent offender, whom you know from your daily work in the community. Equally, you may be called to either a magistrates' court or a Crown Court if you are '**first officer attending**' (FOA) the scene of a crime. It is increasingly likely, for example, that as a result of your routine foot patrol you may happen upon a crime scene such as a burglary, an assault, or murder, or crime scenes involving domestic violence. If that happens, your evidence may well be called. The remainder of this section deals with what you have to do when you get to court.

7.5.1.2 *Likelihood of your going to court*

Your first professional court attendance will probably be at a magistrates' court, even if the offence is serious, because, as we noted above, referral to the Crown Court is made from the magistrates' court. It is possible that if you happen upon a suspicious death (someone comes up to you and tells you that no one has seen Harry McGee for four days and his curtains are still closed, and milk is piling up on his doorstep ...), you may have to give at least preliminary evidence at a coroner's court. The procedure for all courts is more or less the same as far as your part in it is concerned. We'll use, for convenience, your attendance at a magistrates' court. Remember that the court can consist of a 'bench' of three lay magistrates or one **stipendiary** (*paid*) magistrate.

7.5.1.3 *Giving evidence*

Your role in court is to '**give evidence**'. What does this mean? There are four kinds of evidence:

Four Kinds of Evidence

(1) **Spoken** or verbal (often called' oral' evidence)
(2) **Real** (a thing which exists)
(3) **Documentary** (a paper or disc or electronic record)
(4) '**Hearsay**'.

7.5.1.4 *Spoken (sometimes called oral) evidence*

This is the most common form of evidence. A witness will say that 'I **saw** the knife glint as he pulled it out from his sleeve', or 'We could **smell** the alcohol on her breath', or 'I could **feel** the blood trickling down the side of my head after one of them hit me with the bottle'. Although the type of evidence suggests that it is only what you hear, in fact *anything you directly perceive through your senses (see, hear, touch (feel), taste, or smell), is evidence.* You cannot do this on someone's behalf: the evidence must have been something experienced by you.

7.5.1.5 *Real evidence*

This is evidence which exists independently and which can be produced in court. (Though, obviously, if it is a large thing like an articulated lorry or an aircraft, it cannot be produced in court. In such cases, it is usual for the court to visit the thing.) The evidence can be microscopic, such as a single hair or fibre, or it can be bigger, such as an overcoat or sword. It must be solidly existing and self-defining.

'Continuity of evidence', again

One of the difficulties associated in English and Welsh law with 'real evidence' is the audit trail, or 'continuity of evidence' (which we looked at in Chapters 3 and 5) that police forces must observe, from the moment of recovery of the evidence until its production in court. The process of accounting for the evidence in its intact and unmodified form throughout the time from recovery at the crime scene to production in court is to ensure that no malpractice, contamination (deliberate or accidental), or tampering has taken place. Defence lawyers, as we have noted in 2.10.2.1 above, are increasingly driven by irrefutable evidence (such as DNA) into questioning the process of obtaining, securing, and safe-keeping of that evidence. This is why police forces place so much emphasis on the evidence trail. Bitter experience has taught them that a flaw in the process will be exploited and the case could fail. Despite this, every year some trials still founder on poor evidence trails.

7.5.1.6 *Documentary evidence*

This is something written which can be produced in court; ranging from your Pocket Note Book (**PNB**), to a suicide note, to a literary volume (such as in the criminal prosecution for obscenity of Penguin Books in 1960 for the publication of D H Lawrence's *Lady Chatterley's Lover*). For hundreds of years, courts considered written documentation as evidence without general ambiguity (a thing was physically written or it was not). However, with the arrival of the electronic media such as computers and mobile phones, the courts have had to consider digitized forms of documentation and, in some spectacular recent criminal trials, the sending and receiving of text messages on mobile phones. It used to be the case that a document could be authenticated by the characteristics of the handwriting (manuscript), or in a typewritten or printed document by a signature (such as on a cheque or will). In the 'virtual' world of electronic communications, signatures do not exist and occasionally there is no foolproof way absolutely to assign ownership of something which has never been written down externally.

New kinds of 'document'

There are new forms of documentation to accept as well, such as the use of credit or debit cards for online transactions. This is important in fraud cases and in cases of 'identity theft'. Courts live in the real world, despite their occasional appearances of being like *Alice in Wonderland*, and the possession of a computer with images of child pornography will normally be taken to be the responsibility of the user of that computer. The use of a credit card implies a legal transaction with the supplier of goods, and so on. The difficulties which may be encountered are perhaps more at the case-preparation end of court proceedings, where the police and CPS need to establish the facts of ownership of documents, whether physical or electronic.

7.5.1.7 'Hearsay'

'Hearsay' evidence is complex. You will need to study 'hearsay' carefully in addition to what we cover here, because sometimes 'hearsay' evidence *will* be admitted in court (such as a death-bed statement or confession) and sometimes *it will not* (such as the statement by one remand prisoner of what he overheard the accused say to someone else). Essentially, **'hearsay' is what one person says that another person said**, though occasionally it might refer to the existence of something else, such as a piece of writing which has vanished, or a piece of music which was never transcribed. 'Hearsay' is usually inadmissible because it could have been made up: '*he told me that she did it*' is not evidence (though it might be intelligence).

7.5.2 **How to give evidence**

There may be minor variations in your locality from what we are about to describe, but in essence, the giving of evidence is a standard process.

You wait to be called into the court, take the oath or affirmation, and, in a magistrates' court, give a statement of your evidence without prompting. In a Crown Court, your evidence will usually be given through questions from the prosecuting counsel. Put thus baldly and matter-of-factly, it all seems plain sailing, doesn't it? It's actually a bit more complex than that, particularly in terms of your cross-examination and in establishing the sort of impression you want to make. If you look at the second part of the NOS 2J2 (*Present evidence*), you can see the level to which police officers are expected to perform in court. The need for you to be competent here was perhaps not fully envisaged at the first formulation of the PCSO concept. **It is now.** We shall try to make the process of giving evidence clearer by breaking down the process into steps.

7.5.2.1 *The courtroom*

The courtroom, whether a magistrates' court, a Crown Court, or a coroner's court, is a solemn place which exists for a solemn purpose. Indeed, at Crown Court, the surroundings are deliberately ceremonial. There are architectural features with which you should become familiar. The 'bench' upon which the magistrates or the judges sit is elevated above the 'well' of the court. Below the bench sit the Clerks, recorders, and administrators, and facing them are the tiered sitting areas to the right for the prosecution and to the left for the defence. At Crown Court there will be a box of two rows of seats for the jury. In all the courts, there will be a special place where you give evidence, the witness box. It is quite small and not usually elevated beyond a step or two. A magistrates' courtroom is often small and almost intimate, aside from the business transacted there. Sometimes there will be no defence lawyer. Occasionally, business is briskly taken forward with summary judgements and a rapid turnover of cases—many pended (postponed) as well as many dealt with and discharged. A Crown Courtroom is on a grander scale, and may seem dauntingly large. The tendency to use lots of dark wood panelling is now a thing of the past, and whilst it survives in some traditional courts, most are now quite light and airy places.

7.5.2.2 *Who is where?*

Many variations exist in courtrooms but the basic layout, viewed from above, is as shown in Figure 21 below.

This is a schematic or general picture

Don't be misled by our schematic into supposing that all courtrooms will look like this. Some will not conform to this layout at all, some will have variations in where sites are located (some Crown Courts, for example, have elevated galleries where the dock is located, the dock having a separate entrance from the cells). Magistrates' courts will not have provision for juries, and in some courts, space may mean that all participants are jostled up together. (This can be upsetting for witnesses and victims if they come into close proximity with the accused.)

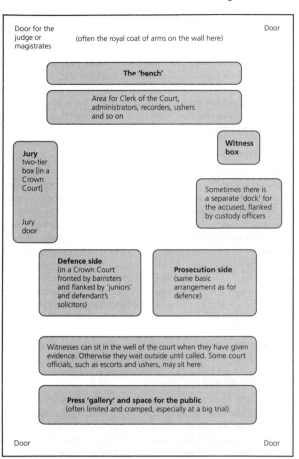

Figure 21: Schematic for general layout of a Crown Courtroom

POINTS TO NOTE

There is no substitute for your going in person to the court and looking at its layout carefully, familiarizing yourself with what is where and who sits where.

Look at the courtroom beforehand

The Clerk of the Court might give you a description of what goes on, as may a friendly usher, but you really should apply to attend in the course of a trial or sitting so that you can see what the court looks like in full flow. What looks like a large echoing space when empty, can suddenly seem really crowded when court is in session. Get along there and see. **Don't leave it until the day you turn up to give evidence.** Note especially where the witness box is and where the doors are that lead in and out.

7.5.2.3 *Who does what?*

When you are called (the technical description is 'summoned to give evidence'), you will wait outside the courtroom until an usher calls your name. During that waiting time (which can be considerable), you are not allowed to speak to another witness or to the defence. Then you enter the courtroom and proceed to the witness box. The magistrates, in ordinary clothes, sit on the bench in a row of three. Sometimes it will be a stipendiary magistrate sitting alone, in which case he or she may be in black robes. The Clerk of the Court sits below the bench and it is he or she who will speak first, asking you whether you want to take the oath or the affirmation (see below). The Clerk may then ask you to confirm your name and role. Occasionally the magistrates may do this, or you may identify yourself when you begin your evidence by saying '*I am Police Community Support Officer [Your Name], Force number 123456*'. Speak in a firm voice, but do not shout.

7.5.2.4 *The players*

To the side is the Crown Prosecution Service (CPS) lawyer who is presenting the case for the prosecution against the accused. He or she will open the questioning (unless you have been invited in a magistrates' court to make a statement). Across from the CPS will be the defence. In a magistrates' court, there may not be a defence lawyer, or there may be a solicitor, depending on the nature of the case. In a Crown Court, each side may have a number of attendees, from junior counsel to solicitors acting for the accused. Behind these two blocks of people will be those witnesses who have already given evidence and possibly members of the Press and media (though in Crown Courts they sometimes have separate seating). Behind them again is the public gallery, though in a Crown Court the public gallery may be in an elevated part of the court reached by a separate staircase and door. Hence the need to go and see for yourself.

7.5.2.5 *The accused*

The other thing for you to note is the presence of the accused, who may sit in the well of the court (below the bench) alongside the defence team, as is increasingly common in magistrates' courts, or in a separate 'dock' in a Crown Court, possibly elevated up some steps, from the cells below. The accused (sometimes more than one person tried at the same time) may be flanked by escort officers of the court, or private security guards, or in the case of some terrorism trials, by armed police officers. Only in the latter case, or when the defendant is known to be violent, will the accused be handcuffed to the escort. You may, if you wish, meet the accused's eyes, but you don't have to look at him or her if you don't want to.

7.5.3 **Taking the oath**

Evidence in any constituted criminal court must be given on oath. **This means that you promise to tell the truth.** If you have no religious faith, you may make an affirmation. There are, as you would expect, variations in the observance of an oath, depending on the witness' faith or non-faith. The important thing is that you **will tell the truth, the whole truth and nothing but the truth**, in the light of your faith or your reason. Christians will swear on the Holy Bible, or occasionally on the New Testament; Hindus will swear by the Holy Gita, Sikhs by Guru Nanak and Muslims by Allah and the Holy Koran; Jews will swear on the sacred Torah (or Scroll) or on the Bible (Old Testament). Some will engage in ritual purification beforehand, or may require an image or picture to be present at the time of taking the oath. All non-believers, some Quakers, Jehovah's Witnesses, and most Buddhists will 'solemnly, sincerely and truly declare and affirm ... '. Some New Age adherents have tried to incorporate pagan rituals into the taking of an oath, but such rituals have been refused to date. The point is that you, the witness, declare publicly and before what you believe and hold most important, that you will tell the truth. It is a properly solemn moment in a solemn undertaking. Be under no illusion, the law takes itself very seriously indeed: **perjury** (*lying on oath*) is a criminal offence with severe penalties.

7.5.3.1 *Giving evidence*

You should have prepared yourself in advance for this moment. You are required to give your account of what you witnessed and to describe what you did. This may be in the form of a simple statement like this (using our fictional town of Tonchester, see map at Figure 23, Chapter 8.2):

Example of a statement

I was on patrol in The Twitten, adjacent to Ogg's College at 1945 on Friday, 8th March. A man came up to me and identified himself to me as Andrew Marvel Phillips, a retired paramedic officer with Tonford Ambulance Trust. He told me that he lives at 19 The Twitten and was concerned because his neighbours, Mr and Mrs Joyce at No 17, appeared to have been having an argument. There had just been a sharp scream and then silence. I accompanied Mr Phillips to the front gate of 17, The Twitten, when the door opened and a male who identified himself as Charles Edward Joyce, came up to me holding a knife by the blade. He said to me 'I have killed my wife. Please help me, I have killed my wife.' He then began to cry and slumped to the ground.

Keep it clear and simple

There are a couple of things worth noting about this evidence: it is clear, logical, and in time (chronological) order. It makes no judgements and offers no interpretations. It simply recounts the facts of what happened. You are not qualified to give **opinion** (expert witnesses, such as doctors and psychiatrists, can offer opinions, such as time of death, cause of death, mental state of the accused, and so on, but you cannot). Confine yourself to spoken testimony, involving what you heard, felt, tasted, smelled, or saw.

7.5.3.2 *Referring to your PNB*

Experienced police officers will sometimes tell you to learn your evidence by heart. **Don't.** It will make you over-rehearsed, too dependent on your memory, and easily jogged off course by questions you did not expect. That said, you are not expected to remember everything and you can consult your PNB to refresh your memory or to quote exactly (refresh your memory now by looking at 5.2 above, on evidence and the PNB). Don't be inhibited about this: the magistrates, judges, prosecution, and defence all rely on written notes. Because you are in a court of law, it is courteous to ask permission of the magistrates or judge to consult your PNB. If your appearance is in a Crown Court, the likelihood is that the prosecuting lawyer will take you through events by asking you questions, like this:

> **Saleh Salim** (CPS): *Now, Officer, what did the accused say to you when you entered the house, having taken away the knife from him?*
>
> **PCSO You**: *My Lord, may I consult my Note Book?*
>
> **Mr Justice Shelby-Dunne**: *Of course you may.*
>
> **You** (consulting PNB): *The accused, Charles Edward Joyce, said, 'I just tried to push her away. I didn't know that I had the knife in my hand. It was just a push and then she was lying on the floor, covered in blood.'*
>
> **SS:** *Thank you. That is in Bundle 3, folio 5, my Lord. We shall go on to show that the victim actually had 27 stab wounds, ladies and gentlemen of the jury, which casts doubt upon Joyce's verbatim 'just a push'. Officer, where was the victim when you entered the kitchen?*

Evidently Mr Joyce has decided to change his story and plead not guilty to murder. The chances are that in a real case of this kind, your PNB entries would actually be disclosed in evidence. Note that the prosecuting counsel refers the judge in the case to your written deposition or statement which will include the PNB entry. In a magistrates' court, the same courtesies apply; you must ask before you refer to your PNB.

7.5.3.3 *Cross-examination*

When the prosecution has finished questioning you, it is the turn of the defence (in a magistrates' court, any defence lawyer present for the accused might challenge your statement). In our 'adversarial system' (see 2.10.2.1), the defence can '**cross- examine**' you about your evidence. Remember the following:

- The defence wants to cast doubt on your evidence
- If the evidence cannot be faulted, the defence wants to cast doubt on your credibility as a witness
- If your credibility as a witness cannot be faulted, the defence wants to undermine your professional standing, perhaps by suggesting that you are incompetent, or corrupt, or prejudiced against the accused
- If that doesn't work, the defence wants to get you angry, confused, demoralized, or bewildered
- If none of this works, the defence wants a delay.

These are tactics, ploys, or tricks of the trade which lawyers use (and have used for many years) in order to get the charges dropped against the accused, or to show that the process was faulty, or to create enough doubt or uncertainty as not to have to answer a case 'beyond reasonable doubt'. Judges are wise to the more blatant stratagems used by the defence, and will intervene if the defence is simply being gratuitously unpleasant to you.

7.5.3.4 *It can be tough in the box*

That said, the court is no place for the faint-hearted: it is a robust place where you will be expected to stand your ground and refuse to be browbeaten; you will be always polite, always calm, always accurate. **It is not easy, and don't let anyone tell you otherwise.** You need a special kind of calm, and you must refuse to rise to any bait dangled in front of you by the defence. Some officers mentally count to three before replying to rude or provocative questions; others concentrate on stone-walling or replying in a deadpan way (sometimes called the '*dead bat*' technique). Be careful though, the judge won't protect you if s/he thinks you are contemptuous of proceedings in the court, and that includes acting as though the defence counsel has a body odour problem. *At all times be calm, glacially in control, and polite.* Here's a sample of what you might encounter:

Example: Dialogue in the Box

Chee Long Sam (defence): *Officer, you allege that the accused was actually holding the knife when you first saw him, isn't that the case?*

You: *He was holding the knife by the blade. I did not consider my safety to be at risk, so I approached and disarmed him.*

CLS: *How good is your eyesight?*

Y: *Adequate to see what I have described, Ma'am.*

CLS: *How long have you been doing this job as a PCSO?*

Y: *Just over two years.*

CLS: *Not much good at it are you?*

Y: *My appraisals say otherwise.*

CLS: *But that's just the police protecting the police. Be honest for a change, Officer. You're prejudiced against my client because he is black, aren't you?*

Y: *No, I am not.*

CLS: *You made up this whole tissue of lies to get at him because of his colour, didn't you?*

Y: *No, Madam, I did not.*

> **CLS**: *And a PCSO is a pretend police officer, isn't it?*
>
> **Y**: *I do not understand what you mean by 'pretend'.*
>
> **Mrs Justice Hertzog**: *This has gone far enough Miss Sam. You are simply insulting the witness. Confine yourself to questions of fact.*
>
> **CLS**: *As your Ladyship pleases.*
>
> **JH:** *Indeed I do. We all know what you are trying to do, but it won't wash. Do you have any real questions for this officer?*

Don't let yourself be provoked

This example of questioning is artificial, a bit desperate, and somewhat theatrical, but it's surprising how many witnesses will get riled up and lose their tempers when prodded in this fashion. It may never happen to you, but if your professional and personal credentials are attacked or undermined in court, remember that it is business, it isn't personal. It is also the case that the prosecution would object to a sustained personal onslaught like this before very long. Most of the time, such an attack merely underlines what a weak case the defence have, if the leading counsel has to resort to such techniques. That fact will not be lost either on the judge or on the jury. In normal circumstances, the defence counsel will take you calmly through your evidence in a logical way, probing for weaknesses and for facts which will be of benefit to his or her client.

7.5.3.5 *Handling questions*

One point we have not yet made is how you answer the questions put to you in court. The convention is that you 'collect' the question from whoever asks it (prosecutor or defence counsel), but you 'deliver' your reply to the judge or the magistrate. This is because you respond to the court, not to the individual. The judge or magistrate may ask you a question directly. If that happens, you simply reply directly. You call a magistrate 'your Honour', 'Sir' or 'Ma'am'; you call a Crown Court judge 'my Lord' (*not* 'M'lud') or 'my Lady'. At the end of giving your evidence, you wait to be told to stand down by the magistrate or judge. You then remain in court until you are discharged, or given direct permission to leave. This is normal practice and is used in case you have to be recalled to clarify a fact or event. You still should not speak to any witness who has not yet given evidence.

7.5.3.6 *Creating an impression*

Judges and juries, together with lawyers for the prosecution or the defence, are only human. Whilst most will be swayed by the logic of your evidence, there is a part of them which may also be influenced by the impression you make on them. This is based partly on your body language (non-verbal communication) and partly on the manner or demeanour in which you give your evidence and respond to questions. If you are easily flustered, lose your thread, use long words when you are a bit shaky about their meanings, lose your temper, snap back at the questioner, or show that you are not taking proceedings seriously, then the impression you create in the minds of all will be negative. However scrupulous the judges, magistrates, and juries may be about the dispassionate facts of the case, if you look, sound and act as though you are shifty and not to be trusted, your evidence may be put aside. It may not be convincing. Your word, however truthful, may carry no weight. If that happens, it could undermine the prosecution case, so that your diffidence, or excitability, or semi-detached attitude, could mean that a guilty person walks free.

The right impression is of professional alertness and calm

Giving evidence is a solemn enough business on its own, but creating the right impression is as important. You want to leave all the court members with an impression of a professional, accurate, and steady person, who presents facts objectively and who was thorough in giving all evidence. In creating such an impression, you do greater good for the image of PCSOs in general and of your Force in particular.

7.5.3.7 *Looking the part*

It follows that in your presentation of yourself at court, you are smartly dressed, properly attired; you have neat hair and polished shoes. The more casual among you may be raising eyebrows at this point. It is a fact, however, that you are expected to be at your smartest when you attend court. Not only is that a compliment to the importance of criminal justice, it is also an external register of the mental and professional smartness which you will show when giving evidence. We do not say that cases will be lost because your shoes are dull and scuffed; what we say is that you are not helping the image of the Force by appearing in that way. On the basis that you probably would not wear a tracksuit to a friend's formal wedding (because you want to pay him or her the compliment of dressing appropriately), so it would be discourteous of you to turn up at court looking anything but the smartest you can.

7.5.4 **Frequency of appearance in court**

We may have given the erroneous impression that you will be attending court once or twice a week. This is not the case. Far fewer charges are heard at magistrates' courts now than used to be the case. This is because, in the wake of reforms suggested in 2000–01 by Lord Justice Auld,[6] fixed penalties and fixed fines can be pleaded to by letter or by direct payment. The offender does not need to go to court unless s/he is pleading not guilty. This was intended to speed up the judicial process. In fact, the sheer number of offences and the increased number of laws has meant that court volume and workload is only modestly decreasing, although, as we have noted throughout this Handbook, the magistrates themselves are concerned about the exponential increase in police use of fixed penalty notices and fines, partly because such actions lack the transparency of the court process and partly because less than half of fines are actually paid.[7] What it does mean is that you will actually be summoned to court less often than in the past but that when you are called, the case being heard is likely to be more serious. This underlines the fact that the presentation of your evidence is even more important than in lesser cases.

7.5.4.1 *Simulated trials and mock examinations*

It is likely that your training included simulation of a court appearance, with mock trials and play-acting at prosecution and defence. We support all such initiatives to familiarize you with a process, but there is absolutely no substitute for being there and seeing it in person. Go to a court and observe.

There are a couple of good books on criminal law and going to court, which you could profitably study; see Fitzpatrick (2005) and Roberts and Zuckerman (2004).

7.5.4.2 *Support for victims and witnesses*

Finally, remember, whilst you grow more used to what happens at court and experienced in the by-play of the adversarial system, newly arrived witnesses and victims will not be familiar with what is going on. In fact, it will be bewildering and very strange to them. Remember how you felt. Then make sure that the support and reassurance you offer the witnesses and victims leaves them with a positive impression of criminal justice, not a sensation that they have been playing in a game where only they do not know the rules.

7.6 **The Future of the Extended Police 'Family'**

The model in Figure 22 below shows the inter-relationship between parts of the extended police family and suggests some complexities in the nature of that inter-relationship (you may notice that the pieces of the jigsaw don't always fit ...). Although warranted, 'sworn' police officers are at the centre of our jigsaw, they do not constitute any longer the whole notion of 'the police'. What this representation shows us is that there are now other members of the police family who dominate some aspects of community life, virtually to the exclusion of the warranted police. An example is in the private provision of security. If you shop in one of the country's smart urban shopping malls, the chances are that the uniforms you will see will be those of private security firms as their employees patrol, record, report, secure, and intervene, just as 'real' police officers would have done, had they been on patrol. The difference is that the private security guards are reporting in to their own centres, not to the police control. One variant has been reported at the University of Surrey, where private security links in with Surrey Police, though the legitimacy of the security function is not at all clear. That said, proctors at the Universities of Oxford and Cambridge have 'policed' the behaviour of students for hundreds of years; Surrey's initiative is by no means new, but the difference appears to be that the Surrey version will 'police' the public as well as students (Pertile, 2007).

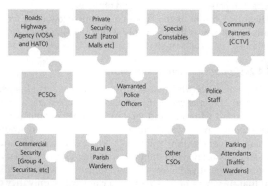

Figure 22: Model of the extended police family

7.6.1 Commercial security: substitutes for police officers?

Senior, experienced police officers will tell you, often with a weary shake of the head, that these private security firms are all very well but that they have neither the experience nor the training of police officers, and that as soon as something happens in the shopping mall, they call for the police anyway. This anecdotal evidence could do with a bit of unpicking: in the event of serious disturbance or the threat of violence, it seems to us that the security guards are perfectly justified in calling the police to deal with a criminal offence. However, when the same security guards use force to expel someone from the mall, the grounds are trickier: under what legitimacy can they do that? What right do they have to use force, whether reasonable or not, and surely their action actually constitutes an assault? (The companies would argue that they are doing no more than a householder would, to eject an intruder.)

7.6.1.1 *Ambiguities in 'private' policing*

(Photograph by Bryn Caless)

Photograph 8: Gated community

Certainly, there seems to be an assumption that the guards can do a 'policing' job within the shopping mall, whether that is the maintenance of order or the provision of first aid. How effectively they do that has yet to be systematically evaluated. The powers through which they can intervene on 'private property' are not clear to members of the public who are invited to enter the 'private property' to spend their money. There are all sorts of ambiguities about legal status and rights here which would occupy a whole chamber of civil liberties lawyers. Instead we invite you to think about what we have outlined in the discussion point below.

Discussion points

What is the legal status of those who carry out a police function on private property?

How does this impact on the 'proper' police function which you and police officers represent?

What training do such private security providers receive and from whom?

Are you confident that they can (a) intervene effectively and (b) ensure the safety of the community when doing so?

Another point to consider is how many of these security providers are locally employed, what checks are made on individuals' backgrounds, and how confident local employers are that there are no criminals among them.

7.6.1.2 *Commercial provision of 'security'*

A related aspect of the 'extended policing family' is **commercial security**. We are used to seeing the big national security companies involved in escorting prisoners, transporting cash and valuables, and providing security patrols and guards for commercial premises. The 'legitimation' of private enterprise in public security has not been without its critics (especially when prisoners in transit abscond, or 'private' prisons are criticized for weak regimes or ineffective containment), but in many ways it has been a stealthy encroachment on traditional policing which has taken place over many years and which is now more or less accepted by all, not least the police, who have never found much job satisfaction in prisoner escorts, courts duty, or the security patrols of commercial premises. However gladly the police yielded space to the commercial providers of security, it is another instance of erosion of the 'traditional' policing role (see Button, 2002).

7.6.1.3 *Roads policing*

In the last few years, policing of the major highways has, in large measure, passed to the **Highways Agency Traffic Officers (HATO)** and the **Vehicle and Operator Services Agency (VOSA)**. They now provide highway patrols and handle most road traffic collisions on the major road arteries (known as the '*fast road network*'). You may have noticed their black-and-yellow chequerboard ('Battenberg') vehicles on patrol on motorways, for example. Some carry signs at the rear of the vehicles saying 'Traffic Officers'. The 'real' police still patrol fast roads, but in much smaller numbers, and often to a specific criminal briefing. Lorry and car checks are still staffed by police officers (with PCSO assistance), though eventually the technical checks themselves may be carried out by Highways Agency HATO or VOSA officials. When empowered to intercept traffic, VOSA is likely to take over this function entirely. Where does this leave the police?

7.6.1.4 *Targeted patrol*

The warranted police have believed for some time now that they should patrol with a purpose if they are going to patrol at all. There is no justification in these days of resource stringency, runs the argument, to mount random patrols on the fast roads network just to act as a deterrent. Instead, traffic police—in ever smaller numbers—are used to target specific wrongdoers and are used in intelligence-led operations to catch known criminals (using the Automated Number Plate Reader (ANPR) scheme). The space thus left on the fast road network has been filled largely by another public service department and the police 'family' is further extended.

7.6.1.5 *Community partners*

The last part of the external elements in the extended police family to be considered is the role of **community partners**. This is best illustrated through the provision in town centres and other public spaces of CCTV monitoring. Most councils now pay for permanent monitoring of key sites and there is an established liaison with police forces to link CCTV coverage with the provision of policing at trouble or 'hot' spots. This relationship is **symbiotic** (*beneficial to both participants*) because the police can rely on others to monitor routinely, whilst councils profit from a targeted police presence. As the night-time economy of most towns and cities expands, so the capability of community partners to help direct police responses (and serve a function as valuable evidence gatherers) will also develop. This not only extends the policing family, but it assigns to other public employees the task of routine monitoring of public (and some commercial) space. Certainly, we are among the most photographed people in Europe, and cannot go shopping without our image being recorded many times.

7.6.1.6 *Legal powers and public status*

The remainder of the pieces in our 'mixed economy' jigsaw are those with legal powers and public status: Special constables, PCSOs, other CSOs, and rural and parish wardens. Most will be familiar to you, either through joint training, Neighbourhood Policing Teams, or through community partnerships, or all of these. Perhaps a word about Specials might be helpful at this point.

The Special Constabulary

The Special Constabulary has been around for a long time. Indeed, at one time, the only legitimate policing to be had was through being either a police cadet (aged 18 to 20), a Special constable (over 18-and-a-half), or a full-time police officer. Specials are warranted officers who perform their agreed policing duties *part-time* (usually in addition to their main employment) *and unpaid*. They therefore have all the powers of a normal police officer and a comprehensive training programme (if of some duration). The days are long gone when Specials appeared only at village fetes to look after the parking; now Specials patrol alongside their full-time colleagues and take part in the full spectrum of policing, and often look on their accumulation of experience as a route into the 'regular' police.

7.6.1.7 *Extending the policing family ever further?*

We have taken you through this model of the extended police family as a pointer to the future. We have noted throughout this Handbook how the traditional views of police officers, and the traditional roles performed by those officers, are all undergoing a process of profound change. The rise of the PCSO and other CSOs and wardens, through partnerships with other agencies and communities, is merely the latest manifestation of what has been going on a long time. It can be seen most graphically by comparing a police force of only 25 years ago with the same police force now.

Discussion points

What specifically do you think will have changed in policing since, say, 1980, in terms of eroding the traditional police role?

A model response

By way of our own answer, we offer the following (which is not definitive, but which gives an indication of how much, generically, has changed)

Taken away	Added
Scenes of crime and forensic investigation: now police staff	High-tech crime, including evidence recovery from computers, and so on
Human resource management, including recruitment, postings, promotion, and selection: all specialist professional staff	Extended responsibility for counter-terrorism (but note role of SOCA replacing police warrant holders)*
Financial management: now sourced with matters like payroll, estates' management, and pensions to police staff	
Information technology: highly specialist engineering and programming, R&D, fault diagnosis, maintenance, etc, now all the province of police staff	
Fast roads policing: partly assigned to Highways Agency	
CCTV monitoring: now largely with councils	
Procedure to charge: now determined by CPS, not police officer	
Routine neighbourhood visible foot or cycle patrol: now largely undertaken by PCSOs	
Road safety campaigns: now largely Highways Agency (DfT) or local partnerships	

Taken away	Added
Prisoner escort, prisoner transportation, guard duties at court: now mainly performed by private security companies	
Estates, vehicle maintenance and engineering, catering, cleaning, ancillary maintenance: now mostly outsourced	
Health monitoring, medical provision, staff safety training, use of protective equipment, much erstwhile specialist police training: either outsourced or passed to qualified police staff	

* The DG of SOCA can determine, apparently, what his staff are warranted to do, dependent upon need; see Police Justice Act 2006.

7.7 **Supervision Issues**

The issue of supervision is a concern in any organization and the police service is no exception. Indeed, at the level of local delivery, the role of the supervisor can often mean the difference between a well-motivated team which knows what it has to deliver to make a difference, and a team which acts dysfunctionally and which may deliver only partially. The introduction of the PCSO into the extended policing family has created some issues for the conventional neighbourhood team supervisor, and indeed, has raised questions about who the preferred supervisor should be. This arises partly because of the 'halfway house' characteristic of the PCSO role—is the PCSO a uniformed civilian or non-warranted police officer? If the first, should PCSOs be supervised by a member of police staff? If the second, should PCSOs be supervised by a police officer, usually a sergeant? (Note that NPIA, in its *PCSO Review*, 2008, recommends a police sergeant as the 'default' supervisor of PCSOs and Neighbourhood Policing Teams in general.) We have already noted in our discussion of corruption (at 7.3 above) that 'intrusive supervision' can be a major deterrent to criminal opportunism. More than that, a good 'skipper' can motivate a team to produce really well and can ensure that each team member is valued. This is especially important in the context of Neighbourhood Policing Teams.

7.7.1 Supervision experience and experience of supervision

Most PCSOs will arrive in the job with some experience of having been supervised; indeed many may have been supervisors themselves. These experiences, both positive and negative, will shape the PCSO's approach and attitude to the process of being supervised. For many, supervision may have been a largely neutral experience, whilst for others, the experience could have been excellent, especially if a supervisor was keen to coach or tutor. For a few, however, the experience may have been one of real worry and concern. There might have been an issue of workplace bullying, or real pressure to conform to a particular type of working practice, or the negative, grinding dreariness of having a supervisor who was constitutionally impossible to please. In other words, the way in which any individual receives supervision is dependent as much upon previous experiences as upon the individual's expectations.

> **Discussion points**
> What experiences of supervision have you had?
> In your experience what factors make a good or bad supervisor?

7.7.2 Defining supervision

What does supervision mean? In his seminal study of social work in 2002, Alfred Kadushin[8] highlighted three core elements of supervision:

- **Administrative**—concerned with the correct implementation of policies and procedures
- **Educational**—concerned with making sure the knowledge and skills of the supervisee are up to date
- **Supportive**—concerned with maintaining the morale of the employee and ensuring that any dissatisfaction or concerns are not manifested in his or her work.

> **Task**
>
> Based on your experience, and using Kadushin's classification, highlight which of the supervisory roles (administrative, educational, or supportive) is likely to be dominant in each of the following PCSO 'problems'.

PCSO Task	Administrative, educational, or supportive
Submission of intelligence reports	
Completion of annual appraisal (also called PDR: personal development review)	
Requests for rest days or leave	
Dealing with personal issues	
Identifying training needs	
Checking the pocket note book (PNB)	
Applying for additional responsibilities	
Need to talk through a work-based problem	
Grievance about treatment	
Assistance with operational matters	
Assessing NOS portfolio requirements	

A model response

Here are our suggestions:

PCSO Task	Administrative, educational, or supportive
Submission of intelligence reports	Administrative; educational if improvement is needed
Completion of annual appraisal (PDR)	Administrative; educational if development points are identified
Requests for rest days or leave	Administrative; supportive if request is for compassionate leave
Dealing with personal issues	Supportive
Identifying training needs	Educational; administrative if there are difficulties with procedures

PCSO Task	Administrative, educational, or supportive
Checking the pocket note book (PNB)	Administrative; educational if shortcomings are noted
Applying for additional responsibilities	Educational; supportive in ensuring your workload is not burdensome
Need to talk through a work-based problem	Administrative; educational; supportive
Grievance about treatment	Supportive
Assistance with operational matters	Administrative
Assessing NOS portfolio requirements	Educational (if supervisor is trained to assess the NOS)

7.7.3 Who should supervise PCSOs?

Within your Force there may be several people occupying very diverse roles with supervisory responsibility for PCSOs. This will vary from force to force and even BCU to BCU. However, the majority of supervisors for PCSOs will fall into one of three categories:

- **Police Sergeant**
- **PCSO Supervisor**
- **Police Staff Employee.**

7.7.3.1 *Sergeant*

Many PCSOs will be supervised directly by a police sergeant who is often located within the Neighbourhood Policing Team or Crime Reduction Team. The sergeant may have a mixed team, including police officers, PCSOs, Special constables, and perhaps parking attendants, to supervise. This may itself create difficulties because of the broad composition of the team and the inherent difficulties in welding many separate elements into a unified team.

7.7.3.2 *PCSO Supervisor*

(See our discussion on potential PCSO ranks in the Introduction.) Some forces have promoted PCSOs to perform a supervisory role (you may hear them referred to as Senior or Supervisory PCSOs); in some cases they may combine this supervisory role with a beat of their own to patrol and manage. As yet, there is no national template to enable this to happen. It is a moot point (at least as far as we are concerned) as to who would make the better supervisor of PCSOs: a 'promoted' PCSO or a career police officer. The police sergeant may be better at bringing diverse individuals together; on the other hand, the experienced PCSO may have a clearer idea about the nature of the job.

7.7.3.3 *Police Staff Employee*

It may be that your supervisor is a 'civilian' (police staff) employee, who has also received the relevant training. Such an individual may therefore have little knowledge of your day-to-day activities, particularly if this is the first time s/he has supervised a PCSO. There is nothing inherently wrong with someone managing a team who has no experience of the detailed work of members of that team, but specifically, *supervisors* need practical knowledge of how a job is done in order to oversee its performance effectively. Managers, operating on a wider canvas and often concerned with resources and targets, may be at more of a remove from the detailed task.

7.7.3.4 *What counts is supervising well*

However, with requisite training, it is the individual supervisor who matters, irrespective of where s/he comes from.

Discussion points

What type of supervisor do you have?

What is his or her role?

Has this affected your experience of being supervised?

7.7.4 Early stages for PCSOs themselves to supervise

Developing PCSOs into supervisors and managers of other PCSOs is still emerging as a topic. Few forces have had PCSOs long enough to determine the supervisory capacity of an individual (with notable exceptions such as the Metropolitan Police), and the common 'default' position is still to utilize police officers as supervisors (some forces use constables rather than sergeants, but there are internal problems inherent in such a practice, since constables are not technically 'supervisors' under Police Regulations). Some of the progress in this subject is going to be down to you. If your experience, clarity of focus, and willingness to put in time to get the best out of people comes to the notice of those above you, you will eventually be given the responsibilities you seek. Our advice is that you **ensure that you receive the right training in supervision** before you move up to running a team.

7.8 **Other Potential Roles and Routes**

There is currently no agreed national structure of ranks that the PCSO can climb, or other forms of promotion or career progression, as is the case for your police officer colleagues. There are, however, extra responsibilities that more experienced PCSOs in particular can assume, including assisting in the training of novice PCSOs. Some of these additional responsibilities may attract extra pay but this is largely down to the policy of your Force, as we noted in 7.7 above.

7.8.1 **Other development**

There may also be opportunities for you to develop in other ways. For example, by:

- Driving patrol cars (after suitable training and perhaps the granting of some additional powers)
- Assuming specialist roles such as 'Transport and Traffic' (as is currently the case with the MPS, but witness HATO and VOSA's emerging role)
- Becoming more involved in the communities that you support (in the kinds of ways described in Chapter 6 of this Handbook).

However, the current lack of a nationally-sanctioned career structure remains of concern to some PCSOs (see, for example, Cooper *et al*, 2006, 49). It seems likely that career development is one aspect of the job likely to change in the near future.

7.8.2 **Route to the regular police?**

A significant number of PCSOs appear to join the police service as a stepping stone to becoming a 'regular' police officer (42% claim to want to do this in the NPIA *PCSO Review*, 2008). There is certainly anecdotal evidence that younger PCSOs in particular may have joined in order to gain life experience in preparation for attempting to join as a police constable (see, for example, the pen pictures of the PCSOs who took part in the ITV documentary 'BEAT: Life on the Street' available at <http://www.itv.com/page.asp?partid=6750> (accessed December 2006)). There is some debate about whether this is a positive or negative development for the police service, given the intention that PCSOs should provide a source of continuity and dependability for their communities. However, if you are one of the 40% or so who aspire to become a warranted police officer in the future, you may wish to bear the following in mind:

- The application and selection process for joining as a police officer is similar to the process you went through to become a PCSO but the former is longer and places somewhat different demands on you. This said, your experience as a PSCO is likely to be of significant benefit in responding to questions about your suitability to work as a police officer.
- The NOS that you achieve during PCSO training are a subset of the 22 units that trainee student police officers also need to achieve during their probation (see Bryant *et al*, 2009). In theory at least there could be opportunities for you to have these accredited as prior learning or 'APL', in order to avoid having to meet the same requirements for a second time. Note at the same time that the number of NOS is likely to reduce for both police officers and for PCSOs.
- Some forward thinkers, in policing and in the academic world, are suggesting that widespread learning could take place in a Foundation Degree for example, **before** any police training is offered following successful application. This would constitute an entrance qualification, of course, which may not be welcomed universally; on the other hand, police training could be reduced to about 20 weeks instead of the 40 or so currently.
- Similarly, some forces are planning to combine parts of the training of PCSOs with the training of student police officers. Hence you may be exempt from the early stages of training. Practice does vary, however.

7.9 **Policing and its Future**

We have looked at some elements of this earlier, particularly matters such as the extended police family, future demography, and the readiness of the police service to embrace radical change. Here we examine what we think will be changes to the nature of policing in the future.

7.9.1 Where do we go from where we are?

If you consider that, up to the early 1980s, the original 'support' staff to the police were mainly typists and filing clerks, the changes to the things police officers used to do and the things that they do now, are quite profound. We think that this has gone in step with reconsiderations about what a police force is for (indeed, whether it is a *force* at all, as we discussed extensively in Chapter 6). The pace of change has been **exponential** (*on an increasingly steep curve*) and we want to look now at some of the factors that we think will help to determine the nature of policing in the next 25 years, and how these factors will impact on you as a PCSO. It isn't crystal ball gazing, nor is it the reading of tea-leaves. This is instead a legitimate, grounded, and realistic appraisal (we hope) of where policing is heading and what will impact on it ('drivers') from outside.

7.9.1.1 *How will being a police officer change?*

The one determinant in the future will be **the possession of a warrant** ('the office of constable'), though there may well be changes to the Crown Servant status of police officers, and more emphasis laid on their being employees of the Police Authority (which currently they are not; only police staff, including you, are employees of the Authority). Police officers may be distinguished from other 'policing' functions—carried out by PCSOs, CSOs, wardens, other government departments, agencies such as VOSA, local council employees, and private security companies—only by what they are empowered to do. Police officers will have the power to enforce the law, to arrest and detain, to use reasonable force. (Some of this exercise of power may be poached by beleaguered politicians and Chief Constables for the PCSO role, but we have already deprecated this as a recourse or default position.)

7.9.1.2 *Police as 'managing directors'*

Police officers may do much more coordinating of the work of others, particularly in neighbourhood team management, where PCSOs, Specials, wardens, volunteers (such as 'Horse Watch' and 'Neighbourhood Watch'), and perhaps even some private companies, will come under the direction of a warranted officer. Delivery of solutions to community problems may well be in a police officer's remit, but in practice this will be delegated by the police officer manager to those who work in the team which s/he manages. In the future, only when the use of warranted powers necessitates a police intervention (such as the use of firearms or with reference to public order) might we see police officers in numbers on the streets.

7.9.1.3 *Managing investigations*

The traditional role of the specialist detective is also changing. Many forces now employ police staff, not police officers, as specialist statement-takers, whose role is to visit witnesses and victims and take statements from them, thus freeing up police detectives to concentrate on the detection and detention of the suspect(s) for the crime. Under the '*Professionalizing the Investigative Process*' (PIP) training, which was begun in pilot forces in 2005, an accredited programme to 'qualify' police officers as detectives is available. We know of some forces that have put police staff on the programme to obtain an investigation qualification. This is not to say that such staff could interview a suspect under caution, but we think that this signals the beginning of a match to the neighbourhood team concept within detection and investigation. There are many jobs within investigation which do not require a police warrant. We have already looked at statement-takers; other areas include victims' and witnesses' support, house-to-house enquiries, research into the background of suspects, including trawls through criminal databases, case preparation, and policy file maintenance. We might also point to the increasingly prominent part played by the recovery of forensic science evidence from crime scenes, where support staff monopolize the role.

7.9.1.4 *Resource pressures drive such expediency*

Managing a team in an investigation may mean that an accredited police detective oversees a team of 'detectives' who are not police officers. As resources become scarcer, and pressures to secure 'brought to justice' targets increase, it seems to us plausible that police forces will respond by cutting their cloth accordingly. Indeed, some commentators have argued that such shifts and changes are inevitable rather than merely possible (Waddington, 2006).

7.9.2 **A diminishing force?**

It is probable that police numbers will grow slowly smaller—in the teeth of opposition from the Police Federation and massaged by politicians to give the best 'spin'—but the fact is that current numbers are not sustainable. Not only can the budgets available to forces not support police numbers at their current level, the **demography, economic climate**, and **lifestyle choices** in the working population are changing significantly too (see below). As we noted in 2.8 above, the popularity of PCSOs with communities may well result in their numbers being increased over time. Unless the funding for PCSOs comes from the government, forces will have to rely on partnership and part-funding, making up any shortfall from their own budgets (as we suggest in the Introduction to this Handbook). Given increasing stringency in the amount of money available (some 82% of all police budgets currently is allocated to salaries and pensions), the probable casualty will be police officer recruitment. This may not have an impact in the short term, except in terms of numbers deploying, but over time, the decrease will have a considerable effect. It follows that forces will configure 'policing' differently, perhaps along the lines of the management teams we have indicated above, to make the most of the resources they do have. Whether police forces will then retain the investigative expertise and crime-solving capability which is normally associated with warranted officers, is not yet clear. There may yet be a return to regional squads of career detectives, managing larger groups of police staff and PCSO investigators, in countering Level 2 crimes and criminals.

7.9.2.1 *Demography, economic climate, and lifestyle choice*

The demography (that is, the age profile of the population) is changing, with greater numbers living beyond 65 than ever before. This has been characterized as the 'greying' of the population. It also means that, as more people reach retirement and live longer, the numbers of the working population who can support those in retirement have fallen. So, in a nutshell, fewer working people are supporting more who do not work. That has an impact on the recruitment pool for the police. Although the starting salary for police officers is fairly attractive, there are competitors, not least of which are the lifestyle choices of young people themselves.

Staying with one employer is likely to be a thing of the past

There is increasing evidence that young people now do not consider a full career with one employer as their 'lifetime of work'. Instead, many are opting to work in public service for a short time, moving on to other things after ten years or so. Additionally, some university graduates in the marketplace may choose to make lots of money in banking or brokering, or in starting up businesses of their own, for the same kind of period. That entre-preneurship plus the period in public service, might then fund a more 'creative' lifestyle which would be less generously rewarded. The economic recession is likely to have only a short-term (say five years') impact; so that the long-term trend is probably to this 'three part career'.

7.9.2.2 There are more choices now, and looser definitions of careers

Whether this becomes a popular phenomenon among gradu-ates or not, is not the point. *The point is that the options to do so are there.* In a diminishing pool of labour, the highly-skilled can call the tune and decide and plan their own futures. Policing is not necessarily going to figure highly among so many counter-attractions, unless there is a rethink of what could be acquired prior to entry, such as a **qualification for entry**, through a degree in policing or in police law or something akin. Those who do opt for a 35-year career in policing might not only be in the minority, they may also be less skilled, and less able to be as eco-nomically mobile as their counterparts elsewhere. Remaining in policing beyond ten years may come to be seen as 'de-skilling' for other jobs or roles.

7.9.2.3 There's only one way in

Policing may have to do something quite radical, in addition to shifting solidly towards becoming a profession, if it is still to attract bright young people to become police officers. That 'quite radical' element will probably embrace **multiple points of entry** to the police service. Where currently the usual way into policing is as a constable, the future may bring people into policing at higher ranks, including at Chief Officer level. It is likely that this will have to be forced on the police service rather than accepted voluntarily by forces, since there is cur-rently very widespread reluctance to open the police up in this way, although the post of Chief Constable for the Civil Nuclear Police Authority was opened up to non-police applicants in early 2007 (and subsequently a career civil servant, Richard Thompson, was appointed as Chief Constable, in April 2007). Where that leaves the PCSO, of course, is still as an ancillary to warranted police officers, but PCSOs may attract more entrants in the second or third stages of their '*portfolio of careers*' than is now the case, as well as PCSOs being a valid alternative to polic-ing in their own right.

7.9.3 What next?

Where policing goes from here, with these options and imperatives, is up to those in command, of course. We are not confident
that those in charge of police forces are thinking radically enough
or quickly enough. Some, like Peter Neyroud at the National
Police Improvement Agency, or DCC Alf Hitchcock, Director of
the National Police Leadership College, are in the forefront of
planning modernization and change, but the changes aired to
date are scarcely earth-shattering. Multiple entry to the police is
not a prevailing option, nor is deliberate progression to a profession with specialized knowledge. Instead, the wearisome debate
is about meeting targets for performance, or responding to Home
Office initiatives. We do not believe that there is either the will
or the belief to embrace radical change at this stage. The alternative, of course, is that changes external to policing may force the
internal reconfigurations that we have discussed. What we can
say with some certainty is that the 'mixed economy' of policing
is here to stay. Indeed, more and more of the core function of traditional policing will be allocated to others who do not have warrants. We can easily envisage a future where the possession of a
warrant is used only when there is a need for serious or prolonged
interference with an individual's human rights.

7.10 Chapter Summary

This has been a less referential and practical chapter than those
preceding it, and this was inevitable, given the subject matter. We
have no monopoly on the vision or the truth of where policing
is going. Indeed, its direction can be very positively or negatively
influenced by those currently in command.

7.10.1 Rise and fall

The last few years have seen the proposal and then the shelv-
ing of amalgamation of police forces. We have seen the rise of
intelligence-led policing and its partial replacement by neighbourhood policing. We have witnessed the formation of SOCA
and the NPIA; the disappearance of the National Crime Squad
and the National Criminal Intelligence Service; the absorption
of Centrex (police training) and PITO into NPIA; an increase in
the accurate recovery of minute forensic evidence, including

mitochondrial DNA; and we have seen the gradual erosion of the traditional role of the police officer in favour of a radical extension of the police family. You are a part of this broad change and flux. At the same time we have encountered an unprecedented number of new laws and statutes introduced by successive governments, we have experienced political initiatives to deal with communities, from the 'Respect' agenda to the use of ASBOs, and we have all tried to come to terms with the meaning of the fear of crime in our communities.

7.10.1.1 *Being a professional*

Stopping to look at the scope and speed of change can leave one slightly breathless, and it is of little comfort to note that many of the initiatives have been false starts and some of the innovations, particularly those master-minded by politicians, lacked contact with reality. To write about the future, then, is to invite ridicule if you get it wrong. Undeterred, we have tried. We have examined the role of professional standards and we have glanced at the work of Professional Standards Departments in police forces. We discussed corruption as openly as we could and we hope that we have given you some insights into why corruption happens and what you can do about it if you encounter corrupt practices among your colleagues. The nature of being a professional in the police family is a central theme in this Handbook, and we paused here to tackle what being a professional means in your everyday duties.

7.10.1.2 *Courts and the criminal justice system*

This was followed by a description of what it is like to go to court and the nature of having to give evidence. We hope that our handy guide will stand you in good stead when you are summoned to attend any of the courts in your Force area.

7.10.1.3 *Extending the police 'family'*

Having dealt with those issues, we felt able to look ahead and to discuss with you the changes which have taken place, and which are continuing to happen, in the extended police family, including what the constitution of that family may be in 10 or 20 years' time. Moving from the general to the very specific, we examined what may constitute supervision of PCSOs in the future, whereupon we looked at other roles and routes for the PCSO, including the transition to being a police officer and what that might entail.

7.10.1.4 *The future*

This brought us, logically enough, to consider the whole future of policing and what is likely to change in the role and function of a police officer in years to come. Time will tell if we're right.

7.10.1.5 *Continuing Debate*

We have come to the end of our attempts to provide insights into the world of policing for the especial benefit of the PCSO, and to the conclusion of our debate and discussion about the sorts of things which PCSOs are being asked to do as they deploy with their police forces. We have emphasized throughout that merely referential concentration on PCSO Powers or the NOS and Behavioural Competences is not enough. **What PCSOs need is a context, a means whereby they can judge the value and the meaning of what they do.** If we have given you that context, we've done what we set out to achieve.

References

C Nicholls, T Daniel, M Polaine, and J Hatchard, *Corruption and Misuse of Public Office* (OUP, 2006).

Notes

1 Lord Nolan, a 'Law Lord' who died in January 2007, chaired the Committee on Standards in Public Life, which sat on and off for the early part of the 1990s. He published his *First Report of the Committee on Standards in Public Life* in 1995; see Bibliography.

2 See eg the discussion in R Bryant (ed), *Blackstone's Student Police Officer Handbook* (OUP, 2006) Ch 5, section 5.4, 'Police Corruption', 99–105, or B Caless, 'Corruption in the Police: the Reality of the "Dark Side"', The Police Journal, Vol 81, No 1, Vathek Publishing, 2008, and B Caless 'Persistent Dark Matter; Police Corruption in the Last Ten Years', *Ethics in Policing*, Vol 1, No 2, 2008. See also J Bennetto, 'Sleeping with the enemy is clue to a bent copper', *The Independent*, 19 May 2000, available as <http://findarticles.com/p/articles/mi_qn4158/is 20000519/ai_n14314433> accessed 26 May 2009.

Another interesting text is G McLagen, *Bent Coppers* (Weidenfeld & Nicholson, 2003) Chs 1, 3, 14, and 16, especially 248–55. Although Graham McLagen tells the story of corrupt Metropolitan Police officers, the lessons are generic. A useful further text is J Miller, '*Police Corruption in England and Wales: an assessment of the current evidence*', Home Office online report 11/03 from <http://www.homeoffice. gov. uk/rds/pdfs2/rdsolr1103.pdf> accessed June 2007.

3 In 2003, a computer operator and an ex-police officer, both Surrey Police, each received a two-year prison sentence for this offence. They had been involved in assisting drugs dealers to avoid detection.

4 Bryn Caless undertook this research in 1999–2000 on behalf of the **ACPO Counter-Corruption Advisory Group**. The data were collected anonymously because of *sub judice* investigations and, in some cases, retirement instead of prosecution of the officers implicated in corruption. The findings were published variously in *Police Review* and by Kent Police, and some profiles derived from Caless' research are in McLagen (n 2 above) 248–55.

5 See Sir John Stevens, *Not for the Faint-Hearted* (Phoenix, Orion, 2005), and ACPO, *Guidance to Chief Constables on a counter-corruption strategy* (Home Office, 2002).

6 See Lord Justice Auld, 'Review of the Criminal Courts of England and Wales' (TSO (Stationery Office), 2001); another useful reference is J Stockdale and P Gresham, 'The presentation of police evidence to court', Police Research Series, Paper 15, Home Office (1995).

7 S Gibb, 'En garde! Magistrates ready for battle over punishments', *The Times*, 26 February, 2009, available from <http://www.timesonline.uk/news> accessed 27 February 2009 and F Gibb, 'On-the-spot fines mean justice is not seen to be done, say critics', *The Times*, 5 May 2009, available from <http://timesonline/tol/business/law/article4622156.ece> , accessed 5th May, 2009.

8 A Kadushin, *Supervision in Social Work* (4th edn, Columbia University Press, 2002).

Chapter 8

Tasks and Knowledge Tests

8.1 **Introduction**

This chapter supports all the other chapters in this Handbook, because this is where you can do your own knowledge checks and test that you really do understand the issues we have discussed in the main parts of the Handbook.

We expect even the seasoned PCSO to test everything s/he can remember through this chapter, because no one can carry all the requisite information in his or her head all the time. The central part of the Handbook is referential, but there are masses of other facts and details to absorb elsewhere in the Handbook and that is why, in this chapter, we offer you the means to look through any test and task reference and establish how much you recall and what you have experienced, as well as suggesting things you should think about.

We have organized the material so that we begin with a general description of **Tonchester**. This is our mythical city in the southern Midlands where we have located many of the practical problems that you might encounter as a PCSO. Our main reason for doing this is that we can give you a 'real' environment in which our examples and illustrations can be based, but it is also to bring together in one place the multiple circumstances, situations, and knotty problems which otherwise would have to be scattered around the country. So Tonchester isn't real but its problems and solutions are.

Following some data to help 'ground' you in the city, we reproduce a letter from the BCU Commander that describes some of the priorities and problems which are dominating local policing agendas. We do this because it is quite common for BCU Commanders to articulate neighbourhood policing priorities to PCSOs and to police officers, and also because again it grounds in a fictional 'reality' the sorts of things you might encounter when you take up a new post (whether or not you are a new PCSO).

Then we present you with a chronological series of tasks and knowledge tests which arise from each of the chapters in the Handbook presented sequentially. You can check the answers and suggested solutions in **Answer sections** which immediately follow the set of questions based on each chapter.

Our intention throughout is to give you some entertaining, but challenging, self-testing, though of course there is nothing to stop you using the texts in this Handbook as group exercises or training exercises with others. What is important is that you enjoy the experience of working briefly as a PCSO in Tonchester, and that you feel stretched by the nature of the questions and tasks which we set you to answer or unravel.

8.2 **Tonchester**

We now introduce you to the city of **Tonchester**, where you will carry out simulations of many of your patrols and tasks, and also introduce you to your BCU Commander, who will set out for you what the policing and reassurance priorities are for your BCU.

Tonchester is the large county town of Tonford (see Figure 23 below), a county between Warwickshire and Northamptonshire, north of London but south of Birmingham. It is a mix of rural and urban, city and industrial town, advanced scientific engineering and the remnants of heavy manufacturing. It reflects faithfully the community tensions, ethnic mixes, age and demographic profiles, employment patterns, poverty and wealth which might be encountered in any PCSO's patrol 'beat' in England or Wales. The map of the city centre is shown in Figure 23 below.

City information

Population: 142,667 (2001 Census)

Cathedral: The Cathedral of St Barnabas and All Angels occupies a site which has had a religious building since at least 890 AD. Most of the present structure dates from the major building period of 1450–1550; though parts were damaged in the Civil War (1642–49), particularly in 1645 when a Royalist Army was besieged and then defeated in Tonchester by Cromwell's 'New

Model Army'. Some parts of the Cathedral, including the West Window and the Great North Door, were subsequently rebuilt in the mid-eighteenth century; at the same time many of the houses in the fine Cathedral Close were erected.

University: Tonchester University had its origins in the late 19th century as a 'Working Man's Evening College', pioneered by the radical Victorian social reformer Sebastian Egdon-Fytchett. For many years the College hosted extra-mural classes in history and politics from Birmingham University. Tonchester College became a University College in 1926 and gained full university status during expansions in 1965–68. The University is particularly well known for its Medical Faculty and teaches the largest number of medical staff, including nurses, outside London and Bristol. Engineering and Social Sciences are also well to the fore. The University has 8,000 full-time students and nearly 15,000 part-time or affiliated students.

Industry and economy: Tonchester is a thriving county town with strong economic bases in tourism and recreation, particularly in the Peak District and Warwickshire's Shakespeare country, which lie to the east and west respectively. There is extensive light industry, mostly located at the Southwoods' Industrial and Science Estate to the south west of the city. Caissons, the steel and plastics manufacturer, has its headquarters in Tonchester and most of the computer casings used across the world are made here. Border Packaging, Sanson's Wire Fencing and Gamboge Flour Mills are the major, long-standing local employers but increasingly, the IT industry and scientific and technical trades are expanding in the city, providing knowledge employment locally.

Social mix: The city centre has mixed economy housing with the lower income sector and housing estates located to the west of the city between the railway and the dual carriageway. Other social and authority-provided housing is found in the Telling and Bone estates to the north-east of Baker Street railway station (not shown on map). The expensive end of the housing market is found in the Cathedral Close, the Georgian Crescent, and roads like Lower Place near the University. Kit's Cut and Semlar Street are known locally as 'Millionaires' Rows' because of the exclusive gated communities there.

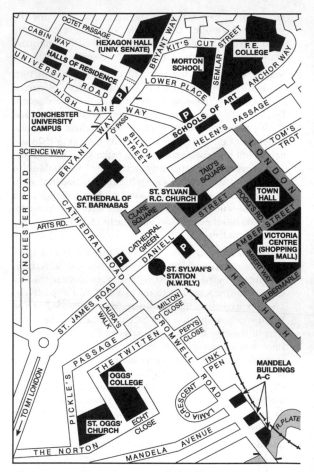

Figure 23: Map of central Tonchester, the 'Midlands Jewel'

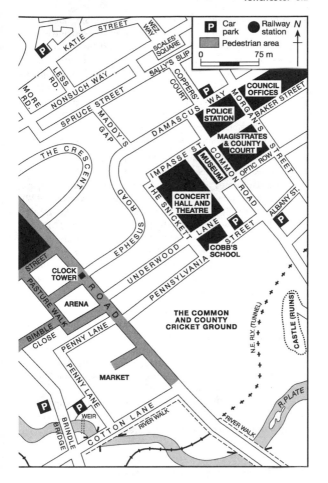

Shopping and retail: Tonchester's largest shopping area is the 'Precinct' between Daniell Street in the north-west and Cotton Lane in the south, bordered east and west by The High and London Road. The whole area was pedestrianized in 2003. The Victoria Complex is a major shopping mall, which was opened in early 2007, and shops which specialize in local leather crafts, jewellery, and fashion accessories are found in Amber Street. Saturday and Sunday trading is carried out at The Market, flanked by stalls in Penny Lane. Pasture Walk is home to dozens of antique shops, specializing in silverware and early furniture.

Civics and amenities: The Police Station is located on Damascus Way, near Baker Street Station (not shown on map). Opposite is the Magistrates' and County Court on Common Road (parts of the interior were designed by Edmund Lutyens in 1927). The Town Hall is off London Road and Amber Street; this fine building was designed by Decimus Burton in 1843. The County Museum Concert Hall and the McReady Theatre are located between London Road and Baker Street Station. Council Offices and Departments are in a new building, Courtauld House, opposite Baker Street Station and adjacent to the Police Station.

Communications: An extensive fast road network serves Tonchester, which is itself located conveniently between the M1, M40 and M5 motorways. Birmingham International Airport is approximately 20 kilometres north of Tonchester, and the area is well served with railways. Alas, the Tonchester/Avon Canal fell into disuse between the Wars and was filled in for housing to be built.

Tonchester has an extensive ring road, competed in 1996, which takes through-traffic away from the city centre, enabling the later pedestrianized areas.

8.3 Discussion Question—BCU Commander's Letter

The following letter from the BCU Commander, Central Tonchester, is the basis of a discussion question which is directly relevant to your job as a PCSO. You have turned up for duty on day one of your new appointment in this BCU. (You may be a new PCSO or an experienced PCSO.)

From:
Chief Superintendent Jennifer Allyse,
QPM, MA,
BCU Commander, Central Tonchester,
Police Headquarters,
Damascus Way,
Tonchester TC2 DF15

Date as postmark
Our ref:/TONBCU/JBA/PCSOltr/09

Dear Colleague,

I am delighted to welcome you as a Police and Community Support Officer on the strength of the Neighbourhood Teams under my command here in Tonchester. It is especially important that you understand what it is that I want from you. Equally, you should be aware of what the City of Tonchester wants from both of us.

First of all, you need to know that the Chief Constable, Jim Harker, has decided that all PCSOs in Tonford Police will have fully designated powers, other than those restricted to traffic wardens. You will be well aware of the challenges which face us in the City, particularly in the economically-deprived residential areas in the south-west and north-east. Recent problems have included unoccupied youths throwing stones at cars and some rather unpleasant racist chanting, particularly at the University and at local football matches. There are also some 'problem families' who have been moved into the estates from Alston and other urban areas to the north of Tonchester. Some groups of youths are coming into the shopping centres and appear to be targeting the elderly for abuse. Groups of youths frequently complain that they are bored and have nothing to do, despite the large and superbly equipped Henperson Sports Centre recently opened on the Common.

Graffiti, petty vandalism and anti-social behaviour abound in the area containing the tower blocks known as Nelson Mandela Buildings A, B and C, which are centres of real social deprivation and evident drugs dealing. Most residents appear too scared to come out except in escorted groups in daylight. By contrast, there have been instances recently of petty vandalism in the Victoria Centre complex. Some shoppers have complained of aggression and drunkenly abusive behaviour by, particularly, groups of girls from Oggs' College off the Cromwell Road. There appears to be a considerable amount of underage drinking in the city centre, judging from reports and CCTV coverage.

The point is that I have pledged to do something about it, and that is where you and the rest of your neighbourhood teams come into the picture. **I want imaginative and long-lasting solutions,** which do not unnecessarily demonize the youth of our city but which do, most effectively, **reassure the general population,** especially those going peaceably about their everyday business. We cannot afford a loss of confidence in local businesses, but that is what will happen if these episodes are not dealt with. Your supervisors are well aware of these local policing priorities. Success in attaining our targets is vital if we are to retain the support of the public in our work and I rely on you to deliver your part in our professional partnership.

Do not hesitate to use your designated powers if you need to. I will back any proportionate and justified use of policing powers, or designated PCSO powers, where the effect is to achieve those outcomes I have described in this letter.

I look forward to meeting you as I visit neighbourhood patrols and would welcome constructive suggestions to improve people's safety and wellbeing in Tonchester.

Yours sincerely

Jenny Allyse

Chief Superintendent JB Allyse
BCU Commander, Tonchester

Discussion points

Having received and read this letter from your BCU Commander, what planning and thinking would you do?
Assuming that your patrol beat extended from Damascus Way police station to Cromwell Road and from Cotton Lane to Bryant Way, what priorities would you be thinking about as you set out on your patrol?

Your patrol takes in most of the shopping 'Precinct' of Tonchester but also goes close to Ogg's College and Cobb's School. You would be mindful of what the BCU Commander said about drunkenness in the city centre, allegedly by girls from Ogg's College. You would probably keep an eye out for any tensions between young people and the elderly using the shopping centres, and you would certainly be looking for any evidence of underage drinking.

Is that enough? In discussion, come up with about five priorities for your patrol period and write them down. Check your responses against what we suggest below.

8.3.1 Answer to discussion question—BCU Commander's letter

There is no right or wrong here, but it depends on how or why you prioritize what you do. We think that you would be mindful of Chief Superintendent Allyse's comment that she wants '*imaginative and long-term solutions*' to some of the city centre problems, and you may indeed have to make allowance for '*adult intolerance*' of the occasional idiocies carried out by bored children. That is not the same as being tolerant of underage drinking, or of graffiti, or of abuse of the elderly. You would need to intervene decisively if you saw anti-social behaviour of that order.

However, what about finding out where children are getting the alcohol? The BCU Commander said that the youths ought to go to the Sports' Centre, but could they? How expensive is it? How might schoolchildren afford an entrance and gym fee on a regular basis? Mightn't it be sensible for you to meet the Henperson's Sports' Centre owners and organizers and explore whether a programme of after-school activities could be offered at a subsidized rate and with proper supervision? You could also talk to the neighbouring schools to see what could be developed, especially if there are some interested parents who could help with supervision. Might there be sponsorship/coaching, supervision, leadership available from sports and health charities and from organizations such as those encouraging cricket and athletics? With the 2012 Olympics in the offing, you might suddenly seem very persuasive to the commercially minded Sports' Centre managers, who might want to show some civic responsibility. Remind them how many parents are members of their gymnasia and sports clubs.

What about a dialogue with city centre traders and shop managers to sponsor such after-school events? They'd see a percentage in paying for that rather than having anti-social behaviour outside their shops and stores, wouldn't they? Not to mention the very positive publicity which they would almost certainly get from such public-spirited support for the community.

So, already you may have the germ of a longer-term strategy to engage with the community, provide alternatives for the children and youths, involve local organizations and enterprises, and seek a 'win-win' outcome. It is worth noting that our suggested solutions show how PCSOs can get results without always resorting to use of designated powers. Making a difference in the community is not always about coercion or punishment; sometimes it can be to do with neatly meeting different needs. These thoughts are part of the 'why?' aspects of understanding.

8.4 Chapter 3—Tasks and Knowledge Tests

Task 1: Legal powers

What do you think that subsection (4) means?

Task 2: Testing what you know about your legal powers

1. Why could the PRA02 be described as a 'catch-all' Act?
2. What four 'occupational' groups can a chief officer designate?
3. What do all four have in common?
4. Who can become a member of a police authority?
5. What is the authority's remit?
6. What does 'under direction and control' mean?
7. What three things should a chief officer be satisfied about before designating someone?
8. What does 'suitable' mean in the Act?
9. What does 'capable' mean in the Act?
10. Why is training described as a two-way contract?

Task 3: Modes of trial and knowledge checks

1. Find out the mode of trial or classification for the following offences:
   - **Failing to give name and address when required**—paragraph 1A(5) of Schedule 4 to the PRA02
   - **Whilst driving a motor vehicle, neglects or refuses to comply with traffic directions given by a PCSO**—section 35 of the Road Traffic Act 1988
   - **Damaging property, etc**—section 1(1) of the Criminal Damage Act 1971

2. Is **'Statute Law'**:
   (a) Law by Parliamentary session?
   (b) Law within Parliament's confines?
   (c) Law in and around Parliament?
   (d) Law by Parliamentary Acts?
3. (a) What is a **Bill?**
   (b) What part of law is the power, for example, to remove vehicles?
   (c) Who makes **byelaws?**
4. Give TWO examples of offences under **Common Law.**
5. What is the common name for **precedents in law** established through appeal or legal argument?
6. What does **SOCRATES** refer to and what case gave birth to both ADVOKATE and SOCRATES?
7. What are 'indictable offences'?
8. What is *'mens rea'* and with what is it linked?
9. What is a **Police Caution** and who can give it? (don't confuse this with the suspect caution).
10. Who could get a **Reprimand?**

Task 4: Powers—dogs (1)

Visit your local authority and identify what land has been designated by them under Dogs (Fouling of Land) Act 1996.

1. Having clearly seen a dog defecate on land that you know to be designated, you approach the person in charge of the dog, and request him or her to remove the faeces. S/he refuses, claiming that s/he was unaware of what the dog had done and will not accept a fixed penalty notice. Mindful of the person's claim to a reasonable excuse, would you go ahead and investigate this person for this offence?
2. In addition to your powers to deal with the problem of dogs fouling, what other preventative measures could you use?
3. What other organizations could you involve to support you?

Task 5: Powers—dogs (2)

Visit your local authority and identify what land is subject to the control of dogs and what offences are included within those dog control orders under section 55 of the Clean Neighbourhoods and Environment Act 2005.

1. You have clearly seen a dog and/or person in charge of the dog, on land that you know to be under a dog control order, commit an

---

offence relating to the control of dogs in your area. You approach the person and point out the offence to him or her and request his or her name and address for the purposes of issuing a fixed penalty notice. What methods and line of questioning will you use to verify the accuracy of his or her details?

2. In addition to your powers to deal with the problem of the control of dogs, what other preventative measures could you use?

3. What other organizations could you involve to support you?

Task 6: Powers—littering

1. Whilst on patrol in Tonchester you receive a complaint from a member of the public that empty fast food packaging is being left each evening on the communal stairs of a block of flats in your area. You visit the flats that evening and are welcomed inside by one of the residents at the main entrance door, which is normally locked. Having climbed the stairs, you are confronted by a pile of rubbish at the feet of a group of youths. Considering the offence of littering under section 87 of the Environmental Protection Act 1990, how will you deal with this situation?

2. In addition to your powers to deal with the problem of littering, what other preventative measures could you use?

3. What other organizations could you involve to support you?

Task 7: Powers—graffiti

1. Whilst on patrol in Tonchester you receive information from a member of the public that nearby youths are spraying graffiti on the walls of a home in which a family of Muslims live. On arrival you stand back at a distance and observe the last words being written of a slogan which reads '**For 7/7 you won't go to heaven, go to hell you muzlem** [*sic*] **murderers!**' Considering your powers to issue fixed penalty notices for graffiti and fly-posting only, which offence(s) would you investigate the suspects for?

2. In addition to your powers to deal with graffiti and fly-posting, what other preventative measures could you use?

3. What other organizations could you involve to support you?

Task 8: Powers—removal of vehicles

1. You are tasked to visit a resident in The Street, Tonchester, who wishes to complain about the incomplete chassis of a car which appears to have been dumped there in excess of a week. In relation

to the enabling legislation contained in Road Traffic Regulation Act 1984 only, consider whether the chassis of a car constitutes a 'vehicle' for the purposes of that legislation, whether you can remove it, and whether this is the correct piece of legislation to use.

2. In addition to your powers to deal with abandoned vehicles, what other preventative measures could you use?

3. What other organizations could you involve to support you?

Task 9: Powers—cyclists

1. A cyclist fails to stop for you while you are on patrol, and you are unable to speak to the person because it was physically impossible to get close to him or her. What means could you use to locate, identify, and successfully prosecute this person?

2. In addition to your powers to deal with the problem of cycling on a footpath, what other preventative measures could you use?

3. What other organizations could you involve to support you?

Task 10: Powers—stopping vehicles

1. The multi-agency team (including roads policing officers, Vehicle and Operator Services Agency staff, Department of Transport staff, HM Revenue and Customs officers) meet for a briefing at Tonchester Police Station to organize the day's operation as part of a campaign of testing vehicles for road safety. You are tasked with stopping vehicles for this purpose and to direct them into a lay-by. You are aware that your health and safety and that of the people around you is paramount. What are you going to consider to do your task as safely as possible?

Task 11: Powers—directing traffic (1)

On the day that an 'operating theatre' abnormal load passes through Tonchester, you are tasked to regulate the flow of traffic at a major junction in the town. You are asked by your supervisor to consider how you are going to give directions to drivers and pedestrians at the junction and, especially, how you are going to maintain health and safety issues. What will be your reply?

Task 12: Powers—directing traffic (2)

Early one morning during the rush hour, the traffic lights fail at a busy road junction in Tonchester. You are tasked to regulate the flow of vehicular and pedestrian traffic at the junction. You are asked by your supervisor to consider how you are going to give directions to drivers and pedestrians at the junction and, especially, how you are going to maintain health and safety issues. What will be your reply?

Task 13: Powers—road checks

1. The purpose of stopping the mechanically propelled vehicle in section 4 of the Police and Criminal Evidence Act 1984 in the majority of cases revolves around indictable offences. What are **indictable offences?** Give examples.
2. What defines a mechanically propelled vehicle? Give examples.
3. When carrying out such a road check and stopping vehicles, what health and safety considerations are you going to take into account?

Task 14: Powers—roads; placing signs

1. Research what signs appertain to the definition of '*object or device (whether fixed or portable) for conveying to traffic on roads or any specified class of traffic, warnings, information, requirements, restrictions or prohibitions of any description*' and note which ones you are likely to be placing.
2. If you have no power to require the name and address of a person who fails to comply with a sign placed by you, what alternative means do you have for dealing with a suspect who commits this offence?
3. What health and safety issues are you going to consider when you are placing the signs?

Task 15: Powers—trespass on a railway

1. What health and safety issues will you consider in relation to the investigation of this offence?
2. In addition to your powers to deal with the problem of trespassing on a railway, what other preventative measures could you use?
3. What other organizations could you involve to support you?

Task 16: Powers—throwing objects on a railway

1. When train drivers report the throwing of objects at railway carriages, but can only give approximate locations for the launch sites, how will you determine the areas from where the objects are being thrown?
2. In addition to your powers to deal with the problem of throwing stones or objects at railway equipment, what other preventative measures could you use?
3. What other organizations could you involve to support you?

Task 17: Powers—driving without care and attention

1. A mechanically-propelled vehicle is defined as any vehicle powered by mechanical means. There are three groups of mechanically propelled vehicles which are not included in the definition. These are listed in section 189 of the Road Traffic Act 1988. What are they?
2. How would you define 'without due care and attention' and 'reasonable consideration'?
3. In most instances when exercising your power to stop and seize what words are you going to use?
4. In addition to your powers to deal with the problem of vehicles being used to cause alarm, what other preventative measures could you use?
5. What other organizations could you involve to support you?

Task 18: Powers—searching premises

1. In addition to your limited power to enter and search premises to investigate licensing offences, what other things should you be considering?
2. If you suspect that such offences are being committed on premises, before you use your power to enter, which other parts of the police 'family' might you consider liaising with?

Task 19: Powers—consumption of alcohol (1)

1. What evidence could you gather to support your belief that the person you are investigating had been consuming alcohol?
2. As a result of the need at the time to inform the person concerned that failing without reasonable excuse to comply with your requirements is an offence, what will you actually say to the person?
3. As a result of the need at the time to inform the person concerned that failing without reasonable excuse to consent to being searched is an offence, what will you actually say?
4. What health and safety considerations should be taken into account when requiring a person to surrender alcohol?

Task 20: Powers—consumption of alcohol (2)

1. What evidence could you gather to support your belief that the person you are investigating was in possession of alcohol?
2. As a result of the need at the time to inform the person concerned that failing without reasonable excuse to comply with your requirements is an offence, what will you actually say to the person?
3. As a result of the need at the time to inform the person concerned that failing without reasonable excuse to consent to being searched is an offence, what will you actually say?
4. When you confiscate alcohol from a person under the age of 18 (who is also clearly drunk), what other factors do you need to take into account?

Task 21: Powers—confiscating tobacco

1. As a result of the need at the time to inform the person concerned that failing without reasonable excuse to consent to being searched is an offence, what will you actually say to him or her?
2. Given that Tonchester youths in the area seem bored and disillusioned, what effect might the confiscation of their cigarettes have on their attitudes to authority? Are other avenues open to you when dealing with this situation?

Task 22: Powers—seizing drugs

1. What are controlled drugs and how are they classified?
2. Who can have lawful possession of a controlled drug?
3. What do controlled drugs look like?
4. What health and safety implications are there in seizing drugs and retaining them for the appropriate disposal?

Task 23: Powers—enforce 'licensing offences'

1. What health and safety issues are you going to consider when dealing with offences that are alcohol related?
2. In addition to your powers to deal with alcohol-related offences what other preventative measures could you use?
3. What other organizations could you involve to support you?

Task 24: Powers—requiring name and address

1. There is no legal requirement for you to warn a person that it is an offence to fail to give you his or her name and address after you have required it when you are designated under paragraph 1A, but rather than enforcement, what persuasive measures will you apply to reach your objective?
2. What process will you go through to verify the identity and address of a person once s/he has given you his or her name and address?

Task 25: Powers—detention

1. What is **reasonable force?**
2. Before reverting to your powers to use reasonable force (if you are designated with them), what other methods of persuasion are you going to use to gain compliance?

Task 26: Powers—search and prevention of escape from lawful custody

Give examples of some of the reasonable grounds for believing that the person may present a danger to him or herself or escape lawful custody.

Task 27: Powers—photograph a person away from a police station

You are investigating a person for trespassing on railway property whom you suspect also of drawing graffiti on buildings in the St Sylvan's area. You have dealt with the person by way of a PND, but the suspect is wearing a full-face balaclava. You are aware that CCTV footage is held at the police station showing instances of a similar nature and you wish to take a photograph of your suspect to check against these images. What will you do now?

Task 28: Powers—to enforce byelaws

1. How will you research the list of '**relevant byelaws**' in your area?
2. If a constable has the power under the relevant byelaw to remove a person from a place, what will you think about when exercising this power yourself?

Task 29: Powers—FPNs for truancy

In 2005 the National Audit Office published a document entitled *Improving School Attendance in England*, * which stated that 'around 450,000 of the 6.7 million pupils in state-maintained schools in England miss school, equivalent to 13 days per year each. These pupils could fill 816 average-sized primary schools plus 252 average secondary schools'.

How are you going to help tackle this problem in your area?

* [See <http://www.nao.org.uk/publications/nao_reports/04-05/0405212.pdf> accessed October 2006.]

Task 30: Powers—'malicious, false and diversionary activities'

1. What types of networks and devices do you think are included in the offence of sending annoying or offensive messages via a public electronic communications network above?
2. If suspects for this offence are going to employ the telecommunications network to contact the police, what parts of your organization can you go to in order to see evidence?

Task 31: Powers—enter and search premises to save life and limb, or to prevent damage to property

1. What are the health and safety implications of using this power? (Refer to 3.2.30 above, to refresh your memory.)
2. Who else could you get support from?

Task 32: Powers—stop and search to prevent terrorist activity

Even though it is an offence to fail to comply with an order, prohibition, or restriction imposed by a PCSO in the area of cordon of a terrorist investigation, that does not stop anybody entering the crime scene if s/he is really determined to do so. What other legislation, if any, could help you in this situation?

Task 33: Powers—require name and address for anti-social behaviour

1. Under section 50 of PRA02 the term 'acting in an anti-social manner' is given the same meaning as in section 1 of the Crime and Disorder Act 1998: causing or *'likely to cause harassment, alarm or distress to one or more persons not of the same household as* [him/herself]'. How would you go on to define *'harassment, alarm or distress'*?
2. At what point does a person start to be sufficiently harassing, alarming, or distressing for you to investigate them and possibly issue a PND under section 5 of the Public Order Act 1986?

Task 34: Powers—disperse and remove to ... places of residence

1. If you remove a person under 16 to his or her place of residence, what further obligations do you have?
2. If you have reasonable grounds for believing that the person would be likely to suffer significant harm if removed to his or her place of residence, what would you do?
3. In addition to directing groups away from a designated area, what offence might you consider investigating them for?
4. Groups, by their very nature, vary in size and this will have an effect on the way you deal with them. What factors should you take into account before deciding to disperse a group?

Task 35: Powers—remove children (breach of curfew) to ... places of residence

1. If you remove a child to his/her place of residence, what further obligations do you have?
2. What is *significant harm*?

Task 36: Powers—begging and associated offences

If your area has people who are persistently begging in the street, what other organizations could you involve to support you?

Task 37: Powers—unlawful supply, possession, and misuse of fireworks

1. In relation to the prevention and detection of firework offences, what other organizations could you involve to support you?

> 2. During peak periods of firework use, what organizations will you
>   consider visiting to lessen the risk of firework misuse?
> 3. What health and safety issues will you consider when investigating
>   offences relating to fireworks?

**Task 38: Powers—threatening, abusive, or insulting
behaviour**

On your way to patrol the area around Nelson Mandela Buildings, you are
met by the Neighbourhood Watch coordinator and his wife and they ask
you to accompany them to their flat on the second floor of tower block
A. Just as you approach the tower block, a window on one of the fourth
floor flats opens and a voice is heard to shout, *'Taking your f***ing
kid for a walk or is it a fancy dress party? Everybody knows you're the
f***ing eyes and ears of the pigs, Mr and Mrs Sherlock f***ing Holmes!'*

Answer the following questions in relation to the offence of using
threatening, abusive, or insulting behaviour likely to cause harassment,
alarm or distress under section 5 of the Public Order Act 1986.

1. Can the offence be committed by the person shouting out from the
   privacy of his or her own flat?
2. If you had been on your own, might you have been harassed,
   alarmed, or distressed?
3. How will you get evidence of the suspect's intentions?
4. If the suspect was drunk, does the court recognize that as a
   defence?

8.5 Chapter 3—Answers to Tasks and Knowledge Tests

Task 1: Legal powers

You might have noted that it allows a chief officer to designate
anyone (support staff) in the Force as a PCSO if s/he so chooses,
but we go on to discuss this in more detail in Chapters 2 and 3.
And not just you, of course: the chief officer can designate powers
to a 'civilian' *investigator* (as distinct from a warrant-holding police
investigator), a *detention officer*, and an *escort officer*; and, if s/he
chooses, one individual can have several sets of powers, effectively
combining more than one role. All roles can be designated within
existing police support staff numbers; temporarily if need be.

The authors' views are captured in the main body of the text, but
you are, of course, at liberty to disagree with them. It might make

a useful **Discussion Point** if you and/or your colleagues are at significant variance from our views.

Task 2: Testing what you know about your legal powers

1. Because the Act pulls together lots of different things to do with policing, some of which are modifications or amendments of preceding legislation, and only a small part of which has to do with PCSOs. The same applies to the Police and Justice Act 2006, enacted in 2007, which tidies up many bits of legislation, including the provision of standard powers to PCSOs, though its primary purpose is to establish a National Policing Improvement Agency.

2. Community Support Officer, investigating officer, detention officer, and escort officer.

3. They are police staff, employed by the police authority specifically.

4. Locally elected representatives (councillors) and, in some Forces, JPs (magistrates).

5. To oversee the work of the Force, its effectiveness, efficiency, and value for money—including the budget—and to ensure that the community can be reassured that its concerns are being listened to.

6. The chief officer can require you to perform to expected and agreed standards.

7. That you are suitable, capable, and have been adequately trained.

8. A responsible citizen.

9. Physical fitness and the mental resilience to do the job properly.

10. The Force trains you and you agree to learn.

Task 3: Modes of trial and knowledge checks

1. **Failing to give name and address when required**—paragraph 1A(5) of Schedule 4 to the Police Reform Act 2002. *Mode of trial and penalty*: Summary—level three fine.

   Whilst driving a motor vehicle, neglects or refuses to comply with traffic directions given by a CSO—section 35 of the Road Traffic Act 1988

   Mode of trial and penalty: Summary—a fine not exceeding level three, discretionary disqualification, and obligatory endorsement with three penalty points, if committed in respect of a motor vehicle.

Damaging property, etc—section 1(1) of the Criminal Damage Act 1971

Mode of trial and penalty:

- If the value of the damage is **below** £5,000
  Summary—three months' imprisonment and/or a level four fine.
- If the value of the damage **exceeds** £5,000 then it becomes an either way offence:
  Summary—six months' imprisonment and/or a fine
  Indictment—ten years' imprisonment.

NB: The offence of **Damaging property** under section 1(1) of the Criminal Damage Act 1971 is unique but remains an **either way offence**, even though it is heard at a magistrates' court only when the value of the property is below £5,000 (see section 22 of the Magistrates' Courts Act 1980). There remain very few other offences where such a demarcation is made in the mode of trial as a result of the value of the property in question. Subsequently, as criminal damage remains an 'either way' offence, it is classed as an **indictable offence**.

2. (d).

3. (a) A proposal for an Act laid before Parliament.
   (b) It is a Statutory Instrument—all the force of law but not requiring a separate Act.
   (c) Local Authorities (but only within their defined boundaries).

4. Theft, assault, manslaughter, murder, rape, burglary, perverting the course of justice.

5. Case law.

6. Suspect descriptors, Observation by a witness of an offence, Clarity of witness' observation, Reasons to remember the suspect, Appearance of the suspect, Time between observation and identification, Errors of fact, Space between witness and suspect (distance); *R v Turnbull* [1976] 3 All ER 549.

7. Indictable offences are all offences that can be tried *either* in a magistrates' court or in a Crown Court (known as 'either way' offences), such as theft, AND all offences that can *only* be tried at a Crown Court, such as murder.

8. 'Guilty mind' + a criminal act ('actus reus') = liability.

9. A formal warning to an adult who has admitted guilt for an offence, delivered by 'a senior police officer'.

10. A juvenile; delivered by a police officer if the first offence is minor.

Task 4: Powers—dogs (1)

1. It would be for the court to decide but under these circumstances being unaware that the dog had fouled would probably not be a reasonable excuse. Therefore the person in charge of the dog should be reported for the offence, and a case file submitted so that a decision whether or not to prosecute can be made.

2. Patrol designated areas to provide high-profile preventative measures. Proactively consult local dog clubs, vets, homes for abandoned dogs, and place reminder posters in each locality. Hand out leaflets in the designated areas to dog owners reminding them of their responsibilities.

3. Consult with local authorities and request further signing and suitable receptacles for the dog excrement in the designated areas.

Task 5: Powers—dogs (2)

1. Using your communications system, request your Control to carry out voters' register checks on the name and address. Ask for a telephone number from the suspect that your Control room can call to verify the existence of the person. Ask him or her to show you identification such as a driving licence, credit card, or utility bill. If the person lives nearby, ask him or her to show you where s/he lives.

2. Patrol designated dog control areas to provide high-profile preventative measures. Proactively consult local dog clubs, vets, kennels, and homes for abandoned dogs. Place reminder posters in each locality if there is an abundance of offences being committed. Hand out leaflets in the areas to dog owners reminding them of their responsibilities.

3. Consult with local authorities and request further signing and suitable receptacles for dog excrement in the areas.

Task 6: Powers—littering

1. Clearly the communal stairs are a place to which the public have access but usually only those people who wish to visit flats there. The offence of littering under section 87 of the Environmental Protection Act 1990 can only be committed in an area which is open to the air, and because the front door of these flats is locked and access is only gained by people living in the flats or visitors, this offence cannot be used to deal with the matter.

2. Increase patrol frequency according to when the problem is most prevalent to act as a preventative measure. On private land in the open air where rubbish is dumped by fly-tippers, inform land owners that they can seek the advice of the local authority, which can bring prosecutions under the Refuse Disposal (Amenity) Act 1978. In blocks of flats, encourage residents' associations to discourage the use of communal areas for eating and to place signs and rubbish bins.

3. Encourage housing associations and local authorities to place signs and litter bins to combat the problem. Visit schools with members of local health authorities to educate people about the health hazards of waste, littering, and discarded food.

Task 7: Powers—graffiti

1. The offence in this illustration is obviously racially or religiously motivated. Therefore, your powers do not extend to issuing a penalty notice for such offences which are aimed at people based upon their membership of a racial or religious group. Such criminal offences should be investigated by the police and prosecuted in court, since much higher penalties can be given to offenders found guilty of racially aggravated offences.

2. High-profile patrolling of areas worst affected. Identification of the purchase point of the resources used to damage or destroy property, such as shops and DIY stores. Employ the use of static or mobile CCTV. Identify the 'tag' (signature) of the graffiti artist through house-to-house enquiries and visits to schools and clubs. Education of people to the effect of criminal damage and the danger to road users from the defacement of signs.

3. If specific but remote places are being targeted for graffiti, owing to a lack of security, consider tracing the owners of property to mend fences and gates. Exchange information between you and owners of property so that they can support any initiatives you or partnership organizations may propose or develop. Ask local shops to support you with information regarding the sale of graffiti artist equipment and suggest to them a sales policy to limit their use. Employ further partnership members, such as local councils, to support initiatives to provide better lighting to darkened areas in order to discourage the causing of damage.

Task 8: Powers—removal of vehicles

1. Even though the chassis is not a complete car, in this section *'vehicle' means any vehicle, whether or not it is in a fit state for use on roads, and includes any chassis or body, with or without wheels, appearing to have formed part of such a vehicle, and any load carried by, and anything attached to, such a vehicle.* A chassis would therefore be included as a 'vehicle'. However, your powers only relate to obstructions which are a matter of urgency that would affect people using a road currently or in the future, thereby preventing situations such as large traffic jams. Situations such as this would be better suited to regulation 5 of the Removal and Disposal of Vehicles Regulations 1986 which give powers to representatives of local authorities to remove or dispose of broken-down, illegally parked, or abandoned vehicles.

2. Be proactive: patrol high-profile areas where a vehicle that was left to remain in a vulnerable place on a road would cause long delays and misery to other people using the road. If particular drivers are continually leaving their vehicles so as to cause an obstruction, display signs at the premises they are occupying or visiting. Send informative letters and announce the likely outcome of removal if they persistently cause obstructions that require urgent resolution.

3. Gain the confidence of local newspapers, radio, and other media to broadcast appeals to members of the public to avoid obstructing vulnerable places. Win the support of local authority representatives who have similar responsibilities to share information and intelligence.

Task 9: Powers—cyclists

1. Increase your local knowledge by making house-to-house enquiries and visiting shops and schools nearby with the description of the cycle and cyclist. The cycle may be distinctive and therefore you could use that as a memory trigger for the people that you ask. Contact your intelligence department and request that other staff in the police family identify the suspect from their local knowledge. Check if there is any CCTV in the area that may have captured the incident.

2. Increase patrol frequency according to when the problem is most prevalent. Visit schools, youth clubs, and local organizations to point out the dangers of riding on a footpath. Consider the adaptation of temporary hazard signs to warn of your presence in the area to detect such offences.

3. Consult with local authorities and request further signing in the areas where the problem is greatest. Request the assistance of other members of the police family to help you to be in two places at once: at each end of a road, for example.

Task 10: Powers—stopping vehicles

- Ensure that the stopping distance is adequate for drivers to pull over, and that there is plenty of space in the lay-by for them to do so. **Ensure that drivers can see you as they approach.**
- Wearing **high-visibility clothing** and your uniform, give clear and obvious hand and arm directions as indicated by the diagrams below from the Highway Code: <http://www.highway-code.gov.uk/signs03.htm> accessed October 2006.
- **Look directly at the driver** of the vehicle you are stopping, to gain good eye contact with him or her.
- Confirm that the driver is aware of what you are directing him or her to do.

Signals by authorized persons

Stop traffic approaching from the front   *To beckon traffic on approaching from the side*

* In Wales, bilingual signs appear on emergency services vehicles and clothing.

High visibility

- Wear high-visibility clothing which has been issued to you personally or lent to you for the duration of the road check.
- Make sure it is comfortable and is the right size for you so that you can still see clearly and move easily.
- Check that cones and signs have been placed, warning drivers that they are approaching pedestrians and parked vehicles.

Layout of the road check

- Check that you personally have an escape route to take should the drivers fail to stop or fail to see you. **Be alert to your health and safety and that of others at all times.**
- Make sure appropriate traffic-calming equipment (such as cones) is in place to slow vehicles down as they approach the road check.
- Clarify your role with your supervisor.

NB—NEVER TURN YOUR BACK TO ONCOMING TRAFFIC!

Task 11: Powers—directing traffic (1)

- To give clear and obvious hand and arm directions as indicated by the following diagrams from the Highway Code: <http://www.highwaycode.gov.uk/signs03.htm> accessed October 2006.
- To look at the driver of the vehicle or pedestrian you are stopping, to gain good eye contact with them.
- To confirm that the driver or pedestrian is aware of what you are directing him or her to do.

Signals by authorized persons

Stop traffic approaching from both front and behind

To beckon traffic on from the front

* In Wales, bilingual signs appear on emergency services vehicles and clothing.

High visibility

- Wear high-visibility clothing which has been issued to you personally or lent to you for the duration of the traffic control.
- Make sure it is comfortable and is the right size for you so that you can still see clearly and move easily.

Communication

Check that your communication equipment is working when you take up your position at the junction and that you are notified when the abnormal load is nearing your location.

Task 12: Powers—directing traffic (2)

- To give clear and obvious hand and arm directions as indicated by the following diagrams from the Highway Code: <http://www.highwaycode.gov.uk/signs03.htm> accessed October 2006.
- To look directly at the driver of the vehicle or pedestrian you are stopping, to gain good eye contact with him or her.
- To confirm that the driver or pedestrian is aware of what you are directing him or her to do.

Signals by authorized persons to stop traffic

Traffic approaching from the front *Traffic approaching from both front and behind* *Traffic approaching from behind*

Signals by authorized persons to beckon traffic on

From the side *From the front* *From behind*

Task 13: Powers—road checks

1. Indictable offences are all offences that can be tried **either** in a magistrates' court or in a Crown Court (known as 'either way' offences), such as theft, AND all offences that can **only** be tried

at a Crown Court, such as murder. To ascertain the mode of trial or classification of an offence you will need to refer to other books in the Blackstone's series, such as *The Student Police Officer Handbook* (2009).

2. A mechanically propelled vehicle is any vehicle that has an engine powered by any kind of fuel including petrol, diesel, gas, or coal. It therefore includes not only motor vehicles that have been designed or adapted for use on the roads, but also vehicles that are designed for use off-road, such as dumper trucks and agricultural vehicles.

3. *The safe stopping of vehicles*
   - To give clear and obvious hand and arm directions as indicated by the diagrams from the Highway Code in the task at the end of the **Power to control traffic for purposes other than escorting a load of exceptional dimensions** and <http://www.highwaycode.gov.uk/signs03.htm> accessed October 2006.
   - To look directly at the driver of the vehicle or pedestrian you are stopping, to gain good eye contact with him or her.
   - To confirm that the driver is aware of what you are directing him or her to do.

   High visibility
   - Wear high-visibility clothing which has been issued to you personally or lent to you for the duration of the traffic control.
   - Make sure it is comfortable and is the right size for you so that you can still see clearly and move easily.

   Communication
   - Check that your communication equipment is working when you take up your position on the road check.

Task 14: Powers—roads; placing signs

1. Signs would include no-waiting cones, Police-Slow, Police-Accident, Diversion, etc.

2. Consider delivering a verbal warning. Even though you have no power you can still ask the person for his or her name and address. Alternatively seek the assistance of a police officer to deal with the suspect.

3. Wear high-visibility clothing at all times. Remember your fast road network training and never turn your back on oncoming traffic. Slow vehicles down in the area before placing the signs and try to create a physical barrier between you and the moving traffic around you.

Task 15: Powers—trespass on a railway

1. Of paramount importance is the fact that railways and railway lines are very dangerous places. High-voltage electricity runs along the railway line either at ground level or overhead. Research your own Force's policy for going on to railway property and do not attempt to go near the railway line until you have been told it is safe to do so by your Control room. The 'lead' is usually with British Transport Police in all matters to do with crimes on the railways.

2. Increase your patrols in areas where trespassing has been reported. If you find damaged fencing, contact the Railway Board relative to the stretch of line in which you find the holes through to the track. Request that the Board mends the fencing as a matter of urgency. Ask the Board to consider lighting such 'hotspot areas' to deter would-be trespassers. Consider visiting schools and youth clubs in the local areas to warn young people of the dangers of trespassing on railway property.

3. Be aware that it is unlikely that any other parts of railway property will be included in this offence as they are not listed, such as station buildings and platforms. You will therefore need to liaise with British Transport Police to find a solution. If there is doubt as to the ownership of various properties which are being used to gain access to the railway, go to local authorities and negotiate to bring organizations together to deal with the problem.

Task 16: Powers—throwing objects on a railway

1. Consider areas which have ready access to and from the scene. Areas more likely to be targeted are those which are fairly discreet or that have an easy escape route. High ground can be of use to suspects as they can see trains approaching from some distance. Bridges are a good place to look, particularly if they do not have safety fencing to stop the missiles being thrown.

2. Increase your patrols along the areas which are more likely to be where the objects are thrown from. Consider monitoring CCTV cameras for the movement of possible suspects. Consider visiting schools and youth clubs in the local areas to warn young people of the dangers of throwing objects at railway equipment.

3. Liaise with British Transport Police to find a solution. Go to the authorities who maintain property adjacent to the railway and request that higher and stronger fencing is erected to deter missile-throwing activities.

Task 17: Powers—driving without care and attention

1. • Pedestrian-controlled mowing machines
   • Other pedestrian-controlled vehicles
   • Electrically-assisted pedal cycles approved by the Secretary of State.

2. 'Without due care and attention' would mean driving in an incompetent manner not normally associated with following the guidelines of the Highway Code, for example. Driving without 'reasonable consideration' would involve causing other road users problems, danger, or anxiety. The stunts pulled by drivers who carry out handbrake turns, 'donuts' (wheel spinning in a circle), and drag racing would therefore be examples of one or both of the above.

3. Examples would include:
   'You have been driving:
   • without due care and attention, or
   • without reasonable consideration for other persons using the road or public place under section 3 of the Road Traffic Act 1988, or
   • on to or upon any common land, moorland, or
   • on any road being a footpath, bridleway, or restricted byway,
   • in a manner which is causing, or is likely to cause or has caused alarm, distress, or annoyance to members of the public.
   I must warn you that if you continue to use the vehicle in the same way or if you repeat the same use on another occasion, I can seize the vehicle under section 59 of the Police Reform Act 2002.'

4. Increase your patrols in areas where such activity has been reported. Speak to the drivers and ascertain their attitude towards the rest of the community, and how much it may be alarming other people. Talk to community members.

5. Liaise with local authorities to consider traffic-calming measures and work with other members of the police family to put an end to the alarm caused by the drivers and riders. Utilize police motorcyclists on large areas of land which are difficult

for you to negotiate. Request local authorities to create pedestrian-only entrances to large expanses of land which cannot then be used by mechanically propelled vehicles.

Task 18: Powers—searching premises

1. Research your local policy for entering licensed premises. It may be that you have to notify a supervisor that you are entering such premises, even if you suspect an offence is being committed and you are in the company of a police officer.

2. The police service is the eyes and ears of the licensing authority. Your Force will probably have licensing officers who have the responsibility for monitoring licensed premises. You will need to keep them informed of your suspicions and intentions.

Task 19: Powers—consumption of alcohol (1)

1. Look at the person's eyes. Are they glazed and do they appear unfocused? Do they wander from the object they are looking at? Do they roll in a lazy manner? Is the person's speech slurred and is s/he unsteady on his or her feet? Does the person's breath smell of intoxicating liquor?

2. Examples might include:
   'I am PCSO [Name] and this area has been designated as a place in which alcohol cannot be consumed. I have reason to believe that you have been/are intending to drink alcohol and I require you to stop drinking now and give me all of your container(s) of alcohol, including the one(s) you have been drinking from. I must inform you that if you fail to comply with my requirements without reasonable excuse, you commit an offence for which you can be arrested.'

3. Examples might include:
   'I am Police Community Support Officer [Name] and I am attached to [Name of police station]. I wish to search you using a power under paragraph 7A(2) of Schedule 4 to the Police Reform Act 2002. The grounds for my search include that this area is designated, that I believe:
   - you are or
   - have been consuming, or
   - intend to consume alcohol here,
   that I required you to surrender anything in your possession that is alcohol or a container for it, and you failed to do so. The

object of my search is to find alcohol or alcohol containers. I must warn you that that failing without reasonable excuse to consent to being searched is an offence.'

4. This may lead to a confrontation and your primary consideration should be for your own safety and for that of any members of the public in the vicinity. Depending on the amount of alcohol he or she has consumed, the person required to give up the alcohol may become belligerent and aggressive. Make sure that you have access to your communication equipment as well as ensuring that you have a free line for exit (as you learned in 5.5.3.5 above). If your local requirements for the disposal of alcohol include tipping it away, be aware that this may represent a considerable monetary outlay for the person concerned, who may not take kindly to you pouring it down the drain whilst he or she is watching. At all times, assess the likelihood that the exercise of your powers may provoke a hostile reaction.

Task 20: Powers—consumption of alcohol (2)

1. There is little problem when the alcohol is contained in a manufactured receptacle which is easily recognizable, such as a beer can or bottle with labels. The situation is slightly more complicated when the person has siphoned the alcohol into a completely anonymous container, such as a 'fizzy' drinks bottle, can, or kitchen vessel. You will then need to supply evidence of the colour of the liquid and the smell. However, *do not* be tempted to taste the liquid.

2. Examples might include:
   'I am PCSO [Name] and this is a relevant place for the purposes of investigating people under 18 or anybody else in their company, who are in possession of alcohol. I reasonably suspect that you:
   • are under 18,
   • intend the alcohol to be consumed by a person under 18, or
   • are with, or have recently been with, a person under 18 who has consumed alcohol.
   I now require you to surrender all of your container(s) of alcohol, including the one(s) you have been drinking from [if applicable] to me. I also require you to state your name and address please. I must inform you that if you fail to comply with my requirements without reasonable excuse, you commit an offence for which you can be detained.'

3. Examples might include:
'I am Police Community Support Officer [Name] and I am attached to [Name of police station]. I wish to search you using a power under paragraph 7A(2) of Schedule 4 to the Police Reform Act 2002. The grounds for my search include that this is a relevant area, that I reasonably suspect you are in possession of alcohol or containers, and that either you:
   • are under 18, or
   • intend the alcohol to be consumed by a person under 18 in a relevant place, or
   • are, or have recently been, in the company of a person under 18 who has consumed alcohol in a relevant place.
I asked you to surrender anything in your possession that was alcohol or a container for it and you failed to do so. The object of my search is to find alcohol or alcohol containers. I must warn you that that failing without reasonable excuse to consent to being searched is an offence.'

4. You must take into account the needs of the young person involved. For example, because there is a duty of care involved, it would be appropriate to arrange for the person to be taken home. If there is no one at home, you will need to contact your supervisor to arrange an alternative. Depending on the age of the person, you may consider informing his or her parents/guardians, so that they are aware. Whilst this may be time-consuming, the outcome of not doing it, and the person suffering harm on the way home alone, could be damaging. If it was a young woman who is drunk, for example, she could be vulnerable to attack or assault if left to make her own way home. Think too about how parents/guardians might react; ensure that there is no likelihood of violence towards the young person. Pay some attention too to whether the alcohol was obtained on the young person's behalf by another, or whether the off-licence or pub where the alcohol was sold made efforts to ascertain the age of the purchaser.

Task 21: Powers—confiscating tobacco

1. Examples might include:
'I am Police Community Support Officer [Name] and I am attached to [Name of police station]. I wish to search you using a power under paragraph 7A(3) of Schedule 4 to the Police Reform Act 2002. The grounds for my search include that you are apparently under 16 years of age, that I saw you smoking in a street (or

public place), and that I asked you to give me the tobacco and you failed to do so. The object of my search is to find tobacco or cigarette papers. I must warn you that failing without reasonable excuse to consent to being searched is an offence.'

2. If the youths are aged 14 or 15, it is not too surprising that they smoke, and many of us may have started experimenting with the habit at this age. The potentially damaging reaction to you exercising your powers may be that you become yet another authority figure not to be trusted. As a result, you may lose your impact on these people, who themselves form a part of the community from which you would want useful intelligence. This is not to say that you condone their smoking, or that you allow them to smoke in your presence, but rather that you offer them a choice, so that they can modify their behaviour. Seizure of their tobacco could give them kudos or street credibility, and you may inadvertently confirm that smoking is cool. Don't lose a chance to tell them about the health damage caused by smoking, and reinforce messages about the positive health benefits of *not* smoking rather than the merely negative. If the children are much younger than 14 to 16, then it would be reasonable to seize the tobacco and inform their parents or guardians.

Task 22: Powers—seizing drugs

1. Controlled drugs are those drugs which the Secretary of State has decided can only be lawfully possessed by people who are authorized to do so. The drugs are controlled because of their effect on the human body if they are consumed and they are categorized into three classes, depending on the severity of effect; starting with Class A containing those drugs which have the most effect, and Class C which contain drugs which have the least effect. The groups are very large but examples in each class are given below with their modes of trial:

Class A
Heroin, Cocaine, and LSD
Mode of trial
Triable either way.

Class B
Amphetamines, Ecstasy, Cannabis leaves and Cannabis Resin (including 'skunk')
Mode of trial
Triable either way.

Class C
Diazepam and Temazepam
Mode of trial
Triable either way.

2. Professional people, such as medical practitioners, postal workers during transportation, police officers, and PCSOs when seizing controlled drugs from another person, can possess them lawfully.

3. Some of the drugs in Classes B and C will look like the carefully manufactured tablets that you receive from your doctor. Most of the others will come in various colours, shapes, sizes, and textures. They will not be carefully manufactured and will be sealed in small brown containers with white tops. They will have been manufactured in very dirty conditions in criminal laboratories. Therefore, any substance you find which you do not recognize, packaged in this way, could be a controlled drug.

4. You must consider your own health and safety and always exercise the appropriate level of care in handling controlled substances. It is always advisable to wear plastic gloves for such searches (these are normally obtained from the custody suite and carried with you for such circumstances) and you should have received training in how to search without risk from 'sharps' (needles or blades). If you haven't, ask your occupational health staff for advice.

Task 23: Powers—enforce 'licensing offences'

1. Alcohol affects different people in different ways. Some are very happy, giggly, and not confrontational. Others are completely the opposite and become aggressive and uncontrollable. There is a lot of scope in between and always the added variant of swinging from one mood to another. Remain constantly on the alert when dealing with such people. Dynamically assess risk as often as possible when dealing with such people, so that you expect the unexpected.

2. Liaise as much as possible with your Force's licensing officer, who deals directly with the licensing authorities, licensees, and licensed premises. Feed information to this officer, especially about where people who commit alcohol-related offences appear to be obtaining their alcohol. Remember that a number of these offences can be committed by anybody, not just those

who are connected to licensed premises; therefore the offence of selling alcohol to a person under 18 could just as easily be committed by a person who 'bootlegs' alcohol from abroad and then sells it back home from his or her car or house.

3. Visit schools and youth clubs in your area to send out the message that drinking alcohol under age is not only unlawful but dangerous. If possible, obtain statistics from your local hospital as to how many young people are admitted as a result of drinking alcohol, and how many are unfortunate enough to have been seriously ill, or who may have lost their lives. Work with local licensed premises to create as many barriers as possible to people under 18 purchasing alcohol.

Task 24: Powers—requiring name and address

1. As an example, use negotiation to try and persuade the person to give you his or her name and address. Explain the consequences of not only committing the offence for which you are investigating him or her, but also of the further offence s/he will commit if s/he does not give you his or her name and address. If you are designated under paragraph 2, S4PRA02, also advise him or her that, in the meantime, s/he may be required to wait with you until the arrival of a police officer.

2. Depending on what system of communication you are using, ask your Control room to check on local databases for the person's details. Ask Control room for voters' register checks on the person's address. Ask the suspect for a telephone number and ask Control room to call the number to verify that the person is who s/he says s/he is. Ask the suspect for identification details, such as a driving licence.

Task 25: Powers—detention

1. There is no definition of 'reasonable force' in any Act of Parliament. Therefore, because it is a question of fact and not a question of law, courts have to make a decision based upon the circumstances. As a guide, you should consider reasonable force in terms of a car which is rolling down a hill towards you. If you want to stop that car from running you over, you will have to use the same force as that with which it is moving towards you. If you want to push the car away from you, then

you not only have to equal the force of the car, but better it **slightly** to get it going in the opposite direction. Similarly, reasonable force consists of matching the force you are met with and using **slightly** more to achieve compliance.

2. You can try tact, diplomacy, and communication skills to negotiate a successful outcome. Outline to the suspect the consequences of making off, and the further offence s/he will commit, and appeal to his/her better nature to remain with you. You may be helped by members of the public should they see that you are in difficulties, but do not rely upon that happening. Try to narrow down the number of escape routes the suspect can take, such as talking to them in shop doorways. But always remember your health and safety and that of the people around you in such circumstances.

Task 26: Powers—search and prevention of escape from lawful custody

The person you detain may:

- continue to put his or her hands in his or her pockets even when you ask him or her not to
- place his or her hands inside his or her pockets, fists clenched as if s/he is holding something
- stand with his or her hands outside his or her pockets, fists clenched as if s/he is holding something
- appear anxious, sweat, breathe at a fast rate, have flushed cheeks, avert his or her eyes in a way that makes you believe s/he will soon use an item to help him or her escape
- have been seen earlier by a witness with an item that you can no longer see on his or her person.

Task 27: Powers—photograph a person away from a police station

Clearly, you are investigating a PND offence and can require a photograph for the purposes of detecting other crime. You should therefore request that the person removes his/her balaclava by saying for example:

'I am PCSO [Name]. I have issued you with a penalty notice for disorder and wish to take a photograph of you to compare with other images in this area of people taking part in similar activities, to establish whether or not you are liable to arrest for other offences. Please remove the item of clothing which is covering your face. Failure to do so may result in me removing the item myself.'

If the person then refuses, you have the power to use **reasonable force** (see answer to Task 25 on using reasonable force to prevent a detained person making off) to remove the face covering yourself.

In similar circumstances where cultural dress is being worn, be sensitive to such issues and, in all cases where the circumstances allow, use a member of the police family of the same gender to remove the item.

Task 28: Powers—to enforce byelaws

1. Go to the website of your relevant body and look for the list of 'relevant byelaws'. Go to your own Force's information databases to see if it is contained there. The criminal justice department of your Force may also hold the list.
2. If a constable has the power under the relevant byelaw to remove a person from a place, then you must only use **reasonable force** (see answer to Task 25 on using reasonable force to prevent a detained person making off) to exercise this power yourself.

Task 29: Powers—FPNs for truancy

Be proactive in your area. Do not take for granted when you see a child or a group of children that they are on a teacher-training day (now called an 'inset day', it used to be called a 'Baker day', which you may still hear), which may well be the excuse if you challenge them. Get a list of school holidays from your local schools as well as their additional (inset) training days. Find out from those schools who are the most likely truants and where they are most likely to be during the school day. Patrol the likely areas where truanting pupils might be 'hanging about'. A recent study showed that there appears to be a causative link between truancy and suspension/expulsion from school and subsequent criminal careers. For example, 176,000 schoolchildren were suspended in 2008, and 86% of under-18 male inmates in young offender institutions had been expelled from school.[1] In other words, truancy and suspension/expulsion can be potent catalysts in turning young people to crime. In partnership with schools and education departments, PCSOs could be in the front line to stop this happening. Therefore it is important that you liaise with local authority personnel who have the responsibility for investigating the truanting/suspended/expelled pupils and their families and exchange information. Lastly, be prepared that, when you challenge the parents of the truanting pupils, they might not be supportive of your efforts (see 5.5 above, on aggression). Another point to make is that, as well as pupils having 'inset' days off school, many schoolchildren today are on 'truncated timetables' (sometimes referred to as '*the golden curriculum*') which limit the time they actually spend in the school grounds. For example, they could be spending a day at college on a vocational course, or they could be on a 'work experience' attachment. The difficulty comes in knowing all the different kinds of timetable, relating to which age groups. Some schools, for example, allow Year 11 pupils (aged around 16) not to attend school except for GCSE examinations during the exam 'season' (May/June). The best solution for you, and to ensure that you get it right, is to make contact with the schools in your area and establish who is on what timetable. This may help you to establish a good rapport with schoolchildren. For example, your popularity rating would soar if you were able to tell any disapproving adult, in the schoolchildren's hearing, that the pupils were on authorized absence and that they are not 'skiving' or 'bunking off'. Of such interventions are enduring relationships made.

Task 30: Powers—'Malicious, false and diversionary activities'

1. This offence does not just apply to the terrestrial systems such as landline telephone networks to include phone calls and faxes, but also applies to extra-terrestrial networks such as mobile telephones and texts. It also includes combinations of both, such as cable TV via a satellite, and e-mails via computers.

2. If suspects use the telecommunications network to contact the police to cause wasteful employment, then consider the use of the **Nuisance Caller Bureau** within your Force, which will have the capability of working with service providers to trace calls that are made. In addition, your Control room will almost certainly be recording all the calls that are made to them, as well as logging the times that the calls are made. You therefore have a very good chance, even with mobile phone technology, of identifying a suspect. Be aware yourself of diversionary tactics as you patrol your area. For example, if you are intercepted by a person who is struggling to find something to say to you but who insists on engaging you in conversation, s/he may be stopping you from walking round the corner where a crime is being committed.

Task 31: Powers—enter and search premises to save life and limb, or to prevent damage to property

1. The health and safety implications are plentiful and can be complex. Consideration must be given to the following:
   - Your Force policy
   - The potential risks and hazards
   - The risk of injury to you
   - The risk of injury or further injury to you and the people around you
   - The risk of insecure or damaged property around you
   - The risk of not achieving your objective as a result of inexperience
   - Your physical capability
   - The extent of your personal safety equipment.

   Remember to stay in control of both yourself and the situation, do not be tempted to do something that will put you in danger because you feel pressured to do something. Remember the Rules of Engagement and the fact that your life is as precious as anybody else's.

2. The fire and rescue services are very well equipped to deal with most emergencies. Use your communications equipment to summon them. In addition, there are other members of the police family who are very well equipped to deal with some emergencies, such as specialist search teams, marine units, and helicopters.

Task 32: Powers—stop and search to prevent terrorist activity

One answer is to use lawful and reasonable force to dissuade the person. The legislation that outlines this lawful force which is available to **everybody, not just police officers or PCSOs**, is section 3(1) of the Criminal Law Act 1967. It states: '*A person may use such force as is reasonable in the circumstances in the prevention of crime, or in effecting or assisting in the lawful arrest of offenders or suspected offenders or of persons unlawfully at large.*' Therefore, once you have pointed out that s/he would be committing an offence by entering the cordon, you can use reasonable force to prevent that crime taking place.

Task 33: Powers—require name and address for anti-social behaviour

1. The meaning of '*harassment, alarm or distress*' is important to your powers in relation to both section 50 of the Police Reform Act 2002 (requiring a person's name and address) and section 5

of the Public Order Act 1986 (which is the offence of causing harassment, alarm and distress). Legislation does not define the terms, just as it does not define the term '*reasonable force*'. The terms are subjective: a question of fact for courts to decide upon and therefore not a question of law. The words should therefore be given their ordinary dictionary meanings:

> **Harassment:** To feel annoyed, persecuted, irritated, or aggravated
> **Alarm:** To feel surprised, frightened, terrorized, or panicked
> **Distress:** To feel suffering, anguish, or misery.

A further note is that it is always important to understand the point of view of the 'victim' of anti-social behaviour. Seeing the situation through his or her eyes constitutes an important part of the PCSO's community role. Whilst such empathy with another's views can seem tepid to some, and whilst it will not always provide a true picture of what is going on, it does help you to understand **why** the person feels harassed, alarmed, or distressed. For example, a call to speak to elderly residents who complain about children playing football in the street (this is a very common complaint) may at first seem trivial and the product of a 'generation gap'. But when you speak to the elderly people, it may be that the real issue is about the ball constantly hitting the house wall and it is this which is causing them alarm. Establishing the perspective in this way reveals the real reason for the complaint. Rather than demonizing the children, your intervention now is about deflecting the activity, not stopping it. Such outcomes can leave both sides satisfied.

2. This will depend almost entirely upon the circumstances surrounding the behaviour of the group or individual. Criminal liability includes not only the criminal act (*actus reus*) but also the guilty mind (*mens rea*). Therefore, you will have to investigate each case to decide whether or not the individual or group **intended** to cause '*harassment, alarm or distress*' which would amount to an offence under the Public Order Act 1986, or whether s/he **caused** '*harassment, alarm or distress*' without intent, in which case you only need to ask for his or her name and address under section 50 of the Police Reform Act 2002.

Task 34: Powers—disperse and remove to ... places of residence

1. You must make a PNB entry surrounding the incident and you have a further obligation to notify the local authority of the removal (refer to your local policy).

2. One person's belief of the likelihood of suffering significant harm is sometimes another person's normal way of life. The standard of your own living conditions may be different from other people's standards. If you have any doubts about the likelihood of an under-16-year-old suffering significant harm if removed to his or her place of residence, then summon the assistance of a police officer who can consider using his or her powers under the Children Act 1989, such as taking the child into police protection.

3. If you had reasonable grounds for believing that the presence or behaviour of that group resulted, or was likely to result, in any members of the public being intimidated, harassed, alarmed, or distressed, then you should also consider investigating them under section 5 of the Public Order Act 1986 (causing harassment, alarm, or distress).

4. The primary consideration must be your own health and safety and therefore you should take the following into account:
   • The numbers in the group
   • The behaviour exhibited; is alcohol involved which might inflame the situation?
   • Do you know the group? Do you have a good rapport with them?
   • Is it a mixed group? Sometimes boys will misbehave in order to show off
   • Are you on single patrol? How far away is back-up?
   • What physical barriers could prevent you withdrawing?

Task 35: Powers—remove children (breach of curfew) to ... places of residence

1. You must make a PNB entry surrounding the incident and you have a further duty to notify the local authority of the contravention of the curfew (refer to your local policy). Local authorities then have a requirement to have a social worker visit the family of the child within 48 hours of being notified about the contravention of the curfew.

2. This is not specifically defined and remains, to a large extent, subjective and a question of fact. However, section 31(1) of the Children Act 1989 gives the guidance 'that the harm or likelihood of harm, is attributable to:

   (i) the care given to [him/her], or likely to be given to [him/her] if the order were not made, not being what would be reasonable to expect a parent to give to [him/her]; or
   (ii) the child's being beyond parental control'.

Task 36: Powers—begging and associated offences

There will be charitable organizations in your area or organizations which can put homeless people in contact with charities, sheltered accommodation, and the like. Liaise with these organizations to find out what criteria they require to be met. Be aware that not all beggars are homeless, nor are all by any means penniless. There are some criminals who make a very good living from asking for money and may well need to be investigated, perhaps for deception offences under the Theft Act. Use your experience and databases in Control room to verify a person's identity. Whilst this does not apply to all beggars, it is worth considering that many people begging are doing so to support a drug habit, or they may be homeless because suitable accommodation is not available for people with mental health issues. Either of these categories may be reluctant to cooperate with an authority figure, so you should consider carefully the manner in which you approach the beggar and you must think about the language you are going to use. If you feel that the situation may become a bit fraught, because the person has been using quite aggressive begging techniques, you may feel that you want back-up before you approach the individual. Alternatively, some cases of begging may be the product of other social factors and a long-term solution might be to consider a partnership approach with other agencies.

Task 37: Powers—unlawful supply, possession, and misuse of fireworks

1. Liaise with local authority staff with the responsibility towards retail and wholesale suppliers and the safe use of fireworks. Contact your local Trading Standards for information on hotspots regarding the sale of fireworks. Seek out your local fire and rescue service and join with them in their campaign against firework misuse. Given that the exemptions regarding the use of some fireworks apply to various faith and ethnic groups, you may be able to develop opportunities to gain access to these groups, and provide them with information on the legislative issues involved. This ensures that your approach is 'community engagement' and is not coercive. It also allows you to identify various groups within the community with whom you need to establish meaningful contacts, which may then go beyond the simple issue of fireworks.
2. Schools, youth clubs, local newsletters, shops, and other retail outlets that sell fireworks are all appropriate areas

in which to spread the crime prevention message. Firework injury statistics can be viewed at <http://www.dti.gov.uk/consumers/Safety/fireworks-policy/statistics/page29032.html> accessed August 2006.

3. The reason why fireworks are categorized and restrictions placed on their sale is because they are potentially life threatening. Whilst investigating reports from people who have been put in danger by their misuse, you could potentially become the target of someone's stupidity yourself. Dynamically assess the risks in the environment that you find yourself in at regular intervals. Do not put yourself in danger.

Task 38: Powers—threatening, abusive, or insulting behaviour

1. Yes, it can. The offence can be committed in a private or public place, so long as the conduct can be seen or heard in public. In the description of the task, the conduct took place in a private flat, but it was clearly observed by the PCSO and the Neighbourhood Watch couple, who were all in a public place outside the block of flats. If the conduct had taken place in the **flat** and could only have been observed in that same flat or another private flat **without** having been observed in public, then no offence would have been committed.

2. Yes, you could be. However, as a member of the police family, you are expected to be harassed, alarmed, or distressed only when the conduct you observe is more than you usually have to put up with in the course of your duty. Whether it rose above that threshold will be a question of fact for the courts to decide and a subjective test of your evidence of being harassed, alarmed, or distressed. If you are in the company of other people, as was the case in this example, then when you are the target of such conduct, evidence can be given by the people in hearing or sight of it.

3. Having cautioned the suspect, manage the conversation (interview) by asking such questions as, 'Why did you do it?', 'What did you hope to achieve by doing that?', 'How many times before have you done that?', 'Who else was around at the time?', 'What do you think the other people made of what you said/did?'

4. No, drunkenness will not be seen by the court to be a defence or an excuse, if it was self-induced. A drunken person will be seen to have acted in the same way as s/he would have acted had

s/he been sober. Difficulties only arise if the suspect can prove that his/her intoxication had been induced by somebody else, for instance that his/her drinks had been spiked. In this case the person may have a defence, but it will be for the court to decide.

8.6 Chapter 4—Tasks and Knowledge Tests

Task 1: Knowledge Check

1. What were NTOs?
2. Identify one of the problems about skills which NTOs were intended to address.
3. Which three NTOs merged to form Skills for Justice?
4. How many National Occupational Standards are there for PCSOs?
5. And how many are there for basic police constable skills?
6. Define what NOS do.
7. What is the term for a whole set of NOS?
8. What are 'performance criteria' and what do they measure?
9. How many core behaviours are there for PCSOs? What are they?

Task 2: Intelligence—knowledge check

1. What is the **NIM**?
2. What is the T&C process?
3. Give an example of a 'systems product'.
4. What are the desired outcomes of the NIM?
5. What does **CHIS** stand for?
6. What legislation governs the use of informants?
7. Give two examples of scrutiny of intelligence operations from outside the intelligence unit.
8. Why is an intelligence report *sanitized*?
9. What goes into an *'intelligence package'*?
10. Can you describe how the intelligence process is *iterative* (it goes around like a circle)?

8.7 Chapter 4—Answers to Tasks and Knowledge Tests

Task 1: Knowledge check

1. National training organizations, standards keepers for the service, and manufacturing industries.
2. Inconsistency in attaining skills, lack of clarity about how competent someone had to be, patchy appraisal processes, lack of rigour in defining skills' standards.
3. Police Skills and Standards Organisation (PSSO), Custodial Care, and Community Justice.
4. 12 (at the moment; this may increase, see 4.2 above).
5. 22.
6. NOS describe competent performance in terms of an individual's work; defining what needs to be achieved rather than what needs to be done.
7. A 'suite'.
8. Performance criteria describe what you need to demonstrate your competence across all the units; these help to define the standard you are expected to reach when competent.
9. Six:
   - **Respect for diversity**
   - **Team working**
   - **Community and customer focus**
   - **Effective communication**
   - **Personal responsibility**
   - **Resilience.**

NB: *'problem solving'* is a core behaviour for police constables, not PCSOs, which is bizarre since problem solving is at the heart of the PCSO's interaction with the community.

Task 2: Intelligence—knowledge check

1. The National Intelligence Model.
2. A scrutiny process which weights intelligence and knowledge and decides on operations against crime and criminality.
3. A criminal database (internal or external) such as PNC or LIVESCAN.
4. Control measures around crime, criminality, and disorder, and the increase of community safety, managed hotspots, arrested or disrupted criminals, and the control of potentially dangerous offenders.

5. Covert Human Intelligence Source.
6. **RIPA**, the Regulation of Investigatory Powers Act 2000.
7. OPSY and an Operations Superintendent in Force, Surveillance Commissioner outside the Force (all are outside the intelligence departments and therefore should be objective).
8. To prevent the identity of the source becoming known and to disguise the circumstances of the intelligence collection.
9. Assessed intelligence, knowledge products, system products and analysis.
10. As we showed in the NIM process diagram (Figure 11 at 4.8.6 above), tasking leads to information, planning, and police operations which in turn throw up new questions and new requirements for intelligence which are tasked to the CHIS, and the circle begins again.

8.8 Chapter 5—Tasks and Knowledge Tests

Task 1: Pocket Note Book

Look at the following pages of a PNB and find the mistakes.

	001
	Bank holiday monday
	Duty 8am to 4 o' clock--------------------
	Patrol the High ~~≋~~ Street

Received task from the

patrol sgt taggart

Commenced patrol to the

High Street

Arrived at the High Street

I mean Lower High Street no

I was right the first time.

Patrolled around the

High street for a little

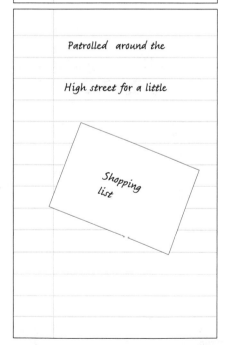

Shopping
list

Task 2: Unsolicited comment

You are on foot patrol in Tonchester one evening, walking along
Katie Street into Less Road on your way back to the police station.
As you turn the corner you are confronted by at least 50 people
of various ages who are gathered (unthreateningly) round a police
patrol car. One of the police officers looks up, sees you, and walks
over to tell you: *'The ambulance has just taken somebody away with
very serious head injuries, my mate's gone with them because we
think the victim may die. Get hold of as many witness details here
as you can.'*

You are then approached by a number of people.

1. What details are you going to take from these people and where are
   you going to record them?
2. One of the people from the crowd walks up to you and says, *'You'd
   better take my details, everybody keeps saying it's the bloke who's
   been nicked sitting in the police car that started it, but I was here
   before everybody else and it definitely wasn't.'*
   - As this information does not appear helpful to the prosecution
     case right at this moment, are you still going to make a note of it?
   - Is it relevant?
   - Will you tell anybody about it?

Task 3: Evidence; unsolicited statement

One evening in Tonchester you find yourself unexpectedly recording in
your PNB the details of a number of witnesses and a summary of their
evidence at a crime scene. Owing to staff shortages, the single-crewed
police officer now requests further support from you. A suspect has
been arrested and placed securely into the back of a patrol vehicle and
you are asked to stand by the vehicle while the police officer transmits
a message to the Control room. While you are standing near the open
window of the vehicle, the suspect says to you, *'He had it coming to
him. He shouldn't have given my mate such a hard time. It's settled
now. I've done what I had to do.'*

What, if anything, are you going to do with this information?

Task 4: Evidence—ground to issue caution

Code C paragraph 10.1 states: *'A person whom there are grounds to
suspect of an offence ... must be cautioned before any questions about
an offence ... are put to [him or her].'*

When will you know that you have the grounds to suspect a person
has committed an offence so that s/he must be cautioned?

Task 5: Possession of exhibits

1. When you take possession of evidence in the form of an exhibit, what is the policy and procedure of your Force for the storage of such property?
2. If the property was in any way perishable, such as foodstuffs, how would you treat it as an exhibit?
3. How are you going to write the exhibit number on the property?

Task 6: Continuity of evidence—video tapes

The reliability and strength of evidence is central to successfully prosecuting any offence. As well as providing continuity at the time of seizure by noting down from whom you took possession of the evidence, what else will you consider doing physically to a video cassette which contains evidential material, so that the recording cannot be erased?

Task 7: Issuing penalty notices for disorder

You may find it helpful to read the *Criminal Justice and Police Act* (sections 1–11), penalty notices for disorder, Police Operational Guidance, March 2005, before answering these questions. It can be seen at <http://police.homeoffice.gov.uk/operational-policing/crime-disorder/index.html/penalty-notice-introduction11> accessed 29 October 2009. Note this is a police operational website and is closed to outside enquiry.

1. Can you consider issuing a penalty notice to a suspect even if you have not directly witnessed the offending behaviour but have the reliable evidence of a witness instead?
2. Can you use a PND when there has been a substantial financial/material loss to the private property of an individual?
3. Is the issuing of a PND appropriate when you know that the suspect has previous convictions for disorder offences, or where you know that s/he has been issued with a number of penalty notices for disorder offences in the recent past, or has been cautioned for such offences?
4. Where you issue a PND and it subsequently comes to light after the incident that a more serious or non-penalty offence was committed on the same occasion, can a charge be brought for the subsequent offence?
   If you issue a PND to a person under 16 years in error, what must you do?
5. In preference to non-physical sources, such as the electoral register or PNC checks, where should you seek documentary evidence regarding age, identity, and place of residence?

Task 8: Issuing a fixed penalty notice

1. When completing an FPN, what sort of writing instrument must you use and what style of writing?
2. Space is restricted on some sections of the ticket; therefore, what words, if any, can be abbreviated?
3. What additional information can be written in the remarks section?

Task 9: Disclosure of evidence

1. If you decide to write your statement in draft first, in order to get the content of the statement in a chronological order and to include everything in the content appertaining to the incident, what will you do with those notes?
2. If you begin to write a statement and find out that, for one reason or another, it is completely wrong, are you going to throw it away in a rubbish bin?
3. Under what circumstances would you write your statement before making an entry in your PNB?

Task 10: Social problems

Look again at the letter from the BCU Commander, Chief Superintendent Allyse, welcoming you to Tonchester and consider all the problems mentioned within this letter. Make a list of what you think they are.

Task 11: Dealing with graffiti

Taking graffiti as an example, devise five questions which you could invite the community members to think about.

Task 12: Knowledge self-test

Let's refresh what you have learned in this section:
1. Define 'problem solving'.
2. What is the major limitation to *coercive policing* (that is, using your designated powers)?
3. What is 'designed-in' crime?
4. What factors may help a PCSO to 'go deeper' for a solution to community problems?

5. 'Homogeneous' means:
   (a) erotic literature,
   (b) one size fits all,
   (c) pasteurized,
   (d) intolerable.
6. Name three ways to engage the community and find out its problems.
7. What might happen when you become familiar with your 'beat'?
8. What are community members most concerned about?
9. What are 'regeneration issues'?
10. What should follow community consultation?

Task 13: Strategies to deal with anti-social behaviour

Taking this situation in the town centre at face value and with no additional information available, write down some practical strategies for dealing with this problem.

Having accessed this information, you can now continue to work on strategies for dealing with the problem. Incidentally, it may be that your investigation of this issue has revealed that youths abusing the elderly was an isolated instance and one that can be monitored in case of repetition. It may be that the whole thing has been exaggerated and taken out of context. It is a sad fact that often groups of youths congregating anywhere will now be labelled as being 'anti-social' merely because of their presence and not because of anything they actually do. Don't take reports at face value. Go and see, judge for yourself, and make sure that any strategies begin with an analysis of the problem. All this must be done before embarking on a mission to make things better. In the scenario you have been given in Tonchester, the effect on the community as a whole could be a lot worse if the youths were wrongly accused of being abusive.

To take our example a stage further, we will suppose that your initial investigations have revealed a concern about youths congregating in the shopping centre from around 15.30 hrs. CCTV footage shows that some of these are in school uniform, although not all. It also shows behaviour which is rowdy at best and intimidating at worst: it involves groups of youths not moving out of the way for shoppers, whistling at girls, jumping on benches, cycling in the centre, running in and out of shops, and generally behaving in a disruptive and faintly intimidating way. Your talks with the elderly, their support groups, and some of the shoppers have revealed that when people remonstrate with these groups, some of the young people respond with abusive remarks. There was a definite feeling among some respondents that this is putting them off shopping in the centre.

8 Tasks and Knowledge Tests

Task 14: Practical applications

Given the information outlined above about the problem, what strategies would you now employ in an effort to deal with it?

Task 15: Practical applications

Given that you have only access to the information provided so far, what strategies would you use for dealing with this situation?

Task 16: Dispute between neighbours

How would you begin to solve the dispute between neighbours Peacock and Drake as given in the example in 5.4 above?

Task 17: Dealing with aggression

Can you suggest what instances of your daily work might bring you into confrontation with another's aggression?

Task 18: Knowledge self-test (aggression)

1. What were *Mohucks*?
2. How many instances of verbal aggression are you, a PCSO, likely to encounter over a 12-month period?
3. Name three 'triggers' or catalysts for aggression.
4. What typifies aggression?
5. When might you encounter aggression arising from defensiveness?
6. What might complicate a drugs user's response to you?
7. What is the golden rule for PCSOs when faced with the likelihood of assault?
8. How many stages do we identify on the spectrum of responses?
9. Which is your 'strong' leg?
10. Define the effects of:
    (a) adrenaline,
    (b) dopamine,
    (c) nor-adrenaline,
    (d) cortisol,
    (e) endorphins.

Task 19: Health and Safety—risk assessment

1. What is the commonest physical risk which we face?
2. 'Counter-intuitive' means:
   (a) arguing in a shop,
   (b) knowing what is going to happen next,
   (c) not trusting to instinct,
   (d) deciding what best suits you.
3. Why would throwing a lifebelt to someone in difficulties in water be preferable to going in to help them?
4. What is a hazard?
5. What does 'risk-averse' mean?
6. What are the three basic kinds of risk assessment?
7. What sorts of risks are each of these:
   (a) serving a court summons
   (b) planning searches of vehicles
   (c) moving desks in your office
   (d) intervening in a quarrel.
8. What does **SPRAIN** stand for?
9. And what does **BEWARE** help us to remember?
10. What are your priorities at a road traffic collision or any accident scene?

8.9 Chapter 5—Answers to Tasks and Knowledge Tests

Task 1: Pocket Note Book (SH)

Answer: find the mistakes on the PNB entry:

Task 2: Unsolicited comment

1. You must record everybody's name, address, and a summary of what they saw, smelled, touched, tasted, or heard to follow the guidelines of **recording, retaining, and revealing.** In addition, to help with the investigation, contact details and dates of birth will be useful.
2. It doesn't matter whether the information appears useful or not to the prosecution case, *you must record the information you are given*. It is **relevant material** because it has some bearing on the investigation and it must be recorded in a durable form and retained. Having recorded such material, you must bring it to the attention of the police officers at the scene. If that is not

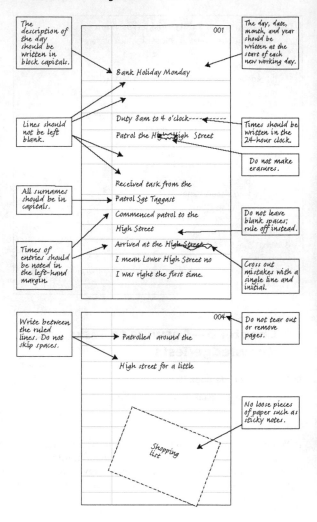

The description of the day should be written in block capitals.

The day, date, month, and year should be written at the start of each new working day.

001

Bank Holiday Monday

Lines should not be left blank.

Duty 8am to 4 o'clock

Times should be written in the 24-hour clock.

Patrol the Hi~~gh~~ High Street

Do not make erasures.

Received task from the

All surnames should be in capitals.

Patrol Sgt Taggast

Commenced patrol to the

Do not leave blank spaces; rule off instead.

High Street

Times of entries should be noted in the left-hand margin.

Arrived at the ~~High Street~~

I mean Lower High Street no

Cross out mistakes with a single line and initial.

I was right the first time.

004

Write between the ruled lines. Do not skip spaces.

Do not tear out or remove pages.

Patrolled around the

High street for a little

No loose pieces of paper such as sticky notes.

Shopping list

608

possible, you must locate the 'officer in the case' at the police station and reveal the information to them verbally or in a written form.

Task 3: Evidence; unsolicited statement

On the face of it, the suspect has made an unsolicited comment. It is significant information about the suspect's personal involvement in the offence and could even be considered as an admission of guilt. Therefore, the comment is a **significant statement**. You should now make a note of the comment in your PNB, make a record of the time it was made, and sign the entry. You should then show the PNB entry to the suspect, and ask him or her to read it over and decide whether it is a true record of what s/he said. If s/he agrees, then ask him or her to sign your PNB to indicate that it is a true record of what was said. After that, remember to reveal this piece of evidence to the arresting officer and/or the investigating officer.

Task 4: Evidence—ground to issue caution

PACE CODE C, Note of Guidance 10A states *'there must be some reasonable, objective grounds for the suspicion, based on known facts or information which are relevant to the likelihood the offence has been committed and the person to be questioned committed it.'*

An example of reasonable, objective (purposeful) grounds would be when a witness has given you the description of a person causing damage nearby and you later see a person causing damage who has the same description. The facts are, in this example, that criminal damage appears to have been committed. This is because of the nature of the damage and the environment in which it took place; because of the suspect by whom it was carried out; and you have a witness, as well as yourself, who has seen the suspect committing it.

On the other hand, having received the description of a person causing criminal damage nearby from a witness, you may locate some people on your way to viewing the damage. The group is some distance away from the site of the damage and does not appear to fit the original description. In this case it would be difficult to find reasonable objective grounds because there is little to connect one or more of the group with the damage, and at this point you do not know whether or not the damage exists, and whether or not it has been criminally made.

Task 5: Possession of exhibits

1. Policy and procedure varies between forces; however, in the majority of cases you will be requested to enter the property into a register at the police station. The register will provide you with a sequential number which will be unique to that property and will allow retrieval of it later. The property will then be placed in a temporary store, sometimes known as a 'transit store', and then a person with the responsibility for the safekeeping of property will take it to a more permanent place.
2. Property which is perishable or very fragile should be photographed by a Crime Scene Investigator and the property left with or given back to the original owner. The photographs will then be evidence of the existence of the property.
3. Depending on the policy and procedure of your Force, there are two or more exhibit labels: those which are durable and can be affixed to property, and those which are affixed to documents.

Task 6: Continuity of evidence—video tapes

Remove the tab at the back of the cassette, which will prevent any new recording taking place and the original recording being lost.

In addition, do not put the cassette into a plastic container or it may 'sweat' and become damp and unusable. Instead, place the cassette in a dry, padded bag, such as the commercial brand for storing fragile items.

Task 7: Issuing penalty notices for disorder

1. Yes, you may consider it appropriate to issue a penalty notice to a suspect even if you have not directly witnessed the offending behaviour yourself but you have reliable witness testimony instead (see paragraph 5.2 PND Police Operational Guidance).
2. No, PNDs will not be used where there has been a substantial financial/material loss to the private property of an individual (see paragraph 6.5 PND Police Operational Guidance).
3. No, a penalty notice may not be appropriate for issue where it is known that the suspect has previous convictions for disorder offences, or where it is known that s/he has been issued with a number of penalty notices for disorder offences in the recent past, or s/he has been cautioned for such offences (see paragraph 7.8 PND Police Operational Guidance).

4. Yes, where a penalty notice is issued for a penalty offence and it subsequently comes to light after the incident that a more serious or non-penalty offence was committed on the same occasion, a charge may be brought for the subsequent offence (see paragraph 8.4 PND Police Operational Guidance).

5. Where a penalty notice is issued in error to a juvenile aged under 16, the Central Ticket Office must be instructed to cancel the notice and refund any moneys paid (see paragraph 9.2 PND Police Operational Guidance).

6. Where possible, documentary evidence (such as a driving licence, credit cards, or membership cards of some kind) as to age, identity, and place of residence should be sought in preference to non-physical sources, such as the electoral register or PNC checks (see paragraph 10.3 PND Police Operational Guidance).

Task 8: Issuing a fixed penalty notice

1. When completing an FPN, you must use capital letters and a ballpoint pen to ensure legibility (see paragraph 5.2 of The Revised Guidance on the Operation of the Fixed Penalty System for Offences in Respect of a Vehicle).

2. With restricted space available on some sections of the ticket, items such as addresses and locations may be abbreviated, but the abbreviation must remain clear (see paragraph 5.4 of The Revised Guidance, ibid).

3. The remarks section may be used to record such information as the offender's occupation or former name. If any abbreviations have been used for addresses or locations, then additional details on expansions of the abbreviation may be added to this section as well (see paragraph 5.5 of The Revised Guidance, ibid).

Task 9: Disclosure of evidence

1. The notes you make as a prelude to writing your statement will have some bearing on the investigation (the defence team may wish to see them for example), therefore they must be retained and you must reveal them to the officer in the case and to the CPS.

2. No, definitely not. Your first and subsequent statements will have some bearing on the investigation, therefore they must be retained and you must reveal them to the officer in the case and/or to the CPS.

3. **NEVER.** This would be evidential suicide. Your statement would become your notes made at the time as well as your statement. There would be such a huge opportunity to make errors and there would be no reason then to make a PNB entry afterwards. Always write down notes which you make at the time of the incident straight into your PNB, and if you can't do it at the time, then they must be made as soon as practicable afterwards. Only when you have written notes in your PNB can you go ahead and write a statement based upon those notes.

Task 10: Social problems

The elements in Chief Superintendent Allyse's letter covered the following concerns:

- Challenges in the economically deprived residential areas in the SW and NE
- Unoccupied youths throwing stones at cars
- Unpleasant racist chanting at football matches and at the University
- 'Problem families' moving in from outside the area
- Groups of youths targeting the elderly for abuse in the shopping centre
- Youths complaining that they are bored
- Graffiti, petty vandalism, and anti-social behaviour in Nelson Mandela Buildings
- Drugs dealing
- Residents too frightened to come out of their houses and flats, even in daylight
- Petty vandalism in the Victoria Centre
- Drunken and abusive behaviour apparently by girls from Oggs' College of FE
- Rowdy, disaffected, and bored youths
- Underage drinking.

Task 11: Dealing with graffiti

The questions might look like this:

1. Have you seen anyone painting graffiti?
2. Have you sold job lots of spray paint recently?
3. Have you seen anyone carrying lots of spray cans or have you seen anyone with paint traces on hands or clothing?
4. Have you heard anyone boasting about writing graffiti?

5. Since we used the anti-graffiti paint on the bus shelter, have you seen anyone with large black paint smudges on clothes or hands?

6. How would you respond to the creation of a special place where people can safely create 'graffiti art'?

7. What are your views on community arts projects?

8. Do you know of any suitable property which would benefit from a community art mural?

9. Are there any parts of the community (such as walkways, walls, or the sides of buildings) which would be better for a good repainting?

10. If any offenders are caught and convicted of spraying graffiti, would you support a community 'sentence', of cleaning it up?

Task 12: Knowledge self-test

1. 'Transforming one set of circumstances into another, preferred state' (Stevens, 1996) but remember that even attempting to solve a problem may give the community the impetus it needs to seek other solutions. We might adapt Stevens slightly, and say 'solving a problem could be bringing a new way of thinking to a set of adverse circumstances'.

2. You can do nothing unless criminal offences have been committed.

3. Crime which is made easier by poor design, such as inadequate or vulnerable lighting, large blank walls which are not overlooked, lifts which do not work, poor communal 'hygiene', such as refuse collection or litter patrols, dense undergrowth beside ill-lit paths (helping the lurker), and so on.

4. Time to consult, listen, meet, liaise, and create partnerships, pre-eminently to 'transcend traditional areas of authority'.

5. (b).

6. Public meetings, surgeries, questionnaires, and mobile police stations (to publicize, among other things, community safety), but also parish and local councils, council offices, local newspapers, radio and occasionally local TV, community sites such as village halls, or community centres.

7. You will know people by name, who belongs to which family, who works where, which car(s) belong(s) to which house, who is having relationship problems, and often who is hard up and who is splashing money around, who hasn't been seen for a while; in short, community intelligence.

8. The physical and social fabric of their own neighbourhood.
9. Graffiti, rubbish, litter, broken windows, unrepaired bus shelters, dog excrement, and so on.
10. An action plan in which all have a part to play, but where you do *not* take it all on yourself.

Task 13: Strategies to deal with anti-social behaviour

At its most basic, the main thing missing from this scenario is some detailed information or intelligence. You need to get this information before embarking on a detailed strategy. Some ways in which you might do this could include:

- Use targeted patrols to assess the situation on the ground
- Review existing police intelligence or crime reports to build up a picture
- Talk to businesses in the area
- Access any available CCTV footage
- Use the mobile police station to speak to people in the town centre, especially those elderly alleged to have been the targets of abuse, to hear their accounts
- Talk to support groups for the elderly to gauge their opinions
- Talk to the youths who congregate in the town centre, build up a rapport with them.

Task 14: Practical applications

Once again this is not an exhaustive list, nor is it one which is merely confined to this particular situation:

- Institute and sustain targeted patrols at the shopping centre to provide a highly visible reassurance presence for the shoppers.
- Set up community safety events at the centre to provide a presence in a less overt capacity. This affords the opportunity to combine presence with a crime reduction initiative.
- Undertake liaison with the businesses in the centre to obtain intelligence and provide support to their staff. Try to identify which of the young individuals appears to be causing the most trouble.
- Establish or improve liaison with the security staff at the shopping centre and the individual businesses. Concentrate upon sharing of information on identified troublemakers, so that CCTV can be used proactively in stopping these individuals entering the shopping centre, rather than merely

recording events. Look at signage that details the use of CCTV and explains what will happen to troublemakers.

- Work with the school to identify the troublemakers as well as exploring possibilities of after-school clubs to provide an alternative place for the youths to meet. There could also be the possibility of working with the school in its 'Personal, Social and Health Education' (PSHE) or 'Citizenship' curricula to work towards greater understanding of the issues facing the elderly community. This could also involve getting elderly people into the school, and involving the school with schemes to support the elderly, to break down barriers between the two groups.

- Talking with the groups of youth to assess why they gather in this area, explaining to them why certain types of behaviour are not acceptable. The welcoming letter from the Chief Superintendent refers to youths not using the new sports centre; we noted earlier that this might be because the entrance and subscription fees are too high. One initiative might be to have reduced entry for schools or subsidized membership, paid for by local businesses. This could also provide an opportunity to work in conjunction with youth groups in helping to identify what the young people lack, specifically in terms of amenities or venues. What about an Internet café?

- Working with all parties on seeking funding for initiatives designed to get these groups off the street and into differing activities.

- Working with elderly support groups to provide practical advice for dealing with such situations, including where they can report nuisance behaviour.

Task 15: Practical applications

- Your first priority must be to take control of this situation and stop the argument escalating. From a suitable distance, you need to establish your presence and ask both parties to stop shouting. You can suggest that it may be possible for you to resolve this issue. However, do not promise absolutely to do this because this may not in fact be possible.

- Ask each party in turn to explain what the dispute is about. Take notes in your PNB because this reinforces your official intervention, and you should make a note of the names and addresses of the individuals involved. You will require diplomacy to ensure that this does not exacerbate the problem, with both parties rounding on you as a common foe.

- Having established the basis of the dispute, ask both parties to retire to their respective houses, explaining that you will be round to each shortly to gain a fuller understanding of the problem. This allows some breathing space and shows that you are prepared to listen to the grievances of both sides.
- Before entering either property, conduct a suitable radio check to establish whether any police intelligence is held on either party. Whilst this may only be a minor neighbour dispute, it could be that one of the parties has a history which may influence whether you decide to seek assistance before proceeding.
- If appropriate, you could speak to any of the onlookers to see if they have any pertinent information.

Task 16: Dispute between neighbours

- Inform Peacock that deliberately winding up Drake is only making the situation worse and therefore needs to stop.
- The matter can be resolved (expensively) in the courts through civil action, but a simple agreement to respect each other's privacy and access may settle the dispute amicably and with considerably less cost.
- If the parties do not live in privately-owned houses, this would be a good time to involve the property owners. It may be that there are clauses in the tenancy agreements that could be used to force each of the parties to back down.
- Look at involving other agencies such as Environmental Health, which could use its experience of such disputes to get a mediator involved. There may be voluntary mediation services that the neighbours may be persuaded to go to.
- Look at increasing patrols in the area to keep an eye on the situation and to ensure that things do not get worse. Don't neglect the possibility that other neighbours could keep an eye on things for you (but avoid commissioning the merely officious local busybody).
- Submit an intelligence report so that if things escalate, an organizational memory exists of the details you have obtained today. Remember that, although this whole issue appears relatively trivial on the surface, there are instances where matters have got completely out of control. There was a case in 2005 in which one neighbour shot dead another over a boundary and hedge dispute.

Task 17: Dealing with aggression

Regrettably, you will encounter aggression in many of the areas where you seek **enforcement**, such as asking people to pick up the litter they've dropped, or telling cyclists to get off a pavement, or acting to stop someone doing something anti-social (such as spraying graffiti). You may also encounter hostility and aggression from parents if you remonstrate with their offspring. The same could be applied to some dog owners, if they are asked to stop their animals fouling. In many cases, it is a case of 'love me, love my dog' (or son or daughter) and people can often be quite wilfully blind to the defects and shortcomings of their children's or dogs' behaviour.

You may also meet aggression which forms as the result of a group mentality, such as a knot of young people who decide that aggression towards you is the better part of otherwise getting into worse trouble. Very often, they don't plan on the basis of consequences, which is sometimes the reason why young people, especially young men aged 16 to 19, find themselves in a spiral of trouble-making, crime, and punishment. You may also become the focus of aggression if you intervene between two hostile groups, such as football supporters, or rival gangs at a club, or between quarrelling families, or members of a family.

Task 18: Knowledge self-test (aggression)

1. Mohucks (named after what people thought the Indian Mohican tribe were like) were urban rowdies, specializing in muggings and assault, in London in the period 1750–80.
2. Five.
3. Any three from **frustration, inarticulacy, anger, defensiveness, desire to escape consequences, under the influence of drink or drugs, guilt, fear** (notably of a stereotype).
4. Any demonstration of anger up to and including assault.
5. Defensiveness is a characteristic response to a PCSO intervening to enforce a law or regulation; it's the 'anyone but me' response.
6. The fear that you, as authority, not only represent punishment but also incarceration, which means not getting the next dosage.
7. Withdraw, call for assistance, and observe from a distance.

8. Six.
9. The natural leading leg for activities (in most people the right leg).
10. (a) 'Fight or Flight'
    (b) 'Clearing the mind'
    (c) 'Emergency energy'
    (d) Cushioning the effects of shock
    (e) 'Feel good' factors or painkillers.

Task 19: Health and Safety—risk assessment

1. Pulling a muscle during exercise.
2. (c), not trusting to instinct.
3. Because rescuing people from water calls for considerable skills and you may not be good enough to do it without risk to yourself or to the person you are trying to rescue (and, indeed, others who may be tempted to follow your heroic if ill-advised example).
4. The potential for harm.
5. Avoiding anything remotely hazardous (even choices, sometimes).
6. Generic, specific and dynamic.
7. (a) Specific.
    (b) Generic.
    (c) Specific.
    (d) Dynamic.
8. Situation, Plan, Risks, Alternative(s), INcrease safety.
9. Biological (or chemical) dangers, Exposure to fire, Weather conditions, Assault or Asphyxiation, Radiological contamination, Effort and Exertion.
10. Preserve life, contain and control the scene (which may be a crime scene).

Notes

1 Reported by Woolcock N and Fishburn, A, 'Expulsion curb condemns unruly pupils to a merry-go-round of disruption', *The Times*, 28 May 2009, 14, and available from <http://www.timesonline.co.uk/tol/news/uk/education/article6375172> accessed 28 May 2009.

Bibliography and References

Note that 'a' and 'b' etc, following a date, refer to more than one publication in the same year with a similar title or the same author. In the body of the text, this is rendered as 'T Smyth, 2006b' for example.

Books and Reports

ACPO, *Guidance on Police Community Support Workers* (Revised June 2005)
_____ *Major Incident Room standard administrative procedures* (MIRSAP) (ACPO, 1999a)
_____ *The Manual of Standard Operating Procedures for scientific support personnel and major incident scenes* (ACPO, 1999b)
_____ /FSS, *Using Forensic Science Effectively* (ACPO/Forensic Science Service, 1996)
_____ /Home Office, Conference: '*Improving Detections: the evidence to shape the future*', (national conference, speakers included Peter Neyroud, David Coleman and Paul Ibrahim), 8–9 June 2004, Birmingham; under the auspices of Association of Chief Police Officers and the Home Office
Adlam, R, and Villiers, P (eds), *Police Leadership in the Twenty-first Century* (Waterside, 2003)
Adler, C, and Polk, K, *Child Victims of Homicide* (CUP, 2002)
Adler, J (ed), *Forensic Psychology, Concepts, Debates and Practice* (Willan, 2004)
Ainsworth, P, *Offender Profiling and Crime Analysis* (Willan, 2001)
_____ *Psychology and Policing* (Willan, 2002)
Aldridge, J *et al*, *Digital Imaging Procedure*, Police Scientific Development Branch, Home Office/ACPO (2002)
Alison, L (ed), *The Forensic Psychologist's Casebook: offender profiling and criminal investigation* (Willan, 2005)
Allen, J (ed), 'Policing and the criminal justice system — public confidence and perceptions: findings from the 2004/05 British Crime Survey' (Home Office Report 07/06, 2006)
Alldridge, P, *Proceeds of Crime* (Hart, 2003)
Alvesalo, A, 'Economic Crime Investigators at work' (2003) 13(2) *Policing and Society* 115–38

Bibliography and References

Amey, P, Hale, C, and Uglow, S, *Proactive Policing* (SCRU, 1996)

Angle, H, Malam, S, and Carey, C, 'Witness Satisfaction: Findings from the Witness Satisfaction Survey, 2002' (Home Office Report 19/03, 2003)

Arnaldo, C, *Child Abuse on the Internet: Ending the Silence* (Berghahn, 2001)

Ashburner, E, and Soothill, K, 'Understanding Serial Killing: how important are the notions of gender?' (2002) 75(2) *Police Journal* 93–8

Ashworth, A, *Serious Crime, Human Rights and Criminal Procedure* (Willan, 2002)

_____ *Principles of Criminal Law* (OUP, 2006)

_____ and Mitchell, B, *Rethinking English Homicide Law* (OUP, 2000)

Audit Commission, 'Helping with Enquiries: Tackling Crime Effectively' Police Paper 12 (HMSO, 1993)

Baggott, M, and Wallace, M, (2006), *Neighbourhood Policing Progress Report*, May, Home Office, Crown copyright

Bean, P, *Drugs and Crime* (Willan, 2002)

Bennetto, J, (2000), 'Sleeping with the enemy is clue to a bent copper', *The Independent*, 19 May 19, available at <http://findarticles.com/p/articles/mi_qn4158/is_20000519/ai_n14314433> accessed May 2009

Bernstein, P, *Against the Gods; The Remarkable Story of Risk*, [on predictiveness and risk management] (John Wiley & Sons, 1996)

Berry, G, Mawby, R, and Walley, L, *The Management and Organisation of Serious Crime Investigations* (Staffordshire University, 1995)

Billingsley, R, Nemitz, T, and Bean, P, *Informers: Policing, Policy, Practice* (Willan, 2001)

Blair, T, Foreword, *Respect Action Plan,* Respect Task Force, January 2006, 1

Bottoms, A, Mawby, R, and Xanthos, P, 'A Tale of two estates' in Downes, D (ed), *Crime and the City* (Macmillan, 1989)

Bottoms, A, and Wiles, P, 'Environmental Criminology' in Maguire, M (ed), *Oxford Handbook of Criminology* (OUP, 2002) Ch 18

Bourlet, A, *Police Intervention in Marital Violence* (Open University Press, 1990)

Bowling, B, *Violent Racism: Victimisation, Policing and Social Context* (OUP, 1998) especially Ch 8 'Policing Violent Racism', 234–84

_____ and Phillips, C, 'Racist Victimisation in England and Wales', in Hawkins, D (ed), *Violent Crime* (CUP, 2003) 154–70

Bradley, R, 'Public Expectations and Perceptions of Policing', Home Office Police Research Series, Paper 96 (1998)

Brain, 'I', 'Policing and the Condition of England' (on the changes in relations between police and public over the last 60 years) (2003) 9(4) *Policing Today* 35–6

Brand, S, and Price, R, 'The Economic and Social Costs of Crime' Home Office Research Study No 217 (2000)

Brantingham, P, and Faust, F (1976) 'A conceptual model of crime prevention' in *Crime and Delinquency*, 22, 284–298

Bratby, L, 'DNA Secrets', *Police Review*, 6 June 2003

Bridges, I, *Blackstone's Police Operational Handbook,* Police National Legal Database (OUP, 2006) especially Ch 11, 606–16 (on PCSOs and their designated powers, close reference to Police Reform Act 2002)

Britton, P, *The Jigsaw Man: The Remarkable Career of Britain's Foremost Criminal Psychologist* (Bantam, 1997)

Brogden, M, and Nijhar, P, *Community Policing: national and international models and approaches* (Willan, 2005)

Brown, A, and Barrett, D, *Knowledge of Evil: Child prostitution and child sexual abuse in twentieth-century England* (Willan, 2002)

Bryant, R (ed), *Blackstone's Student Police Officer Handbook* (OUP, 2006)

Bullock, K, and Tilley, N (eds), *Essays in Problem-Orientated Policing* (Willan, 2003)

Buquet, A, 'Automated Recognition of handwriting and signatures' (2000) 483 *International Criminal Police Review* 10–18

Burke, R (ed), *Hard Cop, Soft Cop; Dilemmas and Debates in Contemporary Policing* (Willan, 2004)

Button, M, *Private Policing* (Willan, 2002)

Buzan, T, *Use your Head* (on mind-mapping) (BBC Publications, 1974)

Byatt, L, 'Forensic Measures', *Criminal Justice Management*, November 2003

Byrne, S, and Pease, K (2003), 'Crime reduction and community safety' in Newburn, T (ed), *Handbook of Policing*, Willan Publishing, Devon, Part III, 'Doing Policing' 286–310

Caless, B, and Spruce, B, 'Police Code of Professional Standards', Chapter 2.3 in Harfield, C (ed) *Blackstone's Police Operational Handbook: Practice and Procedure*, (OUP, 2009)

Caless, B, 'Corruption in the Police: the Reality of the "Dark Side"', *The Police Journal*, Vol 81, No 1, Vathek Publishing, 2008,

Caless, B, 'Persistent Dark Matter; Police Corruption in the Last Ten Years', *Ethics in Policing*, Vol 1, No 2, 2008

Calvert-Smith, Sir D, *The police service in England and Wales: Final report of an investigation by the Commission for Racial Equality* (Commission for Racial Equality, 2005)

Campbell, J (ed), *Assessing Dangerousness: Violence by Sexual Offenders, Batterers and Child Abusers* (Sage, 1995)

Canter, D, *Criminal Shadows; Inside the Mind of the Serial Killer* (TSP, HarperCollins, 1994)

_____ *Mapping Murder; The Secrets of Geographical Profiling* (HarperCollins, 2004)

_____ and Alison, L (eds), *The Social Psychology of Crime* (Ashgate, 2000)

_____ and Alison, L, *Investigative Psychology*, Vol 13, *Profiling Rape and Murder* (Dartmouth, 2002)

Card, R, *Sexual Offences; The New Law*, 2004 (Jordan's, 2004)

Carrabine, E, Cox, P, Lee, M, and South, N, *Crime in Modern Britain* (OUP, 2002)

Centrex (Central Police Training and Development Authority, now part of the National Police Improvement Agency, NPIA), *Wider Policing Learning and Development Programme, WPLDP*, 2005, based on Initial Police Learning Development Programme (IPLDP); version 2 of WPLDP, 2006

Christie, N, *Crime Control as Industry* (Routledge, 2000)

Christmann, K, Rogerson, M, and Walters, D, 'New Deal for Communities: the national evaluation; Research Report 14, Fear of Crime and Insecurity in New Deal Communities' Partnerships', Sheffield Hallam University (July 2003) 12

Clark, D, *The Investigation of Crime: a guide to the law of criminal investigation* (OUP, 2004)

Clarke, C, and Milne, R, 'A National Evaluation of the PEACE Investigative Interviewing Course', Home Office Report PRAS/149 (2001)

Clarke, R, 'Hot Products: Understanding, Anticipating and Reducing Demand for Stolen Goods', Police Research Series Paper 112, Home Office and TSO (1999)

Clements, P, *Policing a Diverse Society* (OUP, 2006)

Cohen, S, *Folk Devils and Moral Panics* (3rd edn, Routledge, 2002)

Cole, S, *Suspect Identities: a History of Fingerprinting and Criminal Identification* (Harvard University Press, 2001)

Coleman, C and Moynihan, J, *Understanding Crime Data: Haunted by the dark figure* (Open University Press, 1996, (reprinted 2003))

Coleman, R, *Reclaiming the Streets; Surveillance, Social Control and the City* (Willan, 2004)

Cooper, C, 'A National Evaluation of Community Support Officers', Summary 2006, Findings 271, Research, Development and Statistics Directorate, Home Office (2006)

_____ Anscombe, J, Avenell, J, McLean, F, and Morris, J, 'A National Evaluation of Community Support Officers' Home Office Research Study No 297, Home Office (2006)

Cope, N, Innes, M, and Fielding, N, *Smart Policing? The Theory and Practice of Intelligence-Led Policing* (Home Office, 2001)

Copson, G, 'Breaking the criminal families' cycle: what works?' (2002) 1(1) *Policing Futures* 1–10

Crank, J, and Caldero, M, *Police Ethics: the Corruption of Noble Cause* (Anderson, 2002)

Crawford, A (2003), 'The pattern of policing in the UK: policing beyond the police' in Newburn, T (ed), *Handbook of Policing*, Willan Publishing, Devon

Davies, A, and Dale, A, *Locating the Stranger Rapist* (HO Police Research Group, HMSO, 1995)

Davies, P, 'Consultation Paper on Standard Powers for Police Community Support Officers and a framework for the future development of powers', Home Office (2005a)

D'Cruze, S (ed), *Everyday Violence in Britain, 1850–1950: Gender and Class* (Longman, 2000)

Denny, P, 'Intelligence-led Policing' (1998) 8(1) *International Police Journal*

Dobash, R, and Dobash, R, *Homicide in the Family* (University of Manchester Press, 2003)

Docking, M, *Public perceptions of police accountability and decision making* (2003, Home Office Online Report 38/03), available from <http://www.homeoffice.gov.uk/rds/pdfs2/rdsolr3803.pdf> accessed 10 January 2009

Douglas, J, and Olshaker, M, *The Anatomy of Motive* (Scribner, 1999)

Drever, J, *A Dictionary of Psychology* (Penguin, 1952 (revised 1969))

Dunnighan, C, and Norris, C, 'The Detective, the Snout and the Audit Commission: the real costs of using informants' (1999) 38 *The Howard Journal* 67–86

Edwards, C (2005), *Changing Police Theories for 21st Century Societies*, The Federation Press, Leichhardt, New South Wales, Australia, particularly Ch. 14 'Control of Policing', and the section 'Police and Privatisation', 311–313, and 'Private Security as Private Police', 314–316; 2005, a second edition of this work is distributed by Willan Publishing, Devon

Ekblom, P, 'How to Police the Future' in Smith, M, and Tilley, N (eds), *Crime Science* (Willan, 2004)

Elliston, F, and Feldberg, M, *Moral Issues in Police Work* (Rowman and Allanheld, 1985), Part 2, Chs 5, 6, and 7

Emsley, C, *Crime and Society in England 1750–1900* (Longman, 2004)

_____ *Hard Men: Violence in England since 1750* (Hambledon, 2005)

Ericson, R and Haggerty, K, *Policing the Risk Society* (Clarendon, 1997)

Farrall, S, and Gadd, D, 'Evaluating Crime Fears: a research note on a pilot study to improve the measurement of the "fear of crime" as a performance indicator' (2004) 10(4) *Evaluation* 493–502

Farrell, G, Pease, K, and Tilley, N, *Repeat Victimization in Context; policy and practice for crime prevention* (Willan, 2004) especially Ch 5, 'Merseyside Domestic Violence'

Felson, M, *Crime and Everyday Life* (Sage, 2002)

_____ and Clarke, R (1998), *Opportunity makes the Thief: Practical Theory for Crime Prevention*, Police Research Series, Paper 98, Home Office, Crown Copyright

First Aid Manual (authorized manual of St John Ambulance, St Andrew's Ambulance Association, and the British Red Cross Society) (Dorling Kindersley, 1987)

Fitzpatrick, B, *Going to Court* (OUP, 2005)

Forensic Science Service, *Scenes of Crime Handbook* (Home Office, 2000b)

Forrest, S, Myhill, AQ, and Tilley, N, 'Practical Lessons for involving the community in crime and disorder problems', Home Office Development and Practice Report No 43 (2005) 16

Foster, R, 'Partners in Crime' (on close relationships between the police and the Crown Prosecution Service) (2003) 9(1) *Policing Today* 25–6

Gaule, M, *The Basic Guide to Forensic Awareness* (New Police Bookshop, 2003)

Gardner, J, *Wartime Britain 1939–1945* (Headline, 2004)

Garland, D, *The Culture of Control: crime and social order in contemporary society* (OUP, 2001)

Gaylor, D, *Getting Away With Murder: The reinvestigation of historic undetected homicide*, Home Office (2002)

George, B, and Button, M (2000), *Private Security*, Perpetuity Press, Leicestershire

Gibb, S, 'En garde! Magistrates ready for battle over punishments' (2009, *The Times*, 26 February, available from <http://www.timesonline.uk/news> accessed 27 February 2009)

Gibb, F, 'On-the-spot fines mean justice is not seen to be done, say critics', *The Times*, 5 May 2009, available from <http://timesonline/tol/business/law/article4622156.ece> accessed 5 May, 2009

Gilbert, N (chair), 'Dilemmas of Privacy and Surveillance—Challenges of Technological Change', Royal Academy of Engineering Report (March 2007)

Girling, E, Loader, I, and Sparks, R, *Crime and Social Change in Middle England: Questions of Order in an English Town* (Routledge, 2000)

Goldsmith, A, and Lewis, C (eds) (2000), *Civilian Oversight of Policing: Governance, Democracy and Human Rights*, Hart Publishing, Portland, Oregon, USA

Goudriaan, H, Wittebrood, K, and Nieuwbeerta, P, 'Neighbourhood characteristics and Reporting Crime: effects of social cohesion, confidence in police effectiveness and socio-economic disadvantage' (2006) 46 *British Journal of Criminology* 719–42

Graef, R, *Talking Blues; The Police in Their Own Words* (Collins Harvill, 1989) Ch 10

Greer, C, *Sex Crime and the Media* (Willan, 2003)

Gudjönsson, G, *The Psychology of Interrogations, Confessions and Testimony* (Wiley, 1992)

Hall, C, 'Social Capital; introductory users' guide', ESDS, Government Office for National Statistics (2005)

Hall, N, *Hate Crime* (Willan, 2005)

Hanmer, J, Griffiths, S, and Jerwood, D, 'Arresting Evidence: Domestic Violence and Repeat Victimisation', Police Research Series, Paper 104 (1999)

Harrington, V, Down, G, Johnson, M, and Upton, C, 'Police Community Support Officers: An Evaluation of Round 2 in Kent, 2004/2005', (O&D, Kent Police, 2005)

Hartfield, C, 'SOCA: A paradigm shift in British policing' (2006) 46 *British Journal of Criminology* 743–61

Bibliography and References

Hawkins, D (ed), *Violent Crime* (CUP, 2003)

Heaton-Armstrong, A, Shepherd, E, Gudjönsson, G, and Wolchover, D, *Witness Testimony: psychological, investigative and evidential perspectives* (OUP, 2007)

Henriques, Hon Mr Justice, 'The role of Forensic Science in the Trial of Harold Shipman' (July, 2003) 43(3) *Medicine, Science and the Law* 185–8

Herbert, C, 'Balancing Act' (on the tensions between government targets and community demands on the police), *Police Review*, 5 September 2003, 25–26

_____ 'A Spider's Web' (on Government performance measures for the police), *Police Review*, 31 October 2003, 20–1

Her Majesty's Government (HMG), *White Paper: Building Communities, Beating Crime* (HMSO, 2004)

Hilbourne, J, 'On disabling the normal' (1973) 2 *British Journal of Social Work* 497–504

Hitchins, P, *A Brief History of Crime: the decline of order, justice and liberty in England* (Atlantic Books, 2003)

HMIC, *Police Integrity—Securing and Maintaining Public Confidence* (Home Office, 1999)

_____ 'Implementation of the NIM at BCU level', Home Office (2002a)

_____ 'Open all Hours, A thematic inspection report on the role of police visibility and accessibility in public reassurance', Home Office (2002b)

_____ 'Civilianisation and the Use of Non-Sworn Police Staff in the Service, Thematic Inspection', Flanaghan, Sir R (2004)

_____ /CPS, *Violence at Home* (a joint thematic inspection of the investigation and prosecution of cases involving domestic violence) (TSO, February 2004)

HMSO, Criminal Justice and Police Act (ss 1–11), *Penalty Notices for Disorder, Police Operational Guidance*, March 2005

_____ *Regulation of Investigatory Powers Act* (RIPA) (now TSO, 2000)

Holdaway, S, *The racialisation of British policing* (Macmillan, 1996)

_____ 'The Forensic Science Service, Fact-sheet: What is DNA?' (2002)

_____ 'Standard Powers for Community Support Officers and a Framework for the Future Development of Powers' (October 2005a)

_____ 'National Community Safety Plan' (2005b)

_____ 'Neighbourhood Policing: Your Police; Your Community; Our Commitment' (2005c)

Home Office, 'Police Community Support Officer: Competency-Based Application Form; scoring key and grading table' (April, 2006a)

_____ 'Revised Guidance in the Operation of the Fixed Penalty System for Offences in Respect of a Vehicle' (April 2006b)

_____ 'Summary of Responses to the Consultation Document "Standard Powers for CSOs and a Framework for the Future Development of Powers" ' (2006c)

_____ *National Community Safety Plan 2008–2011* (2008, Crown Copyright), also available from <http://www.homeoffice. gov.uk/national-policing-plan/national-community-safety-0811> accessed August 2009

Howitt, D, *Introduction to Forensic and Criminal Psychology* (Pearson Prentice-Hall, 2002)

Hudson, B, *Understanding Justice* (Open University Press, 1996 (2nd edn 2003))

Hughes, G, *Understanding Crime Prevention (social control, risk and late modernity)* (Open University Press, 2002)

_____ McLaughlin, E, and Muncie, J (eds), *Crime Prevention and Community Safety* (Sage, 2002)

_____ and Edwards, A (eds), *Crime Control and Community; the new politics of public safety* (Willan, 2002)

Huhne, C, 'Scalpel-sharp intelligence is needed to slash knife crime', *The Times*, 30 March 2009, 26; available from: <http:// www.timesonline.co.uk/tol/comment/columnists/guest_contributors/article5998477.ece> accessed 30 March 2009

Innes, M, *Understanding Social Control (deviance, crime and social order)* (Open University Press, 2002)

_____ *Investigating Murder: Detective Work and the Police Response to Criminal Homicide* (OUP, 2003)

_____ 'Crime as Signal; Crime as Memory' (2004) 1(2) *Journal for Crime, Conflict and the Media* 15–22

_____ 'What's your problem? Signal crimes and citizen-focused problem-solving' (2005) 4(2) *Criminology and Public Policy* 187–200

Innes, M, Fielding, N, and Langan, S, 'Signal Crimes and Control Signals: Towards an evidence-based conceptual framework for Reassurance Policing', a report for Surrey Police, University of Surrey (2002)

Ivkovic, S, *Fallen Blue Knights; controlling police corruption* (on police corruption in the United States) (OUP, 2005)

Bibliography and References

John, T, and Maguire, M, 'Rolling Out the National Intelligence Model: Key Challenges' in Bullock, K, and Tilley, N (eds), *Essays in Problem-Orientated Policing* (Willan 2003)

_____ and Maguire, M, 'Second Round Targeted Policing Initiative: Rollout of the NIM', Report to the Home Office (2003b)

Jones, S, *Understanding Violent Crime* (Open University Press, 2000)

_____ and Newburn, T, *Private Security and Public Policing* (Clarendon Press, 1998)

_____ and Newburn, T (eds), *Plural Policing: a comparative perspective* (Routledge, 2006)

Kemshall, H, *Understanding risk in criminal justice* (Open University Press, 2003)

Kent Police, *Neighbourhood Policing; Handbook for NP teams and managers* (FHQ, Kent, 2006)

Kershaw, C, Nicholas, S, and Walker, A, (eds) (2008) *Crime in England and Wales 2007/08 Findings from the British Crime Survey and police recorded crime* Home Office Statistical Bulletin 07/08 London: Home Office

Knutson, J (ed), *Problem-oriented Policing from Innovation to Mainstream*, Crime Prevention Studies No 15 (Willowtree Press, 2003)

Kleinig, J, *The Ethics of Policing* (CUP, 1996)

Kyvsgaard, B, *The Criminal Career* (CUP, 2003) especially Ch 10 on recidivism, 122–37

Lacey, N, 'The social construction of crime' in Maguire, M *et al* (eds), *The Oxford Handbook of Criminology* (OUP, 2002)

LaFollette, H (ed), *The Oxford Handbook of Practical Ethics* (OUP, 2005)

Lawrence, J, 'Forging a peaceable kingdom: War, Violence and Fear of Brutalization in post-First World War Britain' (2003) 75 *Journal of Modern History*

Laycock, G, *Launching Crime Science* (Jill Dando Institute, UCL, 2002)

Leishman, F, Loveday, B, and Savage, S (eds), *Core Issues in Policing* (Sage, 2000)

_____ and Mason, P, *Policing and the Media: Facts, Fictions and Factions* (Willan, 2003)

Leverick, F, *Killing in Self-Defence* (OUP, 2006)

Linnane, F, *London's Underworld* (Robson Books, 2004)

Lister, S, 'It's a jungle out there: bugs put thousands in hospital' (2009, *The Times*, 26 February, 21)

Loader, I, and Mulcahy, A, *Policing and the Condition of England* (OUP, 2003)

MacPherson, Sir W, *Report of an Inquiry into the Investigation of the Murder of Stephen Lawrence* (Cmd 4262, 1999)

Maguire, M, Morgan, R, and Reiner, R (eds), *The Oxford Handbook of Criminology* (3rd edn, OUP, 2002)

Mark, Sir R, *In the Office of Constable* (Collins, 1978)

Mason, P (ed), *Criminal Visions: Media Representations of Crime and Justice* (Willan, 2003)

Mason, M, and Dale, C, *Analysis of Police Community Support Officer (PCSO) Activity Based Costing (ABC) data: results from an initial review* (July 2008, Home Office, available from <http://www.homeoffice.gov.uk/rds/pdfs08/horr08.pdf> accessed 1 May 2009)

Matthews, R, *Armed Robbery* (Willan 2002) especially Ch 6, 'Policing Armed Robbery'

Mawby, RI, *Burglary* (Willan, 2001)

McConville, M, and Wilson, G (eds), *The Handbook of the Criminal Justice Process* (OUP, 2002)

McLagen, G, *Bent Coppers* (on recent police corruption) (Weidenfeld & Nicholson, 2003) Chs 1, 3, 14, and 16, especially 248–55

McLaughlin, E, *The New Policing* (Sage, 2007)

Mistry, D, 'Community Engagement: practical lessons from a pilot project', Home Office Development and Practice Report No 48 (2007)

Morgan, J, *The Police Function and the Investigation of Crime* (Gower, 1990)

_____ (1991), 'Safer Communities: the local delivery of crime prevention through the partnership approach' ['The Morgan Report'], *The Home Office Standing Conference on Crime Prevention*. August, available from <http://www.mhbuk.com/reports.aspx?sm=c_b> accessed May 2009

Morgan, R, and Newburn, T, *The Future of Policing* (OUP, 1997)

Morris, D, *People Watching* (updated version of *Manwatching*, first published in 1977 by Jonathan Cape) (Vintage, 2002)

Morris, J, 'Removing the Barriers to community participation', National Community Forum (2006) 14

Morton, J, *Supergrasses and Informers: an informal history of undercover police work* (Little, Brown, 1995)

Bibliography and References

Mosse, G, *Fallen Soldiers: Reshaping the memory of the World Wars* (OUP, 1990)

NCF (National Crime Faculty, now part of NCPE, itself within NPIA), *Murder Investigation Manual*, NCF/ACPO Crime Committee (2000, first published 1998)

Newburn, T, 'Understanding and Preventing Police Corruption: Lessons from the Literature', Police Research Series, Paper 110, Home Office (1999)

_____ (ed), *A Handbook of Policing* (Willan, 2003)

_____ (ed), *Policing: Key Readings* (Willan, 2004)

_____ and Jones, T, 'Consultation by Crime and Disorder Partnerships', Police Research Series, Paper 148, Home Office (2002) especially Chs 4 and 5

Newburn, T, Williamson, T, and Wright, A (eds), *Handbook of Criminal Investigation* (2007, Willan Publishing, Devon)

Neyroud, P, and Beckley, A, *Policing Ethics and Human Rights* (Willan, 2001)

NHS: *Accident and Emergency Attendances in England (Experimental Statistics), 2007–08* (opsi, January 2009)

Nicholls, C, Daniel, T, Polaine, M, and Hatchard, J, *Corruption and Misuse of Public Office* (OUP, 2006)

NIM, 'National Briefing Model for the Patrol Function, SOP', Version iv, National Intelligence Model NCIS/Home Office (2002)

Nolan, Lord, *First Report of the Committee on Standards in Public Life* (Cmnd 2850-I, 1995)

NPIA, *Neighbourhood Policing Programme, PCSO Review* (July 2008)

National Police Improvement Agency, available from <http://www.npia.police.uk/en/docs/PCSO_Review_Final_Report.pdf> accessed May 2009)

O'Neill, G, *The Good Old Days, crime, murder and mayhem in Victorian London* (Viking, 2006)

Owen, T, Bailin, A, Knowles J, MacDonald, A, Ryder, M, Sayers, D, and Tomlinson, H, *Blackstone's Guide to the Serious and Organised Crime and Police Act 2005* (OUP, 2005)

Povey, D, and Smith, K (eds) with Hand, T, and Dodd, L, *Police Powers and Procedures: England and Wales 2007/08*, 07/09 (Home Office, Research and Development Studies Directorate (RDSD), 30 April 2009, also available from the Research Development Statistics Internet site: <http://www.homeoffice.gov.uk/rds/index.html> accessed May 2009)

Putnam, R, *Bowling Alone: The Collapse and Revival of American Community* (Touchstone, 2001)

Quinlan, P, and Morris, J, *Neighbourhood Policing: The impact of piloting and early national implementation*, (2008, Home Office OnLine Report 01/08), available from <http://www.homeoffice.gov.uk/rds/pdfs08/rdsolr0108app.pdf> accessed 16 January 2009

Ratcliffe, J (ed), *Strategic Thinking in Criminal Intelligence* (Police Federation, distributed by Willan, 2004)

Rawlings, P, *Policing: A Short History* (Willan, 2002)

Read, T, and Tilley, N, 'Not Rocket Science? Problem-Solving and Crime Reduction', Crime Reduction Research Series, Paper 6, Home Office (2000)

Reiner, R, *Chief Constables; Bobbies, Bosses or Bureaucrats?* (OUP, 1991)

_____ *The Politics of the Police* (OUP, 2000)

_____ Livingstone, S, and Allen, J, 'No more happy endings? The media and popular concern about crime since the Second World War' in Hope, T, and Sparks, R (eds), *Crime, Risk and Insecurity* (Willan, 2000)

Roberts, P, and Zuckerman, A, *Criminal Evidence* (OUP, 2004)

Rodger, N, *The Command of the Ocean* (Penguin, 2004)

Rogers, A, *Teaching Adults* (2nd edn, Open University Press, 1996)

Rogers, C, *Crime Reduction Partnerships* (OUP, 2006)

Rowe, M, *Policing, Race and Racism* (Willan, 2004)

Rowe, M, and Garland, J, 'Have you been diversified yet? Developments in police community and race relations training in England and Wales' (2003) 13 *Policing and Society* 399–412

Sampson, A, 'Lessons from a Victim Support Crime Prevention Project', Crime Prevention Unit, Paper No 25, Home Office (1991)

Sanders, A, and Young, R, 'From Suspect to Trial' in Maguire *et al* (eds), *Oxford Handbook of Criminology* (3rd edn, OUP, 2002) 1034–1075

_____ and Young, R, *Criminal Justice* (3rd edn, OUP, 2006)

Saulsbury, B, Hibberd, M, and Irving, B, *Using Physical Evidence* (The Police Foundation, 1994)

Scase, R, *Britain in 2010* (Capstone, Crown Copyright, 2000) especially Ch 7, 93–106 and Ch 8, 107–13

Bibliography and References

Simpson, K, *Forty Years of Murder* (forensic pathology) (Grafton, 1996 (first published by George Harrap & Co in 1978))

Skinner, T, Hester, M, and Malos, E (eds), *Researching Women and Violence* (Willan, 2004)

Skogan, W, 'Asymmetry in the impact of encounters with police' (2006) 16 *Policing and Society* 99–126

Smartt, U, *Criminal Justice* (Sage, 2006)

Smith, M, and Tilley, N (eds), *Crime Science* (Willan, 2004) especially Ch 4

Sparks, R, *Television and the Drama of Crime* (Open University Press, 1992)

_____ 'Bringing it all back home' in Stenson, K, and Sullivan, R (eds) *Crime, Risk and Justice* (Willan, 2000) Ch 10

Starmer, K, and Hopkins, A, *Human Rights in the Investigation and Prosecution of Crime* (OUP, 2007)

Stenson, K, and Sullivan, R (eds), *Crime, Risk and Justice* (Willan, 2000) especially Part 5, 'The Media, Crime and Risk'

Stevens, Sir J, *Not for the Faint-Hearted* (Phoenix, 2005)

Stevens, M, *How to be a better problem-solver* (Kogan Page, 1996) 9

Tapper, C, *Cross and Tapper on Evidence* (8th edn, OUP, 1995) especially Ch 3, 'Burdens of Proof', 119–75 and Ch 8, 'Similar Fact Evidence', 361–413

Thomas, T, *Sex Crime* (Willan, 2001)

Tilley, N, 'Community Policing, POP and Intelligence-led Policing', in Newburn, T (ed), *A Handbook of Policing* (Willan 2003) Ch 13

_____ (ed), *Handbook of Crime Prevention and Community Safety* (Willan, 2005)

_____ and Ford, A, *Forensic Science and Crime Investigation* Police Research Group, Crime Detection and Prevention Series, Paper 73 (1996)

TSO (The Stationery Office), Police and Justice Bill (later the Police and Justice Act), TSO (2006)

Uglow, S, *Policing Liberal Society* (OUP, 1988)

Villiers, P, *Better Police Ethics—a practical guide* (Kogan Page, 1997)

Waddington, P, *Policing Citizens* (UCL, 1999)

_____ 'Irrelevant Targets', *Police Review*, 16 May 2003, 17

_____ 'Understanding the Theatre of Diversity', *Police Review*, 29 April 2005, 16–18

_____ 'Turning the tide of police criticism', *Police Review*, 26 January 2007, 14–15

_____ Stenson, K, and Don, D, 'In Proportion: race and police stop and search' (2004) 44 *British Journal of Criminology* 889–914

Wade, G, Meguinness, J, and Roberts, L, 'PCSO Training in Kent Police' (January 2007)

Wadham, J, Mountfield, H, Edmundson, A, and Gallagher, C, *Blackstone's Guide to the Human Rights Act 1998* (OUP, 2007)

Wahidin, A, and Cain, M (eds), *Ageing, Crime and Society* (Willan, 2006)

Wakefield, A, *Selling Security: the private policing of public space* (Willan, 2004)

Walker, A, Kershaw, C, and Nicholas, S, 'Crime in England and Wales, 2005–2006', Home Office Statistical Bulletin (2006)

Walters, R, *Deviant Knowledge; Criminology, Politics and Policy* (Willan, 2003)

Ward, R, and Davies, O, *The Criminal Justice Act 2003: a practitioner's guide* (Jordan's, 2004)

Websdale, N, *Understanding Domestic Homicide* (North Eastern University Press, 1999)

Young, J, *Cold War Europe, 1945–1991: a political history* (2nd edn, Arnold (Hodder), 1996) especially Chs 8 and 9

Cases and case law

R v Anthony David Martin [2001] EWCA Crim 2245
R v Turnbull [1976] 3 All ER 549
R v Heggart and Heggart [Nov 2000 CA]

Web, online, and internet articles

Access dates to the website follow the reference.

ACPO (2000), 'Developing an Intelligence-led Approach' <http://www.acpo.police.uk/policies> accessed August 2005

Anti-social behaviour (2004), 'Tackling together' <http://www.together.gov.uk> accessed July 2006

BBC (2003a), 'Crime Fighters: Intelligence' <http://www.bbc.co.uk/crime/fighters> accessed April 2003

BBC (2003b), 'The Forensic Science Service' <http://www.bbc.co.uk/crime/fighters> accessed April 2003

BBC (2003c), 'Intelligence-led Policing' <http://www.bbc.co.uk/crime/fighters> accessed May 2003

BBC (2004), *The Secret Policeman* <http://news.bbc.co.uk/1/hi/magazine/3210614.stm> accessed July 2006

Bell, J (2003), 'I cannot admit what I am to myself', *The Guardian*, 23 January 2003 <http://www.guardian.co.uk> accessed January 2003

Blair, Sir I (2007), response to article critical of PCSOs in *The Daily Mirror* <http://cms.met.police.uk/met/layout/set/print/content/view/full/961> accessed January 2007

Butler, N (2006), 'PCSOs update on recruitment, powers and guidance', ACPO <http://nikki.butler@acpo.pnn.police.uk> accessed September 2006

City & Guilds at <http://www.cityandguilds.com/cps/rde/xchg/cgonline/hs.xsl/uk.html>. BTEC was, until 1996, a sub-degree awarding body called the Business and Technical Education Council. Then its functions were transferred to Edexcel, which has kept the BTEC name but administers all the BTEC programmes, reference at <http://www.edexcel.org.uk/home/BTEC> accessed December 2006

Centrex (2007), 'Neighbourhood Policing', <http://www.centrex.police.uk> accessed February 2007 (from 1 April 2007 <http://www.npia.police.uk>)

Commission for Racial Equality (CRE) news release, commentary on Calvert-Smith's report (qv), CRE investigation into the police and citing the Stephen Lawrence Enquiry 1998, Sir William McPherson's subsequent report 1999, and the BBC documentary *The Secret Policeman* in 2004; all on <http://www.cre.gov.uk/media/nr_050308.html> accessed January 2007

Cooner, M (2000), '*The Value of Communities*', 2000E-Learning Conference, San Francisco, USA <http://www.learnativity.com/community.html> accessed January 2007

Community definitions and consultations from <http://wordnet.princeton.edu/perl/webwn> accessed January2007

Department for Education and Skills (DFES) (2003), *Every Child Matters* (Government Green Paper in response to Lord Laming's Inquiry report into the death of Victoria Climbié) <http://www.dfes.gov.uk/everychildmatters/> accessed June 2006

Easton, M (2006), 'Does Diversity make us happy?' <http://news.bbc.co.uk./1/hi/programmes/happiness_formula/5012478.stm> accessed December 2006

Ford, R, and O'Neill, S, 'Judges to curb costs of complex trials by sacking defence lawyers', *The Times*, 10 August, 2006, 14, and leading article on 17 <http://www.times-online.co.uk/news> accessed August 2006

Gill, P (1998), 'Intelligence-led Policing: "rounding up the usual suspects" again', <http://www.psa.ac.uk/cps/1998/gill.pdf> accessed October 2003

HMG (2004), *'Policing a New Century: a Blueprint for Reform'* <http://www.archive.official-documents.co.uk/document/cm53/5326/cm5326.htm> accessed January2004

HM Inspectorate of Constabulary (HMIC) (2002), 'Training Matters—a thematic inspection report on probationer training in England and Wales', HMIC Robin Field-Smith <http://inspectorates.homeoffice.gov.uk/hmic> accessed July 2006

HMIC (2004), 'Modernising the Police Service—a thematic inspection of workforce modernisation; the role, management and deployment of police staff in the police service of England and Wales', HMIC Sir Ronnie Flanaghan <http://inspectorates.homeoffice.gov.uk/hmic> accessed July 2006

HMSO (1999), 'The Stephen Lawrence Inquiry—Report of an Inquiry by Sir William MacPherson of Cluny' <http://www.opsi.gov.uk> accessed June, July, September 2006

HMSO (TSO, The Stationery Office) (2003), 'Regulation of Investigatory Powers Act (RIPA)' <http://www.hmso.gov.uk/acts/acts2000/20000023.htm> accessed April 2004

Home Office (2001), 'Diary of a Police Officer', Police Research Group Paper, No 149 <http://www.homeoffice.gov.uk/rds> accessed October 2003

____ (2002), *One Step Ahead, a 21st Century Strategy to Defeat Organised Crime*, HMG White Paper <http://www.homeoffice.gov.uk> accessed June 2004

____ (2002), 'Police Community Support Officer Training <http://police.homeoffice.gov.uk/news-and-publications/publication/police-reform/centrex_cso_training.pdf?view=Binary> accessed July 2006

____ (2004), 'Training and Career Development; the National Learning Strategy <http://police.homeoffice.gov.uk/training–and-career-development/national-strategic/index> accessed August 2006

____ (2005), 'Community policing: The Neighbourhood policing programme' <http://police.homeoffice.gov.uk/community-policing/neighbourhood-police> accessed August 2006

____ (June 2005), 'Community Support Officers, strength by Basic Command Unit' <http://police.homeoffice.gov.uk/community-policing/community-support-officers/comm/faqs> accessed August 2006

_____ (2006), 'Good practice for Police Authorities and Forces in obtaining CSO funding' <http://police.homeoffice.gov. uk/news-and-publications/publication/community-policing/ Matched_funding_good_practice? view=Binary> accessed July 2006

_____ (2006), 'Neighbourhood Policing: Progress Report May 2006' <http://police.homeoffice.gov.uk/community-policing/ neighbourhood-police/progress-report> accessed August 2006

_____ (2006), 'Powers that may be designated on Community Support Officers by a chief officer of police' <http://police. homeoffice.gov.uk/news-and-publications/publication/ community-policing/power> accessed July 2006

Kelly, R (January 2007), *Communities and Local Government*, News releases, various articles 'New powers for tenant to tackle anti-social behaviour'; 'What is a sustainable community?'; 'Neighbourhood renewal'; 'The Respect Agenda'; 'Demographics'; 'Liveability'; 'Social cohesion'; 'Economic competitiveness'; 'Social exclusion' all from <http://www. communities.gov.uk/index.asp?id=1002882&Press>, and 1139866, 1127158, 1502147, 1163940, 1164036, 1127160 and 1164035 all accessed January 2007

King, A (2003), YouGOV Poll, *Daily Telegraph* <http:// www.portal.telegraph.co.uk/news/main.jhtml?xml=/ news/2003/09/23/nstate423.xml> accessed August 2004

Ladyman, S (2003), 'Protection of Vulnerable Adults Scheme' (Health Ministry initiative) <http://www.doh.gov.uk/ vulner-ableadults> accessed May 2003

Learndirect (adult learning) <http://www.learndirect-advice. co.uk/helpandadvice/whichcourse/vocqual> accessed December 2006

London Chamber of Commerce and Industry (LCCI) (2004) <www.lccieb.com/Web/lccieb/index.aspx> accessed December 2006

Lund, S (2004), 'Dial a Crime' (on mobile phone crime) *Police Review*, 19 March 2004, 26–7 <http://www.policereview. com> accessed March 2004

MAPPA (Multi Agency Public Protection Arrangements) (2003), 'Protecting the Public from Dangerous Offenders' (on sex offenders and violent criminals, annual report under Criminal Justice and Court Services Act 2000), Home Office Prison and Probation Services <http: //www.probation.homeoffice.gov. uk> accessed November 2004

Meeker-O'Connell, A (2003), 'How DNA Evidence Works' <http://www.science.howstuffworks.com/dna-evidence4.htm> accessed May 2003

Mirror, The, 'The law's a mess', February 7 2004 <http: //web1.infotrac.galegroup.com/itw/infomark/857/38/84983469 w1/purl=rcl_SP00_0> accessed September 2006

MPS (2003), 'History of Fingerprinting' <http://www.met.police.uk/so/100 years/history> accessed May 2003

Myhill, A (2006), 'Community engagement in policing: lessons from the literature' <http://www.crimereduction.gov.uk/policing18.htm> accessed January 2007

Naseby, C (2005), 'National Occupational Standards for the Justice Sector: consultation guidance', Skills for Justice <http://skillsforjustice.com> accessed July 2006

NCIS, 'National Intelligence-led Policing Model', 2000 at <http://www.ncis.gov.uk> accessed October, November, December 2003

NCIS (2004) 'UK Threat Assessment, 2000' <http://www.ncis.gov.uk/ukta/2004/print.asp> accessed 4 July 2004

Open College Network (OCN) at <http://www.nocn.org.uk/about/about-nocn.html> accessed December 2006

Police Federation (2005), 'Row over community officers' role', 6 December 2005 <news.bbc.co.uk/1/hi/england/london/4505040.stm> accessed July 2006

Reid, J (Home Secretary), 'Common values for the Police Service of England and Wales', 6 March, 2007, Home Office <http://police.homeoffice.gov.uk/news-and-publications/publication/commonvalues> accessed March 2007

Skills for Justice, at <http://www.psso.co.uk/printcat.php?ID=289> accessed December 2006

Walker, C (2004), 'Soham Enquiry wants action now' (Sir Michael Bichard's Enquiry into the vetting of Ian Huntley, who was convicted in February 2004 for the murder of Holly Wells and Jessica Chapman), *The Times*, 31 March 2004 <http://www.timesonline.co.uk/Soham> accessed May 2006

Articles, media reports, and ephemera

Bebbington, S, 'Council's £2 million to fund "real officers" ' (on how Gloucestershire County Council prefers to fund police officers, not PCSOs), *Police Review*, 9 June 2006a, 8

_____ 'CSO boost should not affect sworn staff' (the debate whether affording PCSOs would lead to smaller numbers of recruited police officers), *Police Review*, 7 July 2006b, 7

_____ 'Family Unit' (team policing), *Police Review*, 1 September 2006, 16–18

_____ 'Street Smart' (programme for at-risk members of ethnic minority communities in South Yorkshire), *Police Review*, 4 August 2006c, 16–19

Bishton, A, letter subtitled 'CS OH NO', *Police Review*, 25 August 2006, 16

Blears, H, 'Community leaders' (on how constables and PCSOs can work together—the politician's view), *Police Review*, 30 July 2004a, 25

_____ [Police Minister, Home Office], 'Fears unfounded' (letter on funding for PCSOs), *Police Review*, 12 November 2004b, 15

Brinkley, I, 'Working Trends: the Future', *Edge*, 9 June 2004, 25–8

British Crime Survey (no by-line), 'Crime more "stable" ' (on BCS 2005/2006), *Police Professional,* 27 July 2006, 10

Caless, B, 'Numties in Yellow Jackets' (August 2007) 2 *Policing, A Journal of Policy and Practice*

Clark, D, 'Life and Limb' (on Health and Safety law and the police), *Police Professional*, 21 September 2006, 50–2

Country Life, Ten-point Manifesto, ('Bring back the British Bobby'), *Country Life*, 31 August 2006, 72–3

Crawford, A, and Lister, S, 'Patrol with a purpose' (study of PCSO deployment in West Yorkshire Police), *Police Review*, 6 August, 2004a, 18–20

_____ and Lister, S, 'Patrolling with a purpose: an evaluation of police community support officers in Leeds and Bradford city centres', Centre for Criminal Justice Studies, University of Leeds (2004b)

Donnelly, D, 'Policing a 24-hour world', *Police Review*, 12 January 2007, 14

Elder, B, 'CSO critique' (on the 'failure' of the PCSO introduction), *Police Review*, 26 May 2006, 8

Ford, R, 'Tony Martin is a dangerous man, says parole chief' (on the farmer who used 'excessive force' on intruders), *The Times*, 27 May 2003, 9

Foster, P, 'Big Brother surveillance means no one is safe, experts warn', *The Times*, 27 March 2007, 25

Gibb, F, 'Judges to hang up gowns and wigs', *The Times*, 23 September 2006, 39

Gilbertson, D, 'This is the end', *Police Review*, 16 February 2007, 26–7

Graffiti: 'Developers demolish "£100,000 work of art" to make way for flats' (article on 'Banksy', the graffiti artist whose works sell for thousands of pounds), *The Times*, 23 September 2006, 29

Hanna, S, 'Police on the cheap' (front page article on Police Federation hostility to Kent PCSOs) *Kent on Sunday*, 11 June 2006, 1–2

Haynes, C, 'Youth Patrol' (PCSO work in Brighton, part of Sussex Police's *Operation Athlete*), *Police Review*, 5 May 2006a, 20–1

_____ 'Scheme to put staff in response roles' (Northumbria Police on extending PCSO roles to include offender management and intelligence), *Police Review*, 9 June 2006b, 5

_____ 'Community call', *Police Review*, 9 June 2006c, 16–18

_____ 'Authorities hike tax to cover CSO gap', *Police Review*, 16 March 2007, 7

Humphries, P, 'Keeping the beat alive' (neighbourhood wardens, with useful data), *New Start*, 1 September 2006, 14–15

Joyce, P, 'Body of evidence' *Police Review*, 12 January 2007, 18–19

Judd, T, 'Farmer gets life for shooting teenage intruder' (on Anthony Martin, Norfolk farmer), *The Independent*, 20 April 2000, 3

Lund, S, 'Tough Talk' (interview with Jan Berry, Chair of Police Federation, on PCSOs and other modernization issues), *Police*, January 2006, 12

Marchant, C, 'Special interest' (views in favour of including PCSOs in Police Federation membership), *Police Review*, 21 April 2006a, 13

_____ 'A skilled profession' (on how best to deploy the new tranches of PCSOs, in 'mixed economy teams'), *Police Review*, 9 June 2006b, 13

Martis, R, 'CSOs due to "detain suspects by New Year"' (commentary on the HO evaluation of PCSO powers, led by Bob Elder, Police Federation), *Police Review*, 8 October 2004, 7

_____ 'Community links' (on a neighbourhood team, including PCSOs in West Mercia Constabulary), *Police Review*, 30 June 2006a, 17–20

_____ 'Action stations' (PCSOs at Waterloo Station, London, supporting the travelling public), *Police Review*, 21 July 2006b, 16–18

_____ 'Northern Ireland moves a step closer to taking on first CSOs', *Police Review*, 12 January 2007, 8

_____ 'Career Gamble' (on PCSOs' previous careers), *Police Review*, 16 March 2007, 20–2

Mason, G, 'Privatising Custody' (on private companies within the 'mixed economy' of policing), *Police Review*, 1 September 2006, 15–17

McGurran, A, and Johnston, J, 'Tony Martin's story' (on the Norfolk farmer who shot intruders; imprisoned for manslaughter (excessive force)) *The Mirror*, 1 August 2003, 11

Mirror (no by-line), 'Stab Backing' (article on Antonio Caeiro, who stabbed a burglar in his home, example of excessive force) *The Mirror* 18 August 2004, 11

O'Connor, D (HMIC], 'Citizen-focused policing' (on neighbourhood policing teams and the inclusion of PCSOs), *Police Review*, 8 October 2004, 15

_____ *Closing the Gap* (Inspection report on amalgamation of forces) (Home Office, 2005)

_____ 'Authority turns down offer of community support officers' (on Hampshire Police Authority's refusal to employ PCSOs), *Police Review*, 3 December 2004, 6

Pertile, E, 'Force study shows that CSOs can help to reduce crime rates' (on Harrington *et al*'s study in Kent, qv), *Police Review*, 14 October 2005, 10

_____ 'Federation to decide whether to open its doors to police staff' (on admitting PCSOs to membership), *Police Review*, 21 April 2006a, 4

_____ 'Federation closes door to new members' (vote at Police Federation Annual Conference rejects extension of membership to PCSOs), *Police Review*, 26 May 2006b, 7

_____ 'Security guard "cops" to police university', *Police Review*, 16 February 2007

Police Federation, 'Decision time' (the case for extending the police 'family' to include PCSOs) (2006a) XXXVIII (3) *Police* 19–21

_____ Conference Report, 'Vote against opening doors to police "family" ' (2006b) XXXVIII (6) *Police* 7

Police Professional (no by-line), 'Uniformed border-control force announced', *Police Professional*, 27 July 2006, 18

Police Review (no by-line), 'Kent CSOs to be issued with stab vests', *Police Review*, 23 June 2006, 10

PricewaterhouseCoopers, (2006), *ACPO Neighbourhood Policing Survey*, ACPO

Quinlan, P and Morris, J (2008), *Neighbourhood Policing: The impact of piloting and early national implementation*, Home Office OnLine Report 01/08, available from <http://www.homeoffice.gov.uk/rds/pdfs08/rdsolr0108app.pdf > accessed 16 January 2009

Sampson, P, 'Criminal treatment of Community Support Officers', *The Daily Mirror*, 11 May 2005

Shaw, F, 'The Future: Expert view', *Edge*, June 2004, 30–4

Smyth, G, (Police Federation, London Constables' Branch), 'Met constables query confidence in commissioner (*sic*)' (in which Smyth refers to PCSOs as 'gaggles of lost shoppers') (2006) XXXVIII (6) *Police* 30

Tuffin, R, Morris, J, and Poole, A (2006), *An Evaluation of the impact of the National Reassurance Policing Programme*, Home Office Research Study 296, available from <http://www.compassunit.com/docs/hors296.pdf> accessed 10 January 2009

Unison, 'PCSO working group kicks off', *Police Staff* (Unison publication), Summer 2006, 4

_____ 'Unison raises PCSO stab vest fears', *Police Professional*, 10 August 2006, 7

Waddington, P (1999), *Policing Citizens*, University College London (UCL) Press

Waddington, P, 'Turning the tide of police criticism', *Police Review*, 26 January, 2007, 14–15

Wood, J, and Dupont, B (2006) (eds) *Democracy, Society and the Governance of Security*, Cambridge University Press, Cambridge

Woolcock, N, and Fishburn, A, 'School exclusions 'merry-go-round' shows that reforms are failing', *The Times*, 28 May, 2009, 14–15, available from <http://timesonline.co.uk/tol/news/education/article6375172> accessed 28 May 2009

Index

Index

Index

Index

Index

Index

Index